ABSEN

Stefan Collini is Professor of Intellectual History and English Literature at the University of Cambridge and a Fellow of Clare Hall. A leading intellectual historian and cultural commentator, he is a frequent contributor to *The Times Literary Supplement, The London Review of Books*, and other periodicals both in Britain and the USA. His previous books include *Public Moralists* (1991, reissued 2006), *Matthew Arnold: a Critical Portrait* (1994), and *English Pasts* (1999, reissued 2006). He is a Fellow of the British Academy and of the Royal Historical Society.

ALSO BY STEFAN COLLINI

As author:

Liberalism and Sociology: L.T. Hobhouse and Political Argument in England 1880–1914

(with Donald Winch and John Burrow) *That Noble Science of Politics: A Study in Nineteenth-Century Intellectual History*

Public Moralists: Political Thought and Intellectual Life in Britain 1850–1930

Matthew Arnold: A Critical Portrait

English Pasts: Essays in History and Culture

As editor:

John Stuart Mill, *On Liberty and Other Writings*

Umberto Eco, *Interpretation and Overinterpretation*

Matthew Arnold, *Culture and Anarchy and Other Writings*

C.P. Snow, *The Two Cultures*

(with Richard Whatmore and Brian Young)
History, Religion, and Culture: and *Economy, Polity, and Society: British Intellectual History 1750–1950*

Absent Minds

Intellectuals in Britain

STEFAN COLLINI

UNIVERSITY PRESS

OXFORD
UNIVERSITY PRESS

Great Clarendon Street, Oxford OX2 6DP

Oxford University Press is a department of the University of Oxford.
It furthers the University's objective of excellence in research, scholarship,
and education by publishing worldwide in

Oxford New York

Auckland Cape Town Dar es Salaam Hong Kong Karachi
Kuala Lumpur Madrid Melbourne Mexico City Nairobi
New Delhi Shanghai Taipei Toronto

With offices in

Argentina Austria Brazil Chile Czech Republic France Greece
Guatemala Hungary Italy Japan Poland Portugal Singapore
South Korea Switzerland Thailand Turkey Ukraine Vietnam

Oxford is a registered trade mark of Oxford University Press
in the UK and in certain other countries

Published in the United States
by Oxford University Press Inc., New York

First published 2006
First published in paperback 2007

British Library Cataloguing in Publication Data

Data available

Library of Congress Cataloging in Publication Data

Data available

Typeset by Newgen Imaging Systems (P) Ltd., Chennai, India
Printed in Great Britain
on acid-free paper by
Ashford Colour Press Limited,
Gosport, Hampshire

ISBN 978–0–19–921665–9 (Pbk.) 978–0–19–929105–2 (Hbk.)

1 3 5 7 9 10 8 6 4 2

In memory of Luis Castro (23 February 1943–8 April 1999),
most lovable of intellectuals

PRAISE FOR *ABSENT MINDS*

'splendid book'
Timothy Garton Ash, *Guardian*

'Fascinating . . . a provocative and impressive read'
Dominic Sandbrook, *Sunday Telegraph*

'Magnificent'
Jonathan Derbyshire, *New Humanist*

'Fascinating . . . unusual . . . excellent'
James Pierson, *New Criterion*

'A book fully worth not going on holiday for'
Peter Stothard, *Times Online*

'A frequently brilliant survey'
Mark Bostridge, *Independent on Sunday*

'Ambitious, wide-ranging . . . and immensely erudite'
Daniel T. Rodgers, *Journal of the History of Ideas*

'A long book of dazzling short chapters. Richly layered, provocative, and very funny'
Roy Foster, 'Books of the Year', *Times Literary Supplement*

'A rich, subtle, and complex book . . . a constant stimulus to thought . . . and full of witty phrases.'
Robert Skidelsky, *Prospect*

'First rate . . . immensely authoritative, wide-ranging, readable, and often witty.'
Winston Fletcher, *THES*

'Splendidly challenging . . . this book has made me engage in the uncomfortable but salutary task of abandoning some habitual assumptions.'
Bernard Bergonzi, *The Tablet*

Contents

PART FIVE: REPEAT PERFORMANCES

O thoughts of men accurs'd!
Past and to come seems best; things present, worst
William Shakespeare, *2 Henry IV*

Great is the power of steady misrepresentation.
Charles Darwin, *The Origin of Species*

Introduction: The Question of Intellectuals

'Is there such a thing as an English intellectual? It is as well to pose the question from the start, since anyone acquainted with the habits and social position of intellectuals on the continent of Europe must have serious doubts as to whether the same word can reasonably be applied to English conditions.'

I

Perhaps the most common assumption about any book announcing 'intellectuals in Britain' as its theme is that it will be short. Indeed, it is sometimes assumed that such a book should properly belong in the company of treatises on snark-hunting or gazetteers of snakes in Iceland. It will already be evident, however, that the present volume is far from short. I should like to think that this palpable fact may even now be starting the process of calling assumptions about this topic into doubt, a process which the book's contents are devoted to furthering. But at the very least, the untoward bulkiness of the object in hand may cause the reader to pause and focus on what, more exactly, it is about.

This book is about the *question* of intellectuals in twentieth-century Britain. That is to say, it examines the ways in which the existence, nature, and role of intellectuals have been thought about and argued over, including claims about their absence or comparative insignificance. The formulation 'the question of intellectuals' signals in itself the presence of a topic of extended speculation and recurrent debate, something that is at once familiar, troubling, and unresolved. The enduring interest of the topic of intellectuals, considered in general analytical and historical terms, can scarcely be doubted, and it is anyway attested, as I have rueful cause to know, by a dispiritingly voluminous body of scholarly, polemical, and journalistic writing. However, the suggestion that the topic might be a similarly established one when considered in relation to Britain, or that the directly relevant source-materials might be abundant in this case, is likely to be met quizzically even by readers in whom my title arouses a response other than simply the desire to scoff. One of the lesser objects I hope this book will achieve is to document the existence in Britain of a rich tradition of debate about the question of intellectuals: there is indeed an extensive relevant literature, and it may well surprise some readers to learn just how commonly the term 'intellectuals' itself has been employed by British writers. It remains true, of course, that denial of the existence of intellectuals, or of 'real' intellectuals, has been and to some extent continues to be a prominent aspect of national self-definition, but it follows that this tradition of denial must itself then become an object of historical and critical attention. In so attending, I often recur to what I call the 'paradoxes of denial' precisely because there is something intriguing, some kind of revealing tension or betraying unsteadiness, in the way in which various leading intellectual figures have, over and over again, dissociated themselves from the role (at least when so labelled) and have, no less insistently, asserted that the species to which they, according to most classifications, clearly belong is not native to these shores.

'When so labelled'—there is at least part of the rub. Even I have been surprised by the extent to which the history that this book charts has turned on the meanings and resonances of the *term* 'intellectuals'. The very word irritates people. They sense pretentiousness, arrogance: on most of its outings, 'so-called' travels with it like a bodyguard, never far away even if not immediately in view. Those who accept the label can seem rather too self-conscious about their role, a little too intent on parading a conviction of their own seriousness. Even people who deeply value intelligence find themselves more sympathetic than usual to phrases like 'too clever by half'; even those otherwise inclined to jib at the affectation and ruling-class insouciance of 'effortless superiority' find themselves half-guiltily preferring the style evoked by that phrase to the posturing, the self-importance, the tendency to hector or condescend to lesser mortals, of those who may seem only too pleased to describe themselves as 'intellectuals'. As a result, in Britain (I shall return to the non-equivalence of 'Britain' and 'England' below) the term is always having to cope with the resistance its presence engenders, making it difficult for it to move unselfconsciously in the society of other words.

But elsewhere, it is assumed, things are quite otherwise. Intellectuals begin at Calais. If they are true to stereotype, they lose no time moving to Paris. The café is assumed to be the natural habitat of the species; passionate, high-principled debate its preferred nourishment; demonstrating, signing manifestos, and denouncing abuses of power its characteristic activities. And all this in the name of those absolutes—Reason, Truth, Morality, the Rights of Man, the Logic of History—with whom intellectuals allow it to be known they are on first-name terms despite requiring others to accord them the full majesty of their capital letters. This provokes a characteristic British unease, a kind of social embarrassment: comfort is sought and found in the thought that such self-dramatization is hard to distinguish from hubris, an unnecessary courting of the twin fates of tragedy and farce.

Such stereotypes, and the history which has formed them, are inescapably part of the subject matter of a book on the question of intellectuals in twentieth-century Britain. It is their continuing power, after all, that renders the very phrase 'British intellectuals' an oxymoron in some people's eyes. Such people are among those whom I should particularly like to read this book. For cultures, like individuals, can become prisoners of images of themselves, lulled by the sheer repetition of a few pat phrases into believing that they have identified their distinctive nature. Among my larger ambitions for this book is the hope that careful historical analysis might perform one of its appointed tasks here, that of helping to replace such time-worn clichés with something a little knubblier and harder to stack.

II

The question of intellectuals was posed and answered in various ways in twentieth-century Britain. This book attempts to chart some of that variety, but one cluster of responses tended, and still tends, to dominate discussion, namely the claim that in Britain intellectuals have been peculiarly unimportant or even non-existent. It may therefore be helpful, before beginning on the substantive historical account, to isolate this claim itself for preliminary analysis, since its looming negative presence can otherwise prove obstructive. If the longevity of a version of this claim is itself a historical fact of some interest, it can only be said to provide a starting-point in a symptomatic rather than programmatic sense. What seems to me the wrong way to go at this question—the way favoured, it should be said, by most existing accounts—is to take the truth of the claim about the absence of intellectuals in Britain as more or less self-evident, and then to propose various social-structural or other large-scale explanations to account for it. Instead, this book seeks to uncover the larger tradition of debate about intellectuals in Britain, situating the more specific negative claim within that debate. But what, when looked at closely, does this negative claim really amount to?

Since the claim about the absence of intellectuals in Britain is a long-standing and widely held cultural conviction, it cannot be tracked down to a set of definitive statements, still less to a single *locus classicus*. Moreover, if the claim is subjected to any pressure, it frequently retreats to one of several ostensibly more modest positions about the absence of 'real' intellectuals or the comparative insignificance and lack of influence of such native intellectuals as there may be, and so on, positions which in turn involve further clusters of highly questionable assumptions and assertions. The fact that these positions are clearly not all logically compatible with each other is another reminder that we are dealing with a nexus of cultural attitudes here, not a single proposition or argument. For convenience I shall refer to this group of claims as 'the absence thesis', even though 'thesis' risks making it sound too much like a single well worked-out proposition.

In speaking of 'absence', it is important to recognize the structural correspondence between various 'elsewheres' and various 'pasts', those other habitats in which the species is alleged to flourish or to have flourished. In this respect, there is an interesting similarity, especially in the psychological mechanisms involved, between attitudes towards this topic and expressions of that kind of cultural pessimism that sees all the great names (in thought, literature, sport, or any other field) as being in the past, the present being inhabited only by relative pygmies. When faced with a committed proponent of cultural decline, it invariably proves pointless to cite names of contemporary figures who might seem to belong in the company of that distinguished line which is alleged to have come to an end in the previous generation. Mention of any such living figures only provokes squawks of derision: 'But they are not of the same stature as A or B or C,' naming the preferred giants of an earlier age. Among its other failings, this response always forgets that these earlier figures were in fact similarly undervalued by many of their contemporaries in their own lifetimes by comparison to the alleged brilliance of *their* predecessors, and so on. Similarly, when faced with a committed proponent of the claim that there are no 'real intellectuals' in Britain, it will prove unavailing to mention some obvious recent or contemporary candidates. 'Oh', will come the reply, 'but they're not of the same stature as X or Y or Z,' citing the names of some favoured intellectuals from other countries (and, usually, from an earlier generation), among whose names—few things are as certain in this life—will be that of Jean-Paul Sartre. In these cases, argument by enumeration can never make much headway: discussion is too clouded by impressionistic judgements about relative 'stature'. It is the pre-emptive function of the underlying prejudice itself that needs to be examined.

The frequently encountered claim that there are no intellectuals in Britain is generally advanced by those who, were they living in certain other societies, would unhesitatingly be recognized as intellectuals. This in itself should suggest that we are here dealing with something requiring explanation; at the limit it may even imply that we are dealing with an assertion which serves, in the strictest sense of the term, an ideological function—that is, that its systematic misrepresentation of reality furthers some collective interest. Such recurrent and in some ways paradoxical denials also invite scrutiny at the individual level: when an individual insists, repeatedly and emphatically, that something is not true of them, it is hard not to speculate, even without resorting to psychoanalytic theory, about the source of the need to issue such frequent disclaimers. Moreover, common speech has appropriated the phrase 'in denial' to refer to a state of wilful blindness or a condition of being unwilling to recognize the truth of bad news. But why should having some of one's compatriots described as 'intellectuals' be either bad or news? In all of this, the spell cast by the actual word 'intellectuals' is extraordinary, an indication that the term must be serving as a kind of place-holder for a whole collection of cultural attitudes.

As this suggests, one obvious question to ask is: why has the 'absence thesis' mattered—and what is at stake in discussions of it now? It is a topic that invariably excites stronger feelings than the historiographical issue in itself might seem to warrant. In part, this is because it forms part of a long-standing national self-definition: as I shall show, the roots of this thesis can be traced back at least as far as the nineteenth century's Whiggish sense of self-congratulation on England's (as they tended to say) fortunate political history. Some of those who have wished to continue to uphold similar interpretations of British history in the twentieth century have found in the 'absence thesis' one explanation of what they see as the continuing virtues of the indigenous culture, especially its political culture. Those who have wished to challenge this continuity have, in turn, often pointed to the absence of intellectuals as a crucial explanatory element, and have correspondingly lamented it. Indeed, among those whose identity is closely bound up with their carefully nurtured sense of distance from the native culture and its alleged complacency there is sometimes to be found a kind of wilful nostalgia, a yearning for a more exciting state that they have never known. Wading through the laments that in Britain the aristocracy was too adaptable (or the church was too tolerant or the military was too apolitical or the bourgeoisie was too reformist) to produce the need for a properly 'oppositional' intelligentsia, one has to conclude that many British writers on this subject are suffering from a condition that can only be called 'Dreyfus-envy'.

Both groups—insular celebrants and off-shore malcontents—may be irritated by the argument of this book. They each have a great deal invested in assumptions about the 'exceptional' or 'deviant' nature of British history, not least in the matter of intellectuals, whereas my starting-point is that we need to get away from such implicitly binary classifications ('British'/'normal'), and instead attempt to identify both the common features and the specific characteristics of the activities of intellectuals in various societies. For the truth is that each of the major societies is 'exceptional' in its own terms. Familiar claims about 'the peculiarities of the English' can easily be matched by comparable claims about '*Der Deutsche Sonderweg*' or about 'American exceptionalism' or about '*la singularité française*', and so on. Britain is indeed unique—and so is every other country. The question, of course, is whether, when viewed from a series of analytical historical perspectives, Britain emerges as consistently deviant from what can be identified as a broadly common pattern elsewhere. Discussion of the question of intellectuals has been dogged by superficial or lazy invocations of a presumed European 'norm' against which the British case is to be contrasted. It is an important part of my argument in this book that there turns out on closer analysis to be *no* such common pattern elsewhere: almost invariably the implicit content of the contrast is provided by a stereotyped account of the situation in just one country—France. But this, too, helps us to see how the roots of this question have to be traced back to the dominant nineteenth-century story of England's distinctive political development, and, reaching still further back, to the commonplaces of 'national character' upon which that story was partly grounded, given how much that story and those commonplaces were shaped by a series of contrasts with France. Even now, discussion of the issue of intellectuals in Britain is conducted in the shadow of 'truisms' that can in fact be traced back to the writings of figures such as Burke and Tocqueville.

One of the most enduring of these truisms is the claim that 'ideas affect public debate much less in Britain than elsewhere'. On closer inspection, this claim nearly always reduces to the rather less interesting proposition that 'theories do not influence politics in Britain', a culpable narrowing of both terms in the larger proposition. But this does at least serve to bring into focus several of the assumptions that continue to clog discussion of this topic. First of all, it effectively reduces 'ideas' to 'theories', or at least it regards this as the form in which intellectual life has its most significant impact on other spheres of society. But a theory is a highly specific and relatively uncommon intellectual construction in any culture: it involves an extremely high level of abstraction, close logical sequence, and carefully defined or even specially formulated conceptual building blocks. Insights, perceptions, arguments, beliefs, observations, redescriptions, characterizations, judgements, assessments . . . these are among the constitutive features of intellectual life, but they are none of them the same thing as 'theories'.

Similarly, it needs to be recognized that politics is not coextensive with that immensely variegated network of opinion, comment, polemic, and so on that we abbreviate as 'public debate'. It is of course the case that in any complex society, much of its public discussion and reflection will have an explicit bearing on its collective arrangements and the distribution of wealth and power by which these are determined, and so to this extent much of it trenches upon the political, though even here it is clearly not 'politics' in the narrow, news-editor's sense. But there are so many other constituent elements to this public realm, including art, morality, culture, manners, and so on: to take two obvious examples that cannot be assimilated to the narrowly 'political', one only has to consider the importance in the twentieth century of the public expression of scepticism about religious belief or of challenges to conventional sexual morality. And then the verb at the centre of the traditional claim is 'influences', but this suggests only one type of relation, and in only one direction, whereas the reality of such relations needs to be represented by a whole range of verbs such as inform, refer to, reflect upon, compete with, express, derive from, and so on.

This book tries to do justice to this thick texture of relations and to the patterns they formed once the magnetic pull of the concept of 'the intellectual' was introduced into the field. In so doing, it argues that the traditional versions of these long-established truisms are either exaggerated (where not simply false) or not at all peculiar to Britain. What *has* been true is that the idea of British exceptionalism in these matters has flourished in the past two centuries (as, in each of the other countries one might discuss, has the idea of *that* country's exceptionalism . . .). That is an important historical fact in its own right, and it is obviously one that any discussion of intellectuals in Britain needs to take into account, though one must not lose sight of the inconvenient truth that the claim that general ideas have been of no consequence is itself a general idea.

III

It would be possible, and for many purposes desirable, to write historical accounts of various aspects of intellectual life in twentieth-century Britain that paid relatively little attention to the understanding of the term 'intellectuals' or to debates about that role (I hope to return to such work in the future myself). That life has been, by any standards, rich and extensive; such studies would not have to begin by addressing a prejudice that their announced subject matter did not exist. However, this book has, as the title of this Introduction suggests, a more restricted focus—how the *question* of intellectuals has been posed and answered in Britain in the course of the twentieth century—and so it may be as well to make clear at the outset the consequence of this focus as far as the nature and selection of its contents are concerned.

If this book were offering a general history of 'intellectual life in twentieth-century Britain', the reader could expect to find in it discussions of the major intellectual figures of the century, treated in proportion to the quality and importance of their ideas. Were it that sort of book, it might be reasonable to expect to find accounts of, say, the theories of Rutherford or Dirac, the discoveries of Crick and Watson, the thought of Evans-Pritchard or Popper, the work of Empson or Namier, and so on. If originality or profundity were the chief criterion for inclusion, Wittgenstein would arguably merit more space than Russell, and certainly more than A. J. Ayer; if influence on practice were the measure, one could hardly omit Keynes's economic theories; if transforming a whole domain of culture were the requirement, then attention might have to be given to Pinter's plays or Moore's sculptures; and, again, so on. But a book about 'the question of intellectuals' is not a book about intellectual achievement or even 'intellectual life'. It is, rather, a book principally about how this society has understood itself when subjected to the litmus test of dropping the term 'intellectuals' into its public debate. It is thus a book that, from a slightly oblique angle, attends to the mechanisms by which a culture enables some figures to *combine* being recognized as having attained a certain level of intellectual or cultural distinction *with* addressing non-specialist audiences on matters of general concern (these mechanisms themselves are analysed most fully in Ch. 2). For that reason, it is a book that interests itself more in how the term 'intellectual' has been used in Britain, including a revealing reluctance to use it in self-description, than in judgements about the comparative quality of intellectual work. It is a book in which questions about the persistence of forms of social deference or about the power of certain stereotypes of the French or about the making of successful careers or about the nature of a particular periodical's readership bulk far larger than discussions of those ideas which may now strike us as the most original or significant.

By the same token, it is not a book chronicling the doings of leading intellectual figures, full of entertaining vignettes, and constantly seeking to relate 'ideas' to 'politics' in the way that many people seem to feel books about 'intellectuals' should do. Nor will the reader find extended analyses of the social background, political affiliations, and professional roles of 'intellectuals' understood as a social group or stratum. My attempts to characterize the tone and register in which intellectuals in Britain have been written about (largely by other intellectuals) owe more to literary criticism than to political science or sociology, and as a consequence questions of voice, genre, and audience provide more of a focus than either 'political behaviour' or 'social class'. I particularly attend to what has been termed (in a now inescapable but still dangerously metaphorical phrase) the 'cultural authority' of intellectuals, that 'uncommanded response' which their utterances elicit from those who choose to attend to them (this notion is discussed more fully in Ch. 2, below).

For these reasons, among others (including my capacious ignorance), the book makes no pretence to being comprehensive, and I shall be more than usually unmoved by readers or reviewers who complain that this or that important figure is absent from its pages. To illustrate my analytical contentions, I have explored aspects of individual cases—sometimes looking at the working of their particular form of cultural authority, sometimes at their only partial success in reaching a broader audience, sometimes at their command, or lack of it, of certain media or genres. For these purposes, I have deliberately chosen *not* always to dwell on the achievements of those figures who, on almost any definition of the term 'intellectual', might seem to provide the most obvious candidates. Insofar as I discuss particular individuals in any detail, either I have chosen figures who are less celebrated or less highly rated, or I have, with the indisputably famous names (such as T. S. Eliot or George Orwell), concentrated on the surprisingly under-explored question of their attitudes towards the role of the intellectual itself. If I give separate consideration to figures whose roles as intellectuals were in some sense vexed or muted, it is precisely because they thereby illuminate the mechanisms at work more generally.

As I have already suggested, in addressing this topic I am hardly treading on virgin soil; there are many signs that others have passed this way before me. Indeed, it is quite possible that I have now read more articles and essays on the subject of 'intellectuals in Britain' than anyone, alive or dead, has, thus far, ever done. Reading extensively in the literature on any topic, one will, inevitably, encounter a degree of repetition and overlap, but the sheer predictability of so much of the writing in this case is truly awful to behold. In particular, the appetite for such pieces in the broadsheet press and general periodicals appears to be practically insatiable. Intellectuals are to high culture what hem-lines are to *haute couture*: they are, potentially, always news, at least as that commodity is understood by features editors faced with the relentless need to fill their columns. The topic seems to lend itself to eight hundred words of confident opinionatedness with fatal facility. The recent and contemporary prevalence of such pieces in Britain (though not in Britain alone, as I shall illustrate) partly reflects the existential plight of journalism: as print is increasingly challenged by other media as the source of *news*, so the need for columns of more or less readable *opinion* grows; turning out a piece on the theme of 'intellectuals' (especially on their decline or disappearance) might almost seem the would-be columnist's equivalent of passing the driving-test. But in the better exemplars of the genre, this topic can represent an indirect way of meditating on national identity, the intractable task of attempting to sift a distinctive reality out of the historical detritus of image and cliché. And some of this writing surely signals that there is a genuinely important subject here: it is, ultimately, nothing less than the question of whether thought, enquiry, imagination, pursued to the highest level, issue in any wisdom about how we ought to live. Very often, the term 'intellectuals' marks a space in which needs and anxieties are expressed about the relation between the daily round and the ends of life, and about what it might mean, with respect to such matters, for there to be some source of guidance on how to think about them.

IV

The book's overall strategy has seemed to me to call for literary tactics that are varied and discrepant, even at times frankly opportunistic. Some chapters chart usage or analyse concepts; some attend in considerable detail to particular statements or debates; some focus on one individual, some on one medium, some on a given theme over an extended period of time; and there are chapters that look at what might be called a more behavioural form of denial—figures who vaunt the claims of 'speaking out' but do not really seem to do it, or others who are constantly speaking out while denying they have anything to say. And finally, because all such national self-descriptions such as that about the absence or insignificance of intellectuals in Britain are always at least implicitly comparative, there are chapters which ask how this question looks when viewed from a variety of 'elsewheres' in which they do these things differently (or so it is believed). All this makes for a deliberate unevenness of treatment; apart from trusting the reader will come to be persuaded that this is appropriate to the subject matter, I have also divided the book into several clearly separated parts, to try to indicate the rationale behind the major discontinuities in the sequence of chapters. The reader should in addition be warned (or, according to taste, encouraged) that although the book's approach is historical and analytical, it is at times, especially in its closing chapters, more uninhibitedly polemical than may seem quite proper for a piece of scholarly history.

I should, finally, say a few words about scope, sources, selection, and sequence. There are some obvious questions to ask about the book's scope, both geographical and chronological. First, geographical: 'England' or 'Britain'? There is no wholly satisfactory usage here, it seems to me, and that fact itself may be salutary. Once upon a time, historians (and others) confidently said 'England' when they actually meant 'Britain'; once upon a somewhat later time, historians referred, more correctly, to 'Britain', though very often what they had to say did not apply, or applied differently, in Scotland and in Wales. I at first opted, awkwardly but not necessarily more accurately, to write of 'England' throughout: after all, there are real differences in intellectual traditions, social attitudes, educational systems, and so on among the countries that make up 'the United Kingdom of Great Britain and Northern Ireland' (as the relevant political unit has been known since 1922), and where the question of intellectuals is concerned there is a prima facie plausibility to identifying the ideas and values involved as distinctively English. But so to restrict the scope of the book would only offer, I came to acknowledge, a rather artificial purity. For all kinds of intellectual, practical, and political purposes, 'Britain' was the defining entity during this period: the British government made the laws and the British people fought the wars; the British Navy ruled the waves just as the *British* Broadcasting Corporation ruled the airwaves, and so on. (Ireland, always a distinctive culture and for most of this period an independent state, clearly merits, and usually receives, quite separate discussion.) And the inescapable fact is that insofar as there was during this period a shared culture among the constituent elements of Great Britain, as at the level of public intellectual life there clearly was, it was overwhelmingly English in its sources, idioms, and concerns; hard and fast divisions along 'national' lines could not hold. It is for reasons of this sort, no doubt, that 'the question of intellectuals in twentieth-century *Britain*' still sounds more natural to my (middle-aged English) ear, and so where I am speaking of the culture of the familiar political unit or its relevant properties I have used the broader term, even although at other moments I have followed long-established practice and spoken of 'English literature' or 'English irony', as well as of 'English snobbery' or 'English philistinism'. But just as the tradition of 'the lad o'pairts' is quite distinct from the theme of 'the scholarship boy', and just as the meaning of being a 'teacher' was not the same in Swansea as in Surbiton, and just as the need to define, articulate, and preserve a threatened or submerged national identity is experienced by some Welsh and Scottish writers in ways not immediately available to most of the Anglo-English, so one cannot simply assume that the forms in which the question of intellectuals has been posed and answered in what is casually termed (at least by the English) 'British culture' might not be challenged west of Offa's Dyke or north of Hadrian's Wall. I can only hope that, in the light of those challenges, better informed historians will in time supply the necessary correctives.

Second, chronological scope: although I make passing reference to cultural traditions with roots in the nineteenth century or even earlier, this book confines the topic to the twentieth century. There is one very good reason for this limitation: I am only concerned with the question of intellectuals once it emerged as an explicit question, which is to say after the term itself became available, however patchily and unsteadily at first, to conceptualize the issue, and this, as I explain in Ch. 1, only slowly began to be the case after 1900. This restriction does have the incidental advantage of bypassing one of the recurring perplexities of the historian's trade, namely the inevitable tension between two possible vocabularies. The more one tries to confine oneself to terms used by the historical actors themselves, the more one loses a whole range of descriptions and distinctions made available by later terminology; yet if on the other hand one freely deploys such terms, one risks the worst excesses of anachronism and Procrusteanism. By confining my account to the period in which the term 'intellectuals' was used, I hope to have overcome the most damaging consequences of this familiar tension.

The book is based overwhelmingly upon published sources; it is, self-evidently, not a topic that could be addressed principally through use of unpublished material. Articles and essays in periodicals predominate, and I am wholly unapologetic about the extent to which it concentrates on what one scribbler wrote about the writings of other scribblers. Anyone allergic to the necessarily parochial and transient quality of periodical journalism should avoid reading about intellectuals. In some places, I have quoted pretty copiously from writers the exact wording of whose views is crucial, but in general I have made no attempt to document each historical observation with a more or less random sample of quotations. Still less have I felt obliged to cite secondary literature except in case of explicit indebtedness or criticism. I do not imagine that most readers will want any ostentatious assurance about the conscientiousness of my reading.

As I have already allowed, the selection of figures discussed in the book could be seen, from some points of view, as arbitrary or indefensibly idiosyncratic. They have been chosen to be illustrative, and they all, I believe, serve their purpose; further examples could, no doubt, also be found in any given case, but comprehensiveness is not one of my purposes. And although the book is deliberately and persistently revisionist where the accepted clichés of the literature on intellectuals are concerned, it is not an exercise in 'recovery' in the currently fashionable sense. The voices to which it attends were among those most widely heard at the time, and, given my theme, necessarily so. For that reason, few of the figures discussed are women, even fewer were anything but highly educated, most were comparatively successful by conventional standards. I focus on those writings, debates, and episodes through which the dominant understanding of the question of intellectuals in Britain has been most influentially expressed, an understanding that has in turn inflected much of the historiography that is still current on the subject. As a result, I pay proportionately more attention to the pronouncements and careers of a somewhat limited range of established literary and academic figures than any comprehensive history of British intellectuals would be entitled to do, and so I may be thought in some quarters to scant the contribution, even the existence, of various groups defined in terms of their political activism or their provincial location or their working-class origins, and so on. I by no means underestimate the importance of such figures nor their relevance to various other kinds of historical enquiry, but they necessarily play a smaller part in the story I have chosen to tell.

The analytical and argumentative nature of this book has also dictated the following arrangement of the contents. Part One traces the history of the word, its range of meanings, and the structure of the concept informing what has become its dominant, though far from unchallenged, use. Part Two then examines the lineaments of a distinctively British 'tradition of denial', addressing some of the ways in which the question has been addressed across the century, focusing principally on the period after 1945, when, I argue, the claim about the peculiar absence of intellectuals in Britain received its fullest and most explicit formulation. Part Three attempts to set this history in a comparative international framework and to draw out some of the mutual misprisions which have affected the understanding of the place of intellectuals in British and other cultures. Part Four looks in detail at figures whose writings about intellectuals were particularly influential or whose performance, or lack of it, in the role were particularly expressive of the tensions at work in the 'paradoxes of denial'. Adopting a somewhat more experimental mode, Part Five deals with some aspects of recent debate on the topic seen in a series of long historical perspectives; it also reflects, in more polemical vein, on some of the pressures on the role of the intellectual in Britain that are especially marked at the beginning of the twenty-first century.

To conclude this Introduction, we may return to the quotation that serves as its epigraph. 'Is there such a thing as an English intellectual? It is as well to pose the question from the start, since anyone acquainted with the habits and social position of intellectuals on the continent of Europe must have serious doubts as to whether the same word can reasonably be applied to English conditions.' The passage, which comes from a ruminative 'Condition-of-England' survey by Anthony Hartley entitled *A State of England*, published in 1963, offers itself as a useful condensation of what I have called the 'tradition of denial' (and for this reason I return to the book in Ch. 7). However, in so using it, one must not overlook its interrogatory form. The 'question' needs to be 'posed', one may have 'serious doubts' about whether the same word can be 'reasonably' applied, and so on. The author lays claim to a more than average acquaintance with the position of intellectuals in Europe, apparently strengthening the case for answering his own question in the negative. But the question is clearly not just his own: he is invoking a well-established view, while perhaps hinting that it is still worth exploring the answer a little further. I have written this book from a conviction that, since the answers turn out to be so far from straightforward, we need to recognize that it is the *question* itself that is worth exploring further.

PART ONE

THE TERMS OF THE QUESTION

1

The History of a Word

'To the man in the street who, I'm sorry to say,
Is a keen observer of life,
The word *intellectual* suggests right away
A man who's untrue to his wife.'

I

One has, at the outset, to confront a very widespread prejudice. As with most prejudices, this one acts most effectively to shape people's perceptions and responses when they are not wholly aware of it. It is the prejudice that the noun 'intellectual' has a single, relatively clear-cut, referent; that it refers to a type of person who acts in certain specific ways; and that therefore the question of determining whether or not this type of person exists or existed in various societies is, once we clear away misunderstandings about this meaning, a matter of relatively unproblematic empirical investigation. In some respects, this is part of a wider prejudice about the nature of language, namely, the conviction that the meanings of words are given by the existence of those 'things' in the world to which they correspond, and thus that, with any contested term, one can establish 'what the word really means' by stripping away irrelevant or confusing associations until the core referent stands revealed.

This book is not the place to attempt a general consideration of the fallacies embedded in this wider prejudice, but it is important to begin by recognizing that this prejudice is powerfully operative in any discussion of 'intellectuals'. For this is a term with a complex history, and many of the various senses and resonances deposited by that history are still active in the semantic field constituted by contemporary uses of the word. To speak of a 'force-field' of meanings risks being a misleading metaphor, but it does draw attention to the way in which a term exists at the centre of a network of related, and sometimes antagonistically charged, senses. To ask of a series of interlocutors, without any preliminary discussion of the meanings of the term: 'are there intellectuals in all contemporary developed societies?', 'who are the leading intellectuals today?', and 'are you an intellectual?', would inevitably yield far more information about the incidence of different senses and associations of the term than it would about the existence of a certain social role or type of person—indeed, it would probably begin the process of identifying three distinct if overlapping senses corresponding to the three questions. One of the most careful modern accounts of the development of the term concludes that 'the idea of "an intellectual" has remained so fuzzy, ill-defined, and contentious as to be of markedly limited value in the field of cultural history', and this same author goes on to predict that the term will continue

> to be popular, contentious, ill-defined, and used at least as much for praise and abuse as for objective description. In short, 'an intellectual' seems pre-eminently an important category of late-twentieth-century thought that, like the nineteenth-century term 'a gentleman', is more likely to tell us something important about the time in which it was used than about the social phenomenon it was meant to describe.[1]

Although this warning is salutary, and a proper place to begin, the historian cannot rest content merely with charting the evolution of the usage of the word. Since the term has irreversibly entered the common vocabulary even in Britain, one needs to go on to analyse contemporary usage and, on that basis, then make clear the sense or senses in which one is using the term in one's own work. This book does not, after all, simply confine itself to surveying uses of the *term* 'intellectual' in twentieth-century Britain. In discriminating some of the confused or tendentious ways the question of intellectuals has been put and answered, it is inevitably also in part a book about the *concept* of the intellectual and the various aspects of the historical reality during this period which that concept enables us to identify and analyse. My own usage has, therefore, to be situated in relation to the latest stage of the development, the present force-field of meanings which will determine how what I say is understood or misunderstood. This chapter will thus offer a historical account of the evolution of this protean term in English; Ch. 2 will then attempt, first, to discriminate the senses of the term which this development has deposited in contemporary usage, and, second, to analyse the structure of the concept embodied in what has become the dominant usage. Doubtless, no strategy can entirely prevent misunderstanding, but the examples discussed in subsequent chapters will sufficiently indicate the need for some such preliminaries in what has become a highly charged and peculiarly vexed semantic field.

It may, however, be as well briefly to dispose of one foolish but recurrent objection at the outset. One can still occasionally encounter the claim (it is often little more than a cry of pain from an ideological position in distress) that the fact of a foreign word having to be imported demonstrates that the phenomenon referred to has no 'real' existence in British society. As a matter of fact, the implied linguistic history here is simply wrong: even if one believes that the word 'intellectual' came into currency as a response to the use of cognate terms in French and German (a belief which is highly disputable, as we shall see), as a linguistic unit it clearly evolved out of an already established vernacular stock. As a general view about the relation between linguistic development and social reality, the objection is absurd, as even the briefest glance at the development of the vocabulary of modern English would confirm. Neighbouring languages have always been the most fertile sources of linguistic enrichment, and how 'naturalized' or not a particular term seems to be will largely depend upon the moment at which one intercepts the word in its journey from linguistic immigrant to linguistic native. The fact that some of the more fastidious copy-editors still insist that the word 'rôle' wear its circumflex in public can hardly be taken to mean that roles are fundamentally alien to British life. A more immediate comparison with 'intellectual' is provided by the term 'élite', initially italicized and complete with accent in recognition of the importation intact of a foreign word (which in this case seems first to have happened in the early nineteenth century), but then as it becomes domesticated these signs of immigrant status drop away, and it begets children who knew not the old country: in many circles it would now be thought highly elitist to insist on the accent in 'élitist'. The history of the assimilation has an interest of its own, and the earliest stages of it may throw light on some interesting differences in the understanding of social status in the two societies in question. But it would be madness indeed to think that it was somehow inappropriate in the late twentieth century to speak of elites in various quarters of British society. The same, I shall argue, is true of 'intellectuals'.

II

No wholly satisfactory account of the development of the term in English is yet available. The *Oxford English Dictionary*, extraordinary monument and always the first port of call in such circumstances, has in this case failed to record the diversity of usage, and its definitions have not managed to register the complexity illustrated even by its own historical examples. Several modern scholars, notably Peter Allen and T. W. Heyck, have valuably extended the range of such examples as far as the nineteenth century is concerned (and Heyck has more recently made a valiant stab at charting some of the twentieth-century uses), but none of these scholars has, I would argue, come up with an adequate analytical framework which can encompass the variegated history and still unstable contemporary usage of this term.[2] While indebted to these sources, therefore, the following account draws on a broader range of material and attempts a more systematic analysis.

In the course of the nineteenth century, there appeared a variety of linguistic innovations which involved using the established adjective 'intellectual' as a noun.[3] (This development is a common one in English, of course; the evolution of the adjective 'liberal' into a noun provides one particularly well-known instance.) For example, in the early decades of the century one finds the usage 'intellectuals' referring to the faculties of the mind, in particular to their nurture or exercise (as, in an imaginary parallel formation, one might speak of looking after one's 'physicals'). There were also several contiguous usages which clearly trenched on the same field of meaning, as in the slightly ungainly 'intellectualist' to denote someone who particularly cultivated this aspect of life. Among this cluster of linguistic experiments there occurred, in the early and middle decades of the century, the occasional usage of 'intellectuals' as a plural noun to refer, usually with a figurative or ironic intent, to a collection of people who might be identified in terms of their intellectual inclinations or pretensions. These uses had some of the same sense of self-conscious verbal invention or contrivance as might be present in an early twenty-first-century speaker referring to 'the electronicals', meaning perhaps a group of computer enthusiasts or even of leading figures in the electronics industry. One might also compare the similarly experimental frisson evident in the *Pall Mall Gazette*'s reference in 1865 to those engaged in three classes of occupation as 'commercials ... agriculturalists ... industrials'.[4] Inevitably, some of these coinages prosper better than others, and the linguistic history of 'intellectuals' in the nineteenth century is at first a story of false starts comparable to those encountered by 'commercials' and 'industrials'.

The earliest recorded use of the relevant noun in the nineteenth century comes from Byron, reporting in 1813 that various important persons were to be present at an occasion and adding: 'I wish I may be well enough to listen to these intellectuals.'[5] The second example quoted in the *OED* jumps forward to 1884, and consists of the brief and somewhat gnomic phrase: 'the silent person who astonished Coleridge at a dinner of intellectuals'. Interestingly, if one pursues the fuller passage from which this example was taken, one finds it nicely illustrates the slightly arch quality commonly present in this early usage. It comes from A. A. Watts's account of a Mr Joseph Robinson, who

> was a kindhearted and liberal-spirited man, and of a gentlemanlike and handsome exterior. He retained, however, some Yorkshire peculiarities, and was no other than the silent person who astonished Coleridge, at a dinner of intellectuals, by opening his mouth for the first and only time in eulogy of a dish of potatoes with the pregnant utterance, 'Them's the jockies for me.'[6]

One of the earlier examples which presumably escaped the compilers of the dictionary comes from a letter written in May 1852 in which the young Marian Evans described a meeting of leading literary and scholarly persons, and added: 'Mr Chapman read his statement very well and looked distinguished and refined even in that assemblage of intellectuals.'[7] In most of these instances there is a suggestion that the writer intended to exploit a somewhat arch and contrived quality in so using the word, like someone venturing a sly pun or sharing a small private linguistic joke.

There is a little, scattered evidence to suggest that in the closing decades of the century a more stable sense was beginning to assert itself, a sense referring very broadly to someone who cultivated intellectual rather than practical pursuits. The source most commonly cited in recent scholarship to support claims about the growing currency of the noun in the later nineteenth century is P. G. Hamerton's *The Intellectual Life*, published in 1873.[8] However, although the book is full of interest as indicating a heightened self-consciousness about the difficulties and dangers attendant upon the life of the mind, its witness on the matter of terminology seems to me somewhat equivocal. By 'the intellectual life', Hamerton understood a primary devotion to one or more of 'the three intellectual pursuits—literature, science, and the fine arts', each understood in the broadest, or oldest, sense. But the book does not in fact have in mind primarily those who contribute original productions to these fields, so much as those who consume them, those whom he calls 'cultivated persons' or 'men of culture'. In fact, the single or embracing noun which he uses most frequently is 'student', again in the older, broader sense of one who devotes himself to the study or cultivation of one of these branches of learning. And this cultivation may remain a private and inward activity. This emphasis of Hamerton's book comes out in, for example, the chapter (they are each in the form of 'letters' to particular types of individual) entitled 'To the friend of a man of high culture who produced nothing': 'When we lament that a man of culture has "done nothing", as we say, we mean that he has not written books. Is it necessary, is it desirable that every cultivated person should write books? On the contrary, it seems that a more perfect intellectual life may be attained by the silent student than by authors,' and so on.[9]

The significance of Hamerton's terminology has to be gauged in relation to the character of his book. The young man desirous of becoming a 'cultivated person' is the implied addressee, particularly, it sometimes seems, one beset by anxieties about what to eat and how much exercise to take (there is more than a hint of the 'Dear Doctor' or 'agony aunt' column about much of the advice). And it is explicitly addressed to *men*: women appear only in the pleasantly distracting form of wives, for he lays it down that 'with exceptions so rare as to be practically of no importance ... women do not of themselves undertake intellectual labour'.[10] Indeed at times, the book verges on a series of recipes for creating a whole cadre of pub bores ('One of the best ways of interesting and instructing your intellectual inferiors is to give them an account of your travels'), and the tone of the hectoring housemaster is never far away ('Be sure that there has been great moral strength in all who have come to intellectual greatness'). It is as part of this idiom that he sometimes refers to 'intellectual man', sometimes to 'intellectual workers', sometimes to one of a variety of similar constructions to denote those who cultivate the mental and imaginative powers rather than the animal or practical. And just occasionally, when speaking of this type, he uses, somewhat experimentally, the noun 'intellectual': 'In drinking as in eating, the best rule for the intellectual is moderation in quantity with good quality, a sound wine, and not enough of it to foster self-delusion.' Or again: 'It is to this sublime persistence of the intellectual in other ages that the world owes the treasures which they won.'[11] It seems probable that, while his use of the term was, in context, perfectly intelligible to contemporary readers, Hamerton's book neither reflected an established usage nor constituted any very compelling recommendation to adopt it.

Something similar might be said of the isolated example provided by Mark Pattison, the great champion of the somewhat new-fangled and decidedly Germanic notion of 'research' in mid-Victorian Oxford, who observed (somewhat opaquely): 'It is the business of the intellectual to make statements about the things that concern him.'[12] And in 1886 Beatrice Potter (later to be Beatrice Webb) experimented with the term in this sense after she met the Liberal politician and author John Morley, describing him to her diary as 'an intellectual, loving the "order of thought" not the "order of things"'.[13] But Peter Allen surely oversimplifies when he concludes that 'in fact the modern usage [of "intellectual"] is merely a special application of a well-established nineteenth-century idea'.[14] Apart from the fact that 'ideas' and 'usage' need to be distinguished, the available evidence suggests three conclusions here, although it has to be said that the *OED* alerts us to none of them: first, this usage retained its slightly arch or experimental air right up to the closing decades of the century, not yet having become an accepted part of the linguistic furniture to be used unselfconsciously; second, the usage was not particularly widespread; and third, this usage was later largely displaced by the more familiar modern senses. This last point is particularly important: it illustrates a common feature of the development of language whereby, in a kind of Darwinian struggle, neighbouring or overlapping usages which become successfully established drive out some of the more experimental senses that had not yet really gained a hold.

Beyond this, I would suggest that it is clear from the disparate evidence available that the confluence of references in English in the early twentieth century to the French *intellectuels* and to the Russian *intelligentzia* was decisive for the formation of the semantic field within which later uses of 'intellectual' are found, and hence for the subsequent implication that the term referred to an exotic species.

In French as in English there had been nineteenth-century experiments with forming a noun from the adjective *intellectuel*, and in the course of the 1890s the term started to appear with some frequency in descriptions of the bookish and highly educated.[15] Writers such as Paul Bourget and Maurice Barrès used it largely in disparaging ways, but it was the now little-known essayist and novelist Henry Bérenger who 'more explicitly and more frequently than anyone else ... described as intellectuals the overly cerebral young men of the *fin-de-siècle*, and by 1897 he adopted the term to designate educated men who enter politics'.[16] However, the decisive moment for the modern senses came on 1 February 1898. On 13 January Zola had published his famous open letter 'J'Accuse', in which he indicted the military authorities for suppressing evidence and perverting the course of justice in their subsequent investigation of the conviction of

Captain Dreyfus that had taken place four years earlier. The next day, the radical newspaper *l'Aurore* published a short text, entitled 'Une Protestation', endorsing Zola's charges. It was signed by some 1,200 writers, scholars, teachers, and other university graduates, whose names were grouped by their qualifications—'Agrégés de l'Université', 'Licenciés ès lettres', and so on. Georges Clémenceau, in an editorial comment, then referred to this as 'la protestation des Intellectuels', though attention was really focused on the term by the article in *le Journal* for 1 February by the vehemently conservative and patriotic man of letters, Maurice Barrès, who mocked this parade of qualifications and its implied bid for authority, sardonically entitling his own article 'La protestation des intellectuels'. The original was thereafter commonly referred to as 'le manifeste des intellectuels', although it had not, strictly speaking, been a 'manifesto', and its own signatories had not referred to themselves as 'intellectuals'. But the connection established on this occasion between the parade of qualifications and the political intervention was crucial to the subsequent career of the term. As Christophe Charle observes, in the most authoritative recent account, what was new about the Dreyfus manifesto was 'the use that was made there of professional titles or qualifications outside their normal social context, as an argument from authority against another authority, judicial or political'. Although various continuities have subsequently been identified between 'les intellectuels' as baptized during the Dreyfus Affair and their Enlightenment and Romantic predecessors, Charle insists that the role designated by the new term was a response 'to a radically new social and political conjuncture', involving a structural change in the place of the intellectual elite in French society.[17]

Initially, therefore, the term entered common currency in France carrying a freight of mocking and pejorative associations, but, as so often in such cases, those to whom the term was applied came in time to claim it proudly as a self-description. Accordingly, before 1914 usage tended, like so much else in France, to divide along political lines: right-wing polemicists sneered at 'soi-disant intellectuels', while Left-wing commentators deliberately gloried in the attempt to uphold 'les droits de l'homme au nom de l'universel'. The conclusion of the most authoritative scholarship on the topic is that it was in the 1920s that the term came to be used in self-description by those on the right, and that it was in the 1930s that the term passed from these earlier restricted or tendentious uses to becoming 'a widely accepted label'.[18] Given the constant contrast subsequently made in Britain with the supposedly more favourable associations of the term 'intellectuals' in France, it may be worth underlining that the hostility so often associated with English usage was present at the birth of the term in French and has remained available as a potential force of the term ever since.[19]

It was through references to the Dreyfus Affair that the term 'intellectuals' in its plural form seems to have acquired any general currency in English, though it was still usually garlanded with quotation marks to signal its alien origins and to indicate that it was not easy to point to either an existing term or a corresponding reality in Britain (this aspect of British responses to the Affair is discussed more fully in Ch. 3 below). For example, the *Contemporary Review*, commenting on the divisions in French opinion crystallized by the Affair, noted: 'It is the fashion to call the party who are now triumphing—though with sorrow—the "Intellectuals". But whom does this title cover? It cannot be given to all who practise liberal professions.' The last sentence here may represent a somewhat despairing stab at finding an English equivalent, but the author went on to acknowledge that the term did not apply so widely in France either: doctors and lawyers, for example, were notably anti-Dreyfusard on the whole (a line of analysis which indicated that the term was confined to its original Dreyfusard bearers at this point). The core of the category turned out to be restricted to certain sections of the university, those 'who are practised in rigorous methods of study. . . . They have all been Revisionists [i.e. challenging the verdict on Dreyfus], whether they were philosophers, historians, philologists, chemists, or physiologists.'[20] There was no suggestion that such a range of figures would have been described as 'intellectuals' in Britain.

While the French usage clearly came to affect the twentieth-century history of a term which had already known an intermittent, faltering existence in English, the other influential foreign import, 'intelligentsia' (usually spelled thus), could be grafted onto no existing native stock. In its original form, the Russian term has generally been thought to have had a quite specific social referent: 'The Russian *intelligent* was an educated person characterized by an independent position toward the masses or the imperial court.'[21] However, the most thorough scholarly discussion of the topic in English observes that 'none of the definitions given during the past sixty years or so has been found entirely satisfactory, and recent research has clearly shown the vagueness of the term, its many ambiguities, and the strains between the outlook and self-image of those who used it and the social and intellectual reality it is supposed to represent'.[22] Whatever the complexities this points to, in the early twentieth century in Western Europe it was assumed that the Russian term *did* identify a sociologically distinct group who, by virtue of an education that set them apart from an almost wholly illiterate society, were committed to being critical of political and religious authority. Translations from Russian into English in the early twentieth century, especially in the literature of socialism, used 'intelligentsia' to refer to such a social stratum, but once the term was released into the playground of English usage, it came to be used to refer, most often with mocking or dismissive force, to the cultural elite generally (sometimes equated with the 'scribbling' or, more recently, the 'chattering' classes). As we shall see when considering the term's appearances in successive editions of the *OED*, some of the resonances of the original specific sense have continued to cling to the more diffuse and sarcastic usages.

It is hard to know what, if anything, that self-styled 'countryman' Stanley Baldwin had in mind in remarking that 'intelligentsia' was 'a very ugly word for a very ugly thing', but he was obviously confident that, on this as on other matters, most of his compatriots would instinctively agree with him.[23] And A. D. Lindsay—Master of Balliol, Idealist philosopher, a leading Socialist intellectual—clearly had something pretty unpleasant in mind when, in extolling the virtues of Kurt Hahn's new cold-baths-and-cross-country-runs regime at Gordonstoun, he declared: 'It is like the Boy Scout movement, only for adolescents. If we adopted it we might save the universities from producing an intelligentsia.'[24] (There was, of course, a long-standing English view that vigorous outdoor exercise was the best prophylactic against contracting such typically 'Continental' conditions.) But in cultivated circles the term could also be used more neutrally, usually just as the plural for 'intellectual'. A reviewer in 1916, for example, wrote: 'Men of science must realise that unless they take in hand for themselves this work of educating and interesting the intelligentsia it will not be done.'[25] And Virginia Woolf was, by implication, including herself and her friends in the category when she referred, however sardonically, to having met some of her Sussex neighbours: 'I don't think the intelligentzia [*sic*] need fear, either on earth or in heaven, the competition of these simple natures.'[26] By 1965, Sir Ernest Gowers could suggest, not altogether persuasively, that it was 'now an outmoded word with its leftist colouring washed out of it'.[27] In fact, the word continues to be widely used, though it is possibly true that its earlier 'leftist colouring' is much faded. The implication that members of a 'true' intelligentsia are necessarily alienated from and critical of their society remains available for exploitation, but the term is now more frequently used without any such implication. Strictly speaking, the now common phrase 'a dissident intelligentsia' would have been a pleonasm had the term retained its original referent, but the frequent occurrence of this phrase is another indication that the term has largely floated free of its early historical specificity.

It is interesting to note that there was, at the end of the nineteenth century, no equivalent in French for the Russian term *intelligentzia* or the German *Intelligenz* (and translators into French tended to proceed by specifying the range of occupations the foreign terms embraced). As Charle observes: the intelligentsia comprised 'a thin layer of the politico-cultural avant garde, that one finds in France among the the first "intellectuals", but which is nearer to bohemia and to political militants than to fin-de-siècle academics well-placed in society'. ['Une mince couche d'avant garde politico-culturelle, qu'on retrouve en France parmi les premiers "intellectuels" mais qui est plus proche de la bohème et des militants politiques que de nos universitaires fin de siècle bien assis dans la société'.][28] This not only indicates the divergence between the semantic fields of the two terms in French, but it throws an interesting light on commonly accepted contrasts between the situation of intellectuals in Britain and France: whatever other differences there may have been, such contrasts can clearly *not* be founded on the powerful presence in Britain and absence in France of 'universitaires bien assis dans la société'.

Partly as an effect of English-language discussion of French *intellectuels* and the Russian *intelligentzia*, many of the uses of the malleable term 'intellectuals' in the opening decades of the twentieth century displayed two related features. The first was that the plural form came to have both a historical and, it could be said, a semantic priority over the singular; the group identity was defining. And the second was that 'intellectuals' were associated with 'intervention' in politics, especially on behalf of a radical or even revolutionary cause. These, it must again be emphasized, were not the only senses available, and they have not wholly determined the dominant modern usages, but they have lastingly affected the semantic field within which those usages operate.

Another foreign import that subtly affected the semantic field of 'intellectual' was the introduction of the American term 'highbrow' in the 1920s.[29] The term was most famously used by the critic and publicist Van Wyck Brooks in his *America's Coming of Age*, first published in 1915, where he spoke of American culture being disastrously divided between the 'lowbrows'—essentially the philistine business ethos—and the 'highbrows', those who were overly refined and pretentious precisely because excluded from the shaping processes of the national life.[30] This term arrived too late to earn a place in the original edition of the *OED*, but 'highbrow' was defined in the 1933 *Supplement* as: 'A person of superior intellectual attainments or interests; always with derisive implication of conscious superiority to ordinary human standards.' This idea of taking oneself to be 'superior' to others, of affectation or pretension, also remained the informing element in the chief negative use of 'an intellectual'. When this emphasis was to the fore, as it frequently was in the middle decades of the century, 'an intellectual' indicated someone distinguished by a particular form of pretentiousness or self-importance, someone who habitually affects what is felt to be an inappropriately abstract or complex vocabulary or who appears to assert an unjustifiable intellectual superiority. This negative connotation has remained potent ever since.

III

Picking up the chronological thread at the end of the nineteenth century, it is evident that English ears (or at least English eyes) were not wholly unaccustomed to the use of the plural term 'intellectuals' by that date, and thus the noun earned its place in the *New English Dictionary* (the original official title of what has become known more familiarly as the *OED*) when that work began to be published by Oxford University Press from the 1880s onwards. Only one sense was distinguished, and the noun, singular, was defined as 'An intellectual being; a person possessing or supposed to possess superior powers of intellect.' This more or less reflects the occasional pre-1900 usage mentioned above, and the history of the compilation of the dictionary reveals that the relevant fascicle was first published in October 1900, James Murray having completed work on it somewhat earlier.[31] It was, as will by now be clear, a singularly unlucky time to be trying to arrive at an enduring definition of this particular term. It was also unfortunate that later editions of the dictionary retained this as the term's definition even as the additional illustrative quotations began to indicate a greater variety of usage. Moreover, the dictionary's practice of giving brief phrases as examples means that it is vulnerable to the danger of misunderstanding or misrepresenting the resonance of a term in its original setting.

There is a striking example of this in the dictionary's illustrations for 'intellectual' which has, I believe, never been remarked. The fourth and final quotation given under this entry, immediately following that involving our taciturn potato-eating friend mentioned earlier, runs in its entirety: 'Proceeding to refer to the so-called intellectuals of Constantinople, who were engaged in discussion while the Turks were taking possession of the city.' The source is given as *The Daily News* for 30 November 1898. We are not told who, in this incomplete sentence, is doing the referring: was this really just a reference to a group of 'intellectual beings', and if so why are they only 'so-called', and by whom? It is also difficult to understand quite how this could have featured in a news item in 1898, the Turks having 'taken possession of the city' some centuries earlier. These obscurities, one would have thought, might have set some alarm-bells ringing. If one tracks down the original passage in *The Daily News*, one finds that it was in fact reporting a speech given at a dinner in Paris on the previous day by General Auguste Mercier, one of Dreyfus's earliest accusers. This might have raised a further anxiety as to whether the report was simply a literal attempt at translation rather than an example of current English. Trawling through the literature on the Dreyfus Affair, I eventually discovered the original of General Mercier's remarks: 'At the moment when the Turkish army forced the ramparts of Constantinople, the so-called intellectuals of the capital of the Lower Empire were debating theological quibbles. We, too, are undergoing our acute paroxysm of intellectual Byzantinism.' ['Au moment où l'armée turque forçait les remparts de Constantinople, les soi-disant intellectuels de la capitale du Bas-Empire y discutaient sur les arguties théologiques. Nous subissons, nous aussi, notre crise aiguë de byzantisme intellectuel.'][32] The phrase was, of course, a direct jibe at the Dreyfusards, the 'soi-disant intellectuels', who are being accused of prattling idly at a time of grave national danger ('self-styled', rather than 'so-called', may better capture the intended scorn). Constantinople was merely a metaphor: the 'so-called intellectuals' were in fact gathered on the left bank of the Seine. Two weeks later, one of them, Julien Benda, responded by publishing the first of his pro-Dreyfus articles under the title 'Notes d'un Byzantin'.[33]

Once it had appeared in its English form in the *OED*, however, this quotation proceeded to take on a life of its own, as successive commentators reached for their copy of the dictionary as the first move in answering the parlour-game question 'What is an intellectual?' Thus, writing in the *Fortnightly Review* in April 1949, R. D. Charques cited the passage as the 'earliest illustration' of the 'irony or equivocation that belongs to the modern meaning of the term', and went on: 'Clearly, the date of that remark is significant, as significant as its undertone of derision. 1898 marks the distance of a generation from the passing of the Education Act of 1870. We had then, for the first time in our [*sc.* British] history, an entire generation' who had been educated, and so on.[34] An elaborate historical theory of the development of British society begins to be surmised, all, alas, on the basis of a newspaper report of an ironic remark made in French about France.

Interestingly the first edition of the dictionary contained no entry for the term 'intelligentsia', though if one searches under 'intelligent' one finds, as a noun under sense B, 1 ('a person of intelligence') an illustrative quotation from *The Athenaeum* in 1892 that should have been recognized as an attempt to translate the Russian term '*Intelligent*' (and hence be pronounced with a hard 'g', not the soft 'g' indicated in the phonetic gloss at the head of the entry): 'Karpov and Garin . . . depict to us the self-conscious troubles and failures of our "intelligents" in search of rest for their souls.' The term 'intelligentsia' itself is first given in the 1933 *Supplement*, acknowledging the Russian and German derivation and giving the following definition: 'The class of society to which culture, superior intelligence, and advanced political views are attributed.' The conjunction of qualities is interesting here: it seems to rule out, for example, the use of the term to refer to a stratum holding conservative or reactionary political views. Five illustrative quotations are given from the years 1914 to 1924, in which the alien or imported character of the term is usually reflected by being italicized or capitalized, and in which there was frequently some derisive reference to political disaffection ('He told me . . . that he belonged to the Intelligentsia and that he was out to shoot capitalists,' a quotation from 1922 attributed to Mrs Sidgwick). Interestingly, the third edition of the *Concise OED*, first published in 1944, repeated the relevant definition from the full dictionary for 'intellectual', but introduced further slight variation in its definition of 'intelligentsia': 'The class consisting of the educated portion of the population and regarded as capable of forming public opinion.' This registered a move away from the politically radical connotations of the Russian original towards using the term simply as the plural of 'intellectual'. The 1987 *Supplement* then further modified the definition to read: 'The part of a nation, orig. in pre-revolutionary Russia, that aspires to intellectual activity; the class of society regarded as possessing culture and political initiative.' The semi-colon functions as a rather feeble adhesive here, attempting to bind two somewhat different usages together (and 'political *initiative*' seems encompassingly lax). Several new illustrations were added, the earliest from 1907, clearly emphasizing the Russian associations (for example, a reference to the fear that 'there will be a general massacre of the educated bourgeoisie, the so-called "Intelligentsia"'). However, it is not clear that all the later illustrations represent this same sense: one from 1949, referring to the attitudes of Balkan peasants, instances such village worthies as the mayor, the priest, and the doctor as constituting the 'intelligentsia'. This was a common European usage, as translators of Gramsci were to find, but it is not obvious that village mayors and doctors and suchlike tended to provoke the term in English except in a heavily ironic sense.

In passing one may also note, among other works of reference, that when the Fowler brothers produced their standard-setting *The King's English* in 1906, they discussed those neologisms 'which come into existence as the crystallization of a political tendency or movement in ideas'. One such example was 'intellectuals':

> 'Intellectuals' is still apologized for in 1905 by *The Spectator* as 'a convenient neologism'. It is already familiar to all who give any time to observing continental politics, though the index to the *Encyclopaedia* (1903) knows it not. A use has not yet been found for the word in home politics, as far as we have observed; but the fact that intellect in any country is recognized as a definite political factor is noteworthy; and we should hail 'intellectuals' as a good omen for the progress of the world.[35]

Here we may note, first, that this early usage is in the plural, and, second, that the context is political, suggesting the importing of the term from France in the wake of the Dreyfus Affair of a few years earlier. At the same time, the final sentence expresses a curiously pious form of Edwardian optimism, markedly at odds with what was to become the more familiar attitude on these matters of aggressively hard-headed 'realism'. As it turned out, the earliest edition of the *Encyclopaedia Britannica* to acknowledge the term in any form was the eleventh, published in 1910–11, which, as part of the article on 'intellect', contained the following observation: 'A man is described as "intellectual" generally because he is occupied with theory and principles rather than with practice, often with the further implication that his theories are concerned mainly with abstract matters; he is aloof from the world, and especially is a man of training and culture who cares little for the ordinary pleasures of sense.'[36] Although this appears to be offered as a gloss on the adjective, it is clearly meant to be recording a relatively new usage, and uses of the noun in the first two decades of the century commonly reflected this core meaning.

Works of linguistic reference continued to register (some of) these complexities of meaning and social attitude. Discussing 'intellectual' as an adjective, the first edition of Fowler's *Modern English Usage* in 1926 observed: 'An intellectual person is one in whom the part played by the mind as distinguished from the emotions and perceptions is greater than in the average man. . . . "Intelligent" is usually a patronizing epithet, while "intellectual" is a respectful one, seldom untinged with suspicion or dislike.' Revising this entry for the new edition in 1965, Gowers modified this comparison to end:

> 'Intelligent' is always a commendatory though sometimes a patronising epithet; 'intellectual', though implying the possession of qualities we should all like to have, is tainted in the communist ideology by its use in disparaging contrast to 'workers'; elsewhere too it is seldom untinged by suspicion or dislike—called by a leader-writer in the *TLS* 'a rather fly-blown word beloved only of sociologists'.[37]

The quoted phrase may be seen as a neat example of English literary journalism's perennial tendency to kill two birds with one sneer, and that tone is maintained in Gowers's further observation that the sense of 'intellectual' is 'not unlike the definition given by the *OED* Supplement of the colloquial equivalent "highbrow" (US "egghead")' (i.e. the definition quoted below at Ch. 5 Sect. I). This was underlined by the entry for the term in Raymond Williams's (admittedly highly impressionistic) survey *Keywords*, published in 1976, which concluded that up to at least the middle of the twentieth century 'unfavourable uses of "intellectuals" . . . were dominant in English, and it is clear that such uses persist'.[38]

IV

Where recent and contemporary usage is concerned, dictionaries have a near-impossible task: it is like trying to discriminate faces from a series of snapshots taken of a group of very similar-looking actors at various stages of the make-up process. The *OED* and similar reference works have to serve as a starting-point, partly just because there is no more authoritative survey available, but they do smooth out and simplify what has been a complex linguistic history. For there continued to be considerable instability in the connotations of the noun 'intellectual' in the early decades of the twentieth century. Uses which reflected the influence of the imported terms discussed above coexisted with two overlapping but slightly different, and in some ways older, senses. In the first, the term was used to indicate an individual's subjective interest in or commitment to ideas and the life of the mind generally. This tended to assume a certain level of education, but it was not a sociological term, as is indicated by, for example, the lower-middle class character in George Bernard Shaw's 1910 play *Misalliance* who says: 'Oh, don't think, because I am only a clerk that I am not one of the intellectuals. I'm a reading man, a thinking man.'[39] In the second, it was used to refer to a member of the educated class, especially to scholars, writers, and others directly involved in 'intellectual' activities. A notable instance of this usage was occasioned by the notorious manifesto of October 1914, signed by ninety-three leading German professors, repudiating Allied charges of atrocities and affirming their complete support for the German war effort. This was sometimes referred to as 'The Manifesto of the German Professors', but it was also frequently termed 'The Manifesto of the Intellectuals of Germany'.[40] This latter title may have influenced Bertrand Russell's vocabulary when in 1915 he called his protest against literary and scholarly figures lending their authority to nationalist propaganda 'An appeal to the intellectuals of Europe'. In fact, the noun itself appears only once in the text of Russell's pamphlet, when he casually refers to 'philosophers, professors, and intellectuals generally'; more often he speaks of 'scholars' or 'men of learning', and sometimes of 'literary men'. It is the ideal of disinterested enquiry that Russell argues is being betrayed, and it is to the defence of this ideal that he calls 'the intellectual leaders of Europe'.[41] Over the course of several decades, these two senses interacted with the newer or imported uses to produce several subtly different shades of meaning, and since, as I remarked earlier, there is still a widespread prejudice that a word always has a clear and stable meaning, it may be helpful simply to illustrate a little of the variety of this usage.

In the first decade of the century the noun continued to display a self-consciously experimental air, as in the following two examples. Reporting on an address to the student Liberal club ('the Palmerston') at Oxford in 1900 by the 'pro-Boer' Liberal politician, John Morley, *The Contemporary Review* professed to be shocked that criticisms of Sir Alfred Milner were received with 'applause from the "Intellectuals" of the Palmerston (I owe this synonym for the undergraduate to a glowing report in our pro-Boer press . . .)'[42] It seems likely that such currency as the term enjoyed at this date would have involved a rather knowing allusion to the French usage, an echo which for many English ears would only have added to its disparaging force. The second example, however, suggests the experiment was being tried in the opposite spirit. *The Academy*, reviewing the fourth issue of the self-consciously iconoclastic *English Review* in 1909, observed: 'Politically considered, the *English Review* appears to be very mild indeed, though dangerous, in the sense that it is tainted with Socialism . . . . The *English Review* has already and most palpably cast its lot in with a group of authors and journalists who delight, we believe, in being known generally as "intellectuals".' This group stood accused of having 'introduced into journalism and into letters the principle of party'. (The idea that in 1909 anyone could be thought to be doing anything either new or untoward by 'introducing into journalism . . . the spirit of party' is rich indeed.) *The Academy* went on to use 'intellectuals' several times in the next few lines, with evident relish—'There can be no doubt that its [*sc.* the *English Review*'s] sympathies are with the "intellectuals" and that the methods we have indicated are the methods of the "intellectuals".'[43] Both novelty and distaste are suggested by the way this curious verbal specimen is held up for inspection, though the writers represented as so laughably cloth-eared were presumably engaged in the age-old manœuvre of attempting to appropriate a largely negative epithet as a positive self-description.[44]

By the 1910s, the word appeared to be becoming almost fashionable, especially as a way of singling out those of a self-consciously bookish or theoretical disposition. In his 1909 novel *Ann Veronica*, H. G. Wells had the heroine's sister exhort her not to become 'one of those unsexed intellectuals, neither man nor woman' (not a fate that Ann Veronica or any of Wells's other heroines ever seem in any great danger of).[45] The symbolism of the clash between the Schlegels and Wilcoxes of the world was to become a staple theme of English culture, so it is hardly surprising to find Henry Wilcox himself lecturing Margaret and Helen on how 'you intellectuals' are different from 'we practical fellows'.[46] Virginia Woolf, ur-Schlegel in more than one sense, drew upon the same antithesis when, criticizing a third-rate novel in 1918, she observed: 'the conventions of the intellectual are at least as sterile as the conventions of the bourgeois'; and in a diary entry for 1922 she reworked this contrast as a piece of self-description: 'I was struck by the bloodlessness of the philistines the other day at the Rectory [in the Sussex village where the Woolfs had their country cottage]. They seem far less alive than we intellectuals.'[47] Others used it somewhat less evaluatively in referring to those engaged in the life of the mind. For example, in a review in *The Nation* in 1916 of Arthur Clutton-Brock's *The Ultimate Belief*, the reviewer wrote:

> Different men draw widely different lessons from the war. Many, witnessing the complete collapse of Christianity after an experiment of nineteen centuries, call either for a new or no religion. Not a few of our intellectuals, seeing the fruits of philosophy in Germany, a land of philosophers, would cut down this tree of knowledge, leaving bare the place on which it grew.

And the same review later continued: '[Mr Clutton Brock] is primarily concerned with schools and school-teaching, for he rightly observes that a philosophy which can only be acquired by abstruse and complicated ratiocination, carried on by a few middle-aged intellectuals, will not do what is wanted for the common art of life.'[48] In both cases, the reference here seems to be to those who are primarily or even professionally concerned with abstract ideas. The sequence of sentences in the first passage implies that although 'men' in general are likely to express convictions about the role of religion, conclusions about the value of philosophy tend to be the province of 'intellectuals'. In the second passage, the usual suggestion that intellectuals are removed from the ordinary business of life is present, or at least that they are unrepresentative of ordinary human experience, though in this case the possible negative implications of this characteristic are not insisted upon.

As I have indicated, one important dimension of meaning present from quite early uses of the term was the suggestion that 'intellectuals' were those who applied inappropriately abstract or cerebral criteria rather than either accepting traditional standards or recognizing the power of common human passions. For example, E. B. Osborn, writing in 1919 of the work of the popular dramatist Harold Chapin, who had been killed in the war: 'Thus he avoids the fatal mistake of the stern "intellectuals" who would revitalise our drama, but have so far failed because they take too dismal a view of life. Yes, he might have become a dramatic Dickens, if the German bullet had spared him.' Or, writing of Charles Lister in the same book: 'A wider knowledge of men and affairs convinced him of the truth of Jowett's saying, that human beings are not governed by logic, and it was not long before he parted company with the "intellectuals" who think that human nature can be argued into a state of blessedness . . . he never lost his keen and blissful liking for his fellow-creatures,' and so on.[49] In both cases, the excessive emphasis placed on ideas or merely abstract reasoning is held to be the characteristic defect of this self-important category of people. It is noticeable that these and other examples from the 1910s in which the term is decorously draped in a garland of quotation marks all have the air of deliberately referring to a neologism that was enjoying a certain vogue.

A similar self-consciousness was evident in uses that were neutral or even positive in tone. For example, Douglas Goldring in 1917 prefaced his novel with the remark: 'I have tried to give a straightforward account of the spiritual adventures of an average "intellectual" in the first years of the war, and to show how the minds of persons of his age and temperament have become, almost invariably, a battle-ground for opposing influences and conflicting ideals.'[50] The referent here seems to be simply a person of bookish or thinking disposition. A similar usage appears in a discussion by J. H. E. Crees in the following year of the characters in Meredith's novels: 'We associate the intellectual with the town, especially the great town, we naturally assign him a place in some great library or museum into which the hurricane and the frost, the sunshine and the flowers never enter, a place where the atmosphere is deoxygenated or of artificial purity,' whereas in Meredith's novels we 'find that our intellectuals live in "civilised arcadias" ' in the country.[51] The suggestion of remoteness is, of course, present here, but the term appears to indicate more respect than hostility. John Middleton Murry, always a good barometer of literary fashion, was happy to adopt the term in the title essay of his 1920 collection *The Evolution of an Intellectual*.[52] Here, as in most of the examples so far quoted from this decade, there seems to be no implication at all of a public or political role.

In the early decades of the century, a rather different usage of the plural seems to have become fairly common, at least in Socialist circles, to designate a social stratum or class. The class-analysis that was part of the legacy of European Marxism played an important part here, drawing attention to that stratum of 'brain-workers' who helped to furnish the proletariat with ideas and leadership. 'Intellectuals' became one common translation of the German word *Intelligenz*, the educated class who were to be distinguished from both the capitalists and the workers. R. H. Tawney's *The Acquisitive Society*, for example, contained a whole chapter on 'The position of the brain worker', and he urged that in 'the functional society' the obligation of public service would be felt by all those engaged in industry, not just by 'a small *élite* of intellectuals, managers, or "bosses" '.[53] A similar sense, though here leaning more towards a group of exceptionally articulate leaders, is evident in Beatrice Webb's 1918 diary entry: 'The one outstanding virtue of the Labour Party, a virtue which is its very own, not imposed upon it by its intellectuals, is its high sense of international morality.'[54] In American English, in particular, this usage, with its strong German and central-European Socialist derivation, appears to have established itself in immigrant circles in the decade before 1914.[55] The development of the social sciences (again, more marked in the United States than in Britain) encouraged the generalization of this usage in social analysis: for instance, the original *International Encyclopaedia of the Social Sciences* of 1930 contained a long entry on 'intellectuals' by Robert Michels which was largely concerned with questions of the political mobilization of the educated class. The association with Socialism no doubt also encouraged that anyway powerful tendency in British attitudes which assumed that 'doctrinaire' (again, the foreign word for the foreign thing) positions in politics were exclusively the property of the Left. This assumption is present even in the anxiety expressed by the Assistant Director of the Conservative Research Department in 1935: 'I have been told by those in close touch with political movements at the universities today, that our cause is greatly handicapped by the fact that the average undergraduate who is interested in politics has nowhere to turn today but to the *New Statesman* or to the books of the left-wing Socialist intellectuals.'[56] In domestic political debate, 'Left-wing intellectuals' had a familiar cadence to it, while 'Right-wing intellectuals' was only later to emerge from the ghetto of Marxist usage.

But this is to anticipate. For, during the first couple of decades of the century, these various usages not only coexisted, but in each case they retained an air of experimenting with or alluding to a linguistic exotic. The conclusion to a thorough examination of American usage of 'intellectuals' in this period coincides with my more impressionistic survey of uses in Britain: 'During its first twenty years in America from 1898 to 1918, it never won the credentials of full naturalization. Of our sample of thirty-five users, at least two-thirds either placed the word between quotation marks, or prefaced it by 'so-called', or capitalized it in a derogatory fashion.'[57] The negative associations were expressed more pithily by the Socialist writer Mike Gold in 1927, looking back to the milieu of the 'Wobblies' (International Workers of the World) in the 1910s: 'In the IWW the fellow-workers would tar and feather (almost) any intellectual who appeared among them. The word "intellectual" became a synonym for the word "bastard".'[58]

V

These several senses and associations of the noun 'intellectual' could be observed vying for a place in the sun of standard usage deep into the twentieth century, and a heavy escort of inverted commas would often continue to accompany the term on its public appearances. But this slightly fastidious acknowledgement of its *arriviste* status could go along with widely differing understandings of its meaning. For example, in 1926, J. A. Hobson published an examination, surely influenced by Veblen, of the constraints on independent thought, especially as they operated within the modern university. Having indicted professors for their 'class sympathies and reverences' he noted:

> The 'intellectual' is terribly sensitive to the approval and disapproval of rulers and other authorities in the outside world. His strong personal sympathies are engaged in keeping the good opinion of successful practical men. The knowledge that he and his fellows and the intellectual life they conduct are not directly productive of economic values, and are in this sense 'parasitic' on the practical life, feeds the sentiment of deference.[59]

Here, the word suggests those who pursue rather abstruse or specialized intellectual pursuits, as the contrast with 'practical men' in 'the outside world' makes clear, and the general burden of Hobson's charge is that such figures do not 'speak out' on larger political and social matters.

When a few years later E. L. Woodward was recalling his time as a student at Oxford just before the First World War, he also found the now increasingly familiar neologism useful, but understood it in a rather different way. Remarking the lack of concern with the international situation among his generation of undergraduates—'no one bothered much about anything after the battle of Waterloo'—he observed: 'In these years . . . the chief interests of those who would now be described as "intellectuals" were either in social questions or in religion. There was not much interest in foreign affairs.'[60] Though holding the term at arm's length, Woodward presumably found it helpful in identifying a category which might not have been so identified at the time, and the suggestion that this category was made up of those who occupied themselves with larger intellectual and social interests beyond the sphere of their specialized studies. Thus, the kinds of activity which, in Woodward's usage, were constitutive of the category, were, in Hobson's usage, precisely those which intellectuals conspicuously failed to engage in.

The 1930s witnessed a marked increase in the use of 'intellectuals' in English, in part because in that decade issues thrown up by the political life of continental Europe played such a powerful role in structuring domestic political divisions and much of the associated vocabulary was imported as a consequence. As Stephen Spender later put it: 'If a small but vociferous and talented minority of what were called the "intellectuals" (this was the decade in which this term began to be widely used or abused) were almost hypnotically aware of the Nazi nightmare, the majority of people . . . seemed determined to ignore or deny it.'[61] Increasingly, the term's most obvious referent was provided by those writers (poets above all) who publicly espoused a political position; it came to be used readily and relatively unselfconsciously by those young Left-wing writers eager to proclaim their devotion to the cause of 'the proletariat'. Michael Roberts, for example, in introducing an anthology of work by such writers, spoke freely of 'we, the intellectuals and white-collar workers', complained that under the present social system 'the intellectual is turned to a pettifogging squabbler in Bloomsbury drawing-rooms or a recluse "in country houses at the end of drives" ', and announced that 'it is essential that intellectuals should become part of the community, not servants of the financial machine'.[62] John Lehmann, organizer-in-chief of the Left-leaning writers of the 1930s, was unapologetic, writing in a later autobiographical retrospect, about the positions he and his friends had taken up in that decade. He recalled that the outbreak of the war had certainly not invalidated them: 'Our general position, we still felt, had been right: poets, and other creative artists, cannot, if they are to remain fully living people, if they are to fulfil their function as interpreters of their time to their own generation, fail to interest themselves in the meaning behind political ideas and political power.' But he conceded that some of their particular political choices now looked questionable, and certainly that these had earned them a good deal of hostility:

> The intellectuals of the 'thirties were by no means popular at that time [*sc.* 1939–40] with Members of Parliament, influential Civil Servants and Generals in authority. For some obscure reason we were held by many of these—or so it often seemed to us—to be responsible for the mess the country had got itself into, though in fact, of course, all our miserable efforts had been directed towards preventing the mess.[63]

Perceptions of the 1930s intellectuals as literary Bourbons who had learned nothing and forgotten nothing continued for some time to feed a dismissive scorn towards the political *naïveté* and unrealism of the type in general, as well as nourishing the recurrent charge of lack of patriotism.

In some ways, the very preoccupation with political developments in continental Europe made the perpetuation of the 'foreign' connotations of the term even easier, as in Orwell's gibes against those English intellectuals who 'take their cookery from Paris and their opinions from Moscow'.[64] Orwell's remark, and indeed his sustained campaign against the mixture of pretension, dishonesty, and lack of patriotism which he claimed characterized the English 'left-wing intelligentsia', points to the continuing difficulty experienced by those who wished to represent their identity as unproblematically combining the positive features of being both English and an intellectual. Orwell was referring particularly to writers—the 'Auden gang' were his chief target—and subsequent accounts of intellectuals in the 1930s nearly always refer, explicitly or implicitly, to a rather small number of poets and novelists. C. P. Snow was later to complain about how the term 'intellectuals' had come to refer to literary but not to scientific figures, and he quoted the mathematician G. H. Hardy saying to him in the 1930s: 'Have you noticed how the word "intellectual" is used nowadays? There seems to be a new definition which certainly doesn't include Rutherford or Eddington or Dirac or Adrian or me.'[65] Hardy's implicit exasperation with the level of attention accorded a few young poets is understandable, though it would have been interesting to know what he thought the 'old' definition had been. This principally literary connotation was long-lived: it seems, for example, to hover over a remark about the decline in the belief in progress made in 1964 by J. H. Plumb (coincidentally, or not, a close friend of Snow's since the 1930s): 'Although by the middle of the nineteenth century the idea was . . . still held by historians such as Buckle who are no longer fashionable and by many political scientists and sociologists, from Tylor to Spencer, its acceptance by intellectuals, however, became increasingly hesitant.'[66]

Labels and categories are more often applied to others than to ourselves, and this has been markedly true of 'intellectuals'. As Alan Pryce-Jones, for many years editor of the *TLS*, breezily began an article in 1949: 'Nobody likes being called an intellectual.'[67] When, late in her life, Virginia Woolf was once again trying to take the measure of her father and of her distance from him, she observed that 'he was the very type, or mould, of so many Cambridge intellectuals'. She, of course, had reason to mark her own exclusion from this group, as she memorably recorded in *A Room of One's Own*. But to others, Virginia Woolf and her circle epitomized the type: it was in such terms that Ottoline Morrell, touchily sensitive to that circle's condescension, sought to account for 'certain limitations' in a woman who otherwise so much attracted her: 'I think it is living always amongst intellectuals.'[68] By the 1930s the label was used with particular frequency to denote any slightly suspect group, such as 'Bloomsbury', who were thought to be self-consciously rationalist, progressive, and emancipated. For example, Basil Willey, Wordsworthian and Christian moralist as well as Cambridge don, was clearly not including himself when, retrospectively, he spoke of the 1930s (when he had himself been in his thirties) as 'a time when Marxism was greatly in vogue amongst intellectuals', nor when he registered his satisfaction at the way the Nazi–Soviet pact of 1939 threatened to 'put a stop to most of this dilettante Marxism amongst the intellectuals'.[69]

Something similar is at work in the affectionate terms in which John Betjeman, already heavily invested in *not* being rationalist and progressive, tried to explain to his friend, the economist Roy Harrod, the differences in their attitudes towards religion:

> I feel this will shock you, you dear Liberal intellectual old thing. And for every book you can produce which disproves the existence of the spirit, I can produce one which proves it. It boils down to the alternative, materialist or Christian. For intellectuals the materialist standpoint is the obvious one and the easiest. The second is harder, but I hold that it is the most satisfactory, especially when one comes up against injustice, birth and death. But there is no argument. The intellectual is too proud to surrender to this seemingly ridiculous story when viewed from the outside.[70]

'Intellectuals' here picks out a subjective attitude rather than a social group or political role. Intellectuals are represented almost as the prisoners of their own commitment to analytical reasoning; it blinds them to the more intuitive or emotional truths which those not so imprisoned are able to experience in other ways. It is the old charge: the clearly clever risk being merely clever. And on this view of the world, the clever were rarely exemplars of conventional virtue, either. Auden, who knew about being clever and about popular attitudes to it (even if he was not much given to being conventionally virtuous), caught this association in the verse used as the epigraph to this chapter:

> To the man in the street who, I'm sorry to say,
> Is a keen observer of life,
> The word *intellectual* suggests right away
> A man who's untrue to his wife.[71]

The ironic edge to the label remained deeply ingrained, even if not always for the reason Auden suggested. An editorial commentary in *Encounter* in 1955 alluded to this tradition of use when it asked: 'What is it about the English language that gives to the word "intellectual" an ever so fine, an ever so indelible, ironic complexion?'[72] And as late as 1968, T. R. Fyvel noted that it 'is a term that still is not used easily in English discussion about England, except when used with irony in a special English way.'[73] Thirty years later, Sir Peter Hall evidently (if perhaps erroneously) believed that not much had changed when he announced in a 1999 interview: 'I don't want my children to be fed on a diet of dumbed-down international television. We still live in a country where "intellectual" is a pejorative term, and "artist" is suspect.'[74]

However, linguistic change operates at several levels at once. It was particularly during the 1930s that the vocabulary of the nascent social sciences was beginning to have an impact on the idiom of the wider society, and 'intellectuals' was an especially favoured category in the German or (largely German-inspired) American social theory so influential at that time. A notable example of the purely classificatory sense of the term was provided by the translation into English in 1936 of Karl Mannheim's *Ideologie und Utopie*, first published in German in 1929. That social stratum whose business it was to develop and disseminate ideas was at the heart of Mannheim's book (as of his work more generally), and he took for granted that past as well as present societies contained such a group. 'In every society there are social groups whose special task it is to provide an interpretation of the world for that society. We call these the "intelligentsia".' Mannheim does not at this point linger on questions of definition, but it immediately becomes clear that this is effectively just the plural or categorial form of 'intellectuals'. For example, on the next page he speaks of how, in the transition from a medieval to a modern society, 'in the place of a closed and thoroughly organized stratum of intellectuals, a free intelligentsia has arisen.... The intellectual is now no longer, as formerly, a member of a caste or rank ...' and so on. At the same time, Mannheim's usage makes clear that he is referring to a group defined by their primary occupational activity, not by either their political 'intervention' or their affectation of a superior attitude. When, for example, he remarks: 'It is the merit of Max Weber to have clearly shown in his sociology of religion how often the same religion is variously experienced by peasants, artisans, merchants, nobles, and intellectuals,' the term is clearly being used in a neutral, classificatory sense.[75] After 1945, this usage, allowing for all kinds of niceties of definition and a great variety of empirical inclusions and exclusions, became quite standard in the burgeoning social scientific literature, much of it American in origin. The efflorescence of a style of social analysis inspired by the New Left in the 1960s and early 1970s (to which I shall return in later chapters) gave a greater currency to this sense of the term in self-consciously 'radical' circles, whence it was transmitted to a still broader public largely through the rapidly expanding system of higher education.

But, as I have already said, any individual use of such a term may, wittingly or not, draw upon other senses and resonances still active in the language.

For example, in giving a public lecture in 1949, Mannheim's erstwhile colleague at the LSE, R. H. Tawney, warmed to one of his most cherished themes: the need for large, simple truths to be stated in large, simple terms. His topics on this occasion were History and Literature, and at one point he observed with mild sarcasm: 'Both offer ample opportunities for finished exhibitions of the great art of complicating the simple and obscuring the obvious by which the authentic intellectual proves his title to that proud name. I observe these gymnastics with admiration and awe; but a consciousness that the stratosphere is not my spiritual home deters me from imitating them.'[76] This is the classic topos of scorn disguised as false humility, the characteristically English backhanded compliment to one's own down-to-earth style; the sardonic use of 'intellectual' is here readily available for the purpose of disparaging such heady abstractions, and it allows a sense of complacent collusion between Tawney and his listeners.

It is clear that from the middle of the century onwards, these various senses of the term coexisted, the resonances or associations of one sense sometimes colouring the response to the term used in one of the other senses, without the users necessarily being aware of it. And on occasion a given writer could use the word in two different senses without any risk of being misunderstood. A revealing example of this is provided by two essays by F. R. Leavis which were written within the space of three years. In 1958, in one of his several indictments of the later career of T. S. Eliot for having betrayed the poetic talent which Leavis had earlier so much admired, he identified Eliot's regression to 'conventionality' as part of the problem, and then went on to relate this to the fact that 'Eliot is too much of an intellectual.'[77] This could mean that Eliot emphasized pure intellection at the expense of that kind of fusion of thought and feeling that Leavis regarded as the writer's highest form of 'sincerity'. But it could also mean that Eliot was too prone to pick up fashionable ideas, too concerned, perhaps, with striking a public posture rather than seeking to identify and express his own deepest responses to experience. In the paragraph as a whole, there is the related suggestion that Eliot was too cosmopolitan, too little rooted in England. Leavis notoriously insisted on the closest connection between such 'rootedness' and the capacity to experience 'life' in its greatest richness, and the sentences surrounding the remark about Eliot as an 'intellectual' contribute to the sense that there is something simultaneously shallow and un-English about such a role.

But Leavis was drawing upon a different shade of the term's meaning when, in his essay on the Lady Chatterley case, published in 1961, he argued that Mellors, the gamekeeper in Lawrence's novel, is not really 'working-class', as journalistic comment surrounding the trial always assumed: 'He is not only educated, he is an intellectual—we are told of the impressive array of books he has on his shelf.' This is the subjective sense: Mellors is, in the old university slang Leavis liked to quote elsewhere, 'a reading man'. There is, after all, clearly no question of Mellors's political activity or his cultural authority with a wider public. But later in the same essay the capacity of the protean term to support a sneer is seen in the remark that 'in the world of the enlightened and among the intellectuals of the universities and the literary world' the idea of marriage has been forgotten.[78] In the 1960s and 1970s Leavis frequently used 'enlightened' in this sardonic way, and he is happy enough here to trade upon the negative resonances of 'intellectuals' as those who assume a conscious superiority to ordinary people's convictions about right and wrong. Language, it seems, has ways of asserting its power even over its self-appointed guardians.

VI

It was only in the closing decades of the twentieth century that the term 'intellectuals' began to move about freely in (British) English usage without requiring introductions, bodyguards, or identity papers. This fact, a social fact of considerable interest in itself, by no means implies that the term now bears a single unambiguous sense: it remains true, as I have already insisted, that the layers of meaning and association deposited by the earlier evolution of the word are still available in certain contexts. But any attempt to chart usage would have to record not just an enormously increased frequency, but also a very marked preponderance of uses which refer to leading cultural figures, creators of ideas and shapers of opinion. The following examples are not meant to be significant in themselves: they make my point precisely on account of their *un*remarkableness, their now accepted place in the everyday vocabulary of hurried journalism.

When the press reported that before the 1997 election Tony Blair had held a private meeting with '80 intellectuals and business men' (two separate categories one assumes, though it's hard to be sure these days), it was headlined 'Blair urges intellectuals to add weight to new Labour'. The full list of those attending was not disclosed, but the report in the *Guardian* mentioned 'Stuart Hall, Anthony Barnett, John Gray, Geoff Mulgan, Andrew Adonis, and Vernon Bogdanor', all fairly prominent social and political commentators, well enough known to merit being referred to by name.[79] Similarly, when Andrew Marr commented on Blair's efforts to recruit support among leading thinkers and opinion-formers, he, too, spoke of intellectuals in the same way, in this case alleging that, with a few notable exceptions (Berlin, Hobsbawm), the great names had disappeared (Keynes, Hayek, and Gellner were mentioned). After the usual ironic journalistic flim-flam about intellectuals ('the pebble glasses, the cigar smoke, and the grave acts of immorality'), Marr quoted and endorsed Peter Hennessy's claim: 'the real purpose of intellectuals in a society is to hold up evidence and truth to those in power, to provide the inconvenient analysis to those who want the swift and meretricious solution'. Marr described this as an 'unromantic' view of intellectuals, though in fact it is surely the opposite.[80] Certain prominent journalists themselves may also attract the label, especially if they write books or are otherwise associated with general ideas. For example, a profile of Polly Toynbee remarked her increased status in the mid-1990s after having been 'dismissed as an archetypal feminist intellectual during the Thatcher years'.[81]

Less tendentious examples of the way in which this sense of the term has become familiar and unexceptionable were provided by the spate of journalistic tributes which greeted the news of the death of Isaiah Berlin in November 1997. 'Isaiah Berlin, prince of intellectuals, dies aged 88' proclaimed one front-page headline, where he was described as 'the most honoured and deeply admired intellectual of his time', while the same paper's obituary began by referring to him as 'the most famous English academic intellectual of the postwar era', and similar descriptions appeared in other papers.[82] Those whose idiom was formed in an earlier generation, however, remained less confident about the word. In an obituary of Anthony Hartley by his friend and one-time colleague Richard Mayne (b. 1926), Hartley was described as belonging to a group of British journalists who wrote serious works on a wide variety of subjects: 'they were the nearest equivalent to those who, in continental Europe, would be called, unblushingly, "intellectuals"'.[83] The page editor was less given to blushing: the heading to the obituary simply described Hartley as 'writer, editor and intellectual'.

These examples are, self-evidently, drawn from a particular level of comment, and indeed from particular newspapers, whose readerships have particular socio-economic profiles, political inclinations, and so on. The term may be met with less frequently, or encountered only in its derisive form, in, say, *The Daily Telegraph*, and less often still in the tabloid press. But the use of the greater part of the vocabulary of English, or any language, is stratified in this way; the point is simply that the term 'intellectual', and most often one particular meaning of that term, has now taken its place alongside the thousands of other words which are regarded as part of 'ordinary usage' even though they may, for the most part, be used regularly by only a minority of the population.

Two final, highly contrasting, illustrations of dominant usage may, appropriately enough, be taken from instances where claims about the absence or disappearance of 'genuine' intellectuals are at issue. First, for an anecdotal indication of the continuing power of the *belief* that in English, uniquely, the term carries negative associations, one may turn to the diary of that abnormally acute recorder of English speech, Alan Bennett:

> Colin Haycraft [a leading independent publisher] and I are chatting on the pavement when a man comes past wheeling a basket of shopping. 'Out of the way, you so-called intellectuals', he snarls, 'blocking the fucking way'. It's curious that it's the intellectual that annoys, though it must never be admitted to be the genuine article but always 'pseudo' or 'so-called'. It is, of course, only in England that 'intellectual' is an insult anyway.[84]

This last observation is in fact untrue: 'intellectual' is not inherently pejorative in contemporary English, and, conversely, most other languages seem more than capable of deploying the term insultingly, as anyone who has heard a French worker cursing a 'putain d'intello' can confirm. Indeed, it is often certain intellectuals who seem to have most at stake in insisting on the negative force of the term in Britain, thus indirectly glorying in their own heroic defiance of such accumulated prejudice. In this particular instance, it has to be said, Bennett's concluding remark may tell us less about actual usage than about an enduring feature of English self-understanding, a cultural tradition which I shall deal with at greater length in later chapters.

My second example is taken from that recurrent genre, the announcement of 'the death of the intellectual'. It is hard, reading this genre, not to be reminded of Mark Twain's celebrated retort to reports of his death, the more so since these jeremiads are usually launched by those who clearly consider themselves to be auditioning for the vacant role. This particular obituary was posted in the journal *Prospect* in October 1997, when Michael Ignatieff declared that 'the death of the intellectual has left a void in public life'. It was the disappearance, as he saw it, of the 'independent intellectual' that Ignatieff lamented, leaving only 'worthy professors, cultural bureaucrats, carnival barkers and entertainers' (the genre has ancient rights to a certain hyperbole). The body of the article makes clear that he is using the term to refer to those outstanding figures who developed ideas and formed opinion—at one point, for example, Beveridge, Orwell, Tawney, Keynes, Russell, and Berlin are hailed as having 'created the ideas which made liberal social democracy possible'. Like most self-interested users of the term, Ignatieff tries to build a preferred position into its very meaning, as when he laments that 'many intellectuals are sacrificing the intellectuals' historical function of defending the universal against the violence and closure associated with the tribal, national, and ethnic' (it may be pertinent to remark that Ignatieff had recently published a book warning of the dangers of nationalism and ethnicity in just these terms). As so often in romanticizations of the absent intellectual, Jean-Paul Sartre figures as the ideal, though special commendation is, also as usual, reserved for Orwell's supposed independence and outspokenness. But despite the tendentiousness of these polemics, the prevailing sense of the term appealed to is clearly that of the leading cultural figure, the creator of ideas and the shaper of opinion.[85] Whatever the merits of the claim that in Britain this *species* either never existed or is now extinct, there can be no doubt that at the beginning of the twenty-first century the *term* itself is alive and well and living in the English language.

NOTES

1. Peter Allen, 'The meanings of "an intellectual": nineteenth- and twentieth-century usage', *University of Toronto Quarterly*, 55 (1986), 351, 355.
2. Allen, 'Meanings of "an intellectual"'; T. W. Heyck, *The Transformation of Intellectual Life in Victorian England* (Beckenham: Croom Helm, 1982), esp. 11–17, 234–8; Heyck, 'Myths and meanings of intellectuals in twentieth-century British national identity', *Journal of British Studies*, 37 (1998), 192–221. There is a very brief, but

not very helpful, entry in Raymond Williams, *Keywords: A Vocabulary of Culture and Society* (London: Fontana, 1976).

3. It is important to attend to the differences between the noun and the adjectival usage: for example, Heyck's claim that the noun became common in the 1870s and 1880s is not supported by his own examples, which are of 'intellectual' used as an adjective, in such phrases as 'the intellectual life'; Heyck, *The Transformation of Intellectual Life*, esp. 221–39.
4. *Pall Mall Gazette*, 16 Aug. 1865; quoted in *OED*, 'industrial', B. sb. 1.
5. Cited in the *OED*: 'intellectuals', B. 4. i. Bizarrely, Anthony Phelan says the *OED* gives several examples of the relevant use of the noun *before* Byron's remark of 1813, though it is clearly the first instance cited; Anthony Phelan (ed.), *The Weimar Dilemma: Intellectuals in the Weimar Republic* (Manchester: Manchester University Press, 1985), 9.
6. A. A. Watts, *Alaric Watts: a Narration of his Life* (London, 1884), i. 124; cited in Allen, 'Meanings of "an intellectual"', 345–6.
7. Quoted in Gordon Haight, *George Eliot, A Biography* (Oxford: Oxford University Press, 1978 [1st edn., 1968]), 110.
8. P. G. Hamerton, *The Intellectual Life* (London: Macmillan, 1873); see e.g. the use made of the book in Heyck, *Transformation of English Intellectual Life*, 'Conclusion'.
9. Hamerton, *Intellectual Life*, 44, 358.
10. Ibid. 243.
11. Ibid. 354, 18, 52–3.
12. This sentence is quoted in Christopher Kent, *Brains and Numbers: Elitism, Comtism, and Democracy in Mid-Victorian England* (Toronto: University of Toronto Press, 1978), 65 n., citing Mark Pattison, *Essays*, ii. 415, though I have been unable to trace the quotation in this source.
13. Norman MacKenzie (ed.), *The Diary of Beatrice Webb*, 4 vols. (Cambridge, Mass: 1982–5), i, *1873–1892*, 164.
14. Allen, 'Meanings of "an intellectual"', 346.
15. See Venita Datta, *Birth of a National Icon: The Literary Avant-Garde and the Origins of the Intellectual in France* (Albany: State University of New York Press, 1999), esp. ch. 3.
16. William M. Johnston, 'The origin of the term "intellectuals" in French novels and essays of the 1890s', *Journal of European Studies*, 4 (1974), 53.
17. Christophe Charle, *Naissance des "intellectuels" 1880–1900* (Paris: Minuit, 1990), 143, 229 (all translations from the French are my own unless otherwise indicated). See the further discussion in Ch. 11 below.
18. Jean-François Sirinelli, *Intellectuels et passions françaises: Manifestes et pétitions au XXe siècle* (Paris: Fayard, 1990), 68.
19. For examples of hostile uses of the term in French, see Ch. 11.
20. K.V.T., 'The Dreyfus case: a study of French opinion', *Contemporary Review*, 74 (1898), 603, 605.
21. Nicholas V. Riasanovsky, 'Notes on the emergence and nature of the Russian intelligentsia', in Theofanis George Stavron (ed.), *Art and Culture in Nineteenth-Century Russia* (Bloomington, 1983), 3–4; reference in Sheldon Rothblatt, 'George Eliot as a type of European intellectual', *History of European Ideas*, 7 (1986), 50.
22. Michael Confino, 'On intellectuals and intellectual traditions in eighteenth- and nineteenth-century Russia', *Daedalus*, 27 (Spring, 1972), 117–49.

23. Quoted in Brian Harrison, 'Mrs Thatcher and the intellectuals', *Twentieth-Century British History*, 5 (1994), 207.
24. A. D. Lindsay, letter of 1942, quoted in Drusilla Scott, *A.D. Lindsay, A Biography* (Oxford: Blackwell, 1971), 265. See the further discussion of Lindsay in Ch. 20, below.
25. C. D., 'Science and the public', *New Statesman* (15 July 1916), 348.
26. Virginia Woolf, diary entry, 17 Aug. 1920; quoted in Hermione Lee, *Virginia Woolf* (London: Vintage, 1997 [1st edn., 1996]), 432.
27. H. W. Fowler, *A Dictionary of Modern English Usage* (Oxford, 1926), 278; 2nd edn., revised by Sir Ernest Gowers (Oxford, 1965), 290.
28. Charle, *Naissance des "intellectuels"*, 228.
29. This development is discussed more fully in Ch. 5.
30. See Henry May, *The End of American Innocence: A Study of the First Years of Our Own Time 1912–1917* (New York: Columbia University Press, 1992 [1st edn. 1959]), 322–5.
31. See 'Historical Introduction' to the *OED*; see also K. M. Elisabeth Murray, *Caught in the Web of Words: James Murray and the Oxford English Dictionary* (Oxford: Oxford University Press, 1979 [1st edn. 1977]), 281. Heyck, a little casually, dates the *OED* as a whole to 1888, but work on the various volumes was in fact spread over many years (Heyck, *Transformation of Intellectual Life*, 236; this citation, along with many others, is repeated in Heyck's 1998 article, 'Myths and meanings', 205).
32. Quoted in Johnston, 'Origins of "intellectuals"', 43–4.
33. Julien Benda, 'Notes d'un Byzantin', *La Revue blanche* (15 Dec. 1898), 611–17.
34. R. D. Charques, 'The intellectual in politics', *Fortnightly*, 165 (Apr. 1949), 255.
35. H. W. Fowler and F. G. Fowler, *The King's English* (Oxford: Oxford University Press, 1906 [2nd edn. 1919]), 22. The reference appears to be to the 10th edn. of *The Encyclopaedia Britannica*.
36. *Encyclopaedia Britannica*, 11th edn. (Edinburgh: Black, 1910), xiv. 680. Heyck also cites this entry, but he begins the quotation at 'occupied with ...' (having substituted 'person' for 'man') and says this is offered as a definition of 'intellectual' as a noun ('Myths and meanings', 204).
37. *Modern English Usage* (1965 edn.), 289.
38. Williams, *Keywords*, 142.
39. Quoted in Allen, 'Uses', 349.
40. See Stuart Wallace, *War and the Image of Germany: British Academics 1914–1918* (Edinburgh: Donald, 1988), 33–5. The manifesto was reprinted under the latter title in W. W. Coole and M. F. Potter (eds.), *Thus Spake Germany* (London: Routledge, 1941).
41. Bertrand Russell, 'An appeal to the intellectuals of Europe', repr. in his *Justice in War-Time* (London: National Labour Press, 1915), 1, 2, 4, 15–16.
42. F. Edmund Garrett, 'Sir Alfred Milner and his work', *Contemporary Review*, 78 (1900), 153.
43. [Anon], 'Life and letters', *The Academy*, 76 (6 Mar. 1909), 844.
44. Some of the writers in question receive more attention in Ch. 4.
45. H. G. Wells, *Ann Veronica* (London: Fisher, 1909), 99.
46. E. M. Forster, *Howards End* (Harmondsworth: Penguin, 1967 [1st pub. 1910]), 146.

47. Virginia Woolf, review of Gilbert Cannan's *Mummery*, *TLS*, 19 Dec. 1918; repr. in Andrew McNeillie (ed.), *The Essays of Virginia Woolf*, 3 vols. (London: Chatto, 1986–8), ii. *1912–1918*, 345; Anne Olivier Bell (ed.), *The Diary of Virginia Woolf*, 5 vols. (Harmondsworth: Penguin, 1977–84), ii. *1920–1924*, 205 (cited in Heyck, 'Myths and meanings', 206).
48. [Anon] 'Philosophy for the Million', *Nation* (22 July 1916), 495–6.
49. E. B. Osborn, *The New Elizabethans: a First Selection of the Lives of Young Men who have Fallen in the Great War* (London: Bodley Head, 1919), 14, 28–9. I owe this and the preceding reference to my former graduate student, Dr Peter White.
50. From the dedication to Douglas Goldring's novel, *The Fortune*, quoted in Gerald Gould's review, *New Statesman*, 27 Oct. 1917, 89–90.
51. J. H. E. Crees, *George Meredith: A Study of His Works and Personality* (Oxford: Blackwell, 1918), 98–9.
52. John Middleton Murry, *The Evolution of an Intellectual* (London: Cobden-Sanderson, 1920).
53. R. H. Tawney, *The Acquisitive Society* (London: Bell, 1921), 160–1.
54. Beatrice Webb, diary entry, 12 Dec. 1918; quoted in Peter Clarke, *Liberals and Social Democrats* (Cambridge: Cambridge University Press, 1978), 201.
55. See the examples quoted, largely from American Socialist sources, in Lewis S. Feuer, 'The political linguistics of "intellectuals" 1898–1918', *Survey*, 1 (1971), 156–83.
56. J. Ball to Stanley Baldwin, 6 Dec. 1935, Baldwin papers; I owe this reference to Clarisse Berthezène. For further instances of this assumption, see her article 'Creating Conservative Fabians: the Conservative Party, political education, and the founding of Ashridge College, 1929–1931', *Past and Present*, forthcoming 2005.
57. Feuer, 'Political linguistics of "intellectuals"', 182.
58. Mike Gold, 'John Reed and the real thing' [1927], in *Mike Gold: A Literary Anthology* (New York: International, 1972), 153; I owe this reference to Jonathan Sanders.
59. J. A. Hobson, *Free Thought in the Social Sciences* (London: Allen & Unwin, 1926), 53–4.
60. E. L. Woodward, *Short Journey* (1942), quoted in Wallace, *War and the Image of Germany*, 12.
61. Stephen Spender, *The Thirties and After* (London: Macmillan, 1978), 22.
62. Michael Roberts (ed.), *New Country* (London: Hogarth, 1933), 13, 12, 15.
63. John Lehmann, *I Am My Brother: Autobiography II* (London: Longmans, 1960), 27, 30–1.
64. George Orwell, 'The Lion and the Unicorn' (1941), in Peter Davison (ed.), *The Complete Works of George Orwell*, 20 vols. (London: Secker, 1998), xii. 406. Orwell's attitudes to intellectuals are discussed more fully in Ch. 15.
65. C. P. Snow, *The Two Cultures*, ed. Stefan Collini (Cambridge: Cambridge University Press, 1993 [1st edn. 1959]), 4.
66. J. H. Plumb (ed.), *Crisis in the Humanities* (Harmondsworth: Penguin, 1964), 35.
67. Alan Pryce-Jones, 'Intellectuals at sea', *World Review*, 14 (Dec. 1949), 25.
68. Both quotations from Hermione Lee, *Virginia Woolf* (London: Vintage, 1997 [1st edn. 1996]), 69, 576 (Lee's system of references does not allow us to identify the exact date of Woolf's comment; Ottoline Morrell's dates from 1930 or 1932).
69. Basil Willey, *Cambridge and Other Memories 1920–1953* (London: Chatto, 1968), 65–6.

70. John Betjeman to Roy Harrod, 25 March 1939, in Candida Lycett Green (ed.), *John Betjeman: Letters*, i. *1926–1951* (London: Methuen, 1994), 223–5; quoted in Julia Stapleton, 'Cultural conservatism and the public intellectual in Britain, 1930–70', in *The European Legacy*, 5 (2000), 805.
71. W. H. Auden, 'Shorts', *Collected Shorter Poems 1927–1957* (London: Faber, 1966), 190.
72. *Encounter*, 4 (1955), pp. iv, 2.
73. T. R. Fyvel, *Intellectuals Today: Problems in a Changing Society* (London: Chatto, 1968), 15.
74. Sir Peter Hall, quoted in *The Observer*, 28 Mar. 1999, 32.
75. Karl Mannheim, *Ideology and Utopia* (London: Routledge, 1960 [1st edn., 1936]), 9–10, 7.
76. R. H. Tawney, 'Social history and literature', in *The Radical Tradition: Twelve Essays on Politics, Education, and Literature*, ed. Rita Hinden (London: Allen & Unwin, 1964), 184.
77. F. R. Leavis, 'T. S. Eliot as a critic' (1958), repr. in *'Anna Karenina' and Other Essays* (London: Chatto, 1967), 194.
78. F. R. Leavis, 'The orthodoxy of enlightenment' (1961), *'Anna Karenina'*, 238, 241.
79. *Guardian*, 7 Mar. 1996, 2.
80. Andrew Marr, 'Who will fill the intellectual vacuum?', *Independent*, 30 Apr. 1996, 12.
81. 'Weekend birthdays', *Guardian*, 27 Dec. 1997, 18.
82. John Ezard, 'Isaiah Berlin, prince of intellectuals, dies aged 88'; Bernard Crick, 'Obituary: Sir Isaiah Berlin', *Guardian*, 7 Nov. 1997, 1, 20.
83. Richard Mayne, 'Anthony Hartley', *Guardian*, 29 May 2000, 15 (see the discussion of Hartley in Ch. 7).
84. Alan Bennett, 'Diary' (13 May 1987), in *Writing Home* (London: Faber, 1994), 157.
85. Michael Ignatieff, 'Where are they now?', *Prospect* (Oct 1997), 4; a longer version of this article appeared as 'The decline and fall of the public intellectual', *Queen's Quarterly*, 104 (1997), 395–403.

2

A Matter of Definition

> 'We can avoid ineptness or emptiness in our assertions only by presenting the model as what it is, as an object of comparison—as, so to speak, a measuring-rod; not as a preconceived idea to which reality *must* correspond.'

I

There would, as I have already indicated, be little point in trying to legislate about *the* meaning of a term with such a complex history. The literature on intellectuals has been plagued with stipulative definitions which for the most part merely reflect their authors' own sense of what is important or desirable. Alongside the common derogatory uses, there has also been a marked tendency to use the term as an honorific or as a prestigious label, and since many of those who have written about intellectuals are, on some showing or other, candidates for being so described themselves, they are all too likely to build idealized or self-flattering features into their proposed definitions. It may help to avoid these pitfalls if we begin by distinguishing two enterprises that are all too often unwittingly run together.

In the first part of this chapter I shall confine myself to attempting to distinguish senses of the *word*. This is essentially an empirical matter: one records actual usages, however confused or contradictory they may appear on closer scrutiny, and one devises the most economical taxonomy of senses which will account for this variety of usage. In the second part of this chapter I shall then offer an analysis of what I consider to be involved in the *concept* of the intellectual that is represented by one of these senses, the one which seems to me most significant for contemporary discussion. Any such analysis or 'unpacking' of a concept is necessarily selective and contestable: although I naturally intend my account to be recognizable to all users of English and to be likely to persuade them that certain assumptions are implied in the relatively unreflective use of the term in this sense, I recognize that my analysis highlights certain features of the role of the intellectual at the expense of others and is bound, to that extent, to seem to be laying claim to a certain normative force. To put the distinction between the two parts of the chapter in other terms: it would be an absurd and doomed enterprise to hope, by stipulative definition, single-handedly to alter such a large-scale and largely unconscious *social fact* as linguistic usage; I do, however, aspire to alter how we *think* about the role that one form of that usage refers to.

On the basis of various lexicographical surveys, works of other scholars, and my own research for this book, some of which I quoted in the previous chapter, it seems fairly clear that there are now three main senses of the noun 'intellectual' commonly used in English.

The first, which is the most abstract or merely classificatory of the three, may for convenience be called 'the sociological sense'. Here, 'intellectuals' are defined as a socio-professional category within a comprehensive classification of types of occupation. It is assumed that in advanced societies this will be a substantial proportion of the working population, perhaps running, in the largest countries, into millions. The category tries to discriminate those whose occupations involve a *primary* involvement with ideas or culture from those whose orientation and purpose are more directly practical: thus, it will tend to include, say, journalists and teachers, just as it will tend to exclude, say, businessmen as well as manual workers. Attempts to agree upon the limits of the range of occupations to be included under this label have not been very successful—not all sociologists want to use the term to apply to medical researchers or television producers, musicians or dancers, social workers or psychotherapists, and so on—nor has any one attempt to define the term itself met with general endorsement. One of the most frequently cited has been that of the American social scientist, Seymour Martin Lipset: 'all those who create, distribute, and apply *culture*—the symbolic world of man, including art, science, and religion'. But in practice this has come to seem too broad to be helpful. All kinds of occupational groups could be said to be involved in 'distributing and applying culture', but classifying librarians and cameramen, let alone paperboys and tee-shirt designers, as 'intellectuals' might seem to strain against acceptable usage. (Lipset's own gloss on his definition threatened to be disablingly encompassing, since it included not only 'those who distribute what others create', but also 'those who apply culture as part of their jobs—professionals such as physicians and lawyers.'[1]) Nonetheless, some variant of this sense has been extensively used in the (predominantly American) social scientific literature in English, and certain kinds of contemporary academic writing, again predominantly American, continue to treat this as the primary meaning of the term. This sociological sense is pretty clearly *not* the one involved in laments about the 'absence' or 'death' of the intellectual: after all, intellectuals in the sociological sense have never been more evident and it is universally assumed that this social category will only become more numerous still in the future.

The second main sense may be called 'the subjective sense'. This obviously denotes a different type of category, since it focuses upon an individual's attitude to and degree of interest in ideas as measured against an implicit standard of reflectiveness and intellectual seriousness, where it emphasizes a particular commitment to truth-seeking, rumination, analysis, argument, often pursued as ends in themselves. This is the sense usually at work in judgements that a particular individual of one's acquaintance is 'a real intellectual', where there is often an implied contrast with those who may share the same occupational involvement with intellectual matters, but whose want of the right subjective attitudes and purposes excludes them. Membership of the category of 'intellectuals' in the subjective sense cannot, therefore, be read off from any other classification of occupations, social types, cultural roles, and so on, though it would usually be assumed that individuals with this temperamental inclination would find certain kinds of occupation more congenial than others. This is principally a conversational and evaluative sense, though it does also occur in ostensibly analytical or historical accounts. We surely see a version of it at work in, for example, Alan Montefiore's stipulative definition at the beginning of his essay on 'The political responsibility of intellectuals': 'By "an intellectual" I mean here to refer to anyone who takes a committed interest in the validity and truth of ideas for their own sake.'[2] For obvious reasons, this sense tends not to be very useful for historical analysis precisely because it is difficult to isolate any external markers of membership of this category. But it can colour such analysis and, as in the essay just cited, it can allow an author to dwell on a not very sharply delimited subset of the larger category defined in terms of relevant occupational groups. It is also to this sense that the residue of the history of scorn and hostility sketched above most readily attaches itself, where 'intellectuals' are alleged to be people who take themselves too seriously or needlessly complicate and theorize about what for most people is straightforward and natural, and so on. As we shall see, it is important to remember that some of the associations of this negative use may be subliminally at work affecting understanding and response even when the subjective sense is not the one explicitly being used.

The third main sense may be termed 'the cultural sense', since it focuses on those who are regarded as possessing some kind of 'cultural authority', that is, who deploy an acknowledged intellectual position or achievement in addressing a broader, non-specialist public. Here, not *all* those who engage in 'intellectual occupations', even in the narrowest version of that sociological category, nor all those disposed to interest themselves in cultural activities, are termed 'intellectuals': they must also be recognized as having acquired a certain standing in society which is taken to license them, or at least to provide them with opportunities, to address a wider public than that at which their occupational activity is aimed. The preliminary features of this category can be identified fairly easily, though there are deeper complexities which will require more extended analysis. To begin with, there is an element of circularity, or at least of definitional parasitism, in that the 'qualifying activity' has to be recognized as one that is 'intellectual' in some sense in the first place. A businessman or sports personality who offers a general view on some moral, social, or political issue does not thereby tend to attract the label 'an intellectual'. Moreover, it is essential to have some achievement or proficiency in a sphere of activity loosely recognized as 'intellectual' (or perhaps 'cultural') *independently* of the activity of speaking out on public issues. Thus, a novelist or academic who writes an occasional column in a newspaper is likely to attract the label, but a professional reporter with no independent claim to cultural standing may not. At the same time, the 'speaking out' is crucial: a scholar who only addresses other scholars in the relevant specialism, or the painter who only paints, tend not to qualify either. Finally, but most elusively, there must seem to be some connection between the intellectual proficiency and the public role: some notion of being 'good at' handling ideas, of being more reflective, of being able to set issues in a wider frame, and so on. Intellectuals, it has been said, must possess 'a disposition and capacity to discuss and think in an informed way about ideas. . . . There is such a thing as the authority of the intellectual, and it is to be found in that capacity—an authority which, like that of the artist and unlike that of the clergy, depends on the uncommanded response of those it affects.'[3] Whatever its deeper complexities, this third sense of the term is the one implicitly appealed to in most contemporary references to the role or responsibilities of 'the intellectual', as it is of all those repetitive laments about the 'decline', 'death', and 'disappearance' of this species. The named individuals who are so designated are, as a recent analysis puts it, 'the cultural experts or leaders ... [who] speak with some authority on that account'—and this, it is claimed, 'has unquestionably become the predominant meaning of the word in English'.[4]

Usage of these three senses does not constitute a series of strictly concentric circles, since each picks out different *types* of identifying property or marker. But they obviously overlap, and it is usually the case that those termed 'intellectuals' in the third, cultural sense will also tend to attract the label in the two other senses also. Any actual use of the term may, of course, exhibit much less definitional clarity than I am assigning to the three senses here, as is the case with any semantically extensive or variegated word. It is common, for example, especially when referring to whole societies ('President Cardozo is popular among Brazil's intellectuals') for the usage to be a mixture of the sociological and the cultural senses, where the enumeration of the groups within the category will tend to be by occupation, but the examples actually named will nearly always be individuals who enjoy a degree of prominence or cultural standing.

At times it can seem tempting to discriminate a fourth sense which could be labelled 'the political', but there is less compelling evidence here that this has established itself as a separate *sense* of the word in English as opposed to being a frequent *claim* about those whom it is used to designate. However, as was briefly indicated in the previous chapter, it has arguably long been part of the meaning of the dominant sense of the term *les intellectuels* in French, especially in the plural. Here, the defining mark of the intellectuals is that, from a base in activities of recognized 'intellectual' standing, they attempt to 'intervene' in or act upon the political sphere. This sense, too, is parasitic upon some version of the sociological sense—their primary activities have to be classifiable as 'intellectual' in the first place—and even draws upon some of the cultural sense as well—they are at least likely to have already attracted attention beyond their professional group, to have already earned some title to be heard. When spoken of in this way, 'les intellectuels' are commonly seen as a group, in some respects like (to take two different kinds of group) trade unionists or environmentalists, who act collectively in the political sphere.

Thus, in their widely cited work of historical synthesis, Ory and Sirinelli take the Dreyfus Affair to have given the fundamental French sense of the term: 'the intellectual is thus no longer defined by what he is, a function or a status, but by what he does, his intervention in the political field'. ['l'intellectuel ne se définit plus alors par ce qu'il est, une fonction, un statut, mais par ce qu'il fait, son intervention sur le terrain du politique'.][5] Their book and the many other works on the same topic in France tend to be seen as contributions to *political* history; indeed, the history of intellectuals in France has, until very recently, been written almost entirely by political historians, and its centrality to political history is still insisted upon.[6] But one also encounters the same definitional claim in books about intellectuals in France written from a different standpoint. Thus Rémy Rieffel, writing as a self-described sociologist of the media, asks:

> Need one emphasize that in France (and the Dreyfus Affair, the emblematic moment of the crystallization of the term, testifies to this) the intellectual is also defined by his mode of intervention in the business of the community? It is in making his voice heard in relation to certain problems of general interest, it is in taking up his function of '*interpellation*' with the help of an arsenal of weapons (petitions, manifestos, speeches, essays, etc.) that he bears witness to his will to transcend his individual opinion for the benefit of a collective purpose. He is thus one who, drawing authority from his particular competence in some creative or cultural activity, goes beyond his initial role to take part in public debate. The expression 'the engaged intellectual' thus appears as a tautology, a redundant formula: there is, in our country, no intellectual without engagement.
>
> ['Est-il besoin de souligner qu'en France (et l'affaire Dreyfus, moment emblématique de la cristallisation du terme, en fait foi) l'intellectuel se définit aussi par son mode d'intervention dans les affaires de la Cité? C'est en faisant entendre sa voix à propos de certains problèmes d'intérêt général, c'est en assumant sa fonction d'interpellation à l'aide d'un arsenal d'instruments (pétitions, manifestes, discours, essais, etc) qu'il témoigne de sa volonté de transcender son opinion individuelle au profit d'un usage collectif. Il est donc celui qui, s'autorisant de sa compétence propre en matière de création/culture, sort de son role initial pour s'investir dans les débats publics. L'expression d''intellectuel engagé' apparaît de la sorte comme une tautologie, une formule redondante: il n'y a pas, dans notre pays, d'intellectuel sans engagement.'][7]

In this French usage, therefore, intellectuals are not regarded as a category of people who happen to be particularly prone to intervene in politics: the intervention in politics is constitutive of the definition of the category. In practice, however, Rieffel does recognize that some ideas have 'civic consequences' even though their creators do not personally 'intervene' in politics; for this reason, he is not willing to exclude such relatively closeted figures as Lévi-Strauss or Robbe-Grillet from his survey of intellectuals. This is an important concession, since it tacitly recognizes that it is the question of impinging on a wider, non-specialist sphere—making one's voice heard 'in relation to certain problems of general interest' ('à propos de certains problèmes d'intérêt général')—rather than the political activity as such, that is constitutive of the category. Given that discussion of the question of intellectuals in Britain has involved a frequent explicit, and almost constant implicit, comparison with the (supposed) situation in France, the presuppositions embedded in this usage have intermittently affected expectations of the term in English, though without building these expectations into its meaning. Thus, it is, in my view, a perfectly intelligible and coherent use of the (cultural sense of the) term in English to say, as one leading commentator put it: 'An intellectual is not necessarily politically active, but does have a public role . . . an intellectual needs an audience.'[8] A public role is a constitutive part of the *meaning* of the term 'intellectual' in the cultural sense; being politically active is one form which that public role may frequently, but not necessarily, take.

As I have indicated, one should not expect the historical examples of the use of the word in English, such as those cited in the previous chapter, always to instantiate clear-cut distinctions of sense: in any given quotation there is frequently an element of unacknowledged connotative pull from one or more of the other senses, which is why one needs to operate with an awareness of the whole semantic field. Moreover, any particular writer or speaker may be using the term in a playful or ironic or otherwise inventive way, though all such idiosyncratic uses have to trade on one or more of the basic senses if they are to be intelligible. In current usage, identifying which of the three main senses may be in play in any given statement will obviously require close attention to linguistic context as well as delicate discriminations of tone, register, and so on. But as a very rough guide, one can proceed by recognizing which near-synonym may most appropriately be substituted in the statement in question. Where 'brain-worker' (or such related terms as 'professional, technical, and communications staff', 'white-collar occupation', etc.) fits, it suggests the sociological sense; where 'highbrow' (or 'bookish', 'blue-stocking', etc.) could be substituted, it points to the subjective sense; and where 'leading thinker' (or 'opinion-former', 'well-known critic/historian/philosopher', and so on) could be used, it is likely to be the cultural sense.

Once these three senses are distinguished, it becomes fairly obvious which sense I, as an intellectual historian of modern Britain, am primarily concerned with in this book. It would, beyond all question, be perfectly possible to write a book on this topic where the term was consistently being used in the sociological sense. Such a book would be likely to contain a great deal of statistical and empirical information about a substantial segment of the population defined in socio-professional terms, including teachers, journalists, clergymen, therapists, writers, directors, and so on. By its nature, such a book would be likely to have little to say about named individuals; it would be about the analytical units of social structure, to which would be correlated data (it is the kind of book which would unblinkingly use the term 'data' a lot) about distribution of wealth, voting patterns, leisure habits, and so on. This is not that book.

It is much less clear what would be involved in trying to write a book on 'intellectuals' using the term in the subjective sense. It is difficult to see quite what its content would be, unless possibly a book about attitudes towards intellectuality, especially in self-description; in practice it would almost certainly find itself at times slipping into using 'intellectuals' in one of the other two senses. Such a book might, of course, simply content itself with a series of portraits, celebratory or dismissive according to taste, of particularly reflective or intense or bookish individuals. This is not that book, either.

This book, as I explained in the Introduction, is about 'the question of intellectuals' in modern Britain, about why it has been such a 'question' (cf. 'the Irish question', 'the Eastern question'), about what assumptions have underlain assertions about the presence (or, more often, absence) of intellectuals in this society, about how this may be understood as part of a wider history. To the extent that this involves attending to earlier statements about these issues which may not have discriminated at all precisely the sense or senses of the term being used, the following chapters necessarily trench on past discussions of all three senses and of the various approximations and compounds that preceded them. But where I am speaking in my own voice and using the word to characterize the role played by particular individuals, 'intellectuals' are being spoken of in this book in the (now dominant) cultural sense of the term.

It is in this sense that the phrase 'British intellectuals' can still seem to many people to be something of an oxymoron or even a contradiction in terms. No one, after all, could seriously maintain that intellectuals in the sociological sense—members of very broadly defined socio-occupational groups—were not as much part of the social structure of Britain as of any other complex industrial society. Similarly there would be something perverse in proposing that intellectuals in the subjective sense, individuals with a strong personal commitment to thought and reflection, were somehow scarcer in Britain than elsewhere, even if one believed that the culture generally was less hospitable to, or paid less attention to, such individuals than did other cultures. The proposition that in Britain intellectuals have been absent or insignificant or not 'real' examples of the species is a claim about intellectuals in the cultural sense, though this claim is frequently tied up with further claims about the non-existence in Britain of a separate or 'dissident' intelligentsia which acts as a self-consciously collective force in politics, and so on. Behind these claims, or prejudices, lie various unexamined assumptions, both about the role of intellectuals and about the nature of British society, that are the product of a particular history. But before addressing the history of those assumptions, I need to examine more closely what is involved in the *concept* of 'the intellectual' as represented by the cultural sense of the term, reinforced in my sense of the necessity of this task by Wittgenstein's remark quoted in the epigraph: 'We can avoid ineptness or emptiness in our assertions only by presenting the model as what it is, as an object of comparison—as, so to speak, a measuring-rod; not as a preconceived idea to which reality *must* correspond.'[9] Readers should be warned that the following section is more abstract and analytical than any other in the book; those who are impatient to return to the historical story should skip immediately to the beginning of Ch. 3, though they should also be warned that later chapters presuppose the analysis offered in the next section.

II

The essential first step towards clarity here involves recognizing that the term 'the intellectual', when used in the cultural sense, does not refer to an occupational category nor should it be thought of as a fixed characteristic or defining feature of an individual in terms of inclinations and capacities: it is not, therefore, on a par with a socio-economic classification such as 'teacher' or 'writer', nor with a psychological characterization such as 'introvert' or 'verbalizer', nor again with an evaluative characterization such as 'great mind' or 'genius'. Rather, it designates performance in a role or, more accurately, a structure of relations. Given figures act as 'intellectuals' by moving into this structure of relations; their primary social and psychological identities will always be specified in other terms.

In the first instance this structure of relations can be represented in terms of a grid of coordinates. The role of the intellectual, one could say, always involves the intersection of four elements or dimensions:

1. The attainment of a level of achievement in an activity which is esteemed for the non-instrumental, creative, analytical, or scholarly capacities it involves;
2. The availability of media or channels or expression which reach publics other than that at which the initial 'qualifying' activity itself is aimed;
3. The expression of views, themes, or topics which successfully articulate or engage with some of the general concerns of those publics;
4. The establishment of a reputation for being likely to have important and interesting things of this type to say and for having the willingness and capacities to say them effectively through the appropriate media.

Analysing the concept in this way helps to make clearer that the question of how far any specific figure at any one time instantiates the intersection of these four dimensions of the role will always be a matter of degree: being classed as 'an intellectual' is not governed by a simple on/off switch. Similarly, the same individual may over time come to occupy the role either more or less fully: once a certain prominence has been attained, a given figure may never altogether cease to be associated with the role, but they may in effect cease to instantiate it as they come to lose access to the relevant media or cease to have things of general interest to say, and then they begin to drop from view. Of course, the label may become attached in a more or less permanent way to someone who habitually and constantly enters into this role, yet even then this cannot, by definition, be all they do (apart from anything else, there will need to be the 'qualifying activity' which makes them candidates for the role in the first place). More importantly, the extent to which the various conditions are met will vary, and 'extent', again, always involves degree not kind. There will, therefore, always be dispute about whether individuals who meet these criteria only partially or transiently should, for one purpose or another, be classed as intellectuals. Similarly, quite how 'non-specialist' the public in question really is, or quite how 'general' the message may be, will always be matters for judgement in particular cases, questions not resolvable by measurement or formula.

A useful preliminary to further analysis may be the recognition that the description of any given figure as 'an intellectual' (in the cultural sense, always understood) does not necessarily imply praise or approval nor any positive judgement of the 'quality' of that figure's ideas or capacities for expression. What is at issue is a pattern of behaviour in a given historical setting. If a certain figure repeatedly succeeds, on the basis of a kind of creative or scholarly activity, in using a given medium of expression to reach a genuine public to express views on a general theme, then, by definition, that figure is, in that particular context, successfully functioning as an intellectual. Many intellectuals who have become prominent or had a substantial impact may well seem to us (to some of us, at least) to have expressed fatuous or pernicious ideas, but the label may still properly be applied to them. In truth, one cannot help but wonder at the extraordinary, seemingly impregnable, self-confidence manifested by some of those who have most prominently and successfully played the role of intellectual, and indeed wonder at the willingness of certain publics to listen to such noisily self-advertising characters. But that is really just to say that one may, indeed should, be as critical of intellectuals as of any other figures; the term should not be seen as inherently conferring approval. The matter is, of course, not entirely straightforward, since 'broader' or 'non-specialist' perspectives *do* present themselves from many points of view as inherently desirable, and to that extent there may seem to be a kind of positive valence built into the cultural sense of the noun 'intellectual'. But in fact this is no more true of the use of this term than of many others: to refer to someone as, for example, a 'political leader' may indicate that they have attained a position that is associated with qualities of 'leadership', such as energy or decisiveness, but that does not make it a term of approval—energy and decisiveness have marked out some of the most appalling and destructive 'leaders' in history. Similarly with intellectuals, there can just as easily be misleading or inappropriate general perspectives as fruitful or illuminating ones. Getting away from the tendency to deploy the term as a kind of honorific or form of praise (or, conversely, as a dismissive or demonizing label) may be the first step towards undertaking illuminating historical analysis.

Looking a little more closely at each of these dimensions in turn, we may begin with the question of what I have called the 'qualifying activity'. This requires a level of achievement or other recognized standing in an activity which that society values for other than purely instrumental reasons. That is to say, the activity in question is seen *both* as cultivating mental and imaginative capacities beyond the ordinary *and* as issuing in certain kinds of truths or understanding that exceed what is required for merely technical contributions to the practical and economic life of that society. What counts as an example of this activity will be, as with all the other dimensions of the role, historically variable: in 1900, accredited standing as a scholar of ancient Greek texts might have seemed a more obvious candidate than it does now, just as, conversely, a reputation for important work in feminist cultural studies might serve the need now in a way that, obviously, was not available a century ago. Similarly, the criteria for including an activity within this category will vary culturally, as well: for example, in France such standing tends to be accorded to some kinds of actors or singers whereas their peers in several other European countries would not be so regarded unless they had additionally made a mark in some other medium, such as writing books.

Precisely because the role of intellectual involves, on this analysis, a relation with a 'public', the second element in that role has to be access to some medium or channel of expression through which the intellectual reaches that public. In the course of the twentieth century, such media have ranged from pamphlets to paperbacks and from platform oratory to TV profiles. A historical account of intellectuals cannot ignore the changing economics of the relevant media: the pricing and marketing of certain publications will normally determine the publics they reach far more than does the quality of the contents, and of course the successive arrivals of radio and of television (and perhaps now of the Internet) have affected the nature of the stage upon which intellectuals may act. But it was for long true, and may still be so, that the single most important form of these media has, in practice, been the periodical or journal or review, terms which I shall use interchangeably to cover that variety of weekly, monthly, or quarterly publications that fall in the space between books on the one side and newspapers on the other. The history of public debate in Britain since at least the early nineteenth century can be written in terms of the changing fortunes of different types of periodical, from the great days of the heavyweight quarterlies, such as the *Edinburgh* and the *Quarterly*, up to the most recent arrivals, such as the *London Review of Books* and *Prospect*. Periodicals are also important to a remarkably little-studied feature of the growth of an individual's cultural authority that I shall return to below, namely the building of a reputation, creating a standing such that that individual is then invited to hold forth on various topics in other public settings. In these matters, access breeds access, as every embittered 'loner' in history has intuitively known.

Different media or channels of expression reach different audiences: the next important question, therefore, is what does it mean for parts of those audiences to constitute a genuine 'public'? A public, as the term is used here, must have, in some form, the properties of being open, impersonal, and 'non-specialist'. It must be open in the way that membership of a club or trade union is not: in principle, anyone with the requisite degree of literacy and interest may constitute part of such a public. It must be impersonal in the sense that it has to be composed at least partly of people with whom the intellectual in question has not had previous personal connections; one's family and friends may provide a kind of audience, but they do not constitute a genuine 'public'. And it must be, in the relevant sense, 'non-specialist', that is, not constituted exclusively by those engaged in that form of creative or scholarly activity which is the basis for the intellectual's recognized standing in the first place. These conditions, too, are all historically variable, and it may well be that there are moments and circumstances in which one cannot identify a genuine public, defined in these terms, for particular would-be intellectuals.

It is crucially important to distinguish between this analytical concept of 'a public' and the variety of empirical publics. In any given society, there can in principle be a more or less infinite number of publics, even if in practice certain broad groupings will be more important than others. But whether a range of auditors make up a genuine public is not a question of size, and still less should we assume that someone can be regarded as an intellectual only if they succeed in reaching 'society as a whole', as it is often, unhelpfully, phrased. Strictly speaking, it seems unlikely that any message reaches 'society as a whole', and the use of the phrase is surely better understood as indicating a colloquial attempt to gesture towards the characteristics of a public as identified here. Moreover, we should not assume that the publics which accord a certain respect or deference to the activities in question need to be *au fait* with, still less to have mastered, the *content* of that activity; it is enough that it believes the activity to encourage qualities of reflectiveness, analysis, knowledgeableness, and insight so that those who practise the activity are seen to be deserving of some kind of attention. For this reason, the public for whom a particular figure may possess some standing to act as an intellectual will always be partly different from, and usually broader than, the audience at whom the activity which earns that standing is directed.

My analysis is not, therefore, dependent on positing the existence of a single 'public sphere' in any society, the sum of whose participants constitute 'the public'. There are different, partially overlapping spheres of publicness in any complex society, and the 'speaking out' which is held to be characteristic of the intellectual may be addressed in the first instance to audiences that are restricted in various ways. The extensive literature in English that has grown up around Habermas's notion of 'the public sphere' has perhaps been primarily notable as an illustration of the pitfalls involved in taking a phrase out of one very particular conceptual scheme and intellectual idiom, processing it through a kind of academic equivalent of Ellis Island, and then leaving it to make its fortune in the competitive market of American academic discourse. But, more positively, I do think this literature has helped us to think about the relations between the *conceptual* space indicated by the adjective 'public' in a phrase such as 'public debate' and the variety of *empirical* publics who, to different degrees, may participate in such debate.

The third dimension of the intellectual's role—the expression of views, themes, and topics which successfully engage with some of the general concerns of those publics—may not be quite as straightforward as it seems. To begin with, the very notion of 'generality' involves a kind of logical regress: any issue, no matter how large, can by definition be viewed in a 'more general' perspective, and that perspective can in turn be considered in a perspective that is yet more general still. Obviously, what counts as 'general' in these cases is not determined by any single kind of *content*: framing issues in terms of 'justice', 'rights', and so on has, for good reason, been one of the most common ways of bringing a more general perspective to bear in times and places where a particular application of those values might be thought to have special purchase, but even then they are *examples* of such a perspective, albeit extremely important ones, rather than constitutive of it. It should go without saying that a statement or analysis that may be 'general' in relation to one issue may in turn be addressed from a still more general perspective: no one perspective always out-trumps all others. But the characteristic use of the public standing of the intellectual, in the sense being elucidated here, is to license the expression of a view which in some way goes beyond that available from those with a merely instrumental or expert relation to the matter in question. The range of views or ideas which may, in any given historical situation, meet this requirement cannot be specified in advance; *a fortiori*, there is no one set of topics which it is the peculiar business of the intellectual to address.

The fourth dimension of the role, the establishment of a reputation for being likely to have important and interesting things of this type to say and for having the willingness and capacities to say them effectively through the appropriate media, can obviously be properly studied only through specific cases. But even when merely stated in its general form, this dimension does underline how a role requires a *recurrent* pattern of activity. An individual who writes one acclaimed book or makes one important discovery may attract initial attention, but unless they in some way indicate a capacity and willingness to use the relevant media to address other questions on other occasions, they will slip from view. For this reason, as I shall repeatedly emphasize in later chapters of this book, the study of intellectuals is bound to involve, to a degree that would seem irrelevant or perhaps even vulgar for other purposes, the study of the making of careers.

The outcome of the intersection of these four elements is what is usually referred to as the 'cultural authority' of the intellectual. This apparently familiar notion may in fact be conceptually the trickiest of all. Without attempting to resolve the puzzles or complexities at the heart of the concept of 'authority' in the abstract, we may simply recognize that we are dealing with the ways in which certain members of a society may pay attention to, be influenced by, even in some cases defer to, those identified as the prime bearers of certain values or capacities. Where these values or capacities are of a sufficiently general kind, we may distinguish this sort of cultural authority from the mere possession of 'expertise'. A tax accountant or a meteorologist may be deferred to on their specific subject-matters, but that will not in itself earn them the right to be listened to on broader issues. And, increasingly important, the notion of cultural authority needs to be distinguished from mere 'celebrity' or 'notoriety' (a topic I return to in Part Five). Merely being 'in the news' may mean that a person is, often temporarily, attended to, but it does not of itself entail that that person is recognized as speaking on behalf of values which had been acknowledged prior to, and independently of, that individual's rise to newsworthiness. And finally, the kind of cultural authority deployed by someone who successfully occupies the role of intellectual cannot, of course, be a merely individual matter. There has to be some pre-existing disposition in the culture to assign value or standing to the activities in which that figure is seen to be distinguished, and there has to be some pre-existing disposition to be receptive to the expression of views on the topics they address. Some scholars profess to find Pierre Bourdieu's metaphor of 'cultural capital' useful here, though it seems to me to risk importing too narrowly economistic notions of 'competition' and 'positional strategy' into areas of activity better understood in their own terms. In my analysis, 'cultural authority' refers to the *outcome* of the intersection of the four dimensions, and it thus emphasizes the two-way relationship between speaker and publics. This is what I meant earlier by saying that the term 'intellectual' should be understood as describing performance in a role or, more exactly, a structure of relations.

Concentrating on the way in which successfully fulfilling this role involves doing something more, or other, than merely applying expertise also helps to bring out how each individual intellectual is inevitably caught in some version of the following tension: the source of the initial standing or claim to attention will always include distinction in at least one relatively specialized activity, but effective speaking out will always entail going beyond this attested level of achievement or expertise. In other words, the intellectual must, by definition, build out from a relatively secure basis in one specialized activity and simultaneously cultivate the necessarily more contestable perspective of a 'non-specialist'. This structural tension accounts, I suggest, for several recurring features of the polemics which constantly surround the issue of intellectuals. On the one hand, there are the charges of self-importance, of mere windy opinionatedness, of the rank presumption involved in holding forth on some matter on which one has no special credentials to speak (here we are back with the sardonic question which the conservative man of letters Ferdinand Brunetière rhetorically posed to the *universitaires* who signed petitions against Dreyfus's condemnation: 'What right has a professor of Tibetan to instruct his fellow-citizens in matters of morals and politics?'[10]). And on the other, there are the laments that in this generation (always presumed to be the first to encounter this new state of affairs) intellectuals have retreated from public debate, confined themselves to narrow specialisms (in this literature, specialisms are always 'narrow'), abandoned their ancient (hyperbole again) cultural and political responsibilities. Those making either of these charges tend to assume that some special failing of the particular individuals so charged is at issue, but my analysis suggests, rather, that the charges are structural, integral to the concept itself, and dialectically related.

The structural tension that I have analysed also, I think, explains why one meets over and over again, especially but not exclusively in those societies and periods (such as the contemporary United States) in which most of the intellectuals are also academics, a kind of war on two fronts. Faced with the usual media babble about having abandoned the 'public sphere' for the 'ivory tower' (this literature seems irretrievably immured in such cliché), the intellectual affects to bustle about in the world of affairs, confidently unloading opinions on those topics which the editors of features-pages deem to be the issues of the hour. But when caustic muttering breaks out among their scholarly peers—or, more damagingly, juniors—about their having 'sold out' to mere journalism and lost touch with first-hand research, they scurry back to the conference and paper-giving circuit, anxious to shore up the sea-wall of their scholarly reputation. In observing this pattern, one does not have to conclude that they are exceptionally shallow or opportunist: some version of this dynamic, this movement between these two poles, is inherent in the logic of the role itself.

Above all, my analysis here helps us, I believe, to account for a strikingly repetitive feature of the historiography of intellectuals, where, over and over again, one meets the claim that it is in the period under discussion that the generalist has finally yielded to the specialist. This claim is made so often, and about such various historical moments, that one eventually comes to realize that it must be a tension within the concept itself that is at work here: why, after all, is it *this* particular transition which is constantly singled out from among all the many developments that make up the long history of intellectuals in various societies? Moreover, when these accounts are placed end to end there is a cumulative improbability (indeed impossibility, eventually) in taking any of the chronologically later accounts seriously if the descriptions of just this transition in earlier periods are regarded as true.

Thus, if we ask when did 'the retreat into the academy' take place, we find a bewildering array of answers which locate the decisive shift in almost any decade of the twentieth century: contemporary commentators take it to be the distinguishing mark of the present, but their predecessors emphasized the change in the public sphere that took place in the 1950s and 1960s, though *their* predecessors were already complaining about 'the ivory tower' in the 1920s, and in turn *their* predecessors were loud in denouncing the withdrawal from public debate into academic specialism which they discerned at the end of the nineteenth century.

Contraction of horizons, abandonment of public roles, the tyranny of specialism—the laments are formulaic. All this surely suggests something that is both intrinsic and fundamental, less a matter of one specific period and more a structural feature of the role itself. Indeed, it helps to put all these later jeremiads in ironic perspective when one notes that in an influential historiographical account, T. W. Heyck located precisely this shift within the Victorian period itself, even before the term 'intellectual' was established. His thesis, as summarized by a subsequent commentator, was that the move from the early- and mid-Victorian sage to the end-of-century 'intellectual' represented a move from the 'generalist concerned with the moral implications of knowledge' to the academic whose status depended upon 'the possession of specialized expert knowledge', with a consequent loss of contact with a general public.[11] In which case, one can only wonder where, if anywhere, the originary state is to be located—or, rather, to recognize that the search for such a state produces a form of eternal regress, a logical symptom rather than a historical truth.

III

It will be clear that the form taken by each of the elements in my analysis of the concept of the intellectual in the cultural sense may vary in different societies and at different periods—what counts as the relevant kind of 'qualifying activity', what range of media is available and who has access to them, which audiences are susceptible to what kind of appeal, which issues appear to need addressing, and so on. And, taking up the matter from, as it were, the opposite end, one can similarly ask what kinds of contribution the dominant concerns and register of public debate in different societies at different times invite or allow room for. In other words, what this analysis is intended to provide is not any kind of stipulation about what intellectuals 'ought' to do or 'ought' to be like, but, rather, an analytical breakdown of the components of the concept itself, components which will, therefore, be present in some form in all cases. It may help to make this clearer if I contrast my analysis with those stipulative definitions of the intellectual which, in my view, mistake one particular historical manifestation or one preferred ideal for the logic of the concept.

One of the simplest and most familiar of these moves is the claim that 'real' intellectuals constitute a 'class'. A lot of unprofitable semantic skirmishing is possible here, since 'class' is a notoriously slippery term. Of course, where 'intellectuals' is being used in the sociological sense, a version of this claim can be merely trivial, indeed almost circular if one is prepared to say that there are as many 'classes' as there are large occupational groupings. In any strict use of the term 'class' as it comes from the Marxian or Weberian sociological traditions, it is obvious that intellectuals do *not* constitute a 'class'; they might, at most, be said (it would even here be very arguable) all to *belong* to the same class, especially where one is talking of traditional tripartite class structures, but that then becomes an uninteresting classificatory diktat, verging on tautology. When we are not being pressed to use the term with any precision, we do, reasonably enough, talk of 'the intellectual class' just as we may talk of, for example, 'the educated class' (meaning people of a certain *level* of education?) or 'the political class' (meaning people who are directly involved in the exercise of political power?), but in none of these cases is 'class' doing more than providing a convenient agglomerating term. The only interesting question here is whether intellectuals (in the cultural sense) have what might be identified as a 'common interest' (in, for example, protecting free speech), but if they do, it is only in a more or less metaphorical sense that we can then speak of their having a 'class interest'.

Intellectuals may in certain circumstances form a group by virtue of their common interest (in both senses) in matters affecting, say, intellectual freedom and by their common willingness, at certain moments, to attempt to address a broader public about it. But they are not a social group *independently* of such action, still less do they *thereby* constitute a social stratum or class. The problem here usually comes from moving without acknowledgement between the sociological and cultural senses of the term. Intellectuals may indeed be seen as a social stratum in the former sense, but then of course they belong to a far more extensive category than that made up of the few prominent names who have chosen to 'speak out'. Even when, as for example in France in the middle of the twentieth century, a substantial number of individuals may have habitually thought of themselves as belonging to a collectivity, *les intellectuels*, this was in virtue of choices and convictions (and of the degree of attention accorded to the expression of those choices and convictions), not simply of social position.

As I indicated in the previous chapter, the semantic field around 'intellectuals' in English has been much affected by associations derived from the Russian intelligentsia of the late nineteenth century and from the French intellectuals of the first half of the twentieth. In the case of the Russian intelligentsia, there was some ground for regarding them as a class in the full sociological sense, but that only brings out how much the term in its original setting reflected the peculiar position of a small, Westernized educated stratum in an overwhelmingly uneducated, agricultural society. Members of 'the intelligentsia' were precisely identified in terms of their social position, not their expression of particular kinds of view even though they did broadly favour a certain 'enlightened' outlook. By contrast, intellectuals in France in the first part of the twentieth century never constituted a social class as such, though they were heavily recruited from a fairly narrow range of social backgrounds and, more relevantly, shared a high level of common educational experience, leading to a marked sense of group identity and separateness from the surrounding society. But they were identified precisely by their efforts to deploy a certain cultural standing in public debate, not by a sociological position. As a result, principally, of resonances imported from these two traditions, the implication of constituting a separate class always hovers in attendance on all talk of a 'real intelligentsia' or 'real intellectuals', where, as so often, the essentializing adjective should alert us to the definitional sleight-of-hand.

Similarly, it should also be clear that it is not part of the *concept* of 'the intellectual' that persons so described should be 'dissident', 'oppositional', 'marginal', and so on. There are good historical reasons why these characteristics are often associated with the use of the term, but they are precisely *associated* with it, they are not intrinsic to it. It is, of course, true that, insofar as intellectuals address a particular issue from a more general perspective, there is a sense in which they will always be engaged in something which may be described as 'criticism'. The very act of 'placing' an issue, of taking a more analytical or comparative perspective on it, is in effect a form of distancing, a corrective to more limited or one-eyed views, and to this extent all redescription has a critical edge. As this suggests, the values and activities that are accorded this kind of standing will tend to lie somewhat athwart those directing the everyday instrumental processes of society if only because they, by definition, exceed those processes: they involve values that tend to be spoken of as 'ends in themselves'. But putting it like this makes clear that the values involved do not have to be 'dissident' or 'oppositional' in the familiar political sense; what is true is that by representing a realm that cannot be reduced to the instrumental they will always provide the resources for a critique of that instrumentality. (This brings out, from another angle, the distinction mentioned above between the roles of the 'intellectual' and of the 'expert'.) Those possessing this kind of cultural authority, therefore, will tend to find themselves appealing to a set of values which, while acknowledged in principle, may not always be wholly honoured in the practical functioning of the society being addressed.

However, considerable slippage is involved in going on to equate criticism in this generic sense with being 'oppositional' or 'marginal'. For example, in insisting that because intellectuals are committed to 'truth telling' they can never be 'members of a ruling class', Michael Walzer adds: 'Perhaps we should say straightforwardly that marginal intellectuals are the only real intellectuals.'[12] But this is far from straightforward, and it reveals yet again the distorting power of the assumption that intellectuals must be understood in terms of the polarity between criticism and conformity. In support of his claim, Walzer cites Sartre's remark that an atomic physicist is an intellectual only when he signs a petition against nuclear testing. But this, I would argue, is a case where my analysis of the structure of the concept proves more illuminating: it is not because the physicist is *against* something that he would be likely to be so described, but because he is here going beyond his specialist activity and speaking out on a matter of general interest (as Sartre himself, it should be said, appeared to acknowledge in this particular instance[13]). Still less plausible is the old claim that the intellectual stands 'outside' society, wherever that is or could be—a piece of pure romanticization, often implicitly involving self-romanticization. It seems to me one of the virtues of the analysis of the role of the intellectual that I am offering here that it directs attention to the ways in which this is a role constituted *by* and performed *within* a set of historically specific cultural and social relations.

This analysis should also help to highlight what is misleading (at least as far as English usage is concerned) about the common tendency to begin by thinking of 'intellectuals' as *meaning* a social group who intervene in politics. As I have already indicated, this tendency has been strongly influenced by the French example from the Dreyfus Affair onwards, but it essentially involves confusing the contingent and the particular with the necessary and the general. 'Politics', as usually understood in these cases, is only one subset of possible 'general issues', albeit a large and central one. We lose useful distinctions of meaning if we use 'politics' to signify *any* general issues. A figure of acknowledged cultural standing who communicates with a true public on, let us say, the question of the meaning of life and death or on ideals of love and sex is neither acting as a member of a group nor 'intervening' in politics: but that figure may quite properly be described as acting in the role of 'an intellectual'.

It is also important to be clear that the values or standards appealed to by intellectuals in bringing a broader perspective to bear do not necessarily have to be cast in a theoretical form. Such values or standards must, of course, possess some generality if they are to have force, but we should not assume that intellectuals will necessarily draw upon some more or less elaborated philosophical system or speak in what is often now called a foundational or metaphysical idiom. Again, a fantasy about what 'real' intellectuals have 'always' done colours expectations and clouds discussion here. In reality, the idiom in which a broader perspective is brought to bear will vary according to historical circumstance, cultural tradition, and so on. Obviously, the tendency of all argument and all criticism is towards subsuming particulars under more general heads, but no one level of abstraction, still less one cluster of values, is the proper telos of such argument. One current disadvantage of the assumption that the activities of the 'true intellectual' always involve an appeal to 'universals' is the fashionable claim that there are 'no longer' any universals to appeal to or which carry any authority (in the wake of, according to choice, the decline of 'grand narratives', the fall of Communism, the rise of Postmodernism, the flourishing of relativisms, and so on). This then easily yields the latest installment in the repetitive literature on 'the death of the intellectual'. The confusing of contingent historical characteristics with necessary defining properties, a confusion which so dogs this topic, is starkly apparent here.

A similar elision between social realities and political idealizations seems to me present in the claim that 'genuine' intellectuals must be 'unattached'. This usage was at one point relatively common within the confines of sociological theory, especially in the form of that enterprise developed in the United States out of German sources. The most notable instance here was Karl Mannheim, who took over from Alfred Weber the term 'freischwebende Intelligenz', glossed by him in the English translation of *Ideology and Utopia* as 'the socially unattached intelligentsia', an 'unanchored, *relatively* classless stratum'. Mannheim was, broadly speaking, following out the consequences of Max Weber's response to Marx, and in that vein the intelligentsia is for him a theoretically revealing example of what 'a sociology oriented solely in terms of class' cannot properly comprehend.[14] Both his discussion, therefore, and those in the tradition of 'the sociology of knowledge' inspired by him, remain structured by the claims of a class-based sociology even as they wish to contest them.

But more often, assertions about 'the independent intellectual' do not presuppose this, or any other, general sociological theory. When, for example, in 1954 the American critic Irving Howe wished to denounce 'this age of conformity', he pointed to 'the absorption of large numbers of intellectuals, previously independent, into the world of government bureaucracy and public committees; into the constantly growing industries of pseudo-culture', and so on, and especially into the university: 'If the intellectual cannot subsist independently, off his work or his relatives, the academy is usually his best bet.'[15] The easy equation here between subsisting 'independently' and living off one's relatives is almost breathtaking.[16] At the heart of all such claims is an unrealistic or exaggerated idea of 'independence', of being free to be critical because not in the pay of, or dependent upon the good favour of, a patron or constraining institution (being 'critical' or 'oppositional' is again assumed to be built into the definition). But the truth surely is that no one can escape 'attachment' in this sense: freedom from one kind of dependence (on a patron or a government) is only achieved by another kind of dependence (on a family or a public). Still, the ideal of the freelance or 'independent' intellectual retains a glamour which can obstruct further analysis. In recent decades, this notion has most frequently been wheeled out by way of contrast with the situation of those intellectual figures who hold posts in universities, nearly always in disparagement of the conformism or caution of the latter. But, other problems with this description aside, it is never clear why being, for example, shackled to the relentless rhythms of journalism and the need to cater to the tastes of a particular readership (or at least to those tastes as interpreted by an editor or proprietor) should furnish more 'independence' than the relative security and freedom enjoyed by the tenured academic. Moreover, since the claim about the superiority of being 'unattached' is, like most other writing about intellectuals nowadays, frequently put forward by those who themselves work in universities, it also figures as part of the familiar mix of nostalgia and inauthenticity that I have already identified.

These various stipulative definitions and idealizations are, in practice, often found in combination. Thus, for example, when one commentator speaks of 'an intelligentsia of the "classic" type, cohesive, independent and critical of the conventional purposes of its society', we can see several of these moves being made simultaneously. And when this definition is in turn cited as exemplifying the 'strong' or Mannheimian sense of the term 'intelligentsia', used 'to refer to a distinct social stratum with its own ideology and traditions', the problem is compounded.[17] Certain historically specific contingencies are being built into the actual *meaning* of the term. There is also an empirical implausibility in making the requirements so tight: a particular group of associates may be, in some sense, 'cohesive' and have its 'own ideology', but it is hard to see how one might expect 'the intelligentsia' not to comprise a whole tissue of divisions, social and ideological. It is only the shift to speaking of '*an* intelligentsia' that makes it seem allowable to start specifying such demanding criteria for membership. Having then to assume that there are innumerable 'intelligentsias' in any given society, each defined by its cohesiveness and ideology, shows how far we are being asked to move from the established usage of the term.

The examples mentioned here are singled out purely for their symptomatic value; the following chapters will touch on many other cases of authors attempting to build a preferred historical feature into the very meaning of the term. One upshot of such tendentious definitions is that it then becomes impossible to do justice to the sheer variousness of the ways in which the role of the intellectual can be performed. We should not, in other words, *begin* by assuming that if intellectuals in other times and places do not exhibit the characteristics associated with intellectuals in, say, France in the 1950s or Eastern Europe in the 1980s (to take two examples which have been in danger of having paradigmatic status thrust upon them), then they were somehow failing to be 'real' intellectuals. I hope that the fairly extensive analytical framework provided by this chapter will now make it possible to move on to a properly historical consideration of the shape which discussion of 'the question of intellectuals' has taken in twentieth-century Britain, beginning with the roots of the bizarre but persistent idea that intellectuals were an exotic and alien species whose natural habitat was always elsewhere.

These first two chapters have attempted to clarify the terms of the 'question' and to bring to the surface the main determining assumptions that have shaped the way it has been addressed. The chapters in the following sections, which comprise the heart of the book, attempt to look in much closer detail at a representative sample of debates and commentators. But let me here repeat a disclaimer I made in the Introduction: this is neither a narrative history nor a comprehensive survey. The following chapters are deliberately diverse in form and focus: they take a series of soundings using, as it were, different pieces of equipment. The only preliminary conclusion that it may be appropriate to signal at this stage is that, whatever view one takes of the desirability or importance of the *activities* of intellectuals, twentieth-century British culture has scarcely been marked by an absence of discussion of the *issue*.

NOTES

1. Seymour Martin Lipset, 'American intellectuals: their politics and their status', *Daedalus*, 88 (1959), 460.
2. Alan Montefiore, 'The political responsibility of intellectuals', in Ian Maclean, Alan Montefiore, and Peter Winch (eds.), *The Political Responsibility of Intellectuals* (Cambridge: Cambridge University Press, 1990), 201.

3. Bernard Williams, 'Bad behavior', *New York Review of Books* (20 July 1989), 13; Williams was reviewing Paul Johnson's *Intellectuals*, on which see also Stefan Collini, 'Intellectuals in Britain and France in the twentieth century: confusions, contrasts—and convergence?', in Jeremy Jennings (ed.), *Intellectuals in Twentieth-Century France: Mandarins and Samurai* (London: Macmillan, 1993), 219–21.
4. Peter Allen, 'The meanings of "an intellectual": nineteenth- and twentieth-century usage', *University of Toronto Quarterly*, 55 (1986), 347, 349.
5. Pascal Ory and Jean-François Sirinelli, *Les Intellectuels en France, de l'Affaire Dreyfus à nos jours* (Paris: Armand Colin, 1986), 9.
6. e.g. Jean-François Sirinelli, *Intellectuels et passions françaises: Manifestes et pétitions au XXe siècle* (Paris: Fayard, 1990), 12.
7. Rémy Rieffel, *Les Intellectuels sous la Ve République*, 3 vols. (Paris: Calmann-Lévy, 1993), i. 16.
8. Bernard Crick, 'The brains of Britain', *Times Higher Education Supplement* (14 Jan. 1983), 10.
9. Ludwig Wittgenstein, *Philosophical Investigations*, trans. Elizabeth Anscombe (Oxford: Blackwell, 1953), § 131.
10. Ferdinand Brunetière, 'Après le procès', *Revue des Deux Mondes*, 15 Mar. 1898, 446. See Ch. 11 below for a fuller discussion of the original of this celebrated quotation.
11. Heyck, *Transformation*, as summarized in M. S. Hickox, 'Has there been a British intelligentsia?', *British Journal of Sociology*, 37 (1986), 261. Claims about the impact of 'specialization' are discussed more fully in Ch. 20, below.
12. Michael Walzer, 'Intellectuals to power?', in his *Radical Principles: Reflections of an Unreconstructed Democrat* (New York: Basic Books, 1980), 233.
13. Jean-Paul Sartre, *Plaidoyer pour les intellectuels* (Paris: Gallimard, 1972), 12–13; 'A plea for intellectuals', in Jean-Paul Sartre, *Between Existentialism and Marxism*, trans. John Matthews (London: New Left Books, 1974), 230.
14. Karl Mannheim, *Ideology and Utopia*, 137, 130.
15. Irving Howe, 'This age of conformity', *Partisan Review*, 21 (Feb. 1954), 12, 14.
16. The exorbitance of the New York Intellectuals' concern with being 'unattached' is discussed in more detail in Ch. 10.
17. Francis Mulhern, *The Moment of 'Scrutiny'* (London: New Left Books, 1979), 77; Hickox, 'British intelligentsia', 262 (Hickox, it should be noted, expresses reservations about the applicability of this strong sense of the term to the British case). Cf. the similar statement discussed at the end of Ch. 8, below.

PART TWO

FONDER HEARTS

3

Anglo-Saxon Attitudes

'No people has ever distrusted and despised the intellect and intellectuals more than the British.'

I

Cultures, like individuals, can become imprisoned in images of themselves, and so it is with the enduring power of certain images or stereotypes that we need to begin. These images have allowed the familiar claims about the absence or comparative unimportance of intellectuals in Britain to acquire over time the brassy sheen of self-evidence. But the ground for what I am calling 'a tradition of denial' was prepared, sometimes in indirect ways, in the nineteenth century. We need, therefore, to recognize how the earliest versions of these claims were grafted on to a *pre-existing* set of ideas about national identity and the peculiarities of English history and politics (and here it is important to follow nineteenth-century usage and say 'English' not 'British', since the national stereotypes in question were specifically English even though the political entity of which they were supposed to be the animating force was in practice the British state). More specifically, many of the assumptions and prejudices which these claims express turn out to have been present in dominant notions of national identity *before* the term 'intellectuals' and the phenomenon it (unsteadily) referred to entered discussion—for example, those self-congratulatory contrasts with less fortunate nations, especially France, which were such a staple of political argument in England throughout the nineteenth century, pitting stability and practical good sense against revolution and political overexcitability; pragmatic empiricism against abstract rationalism; irony and understatement against rhetoric and exaggeration; and so on. In the negatively characterized half of each of these pairings we can already see the components of what was to become the dominant representation in twentieth-century Britain of (European) intellectuals. In the course of that century, these John Bullish contrasts came to be invoked less frequently and perhaps less confidently, but language is an effective preserving medium, and later usage of 'intellectuals' continued to draw upon such contrasts even when the assumptions behind them could no longer withstand the scrutiny that would follow from their being made explicit.[1]

These attitudes were, in turn, threaded into a still broader fabric of assumptions about the 'unintellectual English'. It would take another, and quite different, book to explore the roots of this cultural trope and to trace its origins back through the nineteenth and eighteenth centuries and perhaps even beyond.[2] It was a characteristic that Bulwer Lytton, writing in the 1830s, could assume that his readers would be disposed to take for granted: 'Our general indifference to political theories; our quiet and respectable adherence to things that are . . . this propensity has for centuries assuredly distinguished us; we have been very little alive to all speculative innovations in morals and politics. Those continental writings that have set the rest of the world in a blaze, have never been widely popular with us.'[3] As his last sentence suggests, this sentiment, for all its claim to be celebrating something reaching back over 'centuries', reflected a peculiarly early nineteenth-century, post-French Revolution, preoccupation. Thereafter, the contrasting experience of Britain and the rest of Europe during this period became a structuring feature of assumptions about English national identity for the rest of the century, and beyond. Suffice it to say that already by the early- and mid-Victorian years (several generations before the period with which I am dealing in this book), the identification of the English people as peculiarly practical, untheoretical, and indifferent or resistant to ideas was so well established that it was available not just for direct affirmation or contradiction, but also for more allusive, ironic, and playful uses. And—particularly telling—even those who wished to deny that it was part of English national character, in any essentialist sense, had to acknowledge its force as a cultural attitude. It was, for example, a familiar feature, in fact almost a constitutive element, in the work of the leading social critics of the period such as John Stuart Mill or Matthew Arnold, each lamenting in their different ways the 'Cimmerian darkness' and 'philistinism' of English culture.[4]

The assumption also surfaced in more oblique, but no less powerful, ways in other kinds of writing. Consider, simply to take one from among so many possible illustrations, the way the truism makes an appearance in J. R. Seeley's plea in the 1860s for the establishment of a properly learned professoriate who would conduct 'research' at the serious level then being achieved by other countries (Germany, most obviously). In a subject such as philosophy, Seeley acknowledged, England had fallen far behind the leading nations of continental Europe, but he argued that there were contingent rather than necessary causes of this state of affairs. 'That barrenness in ideas, that contempt for principles, that Philistinism which we hardly deny to be an English characteristic now, was not always so.' Indeed, in the seventeenth and early eighteenth centuries the English were admired for the boldness and reach of their speculative thinkers such as Locke or Newton. 'It is not then the English character which is averse to thought; we are not naturally the plain practical people that we sometimes boast, and sometimes blush, to be.' But by failing to establish a learned class England had fallen behind in the increasingly specialized world of modern scholarly and scientific enquiry.

The reason for English backwardness is rather that 'in the warfare of thought we have hoped to resist regular troops with volunteers'.[5] There was, we may now feel, surely some risk that the resonance of 'volunteers' might have encouraged Seeley's countrymen to be, contrary to his intentions, entirely content with this state of affairs. But Seeley and his readers could unhesitatingly agree that the English had by now acquired, and were inclined to revel in, a reputation (whether justified or not) for 'barrenness in ideas' and 'contempt for principles'.

Selective uses of these and other stereotypes (they were rarely more than that) recur in various forms of writing in late-nineteenth and early-twentieth-century Britain. The literature on 'national character', a favoured category of academic writing as well as more popular social analysis well into the twentieth century, abounded with such familiar contrasts, though as always they sat alongside other claims about the richness of the English intellectual tradition with which they were not strictly consistent. Ernest Barker's 1927 volume *National Character and the Factors in its Formation* served as a *summa* of received wisdom on the topic (a fourth, revised edition was called for as late as 1948). Although ostensibly addressing its subject in analytical and comparative terms, Barker's book concentrated heavily on the 'English' case, often in the context of a comparison with France. For example, the chapter on 'Language, Literature, and Thought' concluded with an extended meditation on the well-worn theme that 'pure speculative thought, working without conscious regard for time or place, has been rare or infrequent in England.' Barker commanded the requisite Whiggish notes effortlessly: 'If we have shown a gift for practical discussion which has been the very nerve of our practical politics for many centuries, it is the reverse side of that gift that we have shown but little aptitude for the heights of any discussion of abstract principles.' As always, 'we' could found this cherished self-description on a ready contrast: 'We have to admit that the influence which pure thought has exercised on the action and disposition of Englishmen has been less than it has been with the French' (this is 'admit' in the sense of 'boast').[6]

Although it is easy to see how Barker's platitudes could be adapted to the needs of later claims about the relative weakness or absence of 'intellectuals', it is worth noting that his analysis, such as it was, of the involvement of 'our thinkers' in 'practical life' could equally easily be adapted to support the contrary case. When, for example, he is pointing out how 'English historians have been more immersed in affairs', he cites examples such as Macaulay's political career or the fact that Froude 'was a lively publicist as well as historian'.[7] It was indeed the case that nineteenth- and twentieth-century Britain could exhibit a large number of 'thinkers' who were also 'lively publicists' (the variety of Barker's own writings and forms of public engagement could be added to the roster), but of course it was precisely such amphibious activities which were to attract the label 'intellectuals'. As this example reminds us, in the literature on national character Britain's peculiarity was more often supposed to lie not in any absence of public debate or lack of engagement in it on the part of scholars, thinkers, and writers, but rather an aversion to conducting such debate (and indeed the primary intellectual activities themselves) at such a heady level of abstraction as was allegedly the norm elsewhere.

However, that abstraction which we call 'a culture' is made up of a vast congeries of ideas, values, habits, customs, and so on, which are not necessarily all consistent with and functionally supportive of each other. For the purposes of expository argument, we characterize a particular culture in terms of one or more prominent characteristics, but the risk is that subsequent repetition of this description allows us to lose sight of the fact that that culture also comprises quite other, conflicting, even directly contradictory, elements as well. In trying to bring out the main pattern in the carpet, the historian has to try at the same time not to lose sight of the other motifs in the weave. This bland, general truth is particularly pertinent to this topic, since various forms of 'the absence thesis' have in fact coexisted with all kinds of assertions about the glories of English literary, cultural, or scientific achievements, or even about the efficacy in English public life of 'liberal ideals' or of 'men of principle', beliefs which, if elaborated, would lie somewhat athwart the stereotypes of the 'unintellectual English'.[8]

But nonetheless, the stereotype of the pragmatic, low-temperature, abstraction-avoiding English inevitably coloured subsequent discussion. The persistence of this set of national self-descriptions clearly played a significant part in determining the reception of the concept of 'intellectuals' from the turn of the twentieth century, so much so that what we are dealing with here may be seen as part of the modern cultural equivalent of the Whig interpretation of English political history. It has in this respect been an example of those cultural images the very frequency of whose repetition ingrains them beyond the power of rational criticism to dislodge. Such images then function rather in the way that the bric-a-brac of 'heritage' does, immediately recognizable as providing accepted signifiers of 'English life' even though they do not, except as it were in quotation marks or as a form of self-conscious allusion, form part of anyone's actual life. Thus, this familiar stock of images continues to be drawn upon at moments of ostensibly self-reflexive generalizing, such as the writing of articles about the lack of an intelligentsia in Britain and so on, even though these images may remain quite markedly at variance with the reality of behaviour in the society being described.

II

These complexities can be made more vivid by considering the range of terms used in Victorian and Edwardian Britain to refer to those types of figures often later labelled 'intellectuals', and then by asking whether such figures were thought to be in some way less prominent, less influential, or less creative than their counterparts in other countries.

The vocabulary into which the term 'intellectuals' began to make its awkward and self-conscious entrance in the first two decades of the century was already well stocked with words and phrases which could be used in a partially cognate fashion. 'Men of letters' had been perhaps the most widely used term in the mid-Victorian period, though by the end of the century it was beginning to acquire its more restricted sense of reviewers and essayists, even (more critically), book-men, amateurs, mere *littérateurs*. 'Leading minds' and similar terms ('thinkers', 'men of ideas') were common, and there was a growing lexicon of words to refer to scholars, men of science, dons, professors. Artists, writers, 'men of culture', and so on formed another node. There was also a cluster of terms which ran from the deliberately slightly archaic 'moralists' or 'sages', through 'social critics' to more neutral terms such as 'social observers' and (later) 'commentators'. What is particularly interesting for my purpose is to note, first, how contemporaries seemed to experience no difficulty in deploying this extensive vocabulary along-side invocations of the stereotypes of the 'unintellectual English', and second, how figures who exemplified these variously described roles were assumed to be at least as plentiful in Britain as elsewhere. Few admirers of 'the French intellect' were as ardent as John Stuart Mill, yet even in his writings 'the principal leaders of opinion', 'the chief representatives of intellect', and so on were categories that existed on both sides of the Channel, however lamentably the English occupants of those categories were held to have performed.[9]

One of Mill's own most ardent admirers, John Morley, to whom several of these labels were applied at different stages in his long and varied career, nicely illustrates the way in which potentially contradictory elements in a common cultural stock could be called upon for different purposes. In his minor classic *On Compromise*, first published in 1874, he addressed the issue with an degree of self-consciousness unusual in writing on this topic:

> Though England counts her full share of fearless truth-seekers in most departments of enquiry, yet there is on the whole no weakening, but a rather marked confirmation, of what has become an inveterate national characteristic, and has long been recognized as such; a profound distrust, namely, of all general principles; a profound dislike, both of much reference to them, and of any disposition to invest them with practical authority; and a silent but most pertinacious measurement of philosophic truths by political tests.[10]

Morley, a writer who frequently returned to French Enlightenment subjects and who was responsive to the charms of clear and coherent ideas, could not be unam-bivalently enthusiastic about this national characteristic, but he nonetheless held that it was by now a truth beyond contention. And the truth, notice, is not that there was any lack of 'fearless truth-seekers' in England, but more specific-ally that there was a resistance to investing 'general principles' with 'practical author-ity', and—a reminder of the dimension of life that Morley chiefly had in mind—an insistence on putting 'philosophic truths' to 'political tests'. He went on:

> The most obvious agency at work in the present exaggeration of the political standard as the universal test of truth, is to be found in some contemporary incidents. The influ-ence of France upon England since the revolution of 1848 has tended wholly to the

discredit of abstract theory and general reasoning among us, in all that relates to politics, morals, and religion.

He selected 1848 rather than 1789 because he believed, whether accurately or not, that in the later revolution 'the fundamental structure and organic condition of the social union' was called into question by such theories in a way that it had not been in 1789. The ill-considered attempts to 'apply' such theories 'have had the natural effect of deepening the English dislike of a general theory'. But Morley did not conclude from this that the task of bringing 'intellect' to bear on the questions of the day was a hopeless one; quite the contrary. When he was concerned to combat what he saw as the excessive pragmatism of public life in Britain, Morley could still call upon 'the instructed or intellectually privileged class' to provide leadership for the rest in the matter of principles.[11] Reflecting later on the attacks directed at the *Fortnightly Review*, which he edited from 1867 to 1882, he identified his sense of the journal's role in particularly interesting terms: 'The notion of anything like an intervention of the literary and scientific class in political affairs touched a certain jealousy which is always to be looked for in the positive and practical man.'[12] Here he is assuming that the role of the *Fortnightly* was not to be understood in sectarian political terms, though in practice it largely spoke for advanced radicalism, but as a mode of 'intervention' by a single 'literary and scientific class' ('scientific' clearly being used in its older sense to mean any learned or disciplined enquiry)—or in other words, those who were later to be designated 'the intellectuals'.[13] Even though 'class' was being used loosely here, such a sentiment confirmed that growing self-consciousness in the later decades of the century on the part of those who cultivated 'the intellectual life'.

At the same time, other commentators chose to emphasize what could be seen as contrasts with the situation in continental Europe. Writing in 1871, Bagehot quoted Gladstone's recently stated opinion that 'unhappily we scarcely possessed in England the kind of writer who abroad is called a publicist'. (This term, which had still been regarded as a neologism in the 1830s but which was, as we saw above, used unselfconsciously by Ernest Barker in the 1920s, was defined by the compilers of the *OED* at the beginning of the twentieth century as 'A writer on current public topics; a journalist who makes political matters his speciality'.[14]) Bagehot went on to give his own gloss on this category, of which he took Nassau Senior (an edition of whose journals he was ostensibly reviewing) as a native instance. Senior wrote about politics and lived among politicians,

> but he had none of the ties to them usual in England. He was neither a practical politician, engaged in real affairs, nor the editor of a political periodical, nor even a stirring writer addressing a large audience. He devoted much of his time to temporary politics, but he always dealt with them in an abstract and philosophical manner. He always endeavoured to deal with the permanent aspects of them, he addressed only thoughtful men, he was a 'didactic member' of the republic of letters; and this we may suppose is the idea of the publicist.[15]

Bagehot thought that by the time he was writing this, the increased speed of modern life and consequent brevity of journalistic writing had made such a category obsolete anyway (a favourite theme to which he often recurred). On this occasion, he claimed not to find this a matter for regret, preferring to see such men of 'philosophic' ability devoting themselves to some large topic or department of learning rather than squandering their abilities in commentary on the passing political show (Bagehot liked to affect this world-weary tone even though he devoted so much of his own energies to that 'show'). But what is particularly interesting about his characterization of Senior is the way in which he triangulates the role of the 'publicist' with three others which, by implication, had now largely occupied the ground in Britain: the 'practical politician, engaged in real affairs'; the 'editor of a political periodical'; and the 'stirring writer addressing a large audience'. There was some suggestion, in other words, that it was the closeness of such individuals' engagement with affairs that precluded them from addressing 'thoughtful men' in a 'philosophical manner' about contemporary politics, though by implication this possibility, having now disappeared in Britain, remained open in other countries. Viewed from further away, it does not seem hard to identify several figures who filled this role in Britain at the time, unless one interprets Bagehot's criteria in a deliberately rigorist way, but it is true that the *term* 'publicist' did not altogether prosper in Britain.

In practice, as I have argued elsewhere, contemporaries recognized that 'leading thinkers', 'men of letters' and such like had actually played a very prominent part in public debate in Britain in the Victorian period, including in those set-piece moments when particular political issues divided the educated class along lines of moral principle, such as the Governor Eyre controversy of 1867 or the Bulgarian Atrocities agitation of 1876, where the leading figures of the country's intellectual life attempted to throw their cultural authority into the balance in ways which would have been reassuringly familiar even to the most parochial Left-Bank *enragé* of the 1950s.[16] Indeed, the leading authority on the Bulgarian Agitation was later to draw the classic parallel:

> Perhaps only the Dreyfus Affair among political *causes célèbres* can compare with the Bulgarian atrocities agitation for the brilliance of the patronage and the opposition which it evoked publicly among the greatest contemporary names in literature, art, science, and philosophy. Indeed, the intervention of 'the intellectuals' in the agitation may be said to have marked the beginning on a considerable scale in Britain of the phenomenon described by Julien Benda in his *La Trahison des clercs*: the new and historically unprecedented prestige of the 'clerks' in politics in the later nineteenth century.[17]

Here, no striking contrast between Britain and elsewhere, even between Britain and the acknowledged home of 'political intellectuals' is assumed; rather, Britain is acknowledged as participating in, and taking the lead chronologically speaking, in a Europe-wide development. Here, too, the sense of a learned and literary class is strong. (At the time, Morley had made a similar point in the idiom of the day: as the Agitation gathered pace, he remarked to Frederic Harrison that it would be an interesting sight 'to see *Mind* in such force'.) Shannon keeps quotation marks around 'intellectuals' to avoid anachronism, but he has no doubt that this is the appropriate term. A couple of pages later, when referring back to the Governor Eyre controversy of 1867, he refers to the agitation it caused 'among English intellectuals' without even this hesitation.[18]

Returning to nineteenth-century usage, it will be evident that some of the terms I have listed were occupational categories, some cultural roles, some principally evaluative terms. One of the reasons why 'intellectuals' was eventually to take root may in part have been its convenience as a collective term across a range of roles for which no single term existed. The Victorians and Edwardians sometimes spoke of 'the cultivated elite', but that was a broader term, running in to the upper and upper-middle classes more generally, and characteristically emphasizing education, culture, eventually 'the arts'. A precursor of the sociological sense was 'brain-workers' or, even more ungainly, 'workers by brain' (in parallel formation to 'workers by hand'), but that never really caught on outside Socialist circles, until, in the guise of modern sociological theory, it reappears as 'knowledge workers'. And of course there was a whole other range of terms which functioned in the way in which the later subjective sense of 'intellectuals' has done, from such university slang as 'reading man' and on to more ambivalent or pejorative terms such as 'bookworm' and 'bluestocking'.

As this varied vocabulary suggests, there was also by the end of the nineteenth century no little self-consciousness about the various parts now played in the national life by intellectual and literary activity. Even if T. W. Heyck was, in my view, wrong to claim that it had become common in Britain by the end of the nineteenth century to refer to a whole stratum of society by the plural noun 'intellectuals', he was right to chart an increasing anxiety about the effects of intellectual specialization, involving a heightened concern with the nature of 'the intellectual life' and a partial sense of apartness among those who saw themselves as charged with responsibility for 'the intellectual life of the nation'.[19] But these developments were not, for the most part, understood to be peculiar to Britain, and just as the organization of universities and learned bodies frequently involved an attempt to emulate the scholarly achievements of the Germans, so in such matters as the formation of a literary bohemia, partly removed from and at odds with conventional society, Britain was seen to be following a pattern better established in France, as the absorption of the French vocabulary indicated. Although in both these cases the comparison could be framed as a reproach to Britain's backwardness, the differences, such as they were, amounted to differences of degree, not kind.

III

In addition to the various collective categories itemized in the previous section, one further term made occasional appearances alongside this vocabulary, a term whose very existence has sometimes been taken to mark a distinctive national tradition in these matters, namely the ideal of 'the clerisy'. This notion had enjoyed only a very intermittent life since its formulation by Coleridge in the early nineteenth century, and the term never fully established itself in common usage. Indeed, I suspect that its occasional appearance in the course of the twentieth century has usually represented an attempt by those who precisely wished to resist the domestication of the term 'intellectuals' by appealing to a native, and more genteel, alternative. It thus takes its part in the repertoire of denial.

The origins of the term 'clerisy' also indicate something of the continuing dialectic which tends to structure thinking on this topic. The history of the relations between the public and those referred to as 'men of letters', 'sages', or 'public moralists' is a history of need, disdain, and fantasy on both sides; relations, therefore, that have been shot through with ambivalence. And each generation, at least from the late eighteenth century onwards, has tended to see the 'public' of its own time as a corruption of, or decline from, a healthier and worthier public, located in a necessarily vague past. Even in the Romantic period itself, figures such as Southey or Coleridge did not have the untroubled, confident relation to their contemporary public that later admirers tended to ascribe to them.[20] Their use of such literary genres as the dialogue or the letter was an attempt simultaneously to reach the unspecified and potentially limitless audience of print while at the same time recreating some of the intimacy of conversation or correspondence. Similarly, Hazlitt's 'familiar style', which was to serve as something of a model for later generations of critics who aspired to recreate a 'lost' intimacy with an educated readership, was consciously adopted as a voice that was *not* appropriate to the new age; it was an attempt to refashion a mode of address to the reader that was already felt to be archaic. This involved these writers in sharply distinguishing themselves from 'professional' men of letters, demonized figures who were alleged to pursue no goal higher than that of gratifying the fickle tastes of the public created by the 'commercialization' of letters (the charge was to become a familiar one). This was an essential, indeed almost ritualized, move in self-definition: the 'professional' men of letters were complicit with a corrupt commercial civilization, whereas the true social critic wrote out of a sense of considered opposition to the forces that were degrading the quality of life in contemporary society.

It is as part of this ambivalent relation to the public, and the sense of new publics being created by the growth of commercial society, that Coleridge developed the notion of 'the clerisy'. The first appearances of the term are in works which were published posthumously, but which suggest that he used it as early as 1818, though the *locus classicus* of the idea is generally taken to be *On the Constitution of Church and State*, which was completed in 1829–30.[21] There is some instability in his usage of the term: at one point he defined it as the nation's 'learned men, whether poets, or philosophers, or scholars', and at another as the representatives of 'the national church' who were to be 'distributed throughout the country, so as not to leave even the smallest integral part or division without a resident guide, guardian, and instructor'.[22] But the more closely one attends to Coleridge's original conception, the more remote it comes to seem from the functions its later champions have wanted to see it perform. To begin with, the conception is ineliminably religious. It is primarily a means of diffusing *spiritual* cultivation among the population at large; the bulk of the members of Coleridge's clerisy are closer in both role and level of attainment to the local vicar than to leaders of opinion in scholarship and culture. Moreover, Coleridge did not envisage that the clerisy occupied itself with the kind of 'speaking out' which, under whatever description, has been one of the defining activities of those who exercise cultural authority with a general public. Rather, they were to pursue cultivation as an *inward* activity, and hence to influence their neighbours more by example than by writing. The role also had two further features that mark a different kind of distance from later conceptions of the intellectual. First, Coleridge saw the clerisy as being supported by a 'national' endowment; that is to say, not merely that they were to receive something more like a stipend or pension from the state than a salary for employment or fees for services (thereby emphasizing that they embodied a principle counter to the one governing commercial society), but that this was to be acknowledged as a first charge on 'the nationalty', a kind of nationwide tithe, rather than a (revocable) item of government expenditure. Second, he wished them to be as little different from their neighbours in manner of life as possible: they were therefore to be married, living locally, scattered about the country. They were emphatically not to be concentrated in a few great metropolitan or academic centres.

Few of those to whom the label 'intellectuals' has attached itself have corresponded to this role. In some ways, tutors for the Workers' Educational Association and similar bodies in, say, the first two-thirds of the twentieth century came nearer in spirit to Coleridge's notion of how the clerisy should function than have the more glamorous metropolitan intellectuals, even though the generally radical political inclinations of such tutors would have been far removed from his Anglican imaginings. They lived and mixed, they were an example, they inspired; they were even appointed by the equivalent of a diocesan authority (the extramural delegacy of a major university, usually). Some of the early appointments to the new civic universities at the end of the nineteenth and beginning of the twentieth centuries had something of this character, too: they were self-consciously 'missionaries of culture', taking light into dark places. In all these cases a defining aspect of the role was to impart a certain level of self-cultivation.

Of course, these distinctive characteristics of the clerisy ideal have been part of its appeal to more conservative commentators, eager to distance themselves from the insurgent associations of (European) intellectuals, still more of an 'intelligentsia'. T. S. Eliot provides one of the most prominent examples of this response, and I discuss his use of the term in more detail in Ch. 13. By the late twentieth century, the datedness of Coleridge's term had become more clearly a handicap, though it could still figure in ruminations about the distinctiveness of British social attitudes. Taking stock in 1995 of *The Way We Live Now*, Richard Hoggart entitled one part of his book 'Who Needs a Clerisy?'. His argument was that Britain (he more often referred to 'England') did indeed need figures willing to stand up in public debate and defend judgements of value in reasoned terms, figures whom he recognized would be called 'intellectuals' were there not what he detected as a certain resistance to the term. Personally, he hankered after calling such a category a 'clerisy', without tying it at all closely to its Coleridgean original. The frame of reference hovering in the background was indicated by his moving on within a few paragraphs to say: 'the debate about The Condition of England did not die after the mid- to late-nineteenth century,' for it is precisely within the terms of the 'culture-and-society tradition', and its search for a source of 'cultivation' to oppose to the mechanistic logic of commercialism, that the ideal of 'the clerisy' belongs. Returning to the topic in his conclusion, Hoggart feared that late-twentieth-century egalitarianism would have no truck with such airs of superiority: 'Plainly, to hint at the need for some sort of "clerisy" would be to invite instant dismissal.'[23] But not from all quarters, perhaps, for the appeal of this pleasingly cultured term seems likely to remain wherever what I am calling 'the tradition of denial' continues to flourish.

Some commentators have even managed to find an explanation for the absence of 'true' intellectuals in the continuing presence of the clerisy ideal. For example:

> It is important to recognise the crucial distinctions between Coleridge's clerisy and that more modern type of intellectual elite, the intelligentsia, for the continuing orientation of English intellectuals towards the clerisy ideal largely accounts for the persistent absence of a true intelligentsia in England. By proposing an officially recognized 'permanent, nationalised learned order' of intellectuals Coleridge deliberately deprived them of the function of completely independent criticism which is the idea of the classic intelligentsia (in its original Russian sense).[24]

The use of 'deliberately' risks an anachronistic imputation of intention here, but what is more striking in this statement is the exaggeration in the description of the model against which the English situation is described: 'completely independent criticism' could, at best, provide a regulatory ideal; it hardly describes any actual historical situation, in Russia or anywhere else, though the comment is a reminder of the way in which such unhistorical contrasts continue to inform so much of the writing on this topic.

IV

Characterizations of national identity are, by their nature, always implicitly comparative; where the description focuses on a 'lack' or 'absence', this comparative basis starts to become visible and, as it were, structural. As I have already suggested, in the present case the contrast, implicit where not explicit, has been, above all, with France. Once again, this has been grafted onto a broader pre-existing contrast, and again it is one with a very long history. It was already a staple of reflection in literary and theatrical terms in the late seventeenth century, and it was elaborated in cultural and political terms throughout the eighteenth and nineteenth centuries.[25] Indeed, the telling of the national story by the Whig historians of the nineteenth century effectively required the implied, and often explicit, contrast of the French oscillation between revolution and despotism to point its own celebratory moral, and although the practical political conclusions that this contrast helped to illustrate were to lose some of their relevance in the course of the twentieth century, the contrast itself continued to inform reflections on the topic of intellectuals to a quite striking extent. In this sense, the national self-congratulation manifested in Burke's celebration of the lack in Britain of those 'political men of letters' who allegedly helped foment the French Revolution prefigures a good deal of twentieth-century writing on the subject.

For present purposes, it is enough to underline the shaping power of these pre-existing cultural attitudes, and to recall the larger pattern of cross-channel musings into which they have so comfortably fitted: the picture of a centralized and bureaucratized state contrasting with one in which local authorities, voluntary associations, and a host of competing powers have assured a system of checks and balances; the picture of a society given over to sensuous cultivation and sexual licence contrasting with one where plain living and moral rectitude were as intimately linked as cleanliness and godliness (with which they were sometimes confused); and the picture of a culture constantly oscillating between rigid artistic rules and bohemian aesthetic excess contrasting with one in which a certain easy informality in the handling of style and genre was taken to be the mark of fidelity to the rich variousness of human nature. (Contrasts which were still more impressionistic also played their part. Reflecting early in the First World War on French nationalism, the historian and Liberal politician H. A. L. Fisher could assume his readers would readily concur in his observation that 'in England, where the sense of humour is comparatively strong and the dramatic instinct comparatively weak, movements are more easily killed by ridicule than they are in France'.[26])

Within the French historical literature on intellectuals, the Dreyfus Affair has, as we have seen, generally been looked back to as a moment of origin, with the publication in January 1898 of the 'protestation' against Dreyfus's conviction, signed by a long list of those who appended details of their literary standing or academic titles and qualifications, as 'the document on which their public existence is founded'.[27] But while references in Britain to the Affair and its aftermath were eventually to help to put this sense of the term 'intellectuals' into more general circulation, this was not an aspect of the matter that attracted much attention in the British press at the time. Instead, what is striking is, first, the extent to which diverse sections of opinion in Britain were united in the belief that Dreyfus was innocent, and, second, the overwhelming tendency in political and journalistic comment to attribute this gross miscarriage of justice to the long-standing defects of French civilization and the French national character. One might even say, exaggerating only slightly to make the point, that opinion in Britain gave no sign of feeling the need of a distinctive group of 'intellectuals' to take up Dreyfus's cause, since both the original miscarriage of justice and its roots in French 'decadence' were plain for all to see.

Extrapolating from the divisions within French society, one might have expected the bulk of upper-class and official opinion in Britain to rally to the cause of the army and the judiciary and uphold Dreyfus's guilt. But in fact this was far from the case, beginning with the Queen herself who was an ardent believer in Dreyfus's innocence. These convictions appear to have been determined as much by traditional perceptions of the characteristics of England's great defining Other as by any particularly searching analysis of the publicly available evidence. As the most authoritative recent survey of this body of opinion concludes:

> In short, if one synthesizes all the main themes of the British establishment's response to the affair, they amount to a critique of French 'civilization', the victim of its history. Decadent, subject to political instability and panic, lacking a strong and honest political class, a prey to mob violence whipped up by an immoral and uncontrolled press, 'her civilization is shown to be a mere external skin, veneering a body corrupt, decaying and ready to perish'.[28]

Studies of responses to the Affair in the broader periodical press come to a similar conclusion: 'These and other ideas on "national character" and "national psychology" were basic determinants in interpreting the Affair and in inscribing its meanings.'[29] The frequently drawn Whiggish moral pointed to England's good fortune in a history which had entrenched constitutional liberties and the rule of law. Indeed, following wider intellectual fashions of the moment, credit for this achievement was attributed to the 'Anglo-Saxon peoples'—a category that included the United States as well as the white settler colonies, all similarly beneficiaries of a legal system based on the Common Law—whose moral qualities were complacently contrasted with those of devious and decadent 'Latins'.[30] American responses to the Affair were somewhat more diverse, but by and large colluded in this ethnic self-congratulation.[31]

The Affair was followed closely in the British press, where opinion did not divide along the usual political or cultural lines. Leo Maxse, editor of the *National Review*, hardly a radical organ at the time, became a particularly committed crusader on behalf of Dreyfus's innocence, and his journal carried many long articles on the subject. The respectable, indeed distinguished, standing of such 'Dreyfusard' opinion in Britain was well illustrated by the profiles of the two figures who proved to be perhaps his most effective champions with a wider public. The first was Sir Godfrey Lushington, former Fellow of All Souls, former Permanent

Under-Secretary at the Home Office, who wrote, among many other contributions, an extraordinarily long, and long-renowned, letter to the *Times* explaining the procedural complexities of the case (a letter that thereafter figured in the *Guinness Book of Records* for many years as the longest letter ever to have been published in that newspaper.[32]) The second was the distinguished linguist and authority on Armenian (not, alas, Tibetan) manuscripts, F. C. Conybeare, whose 1899 book on the Affair drew upon his extensive range of French informants. Although such British commentators were sympathetic to the Dreyfusards, it is noticeable that they tend to concentrate on the defects of French civilization as a whole rather than drawing attention to the sectional nature of the divisions within France, and there is certainly no overt identification with the newly christened 'intellectuals'.

The generalized Whiggish confidence which was almost second nature to large swathes of the conventionally educated class in Britain at the close of the nineteenth century began to take some hard knocks in the course of the twentieth, but just as it seemed possible that some of the venerable political contrasts might lose their force as the distance from the French revolutionary upheavals and the answering English Burkean adaptations increased, then along came a sequence of episodes and circumstances that reanimated old contrasts and gave them fresh plausibility—the Popular Front in the 1930s, the Vichy regime during the war, the countervailing rise of the *résistants* and Communists, followed by the chronic instability of the Fourth Republic, the whole accompanied by the descant of Existentialism, the continuing political attention accorded to writers and philosophers, and the scandal of Apache dancing in smokey *caves*. The result was that in its own, updated terms, the contrast could be made to seem as illuminating in the 1950s as it undeniably had been in the 1850s. The needs of self-definition drove the accounts in both cases: celebrants of English national identity have always had *une certaine idée de la France*.

Two examples, chosen more or less at random, will illustrate the continuing vitality of this set of contrasts in the middle of the twentieth century. As an example of the self-serving complacency and anti-intellectualism which has tended to accompany the invocation of the French comparison, one could hardly do better than the *TLS* review in 1955 of Raymond Aron's *L'Opium des intellectuels*. The reviewer (in those days anonymous, of course) seized on Aron's highly partisan account of French intellectuals' self-intoxication and utopianism as providing fresh illustration of a well-worn contrast: 'We can reasonably congratulate ourselves', wrote the reviewer, 'that our men of letters and academics either have more sense or are not encouraged to be so silly, but it is an ominous fact that the world is full of intellectuals of the French type.' 'We' have men of letters and academics; 'they' have intellectuals. Aron had, of course, been using the term in the French political sense, but the *TLS* reviewer's usage slides between senses without acknowledgement, as well as seeming pretty much to equate political intervention and silliness. The reviewer endorsed the Tocquevillian contention, elaborated by Aron, that in Britain scholars and men of letters had traditionally been sobered by intimate involvement in practical affairs, a situation that brought rewards as well as responsibilities: intellectuals in France may get a lot of public attention, but they are, the review went on, 'not nearly as much in contact with reality as they are, if they want to be, in the much more closely integrated English society'. (A rough but only slightly unfair paraphrase might be to say that if one had been at school with a chap, one could always get on the phone to invite him to lunch at one's club and find out what was really going on—that special sense of being 'in contact with reality' which had long been second nature to the well-connected in British society.) Similarly, the reviewer hints at the way in which authority would be less readily granted to a potential intellectual in the 'cultural' sense in Britain, where, in dismissive contrast to France, 'the fact that a man has written a good novel means simply that he is a man who has written a good novel'.[33] Throughout, Sartre, predictably, figures as the antitype (this is 1955, remember), and subsequent attitudes towards 'intellectuals' in Britain were, as I have already suggested, enduringly shaped by the attention, some favourable but mostly hostile, stirred by Sartre and his associates in a period when the contrasts between Britain and France in these matters seemed particularly marked.

And for an example in which the complacency is shot through with ambivalence one may turn to Hartley's *A State of England* (the book which provides the epigraph to the Introduction, above).[34] Hartley's opening chapter dwells much on the contrast with 'the continent of Europe', where 'intellectuals, whether they are writers, scientists, artists, or university teachers, live more publicly and dangerously than we do here'. A slight frisson of arousal makes its presence felt in the prose at this point, a hint of the excitement of forbidden pleasures. But the corrective lash of matron's tongue is soon felt, as in the dismissive observation that 'anyone who takes the trouble to be sufficiently thrusting can give himself undue prominence by an aggressive assumption of continental intellectual manners'. And the natural habitat of such manners is not far to seek: even without his references to Sartre and his *confrères*, Hartley's readers knew how to interpret his allusions to 'the feverish discussions in cafés, the irreparable quarrels, the speeches at congresses, the signatures to manifestos' and so on.[35] One soon realizes that in the literature on intellectuals these features operate as familiar symbols in much the same way as, in the literature of the travel brochures, do the beret, the baguette, and the string of garlic.

Although France has undeniably been central to this cultural imaginary, my earlier quotation from Seeley should remind us that other European contrasts have also played their part. One obvious strand was the way in which English culture in the second half of the nineteenth century could at times seem to be labouring under a sustained inferiority complex towards the achievements of German universities. Most of the academic innovations of the late nineteenth and early twentieth centuries sought to justify themselves by invoking this unfavourable contrast, from the establishment of the first university science laboratories in the 1860s and 1870s, through the founding of the British Academy at the turn of the century, and on to the reluctant (and, for a long time, only partial) acceptance of the need for higher research degrees in the 1910s and 1920s. This particular contrast could also on occasion produce some slightly envious musing upon the exalted social status of the figure of 'Herr Professor' in Germany (especially on the part of professors), though more often it issued (especially on the part of those not in universities) in a kind of gruff satisfaction that pedants were not allowed to take themselves so seriously in Britain.[36] Picturing Germany as 'the land of *Geist*' could, after all, easily be inflected with either envious or disparaging attitudes as required. And after 1914 evidence was always to hand to underline that intellectual self-importance rarely travelled without its usual partner, political self-deception. As mentioned in Ch. 1, the notorious 'manifesto of the 93 professors' in support of German war aims in 1914 was sometimes cited at the time and afterwards as 'the manifesto of the intellectuals of Germany', a form of citation that was taken to encapsulate the perniciousness of the partnership.

More broadly, selectively interpreted encounters with a diverse range of European intellectual figures fed an appetite always hungry to have its preferred stereotypes confirmed. For example, there were frequent opportunities in the drawing-rooms and discussion-groups of mid- and late-Victorian London to encounter a diverse range of European exiles and refugees, some of whom were self-described revolutionaries and plotters, some merely itinerant or only temporarily displaced writers and philosophers, and some others figures of acknowledged standing in an international literary or scholarly community. But reports of their volubility and excitability, of the common extremism of their theorizing and their politics, of their frequent assumption that the scribblings of the men of letters could make governments cower and dynasties totter—all this was grist to the English construction of a type perceived as intrinsically alien, a type of 'the intellectual' *avant la lettre*. The encounter with German and Jewish intellectual refugees in the 1930s may have involved a kind of reprise of these themes, a confirmation of the characteristics of a figure who was at once exotic and familiar. And indeed, many of the emigré scholars brought with them an experience to which there was no exact correspondence in British life, the experience of combining the incomparably exalted cultural authority of the German professor with the unthinkably humiliating status of being the despised and persecuted victim of the official creed of one's own country. Such people, their new hosts liked to say, were 'true' intellectuals (and intellectuals, it was frequently assumed, were particularly likely to be Jews). Britain, it was commonly felt, had a long tradition of providing such people with a refuge (in practice the record was inconsistent, of course), but, as with the colourful exotics stared at in zoos, their presence could be turned into a visible reminder that the species to which they belonged was not native to these islands.

A comparative judgement of this type is also implicit in the passage that serves as the epigraph to this chapter, a passage one finds quoted on several occasions in the standard literature on this topic. 'No people has ever distrusted and despised the intellect and intellectuals more than the British.' I suspect this passage—the crisp brutality of its conclusiveness being not the least of its charms—entered the recycling chain as a result of being quoted in Richard Hofstadter's widely used *Anti-Intellectualism in American Life*, where it is credited to Leonard Woolf. In the paragraph in which the quotation occurs, Hofstadter is giving an even-handed consideration of whether anti-intellectualism is more marked in American society than elsewhere: his graceful prose allows him at one moment to appear to question American exceptionalism—'Although the situation of American intellectuals poses problems of special urgency and poignancy, many of their woes are the common experiences of intellectuals elsewhere'—and at another to appear to endorse it—'Perhaps Mr Woolf had not given sufficient thought to the claims of the Americans to supremacy in this respect.'[37]

Actually, if one tracks the Woolf remark to its source, one finds that he, too, is balancing contrasting emphases (as Hofstadter does acknowledge in a footnote). In an article which appeared in *Encounter* in 1959, the 79-year old Woolf was recalling the brilliant figures whom he knew at Trinity at the turn of the century, singling out the philosophers A. N. Whitehead, Bertrand Russell, and G. E. Moore, for the last of whom the article is a kind of obituary tribute. Woolf then goes on: 'It is a remarkable fact—a superb example of our inflexible irrationality and inconsistency—that, although no people has ever despised and distrusted the intellect and intellectuals more than the British, these three philosophers were each awarded the highest and rarest of honours, the Order of Merit.'[38] That does indeed appear to be a singular way of expressing scorn and distrust, though it would be entirely consonant with the case I make throughout this book to find that a tradition of self-satisfied hostility to the *idea* of 'intellectuals' has coexisted with the kind of respect for intellectual activity which is assumed to be characteristic of other societies. In this regard, therefore, Woolf's observation may constitute less of a challenge to 'the claims of the Americans to supremacy' as far as the low status of intellectuals is concerned than may at first appear.

V

In considering the aetiology of the 'absence thesis', it is important to discriminate different stages in its elaboration. They do not form a smooth progression or cumulation, and they are distinguished by markedly different degrees of self-consciousness. The term 'intellectuals', as we have seen, slowly infiltrated itself into educated usage, at first mainly referring to self-consciously bookish or artistic persons, but the substantive discussion of the position and role of such people in English society tended to occur under the rubric of long-standing native preoccupations, such as the forms to be taken by the alliance of 'brains and numbers' in politics, or the mutations in the relations between the writer or artist and an increasingly segmented market, and so on (preoccupations later schematized under the labels of 'Socialism' and 'Modernism' respectively).

It was largely political events in Europe, such as the Dreyfus Affair itself or the Russian Revolution of 1917, which enabled a revivified version of the Whig story to underwrite generalizations about the different role and behaviour of 'thinkers, writers, and scholars' in Britain and on the continent of Europe. The emphasis on 'intellectuals' as an inverted-commas-wearing neologism, and still more the currency of 'intelligentsia' in the 1910s, complete with uncertain pronunciation, then served to draw attention to the foreignness of the phenomenon in question. But, as we have also seen, non-political senses of the term 'intellectuals' continued to predominate during the first part of the century. The situation during these decades was, therefore, a complex one. It was not just that the inherited assumptions about the links between the national distaste (or even incapacity) for abstract ideas and the lack of extremism of the native political tradition coexisted, as usual, with considerable counter-evidence on both matters. There was also the increasing currency of a term, some, at least, of whose uses drew attention precisely to figures existing in all modern societies, Britain included, who made it their business to issue public pronouncements on links between ideas and life in society, including political life. In the course of the 1920s and, especially, the 1930s it became much more common, in Britain as elsewhere, to speak in collective terms of 'the intellectuals' and 'the intelligentsia': the terms became part of the common coin of the political and literary discourses of the latter decade, and indeed tended to reflect precisely the points at which the two discourses intersected. This stimulated a certain amount of explicit analysis, though, as we shall see, it tended to be marked more by forms of ambivalence or hostility than by outright denial.

The 1930s might be expected to occupy a special place in any account of the question of intellectuals in Britain (an expectation which this book deliberately frustrates), not least because that decade came in retrospect to figure as the one period when something like a putatively classic, politically engaged 'intelligentsia' existed and had some impact within British culture. For example, writing in the late 1960s (perhaps the latest moment at which this view could confidently be held), T. R. Fyvel observed: 'The novel feature of the thirties was that for the first time English intellectuals reacted as a class to political events. . . . [F]or the first time in England something like a dissident intelligentsia had been formed.'[39] In fact, of course, there was no sense in which intellectuals had acted 'as a class' in the 1930s: a (smallish) number of writers and academics expressed 'progressive' views, a (smaller) number expressed 'reactionary' views, while a (much larger) number expressed no such views at all. Those in subsequent decades who bemoaned the absence of just such a 'dissident intelligentsia' in Britain frequently evinced nostalgia for what they had come to see as the enviably 'committed' ideological politics of those years, never matched in subsequent decades, an attitude which has fuelled much of the scholarly interest in 'writers of the 1930s'. The pessimistic premise of such nostalgia is displayed in, for example, the later claim that 'the left-wing intellectuals who emerged during the 1930s left no discernible intellectual and cultural legacy'.[40] These accounts depend, as forms of nostalgia always do, on the combination of a highly selective recall with a wildly ahistorical romanticization: however attractive or admirable the personal odysseys of certain individuals may have been, 'left-wing writers' were a small part of the cultural scene as a whole in the 1930s, and there is precious little evidence to support claims about their significant impact on the politics of these years. Bernard Crick was surely right to conclude: 'The famed influence of leftwing intellectuals [in the 1930s] is . . . historically so doubtful'.[41]

What is true, however, is that the experience of the Second World War affected British self-perception on this as on other matters. Indeed, what, in my view, most of the literature on this topic has failed to grasp is that the real heyday of the absence thesis as a fully elaborated position came *after* 1945, and especially in the 1950s. Even then, there were, as I argue throughout this book, different and sometimes conflicting ideas about the nature and role of intellectuals in Britain, but from the middle of the century onwards the claim that the genuine article was not to be found on these shores assumed the status of an orthodoxy. Even the broadly New Left diagnosis of the question, which was to be so influential in the 1960s and 1970s and which perpetuated the romanticization of the 1930s, took many of its terms of reference from the 1950s literature, concurring, on the basis of quite different political assumptions, with the emphasis on British exceptionalism in the matter of 'genuine' intellectuals. The framework laid down in these mid-century decades has been decisive for later historiographical accounts, even though it has been increasingly at variance with actual experience of the position of intellectuals in contemporary British society.

But this is to anticipate. Taking a closer look at representative discussions from the opening decades of the twentieth century, we find few indications of the later preoccupation with 'absence' or 'denial' of intellectuals. Rather, we encounter tangible continuities with that fundamentally confident, albeit sometimes also anxious, Victorian debate on the proper role of the country's 'leading minds'.

NOTES

1. In this paragraph I have drawn upon some phrases from my essay 'Intellectuals in Britain and France in the twentieth century: confusions, contrasts—and convergence?', in Jeremy Jennings (ed.), *Intellectuals in Twentieth-Century France: Mandarins and Samurai* (London: Macmillan, 1993), 199–225.
2. For some starting-points, see Paul Langford, *Englishness Identified: Manners and Character 1650–1850* (Oxford: Oxford University Press, 2000).
3. Edward Bulwer-Lytton, *England and the English* (1833); quoted in Tom Nairn, 'The English literary intelligentsia', in Emma Tennant (ed.), *Bananas* (London: Quartet, 1977), 64.

4. The citation of particular references is otiose here, but for one prominent example of Mill's use of the phrase 'Cimmerian darkness' see 'Coleridge' (1840), in *The Collected Works of John Stuart Mill*, ed. J. M. Robson, 33 vols. (Toronto: Toronto University Press, 1963–91), x. 140; and the *locus classicus* of Arnold's indictment of 'philistinism' is ch. 3 of *Culture and Anarchy* (1869), in *The Collected Prose Works of Matthew Arnold*, ed. R. H. Super, 11 vols. (Ann Arbor: Michigan University Press, 1960–77).
5. J. R. Seeley, 'Liberal education in universities' (1867), in *Lectures and Essays* (London: Macmillan, 1870), 215–16.
6. Ernest Barker, *National Character and the Factors in its Formation* (London: Methuen, 4th edn., 1948 [1st edn. 1927]), 205–6. Barker repeated these claims in similar language in the volume he edited to aid the war effort during the Second World War, *The Character of England* (London: Oxford University Press, 1947).
7. Barker, *National Character*, 205 n.
8. Cf. Ewen Green's recent discussion of the structurally similar claims about the absence of 'ideology' in conservative politics: E. H. H. Green, *Ideologies of Conservatism: Conservative Political Ideas in the Twentieth Century* (Oxford: Oxford University Press, 2002).
9. For some examples, see Giorgios Varouxakis, *Victorian Political Thought on France and the French* (Basingstoke: Palgrave, 2002), 85–6.
10. John Morley, *On Compromise* ([1874] London: Macmillan, 1903), 5.
11. Ibid. 22–3, 212.
12. Quoted in E. M. Everett, *The Party of Humanity: The 'Fortnightly Review' and its Contributors, 1865–1874* (Chapel Hill: University of North Carolina Press, 1939), 324.
13. Later scholars have usually had no hesitation in characterizing Morley's career as that of 'an intellectual in politics'; see e.g. David Hamer, *John Morley, Liberal Intellectual in Politics* (Oxford: Oxford University Press, 1968).
14. *OED*: 'publicist', *sb.*, sense 2.
15. Walter Bagehot, 'Senior's Journals', *Fortnightly Review* (1871); Norman St-John Stevas (ed.), *The Collected Works of Walter Bagehot* (London: The Economist, 1965–), ii. 375.
16. Stefan Collini, *Public Moralists: Political Thought and Intellectual Life in Britain 1850–1930* (Oxford: Oxford University Press, 1991), esp. 144–6, 164–6, 187–8, 230–2; see also Richard Shannon, *Gladstone and the Bulgarian Agitation 1876* (London: Nelson, 1963), and Bernard Semmel, *The Governor Eyre Controversy* (London: MacGibbon & Kee, 1962).
17. Shannon, *Bulgarian Agitation*, 202.
18. Ibid. 216, 204.
19. T. W. Heyck, *The Transformation of Intellectual Life in Victorian England* (Beckenham: Croom Helm, 1982), esp. 'Conclusion: the World of the Intellectuals, 1870–1900'.
20. See the illuminating discussion in Philip Connell, *Romanticism, Economics, and the Question of 'Culture'* (Cambridge: Cambridge University Press, 2001).
21. For further discussion see Ben Knights, *The Idea of the Clerisy in the Nineteenth Century* (Cambridge: Cambridge University Press, 1978), ch. 2; the *OED* also cites the item of his table-talk, attributed to 1832, quoted below.
22. The first comes from his *Table Talk* for 1832, quoted in Knights, *Clerisy*, 41; the second comes from *Church and State*, ch. 5.
23. Richard Hoggart, *The Way We Live Now* (London: Chatto & Windus, 1995), 316, 339.

24. Christopher Kent, *Brains and Numbers: Elitism, Comtism, and Democracy in Mid-Victorian England* (Toronto: University of Toronto Press, 1978), 4.
25. See, among many others, J. W. Burrow, *A Liberal Descent: Victorian Historians and the English Past* (Cambridge: Cambridge University Press, 1981); Gerald Newman, *The Rise of English Nationalism: A Cultural History 1750–1830* (London: Weidenfeld, 1987); Linda Colley, *Britons: Forging the Nation 1707–1837* (London: Yale University Press, 1992).
26. H. A. L. Fisher, 'French nationalism', in his *Studies in History and Politics* (Oxford: Oxford University Press, 1920), 152.
27. Christophe Charle, *Naissance des 'intellectuels', 1880–1900* (Paris: Minuit, 1990), 7; see the discussion at Ch. 1 sect. II above.
28. Robert Tombs, '"Lesser breeds without the law": the British establishment and the Dreyfus affair, 1894–1899', *Historical Journal*, 41 (1998), 506–7, quoting *Blackwood's Edinburgh Magazine* for Oct. 1899.
29. Martyn Cornick, 'The impact of the Dreyfus Affair in late-Victorian Britain', *Franco British Studies*, 6 (1997), 730; see also Cornick, 'Les Grandes Revues victoriennes et l'affaire Dreyfus', *La Revue des revues*, 17 (1994), 53–74.
30. Tombs, '"Lesser breeds"', 509–10; Cornick, 'Impact', 73–5.
31. See Egal Feldman, *The Dreyfus Affair and the American Conscience, 1895–1906* (Detroit: Wayne State University Press, 1981).
32. Cornick, 'Impact', 64.
33. [Anon], 'The role of the intellectuals', *Times Literary Supplement* (16 Sept. 1955), 533–4. The *TLS Contributors' Index* now enables us to to identify the author as the Cambridge historian, Denis Brogan.
34. Anthony Hartley, *A State of England* (London: Hutchinson, 1963); the passage quoted as the epigraph is at p. 25. I discuss this book more fully in Ch. 7.
35. Hartley, *State of England*, 15, 28.
36. See, e.g., the remarks by Harold Nicolson, quoted in Ch. 7 below.
37. Richard Hofstadter, *Anti-Intellectualism in American Life* (New York: Vintage, 1963), 19–20.
38. Leonard Woolf, 'G. E. Moore', *Encounter*, 12 (1959), 68.
39. T. R. Fyvell, *Intellectuals Today: Problems in a Changing Society* (London: Gollancz, 1968), 41, 49.
40. Alan Swingewood, 'Intellectuals and the construction of consensus in postwar England', in Alain G. Gagnon (ed.), *Intellectuals in Liberal Democracies: Political Influence and Social Involvement* (New York: Praeger, 1987), 89.
41. Crick even challenges the assumption that such figures were at least influential within the Communist Party: 'To recruit a few well-known literary intellectuals gave the party prestige, but the party called the tune'; Bernard Crick, 'The brains of Britain', *THES* (14 Jan. 1983), 10.

4

Of Light and Leading

'To require of men, whose knowledge and training peculiarly qualify them to give light and leading to their fellow-citizens, that they shall abstain from active participation in public movements where interests are divided and strong feelings are evoked, is a policy of moral and intellectual mutilation, as degrading to those who are curtailed in their citizenship as it is injurious to the public'.

I

Each week for over seven years before 1914, the question of the role and sense of identity of 'thinkers and writers' in Britain was staged at two regular social gatherings. Both occasions revolved around the production of a weekly periodical; both involved extended, passionate debate about politics and culture; both involved sociability and friendships. Each of the occasions was orchestrated by its own central figure, neither of whom would now appear even in most people's long-list of Britain's leading intellectuals in the twentieth century. The physical location of the two gatherings said much about the contrasting senses of identity involved.

On Mondays, in the late afternoon, the editor of a weekly journal, with some of his regular contributors and one or two aspiring writers, was to be found in the basement room of the ABC restaurant in Chancery Lane. The ostensible purpose of the gathering was to read proofs of that week's issue: the assembled company had tea, they talked and they argued, before moving on to dinner at another inexpensive restaurant, then perhaps to the Holborn Empire ('it removed from us any taint of undue intellectualism which might have been left over from the conclave at the ABC', according to one of the literary aspirants who was to become in time a regular contributor), before ending the evening at the Café Royal, then very much a café. The setting is urban but not stylishly metropolitan; slightly bohemian without being deliberately louche or raffish; and somewhat arty, though more given to criticism than creation and not rich enough to run to collecting. Many of those who attended left testimonials to the value of the gatherings: 'Politics, philosophy, literature, psychology . . . all cultural topics (and in this case *cultural* does not require inverted commas) were discussed.

One could not find so high a level of conversation anywhere else in London; one went away from each discussion with new ideas and new points of view.'

On Tuesdays, at lunchtime, the editor of a different weekly journal, with some of his regular contributors and one or two invited guests, was to be found in a private room of the National Liberal Club in Whitehall Place. The ostensible purpose of this gathering was to have lunch: the formalities were observed, guests were introduced, and then the company fell to discussing current issues, politics above all, sometimes with an eye to the line they would like to take or see taken in next week's issue, sometimes not. The guests might come from several walks of society, though politicians, writers, and editors predominated, and there was a generous sprinkling of foreign notabilities. When proceedings were concluded, they went back to their offices or to their studies, to parliament or to Fleet Street, or on to other, probably less animated but possibly more consequential, meetings. The setting in this case is decidedly metropolitan, at the intersection of clubland, government, and journalism; heavily political, with discussion concentrated on current policy and legislation; and effortlessly well-connected, Cabinet ministers and fêted authors alike coming along as friends or acquaintances of the regulars. According to C. F. G. Masterman, this lunch 'represented something so unique and exhilarating that one would sweep away all other engagements in order to attend', though he was a busy MP and government minister throughout this period.

The two focal individuals in question were, respectively, A. R. Orage, editor of the *New Age*,[1] and H. W. Massingham, editor of the *Nation*,[2] and the similarities and contrasts between them are made all the more compelling by the fact that they each edited their respective papers from 1907 to 1922.

A weekly journal bearing the title the *New Age* had gone through several changes of ownership and identity before it was put up for sale in 1907. The money to buy it was furnished by philanthropists with interests in Socialism and Theosophy (George Bernard Shaw was one), and Orage and Holbrook Jackson were installed as joint editors, bringing out their first issue on 2 May 1907. Orage and Jackson had known each other through the Leeds Art Club before coming to London, and they were both products of the briefly fashionable marriage between aestheticism and Fabianism. But any hope that the older Fabians may have had that they had secured a tame weekly were soon dashed by the independence of the editors, most markedly so after Jackson resigned and Orage became sole editor from January 1908. It was, as its initial advertising proclaimed, 'an independent Socialist weekly', far removed from the conventional party organs; thereafter its masthead proclaimed it 'A Weekly Review of Politics, Literature, and Art'. From the outset, Orage made it a forum for innovation in literature and culture at least as much as in politics. Apart from Orage himself, whose writing was much admired by good literary judges then and later (as in the tribute by T. S. Eliot quoted in Ch. 13 below), the contributors who did most to give the paper its distinctive character in the pre-war years were J. M. Kennedy, deeply versed in European politics and culture and a significant expositor of Nietzsche, perhaps the chief of the paper's presiding intellectual deities, and Beatrice Hastings, one of the relatively few women to make a mark in the journalism of this era. Both Kennedy and Hastings, like Orage himself and many other contributors, wrote under a variety of pseudonyms, in part, perhaps, to conceal the extent to which the paper relied on their contributions; according to one calculation, Orage, Kennedy, Hastings, and A. E. Randall 'wrote approximately one third of the magazine's contents each week' in the years before 1914.[3] Quite soon, T. E. Hulme, the champion of 'Classicism' in literature and ethics, became a leading light, as did Ramiro de Maeztu, who became, along with S. G. Hobson and Orage himself, one of the paper's chief exponents of Guild Socialism. Some of those who were among the most frequent contributors to the paper were not well-known even at the time, and they have since dropped from view almost entirely—this is true of figures such as C. H. Norman, Hulty Carter, and Randall.[4] Nonetheless, despite various changes of tack that were partly due to the temporary prominence of a particular contributor, the *New Age* held fast to its belief that cultural and political matters were fundamentally inseparable, and, as its modern historian put it, in the paper's early years 'the energies of most contributors were devoted to the creation of a coherent Socialist programme for the development of culture as a whole, thus enriching a political theory which tended increasingly to limit itself to economic objectives'.[5] Part of the interest of its heterodoxy lay in the way in which its Classical or 'Tory' philosophy, especially as expounded by Kennedy and Hulme in the years just before 1914, could be used to underwrite a radical social and economic analysis, in which it was hard to distinguish between a neo-medievalizing critique of soulless commercialism and a neo-Nietzschean critique of sentimental liberalism.

The first issue of the *Nation* appeared on 2 March 1907, replacing the ailing *Speaker*, a weekly journal which had attempted to act as the conscience of advanced Liberalism during the previous eight years, notably in its opposition to the Boer War. Massingham, veteran radical journalist, former editor of the *Daily Chronicle* and a renowned parliamentary sketch-writer, was appointed editor of the new weekly. It was his idea that the paper should be edited 'not entirely as a one-man show', so the weekly lunches functioned as informal editorial meetings, which often helped to decide the contents and direction of the following issue.[6] The distinction between staff and regular contributors was not sharply drawn: A. W. Evans worked as the de facto assistant editor for most of this period, with special responsibility for the literary pages, but the four most significant regular contributors who did most, aside from Massingham himself, to shape the voice of the paper, were H. N. Brailsford, L. T. Hobhouse, J. A. Hobson, and H. W. Nevinson. In addition, Masterman, J. L. Hammond, F. W. Hirst, and W. D. Morrison were also frequent contributors.

The *Nation* was a political paper above all, but it did give serious attention to the current literary and cultural scene in a section intended, as Massingham explained, 'for the general body of thoughtful, intelligent readers' and not for experts alone.[7] As Massingham's modern biographer observed: 'During the Massingham years the *Nation* published most of England's significant writers: poets, novelists, dramatists, essayists, critics.'[8] John Galsworthy and Arnold Bennett were particularly closely associated with the paper, and there were contributions from George Bernard Shaw and H. G. Wells, but it also encouraged younger writers and attended to new literary movements: to the *Nation* belongs the honour of the first review of James Joyce's *Portrait of the Artist as a Young Man* (by H. G. Wells, in February 1917).[9] A telling illustration of the overlap between the political and cultural preoccupations of the paper came during the First World War, when its opposition to government policy extended to support of the new generation of anti-war poets in the later years of the war: only four of Wilfred Owen's poems were published in his short lifetime, three of them in the *Nation*.

But just as nearly every significant writer of the period is to be found in the pages of the *Nation* at some point, so, too, do many of same names figure in the pages of the *New Age*. In fact Arnold Bennett, writing under the pseudonym of 'Jacob Tonson', contributed the weekly 'Books and Persons' column in the latter for three years from 1908, one of the major steps along his path to becoming the most powerful arbiter of fate in London literary life.[10] Hilaire Belloc and G. K. Chesterton were frequent contributors, albeit increasingly at odds with the paper's politics, but the particular glory of the *New Age* was its patronage of little-known and experimental writers, publishing, for example, early criticism by Ezra Pound and most of the stories that made up Katherine Mansfield's first collection.

The two weeklies did not simply represent different political points of view—broadly, unconventional Socialism and radical Liberalism. They stood in a different relation to current politics. Regulars at the *Nation* lunch were aware of the paper's power: Liberal politicians could not afford not to read it; its critical analyses of proposed policies sometimes had a direct effect on legislation; and the paper was particularly close to certain key members of the government of the time, notably to Lloyd George, Chancellor of the Exchequer from 1908, and Winston Churchill, who held a series of posts in the years before 1914, including that of Home Secretary. So although the regular contributors wrote as 'thinkers' or 'writers', able to plume themselves on a certain principled independence, they evinced a justified sense of being close to the heart of affairs, conscious of having the ear of an influential public. The *New Age*, by contrast, had to see itself as playing a much longer game, less directed at influencing current legislation, more at getting a hearing for alternative visions of society. It spoke above all to those who saw themselves as 'Socialists', a label embracing a heterogeneous medley of affinities and aspirations at this date, ranging from committed supporters of the fledgling Labour Party to earnest questers after comradeship, inner peace, and oneness with the universe. Once its commitment to Guild Socialism was fully elaborated, from 1911 onwards, it was seen as one of the voices contending for the soul of the growing Labour Party, but it even then retained its distance from day-to-day politicking.

All allowance being made for their distinctive characters, the papers were recognized as in some sense rivals, vying for the adherence of that section of the educated public that cared about ideas, progressive politics, and good writing. They had similar, and probably somewhat overlapping, circulations, and although the *Nation* was clearly the more successful, both relied upon subsidies to keep going. By 1909, the *Nation* had achieved a regular circulation of about 5,000; by the end of the war it stood at about 11,500, which was its peak before post-war economic conditions induced a decline.[11] Reliable figures for the *New Age* are harder to come by: its historian describes it as having a 'fifteen-year average of over 3,000', though also suggesting that in 1908–9 it briefly reached the giddy heights of 22,000 during its short-lived alliance with the independent Socialist MP, Victor Grayson. In 1913 its circulation stood at 4,500; a rise in price helped to depress this to 3,500 the following year, and in its case, too, the post-war economic conditions led to further shrinkage.[12]

Both periodicals evinced a recurrent preoccupation with the question of the proper public role of 'intellect', of the part to be played by 'leading thinkers and writers', by, in short, 'brains', especially in relation to 'numbers', as the Victorian formulation had it. But although their ruminations traced out some themes in common, there were interesting differences of perspective, tone, and (especially significant in this context) vocabulary. In particular, the part played by the *New Age* in putting the term 'intellectuals' into general currency in Britain before 1914 has been largely overlooked in existing discussions of the topic.[13] These two journals repay attention for the purposes of my argument, therefore, for several reasons. First, they illustrate the kind of 'everyday' level of discussion of this question in periodical writing in the first two decades of the century, before it was encumbered by any distinguishing or inhibiting self-consciousness. Second, the juxtaposition of these two journals highlights the coexistence of older and newer idioms, together with their respective political and cultural resonances. And third, contributors to these journals helped to map out, often in revealing ways, some of the main lines of subsequent debate about the responsibility that was assumed to be laid upon 'men of intellect' to 'give light and leading to their fellow-citizens'.

II

Although the *New Age* deliberately cultivated a certain eclecticism, Orage and his closest associates were clear that theirs was a Socialist paper in its handling of cultural issues no less than in its treatment of politics. This doctrinal identity was the determining frame within which the question of intellectuals was raised; it was also this identity that accounted for the frequent appearance in its pages of the term 'intellectuals', used in a political context, at a time when, as we saw in Ch. 1, this was a relatively rare sighting in public discourse in Britain. For it was the class analysis developed in the international literature of Socialism that familiarized readers of progressive publications in Europe and the United States in the first couple of decades of the twentieth century with the notion that nearly all Socialist parties were made up of a (numerically) unequal alliance between 'intellectuals' and representatives of the working class. In this literature, therefore, 'intellectuals' were usually identified as 'middle-class' and as having arrived at Socialism by a process of rational conviction rather than simple class interest. By the same token, intellectuals were also thought of as peculiarly likely to betray or abandon the working class when the going got rough. In this context, the term retained its associations with precious or unrealistic ratiocination, so that positive or neutral appearances of the term could easily give way to more sarcastic or critical uses. A brief sampling of examples (in roughly chronological order) will give some sense of the centrality and, as it were, everydayness of this theme among the *New Age* circle. This will require giving some attention to the texture as well as the context of the chosen quotations.

In one of the first issues under Orage's sole editorship, we find him using the term in a manner which suggested an almost habitual familiarity on both his part and his readers'. Considering, in his 'Notes of the Week', what the fledgling Labour Party gained and lost by not being more overtly Socialist, he concluded:

> In any case, only rarely will middle-class and cultured people identify themselves whole-heartedly with the Labour Party of the present moment. On the other hand, the loss of these intellectuals may be more than compensated by the accession of the Trade Unionists, an accession that might not have taken place had Messrs Hyndman, Shaw, Webb and others been at the head of the Labour Party in place of Messrs Keir Hardie, MacDonald, Shackleton, and Barnes.[14]

Here, 'intellectuals' seem to be equated with 'middle-class and cultured people', though the examples of Hyndman, Shaw, and Webb suggest a somewhat more restrictive application. The context is firmly political, albeit focusing on the role of the 'cultivated'. Something similar is evident in his rumination later that year on the role of the *New Age* itself. It was facing one of its periodic financial crises largely, he suggested, because its 'intellectual pioneering' and 'political pioneering' could never be popular. Still, were the paper to close, he comforted both himself and his readers, he could at least feel that the numbers published in the past eighteen months had been 'worthy of comparison with any paper published in the world. That, I feel, is something for a group, mainly composed of intellectuals, to have contributed to the Socialist movement in this country.' The self-description is unembarrassed, and the only question, perhaps, is how the 'group' is being delimited such that it contains some who are not to be described as 'intellectuals'.[15]

Speaking, in its first year, about the 'slump in reform', the paper facetiously pondered various explanations for the political torpor it claimed to detect, in the course of which it canvassed the possibility that this was a seasonal slump attributable to 'the holiday-making of the intellectuals'. 'The silence and general inactivity of ten thousand of our intellectuals and their retreat to Fabian Summer Schools, the Riviera and elsewhere, do make a large gap in public life which newspapers find it difficult to fill.' When 'intellectuals' are grouped in their thousands in this way, the term is clearly not being used to pick out a few leading opinion-formers: clearly, they are more likely to be attending those Fabian Summer Schools as students rather than teachers.[16]

Another indication of the milieu in which the term was becoming domesticated is provided by an article reflecting on that hardy perennial, 'the problem that confronts the Socialist as to how best he can apply his principles to practical politics'. In the previous week, the *New Age* had quoted from the working-class paper the *Labour Leader*, 'which had inaccurately defined the position of the intellectuals. The argument of that journal broadly was that we (the intellectuals, the middle-class Socialists, the doctrinaires of all schools and classes) are so obsessed with the pursuit of the idea that we fail to appreciate the practical way to compass our end.' Predictably, the *New Age* saw a Labour movement devoid of ideas as even more impractical than this stereotype of the intellectual, a stereotype that nonetheless did not deflect the paper from acceptance of the collective self-description.[17] And this usage extended beyond the editorial columns: for example, we find the paper's art critic, Walter Sickert, in breast-beating mode, declaring that 'I do believe that those of us who are intellectuals owe much more to those who work with their hands than we ever pay.'[18]

But this Socialist-derived vocabulary did not exist in a linguistically sealed compartment, and so it was constantly being melded with the idiom of the wider society. When Will Thorne, secretary of the Gasworkers' Union, wrote to the paper on the issue of popular control of educational endowments, the older English usage was evidently at work in his mind: 'It has often been a wonder to me that the "intellectuals" of the English universities do so little to help the working-class education movement. In Russia young university students often suffer death for the cause of the common people, but here in England they have done nothing . . .' and so on. But a different inflection was present when Sickert sermonized on the duties of the critic, denouncing that kind of critic who 'forgets that the world is not composed only of the tiny circle of intellectuals in the capital who all know each other and each other's opinions'.[19] Two older, less political senses of the term can be glimpsed in the background of these examples.

It is noticeable that although the *New Age* maintained a lively interest in the political and cultural life of other countries, this did not bring in its train any specialized use of 'intellectuals' or any systematic contrasts in their positions in various societies. Thus a letter on the government of India could refer to the problem, long familiar from other parts of the world, 'of finding careers for half-educated young Intellectuals who cannot get a university course and have never had instruction in the industrial arts and sciences to fit them for the alternative of Commerce or Manufacture'. A report on the formation of a new Socialist party in Greece observed: 'It has not started as a popular movement, most of its leaders being "intellectuals" who have studied economics in Germany and France and have come into contact with the Socialists there.' A correspondent from Munich emphasized the Catholic culture of the region, finding it, from an English perspective, surprisingly democratic: 'You see, the priests as a rule are drawn from the masses—are mostly peasants, and they have the grip of the soil, they understand the common needs of the people, while the intellectuals, like intellectuals the world over, are somewhat divorced from the people,' adding: 'And these intellectuals, you will not find them snobbish as are ours.' Sometimes the same contributor could point at one moment to resemblances between British and other European situations and at others to contrasts. Commenting on affairs in Spain, Kennedy quoted Ramiro de Maeztu as saying: '"In Spain the Intellectuals have one grave defect. Do you know what it is? That they are not intellectual at all. They will be the cause of the revolution; not, however, as the result of what they have done, but of what they have left undone."' On which Kennedy commented, a little archly: 'I have translated this fairly literally. Please read between the lines and ask yourself whether the remark applies to any other country.' However, in a later piece, Kennedy reported on the agitations in both Spain and Italy to reform membership of their second chambers, not by appointing 'demagogues' but instead:

> Senators appointed to a very large extent by the Intellectuals. (When I say Intellectuals I mean men who, from a cultural standpoint, are fully developed—Goethe or Leonardo da Vinci, for instance; not the narrow-minded cranks one meets with among the Fabians and other so-called 'advanced' people here.) I am aware that Intellectuals are difficult to discover; but the task need not be approached with utter despair in the Latin countries.[20]

One cannot help wondering whether many of those involved in the appointing process quite measured up to the demanding cultural ideal represented by Goethe and Leonardo, though perhaps this little sally was really just a form of face-pulling at the Fabians. What is most striking is to see the association between intellectuals and cranks, a staple of philistine English commentary throughout at least the first half of the twentieth century, being traded upon in the pages of the *New Age*; a case of the pot calling the kettle black, as far as most contemporaries would have been concerned. Thus, in the following year, one correspondent, remarking how the anti-Socialist polemics of Belloc and Chesterton remained undisturbed by counter-examples of individuals in whom the supposed natural desire for personal property was absent, noted that those two robust champions of English (Catholic) common sense 'invariably describe such "exceptional" people as amiable cranks, intellectuals, or what not'.[21]

All this helped make the term available for various less solemn purposes. For example, we surely see a writer twitting his more stately senior when Arnold

Bennett cited a letter by Sir Henry Newbolt that appeared in the appropriately august pages of *The Times* (Newbolt was in fact only five years older than Bennett, but he already seemed to represent the previous literary generation). Bennett went on to justify giving this letter further attention by saying 'but as an intellectual he [Newbolt] would certainly wish to catch the ear of the intellectuals. Hence I draw attention to his letter in this place.' Referring to Newbolt himself as an 'intellectual' is clearly intended to make him turn a deeper shade of purple, and a little of this arch playfulness may even have been present in Bennett's characterization of the *New Age*'s readership.[22] Edwin Muir may have been representative of one strand within that readership. As a young clerk in Glasgow, he joined the Clarion Scouts, an organization which offered fellowship and cycling to the readers of Blatchford's popular Socialist paper the *Clarion*. He later recorded that within the Clarion Scouts he gravitated to a clique known as 'the intellectuals', and his explanation suggests a possible association or derivation of the label: 'We followed the literary and intellectual development of the time, discovering such writers as Bergson, Sorel, Havelock Ellis, Galsworthy, Conrad, E.M. Forster, Joyce and Lawrence, the last two having been contributed by me, for I had seen them mentioned in the *New Age* by Ezra Pound' (Muir went on to adopt the paper's Nietzscheanism, and launched his literary career by publishing his early poems in its pages).[23] Actually, many of the paper's readers may rather have gloried in the term, and Kennedy surely intended to be neither provoking nor playful when, in one of his regular pieces on foreign affairs, he passingly referred to views held 'among the intellectuals, not necessarily Socialists, who read this paper'.[24]

The question of self-description, at least in 'advanced' circles, is particularly teasing in this period. In a rousing piece defending the morality of a General Strike, written at a time when industrial unrest was mounting in Britain and when Sorelian and Syndicalist ideas from France were starting to attract attention, Orage acknowledged that such action might seem extreme. 'But if the *Spectator*, on behalf of the governing classes, frankly informs us that . . . the custodians so-called of Society have no intention of stirring until the slum-dwellers are driven mad, what alternative have we, who, as the intellectuals, hold the balance between the governed and the governing, but to cry Havoc to the former and let slip the dogs of industrial war?'[25] The rhetorical ambitions of this sentence make it trickier to gloss than many of the examples quoted here, but this spokesman for a stratum that belongs neither to the governing class nor the governed does not seem hampered either by undue modesty or excessive fastidiousness at the application of the label 'intellectuals'. And an interesting instance of how the conventional barriers of gender could also be disregarded if the circles were sufficiently advanced is provided by a letter from Beatrice Hastings citing an article in the small-circulation feminist journal *The Freewoman* in which Rebecca West made some sarcastic remarks about Hastings under the cover of announcing the interest 'to us intellectuals' of the latter's (lightly disguised) appearance in a forthcoming novel. The line between mockery and self-inclusion is particularly hard to draw in this instance.[26]

It is worth remarking that, for all its iconoclasm, one of the ways in which the *New Age* exhibited a real continuity with its Victorian predecessors was in its assumption that debates in the House were still the unquestioned centre of attention. In his 'Notes of the Week', in particular, Orage often commented in detail upon these debates, which he clearly read at length, presumably in the version printed in *The Times*. At the same time, the distance between the *New Age*'s often abrasively Socialist views on the function of the intellectuals and the prevailing liberal pieties about the role of 'men of light and leading' was revealingly illustrated in a piece by William Poel in which he took issue with a *Times* leader on the relation of 'culture' to 'democracy'. *The Times* had rehearsed the familiar argument that the short-sighted, self-interested preoccupations of democratic politics needed the leaven supplied by those who 'to learning and culture and distinction add that elasticity of mind which brings the changing needs of the present into due relation with what is permanent in the human experience of the past'. Such men constitute 'the aristocracy of brains . . . of wisdom that can look beyond the clamour of the moment . . .' and so on (interestingly, *The Times* suggested that the representation of university constituencies in Parliament was a constitutional acknowledgement of this truth). But Poel was fierce that 'culture' as such contributed nothing to politics: 'politics has only to do with "Having" and "not-Having", that is to say, with property and privilege', and therefore everything comes down to the question of which side one is on in this fundamental conflict, a matter of conviction in which 'the plain man' is at no disadvantage by comparison to 'the man of culture'. The latter has no special standing or role here, and the conclusion is unyielding: 'It is for the intellectuals to realise what is now being demanded by the working classes with a persistence which carries conviction. The worker's turn is long overdue.'[27]

One measure of 'reform' by the Liberal government to which the *New Age* was implacably hostile was the National Insurance Act of 1911, largely on the grounds that it singled out the class of wage-earners and then required them to make compulsory contributions. 'Here was a measure which, to the best of our recollection,' Orage inveighed in the following year, 'was opposed by every publicist of standing in the United Kingdom . . . the opposition was unanimous among the minority of the intelligent classes'. But Lloyd George and 'his equally impudent lieutenant, Mr Masterman' simply ignored this; 'they have not even privately set their friends to work to reply to the intellectuals for them', yet nonetheless the Bill survived 'the combined efforts of the workmen and the thinkers'. He then launched into a tirade against the writers and thinkers of Britain who had been bought by the plutocrats' press:

> Of the 'intellectuals' of this country we are now disposed to take a most pessimistic view. They can be bought and sold like sheep. Whether it is a large faith that is lacking in them, or whether the accursed sterilising doctrines of modern thought have corrupted

them, we need not now enquire; but the obvious fact is that none of the great economic powers of the land takes them or their power seriously.

All such figures, he argued recklessly (and in some contradiction to his earlier point about the degree of initial opposition to the Bill), could now be bought: he instanced H. G. Wells, G. B. Shaw, Stephen Reynolds, and Sidney Low who, by contributing to the *Daily Mail*, were simply writing what it pleased Lord Northcliffe to let them write. 'In England, at any rate, no literary man should write for any newspaper under penalty of being expelled from the Republic of Letters. Until this or a similar standard of intellectual taste is established, the intellectual in England will remain what the Insurance Bill has proved him to be—the ineffectual.'[28] Some of this is, of course, the familiar complaint of the self-consciously independent, the voice of the journal with a weekly circulation of 3,000 bouncing barbs off the hide of a newspaper with a daily sale of over 700,000. But it is also an instance of what was to become a familiar dilemma; how, in a widely literate society, was the intellectual to reach out to a broad public without 'selling out' to the dominant media?

Writing in similarly severe vein the following week, Orage lamented the absence of strong, argued disagreement in British politics and journalism alike. Better might have been expected of those whose business is ideas: 'Yet of the hundred or so public writers, journalists, reformers, whom we have challenged to defend themselves against fair criticism, none that we can remember has taken up his pen to defend himself.' This is what underwrites the de facto consensus in parliamentary politics:

The caucus [*sc.* the caucus system in Parliament] is not maintained, with its horrible results, without a general consent, in which our intellectuals share. Indeed, our intellectuals set an example which the caucus merely follows. When the intellectuals in any country decline controversy—which is their sole business, by the way—nobody should be surprised that politicians followed [*sic*] suit.

He speculated that recently fashionable philosophical doctrines which have weakened reason may have contributed to this: 'There will never be anything ripe again in England in ideas, in art, in politics, or in life until our intellectuals stop crying their hasty conclusions as perfected doctrines and resume humbly the way of reason, which is discussion' (which is ripe indeed coming from the paper that probably did most to popularize the ideas of Bergson and Nietzsche in the years before 1914).[29]

For a final example we may jump forward to 1917, a momentous year internationally for the relation of intellectuals to Socialist politics. In an article entitled 'The proscription of the intellectuals', published in September of that year, S. G. Hobson, Orage's chief collaborator in propagandizing for the National Guilds system, blended a familiar medley of ingredients in his reflections on the subject. Hobson began by suggesting that it was disturbing that, at a time when 'more than one intellectual system is undergoing close scrutiny... a phase of suspicion of its intellectuals should be passing over Labour' (note the possessive adjective). He referred to unnamed Labour leaders who had 'recently served notice on the intellectuals that their room is preferable to their company'. This view, he acknowledged, would not be unfamiliar to the paper's readers: 'During the past ten years the *New Age* has been frequently denounced by Labour and Trade Union periodicals, not because its principles and contentions were wrong (they still remain uncontroverted), but because it was written by intellectuals.' But, Hobson countered, 'Labour has been well served by its intellectuals.' He retrospectively conscripted several nineteenth-century figures to this category, from Robert Owen, F. D. Maurice, Charles Kingsley, Thomas Hughes, and Frederic Harrison, right up to the Webbs in the present. 'If these writers and thinkers had never lived, Labour would today be in a more parlous condition than it is. Relevant, too, is to remember that a cloud of intellectuals, not distinctively Labourist, have supplied Labour with a thousand shots for its locker—Adam Smith, Ricardo, Jevons, Mill, and a score of modern writers and thinkers.'

However, Hobson conceded that, despite this strong native tradition, continental Europe had produced many more important thinkers who analysed the social problem from a distinctively Socialist perspective. Organized labour in Britain had, on the whole, been resistant to these European ideas. 'It is, of course, inevitable that, where there is an impatience or contempt for the intellectuals, principles and ideas are ignored. The literature, permanent or periodical, produced by or for the British Socialist or Labour movement is the least knowledgeable and inspired in the world.' Here Hobson fell back on familiar cultural generalizations: 'We must admit that great stretches of Europe show today a reverence for ideas unknown in England.' Apparently partaking in this irreverence, he conceded that 'Labour is in some degree justified in its suspicion of the intellectuals, not, however, because they are intellectual, but because they belong to the oppressing classes.' The danger then becomes the probability that Labour will only listen to those who tell it what it likes to hear. 'The simple fact is that the "intellectuals" whom Labour slavishly follows are the popular writers who think far more of their "public" than the integrity of their ideas.' But the intellectual who lets himself be bullied into saying what the audience wants to hear 'would ipso facto cease to be an intellectual and become a spiritual blackleg'. This was to become a familiar theme, albeit not always so colourfully phrased. Hobson, however, was unwilling to be completely discouraged, and he ends, characteristically, with a positive affirmation that in the future ideas will make their way, even in the British Labour movement.[30] He was not the last British intellectual in the twentieth century to express this hope.

III

In the pages of the *Nation* between 1907 and 1914, the actual term 'intellectuals' occurs far less frequently than in the *New Age*, but the question of the part to be played by writers and thinkers was nonetheless one of its constant preoccupations.

Three (only partially distinct and certainly overlapping) aspects of this theme can be distinguished. The first was marked by a frequent return to the public role allegedly played by the leading thinkers of the mid-Victorian period, and a corresponding insistence that their successors were failing in this task at present. The second centred on laments about the process of intellectual specialization and a consequent fear that universities, in particular, were becoming less rather than more central to national life. And the third took the form of a sustained hostility to 'experts', and especially to any suggestion that, instead of attempting to educate a public to make informed judgements about the complex problems of modern societies, an elite of scientifically trained experts should solve such problems and then rely on skilled politicians to ensure compliance rather than genuine assent. At the root of these three pre-occupations, clearly, was a concern about the form which cultural authority could and should take in a democracy, especially one in which popular media such as the new 'yellow press' appeared to deny any role at all to those who cultivated the life of the mind. A few examples will quickly illustrate the interconnection of the various aspects of this general theme.[31]

Inevitably, one focus of these concerns among the 'New Liberal' publicists who wrote for the *Nation* was the role of the Fabians, by then a conspicuous case of 'applied intellect' in British politics, potential allies in the progressive cause yet in practice a constant affront to true Liberal principles. To L. T. Hobhouse, writing in 1907, they constituted a warning about the dangers of the alliance between expertise and opportunism in politics. 'The little group of middle-class intellectuals, bright young men from the Universities, civil servants, journalists, and artists, who formed the Fabian Society in the early 'eighties had a great opportunity', he declared, since the mid-Victorian orthodoxies were then clearly on the wane. The need had been for 'a clear formulation and spirited application of philosophic principles of social reform', but after a promising beginning, the Fabians turned aside to the lesser activity of trying 'to force progress by packing and managing committees instead of by winning the popular assent'. This opportunism was an aspect of their 'anti-democratic attitude'. Under a Fabian dispensation, 'skilled political engineers are to operate this machinery of government'; 'to construct bureaucracy has appeared to it a more important work' than the one which Hobhouse evidently believed the leading thinkers of the time should undertake, namely 'to educate and to inspire democracy'.[32] Hobhouse returned to this theme the following year in a piece entitled 'Democracy and the expert' (largely a response to a recent article by Sidney Webb). Here he acknowledged that the running of a modern state required 'expertism and a high degree of specialisation', but he argued that Webb's proposals encouraged those with the 'superior trained faculties' to disregard 'the will of the people'. Government would be carried on 'by the superior wills of a virtually self-appointed aristocracy of talent'.[33] Here, apparently, was a nemesis that all little groups of 'middle-class intellectuals' should be wary of.

As it happened, the literary pages of the paper in the following week contained an article entitled 'The dearth of genius', which came at these themes from another angle (the Victorian overlap between politicians and men of letters was still strong in this milieu). Taking up what had become a topical theme, the article looked back to the 1870s, running off a list of 'the giants of those days' in thought, literature, and science (twenty-five names are thrown off in the opening paragraph, all men but for George Eliot), and it then asked who from the present could be ranked alongside them. This trope of pygmies on the shoulders of giants is a constant in discussion of this topic, though not, of course, of this topic alone. The article went on to consider the possibility that this apparent decline actually reflected the changed conditions of intellectual work:

Natural talents are nowadays more rigorously specialised. Our historians are not allowed to roam freely over wide fields of loose literary cultivation like Froude; our Darwin, if we had one, would be chained down to some particular investigation of physical heredity; a philosopher and sociologist who, like Mill or Spencer, took all knowledge for his province, would never emerge from the shades of sciolism. We have the men of genius, but they are working in narrower channels at deeper levels, and their light does not shine forth as it would formerly have done.

However, this was not held to be a sufficient explanation. The truth was that the great men of the 1870s had been 'interpreters of new, large, transforming ideas', but such ideas were notably absent now. One culprit fingered was the 'excessive caution' to be found in intellectual and literary life, and then the piece eased into a mode of analysis that was to become increasingly familiar across the rest of the century:

We are today cultivating, as the best form of modern culture, a type of broad-minded, shallow-feeling man and woman, who move [*sic*] with self-conscious slowness among the intricacies of life, shunning fanaticism and refusing to take risks. Many familiar features of our modern civilisation cooperate with this tendency: the growth of material comfort and security in an age of peace, strong governments, and economic advance. There is also the congestion of ideas and of information, pouring out upon the mind in ways that well-nigh inhibit selection and preclude settled convictions upon issues of critical importance to the inner life. Such conditions are injurious to the emergence and full life of natural genius.[34]

As usual, such an encompassingly gloomy account of 'modern civilisation' has the effect of making it difficult to see how any 'natural genius' could ever spring into life again. We are only in the first decade of the century, and already the giants have departed, never to return.

The relation between a strain of cultural pessimism and the recurring hope of some form of alliance between 'brains and numbers' surfaced in rather different ways in a piece by Hobhouse from the following year. He began by canvassing the usual gloomy contrast with the situation half a century earlier. Now 'the consistent and rational elector of the Benthamite school has become a frivolous and excitable "man in the street", who dissolves the deepest issues into frivolities, and is responsive, too often without knowing it, to the temper and suggestions of a sensational Press.' If this was a tune Hobhouse could hum in his sleep, so was his warning against drawing one fashionable conclusion from it: 'It is no wonder that some of our more daring thinkers, alike among scientists and socialists, have grown impatient of the slow stumbling march of the democratic host, and have encamped with the aristocrats or the bureaucrats under the banner of efficiency.' This is a reminder of how the Edwardian movements for 'National Efficiency', the Fabians at their head, became one of the bugbears of the 'true Liberal'.[35] Hobhouse pointed the more demanding moral: 'One of the leading tasks of the new century must be to bring about, not merely a reconciliation, but an alliance, permanent, heartfelt, and fruitful of good, between the movement towards greater social equality and the new conception of intellectual duty that inspires modern students and thinkers.'

Rather less predictable was Hobhouse's announcement of where to look for this longed-for dawn: 'There is only one place where such an alliance can be effected, and that place is the University.' The slight jolt to one's expectations here is a reminder of how little the *Nation* circle looked to the universities for the ideas that were to move the new democracy, and some of its members, above all J. A. Hobson who both resented and gloried in his exclusion from a university post, were relentless critics of the conformity and dullness fostered by academic life. Hobhouse, erstwhile 'Greats' Tutor at Oxford and now, after a spell as a freelance, professor of the new subject of sociology at the new London School of Economics, did not share his friend's sweeping antagonism, though he could usually be relied upon for a few swipes at Oxford's defensive disengagement from the modern world. But on this occasion the source of his more positive comments was to be found in a report on 'Oxford and Working-Class Education', produced by a joint committee representing the university and various working-class organisations, principally addressing the kind of work carried out by the Workers' Educational Association. Here was a role for 'men of intellect' (and women, too, when they remembered to mention them) that chimed with the *Nation*'s ideal about educating democracy rather than manipulating it, and Hobhouse invested great hopes for the future in 'this new alliance, sealed in the stronghold of lost causes, between scholar and workman'.[36]

The central axis of the *Nation* group, or at least of its informing political and economic thinking, was located in the close friendship between Hobhouse and Hobson, but in accordance with the journalistic protocols of the day, or perhaps of any day, this friendship did not prevent them from reviewing and promoting each other's books. For example, Hobhouse seized the occasion of the publication of Hobson's *The Crisis of Liberalism* to stress 'the need for an apostolic succession of thinking men who will constantly re-state political principles in terms of the living needs of each generation', bestowing on Hobson the ultimate accolade—'the task of Mill is that which Mr Hobson takes up in a spirit worthy of the master'. Along the way, there is the regulation sideswipe at lesser conceptions of the role: 'No man is more free from the Fabian fallacy of conceiving the regeneration of society as the work of a handful of superior persons ordering the lives of a well-drilled population of lifeless units.' Hobhouse then proceeds to elaborate the job-description in general terms:

Can the world be moved without ideas? To this question thinkers like Mr Hobson reply with a clear negative. For them the thinker is no recluse but a man with a living and practical function. He makes no figure on the platform and is little spoken of in the Press, and he may seem to be dealing with words and themes and abstractions rather than the joys and sorrows of living men and women. In truth, in proportion as he can grope his way towards some of those great underlying conceptions which, once clearly grasped and proclaimed, 'make all things new', he is exercising a deeper and more lasting influence on the destinies of the race than the 'able editor' who popularises bits of his teaching or the Cabinet Minister who is ultimately destined to embody some fragment of it in a Bill.[37]

The *Nation* group did not underestimate the value of an 'able editor'—several of those round the lunch-table had performed this role on other publications, and they were genuinely admiring of Massingham himself—but nonetheless credos of this kind about the higher calling of 'the thinker' were common in the journal. In this instance, Hobhouse rhetorically stacks the case against considering such an individual important (he 'makes no figure', is 'little spoken of', seems 'to be dealing with words and... abstractions'), before releasing his prose and letting the paragraph soar to its uplifting conclusion. In such pieces, there is no suggestion that the 'practical function' of 'the thinker' is peculiarly absent or slighted in Britain; on the contrary, it has boasted some of the most glorious exemplars of the role in the past and may, on this showing, continue to do so in the future.

A fortnight later, Masterman considered the apparent puzzle that the greater part of 'the educated classes' were now 'ranged on the side of reaction', instinctively rallying to the support of 'property' (the context was the crisis over the Lords' rejection of Lloyd George's radical budget). But in fact, Masterman pointed out, although this might be true of the majority of the educated middle class, 'the best intellects of the nation' were not to be found on that side of the divide.

Take those men who are in the front rank of uncontested eminence in literature, the first twenty of our living writers and thinkers Not four of them would be found siding with the lords against the people. Nor would the proportion of reactionaries be much greater among the men of science, the leaders of the learned professions (with the exception of the Church), while in those departments of intellectual activity which bear most nearly upon politics, law, history and economics, the condemnation of those causes to which English conservatism has now committed itself is overwhelming in its preponderance. We do not contend that the preponderance of high intellectuality is definitely 'Radical' in its political proclivities. A certain timidity, bred of a lack of sympathy and understanding of the people, commonly prevails in intellectual castes and coteries, precluding our great intellectuals from exercising that powerful and direct influence over the popular mind and movement which is visible in such countries as Russia, France, and even America, not to mention those little countries whose higher rate of progress is primarily due to the larger and freer service rendered by the illumination of the few to the instruction and inspiration of the many. Such fruitful and inspiring leadership is not common here, and we have some reason to complain of the too persistent severance which persists, in what we call an age of popular education, between the advanced intellect of the country and the awakening populace. Perhaps the time is now coming when the free connections may be made by which the riper culture of our Universities and our little groups of philosophers and literary men may be transmitted to inform and stimulate the rude forces of intellectual curiosity which are stirring in our great industrial centres, receiving from them in return a wholesome flow of popular thought and feeling. But this full sympathy between the intellectual leaders and the people lies rather in the future.

This is a rich and revealing passage, albeit a little unsteady in its main argument: representatives of 'high intellectuality' in Britain largely take the popular side in the present conflict, it maintains, yet they are not properly committed to radical causes and play less of a leading role than elsewhere, still being too cut off from the people, though this failing will be overcome in the future. No proper names are put to 'the best intellects of the nation'; instead, certain fields of activity are enumerated—'literature' perhaps in its old sense, made up of 'writers and thinkers'; science; learned professions; and 'those departments of intellectual activity which bear most nearly upon politics, law, history and economics'. Nor is any reason given why the 'timidity' which inhibits 'our great intellectuals' from playing their full part should be any less marked in other countries. Russia and France may have been the obvious comparisons at this date, not many years after the Dreyfus Affair and the Revolution of 1905, though America would have been a more surprising choice (especially to Americans), and it is hard to know which 'little countries' he has in mind. But the structure of concern was by this point the familiar, almost traditional, one of cultural leadership in a democracy, or the relationship between 'the advanced intellect' and 'the awakening populace'. In the remainder of his article, Masterman identified various sources of the unintelligent political apathy and self-interest of the 'educated classes' as a whole, most notably the defects of the 'higher education' they had received, 'from which all that is most vital to the understanding of modern society is excluded', leaving them only with 'a little veneer of literary and scientific culture'. The progressive Edwardian intellectual's frustration with and antagonism to the slow-moving ancient universities finds further expression here, driving Masterman to conclude: 'Surely it is time to do something for the education of our "educated" classes.'[38]

Most of the regular contributors to the *Nation* continued to write occasional pieces for other publications, none more so than the amazingly prolific Hobson who took advantage of the greater space provided by the monthly journals to develop themes adumbrated more briefly in the *Nation*. In a piece that first appeared in the *English Review* at the end of 1909 (and was thriftily republished as part of *The Crisis of Liberalism* almost simultaneously), Hobson held forth in his expansive way on how specialization had gone too far and the pressing need now was for a new synthesis: 'There exists no proper intellectual authority, correlating the work of the innumerable groups of scientific hodmen.' This was something of a double-edged sword for Hobson in particular, since he suffered a disabling allergy to any incarnation of 'authority' that sported a gown and mortar-board. Certainly, the only counter-instance that came to his mind was not an encouraging one: 'We have had, it is true, even in the age of scepticism, little schools of intellectuals who have soared into some loftiness of thought where they have claimed to find the one and absolute.' This was, for knowing readers, an easily decoded reference to the Idealist school of philosophy, here seen as a style of thought, disfigured by its opaque vocabulary, which threatened to eliminate the diversity of experience in its search for a higher unity, a movement which both Hobson and Hobhouse accused of contributing to the general turn-of-the-century reaction. Nonetheless, Hobson could not quite give up the thought that 'intellect' would be more effective in society if it could only somehow be 'coordinated', in a properly liberal and unauthoritarian manner.[39] The universities had failed to provide 'proper intellectual authority'; the only outcome that might have been worse would have been if they had succeeded.

The epigraph to this chapter is taken from another of Hobson's articles on a cognate theme (a piece also reused in *The Crisis of Liberalism*), in this case about the dangers attendant upon large private donations to universities, especially the fear that donors might attempt to restrict free enquiry in the disciplines dealing with social and political matters: 'To require of men, whose knowledge and training peculiarly qualify them to give light and leading to their fellow-citizens, that they shall abstain from active participation in public movements where interests are divided and strong feelings are evoked, is a policy of moral and intellectual mutilation, as degrading to those who are curtailed in their citizenship as it is injurious to the public.'[40] But it is noticeable that, in pressing this case, he never doubts the general role of those 'men, whose knowledge and training peculiarly qualify them to give light and leading to their fellow-citizens', and in this he was representative. For all their hand-wringing about the power of the 'forces of reaction' and the 'sensationalist press', the leading members of the *Nation* group evinced a fundamental optimism about, not just the compatibility, but the inevitable convergence between the advance of science (broadly understood) and the advance of democracy.[41] The barriers which they identified as preventing 'leading thinkers and writers' from providing effective forms of cultural leadership were regarded as contingent and temporary. They still retained an essentially Victorian confidence that 'men of light and leading' were personages of some consequence in the national culture, figures whose standing would be enhanced rather than diminished if they embraced the task of instructing the recently enlarged public that had been created by the advance of democracy and education. Whether they used the term or not, especially in speaking of themselves, they had no doubts about either the existence or the importance in Britain of those who would increasingly come to be termed 'intellectuals'.

NOTES

1. The remark about 'undue intellectualism' comes from Paul Selver, *Orage and the 'New Age' Circle: Reminiscences and Reflections* (London: Allen & Unwin, 1959), 48–9; the testimonial is by Janko Lavrin, quoted in Wallace Martin, *The 'New Age' under Orage: Chapters in English Cultural History* (Manchester: Manchester University Press, 1967), 44.
2. Masterman is quoted from a valedictory article he wrote in 1923, in Lucy Masterman, *C. F. G. Masterman, A Biography* (London: Nicholson & Watson, 1939), 79. For the fullest account of the *Nation* lunch by a participant, see H. W. Nevinson, *More Changes, More Chances* (London: Nisbet, 1925), 212–22; for modern discussions, see Alfred F. Havighurst, *Radical Journalist: H. W. Massingham (1860–1924)* (Cambridge: Cambridge University Press, 1974), 151–5; Peter Clarke, *Liberals and Social Democrats* (Cambridge: Cambridge University Press, 1978), 108–9.
3. Martin, *New Age under Orage*, 125.
4. See Philip Mairet, *A. R. Orage, a Memoir* ([1936], new edn., New York: University Books, 1966), 60.
5. Martin, *New Age under Orage*, 62.
6. Masterman, *Masterman*, 78.
7. Quoted in Havighurst, *Radical Journalist*, 144.
8. Ibid. 156.
9. Noted by Havighurst, *Massingham*, 172.
10. See John Gross, *The Rise and Fall of the Man of Letters* (London: Weidenfeld, 1969), ch. 8; Margaret Drabble, *Arnold Bennett, a Biography* (London: Weidenfeld & Nicolson, 1974), 155.
11. Havighurst, *Radical Journalist*, 154–5, 227, 256, 294.
12. Martin, *New Age under Orage*, 10, 62, 122, 275.
13. In what follows, I have drawn upon the online version of the complete text of the *New Age* for these years made available by the 'Modernist Journals' project at Brown University in the USA (<www.modjourn.brown.edu/newage>, accessed Feb. 2004). This project is at present (early 2004) still very recent and not yet complete, but by making the full text of the journal searchable it has enabled me to confirm my earlier impression, arrived at from other contemporary sources, that the term appeared frequently in the journal.
14. [Orage], 'Notes of the week', *New Age*, 18 Jan. 1908, 221.
15. [Orage] 'And shall the "New Age" die?', *New Age*, 24 Oct. 1908, 501.
16. [?A. R. Orage], 'The slump in reform', *New Age*, 19 Sept. 1907, 324.
17. [Anon.], 'Socialist principles and practical politics', *New Age*, 6 May 1909, 28.
18. Walter Sickert, 'Encouragement for art', *New Age*, 7 Apr. 1910 (Apr. suppl.), 4.
19. Will Thorne, letter on 'Trade unionism and education', *New Age*, 9 June 1910, 140; Walter Sickert, 'The allied artists' association', *New Age*, 14 July 1910. 251.
20. H. V. Storey, 'How to govern India', *New Age*, 31 Oct. 1907, 7; [Anon.], 'The new Socialist party in Greece', 20.5.09, 70; W. R. Titterton, 'Munich, Catholic and Democrat', 7 Sept. 1911, 441; S. Verdad [J. M. Kennedy], 'Foreign affairs', 22 Oct. 1910, 172; S. Verdad [J. M. Kennedy], 'Foreign affairs', 2 Mar. 1911, 414.
21. F. T. Warren, 'Mr Belloc's anti-Socialism explained', *New Age*, 11 Jan. 1912, 258.
22. Arnold Bennett, 'The old Liberal', *New Age*, 15 Dec. 1910, 150.

23. See Jonathan Rose, *The Intellectual Life of the British Working Classes* (London: Yale University Press, 2001), 427–8.
24. S. Verdad [J. M. Kennedy], 'Foreign Affairs', *New Age*, 10 Nov. 1910, 28.
25. [Orage], 'Notes of the week', *New Age*, 20 Oct. 1910, 578.
26. Beatrice Hastings, 'The New Freewoman', *New Age*, 23 Oct. 1913, 775.
27. William Poel, 'Culture and politics', *New Age*, 6 Apr. 1911, 535–8.
28. [Orage] 'Notes of the week', *New Age*, 15 Aug. 1912, 362.
29. Ibid. 21 Nov. 1913, 49–51.
30. S. G. H[obson], 'The proscription of the intellectuals', *New Age*, 13 Sept. 1917, 422–4.
31. The majority of articles in the *Nation* were unsigned. In many cases, it has been possible to ascribe authorship on the basis of a combination of internal and external evidence (e.g. Nevinson kept a detailed diary from which details of authorship can often be gleaned). For identification of the authorship of some of the articles cited below, see also Clarke, *Liberals and Social Democrats*, esp. 309–11, 314, and Christopher E. Mauriello, 'The strange death of the public intellectual: liberal intellectual identity and "the field of cultural production" in England 1880–1920', *Journal of Victorian Culture*, 6 (2001), 1–26.
32. [L. T. Hobhouse], 'The career of Fabianism', *Nation*, 30 Mar. 1907, 182–3.
33. [L.T. Hobhouse], 'Democracy and the expert', *Nation*, 13 June 1908, 375–6.
34. [Anon.], 'The dearth of genius', *Nation*, 20 June 1908, 410.
35. See G. R. Searle, *The Quest for National Efficiency: a Study in British Politics and Political Thought, 1899–1914* (Oxford: Blackwell, 1971).
36. [L. T. Hobhouse], 'Oxford and the people', *Nation*, 6 Feb. 1909, 710.
37. [L. T. Hobhouse], 'The re-statement of Liberalism', *Nation*, 8. Jan. 1910, 614.
38. [C. F. G. Masterman], 'Our "educated" classes', *Nation*, 22 Jan. 1910, 669–70.
39. J. A. Hobson, 'The task of realism', *English Review*, 3 (Nov. 1909), 543–54; repr. as 'The task of reconstruction', in Hobson, *The Crisis of Liberalism: New Issues of Democracy* (1909), ed. P. F. Clarke (Hassocks: Harvester, 1974), 261–76, quotations at 265, 272.
40 Hobson, *Crisis of Liberalism*, 228–9; the Chapter from which this quotation is taken was first published as 'Millionaire endowments', *Independent Review*, 5 (1905), 90–100.
41. Both Stapleton and Mauriello conclude, on slightly different grounds, that this confidence declined sharply after the First World War; Julia Stapleton, *Political Intellectuals and Public Identities in Britain since 1850* (Manchester: Manchester University Press, 2001), 58; Mauriello, 'Strange death of the public intellectual', 19–21.

5

Highbrows and Other Aliens

'What is the cause of this ridiculous diffidence which afflicts intellectuals today? Why should they allow every muddled ignoramus to assert his superiority? Why should they be afraid of betraying their own?'

I

In the course of the 1910s and 1920s, falteringly and rarely in the former decade, more frequently and insistently in the latter, there appeared in English usage a set of related terms expressing social attitudes towards the kinds of people who were sometimes called 'intellectuals', terms which thereby helped to shape the semantic field within which that word was thereafter to function. As I indicated in Ch. 1, the modern senses of 'highbrow', 'lowbrow', and, derivatively and a little later, 'middlebrow' were initially linguistic imports from the United States, though, as so often, there was cognate native stock that made the new terms look like descendants rather than immigrants: Victorian English had, for example, been familiar with 'high-browed' as a term indicating intellectual distinction or nobility of appearance.[1] Two things were particularly significant about the new usage of 'highbrow': first, that it was pejorative, and second, that it presumed a division into antagonistic social groups. From the outset, the language of 'brows' ran together levels of intellectual attainment, types of cultural interest or activities, attitudes towards presumed inferiors or superiors, and social class. However, the presence, and still more the proportions, of all the ingredients were not constant. The dominant tendency was for the terms to be hooked onto the conventional forms of social classification: 'highbrows' were most often assumed to have posh accents and to belong to 'the educated class' (a term which has long outlasted the arrival of 'universal' education), or in other words to be part of the professional and upper-middle classes. The usage of this vocabulary was therefore shot through with class *ressentiment* and a touchiness about being patronized or condescended to, elements which then pervade discussion of 'intellectuals'. In reality, of course, the upper and upper-middle classes were full of 'lowbrows', just as there were always a number of individuals from the lowest social ranks whose interests or attainments could, in all consistency, have led to their being labelled 'highbrows', but although on occasion particular individuals could be picked out in these ways, in general the terms never achieved this degree of descriptive neutrality or freedom from class associations.

In some contexts, from the 1910s onwards, the nouns 'intellectual' and 'highbrow' could be used interchangeably. Two implications of this are worth drawing out for present purposes. First, it underlines that the relevant frame of reference was cultural, not political. 'Highbrows' were certainly not understood to be a group who 'intervened' in politics. Second, although defensive celebrations of the virtues of being 'middlebrow' could draw opportunistically upon strands within the tradition of celebrating the 'unintellectual English', there was for the most part no suggestion that 'highbrows' were an unknown species in Britain. Rather the opposite: something about the affectation of cultural-cum-social superiority implied by the term came to be seen as notably characteristic of contemporary English life, albeit seen in some quarters as an unwelcome growth with shallow roots.

At this point, then, we are dealing with what we may, anachronistically, call the 'culture wars' of the 1920s and 1930s. Various developments had conspired to make the question of the class-related nature of cultural activities a specially sensitive and contentious one in these decades—the cumulative consequences of the Education Acts of the 1870s and 1880s for adult literacy and the markets for various kinds of publications; the increased economic power of a 'new' middle and lower-middle class mainly based in the suburbs and new towns of Southern England; and the complicated, sometimes antagonistic, relation to existing publics of those developments in literature and the arts generally labelled 'Modernism'. (It has even been suggested that these developments 'all conspired to create an office-boy intelligentsia paralleling—and often opposing—the modernist intelligentsia'.[2]) One result of the intersecting effects of these changes was a heightened perception not just that 'culture' needed to be defended against barbarians at the gate—in some form that had been a common trope since at least the early nineteenth century—but that that task now fell to a beleaguered minority whose standards were repudiated and scorned, rather than simply being not shared, by a newly empowered majority. How far the difficulty and inaccessibility of Modernist art and literature contributed to this situation as well as responded to it, and how far it was any kind of deliberate strategy, intended to exclude a 'mass' public, are questions which cultural historians of the period are still disputing.[3] But for the most 'advanced' writers and critics of the 1920s, the reality of some such change was beyond dispute. As John Gross has drawn the contrast with the previous generation of men-of-letters: 'However critical of the established order, men like Shaw and Wells, Bennett and Chesterton put their trust in a popular audience; they might promulgate minority opinions, but not the idea of a minority culture.'[4]

In this context, the language of 'brows' lent itself to the expression of a variety of anxieties and resentments. The *OED*, as noted above, first recorded the relevant senses in its 'Supplement' of 1933: 'Highbrow, *noun*: a person of superior intellectual attainments or interests; always with derisive implication of conscious superiority to ordinary human standards' (with illustrative examples from the 1910s and 1920s); 'Lowbrow, *noun*: one who is not, or does not claim to be, highly intellectual,' and, revealingly, the adjectival form: 'Not highly, or not pretentiously, intellectual; unrefined, coarse, low-class' (again with examples from the 1910s and 1920s). To these were added: 'Middlebrow, *noun*: 'a person of average or moderate cultural attainments', with the adjectival 'claiming to be or regarded as only moderately intellectual' (and in this case the earliest examples are from 1928 and 1929). The blending of social and cultural classifications, the confusion of intellectual interests with intellectual capacity, the ambiguity in the two senses of 'superior', the unsteadiness between 'being', 'claiming to be', and 'regarded as being'—in all these respects the definitions faithfully mirrored the welter of attitudes caught up in this new terminology.

What these parallel entries cannot really register is a fundamental asymmetry in the role of the two main terms. The dynamic of the usage was driven by the notion of the 'highbrow'; 'lowbrow' was the necessary or inferential opposite, but the type so designated attracted far less attention, and the term was much less used in self-description. This analysis is borne out, I believe, by the fact that it took the arrival of the third term 'middlebrow' to transform what had been a rather sporadic and one-sided pattern of name-calling into a fully developed 'battle of the brows' in the late 1920s, complete with two, or perhaps three, 'sides'. From a purely linguistic point of view, 'middlebrow' was obviously a third term waiting to be called on stage once the two extremes achieved some currency, but its burgeoning in the late 1920s represented the cumulative impact of changes in the literary sphere in particular, which contributed to the heightened self-consciousness about the segmentation of the reading public. The 1920s, historians now seem to agree, were the first decade in which we can see 'the development of a specifically middlebrow literature'. McKibbin notes that A. J. Cronin, best-selling interwar author, whose *The Citadel* broke all records for fast sales on its publication in 1937, was actually described in the (admittedly later) *Dictionary of National Biography* as 'a middlebrow writer *par excellence*'.[5] The representative institutions here were the Book Society, established in 1927, followed by the Book Guild in 1930, organizations which were modelled on the American 'Book-of-the-Month Club and which self-consciously promoted what Q. D. Leavis, speaking on behalf of the embattled minority, called 'a middlebrow standard of values'.[6] (For this minority, anxiety about, and resistance to, American cultural influence more generally played a significant part in the 'battle of the brows', and with reason: 'English popular literature was throughout the period subject to continuous and pervasive American influence.'[7]) It had been difficult to use 'lowbrow' in self-description except in a somewhat defensive, arch way; by contrast, 'middlebrow' commentators could now glory in their four-square, middle-of-the-road, downright English status when sneering at the bloodless refinement and European affectations of the highbrow. And as a further indication of what we might call the polemical priority of 'highbrow' over its opposites, it should be noted that the cultural symbol or target around which these latter attitudes coalesced most enduringly in this period was 'Bloomsbury'—a term used and misused so widely that it almost ceased to have any determinate historical referent, but however many individuals were embraced under its capacious canopy and however beneficial or pernicious their role and influence were held to be, it was a term that came to be almost a synonym for 'highbrow'.

If the literary pages of newspapers and periodicals were the chief setting for the battle of the brows, the 1920s also saw the development of an important new medium in Britain's cultural life through which these debates could be further amplified, namely radio. From the outset, the BBC was granted a monopoly, and until the outbreak of the war it consisted of only one 'station', the 'National Programme', which ranged from light music to serious talks, attracting, as a consequence, a diversity of listeners (at the beginning of the war this was renamed 'the Home Service' and was accompanied by a second station, 'the Forces Programme'). What now seems striking is the prominence accorded by the BBC in its early years to the representatives of 'Bloomsbury' as cultural arbiters, especially following the internal reorganization of the Corporation and the setting up of a Talks Department in 1927. One of the earliest such programmes illustrates this point in most startling fashion. On 15 July 1927 a discussion was broadcast on the theme 'Are too many books written and published?' There were just two participants: Leonard Woolf and Virginia Woolf. This pattern of eavesdropping on high-end pillow-talk was extended in June 1929 when the topic of 'Marriage' was discussed by—Harold Nicolson and Vita Sackville-West. (It may partly have been a by-product of the affair between Vita and Hilda Matheson, the Head of Talks, that so many of Vita's social acquaintances were invited to speak in such programmes.) Similarly, to represent rival views on 'art and life' listeners were given a discussion between Clive Bell and Desmond MacCarthy. Figures associated with this particular coterie also gave a disproportionate number of the talks broadcast on cultural topics before the war, and as a result several of them became what one historian has termed 'great essayists of the air' (E. M. Forster was a notable success in this genre).[8] All this reinforced the identification of 'Bloomsbury' with 'culture', a term confidently employed in the period and not yet superseded by the more defensive 'high culture'.

A brief examination of a few representative contributions to the 'battle of the brows' will help draw out what was at stake for the question of intellectuals. One of the figures most often to be found leading a charge in these engagements, indeed a writer whose career can at times seem to have depended upon keeping these antagonisms alive, was J. B. Priestley. (His case also emphasized that highbrows always came from, or sounded as though they came from, the South of England.) Interestingly, one of his early salvoes seems to have predated the currency of 'middlebrow', a term which, once coined, stuck to his name like mud to a hiking-boot. In protesting against 'this "brow" business' in 1926, he distanced himself from both 'high' and 'low', proudly proclaiming himself to be a 'Broadbrow'. Caricatures were the staple ammunition in such skirmishes, and the genre came easily to Priestley: the highbrow 'is the thin sheep with the spectacles and the squeak from Oxford or Bloomsbury.' The herd-like behaviour of sheep was constitutive of the type:

> Never is he discovered finding anything for himself, but always barking in full chorus. Just now he is fussing over the French writers of the eighteenth century, but has a side chapel for the Restoration dramatists. Some time ago it was the Russians accompanied by the Elizabethans. Next year it may be the Spasmodic School of the Mid-Victorian period, and *Aurora Leigh* and Kingsley's *Yeast*, and Bloomsbury alone knows what.[9]

Readers hardly needed this last phrase to recognize how much hostility to that particular nexus of social and cultural attitudes animated Priestley's caricature, a caricature, incidentally, that reveals a level of learning and a eye for literary fashion that rather belied the self-description of most middlebrows. The itemized enthusiasms were not random illustrations: Lytton Strachey was notoriously devoted to French writers of the eighteenth century, and contemporary readers could similarly have decoded the other examples.

In the following year, Leonard Woolf, indisputably a central figure in Bloomsbury however configured, published one of the more notable statements of the contrary view, his Hogarth Press pamphlet entitled *Hunting the Highbrow*. Woolf emphasized that there was indeed a good deal of 'hunting' of this species going on; he instanced two attacks that had appeared in the same week. His response took the form of facetious jocularity, breaking down the species into its variants such as *Altifrons aestheticus* and *Pseudaltifrons intellectualis* and so on (*Altifrons altifrontissimus* he glossed as 'the original, primitive, and real highbrow or intellectual' or 'the intellectual proper, the man who has a passion for the intellect'). Most of his discussion was ostensibly directed to the varieties of aesthetic highbrow; much of it was really devoted to a closely related but slightly different subject, namely why purely popular works of literature (and by extension music and the other arts) die out after a while but the really good work lasts and not merely becomes classic but begins to give pleasure to the popular audience of a later generation. His central conceit threatens to become tedious before the end, but two points are worth noting here. First, there is his rather disingenuous self-description as 'being, if not a highbrow, at any rate on the side of the highbrows'; he knew that in practice he was taken as one of the purest representatives of the species. And second, there is Woolf's passing, but still remorselessly facetious, discussion of why 'the intellectual highbrow is deservedly hated': namely, because he tries to apply his intellect to matters ordinarily governed by prejudice and emotion. This is done most consequentially by 'the intellectual in politics', someone who can, in the right circumstances, have considerable impact; his two topical examples are Woodrow Wilson and Lenin. Woolf, of course, had much more direct involvement with the world of politics than most of his Bloomsbury friends (Keynes excepted), and it is interesting to see how, starting from an attack by the popular novelist Gilbert Frankau on 'highbrows' who don't like a book to have a good story, he can effortlessly slide along the continuum represented by the term 'intellectual' to embrace those rare political figures committed to 'suddenly changing a world based on prejudice and passion into a world based on reason'.[10] It is a moot point whether the Great British Public of the time was more likely to be suspicious of the species if it thought it was represented by Lenin or by Lytton Strachey.

Another indisputable highbrow in the period, sometimes thought of as a Bloomsbury associate though in fact his ties were only those shared by several regular week-enders at Garsington, was Aldous Huxley, and he took stock of the battle at the beginning of the 1930s.[11] 'Today "highbrow" is a term of contemptuous abuse.... In decent Anglo-Saxon society one may not be a highbrow.' Instead, the typical upper-middle-class Englishman and Englishwoman of the period have 'the genuinely upper-middle-class instincts about everything and everybody, including the highbrows, for whom they have a healthily Public-Schooly contempt—mingled, however, with a certain secret and uncomfortable fear'. (Perhaps the element of fear in the strain of *ressentiment* towards highbrows or intellectuals in Britain has not, in general, been sufficiently remarked.) Huxley, like others of his generation, ascribed the new 'stupidity-snobbery' to the perverse effects of universal education. People now despised what, when viewed from a position of exclusion, they once dutifully venerated: they resent the affectations of the cultured the more now that they know from their own experience that 'culture' may actually yield so little satisfaction. The explanation does not seem wholly coherent, given that the typical upper-middle-class Englishman was being put through a form of schooling long before the Education Acts of the 1870s to which Huxley implicitly refers, and, more generally, that the 'highbrow/lowbrow' contrast cut across the conventional 'upper class/lower class' divide. But Huxley clearly shared the conviction of other commentators in the 1920s that the current anti-intellectualism was newly powerful if not altogether new in itself. He nonetheless permitted himself a limited degree of optimism, and in the process willingly accepted the label which others intended as 'contemptuous abuse': 'There is as yet no actual persecution of highbrows. We are safe. [We must hope that] there will always be a few people for whom things of the mind are so vitally important that they will not, that they simply cannot allow them to be overwhelmed.'[12] The alarmist note was characteristic of the period: 'culture' was assailed by 'the masses', and 'highbrow' was one of the verbal arrows which now rained down on the inhabitants of the besieged citadel.

Reviewing Huxley's collection, Desmond MacCarthy, professional bookman and Bloomsbury outrider, took the opportunity to go onto the attack about 'the privilege and advantage of being a "Highbrow"'. In the passage quoted as the epigraph to this chapter, he berated his fellow highbrows for their defensiveness: 'What is the cause of this ridiculous diffidence which afflicts intellectuals today? Why should they allow every muddled ignoramus to assert his superiority? Why should they be afraid of betraying their own?' He did not quite endorse Huxley's explanation for the prevailing hostility: he attributed it rather to the fact that money could now buy its way into any social circle, but 'the only exclusive world remaining today is that of the highbrows'. The catcalls express 'the bewildered misery of those trying to live beyond their intellectual means'. The outcome is that 'those who reveal culture and their faith in it in every line they write, appear to the Many to be fraudulent and pretentious bores—for that is what they mean when they call them "Highbrows"'. But MacCarthy remained serenely confident that caring for 'things of the mind' is the only really satisfying form of life (an assertion not calculated, of course, to make the Many take a more tolerant view of the category to which he proudly assigns himself).[13] In effect, his essay recommends defiantly pinning the label 'highbrow' on to one's well-cut lapel and then sauntering around Gordon Square, caring most beautifully for the things of the mind. These were hardly the terms of a likely peace treaty.

Few people were less inclined to signing peace treaties than F. R. Leavis (except perhaps his wife, Q. D. Leavis). Writing in 1930 of the antithesis between 'mass civilization' and 'minority culture', as he and others tended to categorize the cultural conflicts that came to the fore in the 1920s, Leavis seized on this point of usage: '"High-brow" is an ominous addition to the English language.' Leavis noted that the term had been imported from the United States, as had the Book-of-the-Month Club model, and it was in the promotional literature of the latter's British analogues that he found some of the most disquieting examples of this new usage. 'Distinguished critics attempt to guide the public, but they are often so hopelessly "high-brow" and "precious",' declared the Book Guild which, by contrast, offered to cater 'for the ordinary intelligent reader, not for the high-brows'. It clearly did not help, in Leavis's eyes, that the Book Society's selection panel was made up of the likes of Hugh Walpole and J. B. Priestley, both aggressive proponents of taking the highbrow down a peg or two. Leavis quoted another member of the panel, Miss Clemence Dane, writing in eulogy of fellow-panellist Hugh Walpole, complaining that the modern English novel 'is suffering so severely nowadays from specialists, highbrows, and cranks', and recommending a purgative dose of Edgar Wallace and similar authors. Leavis drew his trademark moral: 'The minority is now made conscious, not merely of an uncongenial, but of a hostile environment.' The possibility of writing in a way that might simultaneously appeal to an elite and a popular audience had now disappeared, he maintained (how far it had actually existed in previous generations is, of course, disputable), and it was predictable that his examples of the current authors who were not just shunned but attacked by middlebrow readers for their inaccessibility should be Eliot, Pound, Joyce, and Woolf, the leading names in literary Modernism.[14]

Since the chief contention of Q. D. Leavis's *Fiction and the Reading Public* was that a unified reading public had been displaced by a series of publics segmented more or less along class lines, it is hardly surprising that she should order her somewhat jejune sociological analysis of contemporary periodical literature into three groups, though surprising, perhaps, that she should so insouciantly declare: 'It will be convenient to call these levels "highbrow", "lowbrow", and "middlebrow".' Perhaps these labels were now inescapable, though a certain unsteadiness in her own use is evident when, in taking the *Criterion* as the representative journal of the first category, she remarks 'it is common even in literary circles to fling the epithet "highbrow" at it'. She, too, drew upon the Book Society and the Book Guild for her most damning examples (Leavis himself may have pinched them from his wife's researches for her Ph.D. in the first place), but she provided far more detail, showing how the best-sellers of the age, such as Warwick Deeping, 'exhibit a persistent hostility to the world of letters which is quite unprecedented', and how they make constant use of the label 'highbrow' to denigrate the denizens of that world.[15] In later years when robustly democratic commentators wished to tar the idea of the intellectual with associations of 'elitism' and 'hypercritical' judgement, the *Scrutiny* circle, with the Leavises at its centre, was nearly always *proxime accessit* to Bloomsbury as a favoured illustration—ironically so, given the Leavises' unrelenting hostility to, and scorn for, the '*rentier* triviality' of 'Mrs Woolf and her friends'.

These debates, it will be seen, peaked in the late 1920s and early 1930s, and if during these years there was one individual, more than any other, whose name sharply polarized attitudes and was most calculated to induce an allergic reaction in the aggressively middlebrow reviewer, it was Virginia Woolf. Her sparring with Arnold Bennett in this vein has become a point of reference for the literary history of the period.[16] Bennett was a Jekyll and Hyde writer, a serious novelist who also cultivated an aggressively middlebrow persona, especially as the author of his enormously influential literary column in the *Evening Standard* from 1926 till his death in 1932. There he constantly sniped at Woolf, now describing *Orlando* as 'a high-brow lark', now labelling her 'the queen of the high-brows', and so on.[17] In Woolf's eyes, Bennett's offensiveness as a self-appointed arbiter of taste was exceeded only by Priestley's, where there was no question of countervailing literary achievement she could respect, but these two were only the most prominent of a whole clutch of reviewers and commentators who found it convenient to focus their hostility to the over-fastidious sensibility and social-cum-cultural superiority of 'the intellectual' in general on this supposedly etiolated and affected, but increasingly successful, author of 'difficult' novels. As she pleaded in a letter to Hugh Walpole in February 1932: 'Anyhow, don't dismiss me as an etiolated, decadent, enervated, emasculated, priggish, blood-waterish, 'ighbrow: as Arnold Bennett used to say', unable, even here, to resist the jibe about dropped aitches. And again a few months later she complained to Ethel Smyth: 'I get so much heckled by journalists for Bloomsbury Highbrowism.'[18]

Priestley finally scaled the peak of his offensiveness with a talk broadcast in October 1932 entitled 'To a High-Brow' (Woolf recorded in her diary that month that she was particularly 'fire[d] up about Priestley and his priestliness').[19] This was responded to the following week by Harold Nicolson in a 'To a Low-Brow', and the exchange then attracted comment in the press.[20] Priestley pummelled his usual cardboard caricature of 'the High-Brow', along the way denouncing MacCarthy and Huxley as purveyors of highbrow 'bunkum', sneering at those 'authors entirely without feeling, who write about human life as an educated wolf might be expected to write about it', and concluding in his best hail-fellow-well-met fashion that one should not be a highbrow or a lowbrow: 'Be a man. Be a broad-brow.' Nicolson offered a pointed and direct rebuttal of Priestley's assertions (and in the eyes of the not-altogether-neutral *New Statesman* he scored a convincing victory), along the way asking rhetorically: 'Has it ever struck you... that there is no equivalent for the words "low-brow" or "high-brow" in any language other than the English language?' On the basis of such evidence, Nicolson apparently concluded with an adumbration of an early variant of the absence-thesis: 'The Anglo-Saxon race is the only race in the world that openly distrusts the intellectual.'[21]

Woolf was driven to a frenzy of irritation by the whole episode, and, writing with that air of tongue-in-cheek whimsy that made her such a deadly satirist, she immediately drafted a response, cast in the form of a long letter to the editor of the *New Statesman*. (Though drafted as a letter, it was never sent, perhaps on Leonard's advice; she intended to revise it for publication as an essay, and 'Middlebrow' was the title she gave it, but it remained unpublished at her death.[22]) 'Will you allow me', she began, 'to draw your attention to the fact that in a review of a book by me your reviewer omitted to use the word Highbrow?' Such an oversight would never be committed by 'that great critic who is also a great novelist' (i.e. Bennett) who unfailingly applies the term to her and who also always helpfully explains which part of London she lives in. But it is the general issue that engages her, and 'since the finest minds of our age have lately been engaged in debating... what a highbrow is and what a lowbrow', she proposes to offer her own contribution. She deliberately revels in the term: the highbrow 'is the man or woman of thoroughbred intelligence who rides his mind at a gallop across country in pursuit of an idea. That is why I have always been so proud to be called a highbrow,' and so on. Roughly speaking, her version of the distinction is that highbrows do the thinking, lowbrows do the living: hence they depend on and need each other. She deliberately, if not altogether convincingly, attempts to disjoin social and intellectual classifications: 'I myself have known duchesses who were highbrows, also charwomen.' The real villains of the piece, of course, turn out to be the middlebrows, wholly committed neither to art nor to life 'but both mixed indistinguishably, and rather nastily, with money, fame, power, or prestige', and it is they who have stirred up this war, especially their spokesmen in the press and the BBC (the 'Betwixt and Between Company').

The informing strategy of Woolf's essay is to call into question all the prevailing assumptions about the relations of intelligence and taste to social background or occupation. Along the way she lands barely coded hits on her usual antagonists, slyly counter-mocking the sneer that Bloomsbury fancy themselves the high-priests of culture: 'to be quite frank, the adjective "priestly" is neither often heard nor held in high esteem'. But beneath the elaborate sarcasms, Woolf's essay was registering the fact that the pejorative usage of 'highbrow' and the caricature associated with it was now a cultural force of considerable power. Woolf might boldly attempt to appropriate the catcall as a positive self-description—'I ask for nothing better than that all reviewers, for ever, and everywhere, should call me a highbrow. I will do my best to oblige them'[23]—but in reality Nicolson had been nearer the mark: the very appearance, still more the prominence, of the language of 'highbrow' and 'lowbrow' was, among other things, an index of recently accumulated resistance and hostility to the idea of the intellectual in Britain.

II

Even once terms become well established in a language, those to whom they seem most naturally to apply may persist in repudiating them. Here we need to consider 'denial' in another sense, where it may be rather a psychological than a sociological pattern that is in play. If the 1920s and 1930s increasingly accustomed English ears to the noun 'intellectuals', they nonetheless seemed at times to remain five syllables in search of an owner. For, by and large, intellectuals were always Other People. Foreigners, principally; or people who lived in Bloomsbury or Hampstead (to those who lived elsewhere); or self-consciously superior aesthetes and irresponsibly radical political theorists (to those who prided themselves on being neither). Certainly, resistance to the use of the label in self-description was not confined to one or two assertively nativist figures. In this respect, any gathering of portraits of prominent intellectuals in twentieth-century Britain might well be subtitled 'Studies in Ambivalence'.

As a way of broaching this aspect of the question, it may be helpful to assemble identikit portraits of imaginary individuals or types who would between them represent almost the entire range of those likely, from about the middle of the twentieth century onwards, to be thought of as 'intellectuals', and then to compare these constructions with the careers of actual individuals. Here are four such types:

The first figure is primarily a poet and critic, though one who turns himself into a significant social commentator, producing quantities of essays and lectures, and for many years editing a general cultural periodical. By both disposition and education he is at ease with European philosophical and critical thinking.

He feels himself to be deeply at odds with the dominant world-view of his society; he espouses a variety of unpopular causes; and he maintains close links with intellectual and literary figures in other countries.

The second figure is a journalist, essayist, and novelist. He lives by his pen, never holding anything like an academic or official position. His novels are self-consciously 'novels of ideas', often expressing an overt political purpose. His angular social criticism attempts to use the existential verities to discomfit all merely fashionable or time-serving attitudes, and he deliberately cultivates the persona of the man of courage and independence, bent on telling truth to power.

The third figure is primarily a philosopher, but one who is a lifelong political activist, even enduring a spell in prison for his dissident activities, and who participates in numerous forms of public protest. He writes a great deal of journalism as well as serious philosophy, and offers his contemporaries moral guidance on issues ranging from money to marriage. His own personal life, too, is appropriately unconventional, even bohemian, something which earns him the hostility of, and further sets him apart from, respectable society.

The final figure is primarily a historian. He is a scholar and writer whose frequently expressed political convictions lead him into controversy; he is a declared agnostic who is at odds for much of his life with the official creed of his country; for part of his career he exists as a metropolitan man of letters, making a living from his books and his journalism. His writing commands a wide readership, not least because of its deliberate propagation of an ideal of national identity. The recognition and honours that come his way give added weight to his support of various public causes.

All four of these portraits may seem to conform to certain familiar (and, therefore, European) models of being 'an intellectual'. They are also, as some readers may already have recognized, perfectly possible descriptions of, respectively, T. S. Eliot, George Orwell, Bertrand Russell, and G. M. Trevelyan. What makes these descriptions of them especially pertinent here is that each of these very different individuals is a prominent example of what I am referring to under the heading of 'paradoxes of denial', that is, leading intellectuals who resist, disown, or otherwise attempt to keep their distance from the label and from those to whom they prefer, disparagingly, to apply it. In the case of both Eliot and Orwell, this is in fact a more central and more complicated feature of their writing than is generally recognized, and for that reason I have devoted a separate chapter to each of them in Part Four. But the broader pattern may be illustrated in the present section of this chapter by considering much more briefly the cases of Russell and Trevelyan.

Many foreign observers would probably have identified Bertrand Russell as the best-known intellectual in Britain in the first two-thirds of the twentieth century. But any reader of the repetitive and under-researched literature on intellectuals would almost certainly have encountered the following comment by Russell himself: 'I have never called myself an intellectual, and nobody has ever dared to call me one in my presence. I think an intellectual may be defined as a person who pretends to have more intellect than he has, and I hope this definition does not fit me.' It is a characteristically perverse remark which has now served several tours of duty as an illustration of the negative connotations of the term in English. For example, when Ernest Gowers was revising Fowler's *Dictionary of Modern English Usage*, he found the remark irresistible as part of his two-edged entry for the noun. It was from Gowers that I took the quotation, in an essay published in 1993, noting his reference to an article by Russell Kirk, 'The American intellectual: a conservative view', published in 1960. There, Kirk introduced the quotation by saying 'Not long ago, someone wrote to Bertrand Russell enquiring...'. My essay was in turn cited in T. W. Heyck in his 1998 article, where he reproduced the quotation, introducing it with the phrase Russell 'is reported once to have said...', and so the chain goes on.[24] In none of the cases was an actual source cited, and Kirk was alone in giving any hint of where and when the remark might have been made.

Only if one happens to light upon the correspondence columns of *Encounter* in June 1955 can a point of origin be traced, and it reveals that Russell never actually 'said' or 'published' this remark. Referring to the recent *Encounter* article on intellectuals in Britain by Edward Shils (discussed more fully in Ch. 6), H. O. Alexander wrote in to report that, 'four years ago', he had written to several 'prominent British intellectuals' specifically asking them 'whether they agreed with this description [of themselves], and inviting them to volunteer some general observations'.[25] The oft-quoted passage was Russell's reply to this enquiry, an enquiry which was surely always likely to provoke the counter-suggestible Russell into such deliberate mischief, and his reply was then quoted in Alexander's letter on this later occasion. The episode dates, it should also be noted, from a period when the contrast between the inflated pretensions of certain French intellectuals and the alleged absence of such posturing in sober, welfare-state-building Britain was most pronounced.

But this one heavily stylized remark cannot be taken to represent Russell's settled view on the question of intellectuals. On other occasions, he was perfectly capable of employing the term in a more positive, or at the least more neutral, way. For example, towards the end of his course of lectures at Caxton Hall in 1915 (subsequently published as *The Principles of Social Reconstruction*), he wrote to a friend:

> As a matter of fact, my lectures are a great success—they are a rallying ground for the intellectuals, who are coming daily more to my way of thinking not only as regards the war but also as regards general politics. All sorts of literary and artistic people who formerly despised politics are being driven to action, as they were in France by the Dreyfus case. In the long run, their action will have a profound effect. It is primarily to them that I am speaking.[26]

It is a curious passage, even apart from its characteristic egocentricity. To judge from the contextual evidence,[27] the 'intellectuals' referred to here primarily meant

Bloomsbury and the young artistic radicals associated with publications such as the *New Age*. It is far from obvious that such people were being 'driven to action', except perhaps for having, in some cases, to stand up for their pacifist beliefs before conscription tribunals. And in any case, Russell's lectures were hardly recommending any conventional form of 'action'. He said himself that in his lectures he was rejecting 'any of the ordinary methods of politics', and in Philip Ironside's persuasive analysis of these lectures (and indeed of the whole of Russell's early social thought), Russell's priority was to establish whatever political and economic arrangements best preserved (or created) the freedom of that artistic and intellectual minority upon whom, Russell believed, all progress depended. If at this point he took 'intellectuals' to refer primarily to 'literary and artistic people', as was not uncommon at that date, then he may, strictly, not have been including himself in the category, though he was certainly not disparaging it.

Similarly, if one jumps forward to 1958, one can find him, when speaking of Keynes and his bold, extra-academic career, insisting that life in universities was too comfortable and protected, producing fearful creatures who could spawn only timid ideas. By contrast, he urged, with his customary provokingness, 'All intellectuals should suffer a certain amount of persecution as early in life as possible. Not too much. That is bad for them. But a certain amount.'[28] It is a moot point whether this remark is sufficiently self-referential for 'them' to be read implicitly as 'us' here, but once again there is no warrant for concluding that Russell was using the term in a particularly pejorative way in this instance. His praise of Keynes in the immediately surrounding sentences is emphatic.

The fact that these last two remarks are separated by over four decades also serves to remind us that in the course of Russell's very long life the meanings and resonances of the term 'intellectuals' had changed. Where it may have been common at the time of the First World War to use it to refer to 'literary and artistic people', there could be no question but that, by the late 1950s, academics were commonly acknowledged to be among the most prominent examples of the category. Russell, of course, was resistant to being embraced in any collective category, including that of 'intellectuals', and to this initial ambivalence is often added a slight sniffiness of tone, as though 'intellectuals' are perhaps intellectually second-rate, publicity-hungry individuals, who may even come close to being not quite gentlemen.

This note may have been most in evidence in the 1930s, when Russell's distance from the fashionable cultural movements of the day was at its greatest. Philip Ironside concludes: 'There is, in fact, every indication that Russell was unimpressed with the achievements of the thirties' intelligentsia, and had, as a consequence, rather lost faith in the intellectuals as a class.'[29] Certainly, by the end of that decade one can find him commenting, in rather critical tones, on the decline of the intellectuals' 'priestly' status consequent upon the spread of science:

> Science, in giving some real acquaintance with natural processes, has destroyed the belief in magic, and therefore the respect for the intellectual. . . . The intellectuals, finding their

> prestige slipping from them as a result of their own activities, become dissatisfied with the modern world. Those in whom the dissatisfaction is least take to Communism; those in whom it goes deeper shut themselves up in their ivory tower.[30]

Here, once again, there is precious little sense of self-identification: intellectuals are, very firmly, Other People.

There are, of course, few easier games than that of quoting Russell against himself: his penchant for making his remarks as lapidary and provoking as possible means that somewhere in his voluminous prose one can usually find him asserting two flatly contradictory propositions on the same topic. An example of the kind of statement that requires supplies of salt to be kept on hand during its reading is his brief article 'The role of the intellectual in the modern world', which was given as an address to the Sociology Club of the University of Chicago in 1938. The opening sentence sets the tone: 'I have been talking a fair amount [*sc.* since arriving in the USA, presumably] and I have become quite adept at talking on subjects of which I am completely ignorant, and I gather that is what is expected of me tonight' (here and throughout the talk one easily imagines that familiar *Hansard* interpolation: 'laughter'). Russell lamented that intellectuals now seemed to have less influence than in 'the good old days'; he went on to lament that they had not actually had much influence then, either; he also lamented that 'the more civilized the world becomes the less it wants to listen to the sages'. It is easy to see why so many of Russell's contemporaries despaired of his glib, self-indulgent facility. But the talk does suggest that, on this occasion and in this mood at least, he could speak of 'intellectuals' in a largely positive way. At one point he glancingly defined the intellectual as 'the man . . . who forms his opinions on evidence', and later: 'One would like, if it were possible, to see some greater influence in the world of those who think about human life as a whole and have some consideration of the ends of life.' This last role he contrasted with that of 'the technician' who is 'the really big man in the modern world'.[31] Russell was not identifying himself with 'the technician': he was placing himself alongside those who 'have some consideration of the ends of life'.

In fact, Russell oscillated, as my analysis suggests intellectuals are always likely to do, between emphasizing his own technical expertise as philosopher and mathematician on the one hand, and, on the other, precisely taking the more 'general' perspective of 'those who think about human life as a whole'. In this oscillation he was acting the part of the intellectual even while repudiating the description. And he most certainly never repudiated his own defining intellectuality. When in 1915, at the peak of his resistance to wartime conscription, Russell wrote 'I feel more allegiance to mathematics than to the state,' he was, as Ironside comments, 'signifying that for the duration his loyalty was restricted to that international community of intellectuals represented for him by such terms as "European culture" '.[32] In one form or other, whether understood as a national 'clerisy' or a cosmopolitan 'intellectual aristocracy', this remained Russell's central allegiance. It may also suggest one reason why, in the eyes of so many self-described 'plain men' in Britain, the loyalty of intellectuals, like that of Jews, Jesuits, and homosexuals, could not be trusted: they could all be seen as owing their primary allegiance to other powers.

There could never have been any question that G. M. Trevelyan, the second of my examples, would have classed himself among 'the intellectuals' (let alone any of the three associated categories just mentioned), even though, as my brief imaginary profile indicated, his career could be seen as displaying several of the classic attributes of that role. As his most recent biographer observes, 'although a member of the intellectual aristocracy, [Trevelyan] had little time for those who thought of themselves as intellectuals'.[33] But why? What kinds of people did he think 'thought of themselves as intellectuals'?

'Bertrand Russell' would be one obvious answer. Although he and Trevelyan were near contemporaries whose education and careers at first followed somewhat similar trajectories, the story of their relationship through the first four decades of the twentieth century was one of growing distance and antipathy. Trevelyan disapproved of Russell's morals, his opposition to the First World War, his pot-boiling writing between the wars, and his consistent lack of pragmatic political judgement. He came to think him (in the appropriately gruff, anti-intellectual idiom) as 'an ass', 'a bloody fool', though apparently by the time they were both in their seventies they were largely reconciled.[34]

One gets a further glimpse of those Trevelyan imagined 'thought of themselves as intellectuals' in an address he delivered in 1944 in honour of his friend John Buchan. Trevelyan made it clear that he admired Buchan because the latter 'despised literary coteries', and avoided 'the squabbles and narrowness to which "intellectuals" of all periods are too prone'. And more generally, as he wrote to his daughter in 1942: 'As to "intellectuals" . . . one of the greatest disappointments of my life has been the decadence of that class (if you can call it a class) of which I first became aware when Lytton Strachey came up to Cambridge.'[35] In both cases, Trevelyan's use of distancing quotation marks indicates his sense, or perhaps just his wish, that the term should not be so readily accepted at face value; 'so-called' is silently present each time.

The contrast with Strachey is perhaps even more revealing than it may at first appear. When he first arrived in Cambridge, Strachey had been rather taken up by Trevelyan, four years his senior, but even at that stage the friendship had not been entirely to Strachey's taste. Too much vigorous walking was involved, for one thing, and he found Trevelyan 'very—I think *too*—earnest'.[36] Thereafter, the meetings of the Apostles became the scene of their differences, and Bertrand Russell later recalled the substance of the conflict thus: 'After my time, The Society changed in one respect. There was a long drawn out battle between George Trevelyan and Lytton Strachey, both members, in which Lytton Strachey was on the whole victorious. Since his time, homosexual relations among the members were for a time common, but in my day they were unknown.'[37] These differences were also to go on to colour their contrasting conceptions of the task of the historian, especially the biographer. Trevelyan's three-volume life of Garibaldi was explicitly cast in the form of biography as epic: Strachey found it interesting 'but tiresomely told'.[38] Conversely, Trevelyan detested Strachey's style of 'debunking', and blamed him for the fashion for 'cheap . . . nasty . . . absurd one-volume biographies'.[39] (Clearly, size mattered.) All the way along, the characteristics Trevelyan ascribed to Strachey could also have doubled as a kind of checklist of all that the hard-working, hard-walking Englishman of his generation found disagreeable about 'intellectuals'.

And how did Trevelyan think that he, one of the leading intellectual figures of his generation, differed from the 'class' of which he was so scornful? Here, the positive form of the checklist might have included: strict adherence to a conventional code of personal morality, especially in sexual matters; 'good sense', 'judgement', and 'public spiritedness', as opposed to 'cleverness', 'silliness', and 'self-indulgence'. Though he was highly critical of most of the members of the Bloomsbury Group, Trevelyan made a particular exception for Keynes precisely because he did possess these qualities, did engage with the world in a serious and responsible way, and exhibited 'immense disinterestedness and public spirit'.[40] Indeed, it comes to seem that it is not the meddling of the intellectuals in public affairs that Trevelyan would reproach them for; if anything it is the opposite, a rarefied or hothouse intellectuality and aestheticism which is precisely *not* chastened by sufficient contact with the world. For most of the twentieth century this was to be a powerful element in British attitudes towards those suspected of 'thinking of themselves as intellectuals'.

A recurring element in this pattern of disdain is the claim that one unfailing antidote to these failings is to remain close to the instincts and good sense of ordinary people. After the Abdication crisis in 1936, Trevelyan wrote to, appropriately, Arthur Bryant: 'And a stand has been made against the view that sexual licence is a natural right of man, a doctrine which half our literary and intellectual leaders have been preaching for the last forty years. I feared they might have converted the country, but clearly they haven't.'[41] The same resonance is evident in the terms in which Trevelyan, in his biography of his father, published in 1932, characterized Macaulay. He remarked that Sir George Otto Trevelyan had referred to Macaulay as, in a very positive sense of the term, 'a common man':

> And indeed Macaulay was the 'man in the street', but with genius, scholarship, statesmanship, and encyclopaedic knowledge added. My father, with a smaller measure of those gifts, was in his innermost nature an aristocrat and an artist. Partly for that reason intellectuals like John Morley, who were jealously indignant at Macaulay's great fame, warmed to the nephew who worshipped him.[42]

Here, lack of kinship with 'the man in the street' is naturally accompanied by the intellectual's characteristic vice of jealousy of another's literary success. The terms in which Trevelyan praised his friends and fellow-historians J. L. and Barbara Hammond expresses, by implication, a sense of how one might be a publicly engaged intellectual figure without being termed 'an intellectual': 'I admire and love the two Hammonds immensely. They are very rare examples of real saintliness of character combined with intellectual and scholarly power and service to the public in the rough ways of the world's arena, and all savoured with great good sense.'[43] These are the authentic tones of Englishness complacently taking stock of its own undramatic moral achievements. Soundness is all.

It is arguable that neither in his histories nor in his contemporary social criticism, such as it was, did Trevelyan consider it part of his role to probe beneath the surface of phenomena; he never really escaped the constraining power of cliché inherent in received descriptions, never tried to formulate new concepts—an activity which expresses the restless play of intelligence in refusing the superficial or the conventional even when the resulting redescriptions and neologisms fail, often for good reason, to take root.[44] The fact that Trevelyan enjoyed such success, both in terms of official or institutional recognition and of popularity with a broad reading public, may be taken as an example of the way in which a denial of intellectuality and the corresponding evasion of difficulty have been damagingly endorsed by some of the dominant strands in English culture. But the distinctiveness here should not be exaggerated. In most comparable societies, not dissimilar tastes have been evinced by the broad reading public, and even in France a charge of this kind is often laid against the kinds of 'society' authors who get elected to the Académie française. What makes Trevelyan an exceptionally instructive figure in this instance, it seems to me, is the way in which he helped to sustain a particular idiom of un- and even anti-intellectual 'manliness' at the heart of historical accounts of English national identity deep into the middle of the twentieth century, firmly attaching to 'intellectuals' the opprobrium of being cliquey, subversive, and self-important; unmanly, untrustworthy, and unhealthy; in a word, foreign.

III

The question of the 'foreignness' of intellectuals can be explored further by means of two rather different devices: first, the views of an outsider, applying 'alien' terminology, and secondly, the views of a representative sample of English people, considering the behaviour of another kind of 'alien'. D. S. Mirsky's *The Intelligentsia of Great Britain*, first published in Russian in 1934 and in English translation the following year, has been neglected by historians, but it deserves more extended consideration since it was perhaps the first would-be systematic survey of the views and careers of leading British intellectuals, explicitly treated as such, in the twentieth century, Part of the interest of the work lies precisely in the fact that it was written by a foreign observer, using a not wholly domesticated vocabulary.

Prince Dimitri Mirsky was one of those intriguing, cosmopolitan figures thrown up by the great dislocations that followed 1914–19 who then made a new life in British literary circles.[45] The son of a Tsarist minister, he lived in Britain throughout the 1920s, making a name for himself as a critic and historian of Russian literature. He became well connected in literary London, writing regularly for Squire's *London Mercury* and Eliot's *Criterion* among other journals, and he published a highly regarded history of Russian literature. But then, at the beginning of the 1930s, he 'converted' to Communism, joining the CPGB in 1931, finally choosing to return to the Soviet Union in 1932. Here he reversed his identity in a more practical way, setting himself up as guide and interpreter of English literature to Russian readers. It was in this role that he wrote his book on 'the intelligentsia', which, as we shall see, did not confine itself to literary figures. Mirsky was thereafter to suffer the typical fate of so many Russian intellectuals in the 1930s: he was denounced in the purges of 1937, dying in a Siberian labour camp two years later.

The Intelligentsia of Great Britain appeared with what amounted to the imprimatur of the Left in the 1930s: it was translated by the self-styled 'Marxist novelist' Alec Brown and published by Gollancz. Mirsky's approach to the topic is governed by his almost compulsively faithful adherence to the orthodox Communist line, complete with confident pronouncements about the impending collapse of capitalism, the revolutionary nature of the proletariat, and so on. But his earlier career in London had left him quite well informed about the recent history of British literary culture, and the powerful distorting lens through which he viewed this culture did at least serve to bring certain features into unusual prominence. His organizing categories were, of course, the tired labels of political propaganda—'reactionary', 'social fascist', 'revolutionary' and so on—but his first-hand knowledge constantly threatened to break through these constrictions. Writing twenty years later, Edmund Wilson, who got to know Mirsky during a visit to Russia in 1935, recognized that in this book 'the categories and conventions of Marxism do, of course, by themselves impose a constraint', but he found it nonetheless 'rather an able and brilliant book', 'full of original insights', and claimed that at the time there had been no comparable guide to 'the main currents and figures of recent English literature and thought'.[46]

In his opening chapter, Mirsky glossed the term 'intelligentsia' as standing for a stratum or class socially independent of the governing class and thoroughly 'critical' and 'dissident' in its views. (As a kind of epigraph to the chapter, the definition of the term from the *Concise Oxford Dictionary* was given—'the part of a nation (especially the Russian) that aspires to independent thinking'—but this was presumably added for the English translation.[47]) Mirsky argued that there had been no signs of such a class in Britain before the 1880s at the earliest, since the leading mid-Victorian intellectual figures were simply integrated into the educated and professional class more generally: 'In short, there were no intellectuals—no intelligentsia—as a special class.' But from the 1880s onwards there were the beginnings of two new kinds of groups who were somewhat detached from the governing classes and more oppositional: first, the aesthetes around Wilde, Beardsley, and company, the beginnings of a properly bohemian literary world; and second, the progressive reformers drawn from the ranks of the new technical and administrative class, epitomized by the Fabians.[48]

Subsequent chapters of the book are then devoted to particular groups ('the Progressives', 'the highbrows', 'the intelligentsia and science', and so on), where in practice he concentrates on characterizing the views of a few well-known figures, such as Shaw, Wells, Russell, Keynes, and company ('Russell is nearly as central for the post-war intelligentsia as Bernard Shaw was for the pre-war one'). Predictably, the main thrust of his argument was that, with the deepening of the 'crisis', there was a polarization among the intellectuals, the bulk of them beginning to tend towards Fascism, albeit initially in the disguise of 'science', as in the case of Wells, or of 'classicism', a jibe at Eliot and the *Criterion* circle. Far fewer prominent intellectuals had yet moved to the opposite pole, and Mirsky is sceptical of the revolutionary credentials of those 'bourgeois' academics who profess to favour the popular cause, such as Cole or Lindsay, and of such gushingly enthusiastic literary johnny-come-latelies as Middleton Murry, then just beginning a new life as a propagandist for Communism. Among leading figures, only John Strachey is unambiguously endorsed as having taken 'the side of the proletariat with complete sincerity and complete loyalty'.[49]

But the book is in some ways more perceptive and original than this account of its rather ritualized political name-calling suggests. It was, for example, alert in singling out social anthropology as 'the sole attempt since political economy arose to produce a discipline of social knowledge', and to accompany this insight with a well-informed brief discussion of Malinowski's work.[50] (His familiarity with recent anthropology may have owed something to his close friendship with Jane Harrison in the mid-1920s.[51]) But perhaps the most original part of Mirsky's tract came in the chapter dismissively entitled 'Religion *etcetera*', where, in addition to familiar denunciations of the 'stultifying power' of organized religion, he included a long analysis of what he called the 'theory of values'. By this he meant that movement of thought, crystallized in philosophy but by no means confined to it, which sought in personal experience, especially aesthetic experience, an alternative method and locus of value to that of natural science. He traced the roots of this back to late nineteenth-century Germany, above all to 'Dilte' (*sic*) and secondarily to Nietzsche, but he shrewdly noted that in the less philosophically inclined culture of Britain, the movement found its influential expression in the work of literary critics, sexologists, and theologians. What Mirsky had captured here was the way in which a powerful strain of philosophical Idealism blended in the 1910s and 1920s with a whole range of current intellectual fads, including a vulgarized form of psychoanalysis, which located value in those intense forms of personal experience which were in some way beyond the subject matter of science. It was in these terms that he understood what he called 'the craze for Croce' in Britain, as a philosopher who could theorize the cultivation of personal experience in a way which suited the needs of that small parasitic ('dividend-drawing') layer of the cultivated elite.

More interestingly, he then suggested that whereas the followers of Croce might be described as 'the right wing of the valueisers', the 'left wing' is 'connected not with idealist metaphysics, but with positivism and agnosticism . . . represented by such writers as Bertrand Russell and I. A. Richards'. It is an indication of the sensitivity of Mirsky's cultural antennae that he should pick up the link between the vogue for Croce's work in the 1920s and the following attracted by Richards's literary criticism, especially *The Principles of Literary Criticism* which Mirsky cited. On the face of things, Richards had attempted to ground his analysis of the distinctive nature of literary experience in a scientific account of human psychology, indeed a neurological account; but Mirsky was, of course, right that it also exhibited a fundamentally idealist valuation of the aesthetic as the category of experience which synthesized the largest number of impulses.[52] On this basis, Mirsky sketched a polemical interpretation of the social role of the teaching of literature, seeing it as taking over the function of religion as a way of diverting attention from the conflicts of class interests, a view of the 'critical revolution' of the 1920s which was only to become at all common in the 1970s and 1980s.[53] For all its crudity and tendentiousness, therefore, Mirsky's book went well beyond the staple fare peddled in Communist pamphleteering.

What also needs to be remarked for present purposes is how Mirsky assumed that his readers would take for granted the inclusion of writers, scientists, philosophers, critics, academics, and others under the label of 'intellectuals' or 'the intelligentsia'. Most British reviewers of the book censured Mirsky for turning against his erstwhile hosts in order, it was assumed, to please his new political masters, but they did not fundamentally object to his identification of the leading groups of 'intellectuals'. The review of the book in the *Criterion* by 'F.C.' (Frank Chapman, a fairly frequent reviewer there), although scornful of the central claim about the increasing 'fascisation' of the intelligentsia and severe on the book's 'poverty of thought, crudeness of manner', and so on, found nothing particularly remarkable in embracing a range of writers and thinkers under this label. Stephen Spender in the *Spectator* was no less severe on the book's argument but conceded that 'it has certain merits as a survey', and he treated its subject-matter as almost hackneyed: the reader soon realizes 'he is moving in the familiar world of pots and kettles which is the world of the intelligentsia, whether in Moscow or London'. In only partial contrast, Raymond Mortimer in the *New Statesman* emphasized the alienness of the book's terminology: 'Its crudities expose Moscow aestheticism in a most unflattering light, and it confirms the suspicion that some official Communist circles at present are rigidly anti-rational.' Ivor Brown in the *Observer* similarly complained that it had been translated into 'the cumbrous jargon so dear to English Communists and almost unreadable by anybody else', though, as Chapman acknowledged, it was hard to know how much of the style of the book in English (the 'typical jargon of the minor Marxist pamphleteers') was due to the translator—Alec Brown came in for some unflattering comment throughout. Even so, none of these reviewers detected anything untoward in the descriptive or classificatory enterprise of the book itself.[54] And indeed, if one were now attempting to draw up a select cast-list of British intellectuals in the first three decades of the twentieth century, one might take issue with certain of Mirsky's inclusions and exclusions, but by and large the same names would reappear. Obviously, both Mirsky and his initial readers had a pretty good idea who would, by the mid-1930s, be recognized as the leading 'intellectuals' in Britain, even when described in an 'alien' terminology.

IV

Finally, as a coda to this chapter, we may jump forwards a few years to consider an episode in which the status of the intellectual as an accepted member of British society—rather than as merely a 'resident alien'—was called into question in a highly specific, but peculiarly consequential, way. There can be few situations in which popular attitudes towards the intellectual are likely to be more starkly and more damagingly expressed than in an English court of law. In the hands of a skilled and merciless advocate, before a jury of 'ordinary' people (bearing the usual collection of extraordinary prejudices), the public image of 'the intellectual' appears almost synonymous with evasiveness, over-elaboration, contempt for the common decencies, and patronizing attitudes towards fellow citizens. In November 1946, one of the figures who had been most readily identified as 'an intellectual' in the previous two decades in Britain faced a jury of his 'peers' (i.e. a selection of people likely to distrust and disapprove of him) in an attempt to vindicate his reputation as an honest man and an upholder of the best political traditions of the country. He lost. 'The endeavour was massive', he reflected afterwards, 'to persuade those in whose hands the decision lay that the "intellectual" was a thing apart in our society, not exactly a pariah, but perhaps the jackal that accompanies the animal who does the kill.'[55]

Only a year earlier, the *New York Times*, a paper not normally given over to sensational or even playful headlines, had on 9 August 1945 felt obliged to inform its readers that, as its headline put it, 'BRITAIN NOT RUN BY INTELLECTUALS'. At first sight this may seem to belong with reports of small earthquakes in Chile as a hot contender for the title of least newsworthy headline in press history, but a clue to why the austere *Times* felt it necessary to give its readers this unsurprising information came in the sub-heading: 'Laski's role minimized'.[56] As this begins to indicate, the story focused on a charge and its rebuttal, in this case the charge that policy under the new Labour government in Britain would be dictated by Harold Laski, Professor of Political Science at the LSE and in 1945 Chairman of the Labour Party. Laski's name had been well known to American readers for some time, but during and after the 1945 election his fame in the United States expanded hugely. Immediately after the poll was declared, the more popular *New York Mirror* had run the headline 'CLEMENT ATTLEE MADE PRIME

MINISTER OF ENGLAND AND THE BOSS IS HAROLD LASKI A PRO-RUSSIAN FIGURE'. He was a favourite bogey with all the anti-Communist American press (essentially the entire press), a reputation as a 'red' dating back to his involvement in the Boston police strike of 1920. But as his biographers observe, 'it was the long biographical profiles of him complete with pictures and cartoons, in the *Saturday Evening Post* and *Life* in 1946 that conveyed true celebrity status'. *Time* carried an equally long spread on him under the heading 'Official Philosopher'.[57] A British intellectual had managed the improbable feat of, briefly, displacing the usual celebrities from the pages of the world's glitziest magazines. His biographers were not indulging in the usual proprietorial hype when they claimed: 'For a time Laski was the most important Socialist intellectual in the English-speaking world.... He was one of the twentieth century's principal public intellectuals.'[58]

Laski had, to a quite extraordinary extent, become an issue in the British general election campaign of 1945 in his own right. The Beaverbrook press decided to run a stream of stories about 'the red professor', the *éminence rouge* behind the avuncular, voter-friendly figures of Attlee and Morrison. In some ways, Laski assisted in his own demonization. He was a frequent and accomplished public speaker, but he did hold many views which were well to the left of the Labour leadership and he could easily be provoked into expressing them. Opinion in the party was divided over whether he was more of an asset or a liability. The Tories sensed the political advantage to be had from concentrating on this unelected theorist of 'extreme' views, representing him as the real dictator of future policy should Labour win. Hecklers pursued him across the country, hoping to goad him into some injudicious and exploitable remark.

This plan seemed to bear fruit in the market-square of Newark on the evening of Saturday, 16 June 1945. After Laski had addressed a meeting of about 1,500 people, a man approached him and asked him two questions (which were, it seems, written on prompt cards, presumably supplied by Tory electioneers). Why had he not served in the First World War and why had he recently openly advocated violence? According to the report carried in the weekly *Newark Advertiser* (a Beaverbrook paper), Laski angrily responded by pointing out that he had been turned down for military service on medical grounds and 'as for violence, he continued, if Labour could not obtain what it needed by general consent, we shall have to use violence, even if it means revolution.' The *Daily Express* took the story over from its regional stable-mate: its banner headline on 20 June was 'NEW LASKI SENSATION: SOCIALISM EVEN IF IT MEANS VIOLENCE'. Laski immediately denied that he had ever spoken the attributed words or that he had at any time in his life advocated violence, and he issued writs for libel against the Beaverbrook newspapers.[59]

The case finally came to trial in November 1946, attracting extensive press coverage in its turn. The Beaverbrook Press had invoked the privilege of having the trial heard before a 'special jury' (composed in this case of five men and two women) drawn from a roll of people with higher property qualifications than was required for basic jury service. 'The special jury was usually invoked when either party to a case deemed the material so complicated that jurors of greater intelligence and education (correlated, it was assumed, with higher economic status) were required.'[60] The case for the defence, led by the most formidable advocate of the day, Sir Patrick Hastings, turned on the claim that even if Laski had not used the exact words attributed to him in the report of the Newark speech, they fairly represented what, on the basis of his writings and other speeches, he generally advocated. To establish this more general case, Hastings took the jury through a large collection of extracts from Laski's writings, arguing that he did indeed advocate 'revolution', albeit usually qualified as 'revolution by consent'.

His cross-examination of Laski himself was a classic of courtroom sneering and innuendo. He constantly badgered Laski to answer yes or no to questions that obviously required a more extended response, and he mocked 'the professor's' over-subtle distinctions. It was the duty of the jury, he several times reminded them, to decide what the various passages meant to 'the ordinary person', and he amply indicated what that understanding should be by his frequent allusions to the French and Russian revolutions. Both Hastings and the trial judge, Lord Goddard (a one-time Tory parliamentary candidate), tried to force Laski to admit that in certain circumstances he did indeed believe that violence was justified. In a vastly prolific writing life now stretching back over three decades, Laski had at various points committed himself to statements which required elaborate contextual interpretation if they were not to seem like advocacy of 'revolution', and elaborate contextual interpretation was precisely what the nature of the adversarial trial system did not allow. Laski's answers were repeatedly interrupted by Hastings, and sometimes by Goddard, and the complexities of meaning he may have intended to convey by sentences written many years ago were scarcely accorded any standing. As Goddard put it towards the end of Laski's five-hour ordeal in the witness-box: 'It will be for the jury to form an opinion, and nobody else, as to what the ordinary meaning of the words used is.'[61]

Addressing the jury, Hastings emphasized the distance separating Laski's beliefs from those of most patriotic Englishmen: 'We have beliefs in many things which Mr Laski does not believe in at all. We believe in law and justice in England; we believe in fairness; we believe in religious beliefs; we do not talk about "the myths of future happiness": we believe in them.' The use of the first-person plural was not the least tendentious feature of this attack; Laski certainly felt that there was a veiled appeal to anti-Semitism involved at some level. Clearly, Hastings was, as Laski's biographers put it, offering 'the jury the spectre of Laski as the callous, unpatriotic intellectual who actually despised ordinary people'. In his directions to the jury, the judge similarly suggested that while Laski had the right to express 'seditious' views, he had a responsibility to consider how they would be understood by 'ordinary people'. The jury did not need to deliberate for long: they judged that the newspaper reports had been 'fair and accurate'. Laski had lost his libel case, and he was in addition ordered to pay all costs.[62]

Although Laski continued to play a part in Labour politics until his death in 1950, the trial had dealt a serious blow to his standing and credibility. Since, very broadly speaking, the conflict between the 'Right' and the 'Left' in the Labour Party at this time could be represented as a conflict between the unions and the intellectuals, the perception that Laski had overplayed his hand as an 'intellectual' and had met his nemesis in the form of the judgement of 'ordinary people', strengthened the case of those, like Bevin, who warned the Party against being led astray by 'over-educated' intellectuals. It was an old refrain in the Party, one which even some of its most highly educated members were not above singing, as when the ever-brisk Hugh Dalton had issued this (unforgivable) complaint about the Party's intellectuals: 'we have too many and too talkative and too scribblish ... these semi-crocks, diabetics and undersized Semites'.[63] Laski was not alone in knowing to whom that last phrase referred.

The story of how he had come to occupy this prominent symbolic role need not be pursued here; the tragic climax of his career is cited simply to illustrate the way in which, at that moment, he served an emblematic function as the 'jackal of the day', having become in a curious way a living distillation of all that was 'un-English' about being an intellectual. But it is worth remarking that although he was stigmatized for being both 'superior' and 'foreign', he had on many matters the tastes of the average educated Englishman of the period. Trollope was his favourite author, and he could sound positively Blimpish in inveighing against 'damn Joyceism or Eliotism or any of those new modern patterns I find so abhorrent'.[64] In his work with the WEA, he stood by the traditional mission of teaching 'humanly enriching' high culture.[65] And he fully shared the English middle-class fantasy of, and identification with, the ideal of the aristocrat and the gentleman against 'the real villain, the philistine businessman': 'I at least would rather have been governed by Lord Shaftesbury than by Mr Cobden, by the gentlemen of England than by the Gradgrinds and Bounderbys of Coketown.'[66] But the modern descendants of the 'gentlemen of England' were not, it turned out, minded to return the compliment. Those who displayed too much damn highbrowism retained, it seemed, a patina of alienness that was not easily forgiven in some quarters. Perhaps there was, after all, something un-English about being an 'intellectual'.

NOTES

1. For the development of the terms in American English, see Lawrence W. Levine, *Highbrow/Lowbrow: The Emergence of Cultural Hierarchy in America* (Cambridge, Mass.: Harvard University Press, 1988), esp ch. 3.
2. Jonathan Rose, *The Intellectual Life of the British Working Classes* (London: Yale University Press, 2001), 420.
3. See, for illustration, Lawrence Rainey, *Institutions of Modernism: Literary Elites and Public Culture* (London: Yale University Press, 1988). For the most emphatic statement of the case for seeing Modernist writers themselves as consciously driven by the desire to

exclude and patronize the larger reading public, see John Carey, *The Intellectuals and the Masses: Pride and Prejudice among the Literary Intelligentsia 1880–1939* (London: Faber, 1992); for reservations about this case, see Stefan Collini, *English Pasts: Essays in History and Culture* (Oxford: Oxford University Press, 1999), ch. 15.

4. John Gross, *The Rise and Fall of the Man of Letters* (London: Weidenfeld, 1969), 211.
5. Ross McKibbin, *Classes and Cultures: England 1918–1951* (Oxford: Oxford University Press, 1998), 478, 484.
6. Q. D. Leavis, *Fiction and the Reading Public* (London: Chatto, 1932), 24.
7. McKibbin, *Classes and Cultures*, 516.
8. The phrase comes from Kate Whitehead, 'Broadcasting Bloomsbury', *The Yearbook of English Studies*, 20 (1990), 121–31 (quotation at 122); on Forster see Mary Lago, 'E. M. Forster and the BBC', ibid. 132–51.
9. J. B. Priestley, 'High, Low, Broad', *Saturday Review* 1926; repr. in *Open House; a Book of Essays* (London: Heinemann, 1927), 162–7.
10. Leonard Woolf, *Hunting the Highbrow* (London: Hogarth, 1927), 10, 40, 46–9.
11. Huxley's career, and the limits of his Bloomsbury connection, are now well documented in Nicholas Murray, *Aldous Huxley: An English Intellectual* (London: Little, Brown, 2002).
12. Aldous Huxley, 'Foreheads villainous low', in *Music at Night and Other Essays* ([1st edn., 1931], Harmondsworth: Penguin, 1950), 133–4, 138, 137–8.
13. Desmond MacCarthy, 'Highbrows', *Experience* (London, Putnam, 1935), 308, 309–11 (the review was first published in 1931).
14. F. R. Leavis, *Mass Civilization and Minority Culture* (1930), repr. in his *For Continuity* (Cambridge: Minority Press, 1933), 32–8.
15. Q. D. Leavis, *Fiction and the Reading Public*, 20, 67–8.
16. The *locus classicus*, of course, is her 1924 essay 'Mr Bennett and Mrs Brown', on which, see e.g., Samuel Hynes, 'The whole contention between Mr Bennett and Mrs Woolf', *Novel: A Forum on Fiction*, 1 (1967), 34–44.
17. See Robin Majumdar and Allen McLaurin (eds.), *Virginia Woolf: The Critical Heritage* (London: Routledge, 1975), 232, 258, for these examples of Bennett's response to Woolf's work.
18. Quoted in Melba Cuddy-Keane, *Virginia Woolf, the Intellectual, and the Public Sphere* (Cambridge: Cambridge University Press, 2003), 22.
19. Quoted in Cuddy-Keane, *Woolf*, 23; for the details in this paragraph I am particularly indebted to Cuddy-Keane's helpful discussion.
20. Priestley's talk was broadcast on 17 October, Nicolson's on 24 October, and the exchange discussed in the *New Statesman* on 29 October.
21. The text of Nicolson's talk appears not to have survived, but Cuddy-Keane cites these extracts as quoted in the *Yorkshire Post*'s column devoted to the exchange ('The intellectual distrusted', *Yorkshire Post*, 25 Oct. 1932;); Cuddy-Keane, *Woolf*, 25. Nicolson was congratulated for his 'victory' in 'A London Diary', *New Statesman*, 29 Oct. 1932, 506–7.
22. Virginia Woolf, 'Middlebrow', *The Death of the Moth and Other Essays* (London: Hogarth, 1942), 113–19.
23. Ibid. 113, 115, 119.
24. Russell Kirk, 'The American intellectual: a conservative view', in George B. de Huszar (ed.), *The Intellectuals: A Controversial Portrait* (Glencoe, Ill.: Free Press, 1960), 309;

H. W. Fowler, *A Dictionary of Modern English Usage*, 2nd edn., rev. Ernest Gowers (Oxford: Oxford University Press, 1965 [1st edn. 1926]), 289; Collini, 'Intellectuals in Britain and France', 203; Heyck, 'Myths and meanings', 205.

25. 'Communications: The British Intellectuals', *Encounter*, 4 (June, 1955), 68–72.
26. Russell to Lucy Donnelly, 10 Feb. 1916; *The Autobiography of Bertrand Russell*, 3 vols., ii. *1914–1944* (London: Allen & Unwin, 1968), 59.
27. See the perceptive discussion in Philip Ironside, *The Social and Political Thought of Bertrand Russell: The Development of an Aristocratic Liberalism* (Cambridge: Cambridge University Press, 1996), ch. 5.
28. Quoted in Ironside, *Russell*, 226.
29. Ibid. 205.
30. Bertrand Russell, *Power: a New Social Analysis* (London: Allen & Unwin, 1938), 44–6.
31. Bertrand Russell, 'The role of the intellectual in the modern world', *American Journal of Sociology*, 44 (1939), 491–8.
32. Ironside, *Russell*, 101.
33. David Cannadine, *G. M. Trevelyan: A Life in History* (London: HarperCollins, 1992), 38.
34. Ibid. 40.
35. Quoted ibid. 44, 45.
36. Lytton Strachey to his mother, Spring 1900, quoted in Michael Holroyd, *Lytton Strachey, A Biography* (Harmondsworth: Penguin, 1971), 146.
37. Russell, *Autobiography*, i. *1872–1914* (1967), 74.
38. Holroyd, *Strachey*, 524.
39. Quoted in Cannadine, *Trevelyan*, 44.
40. Quoted ibid. 39.
41. Trevelyan to Bryant, 27 Dec 1936; quoted ibid. 125.
42. G. M. Trevelyan, *Sir George Otto Trevelyan: A Memoir* (London: Longman, 1932), 152.
43. Trevelyan to Mary Moorman, 18 Jan. 1943; quoted in Cannadine, *Trevelyan*, 45.
44. It is also arguable that David Cannadine's otherwise excellent study of Trevelyan tends rather to collude with these limitations than to expose them; see the fuller discussion in Collini, *English Pasts*, ch. 1.
45. The following paragraphs were initially written before I came across the extremely detailed study by G. S. Smith, *D. S. Mirsky: A Russian–English Life, 1890–1939* (Oxford: Oxford University Press, 2000), which, while helpfully full on Mirsky's life, pays relatively little attention to *The Intelligentsia of Great Britain*.
46. Edmund Wilson, 'Comrade Prince: a memoir of D. S. Mirsky', *Encounter*, 5 (July 1955), 11.
47. According to Smith, 'Brown's translation takes many liberties with Mirsky's text'; *Mirsky*, 237.
48. Dimitri Mirsky, *The Intelligentsia of Great Britain*, trans. Alec Brown (London: Gollancz, 1935), 9, 16–17, 20–1.
49. Mirsky, *Intelligentsia*, 77, 234.
50. Ibid. 179–86.
51. See Smith, *Mirsky*, 96–8.
52. See Stefan Collini, 'On highest authority: the literary critic and other aviators in early twentieth-century Britain', in Dorothy Ross (ed.), *Modernist Impulses in the*

Human Sciences 1870–1930 (Baltimore: Johns Hopkins University Press, 1994), 152–70, 334–8.

53. Mirsky, *Intelligentsia*, 142–56.
54. F. C., review of Mirsky, *Intelligentsia, The Criterion*, 14 (1935), 718–19; Stephen Spender, 'A black pot in search of kettles', *Spectator*, 22 Mar. 1935, 499–500; Raymond Mortimer, 'Books in general', *New Statesman*, 23 Mar. 1935, 420–1; Ivor Brown, 'Comrade Mirsky', *Observer*, 17 Mar. 1935, 8.
55. Harold Laski, 'On being a plaintiff', printed as Appendix to Kingsley Martin, *Harold Laski, 1993–1950: A Biographical Memoir* (London: Cape, 1969 [1st edn. 1953]), quotation at 266. This essay was also published as 'My day in court', *Atlantic Monthly*, 190 (Nov. 1952).
56. *New York Times*, 9 Aug. 1945; quoted in Isaac Kramnick and Barry Sheerman, *Harold Laski, A Life on the Left* (London: Hamilton, 1993), 496.
57. See Kramnick and Sheerman, *Laski*, 495–7.
58. Ibid. 2 (the currency of the term 'public intellectual', as I suggest in Ch. 10, reflects the period of the biography's composition, not of its subject's life).
59. For a full account of the circumstances leading up to the trial, see ibid. ch. 20; see also the briefer account, which differs in a few details, in Michael Newman, *Harold Laski, A Political Biography* (London: Macmillan, 1993), 271–81. For a transcript of the trial itself, see *The Laski Libel Action, Verbatim Report* (London: Daily Express, 1946).
60. Kramnick and Sheerman, *Laski*, 517.
61. Quoted ibid. 527.
62. Ibid. 533–9.
63. Quoted in Ben Pimlott, *Hugh Dalton* (London: Cape, 1985), 251.
64. Mark deWolfe Howe (ed.), *The Holmes–Laski Letters*, 2 vols. (Cambridge, Mass.: Harvard University Press, 1953), i. 1472.
65. Kramnick and Sheerman, *Laski*, 182–4.
66. Harold Laski, *The Danger of Being a Gentleman, and Other Essays* (New York: Viking, 1940), 30.

6

The Long 1950s I: Happy Families

'Never has an intellectual class found its society and its culture so much to its satisfaction.'

I

For all the magnitude of its impact on British society in other ways, the First World War had not in itself marked a major turning-point in the understanding of the place of intellectuals, nor—the much-publicized posturing of aesthetes and upper-class 'rebels' in the 1920s notwithstanding—had it brought about a decisive alteration in attitude in the relations between British society and its leading thinkers, writers, and scholars. The experience of the Second World War, however, together with the social changes which were partly its consequence, has been seen as bringing about an important shift, a perception which has had an enduring influence on discussion of the topic. In the 1930s, the clash of warring isms and the relatively prominent part played by writers in espousing Communism or in supporting the Republican cause in the Spanish Civil War not only made references to 'intellectuals' more common, but also encouraged the thought that the kinds of people who tended to be referred to as intellectuals saw themselves as naturally critical of or estranged from their own society. In these respects, the discourse about 'intellectuals' in Britain could, by the late 1930s, appear to be coming to resemble that found elsewhere in Europe. But the experience of 'total war' modified this perception in several ways. Standing alone, Britain resisted where others crumbled, reinvigorating the traditional emphasis on British exceptionalism as a consequence. The war also required the involvement of a wide range of people—writers, scholars, scientists, and such like included—in practical commitment to the national cause; the foundation of the Welfare State by the Labour government of 1945 went some way towards maintaining this sense of solidarity, at least among the Left-leaning majority. (Interestingly, those who in the late 1940s engaged in the kind of fundamental criticism often alleged to be characteristic of 'real' intellectuals tended to be conservative figures like T. S. Eliot or Michael Oakeshott, attempting to undermine the self-righteous egalitarianism they saw as the official orthodoxy of the day.)

Perhaps one hardly needs to underline the importance for subsequent forms of national self-definition of the very different ways in which Britain and France experienced the war. In France (as I indicated in Ch. 3), the Vichy episode reanimated memories of the Dreyfus Affair, and kept that founding division of French intellectual life at the heart of contemporary consciousness in a way which was ultimately to confer valuable moral capital on the *résistants* and thereafter the Communist Party. In Britain, by contrast, the war and what it stood for in the post-war era effectively gave a new lease of life to a late variant of the old Whig interpretation of English history, where the national character had again displayed its sterling qualities in the defence of liberty.[1] Trevelyan's hugely popular *English Social History* both benefited from and contributed to this development, while the war also provided the occasion for Herbert Butterfield, who had made his mark in the 1930s as a trenchant critic of the 'Whig interpretation', to discover new kinds of relevance in it.[2] Reflecting in 1947 on what he saw as H. A. L. Fisher's pre-war idealism about international cooperation, the historian David Ogg observed: 'That the Channel divides us from a different mentality is an assertion which would find greater credence now than it would have done ten years ago.'[3] Given some of the manifestations of that Continental 'mentality' in the intervening decade, there was clearly cause for self-congratulation in this contrast. Rather than the Sartrean existential dilemmas involved in choosing between betraying one's comrades or seeing one's mother tortured by the Gestapo, the cultural legacy of the war may seem rather to have consisted of a rejuvenated conception of 'the nation as pastoral' and the representative status accorded the down-to-earth decencies of J. B. Priestley.[4]

In literary and cultural terms, the period after 1945 thus saw a self-conscious return to values and forms of expression identified as essentially English, as a reaction against the equally self-conscious internationalism of inter-war High Modernism. One can see examples of this return to the vernacular in much of the poetry and prose of the late 1940s and early 1950s—the names of Philip Larkin and Kingsley Amis can stand in for many others here—and it is not, I think, too fanciful to see a kind of analogue to this development in the vogue for 'ordinary language' philosophy during this period, a philosophical style that evinced some of the same hostility to high-flown or overly abstract ideas, which it often stigmatized as 'foreign'. The fact that this cultural shift coincided with the period during which French intellectual and political life seemed to be more than ever distinguished by the opposite qualities, and that these qualities were displayed on the public stage by such figures as Sartre and Merleau-Ponty who were explicitly referred to (and referred to themselves) as 'intellectuals', went a long way to rejuvenating a contrast which might, before 1939, have been in danger of wearing a bit thin.

Periodization always threatens to be arbitrary, above all in intellectual history, but what I am here calling 'the long 1950s' may be said to have stretched from the late 1940s up to that cultural phenomenon known as 'the Sixties', the beginning of which in Britain may be dated to the years around 1962–3. The Sixties were to see the flourishing of a new idiom for the discussion of the question of intellectuals, grounded principally in European Marxism. That development will be the focus of a later chapter, but I shall there suggest that the New Left diagnoses in the 1960s and 1970s were more intimately bound up with certain influential accounts of the place of intellectuals in British society that had been elaborated in the previous decade than is usually recognized. Indeed, the New Left analyses turn out, on closer inspection, to have inherited many of their assumptions from these earlier accounts and not just, as the standard secondary literature now tends to suggest, to have reacted against them. And at the heart of these accounts, even if only implicitly in some cases, was a structuring polarity between 'integration' and 'alienation' which may seem deceptively familiar but which will require close critical scrutiny.

II

As a kind of overture to the main action of the 1950s, we may briefly consider an essay published by Stephen Spender in 1951 entitled 'The English intellectuals and the world of to-day' (like so many of his contemporaries, Spender tended to allow 'English' still to stand for 'British').[5] Spender seems to be assured of a place in most discussions of intellectuals in Britain, partly because of the (artificial) prominence enjoyed by 'the Auden gang' in accounts of the 1930s, partly because he could thereafter be relied upon to support radical causes, sign protests and petitions, and invoke wider European solidarities with an almost Sartrean readiness.[6] In this short stock-taking piece, Spender began, as such pieces nearly always do, with the current usage of the term 'intellectual'. It 'has come to mean: "a thinking person, often a writer, who has a sense of social responsibility to which he wants to give voice" '. Spender recognized that this was a 'special' or narrow sense, which excluded large numbers of scholars, scientists, and others who might be termed intellectuals in a broader usage, but in beginning with this sense he was accurately reflecting his 1930s experience. Accordingly, his discussion opened by focusing on writers who had expressed overt political views—Wyndham Lewis, T. S. Eliot, Herbert Read, and so on—and then contrasted them with writers of a younger generation who repudiated such public preoccupations in favour of a literature of imagination and personal experience, such as Dylan Thomas and George Barker. But the intensification of the Cold War at the beginning of the 1950s, he argued, has 'suddenly confronted all thinking people with the question of what they really stand for': writers would once again be called upon to 'take a stand'.[7]

Like many of those who have been most readily called 'intellectuals' (not always with flattering intention), Spender had an undentable confidence about presenting his own current preoccupation as the inevitable next step in world history. He talked in his habitually large and confident terms: 'What has happened is that the 1940s were an almost total failure', the years from 1938 to 1950 were 'simply a gap in my development', and so on. The essay is more autobiography than social analysis, one of the steps on Spender's private journey from 'nancy poet' to Cold Warrior; two years later, he became one of the editors of *Encounter*. (And it is significant that he wanted to parade what, at this date, was the ultimate *imprimatur* for his views: 'Shortly before he died, George Orwell remarked to me . . .'.)[8] The piece is interesting largely because of the way it combines a 1930s framework—intellectuals are equated with leading writers who express political views, usually of a radical or oppositional kind—with the beginnings of a characteristically 1950s perspective—intellectuals must recognize that their country stands on the side of freedom against totalitarianism. But that way of putting it may still seem to accept that the situation of the intellectual in Britain conformed to a wider 'Western' model. What was to become more distinctive of the literature on this subject as the 1950s progressed was the insistence on the uniquely close integration of British intellectuals with their parent culture, so close, in fact, that it raised the question of whether there really were any such creatures as 'British intellectuals'.

The year 1955 saw the appearance of the two essays which were to be more frequently cited than almost any others in subsequent discussion of this topic. The first was Noel Annan's 'The intellectual aristocracy' which appeared, appropriately, in a *Festschrift* for G. M. Trevelyan.[9] In this essay, Annan appointed himself the Herald-Pursuivant of the intellectual aristocracy; the piece is a sustained exercise in collective genealogy, complete with interlocking family trees. By this means, Annan illustrated how the elite of a new professional-cum-intellectual class formed itself in the first half of the nineteenth century, and how its descendants came to play leading cultural, academic, and administrative (though not, strictly, political) roles in the late nineteenth and early twentieth centuries. The metaphor of an 'aristocracy' was held to be enlightening because this elite practised 'persistent endogamy' well into the twentieth century, producing a complex web of family relationships among individuals in succeeding generations who had supposedly come to the fore through their personal talents and achievements. Wedgwoods, Darwins, Stephens, Keyneses, Arnolds, Butlers, Trevelyans—these were the names that recurred in this intellectual equivalent of Debrett.

Annan drew an affectionate and entertaining group portrait of this kinship system, and his characterization of an ideal-typical member of that high-minded, public-spirited, somewhat ascetic, largely Cambridge-educated caste in the mid- and late nineteenth century is especially felicitous. But he intended his genealogical charts to serve an explanatory as well as celebratory purpose. The demonstration of this elite's close familial links was designed to account for an ostensibly well-established truism, namely 'the paradox of an intelligentsia which appears to conform rather than rebel against the rest of society'.[10] Once again, one cannot help but be struck by how frequently this kind of thinly binary characterization of the possibilities recurs in this literature. Annan's terminology did not suggest that 'intellectuals' or even an 'intelligentsia' (used here, as so often, simply as the collective plural of 'intellectual') had not existed in Britain—quite the contrary. The Stephens and Trevelyans and Arnolds and company were proposed as constituting a significant number of Britain's intellectuals during this period, but their degree of 'social integration' was assumed to help explain their lack of 'dissidence' and 'alienation'. The implicit contrast, yet again, was with what 'real' intellectuals have been like elsewhere.

But even if one for the moment allows the terms of the supposed 'question' to pass unchallenged (as subsequent references to this essay seem to have done), it is still worth probing why Annan's genealogical researches should be presumed to offer any kind of 'answer'. After all, what his evidence (itself highly selective and unsystematic, as he acknowledges) showed was that, in the course of the nineteenth century, a fairly extended network of families, which produced many of the leading intellectual figures of the time, had a tendency to intermarry. Whether they did so more than comparable groups, or more than might have been expected on the basis of their social contacts, or more than intellectual elites of other countries or other periods were not questions which Annan's examples allowed him to raise: the essay proposed no statistical or comparative analysis, merely the identification of a group of families whose lines of descent sometimes interlocked.

That this could in fact be used to support precisely the opposite conclusion to Annan's is suggested by the way in which the much more systematic and sophisticated researches on the degree of intermarriage among the French intellectual elite at the end of the nineteenth century have been adduced as indicating the formation of a self-consciously separate intellectual stratum, and hence as establishing one of the essential conditions for the development of a corporate sense of 'intellectuals'.[11] For it is worth remembering that although Annan's essay is often cited as demonstrating British intellectuals' close integration into the upper or governing class, it actually suggests something rather different. Their endogamy, such as it was, precisely tended to *preclude* marriage into the really dominant elites of British society such as the aristocracy or the peaks of new money (the latter of which they robustly disdained). Indeed, Annan (rightly) emphasizes their sense of distance from the style of life and the values of the landed and the seriously rich: 'the intellectual aristocracy never confused themselves with the real nobility and ruling class'. Nor was there much traffic in the other direction: as Annan notes, Bertrand Russell was 'the one aristocrat' who 'successfully transplanted himself to the rock-garden of the intelligentsia'. (Russell may have seemed a slightly awkward figure to accommodate to Annan's argument, a difficulty glossed over with the tortuous remark: 'Non-conformity is not a middle-class monopoly and his adopted class owes much to his whig independence of mind.'[12])

Indeed, the more one broods on the explanatory mechanism implied in Annan's account (and it is worth doing so, not just because his essay has been so influential, but because a similar form of 'explanation' has been assumed by so many other discussions of this issue), the more mysterious it comes to seem. Consider, for example, his first formulation of the argument. Members of these families were, he asserts at the outset,

> leaders of the new intelligentsia. Stability is not a quality usually associated with an intelligentsia, a term which, Russian in origin, suggests the shifting, shiftless members of revolutionary or literary cliques who have cut themselves adrift from the moorings of family. Yet the English intelligentsia, wedded to gradual reform of accepted institutions and able to move between the worlds of speculation and government, was stable. That it was so—that it was unexcitable and to European minds unexciting—was in part due to the influence of these academic families.[13]

This passage is a revealing microcosm of a much larger world of assumption and assertion. To begin with, it has to be remarked that it is Annan who calls them an 'intelligentsia' in the first place. At a purely terminological level, therefore, he is responsible for setting up the 'paradox'. Further, it would be straining against any established usage of this term to include under it a large number of the individuals whom he mentions in this essay—colonial governors, society surgeons, senior judges, and even the occasional bishop. These were certainly members of a professional-cum-administrative-cum-academic elite, but the term 'intelligentsia' has never been used as an equivalent for that whole stratum of society. And, of course, he constantly omits—occasionally with acknowledgement, but more often silently—whole swathes of these families where only a few individuals in fact distinguished themselves in cultural and official activities. His introduction of the Wedgwood family is a striking example of this, since he has to admit that he is 'omitting the Master Potters among the Wedgwoods who carried on the craft'.[14] Nor, looking at the matter from the opposite end, as it were, do the names of most of those who might be thought to have made up an 'English intelligentsia' in any given generation appear at all. His roll-call is confined to those who happen to have common ancestors, descendants, or affines. A quite other, and much more ambitious, enquiry would be needed to determine whether the figures he mentions composed a significant proportion of this larger group.

The 'paradox' is then further stiffened by his gloss on what he implies is the usual understanding of the term 'intelligentsia'. *Pace* Annan, it is far from obvious that individual members of an intelligentsia are assumed to be 'shiftless' or indeed that any grouping of them must be a 'clique'. Even more slippery is the implication about 'cutting themselves adrift from the moorings of family'. After all, even his shifty, cliquey members of (European) intelligentsias still *had* families: if 'cutting themselves adrift' means remaining out of touch or rebelling against parental expectations, then there was no shortage of such behaviour among the British families he mentions (Annan concedes in passing that among his cast 'some maintained while others rebelled against the ethos of their fathers').[15] If it means not marrying a partner drawn from the same class or network of families, there is nothing in Annan's essay to suggest that such behaviour was more or less common among professional-class British intellectuals during this period than among their Parisian or Muscovite or Viennese peers.

When, in the next sentence, he moves on to the kind of characteristic that might be argued to be more marked among the British exemplars—for example, being 'wedded to gradual reform of accepted institutions'—he shifts attention to a matter of attitude and belief rather than genealogy. If one were looking for an explanation of the assumed greater prevalence of such an attitude among British intellectuals one would surely have to start with the structure and ethos of the political culture as a whole, perhaps with the bald fact that institutions were in practice more reformable in nineteenth-century Britain than in, say, nineteenth-century Russia. But it is the introduction of the notion of 'stability' that really muddies the waters here. Annan's use of the term seems to blend a form of sociological fixity—members of the same group of families occupying the same place in the social structure across several generations—with a form of intellectual or political moderation—a tendency not to propose dramatic or violent change. The fact that in the last sentence of the quoted passage 'stable' seems to be equated with 'unexcitable' slides us further towards the latter meaning, especially when it is insinuated that (excitable) Europeans habitually make the superficial or predictable judgement that the British intelligentsia is therefore 'unexciting'. (It is again striking how often in this literature one meets the pairing of 'unexcitable', meaning not prone to dramatic or wholesale responses, with 'unexciting', meaning intellectually uninteresting. This again suggests, from a different angle, how this topic has functioned as a kind of figure for, or displacement of, larger cultural attitudes.) In any event, the alleged fact that '*the* English intelligentsia', in the singular, was 'stable' is argued to be 'in part due to the influence of these academic families'. These families, this suggests, were thus only *part* of that 'intelligentsia', but they influenced the rest towards 'stability', and they are said to have done so, it seems, on no better ground than that they themselves had a tendency to marry their friends' sisters.

It is hard to know quite how to go about unpicking this tightly woven nest of assumptions, and it would be unrewarding to try to do so at any length. Presumably, a minor premise of the argument is that close social contact with friends and relatives who are personally involved in running many of the country's major institutions is likely to mean that one's criticisms will take a practical and piecemeal form. There is some plausibility to this, though it hardly seems to apply to such notable scions of the intellectual aristocracy as, say, Christabel Pankhurst or Lytton Strachey or Aldous Huxley or dozens of others whose responses were—sometimes greatly to their credit, sometimes not—far from moderate or practical. Moreover, it is not clear how far the values of this high-thinking and plain-living stratum are supposed to be deviant from those of the larger society. For example, when touching on the Pease family, whose prominent members during this period were Quakers, he remarks that Edward Pease,

Secretary of the Fabian Society, 'is an interesting example of the way in which the Society of Friends breeds that kind of non-conformity which is the life of an intelligentsia'.[16] In the context of the essay as a whole, this comes as a somewhat confusing claim: it seems to imply that the intellectual aristocracy whose pedigree he is compiling have in general displayed such nonconformity. But what exactly does Edward Pease's 'non-conformity' consist in here? After all, joining the Fabian Society hardly seems the most telling way of signalling one's dissent from being 'wedded to gradual reform of accepted institutions'. Pease became the Society's secretary after an unsuccessful career as a stockbroker: are we to assume that his nonconformity lay in his abandoning that career or did it, rather, lie in his dalliance with Mammon in the first place? More broadly, one does not have to search far to find examples of well-connected professional-class intellectuals who were far from 'wedded to the gradual reform of accepted institutions', from John Ruskin and William Morris onwards. And of course the names of prominent British intellectual figures during this period who were *not* part of this kinship network are legion, stretching from, say, Herbert Spencer or John Morley through George Gissing or H. G. Wells to C. P. Snow or Richard Hoggart and beyond.

Undeniably, members of this intellectual elite did come to occupy many influential and prestigous positions, especially in government service and the ancient universities, and they were, at least during the mid- and late-Victorian period, conscious of belonging to a kind of freemasonry.[17] But the key to their sense of identity during that period was something less tangible than family connection as such: certainly, it presumed their membership of a gentlemanly class, economically prosperous and socially esteemed, but it crucially involved personal achievement in intellectual labour or public service. And the explanatory power of kinship is weakened still further when one recognizes that none of these properties necessarily entailed a lack of radicalism or 'dissidence', as any number of examples from Bertrand Russell onwards could confirm. What is true is that most of the members of Annan's intellectual aristocracy displayed a considerable social confidence, a familiarity with other members of this elite, and an assumption of access to the wielders of power. A large number of other members of a putative 'English intelligentsia' during this period did not share these features, or did so to a much lesser extent. Substantial numbers of those who belonged to the comparable elites in other European countries exhibited some not dissimilar characteristics. But by now, the part played by kinship, as opposed to larger questions of political culture and intellectual tradition, in explaining any alleged absence of 'dissidence' among British intellectuals has diminished to near vanishing-point.

And perhaps in the end Annan was not displeased to have exhibited the fact of a certain kind of cultural continuity rather than to have identified a social-structural explanation for it. Such explanations, after all, can have a reductive effect, making epiphenomenal what those involved understand to be essential, and Annan (who was to become Provost of King's College, Cambridge the following year) seemed far from sorry to find the attitudes he had characterized still in rude health. 'Here is an aristocracy, secure, established, and, like the rest of English society, accustomed to responsible and judicious utterance and sceptical of iconoclastic speculation.'[18] By this point, we really are among the clichés of the intellectual equivalent of the tourist industry. This is post-prandial England, rocking gently in the warm complacency of the mid-1950s, appreciatively sniffing the familiar bouquet of Whig history.

III

In the same year, 1955, Edward Shils published in *Encounter* an article on intellectuals in Britain that was also to be widely referred to in the subsequent literature: between them, the essays of Annan and Shils came to represent something of an orthodoxy.[19] Shils's article was the first in a series published in the magazine in the course of 1955 surveying the situation of 'intellectuals' in various countries. *Encounter*, edited initially by Irving Kristol and Stephen Spender, had been founded in 1953, and it was for a while a principal medium through which British intellectuals could reach an educated but non-specialist public. It was supported by the Congress for Cultural Freedom, an American-funded anti-Communist cultural organization, based in Paris; only in 1967 did it become widely known that the source of funds was in fact the CIA, which saw the magazine as a useful weapon in the propaganda war against Soviet Russia.[20] Although the magazine was not narrowly sectarian in either political or aesthetic terms, its pages gave off a distinct whiff of Cold War polemicizing.

Shils's article was a classic case of polemic masquerading as objective description. As with so much writing on intellectuals, his account is explicitly structured around a rather simple polarity between 'alienation' and 'integration'. Both these terms are used in this literature to refer, somewhat unsteadily, to a mixture of cultural attitude and social position, opportunistically emphasizing one or the other to suit a particular case. It is worth pausing to consider why this polarity has figured so prominently in writing on this topic. The phrase 'the alienated intellectual', in particular, has come to be one of those established compounds, like 'the absent-minded professor' or 'the shady secondhand-car salesman', expressing an association that is familiar to the point of pleonasm. The recurrence of this structuring polarity in these discussions surely needs to be seen less as a reflection of objective changes in political attitude or social affiliation among intellectuals and more as emanating from a tension within the role itself, as discussed in Ch. 2 above. Very roughly speaking, intellectuals are, by definition, bringing a more general perspective to bear, and will always, therefore, be potentially at odds with the terms in which business is conducted in their society, thereby positioning themselves at an angle to the practical consensus of that society. But, at the same time, if they are to be listened to, they will be expressing values at least partly shared by their public and commanding channels of expression directed at that public, as well as, of course, participating in the everyday processes of that society in more mundane ways.

In addition, there is the idea, reformulated anew in each generation yet always reflecting a similar and similarly doubtful set of assumptions, that those who inhabit sociological or occupational positions which can be regarded as in some sense 'marginal' or 'extraneous' to the everyday business of society are, ipso facto, naturally prone to hold 'critical' or 'dissident' views. The characterization of the intellectual's standpoint tends, as a result, to oscillate between emphasizing the extent to which they should be seen as 'outside' their society or 'integrated' with it, though both terms are, strictly, misleading. It could be said, speaking again in the broadest terms, that in the 1930s the emphasis in Britain as well as several other societies was on the oppositional, bohemian, or 'alienated' position of the intellectual, while in the 1950s there was the converse preoccupation with the intellectual as 'integrated' within the politically more settled and economically prosperous societies of the post-war period. Perhaps the *locus classicus* of this concern, at least in its American guise, was the symposium carried in *Partisan Review* in 1952 entitled 'Our country and our culture' (discussed more fully in Ch. 10), where almost all the contributors pointed to a new sense of connection and even identification with American society on the part of its intellectuals and a corresponding decline in the idea that 'alienation' was 'the intellectual's fate in America'.[21]

In this vein, the core of Shils's argument was that the period between the wars when 'the English intelligentsia' (membership unspecified) had affected to be 'alienated' from British society had in reality been a brief deviation from an otherwise uninterrupted pattern of healthy integration, to which they had returned emphatically in the post-war world. 'The cranky antinomianism of the twenty years between the wars was more like a digression from the main course of the British intellectual class in its relations with British institutions.' Contemplating the deep normality of the mid-1950s, he was evidently pleased to be able to report (in the sentence that serves as the epigraph to this chapter) that 'never has an intellectual class found its society and its culture so much to its satisfaction'.[22]

Shils embedded this claim in a longer historical narrative which quite closely resembled that given by Annan. In the second half of the nineteenth century, he claimed,

> the union of the intellectuals with the Civil Service, the Church, the Houses of Parliament, the Press, and the leadership of the political parties, through the ancient universities primarily, but also through kinship and through the social and convivial life of London upper-class society, constituted a bond from which few could escape and which no other country could then or has since matched.[23]

The upshot was that even reactions against this state of affairs, in the name of socialism or aestheticism, 'never bred a doctrine or practice of complete alienation'. Such 'alienation' is clearly contrasted with the 'bond' constituted by the social links just referred to, though of course there is no reason why social links should preclude criticism (one's everyday experience rather suggests the reverse). Moreover, it was hardly the case that the social connections alluded to, through family or education, suddenly disappeared in the interwar period; indeed, any survey of the leading writers and intellectual figures of the time has to emphasize the ties of kinship and of school and university experience.[24] But according to Shils this period saw a widespread revulsion among intellectuals from the very idea of Britain: this hostility characterized 'nearly everyone who in the 1920s and 1930s was considered worthy of mention in intellectual circles in Great Britain'. The overstatement here is striking (and what it claims is obviously false), another indication, surely, of the requirements of his binary polarity. But now the *status quo ante* had been restored: 'The re-establishment of amicable and harmonious relations between the intellectuals and British society has really been the unification of the intellectuals with the other groups of the ruling élite', in politics, education, the law, and so on.[25]

Shils cited several factors as helping to bring about this 'reintegration', including involvement in the nation's cause during the war and the establishment of a fairer society post-1945. But the bulk of his essay was actually devoted to a development of a different order altogether, namely the triumph of 'aristocratic-gentry values' within British society. In the nineteenth century, so this argument ran, there had been a thriving bourgeois culture in the great provincial centres, which had also expressed itself in the founding of the civic universities, offering local students a more vocational education in contrast to the residential, humanistic Oxbridge model. But in the course of the twentieth century, the style of life and values associated with, if never strictly confined to, the aristocracy and gentry became the ideal to which the professional and middle classes aspired; as part of this change, the civic universities moved closer to the Oxbridge model and to accepting a subordinate position in a single-status hierarchy. In telling this story, it was the fine grain of perceptions of class and status in mid-1950s Britain which really seemed to engage Shils, the world of *Lucky Jim* and, still more, of the controversy surrounding the significance of that novel.[26] In the end, however, Shils's identification of a dominant social or cultural style reinforces his argument about the lack of 'alienation' among contemporary British intellectuals. 'Outside the China of the Mandarins, no great society has ever had a body of intellectuals so integrated with, and so congenial to, its ruling class, and so combining civility and refinement.'[27]

Although it is pretty evident that Shils is personally drawn to this manner of conducting oneself as an intellectual in contrast to what he dismisses as 'the rancour of rebelliousness', there are moments where a more critical perspective makes itself felt. The dominance of 'gentry' values, he suggests, accounts for 'the narrowness of the range of sympathy and curiosity of the British intelligentsia within its own society'. Their attachment to this single style 'blinds them to

British society in its wider reaches'. 'It makes them less good as intellectuals, among whose tasks—there are many others—is the truthful interpretation of their national society and its culture to their own countrymen and the world.'[28] A much more normative usage of 'intellectuals' is implicit here, one which sits a little oddly alongside his numerous references to the civil service or the Bar as the natural habitat of the British intellectual, and this returns us, inevitably, to the question of the term's meaning.

Neither Shils nor the editors of *Encounter* had thought it necessary to offer any preliminary definitions, but it is not entirely clear what senses of the term are being used in this essay (or, indeed, in the series of essays as a whole). As his usage of 'intellectual class' suggests, Shils at times seems to have in mind something like the sociological sense, as for example in his references to the spread of attitudes through 'the universities, journalism, the Bar and the Civil Service', where large numbers of people defined in occupational terms are involved. But in practice, Shils largely concentrates on two groups, writers and academics, and his more specific observations usually rest on references to named leading figures, almost always literary, where the term is clearly being used in the cultural sense. So, for example, when referring to the 'rebellion of the intellectuals' against bourgeois culture in the 1920s and 1930s, he observes that 'they could not find anything to substitute for it except Bohemianism and an utterly spurious proletarianism'.[29] The names of a few leading writers whose behaviour might fit these descriptions come easily enough to mind, but it would be a strikingly revisionist account of the period which suggested that the inter-war years were marked by a large-scale outbreak of 'Bohemianism' and 'proletarianism' in the civil service or at the Bar.

Shils himself was a sociologist; indeed, his role at, first, the LSE and, later, Cambridge was to act as the acceptable face of international sociological theory in an academic environment largely sceptical of its claims (especially in the second of these locations). But the manner and tone of his essay bore little resemblance to that usually associated with professionalized social science. There were no statistics, no talk of variables and correlations, no reference to recent studies or to the concepts of major sociological theorists. The approach is mildly ethnographic, but his are the observations of one who is personally familiar with what he describes, in fact rather fond of it. He feels no obligation to explain his allusions: speaking of those outside the 'charmed circle' of the Oxbridge-and-London based intellectual class, he refers to the 'thickly scattered Judes and Leonard Basts and Bruce Truscots'.[30] While the first two of these names might not need to be glossed for a transatlantic or cross-channel audience, the third was somewhat *recherché* even in 1955 ('Bruce Truscot' was the pseudonym under which E. A. Peers had in 1943 published an account of life in 'civic' universities entitled *Redbrick University*).[31] In general, it could be said that Shils's essay itself exhibited the cosiness which it celebrated. At one point, he argued that, by comparison to the pre-war period, 'the symbols of hierarchy and authority have found increasing acceptance', and he went on: 'Do the fifties have anything to match the refusal of a peerage by one of the greatest intellectuals of the twenties and thirties, reported in Dr Thomas Jones's correspondence? On the contrary, it can show an avowed anarchist and an ardent exponent of the *avant garde* in art and literature accepting a knighthood.'[32] Of course, writers can, and no doubt frequently do, misjudge their audience, but Shils's implied reader is here evidently expected to know who is being referred to since names are not given for either episode. Presumably, the first refers to R. H. Tawney's refusal of a peerage offered by Ramsay MacDonald ('What harm have I ever done the Labour Party?'), while the second would seem to refer to Herbert Read, knighted in 1953. It is also worth remarking that such examples sit rather uneasily with those explanations of cultural attitudes in terms of social position that are implicit in much of Shils's terminology, since they involve proposing Tawney—Rugby and Balliol, staunch Anglican, the intimate of archbishops and cabinet ministers—as the model 'alienated' intellectual, and Read—Halifax orphanage, Leeds University, assistant curator at the Victoria and Albert Museum—as the representative of social integration with 'the ruling class'.

For all its tendentiousness, Shils's essay was surely right to emphasize that the 1940s had had a considerable impact upon intellectuals' self-definition in Britain (and had thereby, I am suggesting, done something to revivify the traditional contrast with the situation elsewhere). He also identified, albeit again tendentiously, a perception which played some part in this self-definition when he asked rhetorically: 'How can a society which maintains the Third Programme, the Arts Council, the British Council, etc., with their numerous opportunities for the employment of intellectuals, be regarded as lacking in sympathy for intellectual things?' But the implication of his essay—and here I return to the matter of its tone as well as its explicit argument—was that this broad endorsement of their society was to be applauded as a rational response to their circumstances. At one point, elaborating his contrast between the pre- and post-war periods, Shils remarks that the latter had seen 'a downward path for ideology', and this phrase should remind us that his essay belongs in the company of that 'end of ideology' literature which was so fashionable in the mid- and late 1950s.[33] Like that literature more generally, his essay was itself a highly ideological contribution. His scorn for the 'alienated' intellectuals of the inter-war years was manifest: their attitudes were characterized, as we have seen, in terms of 'rancour' and 'rebelliousness', rather than, say, as rationally justified criticisms of their society. Shils's own conservatism became more explicit with time, and it is now perhaps easier than it was in 1955 to see his essay less as an illuminating analysis of the role of the intellectuals in either the sociological or cultural senses in Britain, and more as an Anglophile American's enthusiasm for what he perceived as a society where 'civility' outranked 'commitment' and where as a result intellectuals did not collectively take public stands on political issues.[34]

In subsequent issues, *Encounter* published several letters provoked by Shils's piece. For example, Richard Crossman, Oxford don turned MP (and subsequently both a Cabinet minister and editor of the *New Statesman*), took issue with the narrowness of Shils's range of reference, arguing that it omitted all those who worked within the 'Labour Movement' and were thus never 'alienated' from British society in the past nor given to aping 'aristocratic-gentry' values in the present. Several correspondents remained unpersuaded by Shils that British intellectuals were so at one with their society: 'the great majority of intellectuals', reported one writer, 'continues to be regarded, by the great majority of Britons, either with amused condescension or—more frequently—with contempt'. H. O. Alexander went on to ponder 'the fact that apparently very few people in this country would like to be termed intellectuals', and to wonder why, if intellectuals really had 'reached the enviable status described by Mr Shils' this should be so. Alexander reported that he had himself written to several individuals he regarded as 'prominent British intellectuals', asking them whether they accepted this description. None did (and it was at this point that he quoted the reply from Bertrand Russell discussed in Ch. 5). Another correspondent, the novelist John Wain, while broadly accepting Shils's analysis, registered a protest against the use of 'intellectual' as a noun at all: 'It is a bureaucrat's word, necessary sometimes; but it blankets too many very diverse kinds of people; a sculptor and a marine biologist are both "intellectuals", which is absurd.' Wain's comment reflects the way in which the resistance encountered by the term was fuelled by the unconscious interplay of its different senses and their associations, since it was precisely the convenience of the term when used in its sociological sense that it, like other such sociological categories, could embrace a range of occupations under a single heading.[35]

The succeeding essays in *Encounter*'s short series on intellectuals in various countries did little, whatever their other merits, to stabilize the meaning of the term. In practice, the sense of 'intellectuals' governing each of the essays tended to reflect the traditions in the country concerned, underlining the difficulties of comparing like with like in this case. In discussing the United States in the following number, Marcus Cunliffe plumped squarely for the subjective sense: 'By an intellectual I mean a person of unusual intelligence who, as the possessor of such a gift, has formed the habit of generalising (in words, paint, music or merely at random moments not communicated to others through any medium) about mankind and his world.' In fact, of course, like anyone claiming to be working with this subjective or normative sense of the term, Cunliffe had necessarily to deal with those figures whose expressions of this urge had attracted a certain level of attention from a broader public. And, rephrasing a polarity common to several of the essays in this series (as well as to much other literature on the subject), Cunliffe divided these intellectuals into 'the avant garde', whom he then specified as the 'alienated intellectuals', and the 'clerisy', the term (discussed in Ch. 3) he pressed into service to identify 'the non-alienated intellectuals'. In the body of the essay, these categories, and indeed the term 'intellectuals' itself, were allowed to float around pretty freely. At one point, for example, he spoke of the contemporary versions of the avant-garde and clerisy

NOTES

1. This point is now well illustrated in Julia Stapleton, *Political Intellectuals and Public Identities in Britain since 1850* (Manchester: Manchester University Press, 2001), part III.
2. See Joseph M. Hernon, 'The last Whig historian and consensus history: George Macaulay Trevelyan 1876–1962', *American Historical Review*, 81 (1976), 66–97; Herbert Butterfield, *The Englishman and His History* (Cambridge: Cambridge University Press, 1944).
3. David Ogg, *Herbert Fisher, 1865–1940: A Short Biography* (London: Arnold, 1947), 137.
4. See Simon Featherstone, 'The nation as pastoral in British literature of the Second World War', *Journal of European Studies*, 16 (1986), 155–68; and Eric Homberger, 'Intellectuals, Englishness, and the "myths" of Dunkirk', *Revue française de civilisation britannique*, 4 (1986), 82–100.
5. Stephen Spender, 'The English intellectuals and the world of to-day', *The Twentieth Century*, 149 (June, 1951), 482–8; repr. in George B. de Huszar, *The Intellectuals: A Controversial Portrait* (Glencoe, Ill.: Free Press, 1960), 470–6.
6. Much the fullest and best account of Spender's career is now John Sutherland, *Stephen Spender, The Authorised Biography* (London: Penguin, 2004).
7. Spender, 'The English intellectuals', 482, 486, 487.
8. Ibid. 486–7, 484.
9. Noel Annan, 'The intellectual aristocracy', in J. H. Plumb (ed.), *Studies in Social History: A Tribute to G. M. Trevelyan* (London: Longmans, 1955), 243–87.
10. Ibid. 285.
11. See the work of Christophe Charle and Jean-François Sirinelli discussed in Ch. 11, below.
12. Annan, 'Intellectual aristocracy', 253, 248, 281.
13. Ibid. 244.
14. Ibid. 260.
15. Ibid. 254.
16. Ibid. 265.
17. I have explored their sense of 'freemasonry' in my *Public Moralists: Political Thought and Intellectual Life in Britain 1850–1930* (Oxford: Oxford University Press, 1991), esp. ch 1.
18. Annan, 'Intellectual aristocracy', 285. Forty-four years later, Annan appeared less confident about these continuities. Shortly before his death, he included a highly edited version of this essay in his last book, *The Dons: Mentors, Eccentrics, and Geniuses* (London: HarperCollins, 1999), a version which omitted most of the historical characterization, but which attempted, selectively, to bring the various family trees up to date (he does not acknowledge the alterations and describes himself, misleadingly, as simply 'reprinting' his original essay). In his new conclusion to the piece he reflects that aristocracies can disappear and that 'in the 1960s some of their children who might have been expected to excel abandoned the goal of a fellowship and with a sigh of relief dropped out'. 'Whether the names of these families will continue to appear among the holders of fellowships and chairs [an interesting narrowing of the range of achievement] in the twenty-first century remains an open question' (*The Dons*, 340–1).

19. Edward Shils, 'The intellectuals: (1) Great Britain', *Encounter*, 4 (1955), 5–16.
20. See Frances Stonor Saunders, *Who Paid the Piper? The CIA and the Cultural Cold War* (London: Granta, 1999). For the role of Stephen Spender, the magazine's co-editor throughout this period, see now Sutherland, *Stephen Spender*; and see also the retrospective account by Frank Kermode, the (unsuspecting) literary editor at the time of the revelation, in *Not Entitled: A Memoir* (London: HarperCollins, 1996), 221–42.
21. Reprinted as *America and the Intellectuals* (1953); the quoted phrase comes from Richard Hofstadter, *Anti-Intellectualism in American Life* (New York: Knopf, 1963), ch. 15, representatively titled 'The intellectual: alienation and conformity'.
22. Shils, 'The intellectuals', 6.
23. Ibid. 8.
24. See, most strikingly, the roll-call of school and family connection shared by a wide range of inter-war literary figures in Valentine Cunningham, *British Writers of the Thirties* (Oxford: Oxford University Press, 1988).
25. Shils, 'The intellectuals', 12.
26. For a perceptive analysis of the significance attributed to Amis's picaresque hero, see Blake Morrison, *The Movement: English Poetry and Fiction of the 1950s* (London: Methuen, 1986 [1st edn. 1980]).
27. Shils, 'The intellectuals', 16.
28. Ibid. 8, 14.
29. Ibid. 11.
30. Ibid. 13.
31. 'Bruce Truscot' [E. A. Peers], *Redbrick University* (London: Faber, 1943).
32. Shils, 'The intellectuals', 7.
33. The *locus classicus* was, of course, Daniel Bell, *The End of Ideology: The Exhaustion of Political Ideas in the Fifties* (Glencoe, Ill.: Free Press, 1960).
34. Shils, 'The intellectuals', 10. For a general asessment of Shils's career, see the special memorial issue of *Minerva*, 34 (1996).
35. 'Communications: The British Intellectuals', *Encounter*, 4 (June 1955), 68–72. Further letters appeared in the July issue, 71–2.
36. Marcus Cunliffe, 'The intellectuals—II: the United States', *Encounter*, 4 (May 1955), 24, 25, 32–3.
37. Golo Mann, 'The intellectuals—III: Germany', *Encounter*, 4 (June 1955), 42, 43, 45–6, 49.
38. Herbert Luthy, 'The intellectuals—IV: France', *Encounter*, 5 (Aug. 1955), 5, 12, 13, 14–15.
39. Hugh Seton-Watson, 'The intellectuals—V: Russia', *Encounter* 5 (Sept. 1955), 51.

7

The Long 1950s II: Brave Causes

'There is an intelligentsia in England . . . and it is doubtful if any intellectual class, anywhere, has ever had more natural authority and easy power.'

I

For their series of articles on intellectuals, the editors of *Encounter* had deliberately chosen contributors who, though deeply knowledgeable about the societies they discussed, were, by background or experience, at some remove from them also.[1] That this encouraged at least a somewhat analytical tone becomes more evident when one returns to the run-of-the-mill parochialism about this subject still so evident in pronouncements from members of 'the cultivated elite' in Britain during this period. A short piece in *The Listener* (first given as a talk on the Third Programme) by Harold Nicolson the following year may serve as a representative example of the snobbish and disdainful attitudes which the topic could call forth. The 70-year old Nicolson, former diplomat and MP as well as prolific man of letters (and, most famously perhaps, husband of Vita Sackville-West), was hardly to be looked to for iconoclastic and up-to-the-minute views. Rather, he reiterated the ancient bread-and-circuses wisdom of a governing class: having the people invest their passions in harmless matters such as sport contributes to a desirable political stability. '[I]t is preferable that the general public should be unintellectual rather than intellectual; and that they should spend much of their time, and relieve many internal tensions, by worrying about cricket matches rather than by worrying about what is happening in Cairo or Tel-Aviv.' (1956 was the year of the Suez invasion.) But while commending a tendency towards intellectual apathy in politics, Nicolson deplored (or affected to deplore) the familiar lack of interest by the English in art and 'the things of the mind'. After all, it was this aesthetic inattention which allowed the most frightful things to pass without objection—' the progressive mechanisation of the countryside', 'the abominable approaches to our provincial towns', 'the destruction of Berkeley and St James's squares', and so on.

Even so, Nicolson confessed that he had 'small patience with the intellectual who complains that the grey climate of England is ill-attuned to his genius'.

(Nicolson himself plainly does not belong to the category of intellectuals at a moment like this.) One could, after all, always enjoy 'that solidarity which the sense of being a discarded, disregarded minority imparts'. No doubt Sir Harold Nicolson, society host and official biographer of George V, spoke with special authority about being a member of such a 'disregarded minority'; he at any rate advised intellectuals to fall back on such solidarity in the absence of popular acclaim. In the course of his talk, few of the clichés of mossy, thatched-cottage Englishness were left unturned ('we are above everything a practical race'), and local prejudices were offered as timeless truths, as in the consoling thought that public indifference in Britain had at least one virtue: 'when intellectual or aesthetic matters are regarded as the centre of interest, one is apt to be plagued by the sham intellectual, than whom no more insufferable being walks this earth'. This contrast needed scant elaboration: 'In France and Germany, where the intellectual is much adulated, he is apt to become conceited. I have known French academicians or German professors who have been rendered so self-important by the flattery they receive that they have lost their sense of proportion and no longer realise how ridiculous it is to admire oneself.' Maintaining his own sense of proportion, Nicolson concluded, not altogether logically, that 'on the whole, the intellectual in the English world should be content with his lot'.[2]

Jim Dixon, the anti-hero of Kingsley Amis's 1954 best-seller, *Lucky Jim*, represented, for people of Harold Nicolson's class and generation, a threatening form of discontent. Somerset Maugham notoriously used one word to describe the class and type to which Jim Dixon/Kingsley Amis belonged: 'scum.'[3] The book's success had won its author a lot of attention in the press, in the course of which the distinction between the qualities of the fictional hero and the qualities of his creator was not always respected. Amis traded on this notoriety to make occasional provocative forays into non-literary discussion, and one such statement briefly became the focus for arguments about the question of intellectuals in Britain in the mid-1950s. In January 1957 Amis published a Fabian pamphlet entitled *Socialism and the Intellectuals*. 'Lucky Jim's' later move to the right meant that the somewhat equivocal politics of this pamphlet were to be closely scrutinized.[4] Less remarked has been what it tells us about attitudes towards intellectuals as recorded by a writer who deliberately adopted a straightforward, bloke-in-the-pub tone about such matters.

Amis wrote as a Labour supporter who was becoming disenchanted with politics, but he offered himself as not just an individual instance but as representative of a widespread mood among 'middle-class intellectuals'. He acknowledged that he was using the term 'in a pretty wide sense': in fact it was clearly in what I have called the sociological sense, as indicated by his proceeding to attach a list of occupations—'university, college, and school teachers, perhaps the lower ranks of the civil service, journalists, industrial scientists, librarians, G.P.s, some of the clergy (predominantly the non-conformist sects?), and the various brands of literary and artistic, or arty, intellectual'. The fact that the final example uses the term of which it is supposed to be an illustrative definition suggests that Amis took this group to be the core of the category. This became clearer when he moved on to speak of 'what might be called the intellectual pure and simple... the literary and arty man, the writer in the widest sense, the critic, the journalist, the self-employed intelligentsia if you like'. These were the people who had been notably left-wing in the 1930s ('for this purpose the Thirties can be stretched on until about 1945'), but were so no longer, a change which Amis characterized as one from political romanticism to political apathy. Amis and other 'Movement' writers were, after 1956, sometimes inaccurately bundled together with a different group of writers under the 'Angry Young Man' label, but in this pamphlet, at least, Amis does sound as though he is echoing Jimmy Porter's lament that there were 'no more good, brave causes left'.

Amis's rather shoddy, knockabout pamphlet yields interesting confirmatory evidence on several of the issues discussed in this book, including the question of Orwell's importance in shaping subsequent discussions of intellectuals in England. As Amis put it in the passage from which the epigraph to Ch. 15 is taken: 'Of all the writers who appeal to the post-war intelligentsia, he [Orwell] is far and away the most potent. Apart from incessantly hearing his name spoken, we can hardly pass a month without reading an article on him.' He went on: 'It would be unfair, and also perhaps rather unconvincing, to blame Orwell alone for the present political apathy of the intelligentsia, though I do think him important.' In fact Amis revealed a shrewd sense of Orwell's limitations—'Orwell's insistence that the political game *can* be dirty and dishonest and treacherous, that it *often* is, betrays him into implying that it *must* be a dirty game, that it *always* is'—and he recognized that Orwell went on attacking English intellectuals for their Left-infatuated romanticism even after the political climate had begun to change. By the time of his death in 1950, Amis complained, Orwell was becoming 'a hysterical neurotic with a monomania about the depravity of British intellectuals'. Here, Amis appears to identify himself with the stratum which the term 'the intellectuals' was coming to signify in the decade after Orwell's death: no longer just a few Left-leaning poets, but a large swathe of the well-educated professional class, especially (if one sticks to Amis's selective description) the Welfare-State-supporting, redbrick-university-working, political realists. The writers labelled as belonging to 'the Movement' were, briefly, the laureates of this stratum, and in taking his distance from Orwell's denunciations of the previous generation, Amis was insisting that Orwell's criticisms were no longer applicable, even though, on a broader front, his own characteristic no-nonsense-no-foreigners tone owed more to Orwell than he may have cared to acknowledge.

Amis's pamphlet was also revealing for its unsteadiness—an unsteadiness shared, I have been arguing, with most writers on this topic—on the question of whether he included himself in the category. Ostensibly, he did: 'the intelligentsia—and once more I include myself—doesn't understand economics'. But in practice he often did not: following Suez and the Soviet invasion of Hungary, 'the intellectuals have been up in arms, protesting, helping to pass resolutions, sending letters and telegrams, even demonstrating', though on his own admission he had been doing none of these. Similarly, he spoke in uncertain tones about how intellectuals can no longer identify with half-starved workers because they think them well-paid now, though this was, Amis urged, true of only a minority of workers: 'Your intellectual has never been the man for subtleties of this sort,' though by definition such subtleties had not escaped your Amis. His argument was frankly autobiographical, yet he constantly veered off into speaking of intellectuals as Other People.[5]

For my purposes, one of the most interesting responses to Amis's pamphlet came from Paul Johnson, later editor of the *New Statesman*, later still to move even more comprehensively and noisily rightwards than Amis himself. Johnson identified the potential anti-intellectualism of Amis's pamphlet: he attacked both his quietism and his view that intellectuals are more likely than practical men to get things wrong. Instead, he offered a declaration of faith in reason in politics, invoking the iconic origins of the term at issue: although 'Mr Amis employs the word "intellectual" freely without attempting to define it,' its association with the Dreyfus Affair always recalls those who 'believed that reason was a better arbiter of human affairs than prejudice'. In that founding moment, Johnson reminds those readers tempted by Amis's pessimism, it was 'the intellectuals who eventually triumphed'. Johnson's usage slides into the normative in the familiar way: he builds in 'a sense of justice' (something which 'every true intellectual possesses'), and so 'in this sense, the intellectual is, by definition, politically committed, and his sympathies will always and in all countries be found, in the main, on the side of the rational, progressive, democratic left' (this is one of the many statements by his earlier self about which one would be interested to hear the comments of the later, purple-faced, Johnson). On these grounds, he challenged Amis's ascription of general political apathy to the intellectuals now. That may, Johnson allowed, have been partly true in the late 1940s and early 1950s, but Suez had changed all that: 'Nobody who attended the great Suez demonstration in Trafalgar Square feels the need for another Spain'. And then, hyperbolically: 'Never in modern history has the intellectual element in a nation been so united, militant, and, I submit, successful.'[6] The intellectuals take to the streets and governments fall: for Johnson, the spirit of Dreyfusism was alive and well and living in Trafalgar Square. For Amis, this was just another example of 'political romanticism'.

Looking back to the mid-1950s from the distant vantage-point of 1963, Anthony Hartley (whose *A State of England* is discussed more fully below) recognized a degree of truth in the cosy accounts of the intellectual's position given by Shils and others: 'Indeed, for some years after the war most English intellectuals were reconciled to an astonishing degree with the society in which they lived.' But Hartley believed that, even as this situation was being celebrated, it was about to change: 'It was this pact [*sc.* between the intellectual and society] that came to an end with *Declaration* and the more general outburst of social criticism that took place from 1957 onwards.'[7] The discovery in the second half of the 'long 1950s' that there were some 'good, brave causes' left after all was to call intellectuals into question in sometimes unpredictable ways.

II

The collection of eight essays published in 1957 under the title *Declaration* is indeed an 'outburst', though it is now hard to see much significant 'social criticism' in it. Its eight authors, all under 40, were very far from representing a common position; in fact, 'some were even reluctant to appear between the same covers with others whose views they violently oppose'. They were united only in 'sharing a certain indignation against the apathy, the complacency, the idealistic bankruptcy of their environment'.[8] Those phrases hit the authentically 'Angry' note (in the years after 1956, 'Angry' was a ubiquitous and much-abused classification), and the authors were all figures who had been promoted into the spotlight by the factitious and rather frenzied journalistic efforts of the mid-1950s to identify the spokesmen of 'a new generation'. In practice, the essays were for the most part slight, inconsequential pieces, ranging from thin, mannered personal credos by John Osborne and John Wain to the meta-historical emptiness of Colin Wilson's umpteenth restatement of his ideas about 'the Outsider'.[9] None of the authors, it is true, could be described as 'reconciled... with the society in which they lived', but beyond indicating that they were bored and irritated by that society, none of them (with one exception) seem to have had much to offer by way of illuminating criticism of it.

The collection was, however, distinguished by a bravura piece by Kenneth Tynan, calling for seriousness, passion, colour, and pleasure, in place of the trite conventionality and apolitical gentility of most contemporary British theatre. Speaking of (and perhaps for) 'the young Leftists who have emerged in Britain since the war', Tynan observed that they were different from 'the radical intelligentsia of the thirties' in that they were not in 'filial revolt' against that upper-class into which they themselves had been born. He then went on, in a passage rich in matter for my purposes, to sketch the dilemma the members of such an 'intelligentsia' now found themselves in:

> All of us owe a great debt to semantic philosophy for having taught us to talk sense, and to distinguish always between empirical, analytic, metaphysical, attitude, and value statements. We have been trained to verify what we say, and we know that statements in the last three categories cannot be verified at all. So far, so good: we are less deceived than we used to be. But who are we? Intellectuals, presumably. And here lies the snag. The new philosophy has taught us to eschew moral affirmatives and the use of 'ought', but it has made no impact at all on the great mass of people, who are still as enslaved to vague rhetorical statements as ever they were. We can prove that these statements

are meaningless, but we are forbidden to replace them with social exhortations (attitude-statements) or proposals for a better life on earth (value-statements).[10]

The pedigree here is clearly 'out of Ayer by Larkin' (the latter's *The Less Deceived* had been published two years earlier). The passage is a disarmingly pure expression of the supposed cultural impact of logical positivism on the post-war generation, including the sense of frustrated moral and political impulses which it ultimately generated. But Tynan's frank equation of 'we' and 'intellectuals' was less common. 'We' includes, collusively, his readers as well as fellow-contributors (some of whom would probably have repudiated this conscription), to be contrasted with 'the great mass of people'. 'Intellectuals' were implicitly defined, it would seem, by degree of education, perhaps allied to level of subjective interest in ideas—or, in other words, that older, vague sense of 'intellectuals' which hovers on the edge of other uses, signifying 'the thinking, educated part of the population'. The possibilities of cultural leadership are hinted at, perhaps yearned for: here is where the self-denying ordinance of the verification principle (as popularly rendered) comes in. As a result, the 'intellectuals' seem to be condemned to a Chekhovian sense of uselessness.

In fact, Tynan, by adroit use of a familiar literary device, did manage to work a good deal of 'social exhortation' and 'proposals for a better life' into his essay. It took the form of an imaginary letter to 'the son of a friend of mine who was coming to the end of his three years at Oxford' (evidently still assumed to be the proper form of education even for the new 'classless' generation), sketching some of the characteristics of the society in which he was about to take his place. It offered an ironically amusing and utterly damning account of snobbery, complacency, parochialism, and so on, and briefly gestured towards the countervailing energies waiting to be released in the new generation, whose principal habitat, apparently, is the jazz club ('You could never make a lynch-mob out of them, because the art they live for was invented by negroes'). But 'what they (and you, and I) lack is a rallying-point, social and political . . . They need an organ, a platform to articulate their impatience with convention, with "good taste", with "British prestige", with the use of "emotional" as a dirty word.'[11] This is, implicitly, a help-wanted ad, a request for intellectuals who did *not* find 'their society and its culture so much to their satisfaction'. Tynan strove to fill this role himself in subsequent years, with doubtful success, but he could, more generally, be seen here as asking 'the sixties' to hurry up and begin.

A somewhat more impressive overall level of analysis was evident in the other anthology from this period which was taken to inaugurate a new era of 'social criticism', the collection of twelve essays published in 1958 under the title *Conviction*. The contributors here tended to be of much the same age and from the same variety of backgrounds as those in *Declaration*, but they were largely academics, journalists, and social scientists rather than novelists and playwrights. They were more consciously preoccupied with the state of the Labour Party and the future of Socialism: it was all very much criticism of the Left from within the Left.

References in the volume to 'intellectuals' betray the usual variety of attitudes towards the term. Thus, when, in the peroration of his essay, Raymond Williams invokes the 'transforming energy' of the millions who are shut out from true democracy in their work and lives, he declares that 'the business of the Socialist intellectual is what it always was: to attack the clamps on that energy'. Williams is certainly including himself under this label and, by implication, his fellow-contributors, too. But when Peter Townsend, having invoked the saintly human capacities of his grandmother, goes on to broaden his point, his own self-positioning becomes more equivocal: 'any simple expression of faith in the goodness of man frightens and embarrasses the intellectual. He does not want to be taken for a sucker in public and you rarely find him saying anything so straightforward and naive. He is much too cynical and self-conscious.' This could refer to Other People or it could be the half-guilty self-scrutiny of the scholarship-boy son. But Richard Hoggart was evidently not including himself when he referred to 'the assured narrowness of some intellectuals, a doctrinaire, anti-imaginative, Fabian-sterile single vision', though the phrasing leaves open the possibility that 'some' intellectuals may not be like this. And sometimes the usage varies within the course of a single essay. Speaking autobiographically about doing national service after Oxford, Paul Johnson observed that 'many young intellectuals are driven to the Left by barrack-room discipline'. As it happens, Johnson was not, though it's pretty clear he is placing himself within this category, the category of the highly educated and bookish. But when he was denouncing the snobbery and emulation which shores up the class system, complaining that 'the intellectuals have provided no check on this stampede of Gaderene swine', he was surely referring to those who possessed some cultural authority and appeared not to be including himself.[12]

For my purposes, the most intriguing contribution comes in a subsequently neglected essay by Iris Murdoch entitled 'A house of theory'. The essay is partly of interest because it indicates, from an unusual angle, an awareness that the issue of specialization was now at the heart of the question of the intellectual, partly because it is a somewhat unusual expression of the condition one might call 'Sartre envy'. (Murdoch was more familiar with the French intellectual scene of the late 1940s and 1950s than were most British philosophers of her generation, and she wrote the first substantial study of Sartre to appear in English.[13]) She began with a variant of the sentiment inspiring the essays by her fellow-contributors: 'The socialist movement in this country is suffering from a loss of energy.' She acknowledged some of the general causes discussed by others—the very success of the Welfare State, the impact of greater prosperity on organized trade-unionism, and so on. But she went on to take the discussion into realms unapproached by any of the other contributors, realms populated by names such as Hobbes and Hume, Kant and Hegel, even, passingly, Weldon and Hare. For Murdoch, what was centrally lacking in Britain was what she deliberately called 'theory', systematically connected conceptual explorations of first principles.

She implied (rather than demonstrated) that the Socialist movement had been inspired by such theories in its (unspecified) past, and that such theory is what any radical politics always needs.[14]

In practice, the direction in which such radical theorizing offered to lead looks surprisingly familiar. She urged the need to go back and rethink the very notion of work, and in so doing to return to the ideas in 'our' native tradition, ideas expressed by the Guild Socialists, for example, or indeed to return to 'the point not so very far back at which we retained as a living morality ideas which were common to Marx and to William Morris'. A passing reference reveals how she, like so many in mid-twentieth-century British culture, took the 'catastrophist' interpretation of the Industrial Revolution for granted; 'We have not mended our society since its mutilation by nineteenth-century industrialism'; as ever, the implication is that it was, somehow, whole and unmutilated before that.[15]

Murdoch blames the decline and disappearance of the relevant kind of 'theory' partly on the process of academic specialization in general, partly on intellectual developments specific to philosophy. 'As philosophy is steadily drawn in the direction of logic and becomes increasingly a matter for highly trained experts, it separates itself from, and discourages, the vaguer and more generally comprehensible theorizing which it used to nourish and be nourished by' (this is a variant of Tynan's complaint, but with the larger process of professionalization replacing logical positivism in the dock). There is, as usual with such aerial overviews, some unsteadiness about quite when the rot set in: there are hints that post-war British philosophy is particularly culpable, though also references back to Russell and the beginnings of analytic philosophy, and indeed much further back still to Hume and Kant and projects for 'the elimination of metaphysics'. But wherever its roots should be traced to, its effect is to favour certain sorts of considerations over others in public discussion and political decision. 'It therefore emerges that the choice made by our intellectuals against the development of theories is a moral choice.'[16]

Once again, it is worth asking who 'our intellectuals' are here. Murdoch herself appears not to be one of them: she makes very clear that she sees their choice as mistaken. But the term does apparently include many of her fellow academic philosophers and others who, in looser terms, accept the sceptical, anti-metaphysical tendency of modern analytical philosophy. By limiting themselves in this way, 'our intellectuals' were failing in their task, were reducing themselves, it might be said, to mere experts. 'We cannot live without "the experts". But the true "open society" in the modern world is one in which expertise is not mysterious; and the only way to prevent it from becoming mysterious is continually to subordinate its activities to a lively and *interested* public opinion: and this in turn will languish without "theories".' In this respect, at least, Murdoch was somewhat at odds with her fellow contributors: they may have wanted expertise to be informed by moral passion, but many of them would surely have blinked at the idea that what they needed was 'metaphysics'. She went on to insist on further dangers in the growth of expertise itself: not only was society becoming divided into the experts and the rest, but

> we have now the additional spectacle of the division of the experts into mutually non-comprehending groups. What is needed is an *area of translation*, an area in which specialized concepts and recommendations can be seen and understood in the light of moral and social ideas which have a certain degree of complexity and yet are not the sole property of technicians.

This is a plea for a morally and theoretically informed level of public debate as an antidote to specialization, a theme to which, I have suggested, the logic of the intellectual's position constantly forces a return. In the absence of such debate, there can only be experts, but they lack 'that unifying vision which is needed to prompt more inspired and imaginative uses of technique'.[17] It is a plea, in other words, for intellectuals in Britain to undertake a little more frequently the journey between specialization and its antidote, that journey which is a defining feature of their role.

Yet was this a role that Murdoch herself filled thereafter? In the decade or so following the war, she had seemed to hunger for some creed or body of ideas that would transcend the mundane preoccupations of empiricism. For a while, Existentialism appeared to promise this—and in an exciting, bohemian way, a way that tended to cast one as an intellectual in 1950s Britain—but it was actually a kind of false start for her. Subsequently, partly spurred by her reading of Simone Weil, she moved towards a loosely Christianized Platonism: the good is real, the good is in the world independently of us, the good is known through love. The more she embraced this position, the less engaged she became with public debate in contemporary Britain, raising the question of whether there is something in the Platonist temperament that is inimical to taking on the role of the intellectual, some disposition to find the world, with its messy mixture of the good, the bad, and the indifferent, wanting when judged by the highest ideals.[18] Whatever the truth of this speculation, Murdoch's later career went in other, more purely literary and religious, directions.

The view that British culture in the 1950s was principally characterized by apathy, political apathy above all, was most insisted upon by those on the Left, even though the very increase in the volume of such insisting after 1956 went some way to belying the charge. This strain of criticism was brought to a head in a collection of essays called, appropriately, *Out of Apathy*, edited by E. P. Thompson, who also contributed three pieces to it, including the subsequently much-cited essay 'Outside the whale'.

As one might expect, Thompson's essay was a sustained analysis (and indictment) of the *ideological* components in the 'apathy' of the 1950s, diagnosed as a loss of faith in the beneficent power of collective political action. Less predictable, perhaps, was the extent to which the essay was animated by Thompson's deep preoccupation with the nature and role of intellectuals in

Britain. In fact, the essay begins with the question of why the General Election of 1955 had been one 'in which the great majority of British intellectuals were silent'. The one exception, according to Thompson, was the ageing Bertrand Russell, but he had been treated dismissively even in 'the favourite newspaper of British intellectuals' (*The Manchester Guardian*). Thompson compares this 'ideology of apathy' to 'the disillusion among the radical intelligentsia in Britain in the aftermath of the French Revolution', and he traces the theme of disillusion principally through an examination of W. H. Auden's successive poetic positions, until Auden reached the resignation which 'foreshadowed the attitude which informed the "Natopolitan" intellectual of the fifties'.[19]

However, the literary presence whom Thompson identifies as presiding over the formation of 'Natopolitan ideology' is George Orwell, especially the pessimistic Orwell of the later 1940s. In particular, Thompson finds Orwell responsible for the now widespread tendency to explain away all political commitment as some form of public-schoolboy neurosis: 'By the fifties... novels, plays and theses were written displaying not only Communism but also radicalism as projections of the neuroses of maladjusted intellectuals.... The Natopolitan intellectual was disabled by self-distrust no less than the Stalinist intellectual was disabled by fear of reverting to bourgeois modes of thought.' Thompson recognized that 'only a minority of the intellectuals of the thirties' went through the cycle of faith and disenchantment in Communism, but he insisted that 'the shape of cultural history is decided by minorities'. Even though this phrase confines itself to 'cultural history', it is a striking affirmation of the importance of intellectuals, an affirmation borne out by the rest of the piece and indeed by much else in Thompson's work. He went on to savage the 'official' scholarly line, including the contributions of Edward Shils (a much-noticed article by Shils and Michael Young on the socially-unifying symbolism of the Coronation was treated with some contempt). 'Solemn historians and social scientists assured us that Chinese peasants and Russian sailors would never have revolted if intellectuals had not dropped the seed of maladjustment in underprivileged soil.... The intellectual had no duty to society more important than restraining himself.' And in a reprise of that cruder Marxist idiom to which he could occasionally revert, he indicted practically the whole culture: 'intellectuals may be employed, promoted, neglected in ratio to their acceptability to ruling interests'.[20]

Against this dominant conformism, Thompson sees the beginnings of a 'rebellious humanism' forming itself in the late 1950s, woven together out of various fragile threads. And he urges that the source of the inspiration necessary to coalesce this rebellion into effective political protest is to be found in William Morris (about whom, of course, he had published a large, overtly partisan, book just five years earlier): 'Our greatest Socialist intellectual, William Morris, was a rebel against utilitarianism in every line he wrote.' The terms of praise neatly indicate the indigenous traditions that are preoccupying Thompson (part of that long-standing fault-line that divided British culture in the nineteenth century and after between 'utilitarians' and their allegedly more generous-spirited critics).[21] In fact towards the end of the essay it turns out, rather unexpectedly, that intellectuals in Britain are exceptionally *well* placed to develop an active socialist humanism:

> Is it not possible that British intellectuals work in one of the only well-equipped and peaceable laboratories that are left? Where American intellectuals must struggle against their own sense of isolation, amidst the roar of empty affluence and the constant solicitations of 'organization man'; and where Russian—or even Polish—intellectuals must work under various hazards and constraints? And as the rebels of Hungary and Poland broke the spell upon our will by the example of their protest, may not the success of their rebellion depend in turn upon our own?[22]

In assuming that British intellectuals do not suffer from the 'sense of isolation' and the 'roar of affluence' of their American counterparts, Thompson was presumably thinking of (among other differences) the closer relation in Britain between Left intellectuals such as himself and the Labour movement. Still, the passage places a surprisingly heavy burden on the shoulders of that elusive species, the British intellectuals, since nothing less than the throwing off of both the Soviet and the American yokes seems to depend upon their 'rebellion'. It is curious, too, that he makes no mention here of French or Italian intellectuals, another indication, perhaps, of just how far Thompson was from sharing the almost habitual emphasis on France of most of those who wrote on this subject. And indeed, this distance could be seen as prefiguring what was to become a celebrated clash between Thompson and his younger New Left colleagues in the 1960s, to which I shall turn in the following chapter.

III

Before that, however, we should pause over a book which may be taken to mark the end of the 'long 1950s' where the question of intellectuals is concerned, Anthony Hartley's *A State of England*, which was published in 1963.[23] In the course of the 1950s, Hartley, who had been born in 1925 and educated at Oxford and the Sorbonne, became a leading literary journalist, including a period as literary editor of *The Spectator*, and he rather specialized in Anglo-French cultural comparisons (as we saw in Ch. 3). The fact that I have already cited the work twice is no accident: it is particularly useful for my purposes in providing something of a compendium of journalistic *idées reçues* on the matter of intellectuals from a period which, I have been arguing, was formative for subsequent discussion.

Hartley's book may have been unusual in being so *explicitly* focused on the question of intellectuals: 'I am describing English society in terms of the tensions and perplexities of its intellectuals.' But it was entirely representative of the larger tradition of discourse I have been discussing in structuring its account around the contrast with France. 'Across the Channel intellectuals, whether they are writers, scientists, artists, or university teachers, live more publicly and more dangerously than we do here.' And, as in so many discussions of this subject, his first and chief example, indeed the only proper name mentioned for some pages, is that of Sartre. He then rehearses a selection from among the familiar litany of contrasts. English intellectuals cannot function as 'real' intellectuals because of their preference for living in the country ('Johnson was the last English intellectual positively to revel in his urban existence'); 'intellectual society' exists by 'pretending not to be intellectual at all'; 'it is undeniable that in British public life the word 'intellectual' carries a mildly pejorative sense'; and more in the same vein.[24]

But Hartley's book was also representative in displaying considerable ambivalence about this state of affairs. He was, for example, quick to point out certain merits in this situation: 'If it keeps novelists writing novels instead of addressing mass meetings, and scientists in their laboratories instead of holding forth on subjects about which they are ill-qualified to give an opinion, it may even do good'. This is the traditional scepticism about attempts by others to exercise some form of cultural authority: one wouldn't want novelists and scientists to be—well, doing the kind of thing Hartley himself habitually did, including in this book. The ambivalence passes into sniffy disdain on the matter of acquiring the necessary attention, as in the passage quoted earlier in Ch. 3: 'anyone who takes the trouble to be sufficiently thrusting can give himself undue prominence by an aggressive assumption of continental intellectual manners'. It's those pushy foreign cads again, but we know why (apart simply from being foreign) they do it: 'In general it can be taken that excessive preoccupation with publicity is a sign of declining talent'—an already silly sneer which the use of 'excessive' makes almost tautologous. So, at one moment Hartley appears to be upbraiding English intellectuals for their failure to be the real thing, then at the next he professes himself thankful for this state of affairs: 'I have often denounced the failings of English intellectuals, but how they shine in comparison with the harsh dogmatism and neo-Hegelian nonsense of their continental fellows.'[25]

Hartley's usage of the term 'intellectuals' wobbled among the various senses like a tipsy host at a party trying to find a few words of welcome for everyone. At times, it is sociological ('there are those—doctors, lawyers, journalists—whose work might be supposed to classify them as intellectuals'); at others normative ('true intellectuals must continually be criticizing their own basic assumptions about life'); but in practice he is most often operating with the cultural sense, as the references to Sartre and the noisy novelists suggest. The texture of his prose would seem to offer a positive answer to his own opening question quoted earlier ('Is there such a thing as an English intellectual?'), since he speaks of 'English intellectuals' on almost every page, and refers confidently to such figures as the 'Victorian intellectual'.[26]

However, these figures, insists Hartley, here echoing Annan and Shils, are, unlike their Continental counterparts, closely integrated into the fabric of upper-middle and professional class life. They tend to share 'its mildly liberal views, its occasionally sharp Puritanism, its respect for hard work, and also its knack of bringing influence to bear on national life from the inside rather than the outside.' His example here, not unreasonably, was Keynes: 'He changed our world more than most individuals have changed it, but he did so by being the agitator of the committee-room and the senior common-room rather than of the street corner.'[27] The contrast here relies on unapologetic metonymy: the street corner was hardly the preferred pulpit for intellectuals anywhere in the mid-twentieth century. But, then, Hartley's account is shot through with a contrast, the more powerful when operating implicitly, with a thin parody of the political intellectual, a figure assumed to be constantly on barricades, marches, and 'street corners'.

Hartley's discussion also resumes the accepted chronology of English intellectuals. Bloomsbury 'were the last pre-1914 English intellectuals, the representatives of an age when it was possible to mock the pillars of society with complete assurance that they would not collapse upon the heads of the mockers'. 'The intellectuals of the thirties can be called the first of the ineffectual English liberals (a *persona* which has become more familiar since then)'. The Second World War led intellectuals to reidentify with England, engendering a strong reaction against the thirties generation after 1945. The years since then had seen 'a flight from idealism towards an empiricism which was the more welcome in that ideology had visibly proved itself to be the curse of the twentieth century'. (As usual, 'ideology' is here used to mean 'bad ideologies': idealism fosters 'ideology', but, somehow, empiricism does not.) And Hartley endorsed the received view about the influence of Orwell: 'The "no-nonsense" air of an entire generation comes from Orwell.' Indeed, Orwell, together (a little awkwardly) with Matthew Arnold, emerges as the hero of the book: 'He stands as the last in a long line of English moralists whose judgements have more usually been applied to the living humanity embodied in the Condition-of-England question than to any critique of ethical philosophy.'[28]

Thus, Hartley endorsed the by now familiar view that, compared to the inter-war period, intellectuals in England since 1945 had been more at one with their society. Surveying the cultural scene at the end of the 1950s he made this a complaint: 'So far from being uprooted, young English intellectuals err on the side of being too exclusively interested in the problems of their own society (the present vogue of sociology is one symptom of this).' One is tempted to convert this into a proleptic reversal of the claim Perry Anderson was shortly to make familiar: there are no real intellectuals in Britain because they are *too* interested in sociology. But it seems likely that Hartley did not mean sociological theory in Anderson's sense, but rather the 1950s concern with the empirical sociology of poverty and family structure—in effect, the modern version of 'the condition of England' question. Throughout the book, Hartley oscillates between being exasperated by the failings of the (other) English intellectuals and grateful that the English are not in this respect as other nations are. Thus, English intellectuals are failing to understand and adapt to the changes in English society and are thereby 'cut[ting] themselves off from reality in a way which anyone acquainted with the utterances of French intellectuals over the last ten years will find all too familiar'. Things may be bad, but it would be really alarming 'if there were any clear signs of the development of an intelligentsia in the continental sense of a body of intellectuals placed outside society and inspired by a nihilistic hatred for it and its traditions'.[29] The familiar, ludicrously exaggerated, stereotype of the 'Continental intelligentsia' (where is 'outside' society, why 'nihilistic hatred'?) serves yet again as a device enabling a bit of rather tired national self-definition.

Overall, Hartley's is an attack on what he sees as the Left sentimentalism of talk about culture and class in the late 1950s and early 1960s, 'the fads and whimsies that afflict some of those intellectuals most in the public view'. But this, he concludes, is only part of the story: 'happily, it only touches a minority of what might be called intellectual performers concerned to strut and posture before an audience rather than with the modest and retired pursuit of truth'. But he also charges English intellectuals with not being willing to assume the cultural authority which should be theirs: in taking the part of the oppressed, they end up identifying themselves with the victims rather than frankly accepting the gulf between them. 'If English intellectuals wish to enjoy the proper authority of intellectuals, then they must get over the guilt which leads them to wish to be identified with groups to which they do not belong.' Intellectuals ought to possess 'the authority of thought . . . They are supposed to be able to take a cooler and more general view of things than is available to individuals immersed in the battle of sectional interests.' Somehow, the 'modest and retired pursuit of truth' has to be combined with taking 'the more general view of things': this is yet again the wanting-it-both-ways dialectic of almost all journalistic comment on 'intellectuals'. And of course, no homily or philippic on the subject would be complete without intoning one ritual phrase: those who do not stand up for what they believe, or condemn what they believe to be wrong, are evidence, declares Hartley, of 'a treason of the clerks'.[30]

By this point, his unexamined ambivalence about the role of the intellectual has become positively disabling. Intellectuals in the cultural sense (the sense informing most of Hartley's discussion) are, after all, *constituted* by the relation to an 'audience': the 'retired pursuit of truth', if it does not come out from its retirement to address a wider public, remains within the confines of scholarly or scientific specialism. That Hartley also expects these modest and retiring pursuers of truth to take on this public role is evident throughout the book, including in his peroration. There are those, he affirms, who could still give 'us' what 'we' need, namely 'to listen to sages rather than public entertainers and to philosophers rather than *entrepreneurs*'. So these sages and philosophers must step outside their libraries and their studies, but they must not 'strut and posture before an audience'. The ambivalence constantly generated by the dialectic of the role itself makes its presence felt yet again: chaste intellectual virtue must somehow be lawfully wedded to a willingness to take up wider opportunistic engagements. After all, giving society the thought that it needs is—and these are the last words of the book—'part of the responsibility of the intellectual'.[31] But the *English* intellectual, it would seem, has the additional responsibility of doing this without 'strutting'. And for God's sake, man, keep your voice down.

NOTES

1. For a statement of this deliberate editorial policy, see 'This month's "Encounter" ', *Encounter*, 4 (Apr. 1955), 2.
2. Harold Nicolson, 'The intellectual in the English world', *The Listener* (4 Oct. 1956), 501–2.
3. Quoted Morrison, *Movement*, 59.
4. See Amis's later response in his essay 'Why Lucky Jim turned right', in his *What Became of Jane Austen? and Other Questions* (London: Cape, 1970), 200–11.
5. Kingsley Amis, *Socialism and the Intellectuals* (London: Fabian Society, 1957), 1, 2, 3, 6, 8, 9, 10, 11.
6. Paul Johnson, 'Lucky Jim's political testament', *New Statesman* (12 Jan. 1957), 35–6.
7. Hartley, *State of England*, 55, 57.
8. [Tom Maschler (ed.)], *Declaration* (London: MacGibbon & Kee, 1957), 7–8.
9. See the discussion of Wilson in Ch. 18.
10. Kenneth Tynan, 'Theatre and living', in *Declaration*, 115.
11. Ibid. 122, 128.
12. [Norman Mackenzie (ed.)], *Conviction* (London: MacGibbon & Kee, 1958): Raymond Williams, 'Culture is ordinary', 92; Peter Townsend, 'A society for people', 119; Richard Hoggart, 'Speaking to each other', 124; Paul Johnson, 'A sense of outrage', 206, 213.
13. Iris Murdoch, *Sartre, Rationalist or Romantic* (London: Chatto, 1953).
14. Iris Murdoch, 'A house of theory', *Conviction*, 218, 220. The essay is reprinted in Iris Murdoch, *Existentialists and Mystics: Writings on Philosophy and Literature* (London: Chatto, 1997).
15. Murdoch, 'House of theory', 229, 230. For the broader impact of this 'catastrophist' interpretation, see Stefan Collini, 'The literary critic and the village labourer: "culture" in twentieth-century Britain', *Transactions of the Royal Historical Society*, 6th ser., 14 (2004), 93–116.
16. Murdoch, 'House of theory', 221, 227.
17. Ibid. 232, 227–8, 229–30.
18. This question is raised, in slightly different terms, in relation to Murdoch's fiction, in James Wood, 'Faulting the lemon', *London Review of Books*, 1 Jan. 1998, 13–15.
19. E. P. Thompson, 'Outside the whale', in E. P. Thompson (ed.), *Out of Apathy* (London: New Left Books, 1960), 141, 143, 145, 153.
20. Ibid. 159–60, 167, 170, 174–5, 177.

21. For a fuller account of this 'fault-line', and of Thompson's part in perpetuating it, see Donald Winch, 'Mr Gradgrind and Jerusalem', in Stefan Collini, Richard Whatmore, and Brian Young (eds.), *Economy, Polity, and Society: British Intellectual History 1750–1950* (Cambridge: Cambridge University Press, 2000), 243–66.
22. Thompson, 'Outside the whale', 193.
23. This is the work cited in the Introduction and in Ch. 3, sect. IV above.
24. Anthony Hartley, *A State of England* (London: Hutchinson, 1963), 15, 27, 28.
25. Ibid. 28, 23.
26. Ibid. 29, 40.
27. Ibid. 30.
28. Ibid. 36, 41, 33, 46, 47, 54, 55.
29. Ibid. 239, 230.
30. Ibid. 240–2.
31. Ibid. 244.

8

New Left, New Right, Old Story

> 'The outstanding features – not to speak of the failures – of our national culture can be largely explained by the inability of our native intelligentsia to achieve a detached and self-sufficient group existence that would permit it to sustain its traditions through succeeding epochs, and to keep abreast of European intellectual production.'

I

One aspect of that 'more general outburst of social criticism that took place after 1957' which seemed of relatively minor significance at the time was ultimately to foster one of the most influential and enduring changes in the whole idiom in which the question of intellectuals in Britain was discussed. That year saw the founding of two relatively marginal journals: the *New Reasoner*, representing a splinter group breaking away from the Communist Party after the events of 1956, and *Universities and Left Review*, composed principally of young academics and graduate students connected with Oxford University who wanted to bring together radical politics and cultural analysis as an antidote to the intellectual narrowness of what was represented as the presiding spirit of Fabianism on the Left. In 1960 these two journals fused to produce *New Left Review*, with an editorial board drawn from the two tributary journals, but two years later the 'old guard' was replaced by a younger group, led by Perry Anderson, Robin Blackburn, and Tom Nairn. E. P. Thompson, one of those displaced, later referred to it darkly as a 'coup'; Anderson preferred to remember it, more eirenically, as an 'abdication'.[1] In any event, it was in the pages of this journal in the course of the next decade that an analysis of the historically distinctive position of intellectuals in Britain was to be elaborated, an analysis which was then to set the terms for much of the subsequent discussion of the topic in academic and non-academic circles alike. A defining element in that analysis was the use made of the concepts and explanatory strategies of imported European social theory, especially of radical forms of such theory which had not up to this point had much significant presence in British intellectual life, such as the Marxism of Gramsci or of Luxemburg (or, a little later, of Althusser).

The character of the journal was soon largely set by a series of articles by Anderson and Nairn on the interpretation of the course of British history and its connection with 'the present crisis' ('crisis' was a greatly favoured word).[2] The governing assumptions of what was often referred to as 'the Anderson-Nairn thesis' or, simply, 'the *NLR* analysis', of the distinctiveness of the historical development of Britain were most influentially expounded in Anderson's 1964 article 'Origins of the present crisis', which insisted upon the absence of a 'proper' bourgeois revolution in British history and the consequent ease with which a kind of 'continuism' had muffled both challenges to the established order and any theoretically elaborated defence of that order. This article and its companion pieces in turn provoked debate and counter-analysis. These debates, as Anderson later recalled, 'had at their centre a dispute over the character of the dominant class in Hanoverian and Victorian England, and the nature of the state over which it presided'.[3] They also were quite centrally debates about the question of intellectuals in Britain.

The most celebrated of the responses provoked by the early *New Left Review* analysis issued from the older native Socialist tradition in the form of E. P. Thompson's devastating polemic, 'The peculiarities of the English', first published in *The Socialist Register* in 1965.[4] This was neither the first nor the last time that Thompson clashed with the younger editors of *NLR*. Certainly, there was a marked note of fraternal ardour in many of Thompson's sardonic, telling criticisms: he cut deep, aiming to draw blood.

Thompson's general case, signalled in his title, was that the *NLR* analysis distorted the specificities of Britain's political and economic development to fit, or in practice to reproach it for failing to fit, a conceptual model derived from the historical experience of other European countries. 'There is, indeed, throughout their analysis an undisclosed model of Other Countries, whose typological symmetry offers a reproach to British exceptionalism.' The concepts employed by Anderson and Nairn, particularly concerning what constituted a 'true' bourgeois revolution, a 'true' radical intelligentsia, and so on, proposed as a European norm a pattern which, Thompson rightly insisted, essentially derived from French history. 'It happened in one way in France, in another way in England. I am not disputing the importance of the difference—and of the different traditions which ensued—but the notion of typicality.' (Though entirely right to identify France as implicitly providing the model in relation to a 'proper' bourgeois revolution, Thompson perhaps understated the extent to which Italy furnished the template in relation to political mass mobilization.) Thompson then proceeded to give a persuasive account of how already in the seventeenth and eighteenth centuries the English landowning class was also deeply involved in capitalist enterprise, how Old Corruption was the enemy engaged with by Whig grandees and radical reformers alike, how Victorian England never had a genuinely 'bourgeois state', and so on. He also landed a series of telling punches in detailing the lack of attention paid in the *NLR* analysis to England's distinctively Protestant identity, to the prominence of science in English intellectual life, and to the role of Dissent, as well as convicting Anderson and Nairn for their tendency 'to confuse an empirical idiom with an ideology'.[5]

Thompson's essay is not, therefore, principally focused on the question of intellectuals, but its critical engagement with the *NLR* analysis inevitably issued in a rival account of the place of intellectuals in British history. He particularly took issue with Anderson's charge that 'English intellectuals have not constituted "a true intelligentsia"'. In a characteristically forthright passage, he began to detail the inadequacies of this charge:

> Other countries may have produced a 'true intelligentsia', an 'internally unified intellectual community'; but it is rubbish to suggest that there is some crippling disablement in the failure of British intellectuals to form 'an independent intellectual enclave' within the body politic. Rather, there were formed in the eighteenth century *scores* of intellectual enclaves, dispersed over England and Scotland. . . . Much of the best in our intellectual culture has always come, not from the Ancient Universities nor from the self-conscious metropolitan coteries, but from indistinct nether regions.

Here, as throughout the essay, he went on to discuss a wide range of examples (it would be fair to say that the early *NLR* account was, by contrast, not distinguished by its depth of empirical detail, especially in intellectual and cultural history); in so doing, Thompson strongly projected an identity as a historian who has grappled with the knotty, irreducible variousness of the past in contrast to those whom he represented as being, however adept theoretically, too easily seduced into thinking that the enormous complexity of history could be subsumed under a few overarching concepts.[6]

But Thompson actually shared a good deal of common ground with his antagonists—more, perhaps, than he was always willing to acknowledge. Consider, for example, the assumptions behind the following observation: 'The English experience certainly did not encourage sustained efforts of synthesis: since few intellectuals were thrown into prominence in a conflict with authority, few felt the need to develop a systematic critique.'[7] There are two assumptions here worth drawing attention to, not least because they have suffused so much of the subsequent literature on the topic. The first is the idea that one of the distinguishing marks of 'a real intelligentsia' is to produce 'a systematic critique'; the second is that the impulse to do this necessarily arises out of a conflict with an opposing political force. But to the extent that Thompson relies upon these assumptions (there is much in the body of his essay which tacitly works with more nuanced alternatives), he hamstrings himself in his declared project of providing a more historical and thickly textured account of the British past, principally here its intellectual past. These two assumptions in effect drive one back to the characteristic failing of so much of the literature inspired by the early New Left analysis, namely that of measuring how far 'real' intellectuals exist or offer a 'real' critique of their own society by how far they manage to be (or, more usually, fail to be) Marx or Lenin or Gramsci. The other failings of such meta-historical counterfactuals aside, this emphasis will always tend to overlook the varieties of social criticism engaged in by (to mention merely a few figures contemporary with those European theorists) Ruskin, Spencer, Morris, Hobson, Tawney, Leavis, and many, many more. And it involves, of course, a particularly blatant case of building certain preferred characteristics into the very meaning of the terms 'intellectuals' and 'intelligentsia'.

Thompson also identified the crucial, quasi-Leninist, role in originating and directing political action which the *NLR* analysis tacitly ascribed to intellectuals. Anderson and Nairn treat 'the intellectuals as the embodiment of articulate political consciousness', and others, especially the 'workers', as passive followers. Therefore, since in British history 'the Marxist intelligentsia did not appear, the workers became subject to a tributary stream of capitalist ideology, Fabianism'. But 'an interpretation of British Labourism which attributes all to Fabianism and intellectual default is as valueless as an account of Russia between 1924 and 1953 which attributes all to the vices of Marxism, or of Stalin himself'.[8] By not seeing them as simply the *animateurs* of a revolutionary proletarian movement, Thompson can speak more generously and capaciously about 'British intellectuals' and 'the British intelligentsia', emphasizing that these have been more varied and more effective—and also in some cases more genuinely Socialist—than the Anderson–Nairn emphasis on the absence of systematic Marxist theorizing allowed.

There is more in this essay than I can discuss here; it is a memorably eloquent expression of a native 'Socialist humanism'. But although Thompson effectively challenged the idea that the most fruitful way to approach British history was to arraign it for its failure to match up to a supposed European 'norm', from this distance one can detect a certain ambivalence in his response to the indigenous intellectual tradition: he clearly wanted to rescue neglected Socialist forebears (Morris above all), yet at the same time he could be scornful of what he elsewhere called 'a hostile national culture both smug and resistant to intellectuality'.[9] The extent to which he concurred with some of the *NLR* analysis comes out indirectly when he is discussing, and giving great weight to, the role of religious toleration in shaping British intellectual life. A tacit accommodation between theologians and scientists, each being allowed de facto sovereignty over their respective domains, 'suited very well the mood of those intellectuals in the eighteenth century who, finding themselves to be very little opposed by theological authority, were quite content to leave it alone and get on with the exploration of nature'. There may have been some figures to whom this description roughly applies, but it seems drastically to understate the continuing conflict with theological authority throughout the eighteenth century (and into the next), as sceptics such as Hume or Dissenters such as Priestley could have testified. Nonetheless, an emphasis upon a *relatively* greater level of toleration in Britain was useful for Thompson's well-directed sarcasm. In Britain, natural scientists, he argued, had not had to generalize a case for their own defence because they had been allowed to cultivate their pursuits. 'The intelligentsia of Other Countries have been more fortunate. They have been able to fight their battles with more *panache* and more appeal to Universals because they have managed to preserve Holy Church as a foil to this day.'[10] Thompson here ironizes his antagonists' habitually tendentious construal of this contrast (which may be seen as yet another form of what I earlier characterized as 'Dreyfus envy') but without actually repudiating the underlying historical assumptions on which it rests, and in this the passage is representative of a certain tonal unsteadiness which recurs throughout his essay.

By contrast, Anderson and his associates had not at this date, as Anderson himself later admitted, been much inclined to

> delve into the native past for a more progressive or alternative tradition to counter-pose to the official celebrations of English cultural empiricism and political constitutionalism. For us, the central historical fact which such enterprises always seemed designed to burke or minimize was the failure of British society to generate any mass socialist movement or significant revolutionary party in the twentieth century—alone among major nations in Europe.[11]

'Alone among major nations in Europe': Anderson wanted to condemn precisely what the Whig tradition had celebrated, but in a curious way his account extended the cherished tendency to exaggerate the ways in which Britain stood apart from other countries in Europe rather than drawing attention to how much it, increasingly, had in common with them. And as I have already suggested, this tendency is particularly visible in discussions of the question of intellectuals, discussions which have often functioned as a kind of metonymic place-holder for larger preoccupations about British 'exceptionalism'.

II

Whatever the wider ramifications of this analysis, there can be no doubt that as far as the topic of intellectuals is concerned the key document was Anderson's celebrated essay 'The components of the national culture', first published in 1968. Its impact is not hard to understand: quite apart from the matter of its timing, the essay itself is a bravura performance, brilliantly suggestive and high-handedly schematic in almost equal measure. Any inclination one may now have to regard it indulgently as a youthful *jeu d'esprit* is countermanded not just by its continuing scholarly authority, but by Anderson's own reaffirmation of its claims, albeit chastened by the experience of the intervening decades, in its most recently reprinted form.[12]

In reconsidering Anderson's essay here, it may be helpful to recall three general features of its argument that are not always properly acknowledged. First, and most importantly, we have to recognize that its only partly explicit starting-point remained the assumption that the British case is 'aberrant' when measured against some (Marxist) historiographical norm. Secondly, for all its impressive range, its substance was strikingly academic: 'the culture' was conceived in terms of its constituent 'disciplines' and was explicitly confined to 'the human and social sciences'. Thirdly, it is very noticeable now what a structuralist analysis it was. Anderson was charting 'the geography' of the disciplines, the 'ground-plan of their distribution': spatial metaphors played a large part in his argument, above all the notion of the 'absent centre'.[13]

Anderson's most celebrated explicit claim was that what was 'missing' in Britain was 'the discourse of totality', that is, any attempt to theorize the society as a whole: on this view, the conspicuous absentees in British intellectual culture were Marxism and sociology. A (rather sketchy) historical explanation for this lack was given in terms of the fact that the 'bourgeoisie' had never overtly challenged the aristocratic hold on state and society and so had in turn never been 'forced' to produce an 'official justification of the Victorian social system'. But embedded in this implicitly counterfactual argument was another about the 'failure' of a 'dissident intelligentsia' to develop. And the 'dissidence' is crucial, since Anderson seems at various points to allow that there was some form of intelligentsia (at least if that term is not being used any more demandingly than as a collective plural of 'intellectuals'), as for example when he refers to 'the predominance of literary over visual values in the intelligentsia described by Annan' in the latter's 'intellectual aristocracy' essay.

Some later scholars who have explicitly addressed these issues within the terms set out by Anderson's essay have tended to conflate the 'absence of sociology' thesis with the 'absence of intellectuals' thesis, but that in fact was not the logic of Anderson's original argument. The nub of his actual claim is that no sociological theory developed in Britain because 'the dominant class and its intellectuals' were never really challenged and so never had to formulate a general theory in defence. The kind of challenge he has in mind is pretty clearly that from a 'revolutionary' working-class movement, which would have been furnished with a critical (essentially Marxist) theory of British society by *its* intellectuals. So, sociology is not being regarded as the product of 'dissident' intellectuals but of 'hegemonic' intellectuals (the presence of a Gramscian classification is intermittently visible in the essay). Such hegemonic intellectuals, the essay repeatedly indicates, existed, but were allowed to be as it were indolent or uncreative, because not provoked into a 'defence' of their society. As far as sociological theory goes, their 'failure' is, as his examples reiterate, a failure to be Durkheim or Weber. The use of a counterfactual of this specificity in comparative historical analysis is always fraught with difficulties,[14] but we should at least recognize that the differences between, say, Durkheim and Hobhouse are here supposed to be ultimately explicable in terms of the degree of theoretical and political 'challenge' they respectively had to respond to.

The other claim for which Anderson's essay is well known is his 'white emigration' thesis. He asserted that the great change that had happened by the middle of the twentieth century was that 'the phalanx of local intellectuals portrayed by Annan has been eclipsed. In this intensely provincial society, foreigners suddenly become omnipresent.'[15] It may be proper and charitable to treat this as a piece of symbolism or as a witty aperçu; as any kind of history, its methodological shortcomings are striking. It is described as 'white' emigration because its informing impulse was supposed to be counter-revolutionary: it was largely made up of intellectuals from Austria and central Europe who were seeking to escape social upheavals by identifying with a famously stable society. The contrast is with a 'red' emigration, principally represented by German intellectuals, such as the members of the Frankfurt School, or others who remained committed to the *critical* analysis of their host societies (a familiar binary polarity of another kind lurks here). But Anderson does not distinguish between those who were refugees from persecution by the Right rather than upheaval from the Left (nor between Jews and non-Jews), nor does he distinguish the age at which they left their native countries—those who left as young children surely stood in a different relation to the culture of origin compared to those who had already experienced a political and intellectual life there. His account tended to exaggerate the determining power of the native culture, but only when it suited his case: for example, he alleged an 'elective affinity to English modes of thought and political outlook' in those formed by 'the parish-pump positivism of inter-bellum Vienna', an insinuation which may be convenient when discussing, say, Karl Popper, but would be rather less so if discussing, say, Eric Hobsbawm.

Again, one has to recognize that these European émigrés do not constitute the missing 'dissident intelligentsia', as casual references to Anderson's essay sometimes appear to assume: they are, rather, presented as the functional equivalents and successors to the traditional, 'hegemonic', intellectual aristocracy. But, tantalizingly, Anderson does not treat British culture as entirely incapable of producing 'a dissident intelligentsia'. In fact, he suggests that there were 'two moments in English cultural history' when it seemed that such a stratum might have 'emerged', the 1890s and the 1930s, but 'both were snapped off before they had time to develop'. Again, the suggested historical explanation is highly schematic. For example, the 1890s was 'when bohemianism as a significant phenomenon finally arrived in England—sixty years after its advent in Paris'. But the conjunction of such events as Beardsley's death and the outbreak of the Boer War 'dealt . . . summarily with this revolt', and 'Mafeking submerged the memory of the nineties'. Even leaving aside the implicit teleology which can find in a few green carnations the first signs of the sprouting of an 'intelligentsia', it is hard not to be struck by the wilful holism which sees in the public reaction to the relief of Mafeking an event which is somehow on the same plane of cultural action as the publication of *The Yellow Book*. In any event, the outcome was again an absence: 'In 1900, the harmony between the hegemonic class and its intellectuals was virtually complete. . . . There was no separate intelligentsia.'[16] But here we need to probe a little more just what this intelligentsia was supposed to be dissident about or separate from.

'Dissident', as used here, presupposes the existence of a dominant consensus: it is not so easy to say who should be regarded as 'dissident' if one assumes instead that in any complex culture there will be a whole series of cross-cutting conflicts, disagreements, criticisms. In practice, it also assumes that the consensus will, ipso facto, be politically conservative and the 'dissidents' radical, though again this threatens to conflate forms and levels of difference: in Britain in the late 1940s, as I mentioned earlier, it was figures such as Eliot and Oakeshott who saw themselves as opposing a dominant consensus, but they do not thereby become properly 'dissident' in Anderson's terms. However, it is not just a matter of political or intellectual convictions: not having too close a *social* connection with the governing classes also seems to be a minimum requirement. For example, Anderson returned to Annan's essay to observe that 'many of the intellectuals he discusses were based in Cambridge, then dominated by the grey and ponderous figure of Henry Sidgwick (brother-in-law, needless to say, of Prime Minister Balfour)'. The sneer has a legitimate place in polemic, of course, but perhaps one is not being too priggishly resistant to its playful use by remarking that it is carrying a little too much explanatory weight here. After all, Sidgwick's almost exact contemporary, William Morris, was the son of one of the 250 wealthiest men in England (on Anderson's own much later reckoning),[17] but in his case no one is tempted to read off a lack of dissidence from social position. The well-connected and ever-judicious (but far less well-off) Sidgwick might seem an obvious candidate for the role of *bête grise*, and there was certainly little danger of his death in 1900 being seen as the event which prematurely 'snapped off' the beginnings of a 'dissident intelligentsia' in the 1890s. But even so, his part in shaping the structural relation of intellectuals to British society may not be as simple as Anderson's sideswipe suggests. In practice he was the chief moving spirit in the discussions that led to the founding of the British Academy, officially established in 1901, and although that body has hardly been distinguished by its political or social 'dissidence', its establishment did mark, symbolically as much as actually, a significant step towards the assertion by an intellectual or scholarly stratum of a certain kind of autonomy for itself.[18] Since much recent French scholarship has tended to regard this as an essential precondition for the development of the self-conscious identity of 'the intellectuals' at the beginning of the twentieth century, Anderson's example here risks rebounding on him.

Throughout, Anderson used the phrase 'English intellectuals' very freely, and Annan's essay was his chief acknowledged source when speaking of the nineteenth and early twentieth centuries. (In passing one has to remark how *marxisant* commentators in Britain have simply loved that essay, to which they have imputed an explanatory power in the intellectual sphere akin to that provided by conspiracy theory in the political sphere.) But as Anderson's analysis proceeds, quite what was supposed to be distinctive about the position, or absence, of intellectuals in Britain starts to get blurred. For example, he fairly and generously acknowledges Keynes's stature, but in doing so also concedes that even the aberrant social formation of British society could produce 'genuine' intellectuals. Not only was Keynes's 'theoretical system . . . validated practically', but he 'never hesitated to pronounce outside his subject. . . . He was an intellectual in a classical tradition.' This is a revealing characterization, since we seem for the moment to have left behind questions of dissidence and to be focusing instead on what I have identified as the constitutive logic of the intellectual in the cultural sense, in Keynes's case the movement between the development of his 'theoretical system' and the activity of 'pronouncing outside his subject'. Keynes earns further commendation for the fact that he 'never became a fanatical advocate' of his own society, and so he could be endorsed for remaining 'critical', the hallmark of the 'true' intellectual.[19] 'Fanatical' here is self-defeatingly slack: if not being a 'fanatical advocate' of their society is what constitutes being 'critical', then few English writers or scholars in the twentieth century could be excluded from the ranks of 'true' intellectuals. Nonetheless, Keynes's only failing at this point as a model English intellectual appeared to be that he was, as he famously observed we would all be in the long run, dead.

In 1968 no such disability attended Anderson's other example of a 'genuine' English intellectual, namely F. R. Leavis. Leavis partly earned Anderson's approval because he mounted his criticism of mass society with 'a violent zeal and fury' which 'defie[d] every convention of the British intelligentsia'. Intellectual decorum was apparently as damning as social connection as far as constituting a true intelligentsia was concerned. But it was two other (alleged) characteristics that caused Leavis to be singled out at this point. First, he 'is the only intellectual in this survey to have been significantly affected by Marxism'. And second, 'alone of the thinkers in this survey, he felt acutely aware that something had gone wrong in British culture'.[20] Considered historically, these are extraordinary claims: it is only the circularity of the protective clause 'in this survey' that allows them to be put forward at all, and even then one might want to murmur Laski at the first clause and Tawney at the second, to take only the most obvious examples. Casting the net more widely, the arbitrariness of these claims becomes more pressingly apparent: after all, the number of prominent social critics who, like Leavis, felt that industrialism and 'mass society' were what had 'gone wrong' in British culture were legion. Still, in these few remarks, we see the germ of much subsequent discussion of Leavis and *Scrutiny* by such New Left-indebted scholars as Mulhern, Eagleton, and Baldick, among whom the *Scrutiny* group even came to figure as an English equivalent of the Frankfurt School in its preoccupation with the deadening effects of mass culture; indeed, the major monographic study by Mulhern published in 1979 was to conclude that the Leavisites had constituted precisely the kind of 'radical, dissident intelligentsia' normally taken to be absent in Britain.[21] It is notable that at this point

Leavis's lifelong connection with what in other contexts Anderson would stigmatize as one of the 'governing class's elite educational institutions' is not, unlike Sidgwick's, held against him (that connection was, of course, in part a self-consciously antagonistic one, but in practice Leavis well understood the importance of his Cambridge base to his career and his influence). Needless to add, Leavis fell far short of the ideal, above all because, hampered by his supposed 'empiricism', he was unable to develop a sophisticated *theoretical* critique of his own society. But he was at least 'oppositional': 'Leavis correctly sensed a cultural landscape of much mediocrity and conformity'.[22]

In some ways, Anderson's essay has to be seen as a cry of pain: its prose expresses a reaction, at times vengeful, at times despairing, frequently acerbic, to what many of his generation experienced as the coercive empiricism and stifling 'normality' of the 1950s. On those grounds alone, it surely deserved its subsequent celebrity. But I would suggest that with the passage of time it has become clearer that the chief limitation of Anderson's early work on this topic was that he wrote as a theorist who overestimates the *historical role* of theories, partly because he is so responsive to their intrinsic interest. His conception of 'a culture' is, in practice, framed too exclusively in terms of the Big Names, and the Big Names are confined too exclusively to those who made some original or striking *conceptual* contribution.[23] It is certainly a virtue of his essay that he is interested in the work of such Big Names across a wide range of disciplines and in their synchronic structural relations as well as their diachronic succession. But his is the makeshift intellectual history that always results from arranging a group of 'classic texts' in a satisfying pattern; the thick texture of intellectual life in any given period, as well as the sheer variety of figures, arguments, and issues, are eliminated from the stark geometry of Anderson's 'structure of a culture'. Moreover, his emphasis falls too purely on the *content* of his chosen figures' ideas: we get little or nothing about such figures' roles and styles of performance, about their audiences and modes of address, about the debates they were involved in or the uses to which they were put, about the different levels of abstraction and sophistication at which a 'culture' operates, and so on. In this respect, the essay is premised on an oddly intellectualist mode of explanation. Despite his avowed commitment to sociological analysis, indeed Marxist analysis, Anderson's was in many ways still a Great Man theory of intellectual history.

Paradoxically, perhaps, given its materialist premises, the *NLR* frame of reference directed *more* attention to intellectuals than did other, ostensibly more 'idealist', styles of discourse. It is evident that Anderson himself has always been drawn, perhaps increasingly drawn, to the critical analysis of theories, ideas, large bodies of intellectual or scholarly work more generally; we might also remark that Thompson's first major book was on Morris and his last on Blake. The question of how to *be* an intellectual in what was perceived as an unsympathetic cultural setting had particular existential force, and it was bound to exercise other writers in this milieu shaped by Marxist, and sometimes Leninist, theory. And we should recognize, too, that these writers shared a larger aspiration to replace the familiar, everyday language of social description with a more abstracted, estranging vocabulary: such defamiliarizing and reclassifying is at the heart of the project of 'critique', and their use of the category of 'intellectuals' was part of this purpose. In mid-twentieth-century England, to speak of 'novelists' or of 'dons' was to rest content with the familiar, concrete terms of everyday social description. The *marxisant* use of 'intellectuals', by contrast, achieved what might be called 'the theory effect', calling up a language of systematic social analysis that reveals the 'objective', functional role of familiar occupations and activities.

As I have already remarked, the ostensibly comparative frame of reference of the *NLR* analysis tended in practice to encourage a restatement of the traditional story of British exceptionalism. A good example of how this general line of analysis could be given a paradoxical twist without losing its insistence on the 'pathological' nature of the British situation was provided by Tom Nairn's characteristically provocative essay, 'The English literary intelligentsia', first published in 1977.[24] Nairn begins with an apparently familiar lament about the lack of an intelligentsia in England, but then proceeds to argue that this 'very low profile is deceptive.... To the absence of a prominent "intelligentsia" there corresponds in fact, a singular and powerful presence of intellectuals in the social fabric.' The terms are nowhere defined; the context suggests he is working with a mixture of the sociological and cultural senses of the term 'intellectual'. He sees the role of these intellectuals as wholly conservative: they engage in a form of myth-making which invests imaginative literature with a unique power to apprehend and transmit the essential values of the society while at the same time they resist casting these values into explicitly theoretical terms. This leads him to put forward the striking claim cited in part as the epigraph to Ch. 7: 'In summary: there is an intelligentsia in England, more embedded in and dispersed throughout the social body than usual ... it is doubtful if any intellectual class, anywhere, has ever had more natural authority and easy power.'[25] Before our very eyes, the absence-thesis removes its false beard and stands revealed as its opposite, the little-known Peculiar-Strength-of-Intellectuals-in-Britain thesis. But there are already hints that all may not be as it seems: perhaps having 'natural authority' and 'easy power' are not the attributes of 'true' intellectuals; perhaps the pathology, described in other terms, remains.

And so it proves. In keeping with the broad lineaments of the *NLR* analysis, Nairn traces the peculiar condition of British society back to the absence of an 'authentic' bourgeois revolution, and to the adaptive but essentially conservative response to the twin 'threats' of revolution and industrialism in the early nineteenth century. The ensuing 'ideological work of reaction' was carried on in terms of a romantic, anti-rationalist perspective, and this was alleged to account for 'the particularly large and functional role of the intellectual class in subsequent development'. This is presented as the English ideology, 'romantic-national conservatism ... This peculiar romantic traditionalism *does* fit a separate mode of social evolution, an entry into the modern world which is somewhat different from the developments that became typical.' One cannot help wondering whether this rather sketchily characterized 'romantic-national conservatism' was so uniquely British: it can seem a disturbingly apt label for the dominant cultural tradition in, for example, nineteenth- and early twentieth-century Germany.[26] But the disaggregating effect of paying attention to the diversity of European history would risk losing the informing contrast between the 'typical' and the deviant. And it hardly needs saying that the standard contrast brings in its train immediately recognizable elements: 'So, the weakness and retardation of both Marxism and modern social theory in England were inevitable.'[27]

Another deeply familiar element in Nairn's case emerges in the claim that a key difference between Britain and the rest of Europe was traceable to the fact that the former 'underproduced' intellectuals, but 'overemployed' them. One soon realizes that this is the old Tocquevillian contention: in Britain the intellectuals are involved in making practical decisions, therefore they are not given to the elaboration of their impotent discontent into utopian theories of revolution; Nairn rephrases this, changing the plus sign to a minus along the way. But there are, at last, indications of a New Dawn: 'Rash State-sponsored reforms of Higher Education, in the context of steeper economic decline, have produced something more like the detached and restive intelligentsia of other nations'. This is evidently no moment to be wondering whether one does in fact find 'a detached and restive intelligentsia' in, say, Norway: it is a moment for looking forward to a new era 'by throwing off the suffocating mantle of the English Ideology once and for all'.[28]

In so much of this literature there is a note of muffled rage, a despairing frustration at what is seen as the continuing capacity of British culture to remain 'untheorized' and thereby to 'defeat reason'. Nairn's brisk formulation is representative: 'Sufficient original effort in the theoretical field could undoubtedly solve the problem; but that effort has not in fact been made.'[29] He does not explain why the workers in the theoretical field have hitherto spent their time idling in the long grass, though it sounds as though the new gaffer will sort that out. For all the genuine impulse to wide-ranging comparative analysis which this body of literature provided, it can be profoundly inattentive to the actual details of British intellectual life, content to trade in characterizations that are so broad-brush as to be almost indistinguishable from cliché. Nairn's is one of the liveliest and most amusing contributions to this literature, but one is bound to remark the by now repetitive features: the citing of Annan's already classic piece, the focusing on Leavis as both lost leader and chief villain, the sideswipes at analytical philosophy, and so on. A tradition requires more than repetition for its successful continuance, but repetition undeniably helps give the tradition's precepts an air of self-evidence.

Looking back on his and his *NLR* colleagues' essays of the 1960s more than two decades later, Anderson had to acknowledge that 'tacitly . . . British history and society were analysed as exceptional against an unspoken background of what was taken as typical, derived from French experience'.[30] As I have suggested, this was true not only for what constituted a proper bourgeois democratic revolution, but also for what constituted a properly separate and critical intellectual class. Following the impact of these essays on both Marxist and non-Marxist alike, the whole topic was, perhaps more than ever, defined in terms of a contrast with (an idealized conception of) the French case.

III

One of the most characteristic activities of intellectuals is to engage in debate with each other over the status and role of intellectuals in their society. Britain has had, as my examples up to this point will have indicated, a rich tradition of such debate, one of the recurring motifs of which has been meditations on why, allegedly, Britain has had so little of such debate. The impact of the style of analysis I have just been examining, though ultimately substantial, was both gradual and partly absorbed into or countered by idioms and concerns with deeper roots in British culture. To illustrate this complex layering of a culture, I want now to look at some discussions of the question of intellectuals which were roughly contemporaneous with the *NLR* accounts, but far removed from them in tone and substance.

If one had to imagine the conjunction of speaker, topic, and medium which would best represent this sort of discussion in the two or three decades after 1945, then the hypothetical occasion one would be most likely to construct would involve that prince among speakers (as well as 'prince among intellectuals' as his obituary was to be headed), Isaiah Berlin, addressing that most frequently roasted of old chestnuts, 'the role of the intelligentsia', on that most unapologetically 'highbrow' medium, the Third Programme. In fact, there is no need to construct it since precisely this totemic conjunction occurred in the spring of 1968 (and the text, or at least *a* text, was printed in *The Listener* to prove it).[31] Berlin used his knowledge of Russian culture to anchor the term firmly to its Russian origins. He emphasized the sense of obligation felt by the small stratum of educated Russians in the mid- and late nineteenth century to bring enlightenment to their impoverished, benighted, priest-ridden land. 'This is the kind of phenomenon which, it seems to me, tends to occur in large, socially and economically backward communities, run by an incompetent government and an ignorant and oppressive Church.' And he attempted to make the reference of the term more specific still (and thus, one senses, to try to disqualify it for general use in English) by emphasizing that it did not encompass the whole of the educated class even in Russia: 'the real members of the intelligentsia were the political pamphleteers, the civic-minded poets, the forerunners of the Russian Revolution—mainly journalists and political thinkers who quite consciously used literature, sometimes very poor examples of it, as vehicles of social protest'.[32]

Indeed, Berlin was at pains to circumscribe the term's use more exactly still: it 'does not just mean intellectuals or artists as such; and it certainly does not mean educated persons as such', nor 'does it mean sheer opposition to the Establishment as such'. It specifically involved the belief in science, reason, progress against the overwhelming mass of custom, superstition, and repressive authority. A genuine intelligentsia in this sense 'is generated by truly oppressive regimes', and so there was no question of its members being integrated in or at ease with such a society: 'To the old nineteenth-century intelligentsia the very notion of a class of persons involved in intellectual pursuits—such as professors, doctors, engineers, experts, writers, who in other respects live ordinary bourgeois lives, and hold conventional views, and who play golf or even cricket—this notion would have been absolutely horrifying' ('even' cricket may be expressive of Berlin's characteristic combination of intimacy with, yet distance from, English society). Whatever the faults of government and society in Britain, Berlin contended, no one could plausibly see it as a backward society with a monolithic, authoritarian regime of this sort, 'and that is why one cannot, if the valuable use of the term is not to be hopelessly diluted, really speak of an English intelligentsia', even though 'one can speak of English intellectuals'. Berlin was, implicitly, responding to just such loose usage of the term, but he insisted that his sketch of the contours of its meaning was not an exercise in pedantry: 'Central notions, even labels, which have played a part in human history have some claim to have their integrity respected.'[33]

As an attempt to educate his listeners about the historical circumstances in which the term 'intelligentsia' first arose, the talk is a good example of the kind of *haute vulgarisation* which Berlin did so well. But as an attempt to keep the English usage of the term to this historically accurate sense, it was mere spitting into the wind. This was illustrated with almost vengeful immediacy by the next talk in the series by the sociologist Peter Nettl, entitled 'Are intellectuals obsolete?' (the lexicon of titles for such talks and articles is, it would seem, a painfully limited one). Nettl, as befitted his trade, emphasized that to be an intellectual was to occupy a role: 'the word "role" is crucial, for it is not something innate, a part of one's personality or appearance, but rather a social position, or place in a hierarchy of such positions, which others ascribe to one. So that one cannot decide by oneself to be an intellectual, but has to be regarded or accepted as one.' This elucidation (essentially of what I am calling the 'cultural' sense of the term) was a promising beginning, but Nettl goes on merely to make it the first step in yet another formulation of the 'absence thesis':

> Today, intellectuals in England just don't have the same clearly visible role as in many European countries. It is often said that England does not have intellectuals, that it is an unintellectual country. I think that's a misunderstanding, for we do have plenty of people who act, write, and think as intellectuals, who have that type of personality. What we lack is the social role—at least since Bernard Shaw and the Fabians before 1914.[34]

This raises the intriguing possibility that the absence of this role is not a long-standing feature of British society, but something relatively recent, something lost or mislaid since the First World War. But if 'we' do have people who 'act' as intellectuals, it is not altogether clear what aspect of the role is missing; the implication may be that people are not recognizing British intellectuals *as* intellectuals, in which case the absence thesis seems to operate in an inviolably self-confirming way. There is nothing very surprising in the fact that the Fabians are yet again called upon to play the part of representative British intellectuals, but it is hard to see quite what role Nettl thought they had played before 1914 that they had ceased to play since. In practice, as later historians have shown, there was considerable ignorance about the actual role of the Fabian Society in British politics, to the point where a kind of folk-myth had developed around it, and Nettl may simply be following one standard version of that myth in regarding the pre-1914 Fabians as 'oppositional', but their successors as too close to power (though talk of 'successors' disguises the fact that Shaw and the Webbs remained active, even dominant, in the Society well into the inter-war period). To illustrate the counter-case, where intellectuals occupied a socially recognized 'oppositional' role, he turns to the predictable figure of Sartre. We are back on deeply familiar territory.

In this talk, Nettl is using the term 'intellectual' to refer to those who have achieved this kind of cultural leadership, and he draws a contrast between this and the broader sense by taking issue with T. R. Fyvel's *Intellectuals Today*, published earlier that year (another example of the topicality of the subject). Fyvel chiefly used the term in the 'sociological' sense: 'as a professional term for the strata of higher academics, scientists, and teachers, researchers and top administrators, writers, broadcasters and other communicators and especially the young emerging as a new technical intelligentsia'.[35] (Nettl made it seem as though this was the only sense in which Fyvel had used the term, though in fact Fyvel called this the 'general' sense, and contrasted it with a 'narrow' sense in which 'an intellectual is a person who is fascinated by general ideas and wants them to be as interesting and influential as possible', i.e. more or less what I am terming the 'subjective' sense.[36]) In any event, Nettl, unlike Berlin but in line with much contemporary English usage, referred to this broader class as 'the intelligentsia', reserving 'intellectual' for those who had achieved a certain position of cultural leadership. He was thus able to complain of Fyvel's book, perfectly justly, that its subjects were a random collection of young professional people, not distinguished by their public standing: 'What Mr Fyvel has given us is no more than the views of clever and educated people in very different walks of life on various problems about which they speak with little or no specific authority.' Nettl contrasts this with a recent work in German whose author 'has no hesitation in defining an intellectual not according to his profession but as someone who has the capacity to make himself heard.' He went on to make some astute observations about social change in modern society, especially on the break-up of a single dominant 'high' culture; 'No longer can anyone expect to speak to everyone that matters.' Academic work, too, he noted, is becoming more specialized; it is becoming harder for anyone to speak in universals; there is a growth of technical skills so that the intellectuals will more and more become merely part of a large technical intelligentsia and lose their old critical or prophetic function.[37] It is hard not to feel that we have been here before; they did exist once, they do exist elsewhere, they will soon disappear . . .

In a talk broadcast the following week, Graham Hough addressed the theme of intellectuals from yet another angle. (There may not be many topics on which a succession of talks would be so much taken up with matters of definition, each using the same term in a recognizable but significantly different sense.) Hough began by referring back to the talks by Berlin and Nettl, indicating that he shared the former's more restrictive sense of the term 'intelligentsia' and concurred in the claim that Britain had never had an intelligentsia in this sense. 'I am beginning to wonder, however, whether it is still true that we do not need one.' Hough, that is to say, accepted that British social experience in the nineteenth century had been different from that of most other major European societies. Elsewhere, the intellectual saw himself as having an oppositional role in a way that was not true in Britain: the edge of criticism may have been blunted as a result, but whatever the limitations of the writers and critics of Victorian society, they 'were at least capable of fusing their intellectual activity with the general activity of the world in which they lived'. It was precisely this which Hough felt was no longer possible: intellectual activity seemed to have become more and more a profession or merely a job, disconnected from the life around it (he implied that the preponderant weight of American academia was partly to blame for this). And he suggested that this was somehow linked to the relative lack of protest against the recent follies of the British government, above all that of supporting the USA in Vietnam: compartmentalization had surely gone too far.

> One way out of the impasse would be for those who constitute the raw material of an English intelligentsia to accept their role: to abandon the status of Arnoldian defenders of culture, to accept the distortions and special pleadings that would certainly be involved in any attempt to make the past genuinely available to the present: to accept their role, in fact, as Sartre has accepted it in his brilliant and polemical literary studies.[38]

Hough's is a curious, slightly rambling piece (as he half admits at one point), but it is revealing of an unease felt by someone by no means in the forefront of contemporary radicalism. He was in effect calling upon British intellectuals to accept the compromises and approximations inevitably involved in trying to make their authority tell in public debate. (Hough taught English at Cambridge, having survived being a Japanese prisoner during the Second World War, an experience which appears to have coloured his fierce opposition to the Vietnam War.) His slighting reference to the 'Arnoldian defenders of culture' may partly have reflected the fact that he was a strong anti-Leavisite, but it was principally a plea for intellectuals to be willing to get their hands dirty. His gloss on Sartre's role, however, suggests that Hough was also hankering after a kind of politically committed theoretical work, felt to be absent from British public life, in a manner not altogether unlike Iris Murdoch's in the essay discussed at the end of Ch. 7.

Still less in the forefront of contemporary radicalism at this date (to put it mildly) was Donald Davie, a member, or at least associate, of the coolly iconoclastic 'Movement' group of writers in the mid-1950s, but by the end of the 1960s well on his way to becoming a gruff, curmudgeonly cultural pessimist. In an article in *Encounter* the following year under the established rubric 'Authors and Critics', Davie enacted the much-remarked intimacy of British intellectual life by structuring, if that's not too strong a word, his article around recent comments in *Encounter* on intellectuals by his friend and fellow Movement author Kingsley Amis, and around the earlier talks by Berlin and Hough. The *leitmotif* of Davie's *causerie* was that British society tolerated, indeed nurtured, Antigone-figures, but tended to repudiate Creon-figures and to neglect Ismene-figures: or in other words, it was excessively indulgent towards moralistic critics, with the result that 'the British intelligentsia has virtually no right wing at all . . . the British intelligentsia is a left-wing intelligentsia'. In a move characteristic of the intra-tribal spats so common among commentators on this question, he therefore repudiated Hough's call for British intellectuals to become more politically engaged: 'not only does Britain have, in this deplorable sense, an intelligentsia; it has had one for a long time, at least thirty years'. This would seem to accept the identification of left-wing writers in the1930s as Britain's first 'real' intelligentsia, a common piece of chronology. To the grumpy Davie, this merely revealed that Hough and his ilk accepted that 'intellectuals have a right to be politically irresponsible. As an intellectual myself, I have never understood why any society should be expected to recognize that right, or be reproached for not conceding it.'[39] This is a relatively rare piece of public self-description, the more striking for coming from someone who would have been identified at the time as a man of the Right.

Davie went on to take issue with Berlin, too: he construed Berlin to be arguing that 'British intellectuals have not earned, and cannot claim, the right to that privileged irresponsibility which the Russian intelligentsia could justly claim.' But in reality, Davie counters, 'Britain surely has an intelligentsia in the sense of a body of educated persons who demand and act upon the right to be politically irresponsible', and indeed British society actively 'encourages its intelligentsia and rewards it'.[40] It has to be remembered that Davie, Professor of Literature and Dean of the School of Comparative Studies at the University of Essex, had first-hand experience of what he saw as the costs of such 'political irresponsibility' when trying to confront student 'militants' the previous year. But for present purposes, the interest of his piece lies chiefly in what amounts to its reversal of the absence thesis. Davie takes for granted that there are intellectuals in Britain, and he uses 'intelligentsia' to stigmatize just that kind of collective, public position-taking by intellectuals usually presumed to be 'missing'. In his irritably conservative account, Britain has been peculiarly indulgent to the Antigone-figures, peculiarly lacking in those willing to exercise lawful authority, and still more lacking in those willing to defend its exercise. Thus, when viewed from the wrong side of the barricades in the late 1960s, Britain could be represented as a society which was distinguished by exceptional hospitality to its radical intelligentsia.

One further feature of this short sequence of essays should be remarked here: all four are by academics, yet all four appeared in media aimed at a broader, non-specialist public. In this respect, the essays themselves figure the movement or tension at the heart of the role of the intellectual in the cultural sense. Such media as *Encounter* or the Third Programme occupied that space between technical specialism at one extreme and mass market at the other, a space naturally adapted to raising the question of intellectuals precisely because movement to and fro across that space constituted the role in question. Obviously, features of these particular media reflected the distinctive cultural configuration of that period, but it is always important to distinguish between such period-specific features and the structural characteristics of the space those media define. It is the mistake of cultural pessimists in each generation to confound mutation in the transient, local features with the disappearance or terminal contraction of the space itself.

IV

New Left Review was both a symptom and a cause of changes in the idiom and concerns of British intellectual life in the second half of the twentieth century, changes whose beginnings can be dated to the 1960s and 1970s. Social and cultural historians have abundantly documented many of the underlying shifts in British society: one of the most relevant here is the expansion of higher education. In 1939 there were approximately 50,000 students in higher education in Britain; by 1960 this had doubled to about 100,000; but by 1988 the figure had reached 580,000, and by the end of the century almost one million. There was a corresponding, though far from matching, increase in the number of academics, and the existence of this very large number of teachers, students, and former students created what I have elsewhere termed 'the academic public sphere', a discursive space within which discussion of the question of intellectuals was naturally to flourish.[41]

The exploration and dissemination of ideas derived from the European Marxist tradition was one obvious intellectual component of this development. It had, of course, been something of a (dubious) commonplace that Marxist theory had never really flourished in Britain, but, reviewing the changes that had taken place in the 1970s and 1980s, Perry Anderson remarked in 1990 upon the growth of a new 'radical public sphere' whose 'dominant temper was pervasively, if never rigidly or exclusively, Marxist; and whose influence stretched from slowly increasing positions in colleges and universities and an intermittent presence in the national media, through a numerous undergrowth of its own periodicals and associations, across to allied strands in the performing arts and metropolitan counter-culture'.[42] Less optimistically, Alan Swingewood also commented on the existence by the 1980s of a 'shallow' Marxist subculture in Britain, not organically connected to working-class culture or the political expressions of organized labour, but confined to academics, students, 'and a marginalized radical intelligentsia working within state institutions, local government and the mass media'.[43] The wider reception of diluted versions of this body of thought helped further to domesticate the usage of 'intellectuals', even when the analyses within which such references appeared continued to report the rarity of the species in Britain.

Few figures were as representative of, or as celebrated in, this 'radical public sphere' as Raymond Williams. Writing for a non-specialist audience in 1983, he began, almost inevitably, with the matter of terminology:

> There must be scores of thousands of intellectuals in Britain, yet there are comparatively few who are prepared to admit it. The standard terms of modern analysis are known in English, but are in general disliked and quite often rejected. Thus there are 'educated people', by contrast with the majority, a century after universal education. There are 'learned and scholarly professions'. There is even a 'cultivated minority'. But 'intellectuals', or, worse, 'an intelligentsia': on the whole, no thanks.

Williams linked this historical repudiation of the idea of the intellectual to a cultural resistance to acknowledging the realm of 'general discussion', as opposed to a series of discrete specialisms. There has been no shortage of high-quality intellectual work in British culture, he argued, but 'resistance to an idea of intellectuals was precisely a resistance to the essentially general and critical forms of thought'. (This theme had deep roots within Williams's own work: his identification of 'the culture-and-society tradition' twenty-five years earlier was in effect a marshalling of those predecessors who had attempted to elaborate some form of 'general' perspective.) In focusing on (in my terms) the 'movement' between specialized and general perspectives, Williams accurately reflected what was coming, by this date, to be the accepted understanding of the term 'intellectuals'.

What, on the other hand, constrained his analysis was its reliance on a contrast with a monolithic 'dominant social order' which automatically reproduces itself unless challenged at the right level of abstraction by critical intellectuals. 'General' ideas surely do not stand in some kind of inherently antagonistic relation to a single 'social order': the latter is irreducibly plural, and general ideas are not necessarily to be found 'outside' it. Once again the pitfalls of binary thinking are threatening here. Where Williams seemed on stronger ground was in recognizing that even in Britain the resistance to the claims of general ideas has been only partially successful, and indeed that pressures from within ostensibly 'specialized' discourses has driven them to develop more general perspectives. The activity of the intellectual happens when specialisms 'converge' and scholars 'go beyond their particularities'. Williams was, as usual, programmatically optimistic on this count: 'The emergence of a self-conscious, quasi-American class of intellectuals, as distinct from the English model of local professionalism and general amateurism, is probably already in progress.' (It is interesting that the benchmark here is the USA rather than the usual European suspects.) 'I look for these signs not so much in conscious affiliations, as in moves that really do begin to take us beyond the culture as a congeries of specialisms.' But these changes were taking place 'behind the well-used screens of disparagement and deflection': the need, therefore, was to remove the screens and have the debate in the open. Throughout, the article was replete with the vocabulary of 'struggle', 'pressure', and 'crisis' with which Williams tended to overdramatize his analyses. Nonetheless, the piece was a good example of seriously educative journalism of a kind that ought to have made it harder to repeat the usual tired generalizations.[44]

However, the repetitiveness of the journalistic treatment of this subject remained very striking. Even Neal Ascherson, one of the most thoughtful and best informed of the host of 'commentators' spawned by weekend newspapers, stuttered between ambivalence and cliché when addressing the question of intellectuals. He began with the puzzled cry, 'What is it about the English and intellectuals?', and then went on to cite the latest example of what he called 'an old national riddle: an English intellectual is either not English or else, if his papers are invincibly in order, not an intellectual'. (Old Etonian Ascherson was at this time making much of his Scottish identity, which enabled him to write so quizzically about 'the English' with all the distance and authority of the 'outsider'.) He acknowledged the obvious truth that there are of course numerous intellectuals in England, and so he went on to ask 'What is this pretence that they are invisible—or impossible?' Having posed this very good question, his column, in a manner all too characteristic of the genre, then rather wandered off into a mixture of reminiscence, opinion, and phrase-making. But the thread, in so far as there was one, seemed to be that the English have not thought of themselves as needing the explicit elaboration of national identity which (it is assumed) is the defining task of the intellectual. But now that that identity can no longer be taken for granted, England needs its intellectuals to hold up a mirror in which it can see itself.

Clearly, a pretty narrow sense of what 'intellectuals' are or are for is at work here, but there is also the classic uncertainty about the question of their existence. England, it seems, does have intellectuals, but not, somehow, of the right sort. 'Victorian England was crowded with universal minds. But it did not evolve the European intellectual caste of the nineteenth century and our own times: the thinkers and bards as judges and tribunes of the nation, natural spokesmen for its aspirations.' Since it is not hard to think of a pretty long list of Victorian thinkers and writers who acted as 'judges and tribunes of the nation', Ascherson must have in mind something more specific, perhaps the condition of those central European peoples whose writers were supposed to be articulating a sense of national identity which had not yet achieved political form. This is the romantic ideal: nineteenth-century Ireland, say, can have intellectuals, but not nineteenth-century England. And here the ambivalence starts to flood through the veins of the argument: there is something dull about a country which has not suffered such extremes, some lack of attractive angst or self-scrutiny (though anyone who seriously thinks nineteenth- and twentieth-century England has been marked by a lack of self-scrutiny has simply not been listening). England has, undeniably, 'never known occupation or state terror'; this fact is then parlayed into the historical proposition that it is a 'country which has never feared the extinction of its language and culture, which sees no need for a lay priesthood of men and women to keep the candle of truth burning through dark times'. This, we are being 'reminded', is what 'real' intellectuals do: nothing like a spot of oppression to bring the intellectuals out of the closet. But, *pace* Ascherson, there are surely various gusts of hot air which can threaten to blow out 'the candle of truth': one task of intellectuals in England as elsewhere is to expose the way in which so much discussion of this topic is shot through with this kind of self-dramatizing longing for heroic possibilities.[45]

Another form of this longing can be illustrated from a brief article by the figure whom many regarded as Williams's natural successor within this 'radical public sphere'. In ostensibly discussing Yeats, Terry Eagleton, like so many English writers before him, used Ireland to project a fantasy of what the role of the intellectual ought to be like. Eagleton summarized what Yeats found 'was awry with English culture—empiricist, sentimental, moralistic, slavishly mimetic [this latter of the novel in particular]'. (One cannot help noticing that Yeats is here made to sound like a loyal contributor to *New Left Review* of the 1960s.) And these defects of the culture partly explain the situation which Eagleton finds so regrettable: that English intellectuals do not have available to them the kind of political role as a writer that Yeats occupied. 'It was Yeats's good fortune to have lived in a historical era—that of Irish nationalism—when it seemed possible to reinvent a public role for the poet.' Living in the era of Irish nationalism will not strike everyone as a persuasive example of 'good fortune', but it meets a need for one kind of 'public role'. And that role had to be 'reinvented' because, according to Eagleton, it had been taken for granted by Milton or Blake, but had got lost in Britain somewhere between Shelley and Tennyson. There is a nostalgic fantasy at work here which is, much though Eagleton would disown the comparison, functionally similar to Eliot's yearning for an undissociated sensibility or Leavis's for an organic community. It is also representative of the way in which Ireland has figured for some intellectuals in England as the repressed or unconscious of English life, where agreeably unruly passions, supposedly given no place in orderly England, can preen and strut in full public view.

More generally, there always risks being an element of self-justifying projection at work in these historical gambits: these fantasized other cultures are places where People Like Us are taken more seriously (Ireland, France, Eastern Europe, seventeenth-century England . . .). They are also haunted by a form of nostalgia for a simpler life, including a politically simpler life. But the yearning for simplicity in matters where simplicity is not naturally at home is always a pathology of the intellectual life, a weariness or desire to lay down the burden of potentially endless analysis and criticism, and to be rid of the unglamorous obligation to try to be realistic in identifying the lesser evil. Implicit in Eagleton's essay is the desire for a situation in which public attention is lavished on writers and critics qua writers and critics, but one in which at the same time the writers can feel that they are not being untrue to the demands of their calling if they indulge the gratification of letting out a few uncomplicated visceral battle-cries. It is no doubt common among intellectuals in many societies to feel a degree of distance from, and even hostility to, the possessing classes, the not-intellectuals, the bourgeoisie (to use the scorn-laden French term). But perhaps something particularly marked in Britain is a hostility towards what are alleged to be the *intellectual* traditions of the country, and one source of this has been a resentment that those traditions do not yield a more exciting or gratifying role for intellectuals.[46]

The impact of *marxisant* history and social theory did promote various forms of comparative analysis, even though some of these, as I observed earlier, were largely devoted to explaining Britain's 'deviation' from some presumed norm of capitalist development. Indirectly, this perspective did help to isolate that congeries of attitudes, values, symbols, and practices referred to as 'Englishness' as a subject ripe for critical scrutiny. In the 1980s and early 1990s there followed a minor boom in publications exploring the ways in which the constituent elements of this 'Englishness' have been cultivated and deployed, and even where such analyses have appeared reductively functionalist or historically insensitive, they have stimulated reflection upon the ways in which the different strands in still-enduring images of 'national identity' have been formed and perpetuated.[47] But by the same token, the very emphasis on the 'constructed', ideological nature of such images can encourage both an excessive holism in speaking of how 'a society' functions and also the imputation of sinister agency to an (implausibly unified and powerful) 'ruling class', 'bourgeois state', or similarly conceptualized entity.

One result of these critical, and at first largely academic, developments was that various frequently repeated claims about the nature of British culture were coming to be seen less as objective descriptions and more as elements in the tangled historical growth of those stories it has proved useful for a society to tell itself about itself. One reason why an analysis within a comparative framework of the place of intellectuals in Britain now appears so inviting is precisely because it has become easier in recent years to see the cliché about the absence of intellectuals in Britain as an element in just such an understanding of 'Englishness'.

For all the sophistication of the growing theoretical literature on the subject, in broader public usage in the later twentieth century 'intellectuals' has nonetheless remained one of those terms, like 'single mothers' or 'male ballet-dancers', that acts as a magnet around which social attitudes cluster. The term had, as we have seen, long been associated with gibes about being 'unworldly', 'ineffectual', 'pretentious', and so on. But the rightwards shift in politics and political discourse in the 1980s increased a tendency to use 'intellectuals' as a near-synonym for 'parasites', 'pensioners of the state', and so on. Potentially, deep issues were at stake here about a society's need (or not) for creators, thinkers, writers, and so on, including questions about how such people should be supported. But the polemics of the 1980s did not for the most part address these questions in any analytical or disinterested way. Rather, the topic was exploited opportunistically for political gain, especially as a way of denigrating many of the more articulate among those who were critical of the rapacity and greed of business and financial interests. 'Intellectuals' thus tended to be redescribed as an 'interest-group', whose vaunted commitment to free enquiry and disinterestedness was merely a cover for collective self-interest. In these polemics, an umbilical cord seemed to connect the noun 'intellectuals' and the phrase 'supported at taxpayers' expense'. In partisan terms, intellectuals therefore became stigmatized as simultaneously 'Left' and 'Establishment', forming a 'liberal consensus' against which those few courageous free spirits willing to defend rampant capitalism dared to speak out.

Writing on 'Mrs Thatcher and the intellectuals', the Oxford scholar Brian Harrison provided a dismaying example of this tactic of disparagement. Ostensibly, Harrison was writing as a disinterested professional historian rather than as a partisan, but his article was governed by his animus against what he saw as a slack and prejudiced hostility to Mrs Thatcher by the greater part of Britain's intellectuals. He did not work with any carefully analysed sense of the latter term: the requirement of a certain level of education and learning are mentioned, but so also is a 'lifestyle', a taste for talking about ideas. His narrative conforms to the David and Goliath model, with Mrs Thatcher at the head of 'a pioneering minority on the right' confronting the massed might of 'fashionable opinion'. Thus, the career of Sir Keith Joseph showed 'what a single courageous individual can do to open up tolerance', whereas 'universities were the last place where new ideas could be discussed'. Similarly, Mrs Thatcher herself is represented as a far more impressive intellectual figure than her critics allowed, able to 'recollect . . . her premiership in an autobiographical volume of formidable intellectual reach and grasp'. (Much nearer the mark, surely, was the observation, intended as part of a positive portrait, by her adviser Oliver Letwin, quoted by Harrison: 'She . . . has absolutely no interest in ideas for their own sake.') Harrison does not seem to countenance the possibility that opposition to Thatcher by intellectuals (or anyone else) might have been on grounds of rational dissent from her policies: it is either a snobbish response to matters of accent and appearance, or else 'vested interests were involved'. The cards are similarly stacked in Harrison's account of

Thatcher's clash with the arts world. He finds it quite natural and proper for her to have attacked this milieu given its 'middle-class patronising attitudes and self-righteous self-subsidy'; surely nearer the mark, again, was the observation by Sir Frank Cooper, quoted by Harrison, who reported that Thatcher 'instinctively dislikes anybody who is not helping in the wealth creation process'. And in general, Harrison's prose rejoices in the effects of the Thatcherite revolution: 'the entrepreneur was enthroned, and establishment intellectuals fell from their plinths'. Only once does Harrison acknowledge that in reality 'the conservative leadership after 1975 . . . mobilised one group of intellectuals against another', but in the body of his article he, prominent Oxford academic and commentator, repeats the common trope of speaking of intellectuals as Other People, and his case amounts to little more than a variant on one of the irregular verbs most current within the gutter Toryism of the 1980s: 'I am open-minded, you are self-deceived, he is a publicly-subsidised left-wing intellectual.'[48]

In practice, as many commentators pointed out, the New Right was nearly as much a creation of intellectuals as the New Left, and it is arguable that the think-tanks and policy-study centres set up in the 1970s and 1980s to 'win the intellectual argument' gave certain intellectual figures a greater prominence in Conservative politics than they had ever enjoyed before. However, these figures tended to be drawn from a rather narrow range: economists predominated, followed by policy experts, with a few philosophers and historians in the background. Moreover, the New Right of the 1980s and 1990s was much more allergic to the *term* 'intellectuals' as a self-description than was the New Left, even though its polemics could make intellectuals seem more important in the national life than they had previously been. In comparing the partisan literature on this issue written in the late twentieth century to that produced a generation or two earlier, one is bound to note a shift in the dominant tone from the self-congratulatory or celebratory to the self-excusing or consolatory. But there is also a continuity at work, a continuity which embraces both Left-wing and Right-wing versions. In both cases the claim about the absence of intellectuals may in indirect ways have served the needs of the intellectuals who advanced the claim. For those on the Left, especially the New Left, it has helped to explain their and their predecessors' frustration at what was felt to have been only a limited effectiveness: how much more flattering to have tried to live such a life by participating in demonstrations on the Left Bank rather than by participating in Arts Council panels at the South Bank. But it has also served a need for those conservative intellectuals who have been in the anomalous position of promoting a picture of a pragmatic, tradition-governed people which, were it true, would allow no room for individuals like themselves. The ideological functions of the claim are particularly evident among contemporary Right-wing intellectuals such as Roger Scruton and Paul Johnson, whose doctrinaire denunciations of intellectuals as a virus in the British body politic reveal ever more desperate attempts to disguise the contradictory logic of their own position.

The closing decades of the twentieth century saw a proliferation of academic, especially social scientific, writing about intellectuals both in the United States and in continental Europe, some of which began to find an echoing response in British scholarly publication, notably that carried out under the encompassing rubric of Cultural Studies. But for the most part, this literature has as yet had relatively little impact on that journalistic, belle-lettrist discourse which still jibs at the term 'intellectual' itself, still has recourse to the 'absence thesis' in its most unreconstructed form, still finds the whole topic faintly risible, though also irresistible. It would be impracticable (and anyway unrewarding) to attempt to survey either of these bodies of writing in anything like a systematic way, for which reason this seems a good point at which to halt this particular sequence of chapters. In Part Five, especially in the final two chapters, I shall, instead, use a more selective and informal literary strategy to assemble a kind of layered radiography of the state of the question of intellectuals in Britain at the end of the century.

But by way of transition to the comparative focus of Part Three, let me end with two quotations. For the English translation in 1981 of Régis Debray's *Le Pouvoir intellectuel en France*, Francis Mulhern provided an introduction briefly comparing the situation of intellectuals in France, Britain, and America. Perhaps not surprisingly, the *Scrutiny* group figured prominently in his discussion of the British case, and in the course of characterizing Leavis's ambition (not, it must be said, in terms that Leavis himself would necessarily have recognized) that the discipline of 'English' should 'become the organizing centre of an intellectual elite capable of interpreting the general interest to a society structurally incapable of self-direction', Mulhern glossed this with an additional phrase: 'a centre, that is, of an intelligentsia of the "classic", "French" type'.[49] The quotation-marks around 'French' represent a curious and revealing equivocation here, not unlike those marketing labels that describe a loaf or a cheese as 'French-style'. He could, after all, simply have written: 'a centre on the model of the French intelligentsia', or have referred to 'an intelligentsia of the classic type', derivation unspecified. But his chosen wording suggests an effort to combine a reference to the actual, historical French intelligentsia (whatever is meant by that) with an invocation of an ideal-typical distillation of various historical examples, a 'classic intelligentsia' (whatever *that*, in turn, may be). It was a profoundly representative move, one which signals the presence of certain comparative assumptions that have now floated free from their original historical anchoring.

The other quotation is the one which serves as the epigraph to this chapter: 'The outstanding features—not to speak of the failures—of our national culture can be largely explained by the inability of our native intelligentsia to achieve a detached and self-sufficient group existence that would permit it to sustain its traditions through succeeding epochs, and to keep abreast of European intellectual production.' Placed at the head of this chapter, under a title referring to the New Left, it may have seemed unremarkable, the encapsulation of a view about the pathology governing the situation of intellectuals in Britain which the formidable body of work produced under that particular political and theoretical inspiration has made deeply familiar. The fact that the passage is actually from an American author, writing, as long ago as 1941, about the lamentable situation of intellectuals in the United States and casting envious eyes at Europe should give us pause.[50] For, as its author, William Phillips, indicated in the body of the article, Britain was understood to comprise part of 'Europe' in this respect, and his article takes its place in what has been, as we shall see shortly, a well-established tradition of American observers expressing a somewhat wistful longing for the supposedly more favourable and influential position of intellectuals in Britain. Taken together, these two passages suggest the need to adopt a different kind of view of our subject than that presented up to this point—the view, that is, from elsewhere.

NOTES

1. This episode has subsequently been the subject of several interested retellings: see particularly Perry Anderson, *Arguments within English Marxism* (London: Verso, 1980), 135–7, and the references cited in Gregory Elliott, *Perry Anderson, The Merciless Laboratory of History* (Minneapolis: University of Minnesota Press, 1998), ch. 1.
2. For a list of the major contributions, see Perry Anderson, *English Questions* (London: Verso, 1992), 121.
3. Anderson, 'The figures of descent' (1987), ibid. 121.
4. E. P. Thompson, 'The peculiarities of the English', *The Socialist Register*, 2 (1965), 311–62. The essay was republished, in somewhat fuller form, in Thompson's *The Poverty of Theory and Other Essays* (London: Merlin, 1978), but I have preferred to use the original version since my concern here is with the terms of this debate as they were formulated at the time in the mid-1960s.
5. Thompson, 'Peculiarities', 312, 322, 331.
6. Ibid. 312 (quoting Anderson, 'Origins', 42), 332.
7. Ibid. 333.
8. Ibid. 339, 342.
9. Thompson, *Poverty of Theory*, 109.
10. Thompson, 'Peculiarities', 334, 335.
11. Anderson, *Arguments*, 148–9.
12. Perry Anderson, 'Components of the national culture', *New Left Review*, 50 (1968), 1–57; repr. in *English Questions*, 48–104. See also the further discussion of Anderson at Ch. 20, sect. IV below.
13. Anderson, *English Questions*, 50, 51, 52.
14. Some of which I tried to address, partly with reference to Anderson's essay, in 'Sociology and Idealism in Britain 1880–1920', *Archives européennes de sociologie*, 19 (1978), 3–50; for a fuller analysis of the nature of such counterfactual analysis more generally, see Geoffrey Hawthorn, *Plausible Worlds: Possibility and Understanding in History and the Social Sciences* (Cambridge: Cambridge University Press, 1991).
15. Anderson, *English Questions*, 61.

16. Ibid. 84, 53, 59.
17. Anderson, *Arguments*, 163, citing W. D. Rubinstein, 'The Victorian middle classes: wealth, occupation, and geography', *Economic History Review*, 30 (1977).
18. For an indication of how limited or unsteady this autonomy was at first, see Stefan Collini, *Public Moralists: Political Thought and Intellectual Life in Britain 1850–1930* (Oxford: Oxford University Press), ch. 1.
19. Anderson, *English Questions*, 80.
20. Ibid. 99, 102.
21. Francis Mulhern, *The Moment of 'Scrutiny'* (London: New Left Books, 1979); Terry Eagleton, 'The rise of English', in his *Literary Theory: An Introduction* (Oxford: Blackwell, 1983); Chris Baldick, *The Social Mission of English Criticism 1848–1932* (Oxford: Oxford University Press, 1983).
22. Anderson, *English Questions*, 99, 100, 102.
23. For a parallel comment on Anderson's 'bibliocentrism', see Elliott, *Anderson*, 284 n. 137.
24. Tom Nairn, 'The English literary intelligentsia', in Emma Tennant (ed.), *Bananas* (London: Quartet, 1977), 57–83.
25. Nairn, 'Literary intelligentsia', 58, 59.
26. From a very extensive literature on this topic, see two particularly influential English-language accounts: George L. Mosse, *The Crisis of German Ideology: Intellectual Origins of the Third Reich* (London: Weidenfeld, 1966), and Fritz Stern, *The Politics of Cultural Despair: A Study in the Rise of the Germanic Ideology* (Berkeley: University of California Press, 1961). For a recent reconsideration of this tradition, see Wolf Lepenies, 'The end of "German Culture"', The Tanner Lectures on Human Values, Harvard University, 1999; I am grateful to Wolf Lepenies for allowing me to read the typescript of his lectures.
27. Nairn, 'Literary intelligentsia', 73, 74.
28. Ibid. 82, 83.
29. Ibid. 75, 76.
30. Anderson, *English Questions*, 6.
31. Isaiah Berlin, 'The role of the intelligentsia', *The Listener* (2 May 1968), 563–5; Berlin's talk was also reprinted in Derwent May (ed.), *Good Talk, 2; An Anthology from BBC Radio* (London: Gollancz, 1969), 67–73 (page references are to this version).
32. Ibid. 69, 70.
33. Ibid. 73, 74, 75.
34. Peter Nettl, 'Are intellectuals obsolete?', *The Listener* (16 May 1968), 627, 628.
35. Ibid. 628; quoting T. R. Fyvel, *Intellectuals Today: Problems in a Changing Society* (London: Chatto, 1968), 16.
36. Fyvel, *Intellectuals Today*, 16.
37. Nettl, 'Are intellectuals obsolete?', 628.
38. Graham Hough, 'In dark times' ('Graham Hough takes up the discussion of the role of intellectuals'), *The Listener* (23 May 1968), 661–3, quotation at 663.
39. Donald Davie, 'On Hobbits and intellectuals', *Encounter* (Oct. 1969), 87, 89, 89–90.
40. Ibid. 90.
41. See 'Before another tribunal: the idea of the "non-specialist public"', in my *English Pasts: Essays in History and Culture* (Oxford: Oxford University Press, 1999), 305–26.
42. Perry Anderson, 'A culture in contra-flow I', *New Left Review*, 180 (1990), 45.

43. Alan Swingewood, 'Intellectuals and the construction of consensus in postwar England', in Alain Gagnon, (ed.), *Intellectuals and Liberal Democracies: Political Influence and Social Involvement* (New York: Praeger, 1987), 89.
44. Raymond Williams, 'Intellectuals behind the screens', *Times Higher Education Supplement* (21 Jan. 1983), 11.
45. Neal Ascherson, 'England needs its intellectuals', *The Observer*, 11 Aug. 1985, 7.
46. Terry Eagleton, 'Spooky', *London Review of Books*, 7 July 1994, 8–9.
47. See e.g., R. Colls and P. Dodd (eds.), *Englishness: Politics and Culture 1880–1920* (Beckenham: Croom Helm, 1986); Brian Doyle, *English and Englishness* (London: Routledge, 1989).
48. Brian Harrison, 'Mrs Thatcher and the intellectuals', *Twentieth-Century British History*, 5 (1994), 221, 211, 212, 209, 224, 235, 237, 207.
49. Francis Mulhern, 'Introduction: Preliminaries and Two Contrasts', in Régis Debray, *Teachers, Writers, Celebrities* (London: Verso, 1981); the piece is republished, in slightly modified form, in Francis Mulhern, *The Present Lasts a Long Time: Essays in Cultural Politics* (Cork: Cork University Press, 1998), quotation at 80.
50. William Phillips, 'The intellectuals' tradition', *Partisan Review* (Nov.–Dec. 1941), 483–90; repr. in de Huszar, *The Intellectuals*, quotation at 479.

PART THREE

COMPARATIVE PERSPECTIVES

9

In Their National Habitat

'"And *other* countries", said the foreign gentleman. "They do how?"'

'"They do, Sir," returned Mr Podsnap, gravely shaking his head; "they do—I am sorry to be obliged to say it—*as* they do."'

I

If one were looking for a passage to stand as a concise summary of the views discussed in the previous chapters, the following extract might seem to propose itself as an ideal candidate:

In a country where, very significantly, the usage of the noun 'intellectual' is far from being current, the intellectual milieu seems particularly devoid of any group identity . . . and intellectuals evince a long-standing disposition to remain outside political debate . . . except when acting in the role of experts. . . . What in France appears as a source of social prestige—literary and classical culture, thought, often considered as the highest form of activity, the taste for abstraction and ideas which are so much the traits one knows have given, across the decades, a particular quality to French politics—remain largely absent. . . . Political life is characterized above all by its traditional pragmatism. . . . This absence is naturally reflected in the historiography. There is even to day no history of intellectuals properly speaking . . .

Nearly all the elements are present here in miniature: the unsteadiness in the use of the term itself, the absence of a sense of collective identity, the aloofness from political '*engagement*', the contrast with France, the empiricist or pragmatic tradition, the corresponding lack of a historiography about intellectuals. All this may seem to underline, once again, a version of the 'peculiarities of the English' in this matter.

In fact, the passage comes from an essay on the situation of intellectuals in . . . *Belgium*.[1] What is more, the collection of case-studies in which the essay appeared is full of similar remarks about the relative weakness or absence of 'intellectuals' in other European countries. The essay on Germany, for example, begins: 'There is practically no bibliography on intellectuals in Germany in the strict sense of the French conception of the word, although there is a particularly rich history of intellectuals in this country'. The contribution on Switzerland records 'the relatively weak public presence of intellectuals in this country', and argues that 'in effect, the intellectual does not figure among Swiss social types'. The essay on the intellectual in Denmark concludes: 'His position statements are not considered as oracular utterances. He has an altogether less privileged status than his French counterpart.' Indeed, so common are such remarks in this collection, that one contributor very pertinently wonders: 'Shouldn't one ask oneself whether it is not the French model of the intellectual, respected and listened to in the community, which is the exception, and the more representative figure is that of the intellectual whom one is on one's guard against?'[2]

Even this brief medley of quotations suggests that the 'absence thesis' may look very different indeed when seen from a comparative perspective, thereby providing a salutary corrective to the well-worn clichés of 'British exceptionalism'. As I have argued throughout this book, the bundle of assumptions and claims that go to make up versions of the 'absence thesis' are themselves already implicitly comparative, but by remaining implicit they attempt to profit from comparison without laying themselves open to counter-evidence and correction. When, however, we pause to consider what more exactly 'comparison' means in intellectual and cultural history, we discover that the answer is far from straightforward, and it is worth meditating on this issue for a moment since this topic has been dogged by casual or unreflective uses of comparison at every level.

Cross-cultural historical comparison is at once inescapable and impossible. Any characterization of a style, tradition, or state of affairs alleged to be typical or representative of one society or national history is inherently comparative, including the comparison that is involved in proposing adherence to or departure from a supposed developmental norm. Many of the most familiar terms of historical analysis are in this respect like dead metaphors, concepts whose implicitly comparative frame we no longer notice. This is truer still of those self-descriptions which have become historiographical, and in some cases political, clichés, but which are in effect condensations of a long-running comparative argument—'American exceptionalism', '*Der Deutsche Sonderweg*', '*la singularité française*', 'the peculiarities of the English', and so on.

There is, however, a fundamental difficulty to be faced in all attempts to undertake comparative studies in intellectual and cultural history: the units which are to be compared, whether they be ideas and concepts or identities and roles, are very largely constituted by the terms in which they are described.[3] But any description is in one natural language and not others, and each language slices up reality in partly different ways. I do not mean here to enter into any of the large and complex philosophical issues about the relations between language and reality, nor to deny that many languages have closely corresponding terms which in practice often denominate aspects of reality in broadly similar (or at least apparently similar) ways. I only mean to emphasize the obvious point that the more language-dependent the identification of an entity is, the more the descriptions in different languages will bear traces of the intellectual and cultural traditions of that community of language-users, and the less exactly the place of a single term in a pattern of usage will correspond to those available in other languages. Therefore, since the units or objects of comparison are culturally defined, the exercise of comparison tends to posit a kind of overarching or transcendent category of which each of the national examples is supposed to be a variant or subset; but in practice, this larger category is likely to bear the marks of the national version with which the historian is most familiar. The ostensible 'comparison' then all too easily ends up neglecting the specificity of other cultural patterns in order to fasten on to the presence, or more polemically the absence, of an entity or activity described in terms derived from one particular example.

One could in principle respond to this dilemma by standing pat in one's own language and simply asking whether other societies have the entity which one's own culture refers to by a particular term. Thus, I might be interested in the concept of the 'amateur', as understood in English (itself no straightforward matter, of course), and then go looking at other cultures to find whether they have it or not. However, the tendency of such an approach is either to draw a blank immediately, or, more commonly, to wrench the material targeted for comparison out of the cultural and linguistic contexts that give it meaning and that, ultimately, make it strictly incomparable. As Michel Espagne has very pertinently argued, historians silently presuppose a *tertium comparationis* which is not exactly the concept as found in any one language, but a kind of ideal type or stripped-down version of the putatively common elements in the diversity of thickly constituted originals.[4] Thus, for example, a comparative history which purports to be about what is commonly referred to in different societies as 'la bourgeoisie', 'the middle class', or 'das Bürgertum' will tend to take a different form and come to different conclusions depending whether the author is most familiar with French, British, or German society.[5]

While all the terms involved in such comparisons will derive from individual natural languages, the extent to which their reference is bound up with a particular cultural tradition will vary. One could undertake cross-cultural comparison of a reasonably stable social role (at least for the major European societies in the modern period) such as that of 'soldier' or 'shopkeeper' more easily than of some category which seemed to depend for its definition upon a peculiar evaluative tradition, such as 'gentleman' or 'bohemian'. What needs to be emphasized here is that 'intellectual', as used in English, is in its dominant sense nearer to the latter category than is usually imagined, while at the same time the term has been used to refer to a socio-professional stratum more like the former category. This means that there will inevitably be difficulties in identifying a genuinely common object of comparison independent of the incommensurate evaluative-descriptive vocabularies that partly constitute the candidate objects in each culture. Comparisons, therefore, cannot simply take the form of those binary geographical classifications of countries which do and those which do not have sea coasts or poisonous snakes. Instead, one needs to undertake thick-textured local enquiries that have as their starting-points (1) the appearance of the term (or its linguistic equivalents), situated in its full semantic field, and (2) the existence of explicit or self-conscious reflection in that culture about the nature and occurrence of the roles designated by the relevant terms. What many historians (and others) might regard as the 'actual history of intellectuals' in a given society will necessarily have to wait upon these initial enquiries if it is not to issue in insensitive Procrusteanism. French scholars have been understandably to the fore in promoting the comparative study of intellectuals, but even their work, methodologically self-conscious though it often is, has not wholly avoided these dangers, especially where they have built the idea of 'collective intervention in the political field' into their notion of 'the intellectuals' from the outset.

Intractable as these problems may be at the philosophical level, in practice illuminating comparisons in such matters are undertaken all the time, though they stand a better chance of being genuinely illuminating, rather than merely dazzling, if one's enquiries are at least chastened by an awareness of these conceptual difficulties. The present chapter, together with the others in Part Three, aims not so much to undertake systematic cross-cultural comparisons as simply to indicate how different the question of intellectuals in Britain appears as soon as one replaces the conventional implicit comparison with France with an explicit, and expanded, international context. In my view, what soon becomes clear is that many of the features assumed to be distinctively British are in fact shared, to different degrees, in several other societies, and that while there are varying levels of similarity and difference among all the societies under discussion, if there is a case to be made out for any kind of 'exceptionalism' in the matter it can most persuasively be done with respect to France.

II

Usage of the term 'intellectuals' provides, as I suggested above, the most helpful starting-point. Of course, one may want, once again, to say that the *concept* may have been present in a certain society where the *word* was not used, and that would in turn open up a whole other line of investigation. But for the moment we may begin with a few relatively limited observations about the occurrence of the noun 'intellectuals' in various major European languages, temporarily bracketing off the question of how similar its referents may or may not be.

From such a preliminary survey, what emerges most strikingly, especially in the light of the common assumption that the term has a *uniquely* pejorative force in English, is how strongly such negative resonances are insisted upon in accounts of the dominant usage of 'intellectuals' and its cognates in many other European languages. To illustrate this point, I have compiled the following brief glossary, drawn from recent comparative work on this topic.

Germany: Several sources emphasise that in German the word traditionally had a strongly derogatory force. ' "*Intellektuelle*": in German the term has almost always had a negative connotation or has even been used as an insult ... Today it also signifies, in a more neutral form, a socio-professional category, but it never has the meaning that the term had in France at the moment of the Dreyfus Affair, in the sense of a political commitment.' There is 'a strong tendency in the German cultural tradition which gives a negative connotation to the the term "intellectual" as a carper or a rootless creature.'

Russia: 'in contemporary Russian, the word "intellectual", relatively current as a modifying adjective, is very little used—even if it is more and more—as a noun, and this latter remains the bearer of a strong ironic connotation'.

Sweden: all the terms for 'intellectual' are predominantly 'negative'; in addition, the Swedish word *tyckäre* is used to indicate 'he who always has something to say on a topic, whatever it may be: pejorative'.

The Netherlands: '"*intellectueel*" easily lends itself in Dutch to an ironic usage; the term is 'associated with an unrealistic vision of the world'.

Hungary: *entellektuel* is glossed as 'too clever'; 'these days it is used in an ironic sense'; variations on 'egg-head' are common.

Czech Republic: '"*intelecktuál*", discreditable, almost shameful term'; related terms always suggest someone 'cut off from the reality of things'.

And so on.[6] It is scarcely surprising that Pierre Bourdieu began his article introducing a Europe-wide survey of intellectuals in the mid-1990s by observing: 'In general terms, intellectuals do not have a good press. Everywhere the words for them are almost all pejorative.'[7]

In none of these cases, needless to say, do these brief characterizations tell the whole story. As I have by now established, I trust, in the case of English usage, positive, neutral, and pejorative uses can easily coexist. And merely plotting a semantic field does not tell us very much about the various kinds of statement which the word has been used to make in particular cultural traditions. Still less does it tell us about the social reality referred to: however pejorative the resonances of the *label* in Czech, for example, Havel became to many outside observers a favoured instance of the intellectual as national icon. But even this very brief dip into comparative semantics ought to be sufficient to dispel the ignorant prejudice that it is uniquely in Britain that the word can carry such strongly negative associations. (And although I shall return to the question of the United States in the following chapter, it may be worth including the results of this linguistic survey in the American case as well: 'More than in any other advanced country, the terminology for intellectuals in America is almost exclusively pejorative. Imprecatory, ironic, or insulting terms abound there.'[8]) Not for nothing is the standard German survey of the word's history entitled *The Intellectuals: History of an Insult*.[9]

One conclusion implicit in recent comparative studies though not really developed in any of them is that, hardly surprisingly, the label transplanted itself most readily and flourished most successfully in Romance-language countries or countries most susceptible to French cultural influence. Italy and Spain provide the clearest examples among the major European societies, followed by linguistically affiliated societies elsewhere in the world, such as Quebec, Latin America, Francophone Africa, and former French colonies in Asia. By contrast, in Anglo-Saxon, Germanic, Slavic, and Scandinavian societies and their cultural affiliates the term took longer to establish itself and its negative resonances seem to have remained more prominent.

It should also be said that the accelerated internationalization of intellectual exchange in the closing decades of the twentieth century, and especially the diffusion of the vocabulary of the social sciences, has had the effect of making a more neutral or sociological sense of the term more common in several European languages. For example, the most recent survey of these developments in relation to Germany observed: 'This new interest brought to bear on the intellectual as a type in social history has already begun to have repercussions on the semantics of the term: the predominantly pejorative connotation of the word "*Intellektueller*" is in the process of fading and of being replaced by an accepted usage that is more neutral and technical.'[10] While this development facilitates international comparisons, it also sets traps for the unwary, given the way in which (as abundantly illustrated in the British case) older, far less neutral, senses still pervade the evidence available for such studies and thus help to colour their findings.

To move beyond the term itself and to undertake to compare the *actual* position of intellectuals in different societies would be a far more ambitious project than I can pursue here, though this and the following three chapters attempt to document a little of the *perceived* variation. Where such perceptions are concerned, broader intellectual traditions are in play, often traceable back (as I suggested in the British case at the beginning of Ch. 3) deep into the nineteenth century. In the case of some of the smaller European states, the determining factor was the extent to which they had developed as client cultures of one of the major societies. It also matters in what proportions various countries experienced some of the most relevant common elements in nineteenth-century European cultural life, such as deference to German scholarship and science, susceptibility to French political and artistic radicalism, admiration for English liberty and tolerance, and so on. These histories then shape the broad contours of response to the idea of the intellectual once this begins to be evolved or imported in the course of the twentieth century. In this respect, there might be few better correctives to an exaggerated concentration on the supposed differences between Britain and Europe than to shift the focus away from the usual suspects and to look a little more closely at the history of intellectuals in, say, Norway, Portugal, and Austria.

Even confining oneself to the larger European countries, it is the complexity of the pattern of resemblances and differences in the matter of intellectuals that is most striking. In the following section of this chapter I shall look at the two most pertinent examples of this complexity, Germany and Italy, but as a brief preliminary it may be worth saying that if one were looking to set up a European norm founded on the French model, the prime candidate for inclusion might well be Spain. As Christophe Charle writes in his comparative survey of intellectuals in nineteenth-century Europe: 'Spain is undoubtedly the European country where the process of the emergence of intellectuals as a political force is closest to the French case.'[11] The similarities were partly a matter of the strong cultural influence of France on Spain during this period, partly a reflection of the presence of certain similar structuring divisions in public life, such as that between secular liberalism and the Catholic church. But there was also a marked indigenous tradition in Spain of involvement in politics on the part both of scholars and writers, aided by a flourishing newspaper and periodical press from the 1880s onwards. In practice, the reach of such publications was confined to the relatively small educated class, and in this respect as well as in the way in which many of these writers, often completing their apprenticeships in one of the great European cultural capitals, took up 'literary modes which do not really correspond to the level of development of Spanish society', the situation of intellectuals in Spain at the end of the nineteenth century, surrounded by a largely illiterate, pious, rural population, evokes comparison rather with Russia than with the main West European societies.[12] But the cosmopolitanism of the cultural elite, while it helped to direct their critiques of their country's alleged backwardness, did not seem to produce a radical sense of disconnection from Spain and its fate; rather the contrary. For example, Ramiro de Maeztu, whom we met in Ch. 4 as one of the regular contributors to the *New Age*, initially came to England in 1905 as the London correspondent for an Argentinian newspaper, but despite long residence here as well as close ties with intellectual life in Germany and the United States, his later work focused almost obsessively on the nature of 'Spanishness'.[13]

In Spain the noun 'el intelectual' itself came into use in the 1890s, contemporaneously with its French equivalent; as in France, it made occasional appearances as a way of referring to men of letters of radical views *before* Clemenceau's celebrated intervention in the Dreyfus case.[14] Thereafter, although, as in most of Europe, the label 'intellectual' had been used as an insult by right-wing commentators in the early part of the twentieth century, even they came round to accepting it in self-description.[15] Subsequent discussion of the role of intellectuals in Spain has tended to focus on whether the template was most influentially provided by the so-called 'Generation of 1898'—writers such as Miguel de Unamuno, Ramiro de Maeztu, and Pío Baroja—or by the essayists and scholars who partly reacted against this group and who were then inevitably dubbed the 'Generation of 1914', led by the philosopher and critic José Ortega y Gasset who subsequently established an imperium over intellectual life in Madrid which was rivalled only by Croce's in Naples at much the same period.[16] Most striking in a comparative perspective is the extent to which the public presence of 'los intelectuales' came to be taken for granted in Spain in the first three decades of the century, understood, as in the French case, as collectively bringing the authority of reason and literature to bear on contemporary political issues. Indeed, the ubiquitous *presence* of intellectuals, at least in political debate, rather than any sense of their 'absence', almost threatened to furnish a sense of Spanish exceptionalism in itself. 'Spain is the only country where intellectuals busy themselves with immediate politics,' declared Ortega in 1927, with some exaggeration (and perhaps some misgiving, too), and he is echoed by modern historians of intellectuals: 'Beyond question, in no other European country were they led to play such an important political role.'[17]

The political influence of the press, and of the numerous scholars and men of letters who contributed to it, appears to have been especially marked in the period from the 1890s to the outbreak of the Civil War in 1936. (All these features of the history of intellectuals in Spain have obviously had considerable influence on Latin America, though there, too, one has to be cautious about the oversimplifications involved in continent-wide generalizations.) Clearly, after 1939 the actual historical experience of Spain diverged from that of most of the rest of Western Europe, including France, but although many intellectuals were murdered, went into exile, or prudently retired from involvement in public life during the Franco years, the cultural tradition which sustained them had deep roots and survived this long hiatus. What has in some ways proved more of a challenge to the intellectuals' conventional perception of themselves as a 'counter-power', opposed to the state and the church, has been their closer involvement with liberal and socialist governments since the late 1970s.[18] But in this, too, Spanish intellectuals could be seen as paralleling developments among their peers in France, as well as elsewhere; and something similar can be said about the fact that 'interest in the phenomenon of the intellectual in Spain has burgeoned over the past decade'.[19]

One might essay similarly brief snapshots of the perceived role of intellectuals in several other European countries, each with its own distinctive story. But for the purposes of this chapter it may be more helpful to point to the way that this reiterated distinctiveness can issue in a regular pattern in which claims to 'exceptionality' presuppose a norm that proves to be elusive. To illustrate this claim, discussion of the chosen instances will need to be slightly more extended, even while remaining scandalously brief by the standards of scholars expert in the study of intellectuals in the countries in question.

III

To turn to Germany, by contrast to Latin countries such as Spain, is to turn to the society which figured as France's greatest cultural rival in mainland Europe throughout the nineteenth and much of the twentieth century. The way in which the question of intellectuals has been posed and answered there offers some illuminating points of comparison with the British case, especially because in both countries the doubtful status, or even existence, of intellectuals has been intimately bound up with images and stereotypes of national identity that can be traced back to the nineteenth century and beyond, images which have continued to be powerful even when manifestly at odds with the realities they purport to describe. On the other hand, among the most radical of the relevant differences between the two countries has been the fact that Germany has not enjoyed anything like the institutional and territorial continuities which have allowed the existence and scope of the British state to be silently presumed in so many discussions of national identity in this country. The need, in the absence of such an enduring political entity, to think of Germany as primarily a *Kulturnation* arguably conferred a special prominence on those acknowledged as the principal interpreters of 'culture'. Where the resemblances seem teasingly close in structural terms but dizzyingly different in substance is in the claims made in the course of the nineteenth and twentieth centuries for each country's deviation from what is posited as the 'normal' path of development found elsewhere. In Germany's case, the 'special path' or *Sonderweg* was initially an attempt to represent, in celebratory terms, German culture's escape from the deformations of the materialism and commercialism supposed to characterize both France and Britain. After 1945, the term was chiefly used to point to a different kind of 'deviance'—the result of late state formation conjoined to late industrialization within a culture defined by the legacy of Romanticism, entailing the persistence of pre-bourgeois elites and the weakness of liberalism, the whole being focused on explaining the 'aberration' of the Nazi period. The structural similarities to the British story lay in the ways in which a framework of 'exceptionality/normality' skews perceptions, both negative and positive, encouraging parochialism and helping, with vicious circularity, to perpetuate the kinds of attitudes which were thought to have been part of the exceptionality in the first place. As one of the most recent accounts puts it:

> Debates on the German intellectual field tend to be self-conscious, self-referential, and self-contained. Despite the comparative dimension of the central conceptual pair, *Sonderweg* and Normality, German intellectuals remain inward-looking as well as backward-looking, and caught in the terms of a 'national psychology'... In the German case, the debate is often not even so much about concepts, as about clichés.[20]

However, in the matter of intellectuals, as to some extent with the larger national stories into which ideas about them have been fitted, there have been signs in the closing years of the twentieth century of an increasing recognition of similarities across a number of countries.

In debates about intellectuals, two features of Germany's nineteenth-century inheritance tended to be singled out to account for their presumed distinctiveness. The first was the social and cultural standing of professors, respected for their science or scholarship and their consequent removal from the grubby realities of everyday life, treated as notables in their local communities, and largely recruited from already privileged social groups. German universities had set the pace for most disciplines in the nineteenth century and continued to provide the models for emulation elsewhere. At least up until 1933, the prestige of the German 'Mandarins' was correspondingly high.[21] This intersected with the other much-invoked feature, namely the peculiarly German cultivation and celebration of *Innerlichkeit*, 'inwardness', as the source of the richness and authenticity of German 'Kultur' as opposed to Western (principally French) 'Civilisation', a contrast given iconic expression in the literary duel between the Mann brothers, Thomas and Heinrich, in the course of the First World War.[22] The interplay between these two strands was taken to have encouraged a relation to public affairs that could be described as 'unpolitisch' (unpolitical), and at the same time to have facilitated the dismissal of those 'mere scribblers' who did discuss current events in, inevitably, a vulgar and shallow way. According to at least one authority, 'This fundamental characteristic, which one summarises under the term "apolitical", has remained a constant of the political and intellectual life of Germany'; something similar may occasionally be identified elsewhere, but it is 'a more frequent and recurrent phenomenon in Germany'.[23] It might be thought to have been a characteristic that was largely honoured in the breach earlier in the nineteenth century, since the number of delegates to the assembly in Frankfurt in 1848 who were also professors was very high and much remarked upon in other countries, leading 1848 to be retrospectively dubbed 'the revolution of the intellectuals'.[24] Nonetheless, in the second half of the century the withdrawal of academics from public affairs became much more marked, and by the beginning of the twentieth century it can be argued that there was somewhat less interchange between spheres in Germany than elsewhere, leading Christophe Charle to formulate this contrast with selected 'elsewheres': 'This "retreat from (formal) politics" . . . contrasts with the still frequent exchanges and contacts between the various milieux in France and Britain.'[25] As a result of this combination of circumstances, concluded Charle in his comparative survey of intellectuals in nineteenth-century Europe: 'It is in Germany that the notion of intellectuals understood in the sense of the Dreyfus Affair has apparently had least success.'[26]

When the term 'Intellektueller' first began to be widely used in German in the wake of the Dreyfus Affair, it was applied in the main to the 'scribblers', a derogated French term for a derogated 'unGerman' activity. The true Mandarins preferred to be termed '*die Geistigen*' rather than '*Intellektueller*'. This self-distancing from the term appears to have happened even in the milieu where one would have expected the type so described most to flourish, namely in radical political circles: 'However, by contrast to what was happening in France—and this difference would have weighty consequences for the semantic evolution of the word—in Germany the intellectual arouses distrust, even denigration and contempt, on the part of the Socialist and Marxist left.' As a result, 'in Germany, the intellectual therefore suffers a double attack, from left and right, such that the word has borne since its origins a negative connotation, and in any case it will never become the rallying concept of the left defending the rights of man'.[27] The approach and eventual outbreak of the First World War only exacerbated this situation, in that 'intellectuals' were condemned as (in accordance with the derivation of the label) French and therefore inherently antagonistic to the values of German *Kultur*. 'During the First World War, the word "intellectual" definitely becomes an insult and signifies, in the Franco-German conflict, a traitor to the patriotic cause.' In 1916 a pamphlet was published entitled *Die Deutschland der Intellektueller*, which accused those who bore the label, itself a sign of their arrogance, of importing 'a foreign parasite', and it was suggested that this 'enemy' term should be expunged from the German language.[28]

During the Weimar years, the term started to make something of a come-back, the Expressionists being particularly prone to use it in self-description.[29] But the Nazis' fundamental hostility to intellectuals, in the name of more visceral ideals of *Blut und Boden*, was notorious, as was their close identification of the traits of intellectuals and Jews—rootless, cosmopolitan, irreligious, calculating, and so on. Hardly surprisingly, during the Nazi period 'the word "intellectual" became strictly speaking a term of abuse'.[30] The immediately post-war years saw a concerted effort to reroot notions of rights and 'the universal' in German culture; this historical sequence is surely what accounts for the curious fact that Julien Benda's *La Trahison des clercs* was translated into German for the first time in 1946.[31] But during the years of the Federal Republic after 1949, two related preoccupations dominated public discussion of these matters: first, the question of the alleged *Sonderweg* and the need to explain, and perhaps to accept guilt for, the Nazi episode; and second, the question of the contrast between 'the two Germanies' and the consequent task of building a civic or political identity on liberal and constitutional premises in the West. At the height of the Cold War, it was especially easy in West Germany to associate the very idea of the intellectual with Communism, not least on account of the role of Marxist 'theorists' in East Germany.[32] Nonetheless, by the end of the 1950s, the intellectual figures who were to be most prominent in public debate in the Federal Republic were already in evidence, such as Günter Grass, Martin Walser, Jürgen Habermas, and Hans Magnus Enzenberger, who defined themselves against *both* the culturally pessimistic 'Mandarin' tradition and the 'party intellectual' of the GDR.[33]

The complexities in the position of intellectuals in Germany in the closing decades of the twentieth century were brought out by the juxtaposition of their prominence in the *Historikerstreit* of the mid-1980s and their relative marginality in the process of reunification only a few years later. In the course of the former, historians and social theorists crossed swords in leading general-circulation newspapers and periodicals over the interpretation of the Nazi period, and above all over the extent to which it was or was not on a par with, and even partially to be explained (and thereby excused?) by, the totalitarian excesses of Soviet Russia, with the historian Ernst Nolte taking the lead on the 'conservative' or 'nationalist' side, attempting to liberate German national identity from being defined by the unique unspeakableness of the Holocaust, and the second-generation Frankfurt School philosopher and social theorist Jürgen Habermas figuring as the main spokesman on the 'left-liberal' side, resisting any attempted 'normalization' of the Nazi episode and any resurgent German nationalism that that might be thought to facilitate. (Habermas himself suggested that one outcome of the *Historikerstreit*, a dispute which his side was widely seen to have won on points, was that the role of the left-liberal intellectual had become, adapting the term thrown at his opponents' treatment of the Nazi past, 'normalized'—which, comments Müller, 'seemed to mean that it conformed to French standards'.[34])

But when, only two or three years later, the events which led to the fall of the Berlin wall and the eventual reunification of Germany unfolded, many of these same intellectuals found it difficult to command any general audience for their arguments against, or even just reservations about, reunification. This provoked an inquest after 1991 about the so-called 'failure of the intellectuals'—their failure, that is, to have understood and spoken to the enormous popular enthusiasm on both sides of the wall for the restoration of a single Germany. Once again, claims about the peculiarity of the position of intellectuals in Germany lay readily to hand to explain this 'failure' as also to explain the 'betrayal' of their calling on the part of that majority of East German intellectuals who in one way or another had collaborated with the regime. The elevated expectations invested in *Kultur* as both transcending and compensating for the shoddy manœuvrings of politics once again emerged as the principal culprit.[35] This has been spelled out in a recent volume devoted to the position of intellectuals under the GDR and thereafter in Germany since 1991: 'The presumption of and insistence on the autonomy of culture was justified as a check against state power on one hand [*sic*] and as a counterweight to commerce and industry on the other.' Because of 'the special role of intellectuals as both guardians against the state and as tutors of the nation', their collaboration with the repressive GDR 'destroyed not only the credibility of individual informers and of the whole class of collaborating intellectuals but also the legitimacy of an idea'.[36] In this respect the realities of a unified Germany marked what Wolf Lepenies has polemically called 'the end of "German culture"' as Germany has come closer to seeing itself as one liberal, market-driven, West-European state among others.

As with writing about the position of intellectuals in other countries, one can see a revealing contrast of perspectives at work in the German case. For example, Hans Manfred Bock, writing from within the German academic system and addressing a primarily French audience, emphasizes the long-term causes of the weakness or absence of intellectuals in his country: 'The lack of interest in the phenomenon of the distinctive group of the intellectuals in Germany can be explained simultaneously by the pejorative connotation of the term, the absence of a sufficiently wide public sphere, or the too-intimate integration of the cultural elites with the political class of this country.' As a result, he identifies a continuing pattern of mutual suspicion and hostility between intellectuals and politicians in Germany since 1945: 'From one side on account of an explicit disdain by politicians, for the most part pragmatic and unreceptive to the intellectuals' arguments; from the other side on account of a lack of identification with the West-German state on the part of the intellectuals'.[37] Some of this finds obvious echoes in the literature on Britain, and it is interesting to see the too-intimate integration of cultural elites into the political class being proposed as part of the explanation for the relative weakness or absence of intellectuals in yet another country. One cannot help wondering whether this might not cut both ways, furnishing intellectual figures with superior access and points of leverage, even if inhibiting the growth of a sense of a separate collective identity as a 'contre-pouvoir'. Beyond that, the unresponsiveness of pragmatic politicians to the ideas of intellectuals, for whom they express a certain disdain, may look like part of the definition of the noun 'politician' in more or less any language.

By contrast, Jan-Werner Müller, writing from within the British academic system and addressing primarily an Anglo-American audience, sees the position in almost ecstatically positive terms:

> Only in Germany does one find intellectuals such as Jürgen Habermas occupying the first two pages of a weekly such as *Die Zeit*; only in Germany could a critic literally tearing apart the latest book by Günter Grass make the cover of the country's most important magazine, *Der Spiegel*; only in Germany does one find political scientists regularly publishing popular books on the state of the nation, often with pictures of themselves looking diffident and angst-ridden on the front cover; only in Germany would a random flicking through TV channels inevitably lead the viewer to one of the numerous 'talk shows' in which a small group of intellectuals earnestly debate political-cum-philosophical topics on an almost daily basis. In short, in Germany, unlike in Britain and the United States, it is almost self-evidently legitimate that men and women who have distinguished themselves in cultural and academic matters, should comment on affairs of state.[38]

It is worth saying that these claims about the representativeness within German life of the episodes cited and the uniqueness of Germany in these respects might both be challenged. It is also true that some, at least, of what is being described appears rather to reflect a more general change in the relations between intellectuals and the media in the closing decades of the twentieth century in several countries, and that Müller is, as his final sentence makes explicit, thinking about intellectuals in what I have called the 'cultural' sense here—not the terms in which a French commentator might address the question. And finally, one might observe that the rhetorical insistence of those repeated 'only's, although deployed in this instance to buttress a case about the strength rather than the weakness of the position of intellectuals in Germany, still has the effect of banging the drum of 'exceptionalism' exceptionally loudly.

IV

For the purpose of taking a series of comparative optics on the British case, a particular interest attaches to Italy, the other major European country to be briefly considered, not least because one's initial assumption is that it has stood at the opposite pole from Britain in the matter of intellectuals. Italy, like Spain, has been notably susceptible to French cultural influence in the modern period, and British commentators, remarking the extraordinary imperium exercised by figures such as Croce or Eco, tend to see it as a country in which intellectuals are prominent, well-treated, and effective. But the situation has not presented itself to observers within Italy in quite such positive terms.

Even at the beginning of the twentieth century, the sense of national identity was still fragile and variable throughout the Italian peninsula, and the geographical dispersal of cultural and, to some extent, political life, together with the high Germanic sense of calling of leading academics, meant that intellectuals faced considerable difficulties establishing the conditions for any collective self-consciousness, let alone collective intervention in public life. The standing of prominent individuals such as the independently wealthy Croce was partly a matter of social rather than intellectual distinction. The term 'intellectuals' only began to establish itself in the 1920s, and it was not often used in self-description.[39] But Fascism not only served to mobilize intellectuals both for and against, but also to make the term 'intellectuals' more common on both sides, though intriguingly Croce himself, 'outstanding representative of the anti-fascist intellectual, continued to reject the use of the term'.[40] As in France after 1944, intellectuals in Italy achieved fresh prominence on account of their disproportionate presence among those who had been (or at least managed to claim that they had been) active in the Resistance. 'Italian public life was transformed after over twenty years of fascism, which had enjoyed considerable support, even among intellectuals, by the unusually impressive and widespread mobilisation of the Resistance in 1943–5.'[41] And in Italy, more markedly even than elsewhere, the chief political beneficiaries of their part in the Partisan movement were the Communists, and so Communist-affiliated intellectuals exercised a special *egemonia* in post-war political and cultural life, to use the term associated with the leading theorist of Italian Communism who also formulated one of the most influential analyses of the role of the intellectual, Antonio Gramsci.[42] However, this in turn produced a reaction among the various opponents of the Communists: 'To distinguish themselves from the Communist intellectuals, the word was used with derision by the liberals, as a synonym for blind adhesion to a totalitarian system, denying cultural liberty.'[43] And more generally it became a marked feature of Italian intellectuals that they were closely associated with political parties, with a consequent gain in access to power in some cases but entailing a widespread suspicion that their opportunity to express their opinions depended upon the pleasure of their political masters.

In the closing decades of the twentieth century, Italian culture fully shared in the more general anxieties about the 'mediatization' of the intellectuals, a concern given added urgency by the extent of near-monopoly enjoyed in some sections of the media by the financial and political empire of Silvio Berlusconi. Nor is commentary in Italy immune from familiar laments about the decline and disappearance of the 'major intellectuals'. For example, surveying what he called 'the era of "*opinionismo*"', the editor and journalist Goffredo Fofi mourned the passing in the 1980s and early 1990s of the leading figures who had previously stirred public debate on major cultural issues, as well as, reaching still further back, the absence of the those truly great intellectuals who in the 1950s had been able to take the kind of wider and deeper view that was now so conspicuously lacking. This lack was now palpable, he claimed in 1995, and those few figures who remained, such as Eco or Calasso, 'do not seem to be endowed with the same capacities for provocation or passion as their predecessors'. The cup had now passed to '*l'opinionismo*', 'a kind of national intellectual sport which allows everyone to say what they think, without asking themselves the question of if and when one thinks and on what these thoughts are based. One thus passes imperceptibly from the great scholar from whom one solicits opinions on everything and no matter what, to the most populist television presenter, current or future employee of the Berlusconi channels.'[44]

Perhaps inevitably, this history has issued in the elaboration of what at least one analyst has dubbed 'Italy's exceptionalism' in the matter of intellectuals:

> Unlike intellectuals in other Western countries, Italian intellectuals never were sufficiently prestigious to achieve legitimation independently [*sc.* of their connection with power, especially political parties]. There have rarely been intellectuals in Italy as famous as their counterparts in France, where the history of the country is dotted with the names of the great representatives of culture. Nor does the academic world have the moral and scientific authority which characterizes British universities. And journalists, to choose another example, lack the power conferred on them in the USA.[45]

The historical narrative offered in support of this analysis also emphasizes the peculiarly *un*favourable conditions in which Italian intellectuals have operated. Immediately after 1945 Italian intellectuals embraced 'a merging in the great emancipatory meta-narrative of the Italian Left'; there was no effective cultural sphere independent of politics. With the beginnings of 'modernization' in the 1960s came the 'intellectual as professional', often based in the media and having access to growing mass culture (and therefore suspected by Leftist critics of being 'harbingers of a form of Americanism'). This period also saw a breaking out from the parochial concerns of the earlier generation into a more cosmopolitan role ('organic intellectuals ... were firmly rooted in a national perspective'). The 1980s saw 'the end of Italian exceptionalism.... Italy became more similar to other Western countries.'

These dangers are said to have given rise to 'the neo-corporatist intellectual', a figure investing a certain professional capital in a relationship with political power as adviser, consultant, expert. But still 'the Italian professional market does not offer intellectuals the same possibilities and benefits found in the United States and in the majority of Western countries'. In particular, cultural institutions in the public sphere have been too few or too feeble. So, instead, for these intellectuals 'the political market becomes their form of the professional market'. But their dealings there become less and less a *public* transaction, but rather a private one between the expert and a political body or patron. There is, therefore, a question whether 'this victory of professionalism, along with politics, has not also eliminated everything which differentiates an intellectual from an ordinary expert'. But now a genuine 'public sphere' is developing in Italy, though threatened by collusion between right-wing politics and monopolistic media power. There are even signs of a revival of 'the universal intellectual'. The very complexity of modern life calls for figures who can interpret and provide meaning, figures 'who will take into account the connections between multiple fields of knowledge without referring to any specialized discipline'. But the task of the 'universal intellectual' has changed: 'From the duty of saying the truth independently from the constraints of power', it has now become 'the task of recreating meaning', and providing 'those world-views that political meta-narratives are no longer able to provide'.[46]

I have quoted this analysis at length not because its formulations are all to be accepted without challenge, but because it provides a striking example of the transposition of themes familiar from the British case not just to a quite different setting, but to one normally assumed to offer the strongest contrast where the position of intellectuals is concerned. Reading it, one begins to wonder—at least one should begin to wonder—whether the doubts and exhortations expressed here, wholly familiar as they are in their tone as well as assumptions, should not be seen at least as much as expressive of a broader logic as of a peculiarly Italian situation. On this evidence, the Italian lament would seem to depend upon a highly politicized conception of the intellectual: indeed, Pasquinelli actually says that 'what turns culture professionals (academics, artists, journalists, scientists) into intellectuals is their relationship with power'.[47] I have been arguing that the relationship with politics is only one form of the larger structure implicit in the relevant sense of 'the intellectual' in English usage, that is to say, the reaching out to a public and an issue that is 'general' in relation to the primary activity or initial source of cultural standing. And this, it seems to me, is borne out in the present case by Pasquinelli's emphasis on the contrast between the role of the intellectual and that of 'the expert' and on the need to transcend the limitations of 'specialization'. These are, it turns out, the terms in which every society phrases its laments about how *its* intellectuals fall short of some flourishing condition presumed to be enjoyed by intellectuals elsewhere. The very similarity of the laments surely indicates a shared structural logic rather than a uniquely national condition. And by this point, not much ingenuity should be required to work out where that flourishing 'elsewhere' is normally located.

V

Quite how this common structural logic plays itself out in any given case will obviously reflect distinctive historical circumstances and cultural traditions, but it is worth remembering the disparity almost always to be found between a society's self-understanding and the view of that society from outside. For example, outside observers have enviously pointed to the enormous respect for scholarship in the German cultural tradition, the centrality of philosophy and social theory, the social status of professors; from the inside, commentators have lamented the lack of a liberal public sphere, the institutionalized and conformist nature of so much intellectual life, the mandarin tradition of thinking at a level of abstraction far removed from social reality. From the outside, Russia has been identified as the home of 'the true intelligentsia', of writers who act as the moral conscience of a whole people; from the inside, the backward condition of Russian society, whether in its Tsarist or Soviet forms, has been held to make any kind of critical, sophisticated public intellectual life impossible. From the outside, there is envy and admiration for the way the membership of broader social elites enjoyed by leading intellectual figures in Britain allows access both to political power and to culturally influential media; the view from the inside, as we have seen, is usually some variation on what I have been calling 'the absence thesis'.

If one surveys, however cursorily, the historiography of intellectuals in other European countries, one finds a strikingly similar pattern almost everywhere, namely, an established tradition of regarding intellectuals in the society in question as 'backward', 'marginalized', or simply 'absent'. Even in Germany, clearly France's most powerful cultural rival during most of this period, the comparison is, as we have already seen, constantly drawn in these unfavourable terms. For instance, in a recent survey Manfred Bock, pointing to certain distinctive features of German history, including the central presence of the *Bildungsbürgertum* and the relatively 'late' establishment of a nation-state, argued that these resulted in 'specificities peculiar to the history of intellectuals in Germany since the end of the nineteenth century, which distinguish it from the history of intellectuals in France, but which bring it somewhat closer to a certain number of other countries'. German conditions, he suggested, were 'unfavourable to the birth of a type of intellectual *à la française*, that is to say, characterised by a sense of autonomy and by the recognition of that within society'.[48] In reality, as we shall see, it is far from clear quite what this alleged 'autonomy' really involved, but this is nonetheless a representative illustration of the pattern of citing distinctive features of the national history in order to explain why intellectuals could not have 'emerged' as strongly as in France. In this respect, the situation in Germany (or, as it might be, in Britain) has more in common with that in 'a certain number of other countries'. It is France that provides at once the model and the exception.

The point, of course, is not to propose that there are no significant differences among these various countries in the matter of intellectuals, but rather to urge that the standard binary classification needs to be refined in at least three ways. First, one nearly always finds a contrast between the view from outside, which is prone to emphasize the important or effective part played by intellectuals in a given society, and the view from inside, which tends to offer a more pessimistic or at least sceptical account. Second, the different tropes that come together in the absence thesis can be found, in varying forms, in almost all relevant societies: idealized pasts and idealized elsewheres are rarely in short supply. And third, there is no 'European norm': on the question of intellectuals, there are patterns of similarity and contrast that cut across all conventional classifications of the major European countries. This still leaves open the possibility of there being something genuinely distinctive about the French case, a possibility I shall explore at greater length in Ch. 11. But first, it may be worth considering how this question looks if we start from somewhere that is at once much further afield and considerably nearer home.

NOTES

1. Philippe Bradfer, 'Quelques remarques sur les intellectuels en Belgique', in Marie-Christine Granjon, Nicole Racine, and Michel Trebitsch (eds.), *Histoire comparée des intellectuels* (Paris: IHTP, 1997), 19–22.
2. Ibid. 37, 31, 107, 31–2 (these essays were written in French since they were brought together and published by a scholarly network based in Paris; all translations are my own unless otherwise indicated).
3. In this and the following paragraph I have drawn some phrases from my essay 'Disciplines, canons, and publics: the history of "the history of political thought" in comparative perspective', in Dario Castiglione and Iain Hampsher-Monk (eds.), *The History of Political Thought in National Context* (Cambridge: Cambridge University Press, 2001), 280–302.
4. This argument is more fully developed in Michel Espagne, 'Sur les limites du comparatisme en histoire culturelle', *Genèses*, 17 (1994), 112–21.
5. Cf. Hartmut Kaelble, 'La Recherche européenne en histoire sociale', *Actes de la recherche en sciences sociales*, 106–7 (1995), 67–79. Or as Michel Trebitsch expressed it, summarizing an extensive literature, there is no escaping 'le fait que les comparaisons s'opèrent toujours d'un point de vue national, ce qui les empêche d'élaborer de véritables outils comparatifs et les enferme dans des catégories purement abstraites. Le *tertium comparationis*, la grill commune d'analyse qu'implique toute comparaison, loin de dégager des signifiés commensurables, n'est le plus souvent que la projection sur l'autre d'un point de vue strictement national.' Michel Trebitsch, 'L'histoire comparée des intellectuels comme histoire expérimentale', in Michel Trebitsch and Marie-Christine Granjon (eds.), *Pour une histoire comparée des intellectuels* (Brussels: editions Complexe, 1998), 70.
6. In addition to Granjon et al., *Histoire comparée*, and Trebitsch and Granjon, *Pour une histoire comparée des intellectuels*, both previously cited, I have drawn here upon

Christophe Charle, *Les Intellectuels en Europe au XIXe siècle: essai d'histoire comparée* (Paris: Seuil, 1996), and Michel Leymarie et Jean-François Sirinelli (eds.), *L'Histoire des intellectuels aujourd'hui* (Paris: PUF, 2003). Further material is from the double issue of *Liber: Revue internationale des livres* on 'intellectuals', 25–6 (Dec. 1995 and Mar. 1996), which also contains a helpful series of 'glossaries' of terms relating to intellectuals in the various European languages.

7. Pierre Bourdieu, 'Et pourtant . . .', *Liber*, 25 (Dec. 1995), 1.
8. Loïc Wacquant, 'Misère des academics américains', *Liber*, 26 (Mar. 1996), 1.
9. Dietz Bering, *Die Intellektuelle: Geschichte eines Schimpfwortes* (Stuttgart: Klett-Cotta, 1978).
10. Manfred Bock, 'Un monde intellectuel polycentrique et apolitique. Regards comparatistes sur les intellectuels allemands et les concepts mis en œuvre pour écrire leur histoire', in Leymarie and Sirinelli, *L'Histoire des intellectuels aujourd'hui*, 432.
11. Charle, *Intellectuels en Europe*, 278. 'L'Espagne est sans doute le pays d'Europe où le processus d'émergence des intellectuels comme force politique est le plus proche du cas français.'
12. See John Butt, *Writers and Politics in Modern Spain* (London: Hodder, 1978), quotation at 68–9.
13. See the helpful chapter on 'Maeztu: From Left to Right,' in Donald L. Shaw, *The Generation of 1898 in Spain* (London: Benn, 1975), 75–94.
14. Carlos Serrano, 'Histoire des intellectuels espagnols: panorama d'ensemble', in Granjon et al., *Histoire comparée*, 79. According to Stephen Roberts, it was probably in a letter by Unamuno in 1896 about the trial of Anarchist prisoners in Barcelona 'that the word "intelectual" was first used as a noun in the Spanish language'; Roberts, *Miguel de Unamuno: The Making of an Intellectual* (forthcoming, 2005). I am grateful to Dr Roberts for generously allowing me to read the Introduction to his book before publication.
15. Paul Aubert, 'Comment fait-on l'histoire des intellectuels en Espagne?', in Leymarie and Sirinelli, *L'Histoire des intellectuels aujourd'hui*, 81.
16. For a balanced introduction to 'the Generation of 98', see Shaw, *Generation of 1898*; the introduction to Roberts, *Unamuno*, provides a particularly helpful overview of this historiography.
17. Aubert, 'Intellectuels en Espagne', 63. 'Sans doute ne furent-ils pas conduits, dans aucun pays d'Europe, à jouer un rôle politique aussi important.'
18. Ignacio Echevarría, 'La Culture, entreprise de l'état', *Liber*, 25 (Dec. 1995), 4.
19. Roberts, *Unamuno*, 2.
20. Jan-Werner Müller, *Another Country: German Intellectuals, Unification, and National Identity* (London: Yale University Press, 2000), 280.
21. The classic account is Fritz Ringer, *The Decline of the German Mandarins: The German Academic Community 1890–1933* (Cambridge, Mass.: Harvard University Press, 1969).
22. See, for a particularly illuminating account, the chapter on Thomas Mann's *Betrachtungen eines Unpolitischen* ('Reflections of an Unpolitical Man') in T. J. Reed, *Thomas Mann: The Uses of Tradition* (Oxford: Oxford University Press, 1996 [1st edn. 1973]).
23. Hans Manfred Bock, 'Quelques remarques sur les intellectuels en Allemagne et sur leur historiographie', in Granjon et al., *Histoire comparée*, 38; Bock, 'Un monde intellectuel polycentrique et apolitique', 430–1. But cf. Woodruff D. Smith, *Politics and*

the Sciences of Culture in Germany 1840–1920 (Oxford: Oxford University Press, 1991), 196–8, who distinguishes two senses of the term 'apolitical': the first signifies complete lack of engagement with public affairs, but the second indicates a stance of 'objectivity' or 'non-partisan engagement', and Smith suggests that a good deal of debate about, for example, 'the social question' in Wilhelmine Germany was only 'unpolitical' in this second sense.

24. See the discussion of this description of 1848 in Ch. 12 below.
25. Charle, *Intellectuels en Europe*, 291.
26. Ibid. 283.
27. Hansgerd Schulte, 'Histoire des intellectuels en Allemagne', in Leymarie and Sirinelli, *L'Histoire des intellectuels aujourd'hui*, 30, 30–1.
28. Ibid. 31, 31–2.
29. Bock, 'Histoire et historiographie des intellectuels en Allemagne', 89; see also Anthony Phelan (ed.), *The Weimar Dilemma: Intellectuals in the Weimar Republic* (Manchester: Manchester University Press, 1985).
30. Schulte, 'Histoire des intellectuels en Allemagne', 36.
31. The book was published in French in 1927 and appeared in English translation the following year; see Ch. 12 below for fuller discussion of Benda.
32. Unlike in other Soviet-dominated parts of Eastern Europe, 'there was never in the RDA [i.e. East Germany] a significant opposition to the regime on the part of intellectuals, writers or academics'; Schulte, 'Histoire des intellectuels en Allemagne', 42.
33. Müller, *Another Country*, 8, 39–42.
34. Ibid. 61.
35. See Wolf Lepenies, 'The end of "German culture"', cited in Ch. 8 n. 26 above.
36. Michael Geyer, 'Introduction', in Geyer (ed.), *The Power of Intellectuals in Contemporary Germany* (Chicago: Chicago University Press, 2001), 2.
37. Bock, 'Histoire et historiographie des intellectuels en Allemagne', 79, 102.
38. Müller, *Another Country*, 14.
39. Frédérique Attal, 'Les Intellectuels italiens', in Leymarie and Sirinelli, *L'Histoire des intellectuels aujourd'hui*, 18.
40. Attal, 'Intellectuels italiens', 18. '... figure marquante de l'intellectuel antifasciste, continue de refuser l'usage du mot'.
41. Eric Hobsbawm, *Age of Extremes: The Short Twentieth Century 1914–1991* (London: Abacus, 1995 [1st edn. 1994]), 165.
42. Cf. ibid. 167–8: 'The love affair of French intellectuals with Marxism, the domination of Italian culture by people associated with the Communist party, both of which lasted for a generation, were products of the resistance.'
43. Attal, 'Intellectuels italien', 26.
44. Goffredo Fofi, 'L'ère de l'opinionismo', *Liber*, 25 (Dec. 1995), 5.
45. Carla Pasquinelli, 'From organic to neo-corporatist intellectuals: the changing relations between Italian intellectuals and political power', *Media, Culture and Society*, 17 (1995), 418, 414.
46. Pasquinelli, 'Italian intellectuals', 415, 418, 419, 420–1, 422, 424.
47. Ibid. 413.
48. Bock, 'Histoire et historiographie des intellectuels en Allenagne', 83.

10

Greener Grass: Letters from America

'The so-called intellectuals of the country are simply weather-vanes blown constantly by foreign winds, usually but not always English.'

I

The idea of a 'special relation' between Britain and the United States may have as much, or as little, value in the intellectual sphere as in the political and diplomatic. The linguistic and cultural links have been so intimate that one expects there to be close similarities in the intellectual traditions of the two countries, while the fundamental differences between the two societies suggest no less forcibly that there will be equally profound contrasts at the cultural level. This sense of ambivalent connection was already in place by the beginning of the twentieth century on both sides of the Atlantic: 'Even as consciousness of common cultural traditions joined the continents in the minds of late-nineteenth-century Americans, the contrast between new and old, raw and settled forced them all the further apart.'[1] This dialectic obviously expresses a pervasive tension in Britain's sense of cultural affiliation: Britain forms part of 'Europe' when viewed from across the Atlantic, but the two societies are the core of 'les pays anglo-saxons' when seen from continental Europe (or at least from France, always the most sensitive to Anglophone encroachment). On the question of intellectuals, therefore, the United States offers a differently revealing point of triangulation, figuring not, like France, as a defining opposite, thankfully distant while also sneakingly admired, but more as a younger sibling: bound by early ties and divided by subsequent experience; to be criticized or condescended to, but never entirely repudiated. Just how differently, then, has the question of intellectuals been put and answered in the United States?

The literature on this subject is vast and what follows is deliberately, and quite unapologetically, highly selective. I examine the American discussion simply in terms of the light it can throw upon the British case, and especially on the 'paradoxes of denial' that I have there identified. For these, relatively limited, purposes, the place to start may be with the long-standing American tradition of simultaneously lamenting the marginal or despised status of intellectuals in the United States and envying their (supposed) position in Britain. As with the corresponding British tradition, these attitudes have deep roots, going back long before the term 'intellectuals' established itself in American English. The representation of American society upon which such attitudes depended was, in essence, that made almost commonplace by foreign commentators such as Tocqueville, Arnold, and their successors: America as the first 'new', wholly created society, lacking tradition, aristocracy, culture, and so on. 'Democracy' was a key term in Tocqueville's profound analysis, 'philistinism' a recurring term in Arnold's much more off-hand and opportunistic remarks. The native tradition of commentary domesticated these accounts in various ways, now emphasizing the dominance of the business ethic, now the appeal of populism; at times worrying over the low level of the political class, at others taking pride in the practical bent of the growing number of educational institutions; sometimes celebrating the unparalleled regional and ethnic diversity, sometimes deploring the lack of a dominant capital in which political, social, and cultural elites overlapped. For much of the nineteenth century, what Santayana was later to label 'the genteel tradition' cultivated its ties to old England though increasingly forced to acknowledge that the larger society, fast-growing and ever more diverse, was less and less inclined to let its cultural style be entirely dictated by the upper class of New England. All this has meant that subsequent writing on these topics in America was to be at least as deeply imbued as the corresponding literature in Britain with a sense of the distinctiveness of the country's history and cultural situation, one that was uniquely inhospitable to those whom the twentieth century was increasingly to term 'intellectuals'.

However simplistic or partial these views were (and each element was subsequently to generate a revisionist industry of its own), they coloured the perception of the comparative position of thinkers and men of letters in nineteenth-century America compared to their counterparts in Victorian Britain. And this contrast long survived the period in which it was first formulated:

> To an American looking backward, the English intellectual of the Victorian era appears as *the* intellectual, one who could lay claim to the title and estate by what might almost be regarded as the principle of legitimacy—the unimpeachable right of descent. . . . The English intellectual had, until very recently, that additional mark of legitimacy which stamped a career that was at the same time dignified, remunerative, and socially influential—a unique combination of virtues to which Herr Professor, the feuilletoniste, and the American college teacher could never aspire.[2]

This comes from the mid-twentieth century and hints at a nostalgic idealizing of the British case which was by no means universally shared among American commentators at this point, but it nonetheless fairly indicates an enduring strand of national self-definition. It is worth digressing briefly here to remark how the three types here singled out by Himmelfarb for the purposes of making national contrasts differ from the three cited in the previous chapter from Pasquinelli's article about Italy. Here, the influential and well-connected English intellectual is contrasted with the less exalted condition of the German professor, the French essayist or journalist, and the American academic; in Pasquinelli's case, the relatively low status of the politically dependent Italian intellectual is contrasted with 'the great representatives of culture' in France, 'the moral and scientific authority' of academics in Britain, and the 'powerful' journalists in the United States. As so often, the outcome of comparisons turns on the choice of what to compare, and that choice in turn reflects one's pre-existing sense of the contrasts.

In the opening decades of the twentieth century, the *term* 'intellectuals' rooted itself in the language somewhat earlier and more successfully in the United States than in Britain. As early as 1908 one commentator, referring to in-fighting among Socialist organizations, remarked that 'it is the "intellectuals" who are attacking the "intellectuals" ', and it was in the milieu of radical politics that the term first took hold.[3] A group of politically and aesthetically rebellious young writers in New York in the early 1910s took to calling themselves 'the Young Intellectuals', on which Henry F. May comments: 'As it was used in the teens, the word *Intellectual* associated one with Europe, and particularly with the young heroes of novels from Stendhal to Joyce: the young men fresh from the provinces who had come to the capitals in search of experience and a role in the movement of their time.... Still more daringly, so long as they did not venture uptown, the women could smoke and bob their hair with impunity, and the men could wear flannel shirts.'[4] However, all such questers inevitably suffered from the perception that they were but pale imitations of their counterparts in old Europe, especially in France. As Randolph Bourne, normally disposed to vindicate the values of his home society, observed in 1914: 'Our "intellectuals" will have to sharpen up their knowledge and stiffen their fibre a good deal, it seems to me, before they can take the commanding place of leadership which they fill in France.'[5] That the category was so exclusively composed of young *men* suggested that even in an area where Americans often thought of their society as more advanced than those of old Europe there was no cause for celebration. The writer Mary Austin noted that whatever the term 'intellectuals' meant abroad,

> in the United States it stands for a small group of determinedly young and preponderantly male persons, for the most part engaged in retrieving from the sum of human knowledge such facts as tend to show that we would all be much better off if society were quite other than it is. In the current periodicals where our American Intellectuals are actively in evidence, it is noticeable that there are few women's names, and none that stand out as convincingly, femininely original.[6]

A useful witness on this whole topic is Harold Stearns, an essayist and publicist who made something of a speciality of taking the pulse of America's intellectuals in the late 1910s and early 1920s. Stearns not only used the label very freely—'why should we hesitate to use the term? why should it carry with it a faint aura of effeminate gentility?'—he also urged upon his sceptical compatriots the importance of the role it designated.[7] He resisted the common American tendency to think of college professors as the core of the category, since their professional commitments exercised a constraint upon 'the intellectuals' ideal—the correct and fine one, too—that first and foremost the intellectual must be disinterested, non-sectarian and non-partisan, devoted to no pursuit except pursuit of the truth' (one wonders what professional commitments the academics were assumed to have that conflicted with this ideal). Nor did the much-celebrated achievements of the sciences furnish the true path for the intellectual to follow, since this had resulted in knowledge being subdivided into 'too many unrelated specialisms'; 'the truth of the whole range of human life' was the intellectuals' legitimate bailiwick. But Stearns then launched into a short disquisition on the 'true' sense of the term, revealing once again that the proper models for this valuable activity were to be found elsewhere:

> No, the term intellectuals has come to mean something both broader and narrower; publicists, editors of non-trade magazines, pamphleteers, writers on general topics. In France they are represented by such men as Henri Barbusse, Anatole France, and Romain Rolland; in England, say, by Shaw, Wells, Chesterton, Angell, Massingham, Scott, Brailsford, Wallas and Cole; in America—by such as the reader may nominate.[8]

The placing of that final clause as a calculated hesitation-step could be seen as expressing a proper diffidence about making invidious selections from among one's contemporaries, but it surely has the effect of calling into question the very existence of any American candidates who are on a par with these European exemplars. Those short lists themselves are also revealing in several ways: first, that France and Britain are the two countries chosen to provide the benchmark, assumed to be more similar in this respect than they are different; second, that the illustrative list of English intellectuals is three times longer than that of their French counterparts; third, that both lists, the English especially, lean heavily towards not just literature but journalism (Stearns was not alone, of course, in mingling occupational roles—'editors of non-trade magazines'—with the almost hopelessly circular *omnium gatherum*, 'writers on general topics'). It is doubtful that English commentators of the time would have put full-time editors such as H. W. Massingham or C. P. Scott in any such list, more doubtful still that they would have labelled them intellectuals. But the envious eye is prone to misprisions of this sort, and the undeniable *national* standing, by 1921, of the editors of the *Nation* and the *Manchester Guardian* might well have seemed enviable to any American journalist, even one based in New York.

This constellation of attitudes, involving elements of misperception, envy, and fantasy, particularly formed around the position of writers, assumed to be treated as earthly gods in Europe and derided as unpractical scribblers in America. This perception was expressed in and reinforced by the literary balance of trade, as well as by the patterns of individual migration, far more American writers serving a spell as expatriates in Europe than the other way around. In such cases, the society they left behind was almost inevitably depicted as philistine and parochial, irredeemably mired in money-making (though the strength of the dollar was an essential precondition for their being able to live so cheaply in Europe). Correspondingly, part of the pull of Europe lay in the belief that writers and other intellectuals were more respected and more influential there. As Stearns confidently declared in his essay, 'Where are our intellectuals?': 'The fact remains that in France and England this group has exercised, and is exercising today, enormous influence; it is also the fact that in America today it is exercising no influence at all.'[9]

The cumulative impact of these (and other) attitudes, placed within the wider history sketched at the beginning of this chapter, resulted in the discourse about intellectuals in the United States during at least the first half of the twentieth century being dominated by the theme of the intellectual as 'alienated' from or not 'at home' in American society. And this theme was mirrored in many of the indigenous attitudes towards intellectuals, who were indeed seen as essentially 'foreign' in their affiliations and affectations, still hankering after the cultural perquisites of old Europe. Vernacular anti-intellectualism often fastened on this abject, un-American, dependence: in the 1920s that scourge of 'highbrow' pretension, H. L. Mencken, sneered (as quoted in the epigraph to this chapter) that 'the so-called intellectuals of the country are simply weather-vanes blown constantly by foreign winds, usually but not always English'.[10] This accurately expressed a powerful strain in American attitudes through at least the first half of the twentieth century, though, of course, if one substitutes 'French' for 'English' in this remark, it might also seem familiar from any of the hundreds of off-the-peg dismissals of 'so-called intellectuals' in Britain.

The currency of 'highbrow' from the 1910s and, considerably later, of 'egghead' were similarly expressive of deep egalitarian sentiments in American society, and both quickly came to be used as synonyms for 'intellectual' in its slightly sneering or dismissive form.[11] But the Socialist-cum-social-scientific usage had greater impact in the USA than in Britain, and in the first half of the century it was used fairly commonly as a term of social analysis in both scholarly and journalistic writing. One particular difference from the British usage, reflecting different social conditions, was that the core group designated by the occupational sense of 'intellectuals' came to be that relatively numerous class, the 'college professors', and in the more sustained sociological accounts produced in the middle of the century, academics continued to be at the heart of, and sometimes even coextensive with, the category of 'intellectuals' as a whole. As always, however, the growth of academic specialism generated anxiety and protest and a corresponding emphasis on how the defining role of the intellectual lay in the transcendence of specialism. This view was most forcibly expressed by those who had defined their own careers in opposition to the perceived narrowness of the burgeoning academic disciplines. For example, Waldo Frank asserted in 1940 that 'the intellectual's specialty is the whole', while Lewis Mumford declared the task facing the intellectual was to 'think and live not as "the specialist" but as "the whole man".[12] Within academia itself, various movements and programmes, particularly in the central humanities subjects such as English, History, and Philosophy, took on the burden of sustaining the 'generalist' perspective that was always supposed to be on the verge of extinction, and the champions of these developments were understandably more prone than their opponents to cast themselves as 'intellectuals'.[13]

As we shall see, there has been considerable debate about the extent to which academics have enjoyed status and influence in American society, but one constant of these discussions has been the perception that their counterparts in Europe, and sometimes especially in Britain, have been far more favourably placed in these respects. A recurring emphasis here (we saw an example of it in the analysis by Edward Shils discussed in Ch. 6 above) has been on the personal ties alleged to link British intellectuals to members of the political and social elites, and the consequent sense of cultural centrality and access to power they are supposed to have enjoyed. In this respect, it could be said that precisely that condition of being so closely linked to 'the Establishment' which, according to radical critics, has been one of the elements *preventing* the existence of 'genuine' intellectuals in Britain, turns out, when seen by transatlantic observers acutely conscious of their supposedly marginal or disregarded position in their own society, to be one of the hallmarks of the *possession* of a flourishing intellectual class.

The assumption that intellectuals were more numerous, more influential, and better rewarded in France and Britain than in the United States in the nineteenth and early twentieth centuries may seem to have been in large part justified by the evident facts of American society at that stage of its development. Nonetheless, in the American as in the British and other cases, the power of cultural tradition plays an essential part in my account, continuing to shape attitudes and beliefs long after the original formative conditions have altered or disappeared. The decade or so after 1945 has been represented as something of a turning-point in this respect, directing attention rather to the question of whether intellectuals were not in fact now far more 'at home' in American society (or, in the social-scientific vocabulary of the day, far better 'integrated' with it) than they had been previously. But although this generated a somewhat different mode of reflection, the perception of the United States as a society *peculiarly* inhospitable to intellectuals remained, as we shall see, powerfully active.

II

The group whose own development has been taken to be both largely constitutive of this development and emblematic of the larger fortunes of the intellectual in the United States was that clustered around *Partisan Review* and always known as 'the New York Intellectuals'.[14] (To indicate that this term is the label used to refer to a particular group, rather than to intellectuals who happen to live in

New York, I shall follow the practice of some other scholars in capitalizing the noun.) Quite why this small, highly unrepresentative, group of writers and thinkers should have come to assume such symbolic importance is a question which the vast subsequent literature does not altogether answer.[15] Indeed, this literature itself constantly threatens to exaggerate their significance, and simply by engaging with it at any length one risks appearing to collude with this exaggeration. It is worth remarking at the outset, therefore, that the scope of the cultural authority of this group was severely limited even in its heyday: what played in Greenwich Village bombed in Peoria. The different position occupied by New York in American society compared to that of Paris in France, or even London in Britain, is pertinent here. The volume of attention lavished on them is, as I have already implied, as much a function of the needs and fantasies of later academic authors as a fair reflection of their *national* prominence at the time. (Another group who have received considerable retrospective attention are the Southern Agrarians, who similarly marked the transition from men of letters to academics. One can identify certain points in common here with the '*Scrutiny* group' around F. R. Leavis, but although there may have been some resemblances in the eventual academic influence of both groups, where impact on the wider culture is concerned one is reminded of how much more regional was the role of the Southern Agrarians, and how much harder it was for them to attract the interest of mainstream media for their cultural criticism.[16])

Among the best-known names normally taken to be members or at least affiliates of the New York Intellectuals (relations which could encompass violent attacks on other names on the list) were William Barrett, Daniel Bell, Clement Greenberg, Irving Howe, Mary McCarthy, Dwight Macdonald, William Phillips, Philip Rahv, and Lionel Trilling. From the mid-1930s to the mid-1940s, the heroic phase of the New York Intellectuals' oft-told odyssey, many of these figures made a somewhat precarious living as freelance writers and journalists. Their position was principally defined by the conjunction in their work of a form of left-wing anti-Stalinism in politics and a commitment to European Modernism in literature and the arts. Several of them were Jews, the children of the immigrant generation around the turn of the nineteenth century; many were ex-Communists or Communist sympathizers who 'broke' with the party as the excesses of Stalin's autocracy became apparent in the late 1930s; all were vigorous essayists and polemicists for whom the periodical article was the preferred means of intervention in the intensely local and inward-looking debates among their circle of New York-based bohemian leftists.

Appropriately, therefore, the group's collective existence centred on a journal. Following an early, faltering, phase as a Communist organ, *Partisan Review* was relaunched in 1937, after which it was defined by its attempt to 'combine the functions of a Marxist theoretical journal with those of a little magazine'.[17] In the ensuing two decades, at the end of which period it was already beginning to decline in importance, these two functions came increasingly into conflict, and the journal made its mark in American life more as the voice of a cultural avant-garde than as the mouthpiece of a political vanguard. But to the New York Intellectuals themselves, this cultural role continued to be a form of oppositionality, an expression of their cherished marginality within or dissent from mainstream American culture. 'Rather like their contemporaries, the émigré German Marxists of the Frankfurt School, they had come to view Modernism as one of the few surviving oppositional forces in society, and therefore thought that by helping to preserve it they were performing a radical function.'[18]

Their criticism of and distance from the so-called 'mass society' of the United States fostered a sense of 'alienation' which they took to be the essential mark of the true intellectual. And they generalized the case in a way that should by now be familiar, not merely with respect to the United States. 'During the late 1930s and early 1940s *Partisan Review*'s editors complained repeatedly that the US had failed to evolve a mature intellectual tradition. Throughout the nation's history, they claimed, writers and artists had been baffled and frustrated by the absence of a continuous intelligentsia.'[19] They cast envious eyes on Europe in this respect (continental Europe more than Britain in most of their cases), leading the critic Randall Jarrell to complain that they seemed to think of America as 'a backward Europe', adding that *Partisan Review* was 'barely an American magazine, and always sinks with a sigh of joy into the friendly harbor of Sartre, Camus, Silone, the great European writers'.[20] As intellectuals, their carefully nurtured identity as 'alienated' and their much-vaunted position of 'independence' were held to support and reinforce each other. In practice, their independence meant, as it usually does, dependence on editors and proprietors, and sometimes directly on benefactors. The strains of this position were made manifest when, from 1947, a wealthy backer enabled *Partisan Review* temporarily to quit its Greenwich Village location and move to plusher quarters in midtown Manhattan. For a journal that had defined itself as catering to what long-time editor William Phillips called a 'community outside the cultural market-place', this was unnerving: perhaps it was being co-opted. Fortunately, the subsidies did not last, and it moved back to the West Village some years later, a move which Phillips saw as a resumption of 'its old pure and marginal existence'.[21] But in 1963, it moved again to New Jersey to offices provided by Rutgers, where Phillips was by now a professor. 'Institutionalization' here did literally involve suburbanization, the ultimate nightmare of the properly alienated, bohemian, urban intellectual.

I would suggest that this trajectory is one of the major reasons why the New York Intellectuals have figured so prominently in the literature on this subject, especially but not exclusively in the USA. There could, after all, be little question of the contributions to a few, largely Manhattan-based, small magazines between the late 1930s and the mid-1950s having had a decisive impact on American politics and society. But as I have argued more generally, the structure of the concept of intellectuals constantly generates the lament that intellectuals have retreated from some form of independence into some form of institutional dependence, a retreat seen as simultaneously signalling a move away from engagement with public affairs into private or specialized pursuits. As it happened, the actual careers of the majority of the New York Intellectuals provided handy illustrations of this perennial thesis. Several of the group's leading figures who had been freelance writers in the 1930s and 1940s began to take up posts in universities in the 1950s and 1960s. They have therefore figured as the chief exhibits in many a prosecution case about 'the retreat into the ivory tower', and have frequently been seen as 'the last intellectuals'. With the vastly increased role of higher education in the second half of the twentieth century, and the absorption within it of many who had previously made a living in other ways, the New York Intellectuals assumed the status of having been the last 'independent' intellectuals, which is to say (on the tendentious view often favoured in this literature) the last 'real' intellectuals.[22]

When examined more closely, however, these careers can be seen to have owed more to contingent material circumstances than to any teleology of the 'decline of the intellectual'. They were, as I indicated earlier, nearly all children of that vast wave of immigrants that swept over America at the end of the nineteenth and beginning of the twentieth centuries, the first generation to grow up in America and have access to higher education, most often to New York's City College, 'the immigrants' Harvard'. Several of them were Jewish, conscious of the near-complete exclusion of Jews from faculty appointments at all the most prestigious American colleges and universities in the first few decades of the century. Moreover, they came to adulthood in the Depression years of the 1930s, when regular employment of any kind, including academic employment, was hard to come by. These circumstances changed with the sustained period of prosperity that followed the end of the Second World War: between 1947 and 1960 the gross national product more than doubled; over the same period the number of academics in colleges and universities grew at an even faster rate, up to 380,000 by the latter date. Philip Rahv, one of the defining figures at the very heart of this group, recognized the significance of these changes at the time: 'It is imperative not to overlook so direct and concrete a factor as the long spell of prosperity that America has enjoyed since the War. It has at long last effected the absorption of the intellectuals into the institutional life of this country.'[23] Born in another generation, coming from a different social or ethnic background, growing up in a more prosperous era, they might well have followed more conventional academic careers from the outset. Their moves into academic posts in the post-war year reflected not any 'selling-out' to conformism, but again the circumstances that the vastly expanded universities of this period were more open in their appointment policies and positively eager to recruit figures who had already made a name in some literary or intellectual field.

The key symbolic statement in this long-running preoccupation was undoubtedly the 1952 symposium in *Partisan Review* entitled 'Our country and our culture'.[24] The provoking use of the first-person plural was part of the point: could genuine intellectuals identify with and take responsibility for the culture of their native country? In launching the symposium, the editors of the magazine made clear that they believed a decisive change *had* taken place, and for good reasons, to do with the positive developments in the USA under the New Deal and during the Second World War—the dominant position of the United States in the world, the improved material and social condition of intellectuals in America, the loss of cultural deference to Europe, and so on. But they also clearly expected their respondents to be troubled by this new situation, not least as presaging a possible sell-out to 'mass culture': the United States was assumed to be the primary home of this new cultural form, one which was, furthermore, assumed to be inherently antagonistic to the values and interests of intellectuals. Although the contributors to the symposium expressed a variety of responses to the supposed threat of 'mass culture', they by and large agreed with the premise about a changed attitude towards America. As Lionel Trilling ironically summarized the new orthodoxy: 'For the first time in the history of the modern American intellectual, America is not to be conceived of as *a priori* the vulgarest and stupidest nation of the world.'[25]

The tradition of regarding American intellectuals as alienated from their society was briskly summarized in Irving Howe's contribution:

> The 'alienation' of American intellectuals has at least three major sources: a sense of inferiority felt by earlier generations toward European tradition; a decision, often the result of a radical commitment, to break from official society; and the inheritance of the central experience of modern European writers, which begins with Stendhal's and Flaubert's hatred for bourgeois values, leads to the appearance of a precarious caste of literary intelligentsia, and ends with the cult of aesthetic difficulty and the unappreciated artist working in estrangement from the public.[26]

Two features of this passage call for comment here. First, it is written from an emphatically *literary* perspective: 'intellectuals' are equated with 'writers', and literary bohemia is assumed to be their natural habitat. The many thousands of relatively conventional 'college professors' are not what Howe has in mind. Second, this account foregrounds European Modernism, in its broadest form, as the source of American intellectuals' self-conception, that cultivation of aesthetic form which represents a self-conscious withdrawal from and repudiation of established society. In these respects, the passage not only expresses Howe's own position, but is again emblematic of the way in which, from the mid-century onwards, the trajectory of the New York Intellectuals came to figure as the central reference point for all discussion of this topic in the United States. This trajectory provided the most readily available illustration of the structural contrast between 'intellectuals' (bohemian, unspecialized, addressing public issues) and 'academics' (conformist, specialized, eschewing public issues). This is borne out by the centrality of the New York Intellectuals to the story told in Jacoby's *The Last Intellectuals*, the work which more than any other was to give currency to the term which dominated American discussion of this question at the end of the twentieth century, namely 'public intellectuals'.[27] The term is now routinely retrojected onto earlier periods, principally to refer to those figures who did more than address a specialized or discipline-based public. It is, however, a term which reflects the circumstances not of the 1950s or any earlier period to which it is now applied, but those of the closing decades of the century, where it is principally used to pick out those few academics who enjoy a significant media presence and who use the opportunity to address current political and social issues. At the time, it is worth remembering, no one called Rahv, Greenberg, and company 'the New York Public Intellectuals'.

It should be evident by now that these contrasts, which many American writers have tended to think of as being an expression of distinctively American conditions, are in fact characteristic of all discussion of the role of intellectuals, since they are all manifestations of the tension at the heart of that role—between the specialist and non-specialist functions, between the initial qualifying activity and the 'speaking out', between 'inside' and 'outside'. (Part of the legerdemain successfully practised by the New York Intellectuals was to pass off their small world, which was really its own kind of 'inside', as an 'outside'.) In so far as there was something of a rapprochement between American intellectuals and their society in the middle of the century, it was accompanied from the outset by the anxiety that it would entail the abandonment of the critical function which had by then become historically associated with the role. For example, Irving Howe (again), writing two years after the *Partisan Review* symposium, was a notable dissenter from the happy state of affairs it largely reported, and the founding of *Dissent* was one of the more lasting expressions of his dissidence (it was, after all, Howe who wrote: 'When intellectuals can do nothing else, they start a magazine'[28]). Writing in, naturally, *Partisan Review*, he took issue with what he called 'this age of conformity' in an essay subsequently described as 'perhaps the classic 1950s statement of independent intellectuals'.[29] 'What has actually been taking place is the absorption of large numbers of intellectuals, previously independent, into the world of government bureaucracy and public committees; into the constantly growing industries of pseudo-culture; into the adult education business which subsists on regulated culture anxiety.' As I have already suggested, the sense in which these earlier figures deserved to be called 'independent' requires some scrutiny, but Howe's argument turned on precisely the tendentious contrast which this term built in from the outset: 'For it is crucial to the history of the American intellectuals in the past few decades ... that whenever they become absorbed into the accredited institutions of society they not only lose their traditional rebelliousness but to one extent or another *they cease to function as intellectuals.*'

Howe's essay, it soon emerges, is another lament for the loss of bohemia, with its sustaining sense of principled nonconformity and carefully cultivated independence.[30] But it also revealed the ambivalence towards European models which continued to haunt American discussion of the topic. For example, in a shrewd hit at the kind of conservative cultural politics associated with the second generation of the New Critics, Howe observed that the prevailing emphasis on 'tradition' in current American academic literary criticism expressed 'the provincial American need to be more genteel than the gentry, more English than the English'. Or again, in mourning the passing of the literary avant-garde in America, he declared: 'The *avant garde* first appeared on the American scene some 25 or 30 years ago, as a response to the need for absorbing the meanings of the cultural revolution that had taken place in Europe during the first two decades of the century.'[31] The nativist pride potentially present in the first of these remarks is somewhat undercut by the apparent acceptance that the 'American need' is indeed 'provincial', while the second comment's yearning for the revival of an indigenous avant-garde seems to involve a prior yearning for there to be new cultural movements in *Europe* for it to respond to.

III

In the course of the 1950s and early 1960s, the dialectic between the emphases of 'alienation' and 'integration' was in a sense transposed to the domain of national politics, as the persecution of intellectuals (and others) during the era of 'McCarthyism' was followed by the attention and favours perceived as being lavished on selected intellectuals during the Kennedy administration. This pointed political sequence formed the backdrop (and surely some of the stimulus) to one of the most influential books on this topic, Richard Hofstadter's, *Anti-Intellectualism in American Life*, published in 1963.[32] Hofstadter's book was not narrowly or even primarily about attitudes towards intellectuals as such, but more broadly about attitudes towards what he encompassingly referred to as 'intellect'. (He quoted two somewhat flip definitions of the intellectual—Jacques Barzun's 'the intellectual is a man who carries a brief-case' and Harold Rosenberg's 'the intellectual is one who turns answers into questions'—but showed no sign of distinguishing the sociological and subjective senses which these two examples gestured towards.)[33] Nonetheless, his book helped to give a more sophisticated turn, and much greater historical depth, to a topic which was always in danger of being reduced to a wholly predictable sequence of lifeless types, like one of those elaborate mechanical clocks found on some European town halls, where representative figures take it in turns to enact their stiff-kneed rituals.

Hofstadter identified four main sources of the anti-intellectualism which, in a careful formulation, he found 'pervasive' but rarely 'dominant': Evangelical religion, primitivism, the business ethic, and egalitarianism in politics and education. In an impressive survey, stretching over three centuries of American history, he amply documented the ways these forces had made the United States unreceptive to the claims of what the twentieth century called 'the intellectual'. (Along the way, he quoted a host of pronouncements by representative American figures that would have seemed all too familiar to British readers, looking to explain the 'peculiarly' anti-intellectual qualities of *their* society, pronouncements that could be distilled into Theodore Roosevelt's dictum, reminiscent of a whole procession of Victorian headmasters: 'Character is far more important than intellect to the race as to the individual'.) However, Hofstadter drew an unfamiliar moral from this story. 'Hence, in our own time, those intellectuals whose conception of their role is formed by the history of this society find it strange and even repellent that intellectuals should experience success or have any association with power.'[34] But, he insisted, intellectuals did now enjoy such success and such association, and the last chapter of his book was in some ways a call to American intellectuals to manifest the maturity which such an established position required, rather than deliberately cultivating the adolescent attitude of outsiderness.

Hofstadter cited the 1952 *Partisan Review* symposium as a promising sign in this respect, a sign of, among other things, the fact that America had 'matured culturally, and no longer stood in tutelage to Europe'. But even the supremely self-confident Hofstadter did not find it quite so easy to shake off all traces of such tutelage. He noted that intellectuals in the United States had oscillated between complaining about being disregarded by society and anguishing about being embraced by it, and he went on: 'Among the intellectuals of the Western world, the Americans are probably the most prone to such pricks of conscience, possibly because they feel the constant necessity of justifying their role. British and French intellectuals, for example, usually take for granted the worth of what they are doing and the legitimacy of their claims on the community.'[35] Hofstadter, who was very much an American historian of America, is of course merely falling back on received notions here, but for my purposes it is nonetheless striking that France and Britain, viewed from this perspective, look so similar—and the position of the intellectual in the two countries so similarly secure. Hofstadter may have wanted American intellectuals to recognize their greater 'integration' in American society, and especially to repudiate the new forms of 'alienation' becoming fashionable in the 1960s, but even he constantly implied that all this would be so much easier to do if one were a *European* intellectual.

A counterweight to the relative optimism of Hofstadter's conclusion was provided by a book which expressed one characteristically American form of unease with the figure of the intellectual, Christopher Lasch's *The New Radicalism: The Intellectual as a Social Type*, published two years later. (In an interview almost thirty years later, Lasch acknowledged that the last chapter of his own book was intended to be a rebuttal of Hofstadter's account.[36]) Lasch was not sympathetic to what he saw as the intellectuals' self-created distance: 'these fantasies of omnipotence, together with their concomitant fears of hostility and persecution, spring from the isolation of American intellectuals, as a class, from the main currents of American life'. Implicitly, he positioned himself as one who spoke from within these 'main currents of American life'. But Lasch, too, allowed himself to think that the grass was greener elsewhere, as for example in his aside that an Englishman cannot understand the 'desperation which underlies American radicalism' arising out of the sense of impotence in an anti-intellectual, money-and-mass-communication dominated society.[37]

Lasch recognized that intellectuals had achieved a new prestige by the 1960s. His own epitome of this newly favourable image of the intellectual involved, however, a deliberate display of ironic distance:

> The intellectual was typically a graduate of an Ivy League college; he wore Ivy League clothes with the same casual authority with which he talked about books, wine and women; he had travelled widely, mostly in Europe; he lived in a modern house filled with Danish furniture; his boys had long hair instead of crew cuts; his political opinions, like his other tastes, were vaguely unconventional and 'advanced'; he was always questioning things the rest of us took for granted. In short, he was 'sophisticated'. The older images of the intellectual as absent-minded professor, or again as wild-eyed, long-haired political agitator, were no longer current.[38]

'Things the rest of *us* took for granted'? Lasch went on to make something of a career out of being a critic of 'the liberal elite' from the populist Left, but this is surely a striking instance of constructing an image of the (Europeanized) intellectual in terms which place oneself firmly outside it, the more striking still given that in a later interview Lasch said of himself 'I wanted to be an intellectual, not an academic.'[39]

A central element in Lasch's argument was that intellectuals often affected a more down-to-earth style as a way of assuming the colouring of their hostile environment. He quoted Benjamin Ginzburg on the point:

> In no country of the world is there such a tremendous gap between the values recognized by intellectuals and the values that actually govern political and economic realities. And yet in no country is the intellectual so preoccupied with affecting the course of politics to the exclusion of his intellectual interests. The less power he has of determining conditions, the more passionate, it would seem, is his will-o'-the-wisp quest of political influence.
>
> It is here that the philosophy of Pragmatism is most revealing. Pragmatism has been wrongly called the philosophy of the practical man. It represents rather the anti-intellectualism of the American intellectual, who is overawed by the practical sweep of American life.[40]

There is, of course, culpable oversimplification here as far as the complex philosophical history of Pragmatism is concerned, but in more general terms it accurately identifies a certain kind of pressure on American intellectuals, and goes at least some way towards explaining the emergence of that distinctive American type, the hard-boiled egg-head.

Returning to the wider picture of American intellectuals in the second half of the twentieth century, we need (especially when keeping in mind the contrast with Britain) to remember that most writing on the subject increasingly focused on academics rather than on creative writers. It is also worth remarking that far more of this writing in America has tended to be by social scientists. One notable example here was Seymour Martin Lipset's influential, and subsequently much-cited, attempt to challenge the traditional account of 'alienated' intellectuals in his article, 'American intellectuals: their politics and status', first published in 1959 and later reprinted in abbreviated form (in what was for long the standard anthology on the subject) under the more revealing title 'The real status of American intellectuals'.[41] Lipset's opening sentence announced his theme: 'The supposedly unhappy plight of the intellectuals in America has been a favorite topic for introspective analysis by many in this occupational category.' One notes from the outset the social scientist's tendency to regard intellectuals as an 'occupational category', while 'supposedly' also signals a revisionist intent. In practice, Lipset's case relied upon a brisk summary of 'the facts', which essentially took the form of attitudinal-survey findings, 'demonstrating' that the intellectual was in fact highly regarded. (A more sceptical reading of this evidence might conclude that it showed that some people, when asked, thought they ought to reply that they esteemed the role of college professor.)

Why therefore, asked Lipset, did the American intellectual *think* he (still very much *he* in this period) was so under-appreciated?

I suspect that in large measure his feelings of inferiority derive from his glorified conception of the status of the European intellectual and from his using the European situation as a comparison. Anyone who has ever been in a discussion about the life of an intellectual in this country knows that sooner or later someone will remark that in England, Germany, France, or Italy a writer, painter, composer, or professor really counts. There, such a man is recognized by the public and by the political and economic elites.

Lipset's article went on to touch on several good structural reasons why the American intellectual might justifiably feel under-appreciated: 'the seeming isolation of intellectuals from other sections of the elite', 'their lack of direct contact with political power', 'the egalitarian ethos', 'the fact that there are in absolute as well as proportionate terms more intellectuals in America and they are more widely dispersed geographically than in any other country', and so on. All this contrasted with what was perceived to be the situation 'of his British or French counterpart' (again appearing so similar from such a distance). Lipset clearly felt that he had demonstrated, to his own satisfaction at least, that American intellectuals were not justified in thinking of themselves as marginal or disregarded. However, the emphasis, and still more the tone, of his article might rather seem to embody some of the attitudes against which American intellectuals had traditionally protested. By reducing the issue to such matters as the pay of college teachers relative to other middle-class occupations, and by implicitly urging intellectuals to stop grumbling, Lipset largely sidestepped the key questions about cultural authority, and tended to dismiss international comparisons as an irrelevant distraction.[42]

In both manner and content, Lipset's article was representative of the type of writing which in the middle decades of the century came to dominate the discussion of intellectuals more generally, not just in America. Its informing perspectives were those of the social sciences, especially here the sociological theories of Talcott Parsons and Robert Merton; social survey evidence bulked large, proper names were rare or entirely absent, and the stress was largely on the way 'intellectuals', defined in the broadest socio-professional sense, contributed to the 'functioning' of advanced societies. Among these social scientists, the figure who came nearest to making the topic his own was Edward Shils (already encountered in Ch. 6), who gave the discussion a more Mannheimian, and hence ultimately Weberian, inflection than was common in American social science of the mid-century. Shils' œuvre is an abundant one (his publications span almost 60 years from the mid-1930s to his death in 1995), but the essay which best summarizes the contribution of his sociological perspective to an understanding of the trajectory of intellectuals in the United States was the one entitled, 'Intellectuals and the center of society in the United States', first published in 1972 in his collection *The Intellectuals and the Powers*.

In taking the long historical view, Shils reiterated the standard emphasis on the intellectuals' sense of distance or exclusion from the centre of American society in the nineteenth and early twentieth century:

> From the Jacksonian revolution until the administration of Franklin Roosevelt, intellectuals, particularly literary and humanistic-publicistic intellectuals in the United States, found much to distress them in the actions and culture of the ruling groups of their society. The long persistent, indeed, still lingeringly persistent, preoccupation of American intellectuals—especially literary men and humanistic publicists—with Europe was part of an attachment to a culture in which they thought intellectuals 'counted'.

France and Britain are again bracketed together as societies where intellectuals were integrated with the dominant elites, and Germany was viewed enviously from across the Atlantic as a place where professors enjoyed high social standing and the universities were expected to train the upper civil servants. By contrast, American men of letters saw the public life of their society as dominated by intellectually low-level, corrupt politicians and provincial 'practical men' (in 1931 Edmund Wilson described American politicians as 'a group that seems unique among the governing classes in having managed to be corrupt, uncultivated and incompetent all at once'). The civil service was for long politicized and did not offer a career aspiration for the cultivated classes. 'American intellectuals were pained by their membership in a society, the rulers of which seemed to have no need for them'.[43]

Shils also endorsed the conventional wisdom about the increasing 'integration' of intellectuals from the New Deal and the Second World War onwards, noting the vastly enlarged number of scientists and experts of various types and the growth of higher education, as well as America's changed position in the world.

'From the condition of being peripheral in a society which they believed was culturally provincial, American intellectuals came to see themselves as effective members of the center of an intellectual metropolis.' They were increasingly employed by government and increasingly honoured. All of this was 'a major change for a society which intellectuals had asserted was the society most uncongenial to the life of the spirit of any great society known to history'. Shils acknowledged that there was a continuing strain of critique in American intellectuals' response to their society, focused principally on the phenomenon of 'mass culture', but his own political inclinations start to manifest themselves in the disparaging tone of his treatment here: 'This critique, which had a multiple ancestry in patrician disdain, aesthetic revulsion, puritanical disapprobation, and a high-brow Marxism, did not have a wide adherence.' But even Shils had to recognize that a form of disaffection from American society had again become extremely common in the course of the previous decade.

As was the case with so much of Shils's later writing, a markedly conservative cultural agenda makes its presence felt here: he added his voice to those demonizing 'the sixties' for their lawless self-indulgence and abandonment of the restraining power of tradition. These attitudes ran counter to the 'true' function of intellectuals in modern America: 'The incorporation of the intellectuals into the central institutional system is now integral to the structure of American society.' By retaining, even cultivating, some of their tradition of alienation, intellectuals were now, in Shils's jaundiced view, undermining authority from within. The problem, it seems, was particularly acute in universities: 'It should be observed that the primary culture of the intellectuals is increasingly generated in academic institutions, where there is a delicately poised and not always equally stable balance between, on the one hand, a discipline which acknowledges at least the authority of its own traditions and of the institutions which sustain them and, on the other, a more antinomian and expressive culture.' His unsurprising conclusion was that stability depended upon 'the predominance of that element which accepts an objective discipline'.[44] Shils, as we saw with his discussion of the British case, found the condition of intellectuals in the 1950s (as he perceived it) very much to his taste, and he takes his place among those many other writers on this subject whose analyses turn a specific historical situation into a general prescription.

IV

Up to this point, I have deliberately concentrated on those accounts of America's perceived uniqueness in the matter of intellectuals that date from the middle decades of the twentieth century, the period when, as I have argued, the corresponding absence thesis received its most influential elaboration in Britain. In the closing decades of the century both the actual and the perceived position of intellectuals in the United States have changed considerably, and the volume of literature on the subject has expanded uncontrollably. I shall not attempt here to discuss those changes in any detail, but instead will confine myself to brief remarks about two large matters: first, certain general developments which, it is often claimed, are not only transforming the role of intellectuals in all Western countries, but are making the conditions for the performance of that role approximate more and more closely to those obtaining in the United States; and second, the ways in which, despite this form of convergence, certain traditionally American preoccupations have appeared in new guises in the literature of the last couple of decades.

As we shall see in Part Five, many of the developments which have affected the position of intellectuals in Britain in the closing decades of the twentieth century, especially those found least welcome, are often explained in terms of the growing influence of American culture. In reality, they are the result of large-scale social and economic changes that are affecting most so-called advanced societies, even if the responses which they engender take culturally specific forms. Three of the major changes that are proving consequential for the role of intellectuals may be very roughly characterized as follows. First, an ever-increasing proportion of these societies' intellectual life takes place in, or is otherwise associated with, institutions of higher education and research, with the result that it becomes more and more subject to the excluding imperium of disciplinary specialization. Second, the popular media have become yet more in thrall to the burgeoning celebrity culture, further imposing their agenda on much of the so-called elite media, and many of the mechanisms which control the creation of celebrity now also determine the opportunities for those who attempt to perform the role of the intellectual on a broader public stage. And third, new social groups, sometimes traditionally defined in terms of class, but more often now defined by gender, ethnicity, sexual orientation, disability, and so on, have asserted themselves, have made questions of identity politics central to public debate, and have not been disposed to accept the authority of those marked out by their possession of culture as traditionally defined. The overall tendency of these changes, it is said, is to fragment a previously unified public sphere, to deprive intellectuals of their earlier cultural authority, and to make it virtually impossible to address a genuine public on general issues. In the closing chapters of this book I shall take a closer look at some of these developments as they have played themselves out in Britain, and I shall suggest some reasons for not accepting these alarmist conclusions. But here I would simply remark that these developments have been perceived as operating more powerfully in the United States than anywhere else.

As we have seen, American usage has long made academics the principal members of the category of 'intellectuals', but in recent years there has been a marked intensification of anxiety about the significance of this equation. This heightened level of concern reflects the greatly enhanced position of academia in the

United States in the second half of the twentieth century, including its near-monopoly of many forms of intellectual and scientific activity. The sheer size of American academia now seems to European eyes, like so many statistics about that country, to be extraordinary and strictly incomparable. There were estimated to be 900,000 academics in the United States in 1995 (only slightly fewer than the total number of university *students* in Britain at the time), spread across approximately 3,500 universities and colleges of various kinds. Most universities and colleges before the Second World War were still heavily Christian, but the leading (and many of the lesser) institutions have since been rapidly dechristianized. Value-neutrality replaced religious uplift; funding agencies encouraged the model of science in all fields; the norms of an autonomous professionalism were entrenched. By the end of the 1970s the divide between the principled secularism of academia and the religiosity of so much of American life was well established. Moreover, the conditions and career prospects of the more successful of these academics improved markedly in the second half of the century: 'Between 1940 and 1990, federal funds for higher education increased by a factor of twenty-five, enrolment by ten, and average teaching loads were reduced by half.'[45] The endowments of the major private universities have increased even more markedly; salaries have reflected this prosperity, and there is now a well-established market economy rewarding successful academics, with, at the top of the ladder, a 'star system' more redolent of Hollywood than of ideals of a scholarly community. In addition, the leading institutions have become less local in affiliation since 1945, contributing to the functioning of a nationwide academic public sphere. The discipline and the department are the central, translocal, realities of academic life. In universities, Thomas Bender concluded his recent survey, 'the department remains the basic organisational unit. Very few new departments have been created anywhere since World War II, and even fewer have been abolished.'[46]

Shils, in the 1972 article discussed earlier, concluded that 'the primary culture of the intellectuals is increasingly generated in academic institutions', a tendency that became even more marked in the ensuing decades. As a result, the issue of whether the intellectual has been displaced by the academic, or, conversely, whether the academic is now the new intellectual, dominated American discussion in the closing years of the twentieth century. Indeed, as John Guillory observed in the mid-1990s: 'Intellectuals are supposed to be equivalent in public discourse now to academics.'[47] (There is, of course, a sense in which this can be seen as the familiar American theme of 'alienation' in a new guise: universities, on this view, function as a bigger bohemia.) Writing in 1992, Daniel Bell, one of the few surviving members of the central generation of the New York Intellectuals, lamented that in the contemporary United States 'very few intellectuals remain', at least if one uses the term as Bell does to identify 'those socially unattached individuals devoted solely to the search for truth'. Of course, when one encounters a sociologist, of all people, talking about individuals being 'socially unattached', or indeed when one encounters any intelligent grown-up talking about individuals being 'devoted *solely* to the search for truth', one begins to suspect that these straw men are being stuffed for a purpose. Bell's purpose, broadly speaking, was to indict those within universities for losing touch with 'the larger public'. As a result, he alleged, 'there is no broad intellectual life and broad intellectual public today'. As ever, things are said to be better elsewhere, as well as in the past, and Britain figures among Bell's admired elsewheres. But somehow, as always in articles on this topic no matter where they are written, the one place where 'real' intellectuals are not to be found engaging with a 'broad public' over 'great issues' is here and now.[48]

The perceived 'flight into the academy' has made the trope of 'inside/outside' central to contemporary American discussion of the role of intellectuals, but instead of that latter noun being used (as I use it in this book) to express the movement between these two notional locations, the new usage is more and more equating 'intellectuals' (i.e. academics) with 'inside' and 'public intellectuals' (i.e. academics who also sometimes reach a non-academic audience) with 'outside'. These developments have generated a confused and repetitive polemical literature, but also a rich historiography of more scholarly and analytical accounts. The former has been dominated, for reasons already indicated, by laments over the 'decline' of the public intellectual; in fact, the take-up of the term 'the public intellectual' itself can be seen as expressive of a pessimism about the public reach of 'intellectuals' *tout court*, so there is an unnoticed irony about bemoaning the disappearance of a type that has only just been named. Given the perception that the academicization of intellectual life has gone further in the United States than elsewhere, and given the hoary prejudice that 'genuine' intellectuals must somehow be 'detached' or 'unaffiliated', these polemics have continued to look to Europe for examples of a species alleged to have become extinct at home. Jacoby's influential book encouraged this familiar response: 'Who were the sixties intellectuals?' he asked at one point: 'Probably most were not American: Jean-Paul Sartre, Albert Camus, Frantz Fanon, Herbert Marcuse, Isaac Deutscher, Wilhelm Reich.' (He struck a similar note in his account of the role of the intellectual Left on American campuses: 'A recent survey of philosophic Marxism by an American professor contains chapters on Georg Lukács, Karl Korsch, Antonio Gramsci, Max Horkheimer, Jean-Paul Sartre, and Jürgen Habermas, but only passing references to any American contributors.')[49] However, it should be said that the critics of Jacoby's book—and they were numerous and damaging—partially corrected this emphasis when they pointed out that the very journals and other locations in which their own criticisms were appearing were themselves signs of a far from defunct public intellectual culture.[50] Criticism of the book's premise has also encouraged a more realistic grasp on the sense in which intellectuals are ever 'independent': 'Obituaries for the intellectuals, like Jacoby's, are so persistent a genre because intellectuals have never lived the gloriously independent life so often ascribed to them, and thus must always appear, when observed closely, to be on the point of losing it.'[51]

The book which came to be emblematic of this strand of the discussion—while in its own approach furnishing something of a *reductio ad absurdum* of the whole preoccupation—was Richard Posner's *Public Intellectuals: a Study of Decline*, published in 2001. In practice, Posner narrowed the topic by concentrating on those figures who use mainstream public media to comment on contemporary political issues. Bringing an economistic perspective to this topic, he argued that there are not sufficient 'quality controls' for this to function as an efficient market: all kinds of people get to sound off about current affairs, no matter how ill-informed or misleading their comments prove to be. But the chief reason he believed such intellectuals were now more likely to be ill-informed than in the past was, paradoxically, the growth of universities. More intellectuals are now academics, but the effect of academic specialization is to render them incapable of taking the broad general view required by the role and exhibited by their predecessors: 'the compartmentalization of competence' has meant that 'a successful academic may be able to use his success to reach the general public on matters about which he is an idiot'.[52]

The one element of genuine novelty in Posner's book was that he attempted a rudimentary statistical analysis of appearances in the media. Taking the five-year period 1990–5, he tabulated mentions (of whatever kind) in various mainstream media, including hits on the Web. The outcome, not surprisingly, confirmed the ever-increased power of the media to make reputations, at least where one uses this essentially circular sense of 'reputation'. By this crude measure, the most important public intellectual in the United States during this period was Henry Kissinger, a finding which says much about the news-driven character of Posner's materials. More generally, his survey showed that three-quarters of the living 'PI's' whose reputations were thus measured were academics, confirming his gloomy thesis: 'the market for public intellectuals is becoming dominated by academics at the same time that the growth of academic specialisation has made it increasingly difficult for academics to fill the public-intellectual role'. Posner recognized that figures such as Richard Rorty or Martha Nussbaum may continue to fulfil some of the functions of the public intellectual, for all the 'decline' signalled by his subtitle, but for him, as for so many writers on the subject, the exemplars of the species were always to be found elsewhere, in other times or other places. John Stuart Mill is offered as 'the greatest public intellectual of the last two centuries', and the most frequently saluted figure, who is said to have no true successors in contemporary America, is George Orwell.[53] In short, they do these things better elsewhere: 'Countries with a smaller more homogeneous governing class . . . than the United States will tend to give a more prominent role to public intellectuals.'[54]

The omnivorous appetite of the trend-conscious universities and the power of media 'consecration' also came together in American discussion of the third relevant development, the alleged fragmentation of the public into a series of separate if overlapping identities defined in terms of ethnicity, gender, sexual orientation, and so on. Rethinking the question of intellectuals in terms of identity politics may have thrown up some interesting issues about the need for, and the basis of, identification between members of a public and the intellectuals they are disposed to listen to, especially where it is assumed that beliefs and perceptions are determined by, and even are not fully comprehensible without, certain forms of shared 'experience' which result from a given ethnic or sexual identity. But by and large these developments have led to the restatement of familiar themes in fashionable form. This seems to have been particularly the case with the 'discovery' of a new group of black public intellectuals in the early 1990s. The success of figures such as Henry Louis Gates Jr., Cornel West, and Michael Dyson in simultaneously scaling the heights of the academic profession and continuing to command a non-academic audience among 'the black community' was taken in some quarters to constitute an arresting exception to the general 'decline' of the public intellectual.[55] The sense of speaking 'for' as well as 'to' such an audience was held to be distinctive in these instances: 'black intellectuals are legitimated by their sense of a constituency'.[56] Actually, something similar has been claimed for most of those who have successfully occupied the role of intellectual; what animated this particular version of the familiar claim was, first, the assumption that, in the contemporary United States, black ethnicity constituted an indefeasible and transparent bond between critic and audience, and second that no similarly compelling link with their publics was available to most non-black intellectuals.

Seen in a larger context, the episode reveals itself as another example of the theme of 'the death of the intellectual'. 'One of the few things most intellectuals will agree on in public is that the age of the public intellectual is over,' is the hackneyed, and perhaps intriguingly self-contradictory, opening to the *Atlantic Monthly* piece. If intellectuals have become too professionalized and confined to universities—Berubé speaks of the expansion of academia and 'its gradual incorporation of the American intelligentsia'; Boynton declares 'think of an intellectual today, and chances are he is a college professor whose "public" barely extends beyond the campus walls'—then they have lost that 'natural' relation to a non-specialist public they are assumed once to have had. The search is on for 'public intellectuals' who can restore that link. The wider culture's fascination with certain black writers and scholars is that they seem successfully to combine academic standing with a genuine following among a non-academic audience. Similarly, the central theme in the *Atlantic Monthly*'s article is the relationship between the personal experiences of an individual writer and the needs of some pre-existing group, class, or nation. Gates is quoted as saying: 'It is the birthright of the black writer that his experiences, however personal, are automatically historical'. Lurking here, as so often, is the romantic ideal of being the 'voice of the oppressed'. Strictly speaking, of course, no one's experiences are any more 'automatically historical' than anyone else's; at issue in such a case is the existence of a public willing to grant the truth of Gates's doubtful premise. In the altogether more bracing treatment of the question in *Dissent*, Sean Wilentz remarked the potential racism of lumping these disparate figures together just because they happen to be black, and he also pointed out the ways in which they are beneficiaries of a wider 'celebrity culture'.[57] No less important, it might be added, is the fact that the figures mentioned had made race and their own racial 'identity' the central topic of their academic work. At the heart of the matter, even in this episode, was the question of how, in the peculiarly adverse circumstances of the United States, any academic could ever command any kind of cultural authority with a wider public.[58]

The American scholarly literature on intellectuals-as-academics has, if anything, now surpassed in quantity the traditional French literature on intellectuals-as-political-actors. The most interesting strand in this literature has been that which, rather than uncritically reproducing the misleading and platitudinous contrasts between 'the ivory tower' and 'the real world', has explored some of the ways in which the university, as society's creation, embodies some, at least, of society's values. Historians such as Thomas Bender and David Hollinger have plotted a variety of paths along which this relationship has developed, complicating any simple narrative of 'withdrawal' from the world, while from another perspective cultural critics such as Bruce Robbins have explored the tensions within the contemporary discourse of professionalism.[59] The very idea of 'professionalism' itself involves an implicit contract with a public; the values appealed to both in elaborating such an ideal and in criticizing its deformations are values which cut across any supposed 'inside' or 'outside'. All claims about 'professional autonomy' are claims made *to* someone, and a profession is always in this dialectical relation with a wider public in terms of whose values the legitimacy or otherwise of the claims is validated.

For all the impressive sophistication of this recent writing, it has to be said that an aura of Europe-envy still hangs over public discussion of these themes, a sense that living in a world where the appearance of an occasional professor on television or in the mainstream press is acclaimed as evidence that 'the public intellectual' is not altogether extinct represents a poor second-best compared to a world where (the assumptions linger) intellectuals gather in cafés and on streets, living by their writing, esteemed by a literate but non-specialist public, a cultural and even political force of some consequence. But actually there is here an unlooked-for (and, from each side, largely unnoticed) convergence with the concerns of the school which has come to dominate French writing about intellectuals in recent years, largely under the inspiration of the work of Pierre Bourdieu, which has, in its own terms, paid a great deal of attention to the workings of the French academic world.[60] This body of scholarship tends to work with an economistic model of 'competition in the scholarly (or literary or scientific) field', and it tends to concentrate on systems of education as forms of social reproduction, both aspects indicating its original, but now rather distant, *marxisant* inspiration. But, like the corresponding body of scholarship in the

United States, it reflects a present reality in which institutions of higher education and research seem, simultaneously, to form a larger part of national life *and* to be more withdrawn from that life.

In other words, at the level of scholarly writing *about* intellectuals, as perhaps in the functioning of that species itself, we may be witnessing something of a convergence across hitherto divergent national traditions—which may be merely to say that intellectual life, too, is not without its own form of 'globalization'. But such changes always have the effect of calling into question states of affairs previously taken for granted. In the present case, it should lead us to re-examine what was supposed to be distinctive about the various national traditions in the matter of intellectuals. Or, to put it in the form of a simple question: how did it come to be that throughout the twentieth century the adjective that seemed most naturally to sit alongside the noun 'intellectuals' was 'French'?

NOTES

1. Daniel Rodgers, *Atlantic Crossings: Social Politics in a Progressive Age* (Cambridge, Mass.: Belknap, 1998), 40.
2. Gertrude Himmelfarb, 'Mr Stephen and Mr Ramsay: the Victorian as intellectual', *The Twentieth Century*, 152 (1952), 514–15.
3. Quoted in Richard Hofstadter, *Anti-Intellectualism in American Life* (New York: Vintage Books, 1963), 289 n.; see also the article cited in Ch. 1 above, Lewis S. Feuer, 'The political linguistics of "intellectuals" 1898–1918', *Survey*, 1 (1971), 156–83.
4. Henry F. May, *The End of American Innocence: A Study of the First Years of Our Own Time 1912–1917* (New York: Columbia University Press, 1992 [1st edn. 1959]), 281, 284.
5. Randolph Bourne to Arthur McMahon, 30 Jan. 1914, quoted in Steven Biel, *Independent Intellectuals in the United States 1910–1945* (New York: New York University Press, 1992), 99.
6. Mary Austin, 'American women and the intellectual life', *The Bookman*, Aug. 1921; quoted in Biel, *Independent Intellectuals*, 109.
7. Harold Stearns, 'America and the young intellectual', in *America and the Young Intellectual* (New York: Doran, 1921), 9.
8. Stearns, 'Where are our intellectuals?', ibid. 46–7.
9. Stearns, 'Where are our intellectuals?', ibid. 48. For further general assertions about the weaker place of writers and thinkers in the USA, see H. L. Mencken, 'The national letters', in *Prejudices*, 2nd ser. (London: Cape, 1921 [New York, 1920]), 9–101.
10. Quoted in Ascherson, 'England needs its intellectuals', *Observer*, 11 Aug. 1985, 7 (discussed in Ch. 8).
11. See Lawrence Levine, *Highbrow/Lowbrow: The Emergence of Cultural Hierarchy in America* (Cambridge, Mass.: Harvard University Press), ch. 1.
12. Both quoted in Biel, *Independent Intellectuals*, 226, 231.
13. See e.g. the recurring 'generalist versus specialist' pattern mapped by Gerald Graff in *Professing English: An Institutional History* (Chicago: University of Chicago Press, 1987).

14. There is now a huge literature on this group. I have drawn selectively on the following: Alexander Bloom, *Prodigal Sons: the New York Intellectuals and their World* (New York: Oxford University Press, 1986); Terry A. Cooney, *The Rise of the New York Intellectuals: Partisan Review and its Circle* (Madison: University of Wisconsin Press, 1986); Alan Wald, *The New York Intellectuals: the Rise and Decline of the Anti-Stalinist Left from the 1930s to the 1980s* (Chapel Hill: University of North Carolina Press, 1987); Neil Jumonville, *Critical Crossings: The New York Intellectuals in Postwar America* (Berkeley: University of California Press, 1991); and, particularly useful for my purposes, Hugh Wilford, *The New York Intellectuals: From Vanguard to Institution* (Manchester: Manchester University Press, 1995).
15. The subsequent role of the *reputation* of this group is touched on in Thomas Bender, *Intellect and Public Life: Essays on the Social History of Academic Intellectuals in the United States* (Baltimore: Johns Hopkins University Press, 1993), and Morris Dickstein, *Double Agents: The Critic and Society* (New York: Oxford University Press, 1992); see the discussion of these accounts in Stefan Collini, 'My public is bigger than yours: professors, critics, and other intellectuals', *Journal of the History of the Behavioral Sciences*, 30 (1994), 380–7.
16. See Mark Jancovich, *The Cultural Politics of the New Criticism* (Cambridge: Cambridge University Press, 1993).
17. Wilford, *New York Intellectuals*, 32.
18. Ibid. 61.
19. Ibid. 64.
20. Jarrell to R. P. Blackmur, 1946; quoted ibid. 112.
21. William Phillips, *A Partisan View: Five Decades of the Literary Life* (New York: Stein, 1983), 141, 145.
22. This is very much the emphasis of Russell Jacoby, *The Last Intellectuals: American Culture in the Age of Academe* (New York: Basic Books, 1987).
23. See the reference in the following note, quotation at p. 306.
24. 'Our country and our culture', *Partisan Review*, 19 (1952), 282–326; 420–50; 562–97; cf. Ch. 6, sect. III above.
25. Ibid. 319.
26. Ibid. 576.
27. Jacoby himself certainly claims credit for this usage: 'At the very least it [his book] put into circulation a term, the *public intellectual*, which has travelled far beyond its pages.... As far as I know, I was the first to use this term'; 'Introduction to the 2000 Edition', *The Last Intellectuals* (2nd edn. 2000), p. xvi.
28. Quoted in Mitchell Cohen, 'Introduction', in Nicolaus Mills (ed.), *Legacy of Dissent: 40 Years of Writing from 'Dissent' Magazine* (New York: Simon & Schuster, 1994), 24.
29. Jacoby, *Last Intellectuals*, 82.
30. This lament was relatively commonplace at the time in these circles: see e.g. William Barrett, 'Declining fortunes of the literary review: 1945–57', *The Anchor Review*, 2 (1957), excerpted under the title 'Writers in America', in George B. de Huszar (ed.), *The Intellectuals: A Controversial Portrait* (Glencoe, Ill.: Free Press, 1960), 484–90.
31. Irving Howe, 'This age of conformity', *Partisan Review*, 21 (Jan.–Feb. 1954), 7–33; quotations at 12, 13 (italics in original), 22, 29.
32. 'There was an outpouring of books on intellectuals in the 1950s.... The single most important work, however, was Richard Hofstadter's enormously influential *Anti-Intellectualism in American Life* (1964)'; Thomas Bender 'Recent trends in the

historiography of the intellectuals in the United States', in Marie-Christine Granjon Nicole Racine, and Michael Trebitsch (eds.), *Histoire comparée des intellectuels* (Paris: IHTP, 1997), 166 (Hofstadter's book was actually published in 1963, but awarded the Pulitzer Prize for non-fiction in 1964). All quotations are from the Vintage edition (New York, 1964).

33. Hofstadter, *Anti-Intellectualism*, 26, 30.
34. Ibid. 208, 399.
35. Ibid. 395, 417.
36. 'Interview with Christopher Lasch', *Intellectual History Newsletter*, 16 (1994), 10.
37. Christopher Lasch, *The New Radicalism in America 1889–1963: The Intellectual as a Social Type* (New York: Norton, 1965), 349, 335.
38. Lasch, *New Radicalism*, 314.
39. 'Interview with Lasch', 10.
40. Quoted Lasch, *New Radicalism*, 294–5.
41. Seymour Martin Lipset, 'American intellectuals: their politics and status', *Daedalus*, 88 (1959), 460–86; repr. in shortened form as 'The real status of American intellectuals', in de Huszar (ed.), *Intellectuals*, 510–16.
42. Lipset, 'American intellectuals', 469, 470, 472.
43. Edward Shils, 'Intellectuals and the center of society in the United States', in *The Intellectuals and the Powers* (Chicago: University of Chicago Press, 1972), 156, 159, 160.
44. Ibid. 171, 175, 179, 194–5.
45. Thomas Bender, 'Politics, intellect, and the American university, 1945–1995', *Daedalus*, 126 (1997), 1–38, quotation at 5.
46. Ibid. 30–1.
47. John Guillory, 'Literary critics as intellectuals: class analysis and the crisis of the humanities', in Wai Chee Dimock and Michael T. Gilmore (eds.), *Rethinking Class: Literary Studies and Social Formations* (New York: Columbia University Press, 1994), 112.
48. Daniel Bell, 'The cultural wars', *The Wilson Quarterly* (Summer, 1992), 74–107.
49. Jacoby, *Last Intellectuals*, 114, 167.
50. See the examples cited in Jacoby, *Last Intellectuals*, 'Introduction to 2000 edition', pp. xvii–xviii.
51. Bruce Robbins, 'Introduction', in Bruce Robbins (ed.), *Intellectuals: Aesthetics, Politics, Academics* (Minneapolis: University of Minnesota Press, 1990), p. xv; see also Barry Sarchett, 'Russell Jacoby and the politics of cultural nostalgia', in Jeffrey Williams (ed.), *PC Wars: Politics and Theory in the Academy* (London: Routledge, 1995).
52. Richard A. Posner, *Public Intellectuals: a Study of Decline* (Cambridge, Mass.: Harvard University Press, 2001), 51.
53. Though at one point he does throw out the suggestion that 'Rorty is our Orwell': ibid. 342.
54. Posner, *Public Intellectuals*, 56–7, 353, 12.
55. Michael Berubé, 'Public Academy', *New Yorker*, 9 Jan. 1995; Robert S. Boynton, 'The new intellectuals', *Atlantic Monthly*, Mar. 1995.
56. Berubé, 'Public academy', 77.
57. Sean Wilentz, 'Race, celebrity and the intellectuals', *Dissent*, Summer 1995, 255.

58. Or as Thomas Bender put it, how 'to find some space among nostalgia, politicized group identities, and specialized academic autonomy for the creation of a public culture'; *Intellect and Public Life*, 124.
59. See, among many other works, Bender, *Intellect and Public Life*; David Hollinger, *Science, Jews, and Secular Culture; Studies in Mid-Twentieth-Century American Intellectual History* (Princeton: Princeton University Press, 1996); and Bruce Robbins, *Secular Vocation: Intellectuals, Professionalism, Culture* (London: Verso, 1993).
60. In addition to the numerous studies by Bourdieu himself, such as *Homo Academicus* (Paris: Minuit, 1984), see the works by Charle, Fabiani, Pinto, Boschetti, and others cited in the following chapter.

11

The Peculiarities of the French

'La France passe pour le paradis des intellectuels.'

I

There can be few historical topics on which so many readers of this book are likely to hold such confident opinions as the topic of intellectuals in France. Assertions about French intellectuals' greater legitimacy, prominence, and effectiveness, especially in comparison to their putative counterparts in Britain, have for long figured simply as statements of the received wisdom. Such assertions easily expand into enumerating a whole series of supposedly explanatory characteristics of French society and history, ranging from the republican political tradition or the relatively late development of industrialism, to respect for authors or the teaching of philosophy in schools, usually taking in along the way the geography of Paris and the existence of cafés. Any attempt to engage in a comparative and analytical way with the question of the history and role of intellectuals in France needs to recognize the existence of this great slag-heap of recycled cliché and indestructible prejudice—and then to move on. The venerable parlour-game of cross-channel contrasts is still a seductive one, but the search for historical explanations too easily ends up focusing on a few notable differences abstracted from the detail of their functioning and resonance.[1]

There would be little point here in essaying yet another meta-historical sketch in this manner. Instead, I shall attempt an analysis which, while more limited, may still threaten to tax the limits of a single chapter. I shall ask some of the same questions of the French case as I have of other countries, including Britain: how has the term 'intellectuals' developed, what have been the main stages of the discussion of the question of intellectuals, what forms have the various strategies of denial taken in the French case—have intellectuals been thought to flourish more successfully elsewhere, are they now thought to have died out or at least to have declined in stature, and so on? Traditional British assumptions about intellectuals in France have tended to accept the self-estimation of one or two of the more conspicuous exemplars and then to erect large generalizations on that fragile and unreliable base. But after many years during which most French writing about intellectuals was of a polemical or self-justifying kind, in the tradition of *essayisme*, there has in the last two decades been a remarkable efflorescence in France of research which takes intellectuals as the object of systematic historical examination, and this work now makes it possible to give more carefully framed and properly documented answers to at least some of our questions. One incidental service I hope this chapter may render is to make the main outlines of this body of work better known to Anglophone readers.

It may help to settle the nerves of any readers who are anticipating that I am about to embark on an exercise in wilful revisionism if I say at once that this chapter will *not* conclude that intellectuals have in fact been a negligible or largely derogated presence in twentieth-century France or that intellectuals have attracted less attention there than in other countries. The main aim is, rather, to bring out some of the distinctiveness of the French case, a distinctiveness that illuminates why it has been able to 'pass as the paradise of intellectuals', but that at the same time underlines why it cannot serve as any kind of norm or model against which other cases must be compared. Even the term, 'les intellectuels', has built into it certain expectations or understandings that, when made explicit, cannot be readily transplanted into other traditions. It is particularly important to keep the distinctiveness of these assumptions in mind given that in recent years the comparative study of intellectuals has largely been carried on under the aegis of French scholarship, with the result that, as indicated in Ch. 9, the French sense has tended to structure many of the international comparisons. And by this stage in this book, no reader should need reminding of what Perry Anderson has spoken of as 'the special position of France within the British imagination—the one European country to figure as the intimately alien, alluring Other of the national soul'.[2]

For my purposes, French 'exceptionalism' resides above all in the long-standing and widely held conviction within France itself that it is indeed the natural home of intellectuals. It is not only when seen through foreign eyes, whether envious or scornful, that 'la France passe pour le paradis des intellectuels', as Raymond Aron put it, his characteristic scepticism expressing itself in sardonic hyperbole (is a 'paradise' ever what it seems, and anyway does France only 'pass' for such in this matter?).[3] As I have been arguing in the British case, the existence of a particular tradition becomes what the sociologists would call an independent cultural variable in itself. The constant repetition of a claim about the importance or absence of intellectuals in a given society becomes one determining feature of what the claim purports to describe. The existence of the widely held belief within France itself, from at least the 1930s onwards, that intellectuals played a uniquely prominent part in politics became an element in the French situation that predisposed a certain public to pay attention to the utterances of intellectuals.

In *politics*: this cannot be emphasized too strongly. As I argued in Ch. 2, the sense of the French term itself differs in this respect from its English analogue: in the French usage, to repeat, 'intellectuals are not regarded as a category of people who happen to be particularly prone to intervene in politics: the intervention in politics is constitutive of the category'.[4] Intellectuals have been understood in France to be a *political* force, and they have been written about as part of French *political* history in the twentieth century. By way of preliminary analysis of the sense of the term 'les intellectuels' as it has informed this history, one could begin with the following propositions: 'les intellectuels'

(*a*) possess a sense of collective identity,
(*b*) which is deployed in 'intervening' in politics,
(*c*) in the name of 'universals'.

The fact that this sense established itself so securely in French usage by the middle of the century may in turn be thought to indicate the presence of the following presuppositions:

(*d*) writers, artists, scholars, and thinkers are accorded considerable respect and can expect their views to be listened to;
(*e*) they tend to share a common educational formation that encourages both a sense of collective identity and a separateness from other elites in French society;
(*f*) the ideological divide between Left and Right is all-pervading and overriding;
(*g*) there is a live tradition of expecting the claims of political or economic 'pouvoir' to be contested by a spiritual or intellectual 'contre-pouvoir'.

These features, even expressed in these diagrammatic terms, plainly refer back to circumstances of French life that were especially marked in the early and middle decades of the twentieth century. They could, in their turn, be thought susceptible of the kind of historical 'explanation' I mentioned a few moments ago. Thus, at the risk of slightly parodying the genre, one might say that the prominence of intellectuals in France, and indeed the very currency of the term itself, resulted from the coming together in favourable circumstances of a relatively self-enclosed caste of state-legitimated scholars with the leading representatives of a long-established tradition of writers and men of letters as moral arbiters and prophets, within a sharply divided, chronically unstable, and insistently ideological political culture where republican values could lay claim to the status of universals, set against the backdrop of a relatively underdeveloped economy and a deeply traditional society, a society in which most of the relevant activities were very heavily centralized in Paris, during a period in which the printed word had no real rivals as a form of communication. Actually, each of the separate assertions that make up this more or less familiar account would need to be modified or extended in countless ways when subject to historical scrutiny, but for the moment this thumbnail sketch may serve well enough to indicate at least the general direction in which the specificity of the French case is to be looked for.

Among the more important of the ways in which such a condensed account is bound to be misleading is its implication of stasis, of an enduring, unchanging condition. But the existence of a considerable discursive continuity, at least up until the beginning of the 1980s, here masks some quite fundamental changes in the existence, role, and impact of intellectuals across the century. Since this chapter will not offer anything like a chronological narrative of the doings of intellectuals in France, it may be worth giving a rough indication of some of the main phases in this history. Making all allowance for the inherent crudities and arbitrarinesses of such schemes, one could divide the century into five periods, as follows:

1. *1898–1904.* The Dreyfus Affair was seen, both at the time and above all in retrospect, as so much the originary moment of the intellectuals that it and its immediate aftermath needs to be assigned a period of its own. The term 'les intellectuels' acquired currency during these years, as did practically all the criticisms that were to become the stock-in-trade of French anti-intellectualism thereafter.

2. *1905–34.* The conflict between radical republican 'intellectuels' and their nationalist, conservative, and Catholic critics was temporarily subdued, and eventually tilted in favour of the latter, by the First World War; the immediate post-war years saw a resurgence of Catholicism among French elites and a continuing assault on the legitimacy of 'les intellectuels' (understood to be principally, though not by now exclusively, on the Left).

3. *1934–58.* Although the Second World War marked, needless to say, a massive hiatus in French history in so many ways, there is in fact a continuity in the situation of intellectuals from the formation of the Front Populaire to the ending of the Fourth Republic. This period represents the heyday of the 'intellectuel de gauche', with the Parti Communiste Français (PCF) holding a position of dominance from the Liberation onwards. A particular form of prestige continued to be attached to the public pronouncements of writers and philosophers.

4. *1958–80.* In intellectual terms, the magistrature of the leading 'maîtres à penser' appeared to persist right through this period, from Sartre's existentialist Marxism through the blossoming of structuralism and up to the beginnings of various forms of post-structuralism. But the altered political context accorded such figures less and less of a direct role; the Communist hegemony was beginning to unravel, signalled above all by the (belated) French reaction to Solzhenitsyn's revelations about the Gulags; and new media, especially television, were altering the nature of the public stage.

5. *1980–present.* This period has been marked, most notably, by constant inquests on 'the death of the intellectual' (partly prompted by the actual deaths of the leading figures from the previous periods). French discussion has converged more and more with that to be found elsewhere, especially in its anxieties about the 'mediatization' of intellectuals, and the alleged disappearance of 'grand narratives'.

Partly as a consequence of this elegiac temper, this is the period which has seen the beginnings of a serious French historiography on the subject of intellectuals.

Even this brisk periodization helps to bring foreign, above all British, perceptions of the greater prominence of French intellectuals into slightly clearer focus. There had, of course, as we have seen, been a long tradition of assuming that writers and artists were accorded greater standing in France, and indeed that the political activities of 'gens de lettres' had long been, for good or ill (mostly, to British eyes, ill), of more consequence in the turbulent, unstable public life of nineteenth-century France. As we have also seen, the Dreyfus Affair was followed quite closely in Britain as in other countries, but within a broader concern about injustice, anti-Semitism, and the role of the army, the emergence of intellectuals, so described, was not particularly fastened upon. It was not, I would argue, until the middle decades of the twentieth century, from the 1930s to the 1950s above all, that the image and prominence of 'intellectuals' in France really became established as a fixed point of comparison in British culture. These decades saw the heyday of 'oppositional', collective, public activity on the part of substantial numbers of French intellectuals—the publication of manifestos, the addressing of mass meetings, and above all the signing of petitions and protests. They also saw a whole succession of episodes characterized as re-enactments of the Dreyfus Affair, understood as the mobilization of 'intelligence' to uphold the claims of 'the universal', and these successive invocations of this founding moment helped establish a kind of legitimating pedigree for the actions of subsequent generations of intellectuals, even when the specific engagement in question possessed little of the clarity of the original.

The high visibility of intellectuals in French political life, especially during these key decades, has often been taken by outsiders to indicate that French culture has accorded its intellectuals such standing that they have functioned as the uncontested arbiters of public life. In reality, the situation has nearly always been much more tangled and ambiguous than this casual impression has suggested. Some of the complexity may be indicated by the following four points.

1. The fact that intellectuals have often occupied a highly visible and noisy role in political discussion in France does not mean that they were necessarily more influential than elsewhere, if by that is meant playing a part in determining actual policies. Indeed, some observers within France acknowledged, usually with regret, that what was perceived as the greater integration of elites elsewhere, notably in Britain, meant that individual intellectual figures there often enjoyed more direct access to power or played a more determining role in shaping policy than did their French counterparts, condemned to the futility of self-righteous protest and the staking out of positions that may have been ideologically pure but at the price of being practically impotent.

2. The fact that intellectuals in France have been the beneficiaries of certain cultural attitudes towards education, abstraction, and literature (a fact much

envied, and much exaggerated, by intellectuals elsewhere) does not mean that these attitudes have been uncontested or even always dominant. The audience upon whom intellectuals have been most consistently able to count in France has been in large part made up of other intellectuals. Within the broader society, these attitudes have coexisted with a vigorous and deeply rooted tradition of hostility to intellectuals, and the phenomenon of the anti-intellectualism of the intellectual, often assumed in Britain to be uniquely British (or in America to be uniquely American, and so on), has a long history from the first reactions to the original 'protestation des intellectuels' by figures such as Barrès and Brunetière right through to the present. And, as in the British and other cases, these responses themselves drew on a long French tradition which predated the emergence of 'intellectuels' so labelled, and went back through Tocqueville to early responses to the Revolution itself. As it was already being expressed in the early nineteenth century: 'Nos plus grands malheurs sont venus de l'ambition des gens de lettres, qui, pour faire les gens d'importance, se sont jetés dans la morale et la politique.' ['Our greatest misfortunes have come from the ambition of the men of letters, who, to turn themselves into people of importance, have thrown themselves into morality and politics.'][5]

3. The fact that most French commentators across the first two-thirds or more of the twentieth century either maintained or simply assumed that intellectuals were a more flourishing species in France than elsewhere does not mean that there has been no rival, albeit minority, tradition of insisting on the superiority of the situation perceived to prevail in certain other countries, especially Britain. From such late nineteenth-century admirers of British institutions such as Émile Boutmy, founder of the independent college that became known as 'Sciences Po', through historians such as Élie Halévy (an early professor at Sciences Po), and on to sociologists such as Raymond Aron, there has been a continuous tradition of regard not just for the supposed pragmatism of British politics but also for the role that intellectuals have been assumed to play in British public life. As Aron put it in 1955, at the absolute peak of French intellectuals' self-regard: 'La Grande-Bretagne est probablement le pays d'Occident qui a traité ses intellectuels de la manière la plus raisonnable.' ['Of all Western countries, Great Britain is probably the one which has treated its intellectuals in the most sensible way.'][6]

4. The fact that intellectuals were for long an accepted part of the French political landscape does not mean that the various forms of denial encountered elsewhere have been entirely unknown in French discourse on the question. As we shall see, refusals of the term in self-description have been common, and there has been no shortage of accusations that various prominent figures have been merely 'would-be' intellectuals, or 'false' intellectuals, or pale imitations of the great names of the past. And in the last couple of decades there has been a chorus of writing, some elegiac, some celebratory, about the 'dying out' of the species, especially as a result of the enhanced power of the popular media in an increasingly egalitarian

society (much the same diagnosis, in other words, as is to be found in the discourse of most advanced societies at the end of the twentieth century). As the historian Daniel Lindenberg put it recently, summarizing these various tropes: 'Aujourd'hui on connaît ces têtes de turc inusables: le pseudo-, le "demi"-intellectuel, l' "intellectuel de parodie", l'intellectuel dit aujourd'hui plus généralement "médiatique", donc inauthentique, superficiel.' ['Today we are familiar with these inexhaustible stereotypes: the pseudo-, the "half"-intellectual, the "parody intellectual", those more generally today called "media intellectuals", hence inauthentic, superficial.'][7]

Each of these points will be further developed and illustrated in the rest of this chapter. But they are, I should again emphasize, offered by way of modification and refinement of the traditional perception of the position of intellectuals in French society, not as a refutation of it. The weight or proportionality of these various elements differs in different societies depending on the surrounding circumstances (or as Lindenberg cautions in relation to the French tradition of anti-intellectualism: 'l'anti-intellectualisme n'a pas le même statut en France, où le magistère des intellectuels est un *fait*, que dans des sociétés où ce magistère n'est pas reconnu,' and he cites Hofstadter on anti-intellectualism in America by way of contrast. ['anti-intellectualism does not have the same status in France, where the agency/authority of the intellectuals is a *fact*, as in societies where this agency/authority is not recognized.'][8]). Intellectuals (understood in a certain sense) have (particularly during certain periods) known a standing (of a certain kind) in French society (or at least certain quarters of it) and have had a voice (often an enraged and impotent voice) in political debate (an intensely ideological form of life almost coextensive with the culture as a whole) that has not been matched in the course of the twentieth century by those regarded as intellectuals in other European or North American societies. And as I have already observed, acknowledgement of this fact, in some form, within French culture has in itself been an important part of French distinctiveness in the matter.

None of this, however, justifies the tendency to treat France as the norm or model against which other societies are asked to measure up. Behind this tendency there is, of course, a massive weight of actual history: the Revolution offered itself as the template for modernity, Paris was the 'capital of the nineteenth century', and France was the world's laboratory whether for carrying out successive experiments in democracy or for nurturing every form of cultural avant-garde. In the course of the twentieth century the tendency was further reinforced by those strands of *marxisant* or other Left-inclined historiography which treated France as the vanguard of world history, the first to have a 'proper bourgeois revolution', the exemplar of a fully theorized ideological politics. The residue of these assumptions is still visible in much discussion of the question of intellectuals, but in recent years the historical as well as the political supports of this interpretation have been increasingly eroded. It has become more common to recognize what a socially conservative and economically 'underdeveloped' society France has been, especially during the period from the mid-nineteenth century to the middle or later decades of the twentieth. The comparatively large rural population, much of it still engaged in peasant farming; the absence or belatedness of the 'second Industrial Revolution'; the numbing effect of two world wars; the sclerotic or 'blocked' nature of French institutions; the notably parochial and in-turned nature of French intellectual life—all these features have been better explored in recent years, with the result that the peculiarity rather than the exemplary status of French history has come more clearly into view.[9] The rest of this chapter will touch on some of the complexities of this distinctiveness where the matter of intellectuals is concerned when viewed through the optic of the comparative questions posed elsewhere in this book.

II

As a noun, the term 'l'intellectuel' did not appear in either the *Dictionnaire Larousse* or *Littré*, both dating from the 1870s.[10] It began, as we have seen, to make occasional appearances in French literature, as in English, during the closing decades of the nineteenth century, especially in the course of the 1890s.[11] It tended to carry the pejorative associations of being etiolated, divorced from the world, self-absorbed. It could easily be grafted on to a long-standing conservative discourse about the superfluity of educated men and the ways in which their removal from the responsibilities of carrying on the work of society resulted in the rancorous criticism of the malcontent.[12] But at this stage the term had no inherent political bearing and was not principally used in the plural form.

The fortunes of the word were transformed by its use in the Dreyfus Affair, the episode with which it has ever thereafter been associated. The Affair was the occasion above all others on which the deep cleavages of Third Republic France assumed overt political form, and the fortunes of those political actors dubbed 'les intellectuels' were inextricably bound up with the later reprises of this conflict. For what gave the Dreyfus Affair its defining place in modern French history was the way in which it, like the Revolution itself, made available a template for all similar conflicts thereafter; hence, 'les affaires Dreyfus'.[13] But in so doing, the Affair also carried forward a paradigm of the operation of intellectual authority in politics. After all, what had been so distinctive in the original episode had been not a claim by the signatories of the protest against Dreyfus's conviction to have a contrary view of the facts of the case, but the implication that their view should be accorded a certain respect on account of their academic qualifications or literary standing. Only in a few idiosyncratic cases could it be argued that the link was direct, as, for example, in the case of palaeographers who could be presumed to have a relevant expertise because part of what was at issue in the case was the authenticity of crucial documents (this feature of the case more generally allowed Ory and Sirinelli the nice conceit of describing the Affair as a large-scale 'commentaire de texte'[14]). By and large, however, simply by parading their posts and their qualifications the historians, philosophers, and philologists, as well as the physicists, chemists, and mathematicians, were tacitly making the assertion which has since been regarded as founding the role of the intellectual: their training and attainments in fields quite unrelated to the matter in hand gave them a title to be heard which went beyond that accorded to other citizens, citizens whose involvement in the instrumental business of getting and spending was not thought to give them the same access to 'the universal'.

To speak in this way of 'the universal' still sounds odd to British ears, but in a discourse more inflected by the idiom of philosophy, and especially by the diluted Kantianism that was the house-philosophy of the Third Republic, it was a familiar locution. It represented, in Anglo-Saxon terms, an amalgam of the metaphysical and the moral: truth and justice are instances of the universal; more limited, or local, or temporary, or partisan purposes are not. In this discourse, intellectuals are regarded as 'professionals of the universal'; that is, as constantly engaged in the pursuit of universal values for their own sake by the very nature of their quotidian activities. It was this presupposition that allowed many scholars to argue that they were not dabbling in the grubby factionalism of mere 'politics' by taking their stand over Dreyfus, but, rather, that they were extending their intellectual duty to defend truth and morality. (We shall see in the next chapter how this notion enabled Julien Benda to exempt himself from the strictures he levelled against other 'clercs' of having betrayed their calling by engaging in 'politics'.) Some version of this idea has underwritten the claims of intellectuals in France throughout the century. Towards its close, one still finds a writer such as Maurice Blanchot ventriloquizing the standard conservative complaint about the irrelevance of scholarly or scientific standing to political judgement, and then responding in no less familiar terms: 'Il n'y a pas de spécialité où l'on réussisse sans que cette réussite ne mette en cause un pouvoir de comprendre et de réussir qui relève de l'universel'. ['There is no specialism in which one succeeds without that success calling into question a power of understanding and of succeeding that depends on the universal.'][15] Similarly, in the 1980s the radical sociologist Pierre Bourdieu sounded very much like a latter-day Dreyfusard (not, in this context, a surprising echo) in arguing for 'the corporatism of the universal', that is, for the defence of the collective interests of intellectuals worldwide, on the (very French) grounds that 'the defence of the universal presupposes the defence of the defenders of the universal'.[16] When Bernard-Henri Lévy, the quintessential intellectual-as-media-pin-up, proffered one of the many obituaries for the species to appear in the 1980s, the cause of death he cited was: 'pas survécu au déclin de l'universel' ['not survived the decline of the universal'].[17]

What tends to be overlooked in references to the Dreyfus Affair in general discussion of intellectuals, especially when making a contrast with an allegedly anti-intellectual culture such as Britain, is that the episode was also the occasion for the expression of powerful, well-received, and lastingly influential criticisms of the pretentions of this newly labelled species. As one French historian has recently put it: simultaneously with the appearance of 'les intellectuels' in 1898 's'est développé un anti-intellectualisme virulent et complexe dont la permanence est aussi forte que l'objet même de cette idéologie du rejet et de la dénonciation' ['developed a virulent and complex anti-intellectualism whose persistence is as strong as the actual object of this ideology of rejection and denunciation']. This issued in 'une propagande fondée sur une obsession du nom "intellectuel" synonyme de désordre, de dégénérescence et de trahison' ['a propaganda founded on an obsession with the noun "intellectual", synonomous with disorder, degeneration, and treason'].[18] The contributions of two individuals were of particular significance here: the eminent critic, Ferdinand Brunetière, editor of the venerable *Revue des Deux Mondes* (by this date seen as 'the ante-chamber of the Académie française'), and Maurice Barrès, at the time perhaps France's best-known man of letters of the younger generation.

Barrès entered the fray immediately, publishing a counterblast entitled 'La Protestation des intellectuels!' (complete with exclamation mark) in *Le Journal* for 1 February 1898. As in Britain, the term itself, perceived as a neologism, immediately aroused objections on linguistic grounds, and Barrès was delighted to be able to cite the writer Anatole France on how the noun could only be applied to 'une faculté de l'esprit. Ceux qui ont imaginé d'en faire une qualité des personnes ne savaient pas bien leur langue' ['a faculty of the mind. Those who have imagined to make of it a quality of persons did not know their language well'].[19] (Anatole France's authority may have been a little two-edged for Barrès in this case since he was to prove to be the sole Dreyfusard member of the Académie française.) Barrès went on to offer his own tendentious definition: 'Intellectuel: individu qui se persuade que la societé doit se fonder sur la logique et qui méconnait qu'elle repose en fait sur des nécessités antérieures et peut-être étrangères à la raison individuelle.' ['Intellectual: an individual who persuades himself that society ought to be founded on logic and who refuses to recognize that it rests in fact on necessities prior and perhaps foreign to individual reason.'] This was always to be the classic conservative indictment: the misplaced appeal to abstract logic led to an absurd unrealism. He went on in terms that were to become the stock-in-trade of hostile commentary everywhere: 'Quant à nous, il nous plairait plus d'être intelligent que d'être intellectuel.' ['As for us, we would rather be intelligent than intellectual.'] He also deployed what was to become the common reproach that these 'intellectuels' were trying to set themselves above ordinary people: 'Tous ces aristocrates de la pensée tiennent à afficher qu'ils ne pensent pas comme la vile foule.' ['All these aristocrats of thought like to advertise that they don't think like the base crowd.'] He sneered at 'cette obscure *élite*', mocking the absurdity of the claim to be an 'elite' when they were in large part socially undistinguished scholars and schoolmasters. And the source of this misguided and self-important attitude was the university, which Barrès reproached in terms that were the common coin of right-wing polemic throughout the Third Republic:

Un verbalisme qui écarte l'enfant de toute réalité, un kantisme qui le déracine de la terre de ses morts, une surproduction de diplômés qui crée ce que nous avons appelé, d'après Bismarck, 'un prolétariat de bacheliers', voilà ce que nous avons reproché à l'Université, voilà ce qui fait de son produit, 'l'intellectuel', un ennemi de la société.

[A verbalism that distances the child from all reality, a Kantianism that uproots him from the land of his ancestors, an overproduction of people with qualifications which creates what we have called, following Bismark, 'a proletariat of graduates', that's what we have reproached the university with, that's what makes its product, 'the intellectual', an enemy of society.][20]

Above all, Barrès denied that the self-described 'intellectuels' (though in fact, as noted in Ch. 1 above, the signatories had not used this term of themselves) possessed any relevant authority: their absurd pronouncements only demonstrated 'que le fait de siéger dans une Académie des Sciences ne préjuge aucune autorité particulière pour réviser les travaux d'un Conseil de guerre' ['that the fact of being a member of an Academy of Science or Scholarship does not presuppose any particular authority for revising the work of a War Council']. Their ill-judged intervention confirmed that 'tout théoricien de l'absolu se détruit et nuit dans les affaires publiques' ['every theorist of the absolute harms and destroys himself in public affairs']. The remedy was the traditionalist one of confining oneself to one's station and its duties: 'à chacun son métier et les moutons seront bien gardés' ['each to his own trade and the sheep will be well looked after'].[21]

If there was one contribution to the polemic against the pretensions of the intellectuals that was subsequently to be more frequently cited than any other it was the article entitled 'Après le procés' published in *La Revue des Deux Mondes* for 15 March 1898 by its editor, Ferdinand Brunetière. At this distance, his article is largely known as the source of just one phrase, now quoted in various forms, as in Ch. 2 where it is rendered: 'What right has a professor of Tibetan to instruct his fellow-citizens in matters of morals and politics?'[22] The original occurs as the last sentence of Brunetière's longish article, which was, in best French fashion, divided into three parts: on anti-Semitism, on the army, and a third entitled 'De quelques intellectuels'. He had led up to this conclusion, which in context does not seem quite so baldly reductive, with a rhetorically layered series of innuendoes and ironies, hoping, finally, that the intellectuals will be 'grateful' for his warning of the dire consequences of their individualism. He then concluded:

M'en sauront-ils autant d'ajouter que, dans une démocratie, l'aristocratie intellectuelle est de toutes les formes d'aristocratie la plus inacceptable, parce qu'elle est de toutes la plus difficile à prouver, et que, si j'entends assez bien ce que c'est la supériorité de la naissance et celle de la fortune, je ne vois pas ce qu'un professeur de thibétain a de titres pour gouverner ses semblables, ni ce qu'une connaissance unique des propriétés de la quinine ou de la cinchonine confère de droits à l'obéissance et au respect des autres hommes?

[May they be no less so {*sc.* grateful} if I add that, in a democracy, intellectual aristocracy is the least acceptable of all forms of aristocracy, because of all of them it is the most difficult to prove, and that, if I understand well enough what superiority of birth or of fortune is, I do not see what claim a professor of Tibetan has to govern his fellow men, nor how a unique knowledge of the properties of quinine or cinchonine confers any rights to obedience and respect from other men.][23]

Brunetière was attempting to cut at the root of the intellectuals' presumed authority in a strategy that has never lost its pertinence: how does having attained a certain level of expertise in a scholarly or scientific discipline qualify someone to pronounce on other areas of life? 'L'intervention d'un romancier, même fameux, dans une question de justice militaire m'a paru aussi déplacée que le serait, dans la question des origines du romantisme, l'intervention d'un colonel de gendarmerie.' ['The intervention of a novelist, even a famous one, in a question of military justice seemed to me as out of place as would be, in a question of the origins of romanticism, the intervention of a gendarme colonel.'] The claim to be 'un intellectuel', argued Brunetière, can only be a piece of arrogance; it presumes a general superiority on the basis of what is in fact a limited and perhaps even distorting specialism. Moreover, those who engage in 'intellectual' activities have no monopoly on intelligence.

Si l'intelligence n'est pas sans doute la mesure de l'expérience, ni celle de la fermeté du caractère, ni celle de l'énergie de la volonté, qui sont bien quelque chose aussi, ne conviendra-t-on pas que beaucoup d'intellectuels pourraient être bornés de divers côtés, limités même quelquefois à leur spécialité, diminués encore, et comme rétrécis ou rapetissés par elle?

[If intelligence is certainly not the measure of experience, nor of firmness of character, nor of the energy of the will, which certainly count for something as well, shall we not acknowledge that many intellectuals could be limited on many sides, sometimes even limited to their specialty, further diminished, as though shrunken or reduced by it?][24]

If, therefore, we encourage them to hold forth on larger matters, 'ils ne font que déraisonner avec autorité sur des choses de leur incompétence' ['they only talk authoritative nonsense on things they don't know about']. In any case, most of the disciplines in question cannot claim to be 'scientific' in any significant sense; this is yet another form of pretension, a cover for something else: 'Méthode scientifique, aristocratie de l'intelligence, respect de la vérité, tous ces grands mots ne servent qu'à couvrir les prétentions de l'*Individualisme*,' and individualism he indicts as 'la grande maladie du temps présent'. ['Scientific method, aristocracy of intelligence, respect for the truth, all these big words only serve to cover the claims of *individualism* . . . the great sickness of the present age.'][25]

Many of the main strands of subsequent criticism of intellectuals were already present in these two immediate responses to the founding 'protéstation'.

However, as Christophe Charle has shown, the anti-Dreyfusards very soon had to contest the ground of intellectual authority. In other words, they could not simply take the view that claims to such authority were irrelevant in the case of a military trial, and then content themselves with the support given to the army by the comfortable classes in general. They had to produce their own counter-lists which were headed by members of the Académie française and contained the names of numerous writers and scholars. In one sense, these responses tacitly granted the legitimacy of the intellectuals' intervention. They also helped to domesticate the term itself by suggesting that it was not necessarily confined to those on the Left. This usage remained a point of contention for many years to come. Leading Dreyfusards, such as Jean Jaurès, maintained that the term 'intellectuel de droite' was a contradiction in terms: those so called were nothing more than mercenaries of the pen supporting the established governing class rather than owing that primary allegiance to the absolute standards of truth and morality which was the mark of the 'true' intellectual (and which, for Jaurès and many others, was the property of the Left).[26] But although, for some years to come, conservative moralists and men of letters tended to disdain the label for purposes of self-description, their actual engagement in the Dreyfus Affair had already shown them to be acting in accordance with the logic which the term now described, and by the inter-war years it became common to refer to 'les intellectuels de droite'.[27]

The legacy of the Dreyfus Affair has been as contested as the original episode itself. Indeed, one might say that interpreting its significance became one of the modalities by which subsequent French politics was conducted. But both its actual and its symbolic importance in establishing the role of intellectuals in French *politics* were beyond question. 'Lors de l'affaire Dreyfus, les intellectuels ont revendiqué un pouvoir symbolique et une identité collective sanctionnée par l'apparition d'un mot nouveau'. ['Since the Dreyfus Affair, the intellectuals have claimed a symbolic power and a collective identity sanctioned by the appreance of a new word.'][28]

III

Once one understands that, from the Dreyfus Affair onwards, the role of intellectuals in France has been *defined* in political terms, it becomes important to identify the sense of 'political action' that was involved. That elusive but potent term '*engagement*' did not for the most part connote a commitment to the life of the party official, or the full-time union organizer, or the elected representative. Rather, it involved taking a public stand on major issues of the day, especially those issues which could, in the Manichean terms made available by this political tradition, be seen as clear conflicts between justice and injustice. And a public stand usually meant writing an article, making a speech, or, most frequently of all, signing a petition or protest—'le degré zéro de l'engagement intellectuel'.[29] There was no lack of occasion for such action, partly because of the intense politicization of all areas of French public life for the greater part of the century: affiliating with a particular group, aligning oneself with one side of a given division, even in cultural or intellectual matters, were actions possessed of an unavoidably political character.

In this connection, Rémy Rieffel, writing from the perspective of a sociologist of the media, made a particularly pertinent observation in the course of his large-scale study of intellectuals in the Fifth Republic. He remarked that with the much more frequent appearances of intellectuals in the newly powerful mass media in the last quarter of the century (taking the launch of the celebrated television book programme 'Apostrophes' in 1975 as a symbolic date), they were no longer so reliant on political engagement as a way of becoming known outside their specialized sphere.[30] In other words, Rieffel perceived that, in the first three-quarters of the century, participation in one of the public forms of politics mentioned above (manifestos, articles, meetings, and so on) had functioned as the mechanism of publicity necessary to transform a writer or scholar into 'un intellectuel'. This helps to bring out an underlying congruence with the analysis of the structure of the role of the intellectual that I elaborated in Ch. 2, despite the obvious surface contrast involved in the French tradition's insistence on a political role. It suggests how individuals who did not easily have access to any other means of becoming known to a wider public could do so, and could start to build the reputation necessary to having their views solicited on future occasions, by joining a protest or associating their name with those already more celebrated.

But this highly politicized public life coexisted for much of the century, especially in the key period between the 1930s and the 1960s, with an unstable and frequently discredited political system, or, more exactly, sequence of political systems, which further encouraged intellectuals to remain aloof from the more institutionalized forms of political action. The later years of the Third Republic and the entire span of the short-lived Fourth Republic (1944–58) were notoriously periods of weak and frequently changing governments, vulnerable to public disturbance and pressure; they were also periods when party discipline, never strong in France, was at its weakest, as fragmented groups formed and reformed around interests and ideology. (If the Fifth Republic has appeared to provide less fertile ground for intellectuals the longer it has gone on, that may in part be because it has proved to be a stable and increasingly legitimate regime, but also because its constitutional design deliberately strengthens the position of the executive and makes it somewhat less vulnerable to the winds of political protest.) Arguably, this combination of a pervasively politicized discourse and a lack of direct political involvement was particularly conducive to a kind of 'narcissism of protest'. At the extreme (and the extreme in this sense may have been common), this can lead to a greater concern with one's self-image—with the moral righteousness of one's position or with the theoretical consistency or dialectical ingenuity of one's arguments—than with attempting to influence policy outcomes towards the least bad of the available choices. The fact of intellectuals enjoying a certain kind of political visibility in a given society may not always indicate that the actual conduct of politics is in practice more responsive to the values favoured by intellectuals.

The implicit contrast involved here between the 'expressive' and 'instrumental' values of political action was incarnated in France, during the heyday of that increasingly mythologized creature, 'the French intellectual', by the contrast between the iconic figures of Jean-Paul Sartre and Raymond Aron. 'Le modèle français s'énonce donc selon un schéma binaire incarné par Sartre d'un coté et Aron de l'autre.' ['The French model is thus articulated through a binary scheme embodied by Sartre on one side and Aron on the other.'][31] There is now a large literature on these two figures, especially on Sartre, and I shall confine myself to illustrating briefly how their contrasting styles of address to the question of political action and its effectiveness also drew upon assumptions about the distinctiveness of the position of intellectuals in France.

Writing in the immediate aftermath of a war which had seen France humiliated and occupied, but during which her writers had continued to produce literature that attracted the attention of the rest of the world, Sartre reflected that writers in Britain and the USA had been mobilized and dispersed during the war years, whereas at least many of the French writers had been at home and able to write. He then added, in a curious stab at further explanation: 'Et puis les intellectuels anglo-saxons qui forment une classe à part, coupée du reste de la nation, sont toujours éblouis quand ils retrouvent en France des hommes de lettres et des artistes étroitement mêlés à la vie et aux affaires du pays.' ['And then the Anglo-Saxon intellectuals who form a class apart, cut off from the rest of the nation, are always fascinated when in France they find artists and men of letters closely involved in the life and affairs of the country.'][32] It is difficult to see quite which writers in Britain (to thus confine the comparison for the moment) he thought of as forming a 'class apart', though one can give an intuitive sense to the idea that in France writers were somehow more intimately engaged in the country's affairs. But what is most teasing about the statement is that it comes close to reversing the familiar explanation of the absence or weakness of intellectuals in Britain, namely that they have been *too* closely involved 'in life and the affairs of the country', whereas in France a sense of apartness from and antagonism to the exercisers of political and economic power has generated that collective self-consciousness which underwrites their 'interventions' in politics. But for Sartre, writing in the mid-1940s, the greater political role of writers in France was almost axiomatic.

By contrast, Aron, commenting in the 1950s from his distinctively sceptical liberal position on the French tradition, remarked the sense intellectuals had under the Fourth Republic 'de prêcher dans le désert'. He acknowledged that in France 'la culture générale permet encore de disserter agréablement de politique' ['a general culture may still allow one to dissertate agreeably on politics'], but emphasized how far this self-pleasing practice usually was from issuing in practical proposals. 'En un sens, *l'intelligentsia* est moins engrenée sur l'action en France qu'ailleurs.' ['In a sense, the intelligentsia is less geared to political action in France than anywhere else.'][33] To underscore the contrast, Aron chose, with deliberate provokingness, to reverse the accepted account in a phrase already quoted: 'La Grande-Bretagne est probablement le pays d'Occident qui a traité ses intellectuels de la manière la plus raisonnable.'[34] He conceded that Britain's reputation abroad was rather the reverse, but insisted nonetheless that 'les Britanniques n'en offrent pas moins le même éventail d'opinions, la même galerie d'intellectuels que le reste de l'Europe'. ['Yet the British can offer the same variety of opinions and the same gallery of intellectuals as the rest of Europe.'][35] His further elaboration of this point brings in an interesting set of comparisons: 'Ainsi sont évités et l'anti-intellectualisme militant sur lequel débouche parfois le pragmatisme américain et l'admiration qui, en France, s'adresse indifférement aux romans et aux opinions politiques des écrivains, donne à ces derniers un sentiment excessif de leur importance, les incline à des jugements extrêmes et à des articles au vitriol.' ['In this way the British manage to avoid both the militant anti-intellectualism which American pragmatism sometimes tends to lead to, and the uncritical admiration which, in France, is shown alike for the novels and the political opinions of writers, giving them an excessive sense of their own importance and inclining them to indulge in extreme judgements and vitriolic articles.'][36] Aron was more familiar with the American scene than most of his compatriots at this date, and spoke with some authority on the subject. In the USA, he observed, the typical intellectual is 'non un lettré, mais un expert, fût-il économiste ou sociologue' ['not a scholar or writer but an expert—an economist or sociologist'], and the attached footnote reads; 'Parmi les lettrés, les professeurs tiennent un rôle plus important, dans les discussions d'idées, que les romanciers: à l'inverse de ce qui se passe en France.' ['Among scholars and writers, professors play a more important role in the discussion of ideas than novelists—the reverse of what happens in France.'][37] But his gloss on the favoured status of the writer in France was hardly a positive one: in France, 'le lettré—historien, écrivain, artiste' resents the power of the cultural bureaucrat, but also the necessity of selling his services to the mass media. 'L'homme de culture se sent acculé au choix entre prostitution et solitude.' ['The man of culture feels himself driven to a choice between prostitution and solitude.'][38] It was characteristic of Aron's debunking style to intimate almost in passing that paradise was not all it was cracked up to be.

Aron declared that *L'Opium des intellectuels* was a book 'consacré à la famille dont je suis originaire' ['devoted to the family of which I am myself a member'],[39] but he was in practice shunned and disowned by the majority of his siblings. For the first three decades after the war, he was effectively *persona non grata* with the French intellectual Left: his pragmatism was regarded as reactionary, his indulgence towards liberal economics was beyond the pale, and anyway he wrote for *Le Figaro*, the paper of the industrial and commercial bourgeoisie. (It was noticeable that the reaction in favour of 'liberalism' from the end of the 1970s meant that Aron enjoyed a brief period of more general esteem before his death in 1983.) The contrast between the unyielding (and frequently shrewd) realism of his political analyses and the extravagant (and frequently wrong-headed) romanticism of Sartre's became something of a cultural cliché ('better wrong with Sartre than right with Aron', ran one 1960s student jingle). But in the years after 1944, it was Sartre who had come to be taken as the incarnation not just of what it meant to be a French intellectual but of what it meant to be an intellectual *tout court*.

The Sartre of these years might be described as a Dreyfusard *après la lettre*, so voraciously did he seek out occasions to take a stand on behalf of 'l'universel' against 'le pouvoir', the latter always figured as menacing, corrupt, and 'bourgeois'. It is important to stress 'of these years', since it is often forgotten how unpolitical a creature the Sartre of the 1930s and early Vichy period was; his philosophical and literary work did not present itself as having any political bearing, and in practice he sometimes did not even bother to vote.[40] But from the Liberation until his death in 1980, Sartre was an indefatigable signer of petitions—indeed, he came to be mocked as 'un pétitionnaire de service'—and in his exhaustive study Sirinelli declares that the signing of petitions was 'une pratique dont il [Sartre] fut le champion absolu après 1945' ['a practice of which he [Sartre] was the undisputed champion after 1945'].[41] For example, in the course of the 1960s, there were twenty French intellectuals who signed more than thirty petitions; in the same period Sartre signed ninety-one. In the 1970s, twenty-two such figures signed more than fifty petitions: Sartre signed 120.[42]

It is worth observing here that a petition or manifesto prepared for publication in the press is an inherently paradoxical form. It depends on the contradictory blending of numbers and selectiveness: it is crucial to its impact that it should be seen not just to represent the position of one or two individuals—numbers are of the essence—but at the same time the names need to be recognizable and to carry some form of distinction; the effectiveness of a petition can be undermined by having too many (unknown) names as well as by having too few. Its informing principle is thus what Sirinelli calls 'aristocratic';[43] it displays the logic of 'distinction' lurking within the concept of the intellectual, a logic perhaps more readily acknowledged in France, the country that led the world in abolishing an aristocracy of birth, than elsewhere.

In any event, where Aron spoke in the voice of the political analyst sobered by experience and informed by social science about the relative weights of social, economic, and other factors, Sartre spoke as a 'professional of protest'. But his almost constant public visibility rested on his combining the two most culturally prestigious intellectual roles, that of the writer and that of the philosopher.[44] Over a long career, his own statements about this role were diverse and not always mutually consistent, but probably his best-known declaration of faith, certainly outside France, was his *Plaidoyer pour les intellectuels*, published in 1972 but first delivered as lectures in Japan in 1965. In this short book he offered a quasi-philosophical argument for the imaginative writer as the pre-eminent intellectual. Sartre acknowledged that the fundamental reproach to intellectuals was still essentially that made by Brunetière almost seventy years earlier, but he turned a reproach into a boast that was to become famous: 'l'intellectuel est quelqu'un qui se mêle de ce qui ne le regarde pas' ['the intellectual is someone who meddles in what is not his business'].[45] Writing in the *marxisant* idiom of his later years, he argued that the intellectual is conditioned by the 'bourgeois hegemony' under which he has been brought up and lives, and can therefore gain a perspective on his own society only by in some way adopting the standpoint of those who are oppressed in it. 'Il n'a donc qu'un moyen de comprendre la société où il vit: c'est de prendre sur elle le point de vue des plus défavorisés.' ['It follows that if he wishes to understand the society in which he lives, he has only one course open to him and that is to adopt the point of view of its most underprivileged members.'] This reflects the fact (it is presented by Sartre as a fact) that we do not yet live in the era of 'l'universel', but only of 'celle de l'effort universalisant' ['that of the universalizing endeavour']. As a result the intellectual can now be 'défini comme prise de conscience de sa contradiction constitutive' ['defined as a man who has achieved consciousness of his own constituent contradiction'].[46] His much-quoted conclusion, or at least concluding assertion, was that the imaginative writer, unlike the philosopher or scholar or scientist, is 'necessarily' an intellectual:

Il est *dans son métier même* aux prises avec la contradiction de la particularité et de l'universel. Au lieu que les autres intellectuels ont vu naître leur fonction d'une contradiction entre les exigences universalistes de leur profession et les exigences particularistes de la classe dominante, il trouve dans sa tâche interne l'obligation de demeurer sur le plan du vécu tout en suggérant *l'universalisation* comme l'affirmation de la vie à *l'horizon*. En ce sens, il n'est pas intellectuel *par accident*, comme eux, mais *par essence*.

[*In his professional capacity itself*, the writer is necessarily always at grips with the contradiction between the particular and the universal. Whereas other intellectuals see their function arise from a contradiction between the universalist demands of their profession and the particularist demands of the dominant class, the inner task of the writer is to remain on the plane of lived experience while suggesting *universalization* as the affirmation of life on its *horizon*. In this sense, the writer is not an intellectual *accidentally*, like others, but *essentially*.][47]

Whatever view one takes of the elaborate (and obscure) reasoning which led up to this declaration, it faithfully reflected one strand of the French tradition, possibly the dominant one in the middle decades of the century, in placing the creative writer at the heart of the category of the intellectual. Perhaps one precondition for the flourishing elsewhere (as, for example, in certain Latin American countries) of something like the French conception of the intellectual has been the prior existence of a comparable tradition of according a public role to the creators of literature.[48]

IV

Sartre and Aron were, famously, classmates, both members of the entering class of 1924–5 at the École Normale Supérieure in the rue d'Ulm. Despite their decades of public conflict and mutual hostility thereafter, they were, *au fond*, 'petits camarades', part of one of the most formidable old-boy networks in the world. This detail is not irrelevant to the larger argument of this chapter, since much of the literature on the supposed absence of intellectuals in Britain by comparison to their flourishing condition in France has sought an explanation in terms of the sociology of elites. It has been argued that leading intellectual figures in Britain have been too narrowly the products of a few socially exclusive schools and universities, or too much part of a cultural 'establishment', or too cosily intertwined with the traditional social and political elites, and so on. There are several assumptions embedded in these familiar accounts, some of which I have already subjected to critical scrutiny. For example, there is the premise that 'genuine' intellectuals must be, as though by definition, 'alienated'. Quite what this once-fashionable term means in this context is not clear, but it seems at the very least to connote a sense of not belonging to the dominant groups in society, or at least doing so only in some 'marginal' (the preferred term of the 1980s and 1990s) or even 'excluded' way. A so-called 'elite educational trajectory' is held to be unpropitious for the development of the appropriately 'oppositional' attitudes.

In practice most of those who come to exercise the kind of cultural authority traditionally ascribed to intellectuals are, almost inevitably, likely to be relatively successful products of the established system of elite education. This was particularly the case in the first half or two-thirds of the twentieth century when, even in self-consciously democratic societies such as France or the United States, egalitarian cultural attitudes had yet to unseat the influence of the traditionally prestigious educational institutions. Consider, to take just a single example, the self-described 'Young Intellectuals' in the USA in the 1910s: aspiring to form a bohemian avant-garde in a notoriously levelling and uncentralized society, the members of this group might be assumed to come from diverse educational backgrounds and be unlikely to be the beneficiaries of any form of cultural deference. But as Henry May noted: 'Almost the whole original corps of Young Intellectuals, the new critics who mixed political and aesthetic revolt', were Harvard graduates. 'At Mabel Dodge's salon, on the staff of the *New Republic* and later the *Seven Arts*, Harvard influence was obvious and pervasive.'[49] The truth is that such institutional affiliations in themselves neither preclude nor promote the likelihood of particular individuals assuming the role of intellectuals.

Nevertheless, the bearing of these kinds of assumptions on the French case, the home at once of supposedly 'genuine' intellectuals and of one of the most ferociously selective higher education systems the world has known, requires further investigation.

There has, in the last couple of decades, been a lot of research by French scholars on the formation of intellectual and educational elites in modern France, pride of place going to two massive *thèses d'état* submitted in the same year (1986) by Christophe Charle and Jean-François Sirinelli, representing, broadly speaking, the contrasting influences of the sociologist Pierre Bourdieu in the former case and the political historian René Rémond in the latter.[50] Their fruits were largely published in the form of *Les Élites de la République 1880–1900* and *Naissance des 'intellectuels' 1880–1900* by Charle, and *Génération intellectuelle: Khâgneux et Normaliens dans l'entre-deux-guerres* by Sirinelli. (The 'Khâgne' is the additional year, taken after the completion of the normal lycée course, in preparation for the competitive *concours* for entry to the highly selective 'grandes écoles', in this case for entry to L'École Normale Supérieure, whose graduates are termed 'Normaliens'.) There can be no question here of attempting to summarize these complex studies, which have in turn stimulated further research along similar lines, but they may both be said to support one broad reflection germane to my comparative intent here. Loosely speaking, this work documented in great detail the sense in which there was, at least throughout the period from the 1880s to 1940, though to some extent beyond as well, an intellectual or educational elite in France that felt itself to be partially separate from the other governing elites (economic, social, political), and even formed something of a self-perpetuating caste. The bearing of this contention on French intellectuals' self-confidence and sense of constituting a 'contre-pouvoir' is evident. When Christophe Charle pithily characterizes the Dreyfus Affair as 'the imposition of an issue on the political class by the intellectual class', a certain self-conscious separateness of this 'intellectual class' is obviously an analytical prerequisite.

A few striking pieces of evidence may be cited to indicate the foundations of this sense of group identity. First, the preponderance of teachers in the families of those going on to educational distinction is illustrated by the astonishing statistic that before 1940 one *khâgneux* in three was the son of a teacher of some kind (*instituteur/institutrice* or *professeur*), at a time when all categories of teacher represented less than 1 percent of the French population.[51] In 1961 50 percent of Normaliens were sons of scholars or teachers.[52] (These scholars themselves perpetuate the pattern they study: Sirinelli, now a professor in Paris, dedicates his book to 'mes quatre grands-parents, instituteurs'; Charle, now similarly enchaired, is the son of an *instituteur*; and so on.) Then, the overwhelming majority of those who were to be successful in gaining entry into the grandes écoles undertook their 'classes préparatoires' at four or five crack Paris lycées; a ludicrously disproportionate number did their 'classes prépas' at just two of these schools, Henri IV and Louis le Grand, symbolically located in Paris's

'Latin Quarter' adjacent to the other select institutions they served. For example, of the 294 students who were successful in the *concours* for entry into ENS throughout the 1920s, 176 were prepared at these two Paris lycées alone, with a further thirty-eight coming from two more (Condorcet and Lakanal).[53] These figures mask a considerable amount of upward social mobility, since many of the 'boursiers' at these schools came from modest provincial backgrounds, such as all those sons of *instituteurs* and *institutrices*, and lived in at the lycée while preparing for the *concours*. But Sirinelli's work, in particular, demonstrates the extraordinarily intense and durable social bonds created by this experience, in a strenuously intellectual milieu unmatched even by the most academic of the great English public schools.

Thereafter, graduates of the rue d'Ulm, even though they were part of a small entering class of around thirty each year in 'literary' subjects, played a disproportionate part in staffing French higher education (which at the time included the higher classes in the top lycées). At the beginning of the century, almost a third of each year's teaching posts, which were reserved for those who passed the Agrégation in 'literary' subjects (*lettres, philosophie, histoire et geographie*), were obtained by Normaliens; in 1910, Normaliens occupied 48 per cent of all posts in the *facultés des letters*.[54] Or again, in 1930, two out of every five professors in the provincial *facultés des letters* were Normaliens, and almost three out of every five such professors at the Sorbonne.[55] It is not hard to see how a different sense of identity might be generated in a system, such as Britain's, where a less intensely intellectual experience of higher education was shared by the scions of the various elites (social, economic, cultural), who in turn went on to a greater diversity of subsequent careers. Similarly, although attitudes and values cannot be read off from such social indicators, it is easy to see how it might make a difference when the emblematic (and statistically very common if not actually preponderant) parent was, shall we say, the genteel, Oxbridge-educated parson, on calling terms with the local gentry, rather than the radical *instituteur* or *professeur de lycée*, the implanted representative of the republican state, answerable only to Paris and to Pure Reason.

Nevertheless, the emphasis on the separateness or self-containedness of the intellectual elite can be exaggerated. First of all, one would need to broaden the study to take in the overlap with *khâgneux* who passed into other *grandes écoles*. For example, the École Polytechnique, also a Revolutionary foundation, increasingly formed a scientific and managerial as well as military elite, and a growing number of graduates of a variety of institutions tended to pass a period of time at Sciences Po, where future intellectual, political, and business leaders mingled. But it is also important to remember that although *Normaliens* overwhelmingly entered the higher echelons of the state education system, about 20 per cent did not, and even some of those who began in education later had distinguished careers in other areas of public life. Drawing on a survey of 1680 Normaliens who entered in the years up to 1934, Sirinelli showed that 82 per cent of them had initially pursued a career in education at some level, the overwhelming majority as professors in the universities or higher lycée classes, though quite a few moved out into other occupations later, and some made careers elsewhere from the start. Thus, for example, if one takes the twenty-seven members of the entering class of 1924 (the one which included Aron and Sartre), one finds that the list includes one 'ancien deputé', one 'ministre plénipotentiaire', one 'ambassadeur de France', one 'Inspecteur-général de l'instruction publique', alongside Aron ('Professeur au Collège de France'), Nizan ('publiciste, tué par l'ennemi'), and Sartre ('Philosophe et écrivain'). Or again, among the thirty-one members of the 'promotion' of 1931, one finds, alongside the usual preponderance of university professors and lycée teachers, one 'Ministre delégué à Berlin', one 'ancien sénateur et ministre de l'Education Nationale', one 'expert consultant, Agence de coopération culturelle et technique', two 'Inspecteurs général de l'Instruction publique', and, wonderfully, one 'Président de la République Française' (Georges Pompidou).[56] Clearly, the points of contact or overlap indicated in these cases are largely with the political or administrative elites, not with, say, the worlds of inherited wealth and economic power. Nonetheless, there are both comparisons and contrasts to be drawn with the alumni of Ivy League universities or of Oxbridge colleges. It is far from self-evident that a well-placed Normalien (and there is hardly any other kind) will have had any less direct connection with and access to wielders of power in his society than that imputed to the average Oxbridge swot.

V

It is understandable that so much of this research should have concentrated on the period of the Third Republic, the period which is now regarded as the defining epoch for so many markers of modern French identity.[57] But it is also indirectly expressive of a certain archaic quality in the conception of 'les intellectuels' that itself dates from these years. The smallness of the intellectual elite, the level of deference accorded its views, the dominance of reviews and petitions as means of expression and action, the abstract style of political debate—all these features enjoyed an almost artificial prolongation of life as a result of the conservative and 'blocked' character of French life through the middle decades of the twentieth century. But from the end of the 1950s onwards, French society underwent a period of enforced modernization (much of it, naturally, planned and carried out by a small technocratic elite in Paris), and these and other more global social and economic changes were soon to affect the position of intellectuals. For example, in 1958, only 9 percent of households in France had a television; thereafter, the percentage began to rise dramatically, as in other countries, with familiar consequences.[58] The narrow educational world discussed in the previous section also expanded and changed its character. By the mid-1980s there were *six times* as many students in higher education as there had been in the early 1950s.[59] The relative position of key institutions also shifted: the dominance of the ENS declined somewhat; the ancient Collège de France was revivified with a number of outstanding elections (for example, Aron, Michel Foucault, and Georges Duby were all elected in 1970), so that leading French intellectual figures came to aspire to the 'consecration' of a chair there; and above all the newly founded École des Hautes Études en Sciences Sociales emerged as the academic home for many of the most influential voices in public debate ('Une grande partie des clercs qui sont intervenus dans le débat public, en tant que figures de proue, se sont installés dans cette institution périphérique de l'enseignement français.' ['A large number of the "*clercs*" who have intervened in public debate, as leading figures, have been based in this institution peripheral to French education.']).[60] French intellectual life also lost some of its traditional parochialism, with a much greater openness to developments in 'les pays anglo-saxons', especially the United States, and the translation, often belatedly, of works in idioms that had not previously commanded much recognition, still less prestige, within France, such as analytical philosophy or neoclassical economic theory.

One of the enduring features of the French cultural situation that is still prone to elicit wistful or envious sentiments from observers elsewhere is the apparent overlap or ease of movement between the worlds of academia and of publishing and journalism, allowing serious scholarly works also to engage the attention of a wider reading public. Certainly, the sales of some significant scholarly or theoretical works from the 1960s and 1970s indicated a take-up from some kind of non-academic readership: for example, Foucault's highly abstract *Les Mots et les choses* (1966) sold 100,000 copies; Deleuze and Guattari's opaque *Anti-Oedipe* (1972) over 50,000; Bourdieu's *La Distinction* (1979), over 70,000, and so on.[61] The leading serious commercial publishing houses, above all Gallimard, Grasset, and Le Seuil ('Galligrasseuil'), continue to be powers in current intellectual life in their own right, each sponsoring several series, supporting one or more general periodicals, and in some cases even retaining the services of a house-intellectual or two (as with B-H. Lévy at Grasset and, in a different way, Marcel Gauchet at Gallimard). The publication which, following its launch in 1967, stands at the heart of this milieu is the weekly *Le Monde des Livres*, a national newspaper supplement but one which now exercises significant influence in the making and unmaking of intellectual careers. As Rieffel puts it, with understandable exaggeration: 'Un intellectuel n'existe guère si *le Monde* ne se préoccupe pas de lui.' ['An intellectual hardly exists if *le Monde* doesn't pay attention to him.'][62]

But the existence and cultural power of the audience referred to as 'le Tout-Paris intellectuel' has not been welcomed by all observers within France. Reflecting on 'L'intellectuel et ses publics: les singularités françaises', the liberal sociologist Raymond Boudon sought an economic or institutional explanation for 'l'impression de singularité que la vie intellectuelle française peut donner à l'observateur' ['the impression of singularity that French intellectual life can give to the observer']. Boudon remarked that in the humanities and social sciences France has had an only partly functional mechanism of properly academic publication, peer review, assessment, and reward. Instead, it has too often been the case, in his view, that a properly 'scientific' evaluation and circulation of publications in these fields has been 'short-circuited' by the immediate but superficial response from the governing organs of the larger non-academic market. 'L'existence, prestige, et caractère centralisée du Tout-Paris intellectuel—structure qui n'a pas d'équivalent ni en Grande-Bretagne, ni en Allemagne, ni aux États Unis' makes 'ce processus d'évaluation avec court-circuit, rare dans un pays comme les États-Unis . . . très frappant en France.' ['The existence, prestige, and centralized character of "le Tout-Paris intellectuel"—a structure which has no equivalent either in Great Britain or in Germany or in the United States' makes 'this short-circuited process of evaluation, which is rare in a country such as the United States . . . very striking in France.'] Boudon, who was more sympathetic to an American model of the university and of intellectual activity than has been at all common in France, ascribed many of the long-standing defects of French intellectuals to the seductions of this situation, which encouraged the dominance of 'l'esprit littéraire' over 'l'esprit scientifique', a pattern which in turn he identified as 'la source principale de l'indifférence relative des intellectuels français par rapport à la réalité' ['the principal source of the relative indifference of French intellectuals to reality']. Of course, in the French context, Boudon's piece itself is ideological and polemical in the manner he is denouncing: his examples make clear his disdain for several of those who had experienced considerable *réclame* in the wider world, and his evocation of Tocqueville on 'l'esprit littéraire' and his dismissive remarks about French intellectuals' lack of regard for 'reality' indicate the Aronien pedigree of his article. The piece was something of a covert complaint about the too-ready availability of the role of the intellectual in France. Nonetheless, it both pointed to some often-neglected preconditions for the 'singularité' of that role and itself represented a straw in the wind of change.[63]

Although the term 'l'intellectuel' may seem to have been firmly and unselfconsciously part of current usage in France for at least a century, there had, there as elsewhere, always been those who repudiated the label in self-description. A revealing concentration of denial was produced when in 1974 *Le Monde des livres* attempted to carry out a small survey under the heading 'Des intellectuels, pour quoi faire?' The paper addressed a series of questions to figures whom it regarded as among France's leading contemporary intellectuals, the first of which was: 'Il existe, en France, une intelligentsia nombreuse et qui s'exprime beaucoup. Avez-vous le sentiment d'en faire partie?' ['There exists in France an intelligentsia which is numerous and which expresses itself a good deal. Do you feel that you are part of it?'] The published replies were, inevitably, diverse and often obstructive, but several of the respondents were evidently unhappy with the terms of the question. So, for example, René Etiemble (described by Michel Winock as 'grammairien, romancier, sinologue, antistalinien résolu, chroniqueur aux *Temps modernes*' ['grammarian, novelist, Sinologist, resolute anti-Stalinist, columnist for the *Temps Modernes*'][64]), replied: 'Il y aurait plutôt en France des tas d'*intelligentsias*, sœurs ennemies, plus agitées, caméléonesques, léonines, vipérines et dogmatiques qu'intelligentes. J'espère ne faire partie d'aucune d'elles.' ['In France there are, rather, loads of *intelligentsias*, sibling rivals, more agitated, chameleon-like, leonine, viperous, and dogmatic than intelligent. I hope not to be part of any of them.'] Alfred Fabre-Luce, described as 'homme de lettres et journaliste', kept his distance in no less haughty terms: 'Si l'on convient de désigner, tout simplement, par le mot *intelligentsia* le groupe intellectuel le mieux organisé, je n'ai pas le sentiment d'y appartenir.' ['If it suits some people to designate by the word *intelligentsia*, quite simply, the best-organized intellectual group, I don't feel I belong to it.'] Jean Guitton, 'philosophe, Membre de l'Académie française', was similarly dismissive: 'Je n'ai pas l'impression de faire partie de l'intelligentsia et même je n'ai pas le moindre désir d'être un "intellectuel".' ['I do not have the impression of being part of the intelligentsia and I don't even have the least desire to be an "intellectual".'] And the anthropologist Claude Lévi-Strauss, notoriously reluctant to take the public stage or make political pronouncements, cited Montherlant's mocking remarks about intellectuals whose role it was 'de penser à propos de tout . . . répondre aux enquêtes les plus oiseuses, rédiger des messages, pontifier au hasard, guider leurs semblables dans des directions mûrement choisies en cinq minutes' ['to think about everything . . . reply to the idlest enquiries, compose messages, pontificate at random, guide their fellow-creatures in directions maturely chosen in five minutes']. To which Lévi-Strauss added: 'Si vous vous référez à ce phénomène en disant de l'intelligentsia qu'elle "s'exprime beaucoup", je n'ai pas le sentiment d'en faire partie.' ['If you are referring to this phenomenon in speaking of an intelligentsia that "expresses itself a good deal", I do not have the feeling of being part of it.'][65] It should be said that the chosen sample of intellectuals revealed something of a bias towards literature and journalism, especially, perhaps, those of a rather conservative disposition, and this may have skewed the responses correspondingly. But it also has to be said that the tone as well as the content of these exercises in self-exemption are deeply familiar from other countries.

The decline of 'la singularité française' in the matter of intellectuals received poignant symbolic expression in the coincidence that the first number of the new review *Le Débat*, expressly devoted to the 'liberalization' and 'democratization' of French intellectual life, appeared on the day on which Jean-Paul Sartre died, 15 April 1980. In his inaugural editorial, Pierre Nora announced his own, subtler, version of 'the death of the intellectual'.[66] There are no longer the great 'maîtres à penser' of the past, claiming to speak as tribunes of the voiceless, challenging political power with a countervailing 'pouvoir intellectuel'—and a good thing, too. The present is at once more democratic, more academic, and more 'mediatisée': people can speak for themselves, all topics are subject to the correction of specialist knowledge, there are many publics, with more choices about what they hear and see. There is no longer any place, or need, for the 'despotic intellectual' of the middle years of the century, laying claim to direct the thoughts and actions of fellow-citizens. Nora found this 'un naufrage libératoire, qui a inaugurée la révolution démocratique du pouvoir spirituel et qui appel, en creux, la place d'un intellectuel *dans* l'histoire et seulement dans l'histoire' ['a liberating shipwreck which has inaugurated the democratic revolution of spiritual power and summoned intellectuals to a new historical role: *within* history and only within history'].[67] Of course, in making this the theme for the opening editorial of the most significant new journal to be launched in France for several decades, the piece itself testified to the importance still accorded to the question of intellectuals, even if they no longer exist—in their old form. For Nora clearly believed they did indeed continue to exist and had an essential role to play, only it had to be more modest and more sceptical; less didactic but better informed; less oracular but more communicative. A case, perhaps, of 'L'intellectuel est mort; vive l'intellectuel.'

The 1980s were to see numerous inquests on the theme of 'the disappearance of the intellectual' in France, several of them staged in the pages of *Le Débat* itself. This was one of the many ways in which French reflection on the position of intellectuals came more and more to converge with a pattern discernible in the other major Western societies in these years.[68] The theme of the 'médiatisation' of the intellectuals, their absorption into the world of 'celebrity', has been the burden of several notable jeremiads.[69] Pierre Nora's declaration in 1990 that the need now was 'lutter à la fois contre la spécialisation universitaire et la dégradation journalistique' ['to fight against both academic specialization and journalistic debasement'][70] could, as I shall show in more detail in the final two chapters of this book, serve as something of a motto for discussions of intellectuals almost anywhere at the end of the twentieth century.

In 1990 Jean-François Sirinelli summarized the case that was increasingly made within France by the closing decades of the century, a case whose terms almost exactly matched those made in the other societies we have considered. Intellectuals had been

> progressivement dépossédés du rôle qui fut longtemps le leur. Et ce, sous l'effet d'un triple choc: ces clercs ont perdu leur élément d'identité, la culture, victime d'une définition diluante; supplantés par plus médiatiques qu'eux, ils n'ont plus leur rôle de hérauts; dépouillés de leur coloration idéologique, ils ne peuvent plus, par leurs débats, dégager les enjeux des grandes controverses nationales. Ne constitueraient-ils plus qu'une espèce en voie de disparition, parvenue exsangue et sans voix au bout de la piste?
>
> [progressively dispossessed of a role which for a long time was theirs. And this under the effect of a triple shock: these *clercs* have lost their identity-card, culture, victim of a diluting definition; supplanted by those more media-friendly than they are, they no

longer have their role as heralds; stripped of their ideological colouring, they can no longer, through their debates, identify what's at stake in the great national controversies. Do they not rather constitute a species on the way to extinction, arriving anaemic and voiceless at the end of the road?]

Sirinelli's own assessment disputed this pessimistic diagnosis: the position of intellectuals may have changed, but in a culture increasingly providing 'les nouveautés médiadégradables' there would remain a hunger for more substantial fare.[71] Nonetheless, the sense that France was in this matter coming more and more to conform to a common pattern was strong. This sense of convergence was expressed in a different manner by Pascal Balmand's summary of what had been, at least until the 1980s, 'two French peculiarities: in the first place the existence of a form of politics fashioned by a "culture of conflict" (J. Julliard), replete with a whole procession of Manichean confrontations pursued in the name of absolute values; secondly, and related to this, the special importance attributed in France to the figure of the intellectual'.[72] Writing at the beginning of the 1990s, Balmand, like several other observers, detected the beginnings of a decline in these two peculiarities, and here again are signs that, just as different national political traditions in Europe are in some ways coming closer together, so, too, divergences among the perceived situations of intellectuals in their respective societies are becoming less pronounced.

But that tendency towards convergence, marked in many other spheres of social, economic, and cultural life as well, has certainly not, or at least not yet, effaced all signs of distinctiveness. The death of Pierre Bourdieu in January 2002 provided the occasion for some timely reminders of the continuing vitality of some of the assumptions this chapter has been exploring. In an obituary article in *Le Monde*, Bourdieu himself was quoted as reiterating near the end of his life a central article of faith: 'Ce que je défends, c'est la possibilité et la necessité de l'intellectuel critique. . . . Il n'y a pas de démocratie effective sans vrai contre-pouvoir critique. L'intellectuel en est un, et de première grandeur.' ['What I stand up for is the possibility and the necessity of intellectual critique. . . . There is no effective democracy without real critical counter-power. The intellectual is one, and of the first rank.'][73] With his death, Bourdieu became the most recent candidate for the title of 'the last of the intellectuals'; others will doubtless follow. But for all the elegiac tristesse of that particular trope, there remains in Bourdieu's remark a striking confidence, above all a confidence that the intellectual constitutes a 'contre-pouvoir', indeed one of the first magnitude. Even as this distinctively French tradition is once again being buried by the press alongside the actual burial of one of its most eminent exemplars, these words summon up the ghosts of Dreyfusards, of anti-Fascist intellectuals, of signatories of the petition against French atrocities in Algeria, and an unnumbered host of scholars and writers who had responded across the century to the call to '*engagement*'. More extended reflection on the peculiarities of this tradition surely drives one back to E. P. Thompson's remark quoted in Ch. 8, but now with a fuller understanding of what is at issue where the question of intellectuals is concerned: 'It happened in one way in France, in another way in England. I am not disputing the importance of the difference—and of the different traditions which ensued—but the notion of typicality.'[74]

NOTES

1. I attempted to make this point in a different way in an earlier engagement with this topic: see 'Intellectuals in Britain and France in the twentieth century: confusions, contrasts—and convergence?', in Jeremy Jennings (ed.), *Intellectuals in Twentieth Century France: Mandarins and Samurais* (Basingstoke: Macmillan, 1993), 210.
2. Perry Anderson, *English Questions* (London: Verso, 1992), 288.
3. Raymond Aron, *L'Opium des intellectuels* (Paris; Calmann-Lévy, 1991 [1st edn. 1955]), 229; *The Opium of the Intellectuals*, trans. Terence Kilmartin (London: Secker, 1957), 218 (hereafter, references will give the page number of the French edition followed by that of the English).
4. See Ch. 2 above, esp. Ch. 2, Sect. I.
5. Quoted in Paul Bénichou, *Le Sacre de l'écrivain* (Paris: Corti, 1973), 117.
6. Aron, *L'Opium*, 244/234.
7. Daniel Lindenberg, 'Figures et rhétorique de l'anti-intellectualisme', *Mil Neuf Cent*, 15 (1997), 8.
8. Lindenberg, 'Figures et rhétorique', 7.
9. No set of citations, however extensive, could adequately support this summary account, but for an accessible introduction to the some of the changes that began to transform French society from the 1960s onwards, see Henri Mendras, *La Seconde Révolution française* (Paris: Gallimard, 1988); a revised and modified version of this book was published in English as Henri Mendras with Alistair Cole, *Social Change in Modern France: Towards a Cultural Anthropology of the Fifth Republic* (Cambridge: Cambridge University Press, 1991).
10. François Dosse, *La Marche des idées: Histoire des intellectuels—histoire intellectuelle* (Paris: La Découverte, 2003), 62.
11. There is now an extensive historiography on this, some of which claims to trace the origins of the term back to St Simon at the beginning of the century. For guidance in English, see Victor Brombert, *The Intellectual Hero: Studies in the French Novel 1880–1955* (Philadelphia: Lippincott, 1961); William M. Johnston, 'The origin of the term "intellectuals" in French novels and essays of the 1890s', *Journal of European Studies*, 4 (1974), 43–56; Venita Datta, *Birth of a National Icon: The Literary Avant-Garde and the Origins of the Intellectual in France* (Albany: State University of New York Press, 1999). The best starting-point for French scholarship is Christophe Charle, *Naissance des 'intellectuels', 1880–1900* (Paris: Minuit, 1990). Cf. the discussion at Ch. 1, Sect. II above.
12. Louis Pinto, 'La vocation de l'universel: la formation de la représentation de l'intellectuel vers 1900', *Actes de la recherche en sciences sociales*, 55 (1984), 23–32.
13. Michel Winock, 'Les Affaires Dreyfus', *Vingtième Siècle: Revue d'histoire*, 5 (1985), 19–37. For example, 'la guerre d'Algérie ménage aux intellectuels une occasion de renouer avec la tradition dreyfusienne, entendue comme la protestation contre la

raison d'état'; Michel Winock, 'Les intellectuels dans le siècle', *Vingtième Siècle: Revue d'histoire* 4 (1984), 12.

14. Pascal Ory and Jean-François Sirinelli, *Les Intellectuels en France, de l'Affaire Dreyfus à nos jours* (Paris: Colin, 1986), 28.
15. Maurice Blanchot, 'Les intellectuels en question', *Le Débat*, 29 (Mar. 1984), 7.
16. Pierre Bourdieu, 'The corporatism of the universal: the role of intellectuals in the modern world', *Telos*, 81 (1989), 103 In giving the original of this article as a lecture in Tokyo, Bourdieu may have been deliberately alluding to Sartre having given his celebrated *Plaidoyer des intellectuels* as lectures in Japan.
17. Cited in Jean-François Sirinelli, *Intellectuels et passions françaises: manifestes et pétitions au XXe siècle* (Paris: Fayard, 1990), 335.
18. Vincent Duclert, 'Anti-intellectualisme et intellectuels pendant l'affaire Dreyfus', *Mil Neuf Cent*, 15 (1997), 69.
19. Barrès constantly returned to this point. For example, a year later, in *Le Journal*, 2 Jan. 1899, he insisted: 'L'essentiel, c'est qu'on ne pourra plus dire que l'intelligence *et les intellectuels*—pour se servir une dernière fois de ces barbarismes de mauvais français—sont d'un seul côté'; quoted in Duclert, 'Anti-intellectualisme', 79.
20. French higher education had expanded dramatically in the years since the Franco-Prussian war: there were, for example, four times as many university teachers in 1911 as in 1871; Jean-Louis Fabiani, *Les Philosophes de la République* (Paris: Minuit, 1987), 19.
21. Maurice Barrès, 'Les intellectuels, ou logiciens de l'absolu', in *Scènes et doctrines du nationalisme*, 2 vols. (Paris: Plon, 1925), i. 48, 49, 50, 60–1, 62.
22. The phrase has been so widely cited that Christophe Charle, in his now classic study, could simply allude ironically to the 'professeur de tibétain, cher à Brunetière'; Charle, *Naissance des 'intellectuels'*, 145.
23. Ferdinand Brunetière, 'Après le procés', *La Revue des deux mondes* (15 Mar. 1898), 446.
24. Ibid. 443.
25. Ibid. 445.
26. Charle, *Naissance des 'intellectuels'*, 160–2.
27. For the usage of the term in the years after the Dreyfus Affair, see ibid. ch. 5, and Ory and Sirinelli, *Les Intellectuels en France*, chs. 2–4.
28. Christophe Charle, 'Naissance des intellectuels contemporains (1860–1898)', in Bela Köpeczi and Jacques Le Goff (eds.), *Intellectuels français, intellectuels hongrois, XIIIe–XXe siècle* (Paris: Éditions du CNRS, 1985), 177.
29. Ory and Sirinelli, *Les Intellectuels en France*, 20: 'La pétition est bien le degré zéro de l'engagement intellectuel.'
30. Rémy Rieffel, *La Tribu des clercs* (Paris: Calmann-Lévy, 1993); 2nd edn. entitled *Les Intellectuels sous la Ve* République, 3 vols. (1995), iii. 213.
31. Dosse, *Marche des idées*, 89; for a detailed 'double portrait' that emphasizes their iconic status, see Jean-François Sirinelli, *Sartre et Aron, deux intellectuels dans le siècle* (Paris: Fayard, 1995).
32. Jean-Paul Sartre, 'La Nationalisation de la littérature', *Situations*, II (Paris: Gallimard, 1948), 49.
33. Aron, *L'Opium*, 230–1/220–1.
34. Ibid. 244/234.
35. Ibid. 250/240.

36. Ibid. 244/234.
37. Ibid. 239/229.
38. Ibid. 308/300.
39. Ibid. 11/p. xi.
40. Even during his years at the (highly politicized) ENS, Sartre had been 'incontestablement apolitique'; Sirinelli, *Génération intellectuelle*, 333.
41. Sirinelli, *Intellectuels et passions françaises*, 10.
42. Rieffel, *Les Intellectuels sous la Ve République*, i. 166–7.
43. Sirinelli, *Intellectuels et passions françaises*, 323.
44. This is most fully argued, using notions drawn from the work of Pierre Bourdieu, in Anna Boschetti, *Sartre et 'Les Temps Modernes': une entreprise intellectuelle* (Paris: Minuit, 1985), chs. 2 and 3.
45. Jean-Paul Sartre, *Plaidoyer pour les intellectuels* (Paris: Gallimard, 1972), 12; 'A plea for intellectuals', in Jean-Paul Sartre, *Between Existentialism and Marxism*, trans. John Matthews (London: New Left Books, 1974), 230.
46. Sartre, *Plaidoyer*, 61, 70; *Plea*, 255, 260.
47. Sartre, *Plaidoyer*, 116–17; *Plea*, 284.
48. For an interesting, if perhaps somewhat overstated, account of this French tradition, see Priscilla Parkhurst Clark, *Literary France: The Making of a Culture* (Berkeley: University of California Press, 1987).
49. Henry F. May, *The End of American Innocence: a Study of the First Years of Our Own Time, 1912–1917* (New York: Columbia University Press, 1992 [1st edn. 1959]), 298–9.
50. Christophe Charle, 'Intellectuels et élites 1880–1900', Thèse d'État, Paris I (Panthéon-Sorbonne), 1986; Jean-François Sirinelli, 'Khâgneux et normaliens dans l'entre-deux-guerres', Thèse d'État, Paris X (Nanterre), 1986.
51. Jean-François Sirinelli, 'La Khâgne', in Pierre Nora (ed.), *Les Lieux de mémoire: La Nation*, 3 vols. (Paris: Gallimard, 1986), iii. 589–624.
52. Fritz Ringer, *Education and Society in Modern Europe* (Bloomington: Indiana University Press, 1979), 178.
53. Sirinelli, *Génération intellectuelle*, 68–9.
54. Victor Karady, 'Les Professeurs de la République. Le marché scolaire, les réformes universitaires, et les transformations de la fonction professorale à la fin du XIXe siècle', *Actes de recherche en sciences sociales*, 47–8 (1983), 102.
55. Sirinelli, *Génération intellectuelle*, 158–9, 161.
56. Ibid. Annexe I.
57. This emerges very strongly from the mammoth project of Pierre Nora's *Les Lieux de mémoire*: see particularly Nora's conclusion to the first volume, 'De la République à la Nation'; *Les Lieux de mémoire*, i. *La République* (Paris: Gallimard, 1984), 651–9.
58. Rieffel, *Intellectuels sous la Ve République*, i. 12.
59. In 1950 there were 131,000 university students; in 1986, 861,000; figures from George Ross, 'The decline of the left intellectual in modern France', in Alain G. Gagnon (ed.), *Intellectuals in Liberal Democracies: Political Influence and Social Involvement* (New York: Praeger, 1987), 53.
60. Rieffel, *Intellectuels sous la Ve République*, iii. 30; for the Collège de France, see 36–41.
61. Ibid. 64–5, 79 These figures are for sales over varying periods, mostly of about ten years; they appear to be for sales within France. Such sales for comparably serious

books were not unknown in English-speaking countries at this time, of course: e.g. Walt Rostow's *The Stages of Economic Growth* sold 260,000 copies in English in the twelve years after its publication in 1960; John Brewer, 'The error of our ways: historians and the birth of consumer society', 'Cultures of Consumption' research programme (London: Birkbeck College, 2003), 10. I am grateful to Donald Winch for providing me with a copy of this lecture.

62. Rieffel, *Intellectuels sous la Ve République*, iii. 173.
63. Raymond Boudon, 'L'Intellectuel et ses publics: les singularités françaises', in Jean-Daniel Reynaud and Yves Grafmeyer (eds.), *Français, qui êtes-vous?* (Paris: La Documentation française, 1981), 466, 470, 473, 479.
64. Michel Winock, *Le Siècle des intellectuels* (Paris: le Seuil, 1999 [1st edn. 1997]), 618.
65. The survey is analysed in Rieffel, *Intellectuels sous la Ve République*, iii. 170–1.
66. Pierre Nora, 'Que peuvent les intellectuels?', *Le Débat*, 1 (1980), 3–19.
67. A slightly abridged version of this article later appeared in English as 'About intellectuals', in Jeremy Jennings (ed.), *Intellectuals in Twentieth-Century France: Mandarins and Samurais* (Basingstoke: Macmillan, 1993), 187–98 (quotation at p. 198).
68. For a helpful comparative overview of this theme, see Jeremy Jennings, 'Deaths of the intellectual: a comparative autopsy', in Helen Small (ed.), *The Public Intellectual* (Oxford: Blackwell, 2002), 110–30.
69. For three very different kinds of example, see Régis Debray, *Le Pouvoir intellectuel en France* (Paris: Ramsay: 1979); Hervé Hamon and Patrick Rotman, *Les Intellocrates* (Paris: Ramsay, 1981); B-H. Lévy, *Les Aventures de la liberté: Une Histoire subjective des intellectuels* (Paris: Grasset, 1991).
70. Pierre Nora, 'Dix ans du *Débat*', *Le Débat*, 60 (May–Aug. 1990), 4.
71. Sirinelli, *Intellectuels et passions françaises*, 334–5, 338.
72. Pascal Balmand, 'Anti-intellectualism in French political culture', in Jennings (ed.), *Intellectuals in Twentieth-Century France*, 173.
73. Thomas Ferenczi, 'Pierre Bourdieu, le sociologue de tous les combats', *Le Monde*, 25 Jan. 2002, 29.
74. Thompson, 'Peculiarities', 322; cf. Ch. 8 Swect. I above.

12

The Translation of the Clerks

'We do not realise that we *calculate*, operate, with words, and in the course of time translate them sometimes into one picture, sometimes into another.'

I

La trahison des clercs: this one resonant phrase, whether in its original French form or in translation, has entered the lexicon not just of scholarship but of politics and journalism as well. The contexts in which it appears and the variety of senses attached to it come to seem, once one begins to pay any kind of systematic attention to its use, unsettlingly various. Within the several kinds of writing about intellectuals, its use has become *de rigueur*, even if there seems to be precious little agreement on its meaning. Almost any form of behaviour by almost anyone who might be termed an intellectual seems fated to be characterized at some time or another as an example of *la trahison des clercs*, ranging from irresponsibly washing one's hands of the world's problems to promiscuously getting one's hands dirty in attempting to solve those problems. The phrase has evidently come to encapsulate a whole range of assumptions about and attitudes towards intellectuals, combining the elevation of them into an almost priestly caste with jeering censure of their inevitable folly and self-deception—indeed, it is frequently used to signal precisely the fall from the lofty heights of the one extreme to the squalid depths of the other.

The term was famously given currency by Julien Benda's book *La Trahison des clercs*, published in French in 1927 and in English translation the following year. The book has had classic status thrust upon it: no discussion of the topic of intellectuals can now, it seems, wholly ignore it, and several leading authorities profess to endorse its analysis of the intellectual's role. For example, Michael Walzer, no mean judge of what being an intellectual involves, insisted that 'it remains the best single statement of the critical intellectual's creed', while Edward Said (for once in agreement with Walzer) declared in the first of his Reith Lectures on 'Representations of the Intellectual' that 'there is no doubt in my mind at least that the image of a real intellectual as conceived by Benda remains an attractive and compelling one'.[1] Even those who are less persuaded cite the book as 'the most celebrated sermon concerning the responsibility of intellectuals', 'a major monument of twentieth-century thought', and so on.[2] In a collaborative volume published in 1990 on 'the political responsibility of intellectuals' (which paid special attention to the situation in Eastern Europe), Benda's was the most frequently cited name, ahead of Havel, Sartre, and Marx.[3]

Yet few things are, it seems to me, as indicative of the confusions and stereotypes that dog this topic as the afterlife of Benda's title and the thesis for which it is supposed to stand. This is partly because the phrase itself has acquired a degree of autonomy, with the result that it is now used both by those who wish to complain that intellectuals are failing to 'intervene' in the world and by those who wish to denounce precisely such intervention, and for much else besides.[4] But, more fundamentally, the difficulties arise out of the mismatch between the specifically French circumstances which Benda was addressing and the very different conditions into which his thesis has been parachuted in the English-speaking world. As Wittgenstein reminds us, in the passage quoted as the epigraph to this chapter, 'We do not realise that we *calculate*, operate, with words, and in the course of time translate them sometimes into one picture, sometimes into another.'[5] The problems begin with the task of translating Benda's celebrated title into English, but this, I want to argue, becomes merely a kind of linguistic proxy for the more intractable problems involved in shuttling between French and British cultural traditions. One simple but, as far as I can see, entirely overlooked detail may be taken as emblematic of these difficulties: in this supposedly classic work on the role of the intellectuals, the word 'intellectuals' never appears.

II

Remembered now for just one book (and sometimes only for its title), Julien Benda was an independent man-of-letters who, in a long lifetime (1867–1956), published fifty books and over a thousand articles.[6] Born into a moderately wealthy, wholly secularized Jewish family in Paris, Benda's education fell somewhat short of the paradigmatic cursus: he failed the entrance exam to the École Polytechnique, eventually completing a *licence* in history at the Sorbonne, after a spell at the École Centrale. But he was able, following his father's death, to live for many years off his inherited capital without ever needing to undertake paid employment, and from the outset he identified himself with the life of 'pure reason' in its most unworldly and uncompromised form. His self-description was revealing here: 'Mon drame sera d'être un mathématicien égaré parmi des gens de letters.' ['My tragedy will be to be a mathematician strayed among men of letters.'][7] He became a *dreyfusard* in 1898, though characteristically insisting that this did not represent any involvement in 'politics', but merely the maintenance of eternal and universal values; he seems to have had little sympathy with the plight of Dreyfus himself, but to have believed that it was for 'men of science' to determine truth whatever its political consequences. In the early decades of the century, he was a sharp critic of Bergson and especially of the cult of *bergsonisme*, which he saw as a particularly culpable submission of the tasks of philosophy to the fashions of *le beau monde*; and more generally he upheld a stern classicism in literature and an unbending purism in philosophy, which he always regarded as striving, at its best, to attain the generality and the 'uselessness' of mathematics. Engagement with 'the world', especially in the form of politics, he scorned as the ultimate derogation from the life of the mind lived for its own sake. His own practice, however, was not always obviously compatible with this elevated conception: although he constantly pilloried the 'nationalist passion', this did not prevent him identifying wholeheartedly with the French cause in the First World War on the convenient grounds that for Benda, as Winock ironizes, 'il faut que la cause française coïncide avec celle de la raison pure' ['the French cause has to coincide with that of pure reason'].[8]

In the aftermath of the war, Benda issued sweeping denunciations of those, Maurice Barrès at their head, whom he considered responsible for subordinating the world of thought to the exigencies of political affiliation. In an interview which he gave to the journal *Les Nouvelles Littéraires* in May 1925, Benda sketched the essentials of the thesis with which he was to become identified. He deplored the way

> Les hommes n'ont plus que deux religions: pour les uns, la Nation; pour les autres, la Classe; deux formes, quoi qu'ils prétendent, du plus pur temporel. Ceux qui avaient pour fonction de leur prêcher l'amour d'un idéal, d'un supra-temporel—les hommes de lettres, les philosophes, disons d'un mot les *clercs*—non seulement ne l'ont pas fait, mais n'ont travaillé qu'à fortifier de tout leur pouvoir ces religions du terrestre; les Barrès, les Bourget, les Nietzsche, les Marx, les Péguy, les Sorel, les D'Annunzio, tous les moralistes influents de ce dernier demi-siècle ont été de farouches professeurs de réalisme et se sont glorifiés de l'être, quitte à idéaliser ce réalisme.... C'est ce que j'appelle la *trahison des clercs*.
>
> [Men are left with only two religions: for some, the Nation; for others, Class; two forms, whatever they claim, of the purest temporality. Those who used to have as a function to preach the love of an ideal, of something supra-temporal—men of letters, philosophers, let's say in a word *clercs*—have not only not done it, but they have only worked to strengthen with all their power these earthly creeds; the Barrèses, the Bourgets, the Nietzsches, the Marxes, the Péguys, the Sorels, the D'Annunzios, all the influential moralists of this last half-century have been fierce teachers of realism and have taken pride in being so, even to the point of idealizing this realism.... This is what I call the *trahison des clercs*.][9]

He elaborated this case in the book he first published in four instalments in *La Nouvelle Revue française* between August and November 1927, shrewdly choosing this resonant phrase for its title.[10] The location of its first publication is significant, since the *NRF* had, from its foundation in 1908, carefully cultivated a non-political identity, devoted to literature and culture without taint of partisan polemics. But in the course of the 1920s the journal increasingly acknowledged a congruence between the values it sought to uphold and those claimed by the universalizing radical republican tradition. The tension between claiming to be 'above politics' while at the same time defending certain 'universal values' was at the heart of Benda's book and was to dog all subsequent discussion of the work.

Benda's thesis was in some ways very simple. For 2,000 years, 'jusqu'à ce dernier demi-siècle', there had existed 'cette classe d'hommes que j'appellerai les *clercs*... une suite ininterrompue de philosophes, de religieux, de littérateurs, d'artistes, de savants' ['there existed until the last half-century... that class of men whom I shall designate "*the clerks*"... an uninterrupted series of philosophers, men of religion, men of literature, artists, men of learning'].[11] They were distinguished by being devoted to other-worldly pursuits, and Benda was insistent that this meant that they did not involve themselves with the this-worldly passion of politics. '*Clercs*' were thus those who could say 'Mon royaume n'est pas de ce monde' ['My kingdom is not of this world']. But from the late nineteenth century, according to Benda, some of the leading *clercs* began to abandon the detachment that was their true calling, and to lend their name to the partisan causes of politics, especially nationalist politics. The pinnacle of this 'betrayal' of their calling ('betrayal' may capture the resonance of 'trahison' at this point slightly better than does 'treason') was reached with the First World War, and it is clear from Benda's intellectual biography that his later revulsion from the highly charged partisan emotions of the war, which he had shared at the time, was a determining influence in shaping the argument of his little book, but he broadened it into a general indictment: 'L'âge actuel est proprement l'âge du politique' ['The present age is essentially the age of politics'].[12]

Benda was also proposing a less-noticed claim about a change in the theories and ideas of *les clercs* themselves. From the late nineteenth century there had been movements in philosophy (and philosophy was, implicitly, the core of intellectual activity for Benda) which denied the possibility of 'absolute' and 'universal' ideas, and proposed instead that truth and morality were always local and particular. Under the general heading of 'irrationalism' he lumped together such diverse strands as Nietzscheanism, Bergsonianism, and pragmatism; the House of Reason had been undermined from within, and it was this that facilitated *les clercs*' collusion with 'the realist passion'. Moreover, it was an important part of his case that this betrayal was German in origin. Nietzsche and Treitschke were two faces of the same coin. 'Le clerc nationaliste est essentiellement une invention allemande,' or again, 'la religion du particulier' (as opposed to *les clercs*' proper concern with the universal) is German, and here, too, 'l'enseignement des clercs modernes marque le triomphe des valeurs germaniques et la faillite de l'hellénisme' ['the teaching of the modern "clerks" shows the triumph of Germanic values and the bankruptcy of Hellenism'].[13] Ultimately, the poison spread elsewhere: Kipling and William James are indicted along the way, and there are traces of earlier Parisian infighting in the repeated denunciations of

Barrès and Péguy. But the blame is laid squarely at the door of German culture. There is surely some irony in the fact that a tract ostensibly devoted to denouncing nationalist sentiment in intellectual matters should be so pervaded by an anti-Teutonism commonplace in France in the 1910s and 1920s.

None of this was particularly new, nor, of course, was it a uniquely French diagnosis. In the course of the First World War, commentators in several countries had sought an explanation for the catastrophe in the intellectual developments of the second half of the nineteenth century, especially those inspired by German thinkers. L.T. Hobhouse's *The Metaphysical Theory of the State* (1918) is one of the best-known examples in English of a genre which traced German militarism and 'state-worship' back through Treitschke to Hegel. In fact, three years earlier, Hobhouse had published a much less well-known book whose thesis was closer still to Benda's: in *The World in Conflict* Hobhouse had elaborated the idea of there having been a 'revolt against reason' in the thought of the late nineteenth century, and he singled out as the main progenitors of this disastrous turn several of the figures who were to appear in Benda's indictment—Bergson, pragmatists such as William James, and, above all, Nietzsche.[14] But although this characterization of the trends in late nineteenth-century thought may have been commonplace, Benda cast the argument into a more general form, founding it upon a resonant and polemically forceful conception of the role of *les clercs* in human history as a whole.

In practice, there was, as my earlier comments have already suggested, a tension at the very heart of this conception. Its governing assumption is that the kingdom of *les clercs* is not of this world, and therefore that *any* involvement in politics is a corruption of their pure vocation. But, as an exception to this sweeping interdiction, he allows the *clerc* to 'descendre dans l'arène' if it is purely for the purpose of upholding some universal value such as truth or justice: Voltaire's part in the Calas case is cited approvingly. The covertly partisan nature of Benda's own case is discernible here: in Third Republic France the appeal to universal principles of justice and rights was the ideological property of the republican Left, while the invocation of the particularist values of patriotism and tradition was a hallmark of the conservative Right. Benda's subsequent pronouncements, especially in the course of the increasingly polarized political world of the 1930s, only underlined the asymmetry built into the argument of his most famous book.

From the outset, the work attracted a vast amount of attention in France: writing in the *NRF* in June 1928, Albert Thibaudet remarked that it was impossible to avoid almost daily reference to Benda's book.[15] Between August and October 1928 the *NRF* carried Benda's *La Fin de l'éternel*, which was part sequel to *La Trahison*, part a reply to its critics. Benda had frequently emphasized that 'le clerc peut, et je l'ai dit, descendre sur la place publique sans cesser d'exercer sa fonction' ['the *clerc* may, and I have said so, enter the public arena without ceasing to exercise his function'], and in *La Fin de l'éternel* he reaffirmed, speaking of 'le clerc de gauche', that 'la passion de la justice, plus encore celle de la verité, *ne sont point des passions politiques* et que ceux qui descendent au forum mûs par elles ne me paraissent trahir aucune noble fonction' ['the passion for justice, and even more that for truth, *are in no way political passions* and those who go into the public arena moved by them do not seem to me to betray any noble function'].[16] But what he insisted as vehemently as ever was that the world was divided between the domains of the 'clerc' and the 'laïc': the latter is concerned with the world 'as it is', the former with 'valeurs idéales ou désintéressés', values which are 'universelles, abstraites, intemporelles'.[17] (Traces of this distinction may be visible in a rather unlikely later *clerc*: 'I don't want to publish anything about France. If I publish something about France, I'll strike a pose as an intellectual. I am a poet. For me to defend the Panthers and the Palestinians fits in with my function as a poet. If I write about the French question I enter the political field in France—I don't want that.')[18]

However, not long after publishing his celebrated work, Benda himself seemed to be violating its precepts by such classically unclerkly behaviour as signing manifestos and petitions. In 1931 he signed the 'manifeste contre les excès du nationalisme, pour l'Europe et pour l'entente franco-allemande', and in 1934 he signed a manifesto calling for resistance to Fascism. Reproached with betraying the standards he had set for the *clerc*, he sought to justify himself:

> Ayant récemment signé un manifeste dit 'de gauche', j'ai été accusé de manquer à cette éternité que j'exige du clerc. Je réponds que j'ai signé ce manifeste parce qu'il me semblait défendre des principes éternels. Invité par la suite à signer pour des actes de politique temporelle et concrète, j'ai refusé. Je tiens que je suis dans mon role de clerc en défendant une mystique, non en faisant de la politique. Zola était dans son role de clerc en rappelant le monde au respect de la justice.... On me dit: vous ne deviez pas signer, même pour une mystique de gauche. Vous ne devez être ni de droite ni de gauche. Je réponds que la mystique de gauche est recevable pour le clerc.
>
> [Having recently signed a manifesto said to be 'of the left', I have been accused of flouting that focus on the eternal that I require of the *clerc*. I reply that I signed this manifesto because it seemed to me to defend eternal principles. Invited thereafter to sign for measures of temporal and concrete politics, I refused. I maintain that I am in my role as *clerc* in defending an abstract doctrine, not in taking part in politics. Zola was in his role as *clerc* in recalling the world to respect for justice . . . . People say to me: you should not sign, even for a doctrine of the left [*une mystique de gauche*]. You should be neither of the right nor of the left. I reply that a doctrine of the left is allowable for the *clerc*.][19]

This, as I have suggested, had been the unacknowledged premise of his famous book, but the political events of the 1930s led Benda to become more and more explicit about what political action it was 'admissible' for the *clerc* to undertake. He was more and more drawn in to the anti-Fascist movement, and, of course, as a Jew he had every reason to become a *militant* in this cause. But to the last, Benda never acknowledged any tension in his argument, and when his classic was reissued in 1946 he wrote a long preface in which, even after the necessary *engagement* during the occupation, he reaffirmed the other-worldly vocation of the *clerc*.[20]

III

La Trahison des clercs has come to be regarded, as I indicated earlier, as a classic statement about the proper role of intellectuals; it, especially in English translation, is now established as an obligatory reference-point in modern discussion of the topic. Yet, although the noun *intellectuel* was well established in French usage by the time Benda was writing, it appears in his text in only two places: once when he is citing the attacks made at the time of the Dreyfus Affair by the likes of Barrès, Lemaître, and Brunetière 'intimant aux "intellectuels" de se rappeler qu'ils sont un type d'humanité "inférieur au militaire"' ['intimating to the "intellectuals" that they are a type of humanity "inferior to the soldier"']; and once in a note on the 'prestige' which '*clercs*' might now be thought to bring to the political causes they endorse: 'Des effets comme celui que produisit en France, lors de l'affaire Dreyfus, l'intervention des "intellectuels", ou encore, en 1914, non seulement dans leur pays mais dans le monde entier, le manifeste dit des *intellectuels allemands*, sont des choses dont je ne vois pas l'équivalent dans le passé.' ['The results produced in France by the intervention of the "intellectuals" in the Dreyfus Affair, and those produced by the manifesto of the German Intellectuals in 1914, not only in their own country but throughout the world, are things to which I find no equivalent in the past.'][21] In each case, the term is in quotation marks, citing a specific usage by others; throughout the book Benda himself uses the term '*clercs*'.

The polemical effectiveness of Benda's case was intimately dependent on the peculiar semantic range of the term '*clerc*'. Whilst it could, and can still, be employed to refer to contemporary writers and thinkers, such usage was acknowledged as implying, however playfully, a continuity with the learned and clerical order in earlier periods, especially the Middle Ages. An association with the idea of the contrast between the secular and the spiritual lurked behind the term's modern usage in much the same way as original meanings haunt what are referred to as 'dead metaphors'. Benda converted hovering linguistic potential into polemical argument. Had he in 1927 published a book entitled *La Trahison des intellectuels*, the resonance would have been significantly different. By that date, the plural of the noun referred to the collective exercise by writers and scholars of their cultural authority in the domain of politics. The original *dreyfusard* claim to be doing this in the name of such 'universals' as the Rights of Man still hovered in attendance on occasion, but usage had now decisively surpassed this particular association to encompass *any* such 'intervention'. What seems extraordinary in view of the book's place in all later discussions of 'intellectuals' is the fact that the kind of activity which Benda was condemning as the betrayal of the historic function of the *clerc* had by then become constitutive of the meaning of the peculiarly modern French word, *intellectuels*.

Benda's animus against the role for which *intellectuel* had become the accepted term is particularly manifest in his discussion of what is essentially the problem of the political uses of cultural authority.[22] He objected to what he saw as the new phenomenon of the *clercs* lending their 'prestige' to political causes: it would have been irrelevant in earlier periods, he alleged, if a writer or scholar had 'supported' a war; now, he laments, such endorsement has come to be considered both vital and legitimate. Here and throughout the book, Benda is registering the new pattern of behaviour that the coinage of '*intellectuels*' referred to, but he is in effect ruling out the very activity of 'speaking out' that is constitutive of the main modern sense of the term. As I have indicated, he was not wholly consistent on this, since the exception he makes for the *clerc*'s efforts to uphold truth and reason in the 'lay' world creates a space within which an idealized conception of the *clerc dreyfusard* could appear legitimate. Nonetheless, his argument emphatically repudiates the idea that it is any part of a *clerc*'s proper role to deploy his cultural authority outside his proper sphere. For a true *clerc*, one might say, the greatest treason is to become an *intellectuel*.

This implication of his argument also surfaces in the passage in which he anticipates the objection that figures such as Barrès or Péguy are not really *clercs* at all, but 'gens d'action', and so in their case there is no real question of 'trahison'. But Benda replies that these figures did indeed present themselves as 'clercs' and not as mere 'polémistes': 'Barrès se donnait proprement pour un penseur qui daigne descendre dans l'arène'. (Aldington's rather odd translation of this last sentence suggested a still loftier stance: 'Barrès gave himself out to be a thinker who condescended to the arena'.[23]) Benda rightly emphasizes that in these and similar cases 'c'est à ce titre qu'ils jouissent d'un prestige particulier entre les hommes d'action', and he makes the point more emphatically still when referring to Maurras 'et autres docteurs d'*Action française*':

> Ces hommes prétendent exercer leur action en vertu d'une doctrine due à l'étude tout objective de l'histoire, à l'exercice du plus pur esprit scientifique; et c'est à cette prétention de *savants*, d'hommes qui combattent pour une verité trouvée dans la séverité du laboratoire, c'est à cette posture de clercs guerroyants, *mais de clercs*, qu'ils doivent l'audience spéciale dont ils bénéficient entre les hommes d'action.

> [These men claim to carry out their action by virtue of a doctrine derived from a wholly objective study of history, from the exercise of the most purely scientific spirit. And they owe the special attention with which they are listened to by men of action entirely to this claim that they are *men of learning*, men who are fighting for a truth discovered in the austerity of the laboratory. They owe it to their pose as combative 'clerks', but essentially as *clerks*.][24]

This exactly describes the deployment of cultural authority for which the term 'intellectuel' had become the common label, but Benda pinpoints it as precisely that in which the 'trahison des clercs' consists.

At the same time—and here the central tension or ambiguity of the book comes into play—Benda may be seen as attempting to recall French intellectuals to their *dreyfusard* past. Considered thus, his book was not actually repudiating the *whole* development which the currency of the word 'intellectuel' signified: it was attempting to appropriate the prestige of a cultural tradition in order to legitimate one version of it, that of the withdrawn 'disinterested' thinker or scholar who from time to time acted in the public sphere in order to uphold eternal values of truth and justice. In this way, the book acknowledged no conflict between the ideal of emulating Spinoza, the exemplary *clerc*, and the idealized self-conception of the *dreyfusard* intellectual (in 1938 Benda confessed, revealingly: 'Je voudrais qu'il existât comme une *affaire Dreyfus en permanence*' ['I would like there to be something like a *permanent Dreyfus Affair*']).[25] Benda was in practice always vehemently partisan, but I suspect he became increasingly anxious lest the prestige that properly accrued to the disinterested thinker should be dissipated by too frequent attempts to make that prestige tell in the public discussion of profane matters.

In this connection, the testimony of a hostile witness may be particularly telling. Jean Sarocchi's 1968 book, *Julien Benda: portrait d'un intellectuel* is marked by considerable implicit hostility to intellectuals in general and to Benda in particular, but this makes him especially vigilant in detecting inconsistency and posturing in Benda. Sarocchi suggests, surely rightly, that Benda's career, from the Dreyfus Affair to the Liberation, reveals him to have been a quintessential French intellectual, a ceaseless polemicist, and hence not at all an example of his own definition of a *clerc*. Benda's earlier writings, according to Sarocchi, 'ont le grand mérite de présenter l'intellectuel dans son état original et son ambition nue. *La Trahison* le drape dans la majesté d'une spéculation souveraine. ... Mais le clerc de 1927 est un intellectuel fardé, un intellectuel mûr, qui ruse avec ses appétits' ['have the great merit of presenting the intellectual in his original state and his naked ambition. *La Trahison* wraps him in the majesty of a sovereign speculation. ... But the *clerc* of 1927 is a disguised intellectual, a mature intellectual, who is crafty about his appetites']. Sarocchi accepts, indeed welcomes, the distinction between 'le clerc' (noting that term's 'nimbe médiéval') and 'l'intellectuel', but finds Benda always falling far short of the former status: the disguise is no more than that, and so 'par sa passion politique, par son dédain des chercheurs, par sa coquetterie littéraire, il trahit la cléricature' ['by his political passion, by his disdain for scholars, by his literary coquetry, he betrays the learned class'].[26] Although's Sarocchi's portrait of Benda is somewhat distorted by his lack of sympathy, on this central point about Benda's relation to his own category he is surely right. *La Trahison* is, in this respect, a disingenuous polemic, the tendentious idealization of a category to which, by the very fact of writing such a polemic, the author himself could not logically belong. All of which makes it more puzzling still that contemporary commentators should continue to regard this book as 'the best single statement of the critical intellectual's creed'.

IV

The Englishing of Benda's title caused problems from the outset. When Richard Aldington, a poet and critic who did much to bring French literature to an English-speaking public in the inter-war period, came to translate the book he faced an obvious problem. As I have indicated, the term '*clerc*' was what might be called a 'current archaism' in French: certainly, it was a deliberate choice on Benda's part to emphasize the almost priestly and tradition-sanctioned role he was discussing, but it was an archaism that still had an intelligible meaning and presence in French usage, and is indeed still available for this kind of use today (for example, Jean-François Sirinelli, cited earlier as one of the leading contemporary authorities on the history of French intellectuals, is not at all unusual in frequently writing of 'l'histoire des clercs', 'cette histoire des clercs en politique', and so on.[27]) The same, however, was not really true in English: 'the treason of the clerks' risked suggesting a book about an altogether more Pooteresque social stratum. So Aldington prefaced his translation with a note explicitly addressing this problem of a lack of equivalence, in which he explained that 'throughout the text I have invariably written the word in inverted commas, "clerk", to avoid any possible misunderstanding'.[28] The choice of title for the English translation reflected something of a compromise between this linguistic fastidiousness and the necessary pragmatism of publishing: the edition published by Routledge in 1928 was called *The Great Betrayal*, with the original French title given underneath. Reviewing the book, Herbert Read observed that 'the English title, *The Great Betrayal*, shirks the difficulty of translating the word "clercs"'. Read did not propose a solution, but having acknowledged that the word 'clerk' in English suggested 'banks and insurance offices', he nonetheless used it without further qualification in his discussion of Benda's work—e.g. 'The clerk, then, is the disinterested thinker, the man who pursues his knowledge oblivious of the social and economic tendencies of his time,' and so on.[29]

The editors at the American publishing house of William Morrow in the late 1920s may be partly to blame for initiating a long tradition of misinterpretation of Benda's book in the English-speaking world, though T. S. Eliot may, curiously, also be partly responsible. Unfortunately, no correspondence between Aldington and his publishers seems to have survived, but we can infer that someone in the firm charged with publishing the book in the United States felt that the first English title was an unsatisfactory, and commercially unhelpful, compromise. When the book appeared in the USA in the same year, it was called *The Treason of the Intellectuals*. (For some reason, the Beacon Press edition, published in 1955, was titled *The Betrayal of the Intellectuals*, but the Norton edition of 1969 then reverted to the earlier title, which is the form in which the phrase most commonly appears in English.) It would, of course, be interesting to know whether the eventual title of the American edition had been discussed and rejected by Aldington or his English publishers. There is some evidence, as I indicated in Ch. 1, that the term 'intellectuals' had acquired currency in American English sooner than in Britain. In any event, Aldington's prefatory note on the problem of translating *clerc* was retained in all English-language editions, albeit with one unacknowledged alteration: his declaration that 'in order to avoid a misleading title I have called this translation *The Great Betrayal*' was simply modified by the insertion of the new title, though the point of his 'translator's note' now becomes a little opaque. The rest of the text was reprinted unchanged, save that in the one place where Benda alludes to his own title he is made to say, inconsistently, that 'I dare to call this attitude "The Treason of the Intellectuals".'[30] In fact, as I have remarked, the resonant phrase '*la trahison des intellectuels*' never appears in the French original. But in its American guise, as in all subsequent English-language editions, there could be no doubt that Benda's book was about 'intellectuals'. Not that translation thereafter ceased to perform its own kinds of 'treachery'. In 1994 an article about intellectuals by the German social theorist Wolf Lepenies was translated into English: Lepenies had, almost inevitably, referred to Benda's book, and the translator was therefore faced with a choice about what title to give it in English. Consultation of a library catalogue may have proved unhelpful here: Lepenies is made to say 'Julien Benda's influential work, *The Great Betrayal* (1927), provided twentieth-century thinkers with a definitive slogan.'[31] *Traduttore, traditore*: there may be 'betrayal' of another kind involved here. Certainly, neither Lepenies nor his readers would recognize any 'definitive slogan' in this title.

Bound up with the question of terminology is a substantive issue about the specifically French character of the book's premises and arguments. It is not just that in its preoccupations, allusions, and most of its specific references, Benda's book clearly situates itself in post-1918 French culture.[32] It is, rather, that the character of its argument bespeaks its French provenance in ways that make its absorption into the very different Anglo-Saxon discourse somewhat problematic. To begin with, it is a hymn of praise to the tradition of universalism, held to be pre-eminently, if not strictly uniquely, French. (This assumption was never far below the surface in Benda's writing: for example, in the 1930s, when he was urging the case for European unity, he suggested that, since Latin was no longer realistically available as a common language, French would be the proper choice because of its 'rationality'.[33]) The republican and rationalist ideals officially promoted under the Third Republic had, the biographical evidence indicates, an enormously strong appeal to a wholly secular French Jew of Benda's class and generation. Second, his language suggests something nearer to caste-distinction than to groupings based on inclination or the contingencies of opportunity. This consorts well with both the subjective sense of identity and, in some ways, the objective condition of intellectuals in France, though not at all well with their situation in Britain or the United States. And third, the defining opposite of the *clerc* is *political* power. In this respect, the book reflects the long-standing French preoccupation with *le pouvoir spirituel* or its substitutes, a counterbalance to the secular power of political life. (It is relevant to observe here that when Régis Debray's 1979 polemic *Le Pouvoir intellectuel en France* was translated into English, the chosen title was *Teachers, Writers, Celebrities*, a title which refers to the three 'cycles' of French intellectual life identified by Debray as successively dominant between the late nineteenth and late twentieth centuries. 'The Intellectual Power in France' would not have worked, and even some more idiomatic use of 'intellectual power' in an English title would still have failed to capture the specifically *political*—or, in some ways, anti-political—resonance of the phrase in French.) This antithesis has strong roots in French cultural history, but it also underlines how the force of what was emerging at the time as the dominant French usage of *intellectuel* lay in the attempt to transpose the authority of the *clerc* into the political sphere.

Here again Benda's concerns do not translate easily into British circumstances. The determining geometry in public debate in Britain was not so much the polarity between 'universal reason' and 'political power' as that between 'culture' and 'society'. The recurring preoccupation in Britain, from the early nineteenth century to the mid-twentieth, was (speaking in very broad terms for the moment) to elaborate and make effective values that could check and subjugate the corrosive power of economic calculation. By contrast, from the Dreyfusards to Foucault, the defining mission of the intellectual in France has been represented over and over again as that of challenging the hardened pragmatism of established power in the name of reason and morality—the role celebrated, and perhaps somewhat glamorized, under the phrase 'speaking truth to power'—and for this reason the question of the legitimacy of any given form of political power always lies near the surface.[34] Benda resonates in this tradition, occupying one extreme of what is nonetheless a single spectrum. The awkwardness of the book's transposition to British circumstances is underlined by the fact that Kipling is Benda's sole British example, apparently on the grounds of his 'nationalist' passion; it is doubtful whether anyone in Britain would have thought of Kipling as a *clerc*, still less as an 'intellectual', least of all Kipling himself.

Some of the complexities involved in transplanting Benda's argument in alien soil may have been prefigured by the curious, and apparently unnoticed, fact that the *TLS* carried two different reviews of the French edition of his book within a few weeks of each other. The first, published on 19 January 1928, linked it with Jacques Maritain's *Primauté du spirituel*, as an example of the reaction against nationalism in current French thought. In a slight, almost whimsical piece, the reviewer evidently struggled to find much else to say about Benda's book: she ticked him off for being too dismissive of Barrès, and she (mis)represented the book's argument as a lament about the inevitable worldliness and materialism of mankind, from which only a few great thinkers in the past were exempt. In referring, once, to the *clercs* of the book's title, the review reinforced the monastic association; the term 'intellectual' never appears in the review at all.[35]

Since no editorial correspondence from the period appears to have survived, we may never know for certain what led the *TLS* to take the unusual step of publishing a second review of Benda's book a few weeks later. It is possible that T. S. Eliot, by then one of the paper's most established contributors, suggested it. Eliot had remained a close student of the French literary scene since the year he spent in Paris before the war, and he was an admirer of Benda's earlier book, *Belphégor*, strongly sympathizing with its strictures on the literature of 'sensation' in the name of a more austere 'classicism'.[36] By the late 1920s, however, he was expressing more reservations: for example, in his essay on 'The humanism of Irving Babbitt', which also appeared in 1928, he observed that many social critics have nothing to offer in place of what they criticize, adding: 'M. Julien Benda, for instance, makes it a part of his deliberate programme to offer nothing; he has a romantic view of critical detachment which limits his interest.'[37] In any event, a second review of *La Trahison des clercs*, this time of Benda's book alone, appeared in the *TLS* on 23 February, allusively titled 'Culture and Anarchy', and we now know it to have been by Eliot himself.[38]

Eliot began with a characteristically careful summary of what he saw as Benda's two main theses:

> M. Benda is concerned, first, to show that the modern world, in its politics, tends to become more and more governed by political passions and less and less by political ideas. Secondly, M. Benda considers the attitude of those persons whom he calls *clercs*, a word which we can only translate feebly as 'intellectuals'. Here he brings a grave and specific charge, for he names some of the *clercs*; he accuses them of 'betraying' the cause of speculative thought—*l'art de penser juste*—to the interest of political passions.

Eliot briefly endorsed the first of these claims—unable, along the way, to resist a sly aside on how Benda's case 'constitutes, in effect, a grave criticism of democracy'—and then concentrated on the second. It is difficult to know whether to attach any particular significance to his aside about translating 'clercs' as 'intellectuals'. As I have suggested, 'la trahison des intellectuels' would have had a somewhat different resonance in French than the actual title. Moreover, in the 1920s the English usage of 'intellectuals' still tended to carry the older subjective or normative sense rather than immediately suggesting political intervention as the French term did. Eliot, a personal subscriber to *La Nouvelle Revue française*, was doubtless alert to the polemical force of Benda's choice of terms. Still, dictionaries of the period gave 'scholar' or 'writer' as the translation of the figurative use of 'clerc', and in discussing Benda's book Eliot himself was to use 'men of letters' at least as often as 'intellectuals'. Clearly, the translation of the book for which he called would encounter special difficulties.

Eliot claimed to agree with Benda in principle, but to disagree with the details of his critique, especially with his case against Kipling and against Maurras, two figures for whom Eliot had, on different grounds, considerable respect. But the review exhibited more fundamental misgivings about Benda's organizing dichotomy, that of being either a 'clerc' or 'a man of action'. Eliot, who had, after all, been received into the Anglican communion in the previous year, could hardly be accused of failing to appreciate the value of an appeal to an other-worldly standard. He recognized, however, that in Benda's purist hands this dichotomy becomes 'a counsel of despair, for it advises leaving the regiment of the world to those persons who have no interest in ideas whatever'. Eliot is not willing to see men of letters shut out from the world so completely: characteristically, he preferred to make the distinction between 'those *clercs* who appeal merely to the emotions of their readers and those who appeal, or try to appeal, to their intelligence'. In other words, Eliot, for all his high praise of the book, does not accept the absolutism of Benda's distinction between the clerkly and mundane realms, but calls up a more pragmatic standard against which performances in the role of 'intellectual' can be judged as better or worse.

If it is curious that Eliot should review in the *TLS* a work which had only just been reviewed there, what is more curious still (and apparently unremarked in Eliot scholarship) is that within a matter of months he should publish a second, much longer review-essay on Benda's book, at that point still untranslated, in *The Cambridge Review* in June 1928. (The publication of an essay by Eliot must have represented a considerable coup for this largely local journal; Ian Parsons, who was later to preside over Chatto & Windus's distinguished list in literary criticism, was editor at the time.[39]) Although Eliot later issued several collections of his essays, beginning with the *Selected Essays* of 1932, he never republished this piece, which may have contributed to its neglect by subsequent commentary. In it, he repeated his basic assessment of the book in terms similar to those of his *TLS* review, but he here allowed himself to move away from the work itself and 'to give a summary and tentative account of the way in which the "man of letters", by which we mean either the artist in language, or the *critic* of the artist in language, is involved in practical matters of the day'.

Eliot considered a range of British as well as French writers, including Kipling, Inge, Wells, Belloc, and Shaw, attempting a more complex taxonomy than Benda's binary categories allowed. He showed himself well aware of the basic mechanism at work whereby 'the man of letters', 'having secured a solid reputation for literary ability—say as a novelist—exploits his reputation for the purpose of exerting influence over human beings in other ways'. But he was unwilling to follow Benda in finding this necessarily illegitimate, noting, slightly tartly, that the latter's purist ideal was 'infected with romance'. Instead, Eliot argued that there can be no general guideline about the extent to which the *clercs* should or should not get involved in issues beyond their sphere: what matters is how intelligently they do it, and in Eliot's view the intelligence, or lack of it, that they show in this capacity is likely to be directly continuous with the intelligence, or lack of it, that they show in their purely literary work. He urged that 'it is, in practice, extremely difficult to draw a line between the mere vulgariser of knowledge, of the American type, and the "intellectual" of wide interests. It is furthermore fallacious to group all the intellectuals who may be accused of doing somebody else's business, or of pandering to popular political passions, into one category.' (It is interesting that 'intellectual' seems to carry a broadly positive valence here, and to include some who could not simply 'be accused of doing somebody else's business'). 'The only moral to be drawn', he concluded, 'is that you cannot lay down any hard and fast rule of what interests the *clerc*, the intellectual, should or should not have. All you can have is a standard of intellect, reason and critical ability which is applicable to the whole of a writer's work.'[40] Eliot's brief essay, written in the best provoking manner of his early critical performances, amounts to a shrewd meditation on the question of the cultural authority of the intellectual; a good deal shrewder, to my mind, than the far longer and far more celebrated book of which it is notionally a review (I shall return to Eliot's discussion in the following chapter). In any event, *La Trahison des clercs* was thus initially presented to English-speaking readers by someone who urged those readers to approach the question of intellectuals in a far more pragmatic spirit than that to be found in the work he was reviewing.

By this date, a recommendation from T. S. Eliot carried great weight in British cultural and literary life. As someone whose earliest intellectual work had been given its direction by Eliot's celebrated if gnomic pronouncements on 'the dissociation of sensibility', Basil Willey was more attentive to his master's occasional writings than most, but it is nonetheless striking to find him in 1964 recurring to *La Trahison des clercs* as the book 'which thirty-five years ago Mr T. S. Eliot was telling us all to read' (the lapse of time no doubt acounting for the fact that Willey now remembered it as being by 'M. Jules Benda').[41] Since Eliot's *TLS* review was anonymous, this may seem to equate 'us all' with the readers of the *Cambridge Review*, perhaps not an uncommon slide for Cambridge dons of Willey's generation. In any event, Willey's memory had evidently filtered the message of Benda's book through his own organizing ideas, which by this date were dominated by the belief that he lived in a period of 'dissolving standards and crumbling faiths'. For two and a half millennia, mankind had acknowledged the priority of 'spiritual values': but now 'our civilization—our Christendom' was crumbling, and this 'clerkly tradition' was being lost. In the 1930s it was (surely surprisingly) 'the sociologists, the economic historians and the psychologists' who had between them 'plunged man back into the state of nature', because they had sought to reduce such spiritual values to nothing more than 'rationalized egotisms and power-urges'. In the years since the war, 'M. Benda would have seen signs and portents more disquieting than before.' For the Christian Willey, therefore, the religious associations of 'clerk', the term he used throughout his discussion of Benda's book, were of the essence. The word 'intellectual' makes no appearance. Just as Willey treated Plato and Aristotle as honorary 'English Moralists', so he turned Benda into an honorary Anglican cultural pessimist.[42]

I shall not attempt to chart the reception of Benda's work in any detail here, but two further examples may illustrate the instabilities involved in transporting his argument into the different linguistic and cultural setting of mid-twentieth-century Britain. The first is provided by a substantial article in *The Hibbert Journal* in 1935. Its author R. B. Mowat was a professor of history specializing in international relations, and the main polemical force of his piece was the claim that those scholars and thinkers who endorse *Realpolitik* rather than upholding universal moral ideals in international affairs are guilty of the kind of 'betrayal' identified by Benda. The article was cast in the form of a review-essay of two books, Benda's and one by Reinhold Niebuhr, *Moral Man and Immoral Society*. Benda's book had been published six years before Niebuhr's, but Mowat's article may have been a deliberate act of retrieval: he observed that Benda's book, 'though it has passed through twenty French editions, has received curiously little attention in England'.[43] Mowat perhaps underestimated the level of response in England here, but what *is* so curious is that the article is entitled 'The treachery of the intellectuals' and the phrase '(*"La trahison des clercs"*)' is printed in italics underneath, with a footnote referring to Benda's French title, fully capitalized, accompanied by that of Aldington's translation, *The Great Betrayal*. Quite where the phrase 'the treachery of the intellectuals' comes from is not clear: not only do none of the translations of Benda's book use 'treachery' for 'trahison', but also in the body of the essay Mowat himself does not use the term 'intellectuals', preferring to stick with 'clerks', sometimes with and sometimes without the distancing protection of quotation marks. The egregious title may have reflected editorial realism: Benda's term, *clercs*, was, as we have seen, strictly untranslatable, and in the course of the 1930s 'intellectuals' had become sufficiently established in common usage to offer itself as the least inadequate synonym. Aldington's fastidiousness was already being overwhelmed by the pressure of current usage.

Mowat's decision to use 'clerks' and not 'intellectuals' in the body of the article itself reflected more than a desire to be faithful to the French original, since he, too, wished to appeal to a contrast between the temporal and the eternal. Mowat, unlike Benda, clearly regarded Christianity as still the most potent source of such transcendent values, but, like Benda, he traded on the medieval associations of the term 'clerk' while extending it to include 'clergy, teachers, scholars, scientists, learned men and in general all those who are recognised as leaders of opinion'.[44] His understanding of this category is closer to Coleridge's notion of 'the clerisy' than to the modern conception of 'the intellectuals'. For example, he asserts, as a matter of fact, that since the clerks are not directly concerned with the practical needs of society and it is impossible to assess the value of their services in terms of money, 'they are paid conventional stipends or sums, and in effect are maintained by society, to whose exchangeable value they contribute nothing directly, in order that they may devote themselves to the creation of spiritual values and the maintenance of spiritual standards'. [45] His own criticism of the tendency of modern 'clerks' to depart from their supposedly time-honoured role is wholly unspecific: no treasonous clerks are identified by name. He merely asserts: 'The clerks, in justifying the State when it acts only on motives of interest and self-love, are committing treason against the cause of truth and justice, to serve which is their sole profession.'[46] A Coleridgean critique of the field of International Relations must be something of a rarity, and its curiosity is hardly diminished by taking its organizing concept from the work of a French republican secular Jew.

A different kind of example of the tangled afterlife of Benda's phrase in English is to be found in the unlikely form of Sir Lewis Namier's Raleigh Lecture to the

British Academy, delivered in July 1944. In taking as his title '1848: The Revolution of the Intellectuals', Namier was signalling his disdain for the ineffectual, posturing, 'men of ideas' who were at the head of that year's largely unsuccessful revolutions. But his terminology also betrayed the ambiguous presence of Benda's book. In his introduction, Namier emphasized the role in the events of 1848 of those obsessed by the high ideals 'of reason, logic, sentiment and of a desire... for a better order in government and society'. '1848', he ringingly announced, 'was primarily the revolution of the intellectuals—*la révolution des clercs*'.[47] It is not immediately obvious why Namier added the French phrase: it was hardly, after all, as though 'intellectuals' was a native English vernacular term whose application to European circumstances could be signalled only by an approximate translation (the opposite would have been nearer the truth). One can only assume that Namier wanted to trade on the currency of the term 'la trahison des clercs', and indeed in his peroration, 120 pages later, that phrase itself makes its appearance. He may also have felt that the resonances of the French phrase better captured the continental European associations he had in mind, and thereby underlined that this had not been an affliction from which Britain had suffered. Britain, after all, had been the conspicuous exception in 1848; a badly attended meeting in the rain on Kennington Common did not amount to much of a revolution (and was taken by some to confirm that the weather was always more important than intellectuals in Britain). Namier's conservative Anglophilia underwrote his account in more fundamental ways, too.[48] Indeed, the terms in which he described what 1848 had aspired to attain unmistakably reflected the preferred account of the British polity: 'parliamentary government and political liberty under a constitutional monarchy'. And the outcomes of the revolutions, tragic and squalid by turns, provided him with a text for a familiar Whig sermon: 'The intellectuals, red or pink, had yet to learn that the parliamentary system is based on an articulation of society, and not on levelling it down, and that, with social superiorities discredited and the political structure broken, the field is open, or rather the void is prepared, for plebiscitarian dictatorships.'[49]

This was a moral long familiar to English ears, and most of those listening to the lecture at the British Academy in July 1944, surrounded by the all too visible effects of doctrinaire European politics, probably found much to shake their heads over in Namier's accounts of the role of *naïveté*, betrayal, and cock-up in undoing the 1848 assemblies. But Namier gave the tale his own particular twist and in the process managed to recruit the thesis of Benda's book to a more generally conservative politics. As Namier told the story, reaction triumphed in the end, but this at least prevented the blinkered and high-minded 'professors, doctors, theologians, pharmacists, and philologists' (Herzen's mocking enumeration, quoted by Namier) from enacting any further injustices against the various awkwardly placed ethnic populations of central Europe. In this sense, concluded Namier, 'it prevented the "revolution of the intellectuals" from consummating *la trahison des clercs*'.[50] But what did Namier intend the phrase to refer to in this case? He had concentrated on how the Frankfurt Assembly, in particular, seemed likely to betray various ethnic groups in the German lands through a lethal mixture of high principle and low competence. Used thus, Benda's phrase was given a distinctively Burkean twist: it was not so much that the intellectuals were betraying the purity of their calling but rather that they were betraying the obligations of realism and responsibility imposed upon those who would seek to exercise political power. But in Benda's own terms, no matter how hard-headed and successful the members of the Frankfurt Assembly had been, they would, as 'clercs', have been guilty of 'trahison' by their very participation itself. Unless, of course, they had merely been acting to uphold the 'universal values' of reason and justice—in other words, indulging in what Namier regarded as the most fatuous and self-deceived form of behaviour on the part of that characteristically fatuous and self-deceived species, the intellectuals. In short, the polemical punch of Namier's extremely influential lecture depended upon using Benda's title in a sense which was almost exactly the opposite of the original.

V

As I suggested earlier, the phrase 'la trahison des clercs' has now acquired almost liturgical status in English-language discussions of the question of intellectuals, offering a cadence that can be intoned or chanted in a ritualistic way without intruding questions of exact meaning into the familiar collective rite. It is hardly surprising that Benda's sweepingly polemical little book should have enjoyed such immediate success in France, given the dynamics of French cultural and political debate in the first few decades of this century, but it is less obvious why the book, or at least the idea for which its title has been loosely (and often wrongly) assumed to stand, should also have enjoyed such prominence and longevity elsewhere.[51] To understand its continuing appeal, we need to return to the analysis given earlier of the concept of the intellectual in the cultural sense.

The core of my suggestion here is that the very notion of 'la trahison des clercs' is itself an implicit embodiment of that movement between two poles which is constitutive of the role of the intellectual, though Benda's explicit argument is in one sense a denial of the necessity or desirability of such movement. What Benda appears to provide is an ideal of purity or, in a different but no less revealing metaphor, a gold-standard against which various imperfect performances in the role of 'clerc' can be measured. The ideal appeals in part because it offers a refuge or haven from the wearying, frustratingly imperfect world of cultural and political debate. The cultivation of the life of the mind and the pursuit of truth for its own sake furnish a more impressive and flattering model of intellectual activity than being embroiled in the vulgarities of catchpenny journalism and partisan name-calling. But Benda's seductive metaphors are also misleading. 'Treason', after all, is a term implying membership of a polity, an entity which one 'betrays' to its enemies. Its use in this context conjures up the idea of a separate realm or kingdom to which the 'clercs' belong, a community to which they owe their primary allegiance and which is set over against the practical, political world, for it is to that latter world that the 'betrayal' has been made. At work here is the religious inheritance I mentioned earlier, the secular version of the 'theory of the two swords', which underlies the French concept, much used in this literature, of 'le pouvoir intellectuel'. This cluster of metaphors, therefore, sets up yet another binary polarity. By contrast, we need to recognize that intellectuals are no more *entirely* 'removed' from the world than that world is *entirely* devoid of 'ideas' (that would be to reintroduce the 'culture and society' dichotomy in another form). There can only be one world and nothing in it can be wholly pure.

Moreover, Benda's book expresses a double fantasy. It expresses, most obviously, the fantasy of there being a form of intellectual activity which is entirely divorced from the world, the flesh, and the devil. On Benda's showing, the *clerc* has no interests, no social location, no ego: he (emphatically *he*) is pure reason incarnate. But it also expresses the fantasy that pure thought can be operative in the world without thereby being at all corrupted or compromised. It is the fantasy of a kind of non-political *dreyfusisme*, an upholding of the universals of truth, reason, justice, and so on without actually engaging in any of the messy processes by which such values might be brought a little more effectively to bear on the world. Yet again one cannot help feeling that only a limited and curiously one-sided understanding of the role of the intellectual is likely to be found in the writing of someone whose prose is as pervaded as is Benda's by metaphors of purity and contamination.

The constant invocation of the phrase, and the argument(s) for which it is supposed to stand, is surely testimony not to the cogency of Benda's case, but to the way in which the term encapsulates needs and anxieties invested in the very concept of the intellectual. This is, in my view, borne out by the fact that, as I mentioned earlier, the term is used to refer to two, quite different and even opposite, patterns of behaviour. On the one hand, a charge of 'la trahison des clercs' can be laid when intellectuals are seen to have become overinvolved in practical affairs, to the point where they can be accused of forgetting or 'betraying' their 'true' intellectual function. On the other hand, the term is used no less frequently to reproach intellectuals for failing to act, for failing to become involved, for failing to 'speak out', with the consequence that values they are supposed to uphold are ignored or maltreated. There is obviously considerable looseness of usage here, but it is in my view a revealing looseness, revealing precisely of the way in which the term 'intellectuals' has come to designate the pattern or movement involved in passing *from* the activities which earn an initial cultural authority *to* the activities which deploy that cultural authority outside its specialized sphere. Intellectuals, as that term is now mainly used in English, are, therefore, constantly and, I am suggesting, inescapably vulnerable to the charge of neglecting one or other of the poles of this movement. Part of the appeal of Benda's phrase is that it has floated sufficiently free of his original case to have become equally available for making *both* of these opposite charges.

NOTES

1. Michael Walzer, *The Company of Critics: Social Criticism and Political Commitment in the Twentieth Century* (London: Halban, 1989 [New York: Basic Books, 1988]), 29; Edward Said, *Representations of the Intellectual*: The 1993 *Reith Lectures* (New York: Pantheon, 1994), 7.
2. See Ernest Gellner, 'La Trahison de la trahison des clercs', in Ian Maclean, Alan Montefiore, Peter Winch (eds.), *The Political Responsibility of Intellectuals* (Cambridge: Cambridge University Press, 1990), 17, and H. Stuart Hughes, *Consciousness and Society: The Re-orientation of European Social Thought 1890–1930* (London: MacGibbon & Kee, 1958), 411.
3. See the index to MacLean et al., *Political Responsibility of Intellectuals.*
4. For examples, including some uses 'exactly the opposite' of that intended by Benda, see David L. Schalk, *The Spectrum of Political Engagement* (Princeton: Princeton University Press, 1979), esp. 26–9.
5. Ludwig Wittgenstein, *Philosophical Investigations*, trans. Elizabeth Anscombe (Oxford: Blackwell, 1953), § 449.
6. For an intellectual biography and extensive bibliography, see Robert J. Niess, *Julien Benda* (Ann Arbor: University of Michigan Press, 1956); see also Jean Sarocchi, *Julien Benda; portrait d'un intellectuel* (Paris: Nizet, 1968), Ray Nichols, *Treason, Tradition, and the Intellectual: Julien Benda and Political Discourse* (Lawrence, Kan.: Regents Press, 1978), and Michel Winock, *Le Siècle des intellectuels* (Paris: le Seuil, 1997 [rev. edn. 1999]), 238–46.
7. Quoted in John Kaestlin, 'The splendid isolation of Julien Benda', *Colosseum* 3 (Dec. 1937), 256–7.
8. Winock, *Siècle des intellectuals*, 243.
9. 'Une heure avec M. Julien Benda', *Les Nouvelles Littéraires*, 23 May 1925, quoted in Winock, *Siècle des intellectuels*, 238–9. On Benda's earliest uses of 'les clercs' see Nichols, *Treason*, 73–5.
10. For further details of its publication and reception in France, see Martyn Cornick, 'Catalyst for intellectual *engagement*: the serialization of Julien Benda's *La Trahison des clercs* in the *Nouvelle Revue Francaise*, 1927–1932', *French Cultural Studies*, 4 (1993), 31–49.
11. Julien Benda, *La Trahison des clercs* (Paris: Grasset, 1927), 54; *The Treason of the Intellectuals*, trans. Richard Aldington (New York: Norton, 1969 [first pub. 1928]), 43. Hereafter my citations are to these two editions, abbreviated as *Trahison* and *Treason* respectively.
12. *Trahison*, 43; *Treason*, 29.
13. *Trahison*, 122, 123–4; *Treason*, 100–1.
14. L. T. Hobhouse, *The World in Conflict* (London: Williams & Norgate, 1915); see Stefan Collini, *Liberalism and Sociology: L. T. Hobhouse and Political Argument in England 1880–1914* (Cambridge: Cambridge University Press, 1979), 246–7.

15. Cited in Cornick, 'Catalyst for intellectual *engagement*', 36.
16. Quoted ibid. 36–7.
17. Julien Benda, *La Fin de l'éternel* (Paris: Gallimard, 1930), 130.
18. These are the words of Jean Genet, writing in 1971, quoted by Michael Wood in *London Review of Books*, 10 June 93, 11.
19. Julien Benda, 'L'écrivain et le politique', *La Nouvelle Revue Française* (Jan. 1935); quoted in Jean-François Sirinelli, *Intellectuels et passions françaises: manifestes et pétitions au XXe siècle* (Paris: Fayard, 1990), 87. 'Recevable' is perhaps best translated as 'admissible' (or even 'allowable') here.
20. Julien Benda, *La Trahison des clercs* (Paris: Grasset, 1946), 9–76.
21. *Trahison*, 181, 264; *Treason*, 147, 216.
22. *Trahison*, 264–6; *Treason*, 216–18.
23. *Trahison*, 60–1; *Treason*, 48–9.
24. *Trahison*, 62; *Treason*, 50.
25. Julien Benda, *Un Régulier dans le siècle* (Paris: Gallimard, 1938); quoted in Sarocchi, *Benda*, 13.
26. Sarocchi, *Benda*, 16, 34, 26.
27. e.g. Sirinelli, *Intellectuels et passions françaises*, 11.
28. Julien Benda, *The Great Betrayal ('La Trahison des clercs')*, trans. Richard Aldington (London: Routledge, 1928), Translator's Note, p. vi.
29. Herbert Read, 'Julien Benda, a critic of democracy', *The Realist*, 1 (1929), 18–27, quotation at 24.
30. *Trahison*, 195; *Treason*, 158.
31. Wolf Lepenies, 'The future of intellectuals', trans. Ann T. Gardner, *Partisan Review*, 61 (1994), 116.
32. See the works by Niess, Sarocchi, and Nichols cited in n. 4 above.
33. See Nicholls, *Treason*, 128.
34. See Stefan Collini, 'Intellectuals in Britain and France in the Twentieth Century: Confusions, Contrasts—and Convergence?', in Jeremy Jennings (ed.), *Intellectuals in Twentieth-Century France: Mandarins and Samurais* (London: Macmillan, 1993), 199–225, esp. 209–18.
35. Anon. [Mary Robinson Duclaux], 'Foes of nationalism', *TLS*, 19 Jan. 1928, 39. I am grateful to Dr Deborah McVea of the *TLS* Contributors' Index project for helping me to identify the author of this review as Mary Robinson Duclaux, a frequent reviewer of French works for the *TLS* during this period, on whom see also Derwent May, *Critical Times: The History of the Times Literary Supplement* (London: HarperCollins, 2001).
36. See 'The French Intelligence', in T. S. Eliot, *The Sacred Wood* (London: Methuen, 1920), 44–6.
37. T. S. Eliot, 'The humanism of Irving Babbitt' (1928), in Eliot, *Selected Essays* (London: Faber, 1934 [1st edn., 1932]), 433.
38. Anon. [T. S. Eliot], 'Culture and anarchy', *TLS*, 23 Feb.1928, 118. Dr McVea also confirmed what is strongly suggested by the internal evidence, that the second review was by T. S. Eliot. His authorship had in fact already been noted in David Bradshaw, 'Eleven reviews by T. S. Eliot, hitherto unnoted, from the *Times Literary Supplement*: a conspectus', *Notes and Queries* (June, 1995), 212–15. This item does not at present appear in Donald Gallup's authoritative bibliography of Eliot's writings, but it will do so, I gather, in future editions.

39. T. S. Eliot, 'The idealism of Julien Benda', *Cambridge Review*, 49 (6 June 1928), 486–7; Eliot's review-essay was republished in the *New Republic* later that year (12 Dec. 1928, 105–7), although several passages were omitted. On Parsons' role, see Ian Parsons, 'On being F. R. Leavis's publisher', in Denys Thompson (ed.), *The Leavises: Recollections and Impressions* (Cambridge: Cambridge University Press, 1984), 82.
40. Eliot, 'Idealism of Benda', 488.
41. Basil Willey, *The English Moralists* (London: Chatto, 1964), 18. The opening chapters of Willey's first book, *The Seventeenth-Century Background: Studies in the Thought of the Age in Relation to Poetry and Religion* (London: Chatto, 1934) acknowledged the stimulus of Eliot's historical-cum-metaphysical speculations.
42. Willey, *English Moralists*, 12, 17–19.
43. R. B. Mowat, 'The treachery of the intellectuals', *Hibbert Journal*, 33 (1935), 326.
44. Ibid. 326.
45. Ibid. 327.
46. Ibid. 330.
47. L. B. Namier, '1848: The Revolution of the Intellectuals' (the British Academy Raleigh Lecture on History, 1944), *The Proceedings of the British Academy*, XXX (London: Cumberledge, 1945), paginated separately, 4.
48. On Namier's Anglophilia more generally, see the discussion and the works cited in Stefan Collini, *English Pasts: Essays in History and Culture* (Oxford: Oxford University Press, 1999), ch. 3.
49. Namier, 'Revolution of the intellectuals', 11.
50. Ibid. 123–4.
51. To cite only one recent example: 'It is not by accident that Jules [*sic*] Benda's *The Treason of the Clerks* [*sic*] (1927) is frequently referred to in England; it both puts off and fascinates.' Richard Hoggart, *The Way We Live Now* (London: Chatto, 1995), 300.

PART FOUR

SOME VERSIONS OF DENIAL

13

Clerisy or Undesirables: T. S. Eliot

'This has been called an age of specialization, but it is very much the age of the amateur. . . . There is, in fact, very little respect for authority: by which I mean respect for the man who has special knowledge of some subject of which oneself is ignorant.'

I

T. S. Eliot had very considerable respect for 'authority', especially when it was exercised by people like himself. Much of his prose, above all that written from the late 1920s onwards, explicitly concerned itself with the forms authority, including cultural authority, could and should take in a modern society, a society he notoriously characterized as 'worm-eaten with liberalism'. In the passage which serves as the epigraph to this chapter, his sympathies may seem to lie with the 'man who has special knowledge of some subject' rather than with the 'amateur',[1] and it is certainly true that early in his career he was unremittingly censorious about all forms of intellectual 'slackness' and mere opinionatedness. As he put it in 1918, repudiating a middlebrow attack on 'professionalism' in art: 'an attitude which might find voice in words like these is behind all of British slackness for a hundred years or more: the dislike of the specialist'.[2] Such remarks formed part of his campaign against the debased romanticism of the Georgians and their genteel admirers in literature, in the face of which he wanted to assert a conception of poetry and criticism as severe intellectual disciplines. But when, having established his literary authority, he later ventured into the terrain of the social critic, his references to 'specialists' struck a far more equivocal note. Moreover, the self-description of the position from which he expressed his idiosyncratic political vision was assertively (and, one is tempted to say, flagrantly) 'non-specialist'; indeed, far from being 'professional', the later social criticism is often dismissed precisely for being 'amateurish'.[3]

Of course, in public life in Britain being an 'amateur' has not always constituted a disability, but the social attitudes that have clustered around this term can cut both ways where the role of the intellectual is concerned. At first sight, their tendency would seem to be to strengthen local resistance to any acknowledgement of the need for intervention by 'theorists', 'experts', or other 'highbrows'. 'Amateur' is here aligned with 'character', as in the hallowed preference of the minor (and many major) public schools for 'character rather than brains', just as it can also be lined up alongside those other types that have similarly hardened into cultural clichés, such as the 'all-rounder', the 'man on the spot', and so on. But in the cultural and intellectual sphere, the amateur also figures as the generalist, a role structurally defined by contrast with that of 'the specialist'. Here, the intellectual is the individual who goes beyond the 'merely' professional role (the preserve of the expert or specialist) to speak out on wider matters of concern to a non-specialist public. In this respect, every Professor of Tibetan who protests against the injustice of Dreyfus's conviction does so as an 'amateur'. In these terms, Eliot proves, not for the first time, to be Mr Facing-Both-Ways, disposed to assert the claims of 'authority' against the ignorant and the emptily opinionated, but at the same time looking for ways to trump the authority of 'mere' specialists. It was precisely in his dexterous navigation of these shoals that Eliot displayed a deep, and (I would argue) representative, ambivalence about the figure of 'the intellectual'.

II

It was during the late 1910s and early 1920s that Eliot's ambitious self-fashioning turned an American graduate student in philosophy into literary London's most talked-about poet and critic. The theme of 'the intellectuals' was, as we have seen, only intermittently and equivocally addressed in Britain during these years, but Eliot particularly prided himself at this point on being au fait with the literary and intellectual scene in France, and this may partly account for the occasional appearance of the term in his journalism of the period. For example, when reviewing the English translation of Sorel's *Reflections on Violence* in 1917, he observed that although Sorel hates the middle-class and middle-class democracy, 'he does not hate these things as a champion of the rights of the people, he hates them as a middle-class intellectual hates'. And a few lines later he concluded in his best air of offhand authority: 'His motive forces are ideas and feelings which never occur to the mind of the proletariat, but which are highly characteristic of the present-day intellectual.'[4] Eliot's usage here can seem deceptively modern, though I suspect it draws something from contemporary French Right-wing polemicizing. In both these sentences the term seems to be used to suggest not just a level of education above that of the common people, but a category of person used to expressing general views, with the implication that there is something a little self-important about such people as well as that they are somewhat removed from the realities about which they habitually pronounce.

It is harder still to know quite how to gloss the term as it appeared in another piece of Eliot's writing from the same year:

> M. de Bosschère is in fact almost a pure intellectual; leaving, as if disdainfully, our emotions to form as they will around the situation which his brain has selected. . . . A poet is not an intellectual by virtue of any amount of meditation or abstractness or Moralizing; the abstract thought of nearly all poets is mediocre enough, and often second-hand. . . . A poet like M. de Bosschère is an intellectual by his obstinate refusal to adulterate his poetic emotions with human emotions.'[5]

This passage forms part of Eliot's larger campaign to obtain recognition for poetry, and thereby for its criticism, as the work of a form of intelligence rather than as merely the overflow of powerful emotions or similar reach-me-down Romantic notions. The term 'intellectual' seems here to be being appropriated to refer positively to the category of those who so exercise their intelligence; it allows, but only to repudiate, the possibility that others may think that the hallmark of the species lies in holding forth about general ideas and opinions. As I pointed out in Ch. 1, it is noticeable that here, as in most of the examples drawn from this decade, the term carries no suggestion of a public or political role at all.

As seasoned readers of Eliot's prose will recognize, his statements on this as on other topics often displayed a slightly wilful elusiveness. For example, in 1929 he wrote in a letter to the American theologian and critic Paul Elmer More: 'What I should like to see is the creation of a new type of intellectual, combining the intellectual and the devotional.' Taken out of context, this might suggest a more, as it were, sociological concern than was really intended. In fact, the letter went on to speak more broadly about not separating intellect and emotion, indicating that this was Eliot addressing his familiar concern of 'the dissociation of sensibility' in another guise.[6] In the previous year Irving Babbitt had referred to Eliot's 'numerous following of young intellectuals in Britain and America',[7] a remark that could seem almost calculated to make the fastidious and counter-suggestible Eliot emphasize his distance from such creatures. And again, he could respond sometimes a little sniffily when the label was applied to himself, holding it in the distancing tongs of quotation marks, as when he wrote in *The Criterion* in 1938: 'I do not like to be appealed to as an "intellectual" if it be implied that intellectuals, as a class, have any *special interest* in the maintenance of peace.'[8] In the following year he could refer in passing to 'those who should be the intellectuals', allowing the faint hint of reproach to float free of any positive suggestion for correction, still less of identification.[9] Indeed, many of his remarks about 'intellectuals' are characteristic of a still larger pattern in Eliot's writing, in which he establishes his superiority to the unreflective cant of the day without committing himself to a clear alternative position. One might not be quite justified in adapting the most notorious line from *After Strange Gods* to read: 'Reasons of race and religion combine to make any large number of free-thinking intellectuals undesirable', but it is, I think, revealing both of the connotations of the word in England at the time and of the associations in Eliot's mind—social mobility, destructive criticism, other allegiances—to recognize just how little disruption in his prose the substitution would make at this point. (The original, it is perhaps unnecessary to add, occurred as part of his discussion of the preconditions for maintaining a 'living tradition'. In addition to the familiar prescriptions—'Stability is obviously necessary'; 'The population should be homogeneous'—he added: 'What is still more important is unity of religious background; and reasons of race and religion combine to make any large number of free-thinking Jews undesirable.' The remark would be hard to forgive in any context; to publish it in 1934 was surely particularly culpable.[10])

Nonetheless, Eliot returned with revealing frequency to the question of the exercise of cultural authority by those who were coming to be known as intellectuals, and he did not always set such a determined distance between himself and this category. Moreover, Eliot's more worldly perspective on the role of the man of letters ensured that he was not confined by Benda's kind of self-denying purism. For example, in an essay written three years after his Benda reviews, he playfully observed; 'I suspect there is some taint of Original H. G. Wells about most of us in English-speaking countries; and that we enjoy drawing general conclusions from particular disciplines, using our accomplishments in one field as the justification for theorizing about the world in general.'[11] The use of the first-person plural is not the least interesting feature of this remark. Similarly, in the second Benda review, he had reflected that it may 'happen that a successful writer may be keenly interested in some alien subject, may feel a vocation to write about it, and then he can hardly be blamed for using his reputation to get his writings published and read. I should probably do the same thing myself'. On that occasion, he instanced Arnold Bennett's political views, with which he did not agree, and then acknowledged that 'if I were as important as Mr Bennett I should probably write political articles myself'.[12] Of course, he went on to be at least as important as Arnold Bennett, but perhaps in his later, graver meditations on the desirable form of a modern clerisy this relaxed form of self-inclusion proved less easy to come by. It is not a bad test of any intellectual's account of the general activities of intellectuals to ask whether they could say, as Eliot did here, 'I should probably do the same thing myself.'

There was to be no further substantial discussion of Benda's thesis in Eliot's subsequent published writings, but a revealing characterization of it occurs in an unpublished paper on the idea of the 'clerisy' prepared in 1944 for the 'Moot' discussion group (to which I shall return below). There he wrote:

I cannot find my copy of *La Trahison des clercs,* and I have not read the book since it first appeared. I remember that I did not think it as good as the author's *Belphégor*. My impression remains that Benda was an example of the Cretan Liar, and that he fell into treason while accusing others; but also that he did not distinguish different grades of *clerc*. The higher grades are those, whether philosophers or artists, who are concerned with the word (the discovery of truth or beauty) rather than with the audience, and the lower those who are more concerned with the audience—either to *influence* it or to *entertain* it, or both. (This does not exclude the possibility that a particular lower-grade cleric may be a *greater* man than a particular higher-grade one.) Benda, as I remember, seemed to expect everybody to be a sort of Spinoza.[13]

The calculated offhandedness may owe something to the informal setting, but it allows Eliot to give a sharper and pithier formulation to his main reservation about Benda's position than in his earlier reviews. Saying that Benda seems to expect every *clerc* 'to be a sort of Spinoza' neatly captures something about the book's curiously high-toned unrealism, although it is, of course, the remark about Benda being 'an example of the Cretan Liar' which most interests me here. At first sight, the force of this is intuitively obvious: Benda was, as I suggested, writing an engaged polemic urging that true *clercs* did not involve themselves in engaged polemics. But Eliot's allusion to the Cretan Liar paradox raises interesting questions about his own role, and at the risk of appearing to make too much of this fairly conventional allusion, I shall return to this paradox at the end of this chapter.

III

With a writer for whom the avoidance of vulgarity was such a preoccupation, there was bound to be a good deal of fastidious nose-holding about the elements of self-display and prideful theorizing associated with the *term* 'intellectuals'. And for the later Eliot, any hint that merely human reason (or, still worse, its one-sided exaltation into rationalism) could set itself up as the final arbiter was bound to be treated with a withering ecclesiastical hauteur. Yet at the same time, Eliot, even more than most writers, manifested a strong sense of occupying a position in the public eye, and he was clearly fascinated by the literary means through which cultural authority could be exercised. His prose keeps returning to the question of authority, often in the form of mock-modest disclaimers of any such authority, with a betraying frequency, and, as we shall see, an implicit address to the question of intellectuals is to be found far more often in Eliot's writing than in that of most of his contemporaries in Britain.

In Bruce Robbins's discussion of the paradoxes encountered in late twentieth-century literary critics' description of their public role, where the claim to have access to a therapeutic wholeness is necessarily in conflict with an insistence on the claims of specialized expertise, he acutely observes how such critics engage in what he calls 'rites of propitiation or self-protection', in which they 'impersonate and ventriloquise' the identity of 'the amateur' whose criticism of the disabling narrowness of specialism they most fear.[14] Extending my analysis of the concept of the intellectual developed in Ch. 2, I want to suggest that such 'rites' are in fact an inescapable element in the intellectual's self-description. Since, on my analysis, the intellectual is by definition in constant movement between the poles of specialized cultural achievement and general 'speaking out', no wholly satisfactory public identity can be based on just one of these poles. Hence the various 'rites of propitiation or self-protection', in which modest acknowledgement of being a 'mere specialist' is incorporated in the very act of surpassing such a constraining identity.

One of the most intriguing features of Eliot's public pronouncements in the 1930s and 1940s is the way in which he projects the identity of 'the man of letters' as, simultaneously, the source of a particular cultural authority *and* the name of a position which transcends any one such source of authority. In other words, the label 'man of letters' often serves as the functional equivalent of 'intellectual', except that it also tries to build one, somewhat archaized, occupational role into the model. Robbins speaks of the tension between the ideal of 'wholeness' and 'the necessarily partial place within the division of labour' occupied by the critic,[15] but in Eliot's hands 'man of letters' becomes the least partial of such places, at once an ideal location as well as an actual profession. Yet on some occasions, even this identity can be cut across and, as it were, trumped by the authority of religion. It is when writing as 'a Christian', as he frequently and rather assertively does in the 1930s, that Eliot stakes his claim to the highest of all Higher Grounds. However, what I think one finds on further analysis is that, remarkably, there are times in Eliot's prose when these two identities themselves can appear to be functionally equivalent, in that each is in practice not defined by a particular *content*, but by the *formal* property of taking a more general perspective. In the rest of this section, I shall explore some of the ways in which the instabilities of these identities work themselves out in Eliot's later social criticism and other occasional writings.

The disclaiming of any special competence is one of the recurring tropes of this writing. The opening words of his address to the Anglo-Catholic Summer School of Sociology in 1933 were: 'This is by no means the first occasion on which I have had to speak in public on a subject outside of my competence,' and he went on to cast himself as 'the highly intelligent ignoramus'.[16] He tried to distance himself from the most obviously available role: 'There are, of course, public men for whose opinions on *any* subject there is always a large and interested audience. I have no desire to join this popular profession,' though this is essentially what he did in the course of the 1930s and 1940s. 'I am, as I have already admitted, unqualified to discuss either political science or economics' (although as early as 1927, he had announced in a *Criterion* 'Commentary' that 'we are compelled, to the extent of our abilities, to be amateur economists in an age in which politics and economics can no longer be kept wholly apart'.[17]) Nonetheless, these matters could not entirely be left to the 'specialists'. After all, 'it is perhaps too much to expect of any man to possess both specialised scientific power and wisdom', and the Church was the great repository of such wisdom, especially since 'wisdom seems to be a commodity less and less available in educational institutions; for the methods and ideals coming into vogue in modern education, scientific specialisation on the one hand, and a treatment of the humanities either as a kind of pseudo-science or as superficial culture, are not calculated to cultivate a disposition towards wisdom'. It was surely revealing of the logic of his situation that on this occasion Eliot devoted several pages of his relatively short address to making the preliminary case that Christians 'cannot simply accept or reject the solutions offered by specialised theorists in the world'.[18]

The false modesty of the identity of 'the man of letters' allowed Eliot to disparage the claims to authority of a variety of mere 'specialists'. But when it suited him, he could invoke identities that outranked even this capacious role. For example, in the late 1920s, when pointing out the limitations of 'Humanism' as expounded by the American critic Norman Foerster, Eliot identified as a partial explanation for the shortcomings of Foerster's work the fact that he was 'trained as a man of letters'. 'Mr Foerster and I would probably agree about the prevalent desiccation of the study of philosophy in universities. Nevertheless, there is a philosophic training and it is not the literary training', and his sharpest reproach to Foerster is 'for playing the games of philosophy and theology without knowing the rules'. Whatever the game, Eliot somehow always seemed to know the rules. This essay also contains an interesting prefiguring of his later views about 'elites': 'Humanism . . . is valid for a very small minority of *individuals*. But it is culture, not any subscription to a common programme or platform, which binds these individuals together. Such an "intellectual aristocracy" has not the economic bonds which unite the individuals of an "aristocracy of birth" '.[19] And in the preface to his first (and surely least happy) venture into substantial social criticism, *After Strange Gods*, he even declared himself 'uncertain of my ability to criticise my contemporaries as artists', contending with brazen humility that 'I ascended the platform of these lectures only in the role of moralist.'[20]

On other occasions, the same tropes of mock-humility accompany his assertion of the identity of the man of letters. Thus for example, writing in *Time and Tide* in 1935, he professes to find A. A. Milne, no less, an appropriate writer to consider on questions of war and peace, rather than any of the acknowledged authorities such as Norman Angell, 'because I take him to be a simple man of letters like myself with a sense of public responsibility'.[21] This identity figured in the title of several of his later essays, such as his widely cited 1945 piece on 'The man of letters and the future of Europe', and such essays and addresses are full of disclaimers of the now familiar type, as in his 'leadership and letters' address of 1948: 'As a man of letters, what contribution could I possibly make to the problem of "leadership in a democracy"?'[22] At the same time, these essays do not in practice shrink from assigning the man of letters a fairly extensive jurisdiction, as in his 1945 discussion of regionalist movements: 'The man of letters, who should be peculiarly qualified to respect and to criticize them, should be able to take a longer view than either the politician or the local patriot.'[23]

'Peculiarly qualified' hits a far from modest note, and is again allied to taking the more general view.

From at least the mid-nineteenth century onwards, the 'mere man of letters' has shored up his own cultural authority by disparaging the over-specialized and inward-looking nature of academic scholarship. Eliot was adept at murmuring grave misgivings of this kind, not least about the newly institutionalized study of English literature, but also about other disciplines with a prima facie claim on public attention, such as philosophy. For instance, in writing an introduction to the English translation of Josef Pieper's *Leisure the Basis of Culture* in 1952, he complained that philosophy had become too specialized, too professional, and too prone to try to imitate the natural sciences. And in a move which in the course of the twentieth century has become familiar to the point of being hackneyed, he claimed there was now a 'need for philosophy in an older meaning of the word—the need for new authority to express *insight* and *wisdom*'. For this, the philosopher had to range widely: 'But in an age in which every branch of study becomes more subdivided and specialized, the ideal of omniscience is more and more remote from realization. Yet only omniscience is enough, once the philosopher begins to rely upon science.' What philosophy really needed, he asserted, was to be related to theology. And this in turn underwrote what was so admirable about Pieper's work, namely its address to a wide public: Pieper's influence, wrote Eliot, was 'in the direction of restoring philosophy to a place of importance for every educated person who thinks, instead of confining it to esoteric activities which can affect the public only indirectly, insidiously, and often in a distorted form'.[24] Once again, Eliot comes close to saying that it does not matter *which* religious dogma the philosopher is committed to; what is valuable is the generality of view that *any* genuinely theological perspective brings.

This should remind us that, even when asserting the claims of the 'amateur' man of letters, Eliot did not (as Arnold, for example, repeatedly did) disparage the claims of intellectual abstraction as such. He was temperamentally too drawn to metaphysical and theological construction ever to be indifferent to the claims of the principled and systematic; indeed, part of his cultivated antagonism to the pieties of Whig-liberal complacency consisted in constantly denouncing the merely empirical 'muddling through' which was supposed to be the glory of the English tradition. As a source of principles, religion outranked all opposition. But it is noticeable that Eliot made much of the invocation of principles in general, and rather less of the content of any actual principles.

A good example of this comes in his short article in the *New English Weekly* in May 1939 entitled 'On reading official reports'. The subject ostensibly under discussion is the Spens Report, a report on the state of secondary education by a committee of the Board of Education, chaired by Sir Will Spens. Eliot did not address the substantive proposals in the report, but instead emphasized how any such deliberations would be based on assumptions of which the committee themselves might not always be aware. Such reports can 'only rest upon an uncertain foundation of Liberalism', given the present state of British culture. Any report will be limited by what a range of relevant groups in society already think. 'And it is safe to guess that amongst these innumerable persons there is no majority with any philosophy of life, any political philosophy in the widest and most humane sense, at all.' Once again, a higher ground is being invoked but not really occupied. In effect, the article's readers are simply being reminded of the desirability of being able to relate details of policy to large moral and religious principles.[25]

The coexistence of a disclaimer of competence with an assertion of authority is neatly symbolized by juxtaposing a private letter and a public pronouncement. In replying to a complimentary letter from Keynes in April 1934 about 'my very unsatisfactory lectures' (presumably *After Strange Gods*), Eliot wrote: 'I am glad of your support in my avoidance of the economic problem. That, of course, is what particularly annoys my friends of the Social Credit persuasion but I remain of the opinion that I should not discuss matters about which I am ignorant.'[26] The date of this letter is the most significant thing about it. For only the previous day, a letter had appeared in *The Times*, signed by Eliot and several other fairly well-known literary figures (the list of signatories included Lascelles Abercrombie, Bonamy Dobrée, Aldous Huxley, Hewlett Johnson, Hamish Miles, Edwin Muir, Herbert Read, and I. A. Richards), urging that Social Credit be given serious attention as a possible solution to the perceived maldistribution of wealth under capitalism.[27] This was not just one of Old Possum's little games, and in fact he certainly did not abstain from further forays into economic matters. Indeed, in 1945 he actually sent Keynes a copy of an article he had just published (signed 'Metoikos') in the *Christian News Letter* on the subject of 'Full Employment', adding his usual kind of disclaimer: 'It seems as odd to me as it will to you that I should be writing on this subject.... But I hope that I have stuck to my own weapons on my own ground.'[28] It is worth pausing here to ask what he thought his 'weapons' and his 'ground' were in this case.

First, we have to note that his article takes the form of a response to a view put forward by someone else, in this case an economist who had signed his piece 'Civis': this is always the easiest role for the social critic, a role with special appeal to someone as temperamentally inclined as Eliot was to remaining guarded and elusive about his own views. Second, the title of his essay is 'Full employment and the responsibility of Christians': the issues raised by the second phrase are what really engage his attention. Essentially, he is objecting to 'Civis's' overdrawn picture of the obligation of Christians to make substantial individual sacrifices in order to ensure the success of the proposed policy of full employment (associated, above all, with the names of Keynes and Beveridge). And although Eliot touches passingly on the economic issue, his criticism concentrates on matters of moral and religious principle. 'To some Christians, the scheme for full employment may seem *relatively* good. It may be good on certain assumptions.' In the article by Civis, there is 'a danger of regarding employment as an end instead of a means'. And then, in his final paragraph, Eliot moves closer to home ground. Civis's piece may, because confused, be open to conflicting interpretations: 'Where this happens, the reader is justified in basing his interpretation partly upon the tone in which the author speaks. I find the tone of Civis very disquieting: it evinces a certain imperiousness and impatience.' Such criticism of tone was, of course, one of Eliot's preferred 'weapons'. And yet even here he does not press the point with any ostentatiously literary-critical analysis. Instead, after a few more remarks, he goes on: 'But I believe also that the author raises issues which are beyond the competence of the layman, however skilled in economics, and however sincere, devout, and zealous in his Christianity—issues which are only to be considered by expert and authoritative' (and here it is hard to predict what noun is to come, what kind of 'expert' may legitimately rule on these issues, but in fact the sentence ends) 'by expert and authoritative theological minds'.[29] Again, a Higher Ground is invoked but not really occupied; the position advanced by Eliot's opponent is shown to require certain moral and theological assumptions upon which there has not been adequate reflection. The position is trumped—but without Eliot revealing the content of his own hand.

The choice of classical pseudonyms in this case also tells us something about the position from which Eliot claimed to be speaking. In signing himself 'Civis', the author of the original article made appeal to a culturally validated ideal of 'citizenship'. In choosing 'Metoikos', Eliot might at first sight appear to be alluding to his foreign origins in this particular *polis*, but it seems much more likely that he chose this term to signify the status of not being wholly a citizen because one owed allegiance elsewhere, in this case to the Kingdom of God (at times, it pleased Eliot to present himself as a kind of *Gastarbeiter* in this world). Thus, he concludes his article by objecting that the outcome of Civis's proposals would be that 'the Christian will lose the sense of that loyalty which sometimes conflicts with, and always transcends, that to the State'. 'Metoikos' signals this dual allegiance.

In practical terms, one of the chief means by which Eliot saw the man of letters making a distinctive contribution to public debate was by editing a general periodical, a quintessentially 'non-specialist' activity. As has often been remarked, *The Criterion* under his direction moved away from being a classic literary 'little magazine' in the early 1920s towards an altogether more portentous identity in the 1930s, handing down judgements on most of the major social and political developments of the day. In some ways, such a general periodical performed, as it were collectively or institutionally, the role increasingly coming to be designated by the noun 'the intellectual'. Alongside Eliot's well-known rulings on the function of the editor of such a journal, one may set this little-known but revealing obituary comment on Michael Roberts, who had been one of the *Criterion's* most valued contributors, not least on modern poetry:

> But he was not a specialist; his interests were too wide for limitation to a particular pedagogical subject, and too well coordinated to be pursued independently of each other.

He would have made an admirable editor of a review of ideas; indeed, had 'The Criterion' continued, he was the only man junior to myself of whom I could think for the editorship.[30]

There is a disinterested matter-of-factness to the implicit self-description here. Overlapping with this role was that of the writer of 'occasional or periodical commentary', a topic, Eliot coyly acknowledged in 1935, 'to which I have given some attention', and here he singled out the two outstanding practitioners he had known as Charles Whibley and A. R. Orage. There is again an element of idealized self-description in his praise of them, as well as the familiar trope that something deeper than mere professional technique is at issue. Writing about Whibley in 1931, he praised his range and his conversable style, and went on: 'It is in such ways as I have indicated, not aspiring to any literary dictatorship or pontificate, or to academic or extra-academic honours, and never caring to express his mind except on what really interested him and excited his admiration or indignation, that Charles Whibley made and holds his place in literary criticism.[31]

The true 'amateur', we are being reminded here, does not write to gain some purely 'professional' advancement. Similarly, when praising Orage four years later, he acknowledged his mastery of the role: 'The ideal commentator must be attentive to current events, with an amused attention to the *faits divers*, as well as to the headlines, and must be sensitive to the symbolic importance of the petty, as well as to the insignificance of the sensational.' But at the end of his portrait, Eliot seems to sense that he may be giving the impression that there is nothing more than an occupational skill involved here, for he adds: 'And he had what seems to me the completing virtue of the commentator: one feels even in his comments that he is not merely the *professional* commentator.'[32] Hovering over such judgements is the suggestion that it is by such qualities that the 'true intellectual' is distinguished, in sharp contrast to the brassy noise-makers to whom the label was most readily applied.

Eliot repeatedly insisted—here sharing the cultural pessimism so widespread among the educated classes in the inter-war years—that serious critical commentary in this vein could now only be aimed at a small public. The valedictory editorial in which he announced the closure of the *Criterion* declared that 'the continuity of culture' would henceforth have to be maintained by 'a very small number of people indeed', and that therefore the 'little review' would be the essential vehicle, having displaced the older general cultural periodicals which had managed to reach a broad public.[33] And again, in contrasting the scale of success enjoyed by earlier writers such as Bennett and Wells with the more limited popularity of his own contemporaries, he laid it down that 'the serious journalism of my generation is all minority journalism'.[34] Needless to say, there was more than a dash of self-justification in these remarks, but the practicalities of reaching different publics did seriously preoccupy Eliot. Consider, for example, his reflections on this theme in writing in 1941 to his friend and fellow 'Christian sociologist' Philip Mairet about the question of preparing talks for radio:

No-one could be more lucid than you in the form of exposition of a N.E.W. [*New English Weekly*] leader or note; but I think that for transference to the people your thought needs an intellectual middleman to dilute it. There, I feel, we suffer from a considerable handicap: where are the men who are intelligent enough to understand your thinking but yet superficial enough to be able to translate it? My danger is not so much of being unintelligible to the mob (and in the mob I include the people at Malvern etc) but as being taken as having said something else—possibly the opposite of what I mean. Vidler tells me that our letter to the *Times* was taken in some quarters as meaning that we were reactionaries: yet if the only alternative to suffering that injustice is to be a member of the 1941 committee.... The whole question of popularisation of ideas (and the avoidance of perversion of them) deserves our consideration, and I don't know how to begin.[35]

This passage stacks 'the people', 'radio', 'the mob', and 'popularization' on one side of the divide, and 'thoughts', 'thinking', 'ideas', and 'us' on the other, recalling the distinction made in his second Benda review between 'the mere vulgariser of knowledge, of the American type' and 'the "intellectual" of wide interests'. Certainly, Eliot's own writing in the genre of commentary implied a select and sympathetic audience ('readers of *Christendom* do not need to be reminded that the agricultural community is the most stable'[36]), a feature that was particularly marked when he was writing for assertively Christian publications. For example, in the summer of 1940 he stood in for J. H. Oldham as editor of the *Christian News Letter*, and his editorial commentaries have a distinct air of whistling loudly to keep up the morale of the (Christian) troops, as in his wilful comment on Dr. Salazar: 'His interest and importance for us is that without being in any dubious political sense pro-clerical, he is a Christian at the head of a Christian country.'[37] But as this reminds us, in the course of the 1930s Eliot had involved himself more closely in the work of explicitly Christian organizations, and in these and other settings he increasingly cultivated the identity of the committed Christian social commentator, an identity which requires fuller analysis.[38]

The best known expression of this identity was his little book, first given as lectures at Corpus Christi College, Cambridge, entitled *The Idea of a Christian Society*. The book's explicit preoccupation is with the role of Christians in a no longer wholly Christian country; more obliquely, it is also a meditation on the theme of cultural leadership in a modern society. From its title onwards, this is the most Coleridgean of Eliot's works, and nowhere is this more evident than in its preoccupation with what it tries, not always successfully, to resist calling 'the clerisy' (an attempt to revivify Coleridge's term had just been made by Middleton Murry in *The Price of Leadership*, cited by Eliot).[39] In sketching the components of his Christian society, he distinguished the small, self-conscious 'Community of Christians' from the larger, and largely unreflective, 'Christian Community': the former were to be 'the consciously and thoughtfully practising Christians, especially those of intellectual and spiritual superiority'. Having emphasized that they could not be the kind of vocational body that Coleridge had had in mind in his idea of a 'clerisy'—to which university teachers and parish priests belonged by virtue of their offices—he went on:

> The Community of Christians is not an organisation, but a body of indefinite outline; composed of both clergy and laity, of the more conscious, more spiritually and intellectually developed of both. It will be their identity of belief and aspiration, their background of a common system of education and a common culture, which will enable them to influence and be influenced by each other, and collectively to form the conscious mind and the conscience of the nation.

If one replaced the first phrase in this passage with the phrase '*Christian intellectuals* are not an organisation, but...', the rest of the passage would seem a natural gloss, concluding with the defining role of intellectuals, 'form[ing] the conscious mind and the conscience of the nation'. Indeed, as Eliot goes on to lament increasing specialization yet again, he observes that literature, theology, politics, and so on are all seen as separate, even by (in a phrase quoted earlier) 'those who should be the intellectuals'. But this term leads a troubled life in this book, as elsewhere in Eliot's writing. Having insisted that 'the Community of Christians' would contain 'both clergy and laity of superior intellectual and/or spiritual gifts', he continued: 'And it would include some of those who are ordinarily spoken of, not always with flattering intention, as "intellectuals".' At the same time, Eliot insisted it was essential that the Community of Christians should not become any kind of separate intellectual caste: it was desirable that 'ecclesiastics', 'politicians', and 'those who are ordinarily spoken of... as "intellectuals"' should mix.[40] This kind of social integration had, of course, long been the reigning model (and to some extent practice) in Britain—as compared, predictably, with France—and the lack of 'flattering intention' in the common use of the label 'intellectuals' partly referred to the self-important sense of apartness this term was taken to connote. In Victorian Britain, the man of letters and the don, like the higher ecclesiastic and the politician, were largely seen as gentlemen among gentlemen. An ambivalence towards this model is frequently discernible beneath the smooth surfaces of Eliot's prose, and *Idea* is one of the places where his distance from comfortable English assumptions is occasionally evident.

Having insisted on the value of religious orders in his conception of a Christian society, he then adds a sentence which at first appears to be a non sequitur: 'And, incidentally, I should not like the "Community of Christians" of which I have spoken, to be thought of as merely the nicest, most intelligent and public-spirited of the upper middle-class—it is not to be conceived on that analogy.'[41] The sentence, with which the paragraph ends, is formally characteristic of much of Eliot's prose, from the apparent offhandness of 'incidentally' to the abruptness of the last clause and the tacit withholding of further explanation. When an author disclaims any intention of saying or meaning something, there is always some significance to why it is *that* something, out of the limitless somethings he is not saying, that he chooses to disown. Why should Eliot choose at this point to distance himself from this particular possible misinterpretation? The immediately preceding and succeeding sentences defend—his tone hints at the pleasures of snubbing fashionable prejudices—the role of celibate and contemplative religious orders. The implication could be, therefore, that rather than the social interpretation of his category that he repudiates in the quoted sentence, he is summoning a more unworldly, less conventional set of beings into existence. But those in religious orders clearly constitute only a tiny fraction of the individuals who make up Eliot's 'Community of Christians', so they can hardly be thought to provide the positive illustration of the term that would seem to be necessary to prevent the slackly conventional assumption from usurping it. Yet the incongruously archaic image of the cloistered, celibate monk does figure what Eliot hints is missing in the conventional conception, something to do with giving priority to one's relation with God. And, at the risk of appearing to try to extract too much from this one sentence, I suggest that Eliot's mind moves instinctively to repudiate *this* particular conception precisely because the 'most intelligent and public-spirited of the upper-middle class' had in fact been the source of so much of the reforming and morally earnest activity in English society for several generations.[42] This is the contrast that comes to his mind because he wants his 'Community of Christians' to represent a more strenuous ideal, one carried by a heterogeneous group of individuals who are less at ease in Zion than the traditional leaders of English opinion. But even this position, as we shall see in the next section, was to be modified as he moved further and further away from vesting cultural leadership in a stratum of intellectuals and more and more towards wishing to see it exercised by a traditional governing class.

IV

It would be interesting to know whether the dozen churchmen, academics, writers, and public figures who gathered at High Leigh in Hertfordshire in April 1938 for a weekend of discussions would have been more resistant to describing themselves as belonging to 'the intellectuals' or to 'the governing class'. They were perhaps representative of the larger configuration of English culture in their combination of these two identities and their repudiation of both labels. Their own primary self-description was that they were an informal gathering of Christians. The meeting was a natural extension of the various organizations of clerics and laymen which had flourished in the late 1930s, including the 1937 Oxford Conference on Church, Community, and State, and its later off-shoot, the Council on the Christian Faith and the Common Life. Eliot was an active participant in these groups, and when in 1939 the *Christian News Letter* was established to promote their ideas, he became a member of the small editorial board. The editor was J. H. Oldham, a churchman with a talent for organization, and it was he who instigated the series of weekend discussions that became known as 'the Moot'. These lasted, irregularly, until 1947, and were to be the setting in which Eliot elaborated his later ideas about the role of cultural leadership in a modern society.[43]

Over the nine years of their existence, the meetings were attended by a total of thirty-five people, though usually only twelve or fifteen were present at any given meeting. Apart from Oldham, the most regular members were the churchman and broadcaster the Revd Eric Fenn; H. A. Hodges, Professor of Philosophy at Reading University; Karl Mannheim, refugee Hungarian-German sociologist at the LSE and then, until his death in 1947, Professor of Education at London University's Institute of Education; Sir Walter Moberly, prominent Anglican layman, formerly Vice-Chancellor of Manchester University and the long-serving Chairman of the University Grants Committee; the Revd Gilbert Shaw, Warden of St Anne's House, Soho, a 'centre of Christian discourse'; Alec Vidler, Warden of St Deiniol's Hawarden, and later Dean of King's College, Cambridge; and Eliot himself.

The group's early discussions focused on what kind of 'action' they should be aiming at and whether they should proceed to establish a formally constituted 'order'. The tenor of the proceedings is caught by Mannheim's declaration at the Moot of July 1940: 'We need a small committee composed partly of intellectuals and partly of parliamentarians which meets weekly and watches changes in the situation. It would be without public responsibility, but it would advise people. This would become the nucleus of "the Order".' (It seems as though it may at times have been necessary to restrain some of the more zealous members on this matter; as the minutes of the same meeting tersely put it: 'The suggestion of a badge was premature.'[44]) The discussions also evinced considerable dissatisfaction with the high level of specialization in academic disciplines, even to the point of reproaching the 'Modern Greats' (i.e. PPE) course at Oxford for failing to provide sufficient coordination between its constituent disciplines.[45] Mannheim, who attended every meeting from the second in September 1938, soon assumed a leading role in the group, and proceedings were often largely given over to discussion of his sociological ideas about cultural leadership and 'planning for freedom'. Eliot, whose own early contributions were relatively spare (at least as recorded in the surviving minutes and papers), became increasingly involved in a dialogue with Mannheim, a long-running creative disagreement that turned principally on the understanding of 'culture' and the role of 'the clerisy'.

Eliot and Mannheim do not make an obvious couple.[46] Although specialist scholars have long been aware of the links between them, the significance of the relationship for our understanding of Eliot's place in the intellectual history of the period has not, perhaps, been fully appreciated. In 1935 Mannheim, who had fled Germany two years earlier and taken up a teaching post at the LSE, published *Mensch und Gesellschaft im Zeitalter des Umbaus*, which appeared in revised and enlarged form in 1940 as *Man and Society in an Age of Reconstruction*.

It was in this and other work from the late 1930s and early 1940s that Mannheim elaborated his notion of 'planning for freedom', an analysis in the abstract conceptual language of German sociology of the need to supersede laissez-faire individualism with democratic planning. Mannheim was working, broadly speaking, within a post-Weberian framework which focused on how something more than the affectless link of individual rationality was needed to hold modern societies together. Here he looked to the role of 'the intellectual elite' to be the formulators and disseminators of the 'values' which would provide the requisite social glue, and in the course of the 1940s he became increasingly preoccupied with the ways in which this elite could be effective under the conditions of 'mass society'.[47] Eliot would seem to have met Mannheim at the second 'Moot', to which the latter had been introduced by his fellow emigré Adolf Löwe.[48] It is clear from surviving accounts that Mannheim became a focal figure at meetings of the Moot, and several of Eliot's contributions took the form of direct or indirect responses to his ideas.[49] It seems possible that these discussions directly affected Mannheim's own thinking. In his notes for a never-published study of 'intellectuals', Mannheim discussed the emergence in England of the social type of 'the gentleman', who, though he did not pursue abstract speculation for its own sake, was nevertheless conscious that his greater knowledge and culture gave him a responsibility towards the larger public. For this reason, Mannheim became convinced that structural problems of 'mass society' would be less destructive in England than elsewhere, and that there was a correspondingly greater chance of permeating this influential elite with his own ideas. Rather than having to face the problem, intractable in the circumstances of most European countries, of how to bring 'the intellectuals' to power, the task in England seemed to Mannheim to be rather that of bringing the intellectually inclined 'gentleman' to recognize his role as a member of the 'planning elite'.[50]

At first, Eliot broadly endorsed Mannheim's analysis of the ways in which cultural leadership in an age of 'mass society' had still to be exercised by cultivated minorities, but he found both the secular frame of Mannheim's account and its tendency to recommend the 'organization' of 'values' deeply uncongenial. Mannheim wanted a systematic theoretical structure within which the analysis of individual problems could be located, whereas Eliot (and, it would seem, most other members of the Moot) inclined rather to the pursuit of individual intuitions and practical suggestions.[51] There were similar differences over the conception of an 'order' with which the Moot had begun. Mannheim, characteristically, favoured the establishment of a highly organized group committed to collective action; Eliot was among those who thought it more appropriate to confine their activities to discussion and informal contacts with influential members of the surrounding, largely secular, society. Eliot also deprecated the notion that they should have an agreed body of ideas to promote: 'It is not the business of clerics [*sc.* members of a clerisy] to agree with each other; they are driven to each other's company by their common dissimilarity from everybody else, and by the fact that they find each other the most profitable people to disagree with.'[52]

Publicly, Eliot treated Mannheim's work with considerable respect. Reviewing *Man and Society* in 1940, he endorsed its premise that 'for better or worse, we have a "mass" society, and if we do not study how to use the techniques for good, then we must certainly be prepared to see them used for evil'.[53] He recognized that this analysis focused attention on the role of the 'elites', but he was sceptical of Mannheim's faith in the selection of elites in a mass society on the basis of aptitude and achievement alone. When he reviewed Mannheim's *Diagnosis of Our Time* three years later, he also raised doubts about the adequacy of sociology as a basis for the understanding of society.[54] In effect, Eliot was reserving for the 'man of letters' the mantle of 'the generalist', not imprisoned by a particular professional idiom and standpoint. In his obituary notice of Mannheim in 1947 he gracefully avoided these differences, but in private he could sometimes be more forthright: 'Of the numerous central Europeans here,' he wrote to Allen Tate in March 1945, 'there are two I recommend: Eric Meissner and Michael Polanyi. Most of the others hold views which I distrust. Karl Mannheim is a very good fellow, but if you have read his "Man and Society" (Harcourt publish it, I think) you will know that I regard his ideas as dangerous.'[55]

The Moot records reveal two recurrent features of Eliot's response to Mannheim: first, he tried constantly to substitute terms and observations drawn from England's distinctive social circumstances in place of Mannheim's general sociological categories; and secondly, he pointed to ways in which Mannheim's examples of the working of *elites* in a democratic society presupposed advantages enjoyed by a dominant *class*. An undercurrent in Eliot's response (which occasionally surfaced in public comment, as in his review of *Diagnosis of Our Time*) was his scepticism about sociology's scientific pretensions; both 'the man of letters' and 'the Christian' were, one is again reminded, identities that offered to transcend (and trump) the limitations of the kind of scientistic and mechanical understanding of society which Eliot saw as currently gaining authority with the wider public.

As I have suggested, all the Moot's discussions bore, in one way or another, on the issue of cultural leadership in a modern society and hence, indirectly, on the question of intellectuals. It was a question in which Eliot manifested a keen interest, although without, for the most part, taking the lead. However, there were two occasions when his views on this topic were explicitly the focus of the Moot's debates. The surviving records largely consist of summaries of the proceedings, but they also contain two typescript discussion-papers by Eliot, entitled 'Notes on Mannheim's paper' and 'On the place and function of the clerisy', dating from January 1941 and December 1944 respectively, in which he took issue with Mannheim's ideas directly.[56] The first of these contains one of his earliest attempts, here in explicit contrast to Mannheim's usage, to grapple with the concept of 'culture':

> I cannot find that I have ever associated 'progress' with what I mean by 'culture'. I mean by the latter, something which is always decaying and always has to be reborn: we try to

preserve something which is essentially the same amidst extreme superficial changes. I do not mean by culture the extension of popular education and of refinement of manners: these forms of progress may even be, in practice, inimical to culture. What I mean by it may be something peculiar to myself: but I think that the point that it does not mean quite the same thing here that it does in central Europe is perhaps worth making.[57]

The first published fruits of this train of thinking appear in his articles 'towards a definition of culture' in the *New English Weekly* in January 1943, where, against the implicitly Mannheimian notion of the role of the intellectual elite in promoting culture, he argues that 'there is no "culture" without "a culture"'.[58] Nor, in his later paper, would Eliot accept that 'culture' is the preserve of the clerisy: 'The maintenance of culture is a function of the whole people, each part having its own appropriate share of responsibility; it is a function of classes rather than of elites.'[59] By these standards, his own earlier notion in *Idea* of 'the Community of Christians' begins to look rather like the kind of self-selected *elite* he was now deprecating.

For the meeting in December 1944, Eliot's paper entitled 'On the place and function of the clerisy', a response by Mannheim, and Eliot's reply to that response, were all pre-circulated.[60] Eliot roughly defined the clerisy as 'at the top, those individuals who originate the dominant ideas, and alter the sensibility, of their time', though he added that there was also a lower stratum of membership made up of those involved in disseminating such ideas. He again showed his preference for employing the label 'men of letters' ('using that term as loosely as possible'), though in deference to his title he also used the rather awkward 'clerics'. Throughout, he implicitly contested any attempt to sacralize or institutionalize intellectuals (a term he studiously avoided here) or to expect them to form a self-contained caste acting in concert for objects of their own: 'Agreement and common action can only be by particular groups of clerics, and is most effectively exercised against some other groups of clerics.' More generally, as we have seen, Eliot was not willing to posit the existence of 'elites' divorced from the larger units of 'class'. In England, he argued, the clerisy has by and large been part of the upper-middle class, although its members have been conscious of their sense of distance from the core of that class and have often been highly critical of it. 'To some extent, therefore, there is, and I think should be, a conflict between class and clerical elite. On the one hand the clerical elite is dependent upon whatever is the dominant class of its time; on the other hand, it is apt to be critical of, and subversive of, the class in power,' and he instanced the French Philosophes, and 'such men as Carlyle, Ruskin, and Arnold in the upper-middle class Victorian era'.

Distinguishing at one point those 'clerics' who have some secure employment devoted to pursuing their intellectual activities from those who get their living by other means or none at all (casually designating them as 'employed' and 'unemployed' clerics respectively), he pronounced that the ideal was a balance between these two groups. Having too many 'employed' clerics risks uniformity and excessive state patronage: 'On the other hand an excess of unemployed clerics is apt to be unsettling: when society produces a large number of unemployed clerical small fry, we have what is called the *intelligentsia*, expressing its discontents in subversive movements and, in Cairo and such places, overturning trams.' This struck that condescending English tone which this particular naturalized American was so good at (but, my dear, what can you expect—in *Cairo*!), not least in assuming that those 'unemployed', in his special sense, would be bound to have 'discontents' that could not be addressed in any way except through civil disorder.

The most obvious aspect of Eliot's attempt to align himself with the native tradition lay in his somewhat wilful preference for the term 'clerisy' itself. Its Coleridgean ancestry and religious overtones were evidently part of the appeal, but he also wanted to resist the 'Continental' associations of an imported vocabulary. Writing in the *New English Weekly* in 1943, he referred to the question of 'the formation of "elites" in democratic or mass society', and quoted Mannheim on the 'sociology of the intelligentsia', but then appended the following footnote: 'I am not very happy with the word "elite", but it seems to me preferable to the word "intelligentsia', which might be preserved to denote intellectual groups in Russia during a particular period of change.'[61] Or as he put it in his reply to Mannheim's comments on his 'clerisy' paper: 'I agree that your term "intelligentsia" comes nearest to mine; it is only the term itself I am not happy with, because it is apt to carry with it more or less conscious connotations of a particular group in a particular country during a particular period of time.'[62]

Eliot could have what he regarded as fruitful disagreement with Mannheim only because there was so much about the nature of modern societies, and the need for cultural leadership within them, on which they agreed. (It is worth remarking that one of the earliest and most critical responses to Mannheim's account of the intelligentsia had come from E. R. Curtius, the presiding spirit of *Die Neue Rundschau*, one of the European periodicals with which the *Criterion* was most closely identified in the 1920s. Curtius had been critical of Mannheim's sociologism, and had stood up for the traditional notion of *Bildung*, grounded in philosophy and literature.[63] One might have expected Eliot to follow a similar line, but he in fact took Mannheim's sociological analysis more seriously than that.) Moreover, it is clear that the Moot's discussions were premised on the assumption that it was for a cultural elite to decide what 'the people' needed—and then to give it to them. The model of cultural leadership present in the various proposals was that of an already established elite using its position and resources to propose 'values' *to* the great bulk of the population, not to engage in discussions *with*, still less to receive instruction *from*, them. It is this premise that allows Eliot to use such phrases as the following without any suggestion of self-consciousness: 'The necessity for the re-education of the people's sense of values, from above, is one of immediate importance'. When he went on to say that, once the war was over, 'we shall be told . . . that we have allowed the people to sink into a state of physical, moral and cultural deterioration', the responsibility for these things lies clearly with the 'we' who belong to this elite.[64]

There is also in the Moot papers a revealing letter from Eliot, dated 31 October 1942, which was apparently circulated for discussion at the meeting of 10 December that year. In it, Eliot reports his response after having read Fred Oliver's *Endless Adventure*: one of the themes discussed by Oliver was that of 'the relation between the politician and the intellectual'. Oliver, observed Eliot:

> gives some pages to mocking the purveyors of ideas, most of whom are branded as *speculatists*. But later, in reviewing the history of the nineteenth century and the policy of that Liberalism that is largely his own background, he mentions (p. 185) Carlyle, Ruskin, and Arnold in such a way as to suggest that Britain might have profited by their unheeded admonitions. In short, he seems to me to waver between the view of the intellectual as negligible and of the intellectual as merely *neglected*, according to the particular group towards which he happens to be directing his attention. . . . [These difficulties] indicate the profundity of the problem, rather than any simple defect in Oliver's thinking. We, I take it, approach these problems as Christians and as intellectuals respectively; Oliver is attempting (and it is no mean attempt) to put himself at the opposite point of view. . . . (Of course his 'anti-intellectualism', if it may be provisionally called that, is itself, as any anti-intellectualism on a conscious level must be, itself [*sic*] an intellectual attitude; nor does he, in effect, repudiate his Christian ancestry).[65]

As ever, Eliot does not definitely come down on one side or the other of the supposed 'problem', though he apparently does not endorse Oliver's initial 'anti-intellectualism'. Nor is it obvious what it meant for Eliot and his fellow members of the Moot to 'approach these problems as Christians and as intellectuals respectively'. It is characteristic that on one of the relatively few occasions when Eliot includes himself in the category of 'intellectuals' he should be making a point about the subordination of this identity to that of being a Christian.

V

When Ezra Pound observed in 1930 that Eliot had 'arrived at the supreme Eminence among English critics largely through disguising himself as a corpse',[66] he was voicing, with calculated excess, what was to become a staple criticism of the prose written in the second half of Eliot's career. The nub of the charge, for charge it certainly was, lay in the suggestion that Eliot had allowed his gifts to be stifled by his deep need for order and social status, with the result that in his later work creativity had been mugged by respectability. The disturbingly avant-garde poet and iconoclastic critic had become 'Mr Eliot', 'the Pope of Russell Square' (the location of the offices of Faber & Faber where his editorial role enabled him to exercise so much influence and patronage). On this view, the later prose was all of a piece with that 'Mr Eliot' recalled in numerous memoirs, always impeccably dressed in dark suit and correct manners, murmuring grave and judicious misgivings about the contemporary world, the pain and vulnerability that had fired his most brilliant poetic innovations now hidden beneath a protective veneer of exaggerated politeness and stiff syntax. In the years during which most of his social criticism was written (roughly, 1933–48), the regular rhythms of his life were built around acts of religious and social ritual—morning services at St Stephen's, Gloucester Road, where he was a churchwarden, lunch at familiar clubs, tea in his office with an aspiring writer or contributor to *The Criterion*, and eventually the retreat into the closely guarded privacy of the bare rented rooms in which he lived and where he could be alone with his bare rented soul.

'Disguise', of course, is what intrigues us, with its promise of a person behind the persona, and literary critics tend to scan the later writings for those moments when the mask slips, when we are allowed, almost despite itself, a glimpse of the most powerful literary intelligence of English Modernism, before the prose once again smoothes its hair and tightens its tie. In this vein, the later social and political writings have been regarded as possessing at most a certain biographical interest, but by and large literary scholars have returned from the encounter with them expressing a combination of impatience and bafflement. Indeed, even some contemporary readers clearly wondered whether Old Possum was not just playing a new game: reviewing *Notes Towards the Definition of Culture* in *Scrutiny*, David Pocock remarked: 'It is in fact the major difficulty that confronts anyone trying to write about his later prose works, to discover just how seriously Eliot takes himself or intends to be taken', adding 'it is difficult to associate this later Eliot with the author of the earlier critical essays'.[67] Of course, a writer might fail to measure up to a young Scrutineer's standard of 'seriousness' without thereby being convicted of excessive levity or dissimulation, but there is a disquieting continuity between Pocock's wondering how 'seriously' Eliot intended these writings to be taken and the puzzlement of subsequent critics that they were in fact taken so 'seriously'.[68]

The alleged falling-off in Eliot's later prose can, I think, be addressed in another way. The Higher Ground serves as a point of intellectual advantage as well as moral superiority. Eliot's prose had always—insolently at first, deftly at his best, somewhat ponderously later—presented itself as being written from such an eminence. The shift from his literary-critical to his social-critical prose is partly a chronological development, partly a widening of the prospect surveyed from his always lofty vantage-point, but above all it marks a modulation of tone. The spiky ironies and wilful obliquities of the early essays are increasingly displaced by a blander, flank-guarding discursiveness. There is less irritation but more pessimism, sometimes a slightly stagey, noble-stoicism-in-the-face-of-human-folly kind of pessimism.

But some of this blandness may be the necessary price to be paid for occupying the role of man-of-letters as intellectual, the natural tonal expression, as it were, of the ever-receding horizon of the 'generalist' perspective. The structural difficulty facing any social critic who adopts this perspective is to make it yield any determinate content in specific cases. Its natural logic is to confine itself to asserting broad principles. Where specific economic or social proposals are at issue, the 'mere man of letters' is caught between deferring to the claims of expertise and falling back into the vacuously gestural. For the later Eliot, Christian dogma is supposed to provide the content, but in practice, as we have seen, that usually turned out to mean little more than the assertion of the desirability of acknowledging the claims of Christian dogma. At crucial moments, Eliot's prose tended, we might say, adapting actors' slang, to 'corpse'.

This discussion should have made clear why I can only partly agree with a generally perceptive remark by William Chace:

> Faith, for Eliot, was less a positive doctrine than a means by which he could retire from all conflict. Searching throughout his career not for a middle way, but for an escape from all confines, he found in faith something appropriate to his wish to be both inaccessible and silent. Faith could simply be announced, not explained, and could at the same time reduce politics to the utterly trivial or the outright heretical.[69]

Describing Eliot as wishing to 'escape from all confines' surely hits a false note: he wished to combine the satisfactions of endless elusiveness at one level with the security of given, impersonal limits at another. More than many people, he needed to be bound, but he did not at all experience that as being confined. Similarly, he wished to stand above conflict rather than to retire from it: the various forms of such 'conflict' engaged his attention, but he needed to find a way to address them without being classified *within* their terms; to address the conflict without, quite, being of it. And finally, it does not seem exactly right to say that he needed to reduce politics to the 'utterly trivial'. Rather, he sought a position from which the merely transient could be at once engaged with and disowned: where all mundane things are 'trivial', politics can actually be allowed to be quite important.

But Chace's comment does in passing touch on a central contradiction in Eliot's later career: he aspired to play the role of the intellectual, yet he also evinced a deep desire to be 'both inaccessible and silent'. As silent as—the grave, one might say, the proper home of a 'corpse'. Eliot was therefore caught in his own version of the 'paradoxes of denial' that I have been suggesting recur in discussions of the question of intellectuals in Britain by those who were themselves playing the part of intellectuals. 'Silence', in the relevant sense, was not just a temperamental inclination of Eliot's; in a stable, traditionally governed society, there would simply not be much of a general kind to say. But intellectuals are, by definition, those who feel compelled to 'speak out'. Put another way, Eliot faced a double dilemma. The ideal society he celebrated had, in its purest form, no need of intellectuals; and the actual society in which he lived habitually denied the existence of its intellectuals. In either case, intellectuals were foreign bodies.

Being foreign was a disability that Eliot worked assiduously to overcome, whether in emphasizing his East Coker ancestry, or in becoming both a British citizen and an Anglican, or in cultivating a conservative formality in dress and speech. His exceptionally acute ear was attuned to the native strain of derision in uses of the noun 'intellectuals', yet on this as on other matters, his status as a 'metic' included, Eliot could almost be said to have raised the cultivation of ambivalence to one of the fine arts. Consider, for example, his obituary assessment of John Maynard Keynes, published in the *New English Weekly* in 1946. Eliot recalled that when he first met Keynes over twenty-five years earlier, he was immediately struck by his 'intelligence', adding, with characteristic artifice, that it was 'the French rather than the English associations of the word' he had in mind. He went on:

> Certainly, Keynes was quite English, and, in any sense of the word, an "intellectual". That is to say, he was born into, and always lived in, an intellectual environment; he had intellectual tastes; and he had—what is not always denoted by "intellectual"—an intellect. But his mind was also intelligent: it was highly sceptical, and free from the bias of enthusiasm; furthermore, it was a free mind, in that his interests were not limited by the activities in which his talents were supreme. A sense of humour, a lively but kindly curiosity about human beings, and a love of society and good conversation, combined to prevent him from becoming either a doctrinaire or a scholarly recluse.[70]

One curious feature of this passage is the way Eliot, having begun by saying that Keynes was 'in any sense of the word, an intellectual', manages to praise him for *not* having those traits commonly associated with 'intellectuals' in at least one major sense of the word. Yet at the same time the passage does also hint at a positive conception of the role of the intellectual by situating it between the two alternatives indicated in its concluding phrase. Keynes was neither 'a doctrinaire' nor 'a scholarly recluse': these terms line up pretty exactly with the corresponding phrases in the preceding sentences: 'the bias of enthusiasm' on the one hand, and being 'limited by the activities in which his talents were supreme' on the other. The reader is left feeling that there *is* an admirable role to be filled here, but that it is perhaps not often filled by those commonly called 'intellectuals'. Keynes, the passage intimates, rises above the failings of the type thanks to his unshaken possession of native strengths. He may have been 'an intellectual', but the important thing is that he was (Eliot all but permits himself the sly oxymoron) an *English* intellectual.

And it is here that we need to return to the paradox of the Cretan Liar. This paradox was famously made the centrepiece of the 'theory of Types' in Bertrand Russell and A. N. Whitehead's *Principia Mathematica*, published in 1911. Epimenides (a Cretan) says: 'All Cretans are liars.' The paradox is normally stated as follows: either the statement is true, in which case the maker of the statement is *not* a liar, but therefore what the statement asserts is false, and hence his making of that statement is self-contradictory; or the statement is untrue, in which case the maker of the statement *is* a liar, but in that case the statement he makes is not to be believed, and so his making of it once again involves a form of self-contradiction. Russell's attempted resolution of the paradox (by means of a distinction between first-order and second-order statements) need not be pursued here;[71] my interest lies in the more pragmatic issue of what forms of general descriptions of intellectuals *by* intellectuals may involve some similar element of disabling self-contradiction. For this purpose it is important to note two things: first, that the identity of the speaker is vital—for a non-Cretan to assert the proposition would involve no self-contradiction; and second, the vast majority of general statements about a category to which the speaker belongs do not involve any self-contradiction either. To be examples of the Cretan Liar paradox, they must be statements which, if true of the class to which the speaker belongs, cannot be made by that speaker without self-contradiction.

Benda may indeed be caught in some such self-contradiction (as may Orwell in a different way, as I shall suggest in Ch. 15), but Eliot—the Eliot who had been able to acknowledge 'I should probably do the same thing myself' and who had identified the Cretan Liar in Benda—may at first sight appear to escape it. Or does he? In his later social criticism, Eliot thinks society should be guided not by intellectuals who happen merely to have achieved some kind of individual eminence, but rather by those figures who combine such eminence with a background in a traditional indigenous ruling class. Eliot wishes society to be guided by this view of his, but Eliot himself is not in fact a member of such an indigenous ruling class. This, we may say, is where disguising oneself as a corpse comes in. The figures who had traditionally exercised this kind of collective cultural authority in English history were all, in Pound's sense, 'corpses'. In some ways, the animating pathos of the middle and later years of Eliot's life was his struggle to become a type of person which one could only truly be if one had not had to struggle to become it. (Here, the question of intellectuals is only a metonymic expression of a profounder tension in Eliot's life.) This shifts the focus of the familiar paradox: the question now becomes not whether Eliot is, as it were, a *liar*, but whether he is genuinely a *Cretan* in the first place. Or, in the terms in which he had praised Keynes: Eliot was an intellectual, but was he an *English* intellectual? Denial of another kind was at work here, entailing paradoxes of its own.

But even that may not be the right note on which to end, not least because the later Eliot was prone to insist on his identity as a (restored) Christian even more than his identity as an (adopted) Englishman and certainly more than his identity as an (ambivalent) intellectual. And this can produce a disquieting sense in reading his later prose that most of the issues it treats belong to a shadow world. The union in Eliot of deep religious faith and deep intellectual scepticism occasionally expressed itself in the studied implication that this world is a theatre of mere appearance; England may be 'now and history', but reality is eternal and spiritual. The reader's disquiet is intensified by the recognition that once Eliot became a famous figure, his private as well his public utterances become guarded and mostly tactical, giving the relevant correspondent or public as much as was needed to maintain the relationship, always holding something in reserve. The courtliness seems to have become a mannerism, a way of staging himself as the polite and thoughtful Great Man who allows us to sense that celebrity has its burdens and its constraints. And just occasionally we are reminded that Ol' Possum is still there, lying lower than ever, and never to be taken entirely at face value.

W. H. Auden seems to have felt something of this disquieting sensation when reviewing Eliot's *Notes Towards the Definition of Culture*. Auden remarked the gracefully fatigued tones in which Eliot expressed his distance from mere earthly matters, including politics: 'Whig? Tory? All flesh is grass.'[72] But perhaps this was merely the most general of those increasingly general perspectives from which Eliot sought to outrank the claims of the 'specialist' and the 'doctrinaire': after all, Higher Ground doesn't come any higher than this, viewing all things from the moment at which we are lowered into the ground. Or, as it was almost put by the intellectual whom Eliot so admired, in the long run we are all corpses.

NOTES

1. T. S. Eliot, 'The idealism of Julien Benda', *Cambridge Review*, 49 (6 June 1928), 486–7.
2. T. S. Eliot, 'Professional or . . .', *Egoist*, 5 (1918), 61.
3. e.g., 'The moral vision is severely attenuated, the accompanying political thought unexamined and amateurish'; Michael Long, 'The politics of English Modernism: Eliot, Pound, and Joyce', in Edward Timms and Peter Collier (eds.), *Visions and Blueprints: Avant-Garde Culture and Radical Politics in Early Twentieth-Century Europe* (Manchester: Manchester University Press, 1988), 105.
4. Anon. [T. S. Eliot], 'Review of Georges Sorel, *Reflections on Violence*', *The Monist*, 27 (1917), 478. Eliot is identified as the reviewer in Donald Gallup, *T. S. Eliot: a Bibliography* (New York: Harcourt, 1969).
5. T. S. Eliot, 'Reflections on contemporary poetry' [review of *The Closed Door*, by Jean de Bosschère], *Egoist*, Oct. 1917, 133.
6. T. S. Eliot to Paul Elmer More, 3 Aug. 1929; P. E. More Papers, Firestone Library, Princeton.
7. Quoted in John D. Margolis, *T. S. Eliot's Intellectual Development 1922–1939* (Chicago: Chicago University Press, 1972), 115.
8. T. S. Eliot, 'Editorial', *The Criterion*, 17 (Oct. 1938), 65.
9. T. S. Eliot, *The Idea of a Christian Society* (London: Faber, 1939), 40.
10. T. S. Eliot, *After Strange Gods: A Primer of Modern Heresy* (London: Faber, 1934), 19–20.
11. T. S. Eliot, 'Thoughts after Lambeth' (1931), in Eliot, *Selected Essays*, 361.
12. Eliot, 'Idealism of Benda', 486; see the fuller discussion of his two reviews of Benda in Ch. 12, above.
13. T. S. Eliot, 'On the place and function of the clerisy', 4; this paper was prepared for a discussion at the Moot on 10 Nov. 1944; the typescript is now in the A. D. Lindsay

papers (L215) in the library of the University of Keele. For the records of the Moot, see below, n. 43.

14. Bruce Robbins, *Secular Vocations: Intellectuals, Professionalism, Culture* (London: Verso, 1993), 74.
15. Ibid. 75
16. T. S. Eliot, 'Catholicism and international order', *Christendom*, 3 (1933), 171–84, quotations at 171, 172.
17. T. S. Eliot, 'Commentary', *Criterion*, 5 (1927), 283.
18. Eliot, 'Catholicism and international order', 173, 174.
19. T. S. Eliot, 'Second thoughts about humanism', (1929), in *Selected Essays*, 448, 451.
20. Eliot, *After Strange Gods*, 12.
21. T. S. Eliot, 'Mr Milne and war', *Time and Tide*, 16 (26 Jan. 1935), 124.
22. T. S. Eliot, *Leadership and Letters*, address at Milton Academy, 3 Nov. 1948 (London: Cumberledge, 1948), 5.
23. T. S. Eliot, 'The responsibility of the man of letters in the cultural restoration of Europe', *The Norseman* (1945); repr. as 'The man of letters and the future of Europe', *Sewanee Review*, 53 (1945), 335.
24. T. S. Eliot, 'Introduction' to Josef Pieper, *Leisure the Basis of Culture* (London: Faber, 1952), 11–17, quotations at 11, 13, 16.
25. T. S. Eliot, 'On reading official reports', *New English Weekly* (11 May 1939), 61–2.
26. Eliot to J. M. Keynes, 5 Apr. 1934; Keynes papers, King's College, Cambridge
27. See *The Times*, 4 Apr. 1934.
28. Eliot to J. M. Keynes, 23 Mar. 1945; Keynes papers, King's.
29. 'Metoikos' [T. S. Eliot], 'Full employment and the responsibility of Christians', supplement to *The Christian News Letter*, 230 (28 Mar. 1945), 7–12.
30. T. S. Eliot, 'Michael Roberts', *New English Weekly* (13 Jan. 1949), 164.
31. T. S. Eliot, 'Charles Whibley', (1931) *Selected Essays*, 466.
32. T. S. Eliot, 'Views and Reviews', *New English Weekly* (7 Nov. 1935), 71–2.
33. T. S. Eliot, 'Editorial', *Criterion*, 18 (1939), 274.
34. T. S. Eliot, 'Journalists of yesterday and today', *New English Weekly* (8 Feb. 1940), 237.
35. Eliot to Philip Mairet, 21 Feb. 1941; Mairet papers, HRHRC, Austin, Texas. The 'people at Malvern' refers to the Anglican conference on the future role of the church, held at Malvern in 1941; for the letter referred to, see *The Times*, 14 Jan. 1941, 5.
36. T. S. Eliot, 'The English tradition; some thoughts as a preface to study', *Christendom*, 10 (1940), 105.
37. T. S. Eliot, 'Portugal', *Christian News Letter*, 42 (14 Aug. 1940).
38. In the following paragraphs I have reproduced or adapted some sentences from my essay 'The European Modernist as Anglican moralist: the later social criticism of T. S. Eliot', in Mark S. Micale and Robert L. Dietle (eds.), *Enlightenment, Passion, Modernity: Historical Essays in European Thought and Culture* (Stanford: Stanford University Press, 2000), 207–29, 438–44.
39. Eliot, *Idea*, 35, 74; see also the discussion in Ch. 3, above.
40. Ibid. 42, 40, 35, 37.
41. Ibid. 60–1.
42. For a reassessment of the role of this stratum, see Susan Pedersen and Peter Mandler (eds.), *After the Victorians: Private Conscience and Public Duty in Modern Britain* (London: Routledge, 1994).

43. The proceedings of the Moot, and their importance for Eliot's development, have been largely neglected by scholars, with one notable exception. The exception is the Oxford D.Phil. thesis by Roger Kojecky, published in revised form as *T. S. Eliot's Social Criticism* (London: Faber, 1971). Kojecky was clearly given access to Moot records which seem to be no longer available to scholars; from his acknowledgements one might infer that Helen Gardner facilitated access to papers held by the Eliot estate. I have consulted the material that is accessible, above all the papers of Sir Fred Clarke, at the Institute of Education in London, and the papers of A. D. Lindsay at Keele University (Clarke was initially a fairly regular member of the Moot; Lindsay was invited to join but seems never to have attended meetings). The Moot papers in the Clarke collection only cover the years 1939–42; some of these papers are duplicated in the Lindsay papers, which also contain items from later meetings, including the paper on 'the clerisy' referred to at n. 13 above.
44. Moot papers, 12–15 July 1940; Clarke collection.
45. Moot papers, 9–12 Feb. 1940; paper 17 by Adolf Löwe; Clarke Collection. See also the references to PPE in Ch. 20, below.
46. This and the succeeding paragraphs on the Moot again draw upon my essay 'The European modernist as Anglican moralist' cited in n. 38 above.
47. The best account of the development of Mannheim's thinking on this topic is David Kettler, Volker Meja, and Nico Stehr, *Karl Mannheim* (London: Tavistock, 1984), 129–50. See also Gunter W. Remmling, *The Sociology of Karl Mannheim* (London: Routledge, 1975); A. P. Simonds, *Karl Mannheim's Sociology of Knowledge* (Oxford: Oxford University Press, 1978); and Colin Loader, *The Intellectual Development of Karl Mannheim* (Cambridge, Cambridge University Press, 1985).
48. See Loader, *Intellectual Development*, 151.
49. See e.g., Alec R. Vidler, *Scenes From a Clerical Life: An Autobiography* (London: Collins, 1977), 116–19.
50. Quoted in Kettler et al., *Mannheim*, 137–8. Unfortunately, the date of the composition of these notes is not given.
51. Kettler et al., *Mannheim*, 154.
52. Eliot, 'Place and function of the clerisy', 3; see n. 56 below.
53. Eliot, 'Review of Mannheim's *Man and Society*', *Spectator*, 7 June 1940, 782.
54. Eliot, 'Planning and religion', *Theology*, 156 (1943), 102–6.
55. Eliot to Allen Tate, 13 Mar. 1945; Tate Papers, Princeton. Eliot's letter supplementing Mannheim's obituary appeared in *The Times*, 25 Jan. 1947, 7.
56. Copies of both these papers are to be found among the Lindsay papers; only the former is in the Clarke collection; the text of the latter paper is reproduced as an appendix in Kojecky, *Eliot's Social Criticism*, 240–8.
57. Eliot, 'Notes on Mannheim's paper', 2; Moot Papers, Clarke Collection.
58. Eliot, 'Notes towards a definition of culture I', *New English Weekly*, 21 Jan. 1943, 117.
59. Eliot, 'Place and function of the clerisy', 3.
60. Eliot's paper is dated 10 Nov.; Mannheim's response 20 Nov.; Eliot's reply 24 Nov.; Lindsay papers, L215.
61. T. S. Eliot, 'Notes towards a definition of culture, III', *New English Weekly*, 4 Feb. 1943, 136.
62. 'T. S. Eliot, 'Comments on Mannheim's letter', 1; Lindsay papers.

63. E. R. Curtius, 'Die Soziologie und ihre Grenzen [Sociology and its limits]', *Neue Schweizer Rundschau*, 22 (1929), elaborated in his *Deutscher Geist in Gefahr* [German Spirit in Danger] (1932); see the discussion in Remmling, *Sociology of Mannheim*, 74–5.
64. T. S. Eliot, paper entitled 'Some notes on Social Philosophy' prepared for the Moot meeting of July 1940; file 17, paper 123, Moot papers, Clarke Collection.
65. Letter from T. S. Eliot, 31 Oct. 1942; Moot papers, file 15, paper 92; Clarke collection.
66. Quoted in William Chace, *The Political Identities of Ezra Pound and T. S. Eliot* (Stanford: Stanford University Press, 1973), 221.
67. David Pocock, 'Symposium on Mr Eliot's "Notes" (III)', *Scrutiny*, 17 (1950), 273, 276.
68. Cf. Long's puzzlement that Eliot's later social criticism 'was, in English literary-critical circles, widely felt to constitute a challenging intellectual vision'; Long, 'Politics of English Modernism', 103–4.
69. Chace, *Political Identities of Pound and Eliot*, 207.
70. T. S. Eliot, 'John Maynard Keynes', *New English Weekly*, 16 May 1946, 47.
71. See Ray Monk, *Bertrand Russell; The Spirit of Solitude* (London: Vintage, 1997 [1st edn., 1996]), 188–9.
72. W. H. Auden, 'Port and nuts with the Eliots', *New Yorker* (23 Apr. 1949), 96–7.

14

Professorial Cackling: R. G. Collingwood

'Between the idea
And the reality
Between the motion
And the act
Falls the Shadow.'

I

In the Epilogue to his *An Essay on Metaphysics*, published in 1940, R. G. Collingwood defended the action of 'offering to the public what might seem essentially an academic essay, suitable only for readers who are already, like myself, committed to an interest in metaphysics', and he concluded, with memorable rhetorical excess:

> The fate of European science and European civilization is at stake. The gravity of the peril lies especially in the fact that so few recognize any peril to exist. When Rome was in danger, it was the cackling of the sacred geese that saved the Capitol. I am only a professorial goose, consecrated with a cap and gown and fed at a college table; but cackling is my job, and cackle I will.[1]

This passage asks to be read as the classic credo of the academic as intellectual: although the work done in one's professional capacity may appear to be somewhat technical or abstruse, it is in fact, so goes this plea, animated by larger concerns: such work is, it turns out, an attempt to address the fundamental roots of current ills. Nor are those ills inconsequential: nothing less than the 'fate of European civilization' is at stake. As a result, what might '*seem* essentially an academic essay' begins to acquire the dignity of a heroic gesture. In this particular case, the apocalyptic register, the classical allusion, and the feisty challenge are all characteristic of the final phase of Collingwood's writing more generally (he was to die in January 1943 at the comparatively early age of 53). But all this may only seem to strengthen the case for seeing him as an example of that species usually thought to be more common elsewhere in Europe—the philosopher whose enquiries into the deepest metaphysical questions are simultaneously a mode of political 'engagement' in his own society.

Collingwood does indeed provide an interesting test-case for any discussion of the question of intellectuals in twentieth-century Britain. A figure of undoubted intellectual distinction, he was one of the most original and creative English-language philosophers of the mid-century, and a scholar with an exceptionally wide range, spanning the practice of history and archaeology as well as several branches of philosophy. Moreover, he is far from being a forgotten worthy, one of those figures whom it requires a considerable act of historical imagination to see as possessing any but a narrowly local significance; to the contrary, his reputation may stand higher at the beginning of the twenty-first century than at any time during his life. What, above all, makes him seem an inescapable figure in any account of twentieth-century intellectuals is the fact that the book which bears the title *An Autobiography*, one of the most widely read of all his works, is largely given over to a forthright justification of the scholar's public role. Though it does not use the actual term, the book can be read as in effect a vindication of the philosopher as intellectual. And yet, as I shall suggest, Collingwood's is a far from straightforward case, and one which, for that reason, illumines the mechanisms by which, through the interaction of medium, message, audience, and reputation, cultural authority operates, or fails to operate, in a given situation. Rather than being a prize exhibit in a gallery of leading intellectuals in twentieth-century Britain, Collingwood may at first appear to be an intriguing example of that little-considered species, the intellectual manqué. However, viewed against the backdrop of conventions and expectations governing his milieu, he emerges as a representative of a different and less obvious form of denial.

II

In many ways, Collingwood's could be seen as a model academic career, at least until its final phase. His precocity was recognized by election to a Tutorship at Pembroke College, Oxford even before the announcement of his First in 'Greats' in the summer of 1912. He remained at Pembroke, a period of war service in naval intelligence apart, until 1935 when he was elected to the Waynflete Chair of Metaphysics which was attached to Magdalen College. Though always rather a remote figure, preoccupied with his own work, he was a sought-after teacher and successful lecturer. Throughout these years as a college tutor, he pursued his unusual dual career as both a philosopher and an ancient historian-cum-archaeologist; his bibliography lists over 120 publications on the history and archaeology of Roman Britain between the years 1913 and 1938, some in the publications of local archaeological societies, but many in the leading scholarly journals. His work in both philosophy and history met with considerable scholarly recognition: by the mid-1930s (when he was in his mid-forties) he was an Oxford Professor and a Fellow of the British Academy. Seen externally,

Collingwood's career appeared to conform quite closely to the prevailing academic norms, distinguished by its success in more than one field, perhaps, but not by any heterodox conception of his role or wayward public behaviour. By his actions and statements in the last few years of his life, however, he appeared to break out of this conventional mould, and part of my purpose here is to try to assess the adequacy of his own characterization of the role he played in that final period. This requires *un peu d'histoire*.[2]

In February 1938, a few days before his forty-ninth birthday, Collingwood suffered a stroke. There had been serious worries about his health for some time: as early as 1932 he had needed a period of recuperation after a breakdown. Now the doctor ordered a complete change of scene. Oxford gave him an entire year's medical leave from his duties, and Collingwood's immediate instinct was to turn to what had always been scenes of happiness and vigorous activity for him: first, the sea, as he single-handedly sailed his own yacht along the English Channel; and then the Lake District, where he had grown up in the shadow of the area's presiding literary deity, John Ruskin (whose friend and last secretary Collingwood's father had been).

Collingwood might well have died that February day in 1938. In fact he lived on for almost another five years, until January 1943, having finally resigned his chair in 1941. To ask what his subsequent reputation would have been *had* he died at the earlier date is, in his case, an unusually revealing, if also exceptionally intractable, counterfactual question. For the figure that Collingwood now cuts in the history of philosophy and in intellectual history more generally is to a considerable extent the result not just of what he wrote in those last five years, but, in a curious way, of the manner in which his deteriorating health, his circumstances, and the rapidity of his composition conspired to produce a particularly tangled bequest of published and unpublished material.

It could hardly be said that his earlier years had been unproductive. Apart from his extensive publications on the history and archaeology of Roman Britain, including the jointly authored book on the subject in the Oxford History of England series, he had several major books and shorter studies in philosophy to his credit, notably *Speculum Mentis* (1924), *An Essay on Philosophical Method* (1933), and *The Principles of Art* (1938). Not only was his philosophical work substantial enough to secure him his Oxford chair, an election no more controversial than most elections to Oxford chairs of philosophy, but he had made himself the leading authority on Romano-British inscriptions. Nonetheless, all of this would surely have earned him only a small footnote in the more conscientious surveys of twentieth-century British philosophy and academic scholarship.

Though he always repudiated the label of 'Idealist', Collingwood recognizably belonged to that school which, broadly speaking, took its inspiration from Hegel's critique of Kant. This school achieved something approaching a dominant institutional (if not intellectual) position within British philosophy between about 1880 and 1920, with its strongest centres in Oxford and the Scottish universities. But even in Oxford it was increasingly challenged in the first two decades of the century by the 'Realist' school, led by John Cook Wilson, who insisted on the existence of a reality independent of the mind's knowledge of it. Collingwood later labelled this school 'the minute philosophers', presumably on account of their focus on the primacy of close destructive criticism, often based on details of everyday linguistic usage, and their consequent tendency to be sceptical of the constructive power and positive social role of philosophy.

Collingwood was self-consciously, even wilfully, a philosophical loner, but his affinities with the British Idealist tradition (and still more with its Crocean Italian cousin) were manifest, and by the 1930s his situation could seem to involve some of the pathos that attaches itself to an epigone who has missed his historical bus. The coming generation of Ryle, Austin, Ayer, and company treated him respectfully, but their politeness confirmed rather than disguised the fact that he was no longer regarded as a philosophical antagonist with whom disagreement promised to be fruitful. Nor was he one of those figures who could compensate for professional neglect by basking in a wider celebrity, for he had cut no kind of public figure: as I shall show, he wrote practically nothing for the newspapers and wide-circulation periodicals of general culture, having none of the reputation with the non-academic public enjoyed by figures such as Russell or Joad, nor was he the *éminence grise* to fashionable aesthetic movements as G. E. Moore was to the Bloomsbury group. If the members of the third and fourth generation of British Idealists did not, in purely philosophical terms, rank alongside Green, Bradley, and Bosanquet, they had at least usually made some mark on their times through their involvement in social reform, educational administration, or other good causes. Collingwood had not followed that route, and so had he died in 1938 his publications and his institutional position might well have ensured that his name was as familiar to later generations as that of such luminaries as, say, H. H. Joachim or J. A. Smith.

As things have turned out, what Collingwood has been principally known for during the past half century is his work in the philosophy of history, a topic on which he had published comparatively little by 1938, though one on which he had, it is becoming increasingly clear, already written a considerable amount. The book on which this reputation almost entirely rests is *The Idea of History*, published in 1946 three years after Collingwood's death, edited by his former pupil T. M. (later Sir Malcolm) Knox, Professor of Moral Philosophy and subsequently Principal of St Andrews. The book has become something of a classic in a field not over-supplied with classics written in English, but for my present purposes it is important to remember that this standing was, of course, entirely posthumous.

Had Collingwood died in February 1938, then, he would now have had little claim on the attentions of the historian of intellectuals in Britain, whatever stature he might finally have been accorded by historians of philosophy. Even his most ardent admirers have to concede that he enjoyed only a 'modest reputation during his own lifetime', and my analysis here is confirmed, unwittingly, by one such scholar who observes that, at the time of his death, 'Collingwood was better known and more highly respected, among the more general audience to which he addressed himself, for his archaeological achievements' than for any of his other writings.[3] To take the measure of Collingwood's other attempts to address this 'more general audience' in the final years of his life, we have to return to the politically (and, for Collingwood, philosophically) charged months around the Munich crisis of 1938.

Collingwood's doctor was evidently a shrewd man, for in ordering his patient to take leave from his teaching post, he (according to Collingwood, at least) positively recommended him to carry on writing. Perhaps this was no more than an acknowledgement of the impossibility of breaking what had by now become a compulsive habit—Collingwood used to write out his lecture courses in full every year as well as drafting a great deal of other material he never published—but perhaps the doctor privately reckoned that Collingwood had better seize every opportunity to put his literary house in order. In any event, this particular patient responded to these unusual orders in an equally unusual way. First, in the course of a few weeks spent by Coniston Water that summer he wrote his autobiography, which, after some alarums (to which I shall return), was published by Oxford University Press in the following year. This, the most readable of his books, is something of a snare for the unwary, less a reliable account of his life and more a polemic written in the shadow of war and the likelihood of an early death.

Turning to the sea again, he then took ship for the Dutch East Indies. Captains of merchant steamers do not normally cut a large figure in the history of philosophy, but in the Preface to his *Essay on Metaphysics*, Collingwood offered his celebrated acknowledgement to the master of the M. V. *Alcinous* who 'rigged me up an open-air study on his own Captain's Bridge where I could work all day without interruption, and thus made it possible for me to write the first draft of the book during a voyage from England to Java under perfect conditions'. It was characteristic of Collingwood's mixture of confidence and intellectual isolation that his idea of 'perfect conditions' included neither library nor interlocutors.

Collingwood had sailed from England in late October 1938, returning in early April 1939, the outward and return journeys each taking approximately a month. During this period he not only wrote the book on metaphysics, but he also started work on a manuscript entitled 'The Principles of History', though he found that he got bogged down and decided to abandon it temporarily. In recent years it has become clear just how high were the hopes Collingwood had entertained for his projected book on the philosophy of history. For example, he wrote to his son in February 1939 from the East Indies: 'I have begun writing "The Principles of History", which will go down to posterity as my masterpiece,' and to a friend he described it as 'the book which my whole life has been spent in preparing to write'.[4] On that view of the matter, his life was never quite to arrive at its *telos*. He returned to his teaching duties in April 1939, and then spent much of the last two fully active years of his life writing *The New Leviathan*, which was published in 1942. *The New Leviathan* is a big book, and this, together with his other commitments and his declining health, seems to have prevented him from returning to the book on the philosophy of history which he had started in Java.

The decision to devote his remaining energies to a work of political philosophy reflected Collingwood's sense of the urgent need to address the crisis threatening what he, in the idiom of the time, called 'civilization'. For all his commitment, in the older Idealist manner, to engaging with the large questions of religion and philosophy, Collingwood's writing up till this point had adhered to the chaste standards of academic scholarship and had for the most part not directly addressed topical issues of politics and public affairs. But in the final phase he was possessed by an urgent desire to make philosophy into an effective public weapon against the various evils he believed were threatening Europe (like so many of his contemporaries, he tended to speak of 'Europe' and 'civilization' more or less interchangeably), and here the key text is *An Autobiography*.

The story this seductive little book tells is something of a 'conversion narrative' or even a kind of 'coming out': I too, it seems to say, used to cultivate my professional garden, but now I acknowledge my true nature as an instructor of *le grand public*. The book is certainly not marked by any academic reticence, and its outspokenness reaches a kind of climax in the final chapter (this was what provoked alarums within Oxford University Press). This chapter contains a swingeing attack on the allegedly craven attitude taken by both the government and the press in Britain towards the anti-Republican forces in Spain. And his discussion of the debate in 1938 over the adequacy or otherwise of the government's rearmament programme exhibits the cadences of the classic conspiracy theory, hinting darkly at how a conflict between 'a Fascist cabinet and the parliamentary constitution of the country' was 'hushed up in the government newspapers', while in speaking of the larger policy of appeasement he insists 'the country has been tricked'.[5]

The language of tricks, swindles, and rackets, as well as the implicit identity of the lonely, unpopular truth-teller, are uncannily reminiscent of the exactly contemporaneous writings of George Orwell. But this is Orwell without Orwell's grasp on social realities, and in the closing paragraphs of the book, Collingwood's private obsessions bulk disproportionately large. 'I know now that the minute philosophers of my youth [i.e. the Oxford 'Realist' school of Cook Wilson et al.], for all their profession of a purely scientific detachment from practical affairs, were the propagandists of a coming Fascism.' The Realists had in effect 'train[ed] up a generation of Englishmen and Englishwomen . . . as the potential dupes' of the sinister manipulators of public opinion.[6] In short, Cook Wilson, Prichard and the rest of them were responsible for Munich. It is not hard to see why the Delegates of the Oxford University Press might have murmured the odd reservation.

One can also see why, readable and engaging though the book is, it is somewhat problematic considered as an autobiographical record. Its preface famously declared that 'The autobiography of a man whose business is thinking should be the story of his thought,' but it was, inevitably, more a new instalment of his thought than an accurate narrative of its past; he was still thinking, but now more angrily than ever. The pugilistic note rises to a crescendo in the book's closing sentences: 'I know that all my life I have been engaged unawares in a political struggle, fighting against these things in the dark. Henceforth I shall fight in the daylight.'[7] 'Unawares' gives the game away: Collingwood now wishes that this political purpose *had* governed his work earlier in his life, and so he rearranges things to suit the implicit teleology. In reality, the philosophical and scholarly writing of his earlier years had, as I have already observed, more nearly conformed to the canons of academic detachment then endorsed in British universities, though one can in retrospect catch glimpses of an aspiration to make philosophical thought tell on the world beyond the walls (nor should one forget that when his friend Guido de Ruggiero was imprisoned by the Fascist regime in Italy, Collingwood translated his *History of European Liberalism* as a gesture of solidarity). Perhaps his own insistence in *An Autobiography* on the magnitude and recentness of this shift in his outlook helps to account for the book's sublime unawareness of its own Oxford parochialism: Collingwood constantly berates his colleagues for their shortcomings, especially their lack of involvement in the world, but it is always his *colleagues* upon whom his critical attention is fastened, those 'thirty or forty professional philosophers in Oxford'[8] whose opinions clearly mattered to him enormously for all his proud declarations of complete intellectual independence. (In these terms, his life's project of bringing about a '*rapprochement* between philosophy and history' can also be seen to owe a good deal to the distinctive requirements of the Oxford 'Greats' school.)

Like the majority of critics, he wrote most effectively and discriminatingly about the things he knew well, as in his detailed and cogent attacks on the pretensions of scientific psychology, the vogue discipline of the inter-war period. Here he could draw on his Idealist inheritance to unmask the 'modern pretence' that the mind could be reduced to the workings of appetite and sensation, upholding instead 'the sciences of mind proper, logic and ethics, the sciences of reason and will'. As in his writings on history and art, Collingwood is at his best when exposing the limitations of natural scientific models for understanding what is distinctive about human action. But in his late writings, Collingwood is not always at his best. Even one of his most measured and sympathetic modern admirers speaks of his 'stridency of manner and unevenness of performance', and he also concedes that 'Collingwood's writings are . . . sometimes disfigured by an apparent arrogance or intransigence.'[9] But then Collingwood was a philosophical obsessive, as perhaps true philosophers have to be, locked in an inner conceptual struggle from which little could deflect him. 'When I am unwell, I have only to begin work on some piece of philosophical writing, and all my ailments are forgotten until I leave off.'[10]

Contemporaries had long remarked Collingwood's absorption in his work and his consequent removal from the world: this is what made his late declarations of political purpose, above all in the autobiography, all the more striking or perturbing, leading to attempts to explain them away as the results of ill health or even, improbably (and entirely on the basis of his having grown a beard), of a late conversion to Marxism.[11] But there was, I would argue, something more than personal involved here, and that in two ways: first, Collingwood provides yet another example of the way in which the ambivalence about specialization that is built into the scholar's role tends to issue in proud declarations of a broader social justification, declarations that are unaccompanied by any sustained attention to the actual processes of dissemination; and secondly, the form taken by his desire to 'fight in the daylight' may itself be seen to be part of a larger cultural style, one that is particularly easy to misread. A closer look at Collingwood's late 'cackling' is in order here.

III

One of the several inadvertently revealing moments in *An Autobiography* comes when Collingwood has been summarizing the development of his thinking about the nature of historical knowledge (including his celebrated demolition of 'scissors-and-paste history'): he felt that by the early 1930s he had reached the point at which 'the main problems are now solved', but he had not yet published the fruits of his thinking. 'By this time', he recorded, 'I had in my head a great deal which I believed the public would value; and the only way of giving it to the public was by writing books.'[12] But it is not at all clear who this 'public' was nor why he thought it would 'value' his thoughts on this relatively technical subject (nor, indeed, why 'writing books' was the *only* way to reach it).

It is hard to know what public Collingwood's philosophical books *did* reach. They were published by Oxford University Press, usually in editions of 1,000 or 1,500 copies; none was reprinted during his lifetime (their standing, such as it has been, has come subsequently, spurred by the success of *The Idea of History* above all).[13] It was a public which could, at least in part, be thought of as non-specialist, especially since the readership for works of philosophy that could be called strictly 'professional' at this point was very small. The civic universities in England were enduring very straitened times in the 1930s: where philosophy departments existed, they often consisted of a professor and a couple of assistants. Numbers were somewhat greater in the four Scottish universities, but only at Oxford was there any significant concentration of academic teachers of philosophy. A modern calculation suggests that at the beginning of the 1950s, by which time there had been considerable university expansion, there were 'about two hundred philosophy teachers in England . . . (a quarter of them in Oxford)'.[14] Some copies of Collingwood's books were also sold to scholars and libraries abroad, but nonetheless the strictly 'professional' market in philosophy was at this time tiny.

Without selling in any great numbers, therefore, Collingwood's philosophical books did presumably reach a very small public which was, under one description, 'non-specialist', and the fact that they were sometimes reviewed in the general cultural weeklies and quarterlies may be seen as confirming this. It was a public which, at its largest, may be thought of as some combination of, on the one hand, the readers of *Mind* and members of The Royal Institute of Philosophy (founded in 1925 with the aim of making philosophy available to a wider, non-student, public), and on the other, readers of the weighty cultural periodicals such as *The Criterion* and *Scrutiny*. Certainly, the aim of trying to reach such a public was a recurring feature of Collingwood's rhetoric of self-justification (though not, as I have repeatedly insisted, of his alone). The Preface to *The Principles of Art*, for example, contains a representative specimen of the genre: 'Everything written in this book has been written in the belief that it has a practical bearing, direct or indirect, upon the condition of art in England in 1937, and in the hope that artists primarily, and secondarily persons whose interest in art is lively and sympathetic will find it of some use to them.'[15] Such statements of intent are a recurring expression of the logic of the social position of academics in the humanities; Collingwood was particularly given to them as a way of emphasizing his distance from, and independence of, the professional community by which he, in turn, felt neglected.

Print was, of course, still the unchallenged medium (apart from actual lectures and addresses): in the inter-war period radio was only slowly coming to be taken seriously by the educated class, and the age of the telly-don was almost unimaginable. The absence of such media did mean that lectures and addresses were correspondingly more important, and they were one means of associating one's ideas with a particular personal manner and even appearance, qualities which would otherwise be unknown outside one's immediate circle. Collingwood, however, a few addresses to local archaeological societies apart, did practically no public speaking of this sort, and took no part in the kind of broader educational or political activities that made, for example, Tawney or Lindsay known to quite diverse sections of the population.

From this point of view, an analysis of the complete bibliography of Collingwood's writings is revealing. He wrote, of course, for professional philosophical journals, such as *Mind* and the *Proceedings of the Aristotelian Society*; wearing his other hat, he also produced numerous specialized articles for the *Journal of Roman History* or, less purely professional but still more arcane, *The Proceedings of the Cumberland and Westmorland Antiquarian and Archaeological Society*. But apart from these specialized publications, the one 'general' periodical for which Collingwood wrote with any frequency (in this case almost entirely as a book reviewer) was the *Oxford Magazine*. It is true that Oxford bulked larger in the national culture in the inter-war period than it does now, the conception of 'the national culture' shared by those with some connection with Oxford having at that point been less successfully challenged by notions of plural 'cultures'. Still, book-reviews in the local parish magazine, even of a parish with such more-than-local significance, represent a somewhat muted form of 'public' intervention. This is not, of course, to imply that all academics either were or ought to have been devoting their energies to attempting to address such wider publics; it is, rather, to try to identify more precisely what Collingwood's career tells us about the mechanisms for successfully reaching such publics in a given historical situation. Collingwood, after all, repeatedly declared towards the end of his life that this was what philosophers should try to do and what he had, at least in implicit or indirect ways, aspired to do. Moreover, Collingwood had an exceptional intellectual range: precisely because he could speak with authority not just on the different branches of philosophy, but on art, religion, and history as well, he was unusually well placed to comment on specialized work in these areas from a wider perspective. It is in this context that the fact of all those reviews appearing in the *Oxford Magazine*, rather than in the likes of the *New Statesman* or *Time and Tide* or even the *Times Literary Supplement* (though special considerations applied there on account of its practice of anonymity), starts to acquire some significance.

Even so, to overemphasize this significance might be to fall prey to one kind of anachronism here. For it was surely the case that circumstances of upbringing, education, and social experience made it much more natural for inter-war Oxford dons (likely, in the nature of the case, to be the products of late-Victorian and Edwardian society) to assume that the 'public' which really counted was a very small one, a 'public' which could be encountered in person at high tables, at weekend house-parties, on the governing councils of learned and public bodies, and in the reading-rooms of clubs and professional associations (some, at least, of which scenes of social contact remind us of the difficulties women were likely to have in becoming accepted members of this elite). Something like this surely sustained those numerous small publications, such as *Christendom* or *The Criterion*, which carried weight in their particular circles, and were to that extent effective not just in articulating certain (self-described) 'unpopular' views but also in establishing and furthering individual reputations. These publications are in this respect the print equivalent of those groups of conventionally suited gentlemen who met in the sorts of discussion- and dining-clubs which seemed to proliferate in the years before the Second World War and who still managed to think of themselves as 'the country'—or at any rate as the part of it that really mattered.[16] Collingwood may himself have been something of a recluse and dismissive of conventional socializing; but maybe just because he moved so little in circles of power and influence he was the more inclined to take the established channels of expression for granted: a truth laid out in the *Oxford Magazine* could seem like a truth made powerful in the world.

IV

After completing his autobiography, with its ringing affirmation of the philosopher's public role, Collingwood lived to publish two large philosophical works: *An Essay on Metaphysics*, written, as we have seen, largely during his East Indian voyage, and *The New Leviathan*, written in London and the country during the early years of the war (in both cases his isolation from his peers was almost complete). His own sense of the informing purpose of such works was most succinctly stated in a letter written to an archaeologist friend early in the war: 'When the war broke out I saw that the whole business was due to the fact that everybody concerned was in a completely muddled condition about the first principles of politics and, examining my own mind, I saw that I had plenty of ideas which it would be a public service to state.'[17] The casual excesses of his language betray the rationalistic perspective he brought to the understanding of contemporary political and social processes—the 'whole' business, 'everybody' concerned, 'completely muddled', and so on. However much one may admire the attempt to trace the roots of political ills to confusions over 'first principles', there is more than a hint of the *déformation professionnelle* of the philosopher here in assuming that a brisk dose of clear thinking will be a sufficient remedy. Certainly, it is hard to see any directly illuminating connections between 'the whole business' of the war and the lengthy discussion of Kant on transcendental analytics and similar topics in the body of *An Essay on Metaphysics*. That they were, somehow, present to Collingwood's mind was indicated in his spikily defiant closing paragraph about 'cackling' quoted at the opening of this chapter, and yet it must be doubtful whether many inhabitants of the modern Rome were alerted to danger by this particular professorial goose, trying to make itself heard above the cackle of Messerschmitts and Doerniers.

Quite what 'public service' was being performed by stating the ideas expressed in *An Essay on Metaphysics* would be hard to say without recourse to those conventional notions of the broader social role of specialized intellectual enquiry which Collingwood seemed at this point to be repudiating. The book contains his most fully worked-out statement of his idea of metaphysics as the study of 'absolute presuppositions', those notions which lie deeper than propositional statement and which are their foundation, notions which are implicit in practice and not always amenable to being explicitly formulated by those engaged in the practice. Since Collingwood seems to have maintained that such presuppositions could not meaningfully be said to be true or false, there has long been a question about whether he was here turning metaphysics into a form of intellectual history, the charting of successive cultural *Gestalts*, and, more generally, whether in the last five years of his life Collingwood had effectively dissolved the distinction between philosophy and history (as Knox, disapprovingly, implied that he had). It was certainly part of the thoroughgoing historicism of this final phase of his thought that he did not believe, in Kantian manner, that the preconditions of 'our' practices of enquiry were universal and timeless—absolute presuppositions are always changing. Almost alone among philosophers in Britain at the time, Collingwood came to believe that philosophy had to be undertaken historically, but not, it would seem, that philosophy thereby became a subfield of the discipline of history. Reflection on the presuppositions of enquiry in the past, as well as of those in the present, equally involves the aim, which can never be completely realized, of making an inchoate set ot presuppositions coherent. Some critical standards not internal to the absolute presuppositions themselves could, his best modern commentators suggest, be appealed to as a way of staving off complete relativism.[18]

Relativism is the last charge anyone could bring against *The New Leviathan*, as is indicated by its grandly declarative subtitle: *Man, Society, Civilization and Barbarism*. Nor could the book be accused of limited ambition: its aim was nothing less than to bring Hobbes 'up to date', to show how the relations between 'man' and 'the state' were to be understood in the twentieth century. The editor of the modern edition, though inclined to make some large claims for the book's value as a work of political philosophy, has, reluctantly, to concede that its alleged importance has been almost wholly overlooked in the half century or so since its original publication.[19] Its neo-Idealist approach was profoundly out of step with the protocols governing the practice of analytic philosophy in the post-war decades, and even now it requires an effort to recognize its confidently taxonomic style as a form of philosophical argument. It is a curiously assertive work, carried along by a kind of definitional high-handedness: 'Civilization is a thing of the mind; an inquiry into its nature, therefore, belongs to the sciences of mind, and must be pursued by the method proper to those sciences,' and so on.[20] To find a work of comparable scope and idiosyncrasy, one would have to jump forwards thirty years to Michael Oakeshott's much more elegantly written *On Human Conduct*, both books hinting at the possibility of an Englished Hegel, where the domineering will of '*der Staat*' is softened into the quieter civilities of 'voluntary associations'. The comparison is a reminder of the several close intellectual affinities between Collingwood and Oakeshott, the full extent of which have still, it would seem, to be properly charted. It is also a reminder that even the relatively cloistered Oakeshott made many more recognizable contributions to political polemics, ranging from his targeted assaults on 'collectivism' in the late 1940s to his wide-ranging denunciation of 'rationalism in politics'.

The New Leviathan was in one sense the ailing Collingwood's war effort, an attempt to do his bit in the only way he knew. But for all its topical denunciation of 'German barbarism', it is hard to identify, in its procession of bare abstractions, any compelling insights into the particularity of actual societies in the middle of the twentieth century. One cannot help remarking the gap which separated the stirring credo of the 'engaged' philosopher given in *An Autobiography* from the professorial austerities of the two works which followed. Publishing large philosophical tomes with the Oxford University Press suggests a very restrained, and oddly conventional, form of 'cackling'. And here Collingwood may, for once, have been a more representative figure than he was usually willing to allow, cultivating the familiar academic genres without perhaps attending sufficiently closely to the mechanisms by which the fruits of scholarly labour might be made effective in the wider society.

Moreover, Collingwood's understanding of, and hence engagement with, his own society, was, like that of so many of his educated contemporaries in inter-war Britain, fatally hamstrung by a too easy acceptance of the idea of cultural decline. From his first major work, *Speculum Mentis*, published in 1924, in which he spoke of individualism as the 'disease' of modern society, up to *The New Leviathan*, he inveighed against the 'soullessness' of industrial civilization and mourned the loss of the unifying power of religion. 'What is wrong with us is precisely the detachment of these forms of experience—art, religion, and the rest—from one another; and our cure can only be their reunion in a complete and undivided life.'[21] The sentiments, if not the phrasing, are akin to Eliot's laments about 'the dissociation of sensibility' (Collingwood was an occasional contributor to the *Criterion*): the Renaissance and the scientific revolution of the seventeenth century are, as usual, fingered as the culprits, a misguided scientism as the outcome. Similarly, *The Principles of Art*, published in 1938, includes a sustained philippic, worthy of Leavis at his most irascible, against the decline of taste in modern society, with its 'insatiable craving' for cheap 'amusements'.[22] His writing contains several asides about agriculture as the only possible basis for a sound society, together with frequent echoes of the 'Lake District plus uplift' school of social thought, extolling 'the deep primitive, almost unconscious emotion of the man who, wrestling with the earth, sees the labour of his hands and is satisfied'.[23] And behind it all stands Ruskin, the great, untamed Jeremiah of industrial civilization, the great nostalgist for the harmony between heaven and hands supposedly exhibited by the medieval mason. Though not normally placed in this company, Collingwood surely belongs in these respects on the conservative wing of the so-called 'culture-and-society' tradition, with its deep yearning for the modern world to go away.

This limitation was especially damaging where the question of the kinds of public reached by different media was concerned. Like so many of his culturally conservative contemporaries, Collingwood saw the arrival of a popular press as an unmitigated evil, a Fall from the timeless Eden represented, it usually transpired, by the newspapers and periodicals of the high Victorian period.

> The newspapers of the Victorian age made it their first business to give their readers full and accurate information about matters of public concern. Then came the *Daily Mail*, the first English newspaper for which the word 'news' lost its old meaning of facts which

a reader ought to know if he was to vote intelligently, and acquired the new meaning of facts, or fictions, which it might amuse him to read. By reading such a paper, he was no longer teaching himself to vote. He was teaching himself not to vote; for he was teaching himself to think of 'the news' not as the situation in which he was to act, but as a mere spectacle for idle moments.[24]

For all this passage's rhetorical brio, as cultural history it is blinkered and tendentious. There were plenty of publications in the Victorian period which provided more varied fare than reports of parliamentary debates, and Collingwood is simply refusing to recognize the diversity of functions which a modern newspaper fulfilled.[25] In its untroubled confidence about what is and is not of 'public concern', the passage is essentially reproaching all other papers for failing to be (an idealized version of) *The Times*, and behind the closing sentence one may detect a hankering for the conditions of the ancient city-state, a small-scale deliberative community (of those qualified for citizenship), rather than any serious engagement with the realities of mass democracy. His grasp of the mechanisms of modern politics suffered from a similar misplaced purism and lack of realism, as, for example, in his condemnation of Lloyd George for appealing to voters' pecuniary self-interest in recommending the social legislation of the Asquith government: 'Mr Lloyd George became to me a landmark, second only to the *Daily Mail*, in the corruption of the electorate.'[26] These were not, of course, unusual views among members of the traditionally educated classes before 1914; for someone attempting to be a 'gloves off' philosopher in 1938, however, they were surely a severe handicap.

Since my argument is that Collingwood furnishes an instructive example in how filling the role of an intellectual in the cultural sense is always a matter of degree, not a once-and-for-all identity, it is important not to overstate a case in either direction.[27] In his last years, Collingwood did 'speak out' on certain matters, the publication of his controversial autobiography being not the least of the evidence to be cited here. His hostility to what he saw as the linked evils of the policy of appeasement and the quietism of professional philosophers was expressed in other ways, too. According to one of the best-informed of his modern admirers, 'Collingwood wrote to the *Times* to complain about the political complacency of many Oxford philosophers and visited the Labour Party headquarters to persuade its leaders to reject appeasement.'[28] He strongly supported A. D. Lindsay's celebrated anti-appeasement candidacy in the 1938 Oxford bye-election, writing to him:

My dear Lindsay—I am leaving for the East tomorrow but I cannot go without sending you my deepest good wishes for your success in your candidature. I do not think that the country has ever in all its history passed through a graver crisis than that in which it is now involved. I am appalled by the apathy with which our situation is regarded by a great many of us, and by the success which the Government has had in keeping the country as a whole from knowing the truth. Your candidature shows that the spirit of English democracy is not extinct. I hope that it still survives among those who have to vote next week.[29]

This displays undoubted strength of conviction and fighting political spirit. All the same, he *was* 'leaving for the East tomorrow', and although the state of his health obviously imposed its own imperatives, the outcome was that even on this issue Collingwood played no part on the public stage.

A similar balance needs to be struck in examining what ought to be one of the prize exhibits in the case for Collingwood in the role of intellectual, his essay entitled 'Fascism and Nazism', published in 1940. To the text as printed in *Philosophy*, Collingwood appended a note saying that the piece had been written 'immediately after reading Mr Joad's *Appeal to Philosophers*'.[30] Joad's article, which had initially been an address to the Aristotelian Society at its meeting held in Cambridge in February 1940, was a call to philosophers to return to 'the practical concerns' which had been, he contended, at the heart of 'the classical tradition in philosophy'. The article is a pretty standard example of the dialectical relationship between specialization and laments-about-specialization that I touched on earlier and shall return to in Ch. 20. The war provided the heightened atmosphere favourable to the 'generalist' case, and in any event the broad position was one with which Joad, arch-popularizer and early radio don, was already intimately, perhaps even damagingly, associated. Not surprisingly, he seized on some statements from Collingwood's recently published autobiography which he found gratifyingly congenial on this score, and Collingwood in his turn then broadly endorsed Joad's plea.[31]

One of the striking features of the short essay which Collingwood published in response was just how little it rested on the authority of 'the philosopher'. Ostensibly, it is an enquiry into the nature of Fascism and Nazism, but in practice it is an assertion of the historical and spiritual centrality of Christianity to European civilization. This was a prominent theme in much anti-Communist as well as anti-Nazi cultural analysis in the 1930s, and one which Collingwood went on to endorse most emphatically in *The New Leviathan*. Quite how to characterize the status of Collingwood's remarks on this occasion, however, is not altogether obvious. The reader (the reader of *Philosophy* in 1940) is asked simply to accept the truth of such meta-historical statements as 'the vital warmth at the heart of a civilization is what we call a religion'.[32] The style is assertive rather than analytical, and historical evidence is conspicuous by its absence. In so far as there is a more specific thesis to the essay, it is the claim that the fundamental reason why Fascism and Nazism have flourished in Italy and Germany is the underlying strength of 'Paganism' in these countries, Christianity having put down only shallow or relatively recent roots there. In itself this is, to put it mildly, a debatable claim, and in his writings of this period Collingwood, like Eliot and several other spokesmen who trumpeted Christianity as the antidote to the dictators of both left and right, seems to underplay the link between Catholicism and Fascism in Latin Europe. But again the lack of any sociological analysis of the support for these movements, or of any mention of the specific political means by which they had come to power, or indeed of any reference to actual events of the 1930s, is striking.

However, perhaps anachronism threatens from another quarter here—and this bears on the question of the limited extent to which Collingwood can be said to have played the role of the intellectual in this setting—for we have to acknowledge the possibility that some members, at least, of the 'cultivated elite' in the 1930s did actually take this highly intellectualist meta-historical account pretty much for granted. To a certain, restricted, readership these may have seemed vital truths, in urgent need of restatement, a task to which a scholar of Collingwood's standing brought an appropriate cultural authority even if not (as it may seem now) much in the way of directly relevant knowledge. Thus, when Collingwood writes that 'the union between philosophy and history is what will save Europe', indeed that 'nothing else can', one has to try to imagine why this might not have seemed to the implied reader to be at best vapid, at worst a kind of intellectual *folie de grandeur*. Though written in the summer of 1940, he seems to be treating Panzer divisions and bomber squadrons as epiphenomenal, mere symptoms of the spiritual disease which had been gnawing away at the heart of 'Europe'—where that term did not conjure up armed states and competing economies, but some idealized cultural or spiritual entity, only fully manifest in the works of Dante, Rembrandt, Racine, Kant, Beethoven, and their (few) peers. The implication is that the only way in which Europe could be 'saved' would be by recovering or repossessing the spirit at the heart of such imaginative achievements, a repossession that would entail acknowledging and attempting to sustain the religion of which such creations were, if sometimes unknowingly, the fruit. When placed in the company of the increasingly professionalized analytical philosophers of the inter-war period, Collingwood can seem an eccentric figure; but placed alongside contributors to *The Criterion* or the self-described 'Christian sociologists'—alongside, indeed, figures such as T. S. Eliot or Christopher Dawson—he can be seen as expressing something of an anti-utilitarian, anti-'pagan', consensus.

V

Collingwood's œuvre has continued to be enlarged by the publication of material left in manuscript at his death. While this will, quite properly, affect the scholarly interpretation of his ideas, it obviously has no bearing on his public standing in his lifetime, and, indeed, it may not greatly modify the more general appreciation of his work. It seems likely that for most readers the two works by which Collingwood has long been best known—the autobiography and the *Idea of History*—will remain the most widely read, and with good reason. It was in these two books that he came nearest, albeit largely posthumously, to realizing his ideal of persuading a wide readership to think seriously about the distinctiveness of history as a form of knowledge. As he put it in a 1937 review, 'the advent of history, in the full modern sense of the word', took place in the course of the nineteenth century. 'But it was a change to which English philosophers, sunk in their traditional obsession with the methods and principles of natural science, were blind, and for the most part are still blind. Apart from two or three books, the whole vast literature of English philosophy in the last century contains no reference to this event, no attempt to estimate its significance or analyse its implications.'[33] As in so much of Collingwood's later writing, the combative exaggerations ('sunk in', 'obsession', 'no reference') risk alienating as much as persuading the uncommitted reader. But in this case, Collingwood may have been accurately pinpointing what his own most enduring contribution would prove to be.

There is an undeniable drama in the way in which this intellectually lonely man drove himself on, in the face of professional indifference and ill health, to try to work out the full implications of this 'great event in the history of the world', as J. B. Bury had called the 'advent of history'.[34] His efforts could at times seem arrogant, opaque, or even misguided, but perhaps he has had his posthumous reward as, first, his work almost single-handedly kept alive an anti-positivist understanding of history through the dark days dominated by the narrow sympathies of analytic philosophers and the brisk empiricism of political historians, and then, more recently, as he has come to be seen as the presiding spirit of a remarkable efflorescence in the English-speaking world of enquiries into the nature and scope of historical understanding. After returning from the East Indies in April 1939, Collingwood wrote to a friend of the start he had made on 'The Principles of History': 'If I can finish that, I shall have nothing to grumble at.'[35] Although he never did finish it, he might still have felt, contemplating his extraordinary standing in the philosophy of history today, that, on that score at least, he had nothing to grumble at. Just how effective his 'cackling' had been, however, is altogether more open to question—or, in Eliot's terms, 'Between the idea | And the reality | Between the motion | And the act | Falls the Shadow'.[36] Part of the fascination of Collingwood's career to the historian of intellectuals in Britain lies in the difficulty of deciding how far he represents a confident, well-placed academic culture which, in the pre-war period at least, felt no need to accommodate itself to the role increasingly referred to as that of 'the intellectual', and how far, for all that career's philosophical and scholarly achievement, it exhibits one distinctively British way of being an intellectual manqué.

NOTES

1. R. G. Collingwood, *An Essay on Metaphysics* (1940), rev. edn., ed. Rex Martin (Oxford: Oxford University Press, 1998), 343.
2. Some sentences in the following paragraphs draw upon my 'When the goose cackled', *TLS*, 27 Aug. 1999, 3–6.
3. David Boucher, *The Social and Political Thought of R. G. Collingwood* (Cambridge: Cambridge University Press, 1989), 21, 23.
4. Collingwood to his son, 14 Feb. 1939, quoted in Jan van der Dussen, *History as a Science: The Philosophy of R. G. Collingwood* (The Hague: Martinus Nijhoff, 1981), 61; Collingwood to Gerald Simpson (late spring 1939); quoted in editors'

introduction to R. G. Collingwood, *The Principles of History*, ed. W. H. Dray and W. J. van der Dussen (Oxford: Oxford University Press, 1999), p. lviii.

5. R. G. Collingwood, *An Autobiography* (1939), new edn. with intro. by Stephen Toulmin (Oxford: Oxford University Press, 1978), 165, 166.
6. Ibid. 167, 48–9.
7. Ibid. 167.
8. Ibid. 85.
9. W. H. Dray, *History as Re-enactment: R. G. Collingwood's Idea of History* (Oxford: Oxford University Press, 1999 [1st edn. 1995]), 30.
10. Collingwood, *Autobiography*, 117.
11. See the entry by T. M. Knox in the *DNB 1941–50*, 168–70; and the obituary notice by R. B. McCallum in the *Proceedings of the British Academy*, 29 (1943), 464–8.
12. Collingwood, *Autobiography*, 117.
13. See D. S. Taylor, *R. G. Collingwood, A Bibliography* (New York: Garland, 1988).
14. Jonathan Rée, 'English philosophy in the fifties', *Radical Philosophy*, 65 (1993), 6.
15. R. G. Collingwood, *The Principles of Art* (Oxford: Oxford University Press, 1938), p. vi.
16. For Collingwood's own participation in such groups in inter-war Oxford, especially those concerned to apply or revive a Christian perspective, see James Patrick, *The Magdalen Metaphysicals: Idealism and Orthodoxy at Oxford 1901–1945* (Macon, Ga.: Mercer University Press, 1985); for the increased importance of such a Christian perspective more generally in the 1930s and 1940s, see my 'The European Modernist as Anglican moralist: the later social criticism of T. S. Eliot', in Mark S. Micale and Robert L. Dietle (eds.), *Enlightenment, Passion, Modernity: Historical Essays in European Thought and Culture* (Stanford: Stanford University Press, 2000), esp. 211–21.
17. Collingwood to O. G. S. Crawford, quoted in the editors' introduction to Collingwood, *Principles of History*, p. lx.
18. See Rex Martin's introduction to Collingwood, *Essay on Metaphysics*, esp. pp. xxx–xxxviii. In this paragraph I have drawn on some phrases from the entry on Collingwood in *The Oxford Dictionary of National Biography* (Oxford: Oxford University Press, 2004), jointly written by Bernard Williams and myself.
19. R. G. Collingwood, *The New Leviathan, or Man, Society, Civilization, and Barbarism* (1942), rev. edn. with Introduction by David Boucher (Oxford: Oxford University Press, 1992), p. xiv. The revised edition includes additional material from the Bodleian manuscript hoard, notably the text of Collingwood's 1940 lectures on 'Goodness, rightness, utility', which display, from another angle, his continuing antagonistic preoccupation with the work of Prichard, Ross, and the Oxford 'Realists'.
20. Ibid. 280.
21. R. G. Collingwood, *Speculum Mentis, or The Map of Knowledge* (Oxford: Clarendon Press, 1924), 36.
22. Collingwood, *Principles of Art*, 96–7.
23. Quoted from an unpublished essay entitled 'Man goes mad', in Boucher, *Social and Political Thought*, 235.
24. *Autobiography*, 155.
25. For evidence on both these points, see Matthew Engel, *Tickle the Public: One Hundred Years of the Popular Press* (London: Gollancz, 1996), 21–43.

26. *Autobiography*, 156.
27. As, it may be felt, some of his modern admirers sometimes do. Consider, for example, this report of Michael Foot's remarks at the opening of the Collingwood centre at the University of Swansea: 'Mr Foot suggested that Collingwood reminded him of Aneurin Bevan, who was similarly disposed to philosophical arguments and their application to practical problems. He suggested that Bevan had certainly read Collingwood and learned much from him.' David Boucher, 'Editor's Introduction', *Collingwood Studies*, 1 (1994), pp. ix–x.
28. Boucher, 'Editor's introduction', *Collingwood Studies* 1, p. x.
29. Quoted in Drusilla Scott, *A. D. Lindsay: A Biography* (Oxford: Blackwell, 1971), 251.
30. R. G. Collingwood, 'Fascism and Nazism', *Philosophy*, 15 (1940), 176; the essay is reprinted in R. G. Collingwood, *Essays in Political Philosophy*, ed. David Boucher (Oxford: Oxford University Press, 1989), 187–96.
31. C. E. M. Joad, 'Appeal to philosophers', *Philosophy*, 15 (1940), 400–16.
32. 'Fascism and Nazism', 187.
33. R. G. Collingwood, review of R. Klibansky and H. J. Paton (eds.), *Philosophy and History: Essays Presented to Ernst Cassirer*, in *English Historical Review*, 52 (1937), 141, 146.
34. Quoted by Collingwood in his review of *Philosophy and History*, *EHR*, 142.
35. Collingwood to Gerald Simpson (late spring 1939); quoted in editors' introduction to Collingwood, *Principles of History*, p. lviii.
36. T. S. Eliot, 'The Hollow Men' (1925), in *Collected Poems, 1909–1962* (London: Faber, 1963), 91–2.

15

Other People: George Orwell

> 'Of all the writers who appeal to the post-war intelligentsia, he is far and away the most potent... apart from incessantly hearing his name spoken, we can hardly pass a month without reading an article on him.'

I

No major writer in English can have used the terms 'intellectuals' and 'intelligentsia' as frequently as George Orwell. Anyone who has read extensively in Orwell's essays and journalism will recognize his tendency to flog his hobby-horses unmercifully, and on few subjects was he as finger-jabbingly insistent as on the alleged failings of 'the intelligentsia', more especially 'the Left intelligentsia'. In general terms, his denunciations of the dishonesty and slavishness of intellectuals are well known, though in all the abundant literature on Orwell there seems to be no proper analysis of the development and content of his views on this topic. Apart from the intrinsic interest of such an analysis, there are three further reasons for exploring this topic more fully here. First, Orwell's writings are a particularly rich source for evidence about the availability and uses of the key terms and about the attitudes attached to them. Indeed, his preferred plain-man persona tended to make him more representative of ordinary usage than might be the case with a writer whose vocabulary was drawn from more recondite sources, whether of learned discourse or individual inventiveness. Second, Orwell probably did more than any other single writer in the middle of the twentieth century to shape and harden attitudes towards intellectuals in Britain. His iconic status both as the courageous truth-teller and as the champion of the individual in the face of the totalitarian tendencies of modern states has meant that his writings have helped to shape a semantic field in which freedom, honesty, and plain speech are contrasted with tyranny, ideological fashion, and pretension, and in which the term 'intellectuals' is strongly associated with the latter of these two poles. Third, Orwell also provides a notable example of the larger pattern or problem I have already identified, namely the fact that nearly all extended attacks on intellectuals as a category are by those who, in at least some senses of the term, would have to be classified as other intellectuals. This always raises, or should raise, the question of where the critics situate themselves and on what grounds they claim exemption from the strictures directed against their fellow-intellectuals. Orwell has been described as possessing a marked talent for 'rubbing the fur of his own cat backwards'.[1] This is normally understood to refer to his being a critic of the Left from within the Left, but it may also serve as an apt description of his relations with (other) intellectuals.

Although Orwell's hostility to intellectuals has largely been taken for granted, the tensions in his position have attracted occasional comment, both during his lifetime and since. For example, when Victor Gollancz published *The Road to Wigan Pier* as part of the Left Book Club, he felt obliged to write a Foreword which attempted to disarm some of Orwell's more stinging criticisms of the Left. In the course of this uncomfortable exercise, Gollancz suggested that Orwell should be seen as struggling with two conflicting compulsions: on the one hand the dictates of his conscience force him towards socialism, while on the other he experiences 'the compulsion to conform to the mental habits of his class'. Seeking to illustrate this, Gollancz went on: 'For instance, Mr Orwell calls himself a "half intellectual"; but the truth is that he is at one and the same time an extreme intellectual and a violent anti-intellectual'.[2] When Orwell eventually read this Foreword (after the book had been published while he was in Spain), he wrote to Gollancz to say that 'I could have answered some of the criticisms you made'.[3] It is not hard to imagine some of the answers Orwell might have given—about, for example, his descriptions of working-class life—but it is more difficult to see how he might have responded to this particular observation, since it offers a characterization whose truth he could not easily have acknowledged. I shall return below to the passage in which Orwell referred to himself as a 'half-intellectual', where we have to consider what he thought was involved in being a 'whole intellectual', but for the moment the suggestion of a tension between being 'an extreme intellectual and a violent anti-intellectual' offers one fruitful point of departure.

Almost fifty years later, Bernard Crick, discussing Orwell's slashing attack in *The Lion and the Unicorn* on the lack of patriotism among intellectuals in Britain, wagged an admonitory finger at the reader: 'Notice that Orwell did not denounce intelligence or possibly intellectualism, only the behaviour of a specific kind of intellectual. He was no anti-intellectual as such, only against most of the self-styled intellectuals of the 1930s vintage.'[4] Amid the flood of indulgent and unanalytical biographies of modern literary figures, Crick's stands out for its consistently tough-minded scepticism about the status of much of the 'evidence' for Orwell's life,[5] but this is an uncharacteristically slack passage. To begin with, the phrase 'or possibly intellectualism' is as awkward syntactically as it is curious substantively. Moreover, saying that Orwell 'did not denounce intelligence' is to make a show of fending off a charge which is anyway too implausible to stick: many, perhaps Orwell among them, have found ways to express their anti-intellectualism without 'denouncing intelligence'. The real issue here is whether

Orwell legitimately criticized various figures in the 1930s whom he also, contingently, classed as 'intellectuals', or whether classing them as 'intellectuals' was an essential part of his charge against them. Since at least some of the evidence that I shall examine below supports the second of these interpretations, I suggest that, *pace* Crick, the question of Orwell's possible 'anti-intellectualism' remains open.

One or two of Orwell's more celebrated, or more notorious, criticisms of British intellectuals have made frequent reappearances in the essayistic and journalistic literature on this topic in recent decades, but the publication in 1998 of the final eleven volumes of the extraordinarily thorough *Complete Works* now makes it easier to establish both the chronology and the diversity of Orwell's critical remarks. Drawing on this newly accessible material, I want at least to address the questions that need to be asked in any fuller consideration of Orwell's place in my larger story. When did intellectuals first figure in Orwell's demonology? Whom did he have in mind? What did he reproach them with? Did his attacks on them change over time? What part did these attacks play in the economy of his thought and sensibility as a whole?

II

In the evolution of the 'George Orwell' who famously declared in 1946 that 'what I have most wanted to do throughout the past ten years is to make political writing into an art', it is generally agreed that the crucial transformation took place around the years 1936–8, beginning with the journey to the north of England that resulted in *The Road to Wigan Pier*, and ending with the publication of *Homage to Catalonia*, his account of his experience in Spain.[6] One can date the beginnings of his dismissive jibes at intellectuals to this same period. Up until then, he might easily have been classed as a familiar type of minor intellectual of the period: he had pungently expressed the struggling writer's stylized hostility to society, one of the central themes of his early fiction being the tyranny of 'the money God', and *Burmese Days* had attempted to expose the canker of injustice that lay at the heart of all relationships conducted under the sign of imperialism. In his writing, and still more in his manner of presenting himself in the literary world, such as the circle around *The Adelphi*, to which he began to contribute in the early 1930s, he had also emphasized his distance from the metropolitan world of letters, ostentatiously cultivating his down-and-out image. He freely expressed his outsiderish antagonism to the 'snooty refined books...by those moneyed young beasts who glide so gracefully from Eton to Cambridge and from Cambridge to the literary reviews'.[7] But before the writing of *The Road to Wigan Pier* in the second half of 1936, there is no sign that these various aversions and personae had yet gelled around the idea of systematically denouncing 'intellectuals'.

Cyril Connolly later recalled, as a partial explanation of the fact that he and Orwell, friends at Eton, had not met again until some six years after the latter's return from Burma in 1927: 'When Orwell came back from Burma he did not care for Oxford and Cambridge intellectuals, the easy livers, "the Pansy Left" as he called them.'[8] Although Crick cites this comment at the point in his narrative when Connolly and Orwell did meet again, namely 1933, it is taken from a reminiscence that was written much later, and so it seems likely that Connolly was recalling phrases that he heard Orwell use, in speech or writing, in the later 1930s and 1940s. Orwell may well have been hostile to all kinds of 'easy livers' on his return from Burma, but it is unlikely that 'the Pansy Left' figured among his targets, since that phrase only acquired its referent with the rise to cultural prominence of 'the Auden circle' in the course of the 1930s. Certainly, there is no mention of Auden and Spender and their associates in Orwell's writing before 1936.

But it is equally important not to assume that Orwell's antagonism to intellectuals only developed as part of his later hostility to Communists, Russophiles, and other fellow-travellers. Notoriously, his political experiences in Spain, specifically the attempt by the orthodox Communists to suppress the anarchist-Trotskyist POUM with whom he had fought, played a crucial part in opening his eyes to the pernicious tendencies of political ideologies to exact loyalty at the expense of truth (as he always saw it). But the chronology of his writing suggests that many elements of his tendentious picture of intellectuals were already in place before he arrived in Spain. Orwell submitted the completed manuscript of *Wigan Pier* in December 1936, shortly before leaving for Spain, and the controversial second half of that book is laced with jibes at intellectuals which do not at all derive from the machinations of international Stalinism. In this relatively early work we can already see the how the interaction between his cantankerous writing persona and certain strains in English culture seemed very naturally to issue in a stylized hostility towards 'intellectuals'.

The keynote of the second, autobiographical half of *Wigan Pier* is honesty about one's class location. Orwell, constantly positioning himself as the one voice willing to acknowledge the unwelcome, ineliminable truths of social behaviour, insists that even if one attempts to throw off the inherited opinions of one's class, one will still retain at a deeper level its tastes, attitudes, and way of life. 'A middle-class person embraces Socialism and perhaps even joins the Communist Party. How much real difference does it make?'[9] It is within this structural dynamic that 'intellectuals' can be treated practically as a synonym for those who are in this state of bad faith about their real class position. 'Not only the *croyant et pratiquant* Socialist, but every "intellectual" takes it as a matter of course that *he* at least is outside the class-racket . . .' Broadening the assault, he argues that this falseness about class position goes along with a volatility or fundamental insincerity of opinion.

This is the inevitable fate of the sentimentalist. All his opinions change into their opposites at the first brush of reality. The same streak of soggy, half-baked insincerity runs through all 'advanced' opinion. Take the question of imperialism, for instance. Every left-wing 'intellectual' is, as a matter of course, an anti-imperialist. He claims to be outside the empire-racket as automatically and self-righteously as he claims to be outside the class-racket. Even the right-wing 'intellectual', who is not definitely in revolt against British imperialism, pretends to regard it with a sort of amused detachment.[10]

Many of the elements in Orwell's later assaults on the intelligentsia are already present in this early riff—the lack of contact with 'reality', the tendency to hold one's fashionable views 'automatically' and 'self-righteously', the pretence at a stance of detachment, the insincerity, the 'sogginess' ('soggy', 'soft', and cognate terms cluster around 'intellectuals' in Orwell's writings), and so on. At this date, in contrast to most of his later diatribes, there is no suggestion that the intellectuals are confined to 'literary' figures, nor any question of their being forced into duplicity by slavish adherence to the official Soviet line. Indeed, in this passage they are not even exclusively left-wing. They are identified, rather, by their self-consciously superior views, their sense of their own distance from the common prejudices of the vulgar. Like the middle-brow press of the period, Orwell is not above playing to the gallery by trading on the sneer that lurks behind the quotation marks around 'intellectual'. The sequence of associations that moves through 'so-called' to 'pretentious' to 'dishonest' was at the core of his allegations. With this range of associations in place, he could later press on more briskly. 'I have pointed out that the left-wing opinions of the average "intellectual" are mainly spurious.'[11] This is a fine example of the tendentiousness so often present in Orwell's celebrated plain speaking. 'Pointed out' is mere bullying here as a way of referring to a general, unsubstantiated (and perhaps unsubstantiatable) charge, and 'mainly' is meant to indicate that the charge was supported by some careful discrimination among the views thus indicted.

All this suggests that the most teasing (and, I have to say, most neglected) feature of this section of *Wigan Pier* is the question of where Orwell positions himself, where he is speaking from in his strictures on Socialist intellectuals. One way to approach this is by considering another aspect of the book that made it such an awkward recruit to the ranks of the Left Book Club, namely its explanation of why the 'normal' middle-class person was put off by Socialism. The nub of Orwell's argument here was that 'as with the Christian religion, the worst advertisement for Socialism is its adherents'. At this point, clearly, the authorial voice is not locating itself among those 'adherents', and this sense of distance increases as he warms to his theme. 'There is the horrible—the really disquieting—prevalence of cranks wherever Socialists are gathered together,' and then, notoriously, 'One sometimes gets the impression that the mere words "Socialism" and "Communism" draw towards them with magnetic force every fruit-juice drinker, nudist, sandal-wearer, sex-maniac, Quaker, "Nature Cure" quack, pacifist and feminist in England.'[12] The use of such incantatory hyperbole is one of the polemicist's time-honoured weapons, but a characteristic limitation of Orwell's writing becomes evident if we juxtapose this passage to, say, one of

Nietzsche's wonderful tirades about how the man who has become truly free 'spurns the contemptible sort of well-being dreamed of by shop-keepers, Christians, cows, women, Englishmen, and other democrats'.[13] Both lists want their flagrant outrageousness to be at once registered and forgiven, but Nietzsche's list was genuinely provocative precisely because it ran so counter to received sensibilities. Its offhand inclusiveness was shocking because, beneath the exaggeration, a wholly new moral perspective was being hinted at which cut across established categories. By contrast, Orwell's list, for all its deliberate comic or rhetorical effect, is in fact a compendium of widely accepted middle-brow prejudices. Orwell tries to repeat the effect in subsequent paragraphs, and it is an indication of the conventional status of his lists that he can even at one point simply round off an abbreviated version with 'etc.'. In attempting to ridicule middle-class supporters of Socialism, he emphatically endorses the popular notion of the 'crank'. A 'crank', he went on to spell out, is by definition 'a person out of touch with common humanity'. Precious little challenge there to received notions of 'common humanity'.

But, one needs to ask, since Orwell acknowledges that he has himself moved in the company of such people by attending ILP branch meetings and the like, how it is that he treats himself as exempt from these strictures? He freely mocks those who attend 'summer schools', but we also know that during the writing of *Wigan Pier* he lectured at the Adelphi summer school himself (on 4 August 1936).[14] One whole chapter of the book is devoted to lecturing (the verb seems just, much though Orwell would have hated it) his fellow-Socialists on the reasons for their failure to convert the great mass of the population to their cause. By implication, the vantage-point from which he is doing so is that of someone who is more in touch with 'common humanity' than are most Socialists, someone who is definitely not a 'crank'. And just as his prose never offers itself as expressing what 'we cranks' are like, so he never seems to be speaking from the point of view of 'we intellectuals'. Orwell's writing in general made inauthenticity or bad faith the fundamental fault of the intellectuals, but that writing was itself shot through with a systematic inauthenticity of its own in consistently positioning him outside the group to which, by the very fact of his writing, he so clearly belonged.

Only in a couple of places is his own affinity with the objects of his criticism allowed to surface. The first comes in his famous account of the dependence of the comfortable classes on the miners.

In a way it is even humiliating to watch coal-miners working. It raises in you a momentary doubt about your own status as an 'intellectual' and a superior person generally. For it is brought home to you, at least while you are watching, that it is only because miners sweat their guts out that superior persons can remain superior. You and I and the editor of the *Times Lit. Supp.*, and the Nancy poets and the Archbishop of Canterbury and Comrade X, author of *Marxism for Infants*—all of us *really* owe the comparative decency of our lives to poor drudges underground.[15]

'Intellectual' here seems to be used in a fairly neutral way, perhaps just indicating someone engaged in intellectual pursuits rather than manual labour, though yoking it to 'superior person' keeps up the ironizing tone. But what is the function of the bizarre list in the final sentence? A couple of prominent cultural roles, a group of nameless poets, a hypothetical pseudonym, and 'you and I'. These are not the components of any pre-existing social or cultural category; on the face of things the heterogeneity is merely intended to underline how extensive society's debts to 'the poor drudges underground' actually are. But in that case what is striking is the absence of the more obvious groups who depend on such labour, all the wealthy owners of capital and drawers of dividends and so on. But there the economic relation is apparent and inescapable. What Orwell seems to be looking for are types who may be most prone to *forget* their dependence because they think of themselves as engaged in activities that far transcend the material world. That, he implies, is one of the marks of the 'intellectual' referred to in the first sentence—and so intellectuals are associated with yet another form of evasion and dishonesty. Although 'you and I' are placed in this category, the mere fact that 'I' am pointing this out shows that 'I' have at least begun to free myself from the illusions in which the others in this list are still trapped.

More intriguing still, partly because even less under control, is the passage in which he discusses the 'softness' of the world which Socialism promises for the future. Orwell argues that the ideal of a machine-dominated, effort-free utopia repels potential converts to Socialism, and rightly so, since no one could want to live in a condition of such 'softness'. Thus, he insists, we (here implying 'we Socialists') need 'to make clear what we mean when we say that we "want" this or that. I am a degenerate modern semi-intellectual who would die if I did not get my early morning cup of tea and my *New Statesman* every Friday. Clearly I do not, in a sense, "want" to return to a simpler, harder, probably agricultural way of life'. But 'in another and more permanent sense' he claims he does want that, or at least wants some of the features of that simpler life.[16] Now, obviously Orwell is playing with a little self-ironic hyperbole here—'degenerate', 'die', the detail of the *New Statesman*, and so on—but I suspect it is the unresolved problem of how to represent his own subject-position that leads him to opt for the awkward and evasive self-description as a 'semi-intellectual'. Does he want these things or not? Does he share the inherent faults of the 'intellectuals' or not? 'Semi-intellectual' is, I suggest, a semi-acknowledgement that he cannot really address, let alone answer, these questions in these terms while still continuing to berate intellectuals.

The other obvious question to ask of Orwell's attacks is: which actual historical figures were supposed to be examples of this category, to the extent that it was more than a piece of generalized social swearing? There is a notable scarcity of proper names in Orwell's book, but a few obvious suspects do make discreet appearances, and they fall into roughly two categories: Socialist thinkers and political theorists on the one hand, fashionable young poets and writers on the other. Orwell manages to extend his general loathing of the middle-class *pretence* of egalitarianism into a point against Socialist theory itself. 'If you secretly think of yourself as a gentleman and as such the superior of the greengrocer's errand-boy, it is far better to say so than to tell lies about it.' The 'gentlemanly' prose of Socialist theorists betrays their true position here since it is 'always completely removed from the working class in idiom and manner of thought', and by way of illustration he instances 'the Coles, Webbs, Stracheys, etc'. In somewhat similar vein, he attacks Shaw's plays for showing no real understanding of working-class life, despite Shaw's lifelong profession of Socialism, and he also suggests that Beatrice Webb's autobiography (*My Apprenticeship*, presumably) 'gives, unconsciously, a most revealing picture of the high-minded Socialist slum visitor'. *Wigan Pier* is laced with jibes at 'the intellectual, book-trained Socialist' (including further sideswipes at Shaw), all reinforcing the suggestion that a 'Socialist intellectual' is, *ipso facto*, involved in a form of pretence and self-deception.[17]

As far as fashionable writers were concerned, most contemporary readers of *The Road to Wigan Pier* would, presumably, have read the phrase 'Nancy poets' as referring to Auden and Spender and their circle; this may be the first mention in Orwell's writing of what was to become a favourite target. He allowed himself to be still more explicit when discussing the question of the failure of Socialism to have produced any great literary works (a question, incidentally, only likely to be raised in the first place by someone who was something of a literary intellectual). 'A whole generation has grown up more or less in familiarity with the idea of Socialism; and yet the high-water mark, so to speak, of Socialist literature is W. H. Auden, a sort of gutless Kipling, and the even feebler poets who are associated with him.'[18] Auden served as Orwell's favourite whipping-boy in the late 1930s, and it is telling that the charge against him here should be a lack of 'guts': in stressing his own distance from the aesthete or intellectual, Orwell all too often allowed his idiom to fall into that of the opposite social type, more public-school bully than man-in-the-street.

One of the most familiar and at the same time most tiresome features of Orwell's prose is the way he constantly tries to underline his own independence of all literary 'rackets': only the misfit or outsider is free enough to see, and still more to tell, the truth. *Wigan Pier* again provides one of the earliest examples of the way in which 'the intelligentsia' figures as the opposite of this position of lonely authenticity. It comes in the passage where he is expressing his scorn for that kind of 'proletarian intellectual' who escapes from his working-class origins via success in 'the literary racket'. This process, he asserts, is inherently corrupting.

> For it is not easy to crash your way into the literary intelligentsia if you happen to be a decent human being. The modern English literary world, at any rate the highbrow section of it, is a sort of poisonous jungle where only weeds can flourish.... In the highbrow world you 'get on', if you 'get on' at all, not so much by your literary ability as by being the life and soul of cocktail parties and kissing the bums of verminous little lions.[19]

It is an ancient refrain, of course, which does not make it wholly untrue; but Orwell's vehemence depends upon the implication that he remains well outside this 'highbrow' world, though in reality he was 'getting on' not at all badly by 1937, given that *Wigan Pier* was the fifth book he had published in five years. But acknowledging that he was fully part of this 'literary world' would have been as disabling for his criticisms of it as would including himself in his target category of 'intellectuals'.

One interesting acknowledgement of the extent to which Orwell was conscious of this need to cultivate and accentuate his distance comes a couple of years later in a letter to Stephen Spender where Orwell in effect apologises to Spender for having attacked him as 'a parlour Bolshevik' before he had met him. Having candidly explained what he had taken Spender to represent (indifferent poetry, Communist sympathies, and being 'a sort of fashionable successful person'), he went on: 'I don't mix much in literary circles, because I know from experience that once I have met and spoken to anyone I shall never again be able to show any intellectual brutality towards him, even when I feel that I ought to.'[20] 'Brutality' is, of course, characteristically brutal here, as is the assumption that all those who do mix in literary circles thereby pretty much disqualify themselves from practising objective criticism (Orwell tended to make destructive criticism rather than, say, appreciation the distinguishing mark of 'objectivity'). He here elevates into a policy what others might put down to lack of inclination or opportunity, underlining his susceptibility to weakness like a determinedly chaste girl who confides how easily her virtue would yield given half a chance. And in a sense Orwell's virtue *did* so yield, in that once he had met Spender he did stop attacking him in print. As he wrote to Connolly twelve days later, after Spender had visited Orwell in hospital: 'Funny, I had always used him and the rest of that gang as symbols of the pansy Left, and in fact I don't care for his poems to speak of, but when I met him in person I liked him so much and was sorry for the things I had said about him.'[21] Orwell hated the *idea* of someone like Spender, rather than Spender himself—and his name for that idea was 'an intellectual'.

This counterposing of his own greater involvement with the world of action and 'guts' to the effeminate preciousness of 'the pansy poets' is particularly evident in Orwell's furious response in August 1937 to the circular sent by Nancy Cunard on behalf of *Left Review* asking writers to say which side they supported in Spain (a collation of the replies was published later in the year as *Authors Take Sides on the Spanish War*). 'Will you please stop sending me this bloody rubbish....I am not one of your fashionable pansies like Auden and Spender, I was six months in Spain, most of the time fighting, I have a bullet-hole in me...' and so on.[22] In fact, some of those who responded to the enquiry had also fought in Spain, but the contrast invoked in this letter had by now sent down deep roots in the literary persona of 'George Orwell'.

One of the ways in which Orwell expressed his very considerable aggression was in his attacks on the self-indulgence of those who, from positions of safety and comfort, held forth about the need for some kind of action. There are times when Orwell can seem like a late example of the classical republican tradition, with its strong preference for collective austerity over private indulgence, and its insistence on the ethically formative value of physical participation in the business of defence; his later spell in the Home Guard during the Second World War constantly threatened to acquire the dignity of service in a citizen militia. He certainly had his share of that tradition's tendency to become coercively moralistic, but his idiom was more demotic and, in its way, more genuinely democratic, which only increased its intolerance of those who spouted high-flown ideas about what ought to be done. Orwell's was partly the footslogger's complaint against the generals and partly the man-on-the-spot's disdain for the desk-wallah, two registers with powerful purchase in English life. But it was also, surely, that sense, familiar from time to time to any writer, thinker, or journalist, of utter weariness with the unending round of opinion and counter-opinion, the desire to break out of the circle of mere words. For the most part, of course, Orwell expressed this desire in yet more words, an irony he never fully acknowledged, but he *had* fought in Spain, and this gave him a frequently played trump card against those who called for action from a safe distance.

One of the most celebrated occasions on which he played this card was his snarl in 'Inside the whale' at Auden's poem 'Spain', with its apparently untroubled 'acceptance of guilt in the necessary murder'. 'Mr Auden's brand of amoralism is only possible if you are the kind of person who is always somewhere else when the trigger is pulled.'[23] But Orwell had in fact already singled out this line two years earlier in a little-known piece which reveals the dynamic of the charge even more clearly. Writing on 'the political crisis' in *The Adelphi* in December 1938, he remarked that there seemed to be more prominent publicists in England than in France who were now calling for war. 'A type that seems to be comparatively rare in France is the war-hungry middle-class intellectual.' Characteristically, his proposed explanation for this is the experience of obligatory military service in France, which has the effect of making adult males more realistic about the nature of war. 'One could not possibly say the same of the English intelligentsia.' They have no conception of the peculiar horribleness of modern war, and probably do not even anticipate having to serve in it. '. . . [T]hese people, who have been born into the monied intelligentsia and feel in their bones that they belong to a privileged class, are not really capable of foreseeing any such thing', and then, scenting his prey: '. . . it is, of course, precisely because of the utter softness and security of life in England that the yearning for bloodshed—bloodshed in the far distance—is so common among our intelligentsia. Mr Auden can write about "the acceptance of guilt for the necessary murder" because he has never committed a murder . . .' and so on.[24] Perhaps no professional writer could emerge from a genuinely 'complete' edition of his work without seeming somewhat repetitive, but bringing together the scattered writings of Orwell the busy, and mostly penurious, journalist makes strikingly clear just how few qualms he had about lifting whole sentences and paragraphs from himself without acknowledgement. Much of this earlier article is repeated almost verbatim two years later in 'Inside the whale', though he now makes more of his own superior qualifications: 'It so happens that I have seen the bodies of numbers of murdered men. . . . Therefore I have some conception of what murder means. . . . To me murder is something to be avoided. So it is to any ordinary person.'[25] Once again Orwell's prose colludes with the conventional antinomy: his is the voice of the 'ordinary person', and represents what is morally healthy; Auden's is the voice of the intellectual, and represents what is morally unhealthy. The equation 'an intellectual and *therefore* morally unhealthy' lurks only just below the surface.

III

In characterizing and assessing Orwell's social criticism in general, of which his attacks on intellectuals form a part, it is important not to attach excessive significance to some of the more quotable passages of *The Lion and the Unicorn*, especially its first section, 'England Your England', which has often been reprinted separately. This pamphlet was written 'at great speed' in the Autumn of 1940, amid the heightened emotions of the Battle of Britain, and written with deliberate propagandistic intent.[26] When at the end of his life Orwell was leaving instructions for future editions of his works, he expressly desired that this pamphlet, along with its later companion 'The English People' and his two earliest novels ('potboilers' he called them), should not be reprinted. The pamphlet was written at the peak of his conviction that the war would bring, or could be won only as a result of, a social revolution in Britain, and he passionately expounds his provoking thesis, namely that Socialism, far from being incompatible with 'the English genius' is in fact its consummation. It is as part of his epigrammatic survey of English social structure that he draws one of his most memorable sketches of 'the intelligentsia', giving them a far more significant place in British society than most observers would have done then or since. One of the challenges posed to the critic by Orwell's writing is that of deciding quite how seriously or literally to take many of his more polemical and journalistic flourishes. In the present case, it may be helpful not only to read his rhetorical exaggerations symptomatically rather than literally, but also to recognize how he is giving his own distinctive twist to a vocabulary and attitude with deep roots in the culture.

His portrait is structured around a dialectical relationship between 'the blimps' and 'the highbrows'. These are explicitly treated as stereotypes—'the half-pay colonel with his bull neck and diminutive brain', 'the highbrow with his domed forehead and stalk-like neck'—and the discussion never really escapes the constraints of such conventional and diagrammatic thinking. At the outset, it seems to be casually assumed that 'highbrows' may be equated with 'the left-wing intelligentsia'. But Orwell then offers a breezy defence of this assumption. 'It should be noted that there is now no intelligentsia that is not in some sense "Left". Perhaps the last right-wing intellectual was T. E. Lawrence. Since about 1930 everyone describable as an "intellectual" has lived in a state of chronic discontent with the existing order.' And he goes on to explain why intellectuals were necessarily in this position:

> In an England ruled by people whose chief asset was their stupidity, to be 'clever' was to be suspect. If you had the kind of brain that could understand the poems of T. S. Eliot or the theories of Karl Marx, the higher-ups would see to it that you were kept out of any important job. The intellectuals could find a function for themselves only in the literary reviews and the left-wing political parties.[27]

It is often difficult to judge just how far Orwell is ventriloquizing or even ironizing such statements by his use of a markedly demotic register and how far this simply represents his own writerly preference for homely, everyday speech. 'Brain', rather than, say, 'mind', mimics one detail of popular attitudes towards intellectuals; 'higher-ups' strives even harder for the view-from-the-ranks effect. Ostensibly, the passage mocks those distinguished by their 'stupidity', yet it comes close to colluding with the sneer in 'clever' and with the suggestion that noisy futility is all that one can expect of intellectuals. Orwell, the much-lauded master of the plain style, can display a disabling unsteadiness of tone at times, especially those times when his own identity as an intellectual is kept cowering in the background by his simulated middlebrow dismissals of 'intellectuals' as a category.

In *The Lion and the Unicorn* the hostility is unchecked by any explicit acknowledgement of identification. Intellectuals are marked by their 'carping', 'the irresponsible carping of people who have never been and never expect to be in a position of power'. They (always *they*) display 'the emotional shallowness of people who live in a world of ideas and have little contact with physical reality'. Moreover, 'underlying this is the really important fact about so many of the English intelligentsia—their severance from the common culture of the country'. He then embarks on a set piece which has become a minor classic of denigration.

> In intention, at any rate, the English intelligentsia are Europeanized. They take their cookery from Paris and their opinions from Moscow. In the general patriotism of the country they form a sort of island of dissident thought. England is perhaps the only great country whose intellectuals are ashamed of their own nationality. In left-wing circles it is always felt that there is something slightly disgraceful in being an Englishman and that it is a duty to snigger at every English institution, from horse-racing to suet-puddings. It is a strange fact, but it is unquestionably true, that almost any English intellectual would feel more ashamed of standing to attention during 'God Save the King' than of stealing from a poor box.[28]

Couched in a different idiom, such an emphasis on the 'alienation' of the intellectuals might be wholly positive, yet every detail of Orwell's portrait is plainly intended to intensify the reader's distrust of such 'unnatural' behaviour. The strictly superfluous references to such details as cookery, horse racing, suet puddings, the national anthem, and poor boxes are intended to conjure into existence the very shared life of the community from which he is suggesting the intellectuals are isolated. Similarly, in saying that they take their cookery from Paris and their opinions from Moscow he first of all makes them seem rather slavish followers of fashion and snobbery; second, he thereby manages to reduce their politics to the level of a fashion like cookery; and third, he impugns their independence of mind—to 'take' one's opinions in this way is to allow oneself to be dictated to. And even the choice of a verb like 'snigger' contributes to this sense of distance: it suggests something unmanly, cowardly, mean-spirited. Other people snigger; one does not snigger oneself. And of course by concentrating on the way the intellectuals are 'ashamed' of being English and would be 'ashamed' of standing up for the national anthem, he makes them seem vain and shifty about things which the plain man would naturally feel proud of.

Notoriously, *The Lion and the Unicorn* paints an over-cosy picture of the society in which the 'plain man' feels a natural pride. 'A family with the wrong members in control... is as near as one can come to describing England in a phrase.'[29] The 'wrong members' are, in the stereotypes which Orwell is using here, the Colonel Blimps, and these social stereotypes also play a part in explaining where the intellectuals have gone wrong. They could not bear a society run by Blues and Blimps, he is suggesting, and so they repudiated its values; but the result of this was a 'severance from the common culture of their country', which has distorted their responses. And since they were thereby excluded from playing any part in the running of their society, they were left to denounce it without being sobered by the responsibility of power. Thus, Left-wing intellectuals had become self-indulgent and posturing.

Again, the implied contrast is that of responsibly facing up to the unpleasant realities, and of course Orwell is tacitly identifying himself with this position. Similarly, the same persona is being implicitly contrasted in the swipe (cited a moment ago) at those 'people who live in a world of ideas and have little contact with physical reality'. It may be relevant to recall that Orwell made rather a point of the fact that he *did* do woodwork and grow things in his garden and so on, but in the light of this sort of comment one is half inclined to think that he did these things less out of natural inclination than from a principled commitment to being somebody in contact with physical reality—a commitment, in other words, to not being an intellectual. Since by definition 'George Orwell' did not exist except as an author, there is something almost poignant in his attempting to bolster his plain-man credentials in this way, the better to denounce the inherent deceitfulness of the (other) intellectuals.

Some of the same themes surface in Orwell's 1942 essay on Kipling, which took as its starting-point T. S. Eliot's *A Choice of Kipling's Verse*. The main ground of Orwell's sympathy for Kipling here was that, by emotionally identifying with the ruling powers, he made himself susceptible to the ethic of responsibility: he had at least to consider what ought to be done, whereas an oppositional writer has the luxury of merely protesting. Orwell could not resist generalizing the point: 'Where it is a permanent and pensioned opposition, as in England, the quality of its thought deteriorates accordingly'.[30] Orwell's urge to advertise Kipling's merits was his usual reflex response to the fact that, by this date, Kipling was largely sneered at in cultivated circles. But the case of Kipling did partly call into question the superficial social categories with which Orwell was prone to work. Kipling is Orwell's prize example of his celebrated category of 'good bad poetry'. That Eliot should think Kipling worth republishing, Orwell reflected, attests to Kipling's curious appeal to a highly cultivated as well as to a popular audience, and then, abruptly: 'The fact that such a thing as good bad poetry can exist is a sign of the emotional overlap between the intellectual and the ordinary man. The intellectual *is* different from the ordinary man, but only in certain sections of his personality, and even then not all the time.'[31] The paragraph immediately returns to the nature of Kipling's verse, but this slightly throwaway admission is interesting, not least because the coiner of 'good bad poetry' cannot plausibly continue to align himself with that 'ordinary man' who does not find Kipling's poetry 'bad' in any sense.

IV

As Orwell's polemics against 'the intellectuals' gathered momentum from the late 1930s onwards, one theme came to predominate to the point where, by the late 1940s, it could seem to be practically his only theme. That theme is the necessary dishonesty involved in consistently upholding the cause of the Soviet Union on ideological grounds. In the mid-1940s he claimed that 'I have never fundamentally altered my attitude towards the Soviet regime since I first began to pay attention to it some time in the nineteen-twenties.'[32] Whatever the accuracy of that retrospective view, there is no doubt that his sense of the damage done *within* English intellectual and literary life by support for the Communist line changed very considerably during these years. Writing in 1946, he observed that:

> Fifteen years ago, when one defended the freedom of the intellect, one had to defend it against Conservatives, against Catholics, and to some extent—for in England they were not of great importance—against Fascists. To-day one has to defend it against Communists and 'fellow travellers'. One ought not to exaggerate the direct influence of the small English Communist party, but there can be no question about the poisonous effect of the Russian *mythos* on English intellectual life.[33]

There is, however, considerable continuity with his earlier attacks, especially in the way he constantly suggests that slavish adherence to a doctrine backed by the sanction of either party or fashion is inherent in the very idea of the 'intellectual'.

In the course of the war this hardened further into the charge that the intellectuals were *peculiarly* prone to the kind of mental dishonesty characteristic of totalitarianism. The general public 'are at once too sane and too stupid to acquire the totalitarian outlook. The direct, conscious attack on intellectual decency comes from the intellectuals themselves.' Indeed, he manages to suggest that the constant element is the self-deception itself, not the content of the belief: 'It is possible that the Russophile intelligentsia, if they had not succumbed to that particular myth, would have succumbed to another of much the same kind.'[34] And he also implies that this tendency is not merely a recent development, but has long been present in the species; in rehearsing his familiar diatribe against 'power-worship' among intellectuals, he contends that 'the countless English intellectuals who kiss the arse of Stalin' are no different in this respect from 'the older generation of intellectuals, Carlyle, Creasey and the rest of them, who bowed down before German militarism'.[35] It may be worth noting that when he had written about Carlyle in 1931 he had criticized him as a 'literary egoist', but he had not referred to him as an intellectual.[36] Only later did he retroject the label onto precursors of those who so infuriated him in his own time.

Throughout this period, Orwell conducted something of a guerrilla war against what he regarded as the house journal of this 'Russophile intelligentsia'. In his profile of 'Britain's Left-Wing Press' for an American readership in 1948, he remarked: '[O]ver a period of about 20 years *The New Statesman* has probably done more than any one thing—certainly more than any one periodical—to spread an uncritically Russophile attitude among the British intelligentsia.' He mentioned that apart from its editor, Kingsley Martin, 'many well-known left-wing publicists are or have at some time been associated with it: Leonard Woolf, H. N. Brailsford, John Strachey, Harold Laski, J. B. Priestley, R. H. S. Crossman and others'.[37] These would be good examples of the kind of people he constantly attacked as 'left-wing intellectuals' after the war, where there is something of a shift away from the *writers* whom he had earlier pilloried as 'parlour-Bolsheviks' and towards political theorists, political activists and (in the increasingly domesticated American term referred to in Ch. 3) 'publicists'. (He made something of an exception of R. H. Tawney, who was personally kind to him and visited him when he was confined to hospital in 1949; he described Tawney as 'one of the few major figures in the Labour movement whom one can both respect and like personally'.[38]) He was quick to identify any figures whom he believed to be 'crypto-Communists' or 'fellow-travellers', as in the notorious list he handed over to his friend in the Foreign Office's Information Research Department.[39] One test he applied was their participation in or attitude towards the international 'Congress of Intellectuals' held in Wroclaw in August 1948: this was in practice a Communist-front event, and the choice of title would not have lessened Orwell's suspicions about the intrinsic connection between 'intellectuals' and this kind of politically motivated deception.[40] As will become clear from my discussion in the following chapter of A. J. P. Taylor's role in the

Congress, this was another example of Orwell's rush to judgement being insufficiently controlled by the evidence.

Although in the mid- and late 1940s Orwell continued to rail against the intellectuals' subservience to Soviet Russia, it is worth remarking that he did also come to acknowledge the potential, and even on occasion the actual, role of intellectuals in defending liberty against the encroachment of totalitarian states. For example, in an interesting piece on 'Poetry and the microphone' (probably written in late 1943) he argued that the sheer scale of the war effort had forced the British government to recruit oppositional intellectual figures for such purposes as making radio programmes, figures who had then discovered a certain freedom in the interstices of a large bureaucratic machine. He drew an optimistic moral from this: 'It means that in countries where there is already a strong liberal tradition, bureaucratic tyranny can perhaps never be complete. The striped-trousered ones will rule, but so long as they are forced to maintain an intelligentsia, the intelligentsia will have a certain amount of autonomy.'[41] (According to Crick, this piece 'turned into yet another defence of the intellectuals, more like his defence of Henry Miller than his near-rejection of them in *The Lion and The Unicorn*'.[42] It is hard to read 'Inside the whale' as 'a defence of the intellectuals' in any general terms, and it is not otherwise clear what Crick's 'yet another' might refer to.)

Or again, in the 'Afterword' to the German edition of his four articles on 'The intellectual revolt' (entitled 'The revolt of the intellectuals' in the German version), written in April 1946, he discussed how 'the growing power of the State produces... considerable dismay, particularly amongst those for whom only ten or twenty years ago Socialism was the guarantee of progress'. Although the general public might still believe in central planning as the route to prosperity, 'writers, artists, scientists and philosophers' were expressing reservations. In the articles themselves, written in February 1946, Orwell identified four groups who, in their different ways, shared this reaction against planning and 'the machine age': he labelled them the Pessimists, Left-wing Socialists, Christian Reformers, and Pacifists, and he instanced a wide range of individuals as illustration (Eliot, Russell, Hayek, Huxley et al.). In the 'Afterword' he observed: 'The antitotalitarian tendencies described are not evenly distributed among the intellectuals. Writers and artists reject the centralised State much more decisively than do scientists and engineers' (in his pre-war attacks, by contrast, it was the culpability of writers and artists in particular that he had insisted upon.) On this occasion, he allowed himself an uncharacteristically optimistic conclusion. He contended that 'all intellectuals', whether they favour centralization or not, want to humanize the workings of modern societies and are united in 'opposition to the tyranny of the State. That so many minds in so many countries agree on this leads one to conclude that centralisation and bureaucratic controls, however much they may thrive today, will not be permitted unlimited growth.'[43] In other words, there are signs that as Orwell came, in the course of the 1940s, to worry about the bureaucratic tendencies of modern states in general even more than about particular ideologies, he grudgingly recognized that intellectuals could, in principle, be one of the chief forces for resistance.

He also occasionally singled out individual intellectual figures for praise, but in emphasizing their singularity he in effect removed them from the collective category of 'intellectuals'. For example, in a favourable review of Bertrand Russell's *Power* in early 1939 he, rather surprisingly, commended Russell for having 'an essentially *decent* intellect... which is far rarer than mere cleverness' (Russell usually attracted exactly the opposite description). The terms of Orwell's praise indicate the sense of affinity: 'Few people during the past thirty years have been so consistently impervious to the fashionable bunk of the moment.' Russell, in other words, was another honest, lonely man, and they, by definition, have to be few and far between. Actually, Orwell does at this point allow himself to posit the possibility of a category of intellectuals that was at once collective and admirable, but only by placing it safely in the past: 'Where this age differs from those immediately preceding it is that a liberal intelligentsia is lacking.'[44] Though this is offered as a lament, one is bound to wonder whether Orwell didn't at some level prefer it that way.

More generally, he could on occasion allow that some types of intellectuals were preferable to others. For example, although he professed a personal dislike for the long-running radio programme 'The Brains Trust', he admitted that it did at least promote open discussion of ideas, and noted that it was for that reason 'the object of endless attacks by right-wing intellectuals of the G. M. Young—A. P. Herbert type (also Mr Douglas Reed)', who share the views of 'the Blimps'. Feeble as the programme might be in its present form, 'just think what the Brains Trust would have been like if its permanent members had been (as they might so well have been) Lord Elton, Mr Harold Nicolson and Mr Alfred Noyes' (all prominent conservative intellectual figures).[45] More strikingly still, in a 1944 review of Noyes's end-of-civilization-as-we-knew-it jeremiad *The Edge of the Abyss*, he even finds a good word to say for the 'anti-Fascist intellectuals' of the pre-war years whom he normally scorned. Having noted Noyes's sweeping condemnation of the decline of moral standards in the modern world, he went on:

> Then there is the question of the amount of blame attaching to 'the highbrows' ('our pseudo-intellectuals' is Mr Noyes's favourite name for them) for the breakdown of moral standards. Mr Noyes writes on this subject in rather the same strain as the *London Mercury* of twenty years ago. 'The highbrows' are gloomy, they are obscene, they attack religion, patriotism, the family, etc., etc. But they are also, it appears, in some ways responsible for the rise of Hitler. Now this contradicts the facts. During the crucial years it was precisely the 'pseudo-intellectuals' whom Mr Noyes detests who cried out against the horrors of Fascism, while the Tory and clerical Press did its best to hush them up.[46]

Orwell here shows himself considerably less willing to collude with the common anti-intellectualism of the conservative press. He may have relished 'rubbing the fur of his own cat backwards', but if an outsider's hand attempted any such rubbing it was firmly smacked away.

It is also true that Orwell did not, in practice, always stand aloof from organized groups of intellectuals where he thought they were genuinely trying to defend liberty, especially once the Cold War started. The discussions he held with Arthur Koestler and others at the beginning of 1946 about founding a new 'League for the Rights of Man' could be seen as an example of the most classical kind of public activity by intellectuals.[47] Orwell himself recognized that they needed to be drawing up lists of 'intellectuals and publicists' in other countries sympathetic to their (anti-totalitarian) way of thinking.[48] In this context one should also mention his role in supporting the establishment of new periodicals, such as Humphrey Slater's *Polemic* in 1945, in which Orwell published several of his best essays (I return to the identity of this journal in Ch. 17).

It was in response to one such piece, 'The prevention of literature' (which appeared in *Polemic* in January 1946), that the literary journalist (and one-time Communist) Randall Swingler remarked the 'sense of martyrdom' evident in Orwell's obsessive attacks on 'the pro-Soviet orthodoxy': 'Orwell's posture of lonely rebel hounded by monstrous pro-Soviet monopolists has a somewhat crocodile appearance.' But in reply Orwell insisted that even if, in the late 1940s, it were going to become more common to draw attention to the defects of the Soviet regime, it had been a decidedly unpopular and professionally unprofitable role in the previous few years: 'During the past four or five years it has been extremely difficult even to get anything of anti-Russian tendency into print.' He itemized the kinds of obstacles he had faced, particularly the difficulties he had had in trying to find a publisher for *Animal Farm*, and emphasized that in Britain the chief censoring force was 'public opinion inside the literary intelligentsia'.[49] Orwell was by no means inventing the difficulties he had faced, as the surviving evidence of the pusillanimous behaviour of several publishers over *Animal Farm* makes clear, but Swingler's comment on Orwell's 'sense of martyrdom' points to some more general features of his attacks on intellectuals which require fuller analysis.

V

Orwell's constant idealization of the true writer as a lonely rebel rests upon an implicit binary opposition between 'individual integrity' and 'collective self-deception'. In Orwell's usage, 'intellectuals' is the term used to describe those who represent the latter pole. His essays disclose a revealing association of ideas here, most baldly displayed in 'Inside the whale'. Just as he is there warming to his habitual theme of how 'the discipline of a political party' is fatal for a writer, the paragraph veers towards a more encompassing reflection on the roots of creativity, especially the need for a kind of intellectual honesty. He then, somewhat abruptly, asks: 'How many Roman Catholics have been good novelists?', and, by way of an answer, goes on to assert that 'The novel is practically a Protestant form of art; it is the product of the free mind, of the autonomous individual.'[50] Orwell, richly endowed with native prejudice, was always happy to fan the flames of traditional English anti-Catholicism, representing the Inquisition as the continuing essence of the Church; he never missed an opportunity to attack such columnists as 'Beachcomber' as well as more obvious targets such as Chesterton, for the 'sinister' influence of their Catholicism on their views.[51] Here, this licensed his strikingly tendentious contrast with Protestantism, a creed which at times has exacted a comparable orthodoxy of its own. But what rouses Orwell on this occasion is that element in the standard post-Reformation representation of Protestantism as the religion of individual conscience, which, in a characteristic elision, Orwell equates with the 'free mind'. The extent to which Protestantism might be a collective enterprise is glossed over, and the idealized emphasis on the individual slides over into the fostering of 'creative autonomy'.

Lurking here (and in the many similar remarks elsewhere in his essays) is a point about the assumed naturalness of the alliance between three properties vital to Orwell's moral economy: trustworthiness, patriotism, and the unmediated good sense or conscience of the individual. Orwell was not above appealing to the old suspicion that the Catholic and the Communist owe their prime allegiance to a foreign power. The logic of their position within English society, therefore, however much it may be disguised by social convention, is that of the spy. The cumulative effect of Orwell's repeated charges and innuendoes rather suggests that intellectuals belong in the same category.

As always in Orwell's writing, the deeper implication is that genuine intellectual integrity only exists, only *can* exist, outside collective or institutional structures. The locus of value is always in the integrity of the unsystematic intuitions of the resistant individual, of the outsider. It is significant that Orwell almost always speaks, by contrast, of 'intellectuals' in the plural. The very fact of number, that they can be referred to as a collectivity, counts against them. Ultimately, for Orwell, anyone who can be included under a plural term is *thereby* suspect.

The unstated premise here is that, since 'spontaneity' is essential to imagination and 'intellectual honesty' is essential to 'literary creation', so 'party discipline' (of whatever kind) must be fatal to writing. It is noticeable that in these tirades there is a constant slide between the dangers of upholding a position which one knows to be false and the dangers of subscribing to *any* view which is shared by an organization or group. The implication is that the latter will always eventually involve the former. More profoundly, and perhaps more representatively, Orwell speaks as though to write out of the convictions that *he* happens to have involves no constraint on spontaneity and literary creativity, whereas to write out of convictions that others, especially any group of organized others, might have will inevitably involve putting checks to that spontaneity, the first step towards intellectual dishonesty. We here touch something very deep about Orwell's kind of individualism, namely the assumption that the view of the world held by the loner or misfit is in some way raw and unmediated, not guided by ideas, still less by theories. It is then a very short step indeed to regarding such a view as 'objective' and, ultimately, true *precisely because* it is held by a recalcitrant non-joiner.

Any elaborated defence of 'common sense' is, at bottom, a deeply theoretical exercise. Orwell never attempts such an exercise; his inclinations were too unphilosophical even to be properly anti-philosophical. For example, although he admired Bertrand Russell politically, he found even *his* exceptionally lucid philosophizing deeply alien. Citing a passage of logical analysis from Russell's *Human Knowledge: Its Scope and Limits* in a letter to Richard Rees in March 1949, Orwell commented: 'But I never can follow that kind of thing. It is the sort of thing that makes me feel that philosophy should be forbidden by law.'[52] Next to the entry on Russell's book in his list of reading for 1949, Orwell had written with laconic expressiveness: 'Tried and failed'.[53]

The limits of his intellectual sympathy for abstract reasoning come out even more clearly in his response in the years immediately after the Liberation of France to the period's most fashionable intellectual and literary figure, Jean-Paul Sartre. Orwell reviewed the published text of *Huis Clos* with a kind of baffled respect in *Tribune* in 1945,[54] but it is clear that his judgement of Sartre became more dismissive the more he read. For example, in the course of reviewing a book of essays on contemporary 'philosophical novelists' he observed: 'As an exponent of Existentialism, M. Sartre must, of course, be judged by his fellow-philosophers; but as a novelist and political essayist he gives the impression . . . of being one of those writers who set on paper the process instead of the results of thought, and, after many pages of feverish cerebration, end by stating the obvious.'[55] By the time he received *Portrait of the Anti-Semite* for review, his opinion had hardened still further: 'I think Sartre is a bag of wind and I am going to give him a good boot,' he told Fredric Warburg, Sartre's English publisher, and he repeated the sentiment in a letter to Julian Symons: 'I doubt whether it would be possible to pack more nonsense into so short a space. I have maintained from the start that Sartre is a bag of wind, though possibly when it comes to Existentialism, which I don't profess to understand, it may not be so.'[56] The review itself clearly failed to engage with the theoretical nature of Sartre's writing: Orwell concluded that 'in spite of much cerebration', the book contained 'little real discussion of the subject, and no factual evidence worth mentioning'.[57]

Instead, therefore, of engaging with the claims of philosophy, Orwell's prose fell back upon a kind of tight-jawed obdurateness which effectively classified *any* conceptually elaborated idea or position as inherently pretentious and distorting. If the individual was sufficiently determined to be honest, then not only was any body of ideas derived from systematic theorizing unnecessary; it was, by the very fact of possessing the fatal, and linked, characteristics of being abstract and collective, bound to be a hindrance to true perception and unfettered expression.

We have finally, therefore, to return to the question of how Orwell accounted for his own exemption from the charges he laid at the door of (other) intellectuals.

His essays and journalism contain frequent casual remarks and asides indicative of his noticeably unsteady positioning of himself in this respect. The interest of many of these remarks lies precisely in their glancing, habitual nature. For example, in a book-review in 1940 he claimed that 'the brutal side of public-school life, which intellectuals always deprecate, is not a bad training for the real world.'[58] In practice, the author of 'Such, such were the joys' was not above deprecating it himself, but as usual this did not lead him to any ready acknowledgement of his membership of the class of 'intellectuals'. Similarly, in a review of Edmund Blunden, he went out of his way to speak up for the virtues of cricket, at least at the village level, in the face of denunciations of the game by 'Left-wing writers'—not, as it might more accurately have been put, by '*other* Left-wing writers'.[59] And he constantly proclaimed how he did not share 'the general Russophile feeling of the intelligentsia', and hence was free to point out that 'the servility of the so-called intellectuals is astonishing'.[60]

His 'London Letters' to *Partisan Review* during the 1940s are a rich source here, since the genre sometimes required him to explain how he was not part of some feature of the British cultural or political scene which he was describing for a foreign audience. For instance, a 'London Letter' from the spring of 1941 offers an example both of how at this date Orwell tended to use 'intellectuals' to refer chiefly to writers who took some political stand, and of how at one level he half identified with this group even though constantly denouncing them.

> During the Spanish civil war the leftwing intellectuals felt that this was 'their' war and that they were influencing events in it to some extent. In so far as they expected the war against Germany to happen they imagined that it would be a sort of enlarged version of the war in Spain, a left-wing war in which poets and novelists could be important figures. Of course it is nothing of the kind. It is an all-in modern war fought mainly by technical experts (airmen etc) and conducted by people who are patriotic according to their lights but entirely reactionary in outlook. At present there is no function in it for intellectuals.[61]

The last sentence hints at the kind of satisfaction it always gave Orwell to see 'the intellectuals' taken down a peg or two and thereby to demonstrate his own greater realism. Yet he had arguably been one of the novelists or left-wing intellectuals who had thought of the war in Spain as a 'leftwing war'. By 1941, however, his identity as the scourge, *from outside*, of the 'lying propaganda' and 'horrible atmosphere of orthodoxy' of the pro-Communist, Popular Front intelligentsia was at the centre of his political writing.

In a 'London Letter' written in the winter of 1944, he took stock of how his and most other commentators' predictions earlier in the war had been proved wrong. In the early years of the war he had constantly insisted (*The Lion and the Unicorn* is merely the best-known instance) that Britain could win the war only by turning it into a 'revolutionary war', overturning the capitalist order in Britain and replacing it with Socialism. He recognized that he had been more optimistic than many observers, including having been more optimistic about the chances of military success. What is interesting (and in its honesty admirable) is his attempt to explain why he deviated from the views common among 'the left-wing intelligentsia'. The chief reason, he thought, was another example of how much people's perceptions, including his own, were coloured by what they wanted to see. He wanted to see England both victorious and reformed and this led him to predict both, accurately so on the first count, not on the second. He went on:

> I could be right on a point of this kind, because I don't share the average English intellectual's hatred of his own country and am not dismayed by a British victory. But just for the same reason I failed to form a true picture of political developments. I hate to see England either humiliated or humiliating anybody else. I wanted to think that we would not be defeated, and I wanted to think that the class distinctions and imperialist exploitation of which I am ashamed would not return.[62]

In itself the passage is a good example of the merits of Orwell's political journalism, but in the present context it is revealing of his own sense of distance from the intuitions of most intellectuals. He is, in another form, yet again claiming the high moral ground against other intellectuals. He presents himself as being more like the ordinary man in his patriotism, not corrupted by fancy foreign ideas or pathological reactions against his own background (though in truth he had plenty of the latter). The fact is, he continued, that 'in one form or another almost everyone is a nationalist. Left-wing intellectuals do not think of themselves as nationalists, because as a rule they transfer their loyalty to some foreign country, such as the USSR, or indulge it in a merely negative form, in hatred of their own country and its rulers.' Love of country, intellectual honesty, and emotional maturity are again figured as intrinsically related qualities, qualities which Orwell again represents himself as having and the (other) intellectuals as lacking.

The fact is that the terms of Orwell's social criticism allowed him no structural or systematic explanation of his difference from 'the average English intellectual'; his writing can only suggest that the difference is, at bottom, a matter of honesty and moral effort. 'I believe that it is possible to be more objective than most of us are, but that it involves a *moral* effort. One cannot get away from one's own subjective feelings, but at least one can know what they are and make allowance for them' (or again, in his 'Notes on nationalism', the only way to free oneself from the biases of nationalism is to make what 'is essentially a *moral* effort', but few contemporary writers seem capable of this).[63] Collective vice is constantly contrasted with solitary virtue, and once again he comes close to endorsing that cliché of Blimpish culture: character is more important than intellect.

In reading Orwell's essays and journalism of the late 1930s and 1940s, one is bound to remark the absence of any reference to the cliché that intellectuals somehow do not exist in Britain. Most of the time, it is true, Orwell manages to stigmatize them as essentially 'unEnglish', especially as they take their doctrinaire ideas from foreign sources. But there is no question about their existence, or about the normality of referring, however dismissively, to 'the English intelligentsia'. He had a liking for the term as a kind of sneering or diminishing label, but the exchanges and controversies in which he engaged suggest that the term and the idea were far from uncommon features of journalistic and political polemic in the 1930s and 1940s. Paradoxically, he may even have helped accustom English readers to regard as a familiar feature of their society the very category he attacked. In any event, this raises from another angle the question discussed earlier of whether the 'absence thesis' in its recognizably modern form is not largely an idea which was revived and burnished in the course of the 1950s, especially in terms of the contrast with the France of Sartre and Camus.

For all the directness of Orwell's attacks on intellectuals, one is nonetheless left, as so often when encountering exaggerated, obsessive behaviour, with the feeling that there must be more than meets the eye here, that the purported object of criticism cannot quite be the real one. In some ways, this sense of displaced hostility or anxiety is a recurrent feature of the more or less continuous criticisms made of writers and journalists, especially those of radical leanings, stretching from (to go no further back) the conservative Romantics' denunciations of 'mere opinion' right up to contemporary dismissals of 'the chattering classes'. This repetitive litany expresses a distaste for, even a weariness at, the unending circulation of 'views', 'comment', 'ideas', 'theories', 'opinions', and so on. Reading these laments, one detects—it is particularly marked in Orwell, but not of course in Orwell alone—a deep yearning for a state of affairs that is quiet, settled, solid, genuine. In all this, the contemporary world is figured as being marked by the opposite of these qualities. What has to be recognized, therefore, is that intellectuals—the noise they make, the discord they express, the attention they attract—are taken to be one striking embodiment of the distressingly open-ended nature of modernity, just as they are at the same time expressive of what is presumed to be the increasing removal of life from its anchoring in the natural and material world. This helps explain why there is no place for such parasitic, opinionated creatures in that archaic ideal commonwealth the half-memory of which always lurks behind the political criticism of Orwell the antique moralist. In this kind of dream of an English Eden there is neither need nor room for those who only stand and carp. In so far as Orwell indulged this strain in himself—and it was, of course, partially offset by other, less culpable strains—he encouraged an undiscriminating hostility to intellectuals as such, and he was then surely guilty of that most unlovely and least defensible of inner contradictions, the anti-intellectualism of the intellectual.

NOTES

1. Bernard Crick, *George Orwell: A Life* (Harmondsworth: Penguin, 1982 [1st pub. 1980]), 18.
2. Gollancz's 'Foreword' is reprinted as an appendix to *The Road to Wigan Pier* (1937) in Peter Davison (ed.), *The Complete Works of George Orwell*, 20 vols. (London: Secker, 1998), v, quotation at 221. Hereafter references to this magnificent edition will be by volume and page number.

3. Orwell to Gollancz, 9 May 1937; xi. 22–3.
4. Crick, *Orwell*, 404.
5. I attempt to support this judgement in 'The grocer's children', *TLS*, 20 June 2003, 3–8.
6. 'Why I write', *Gangrel*, summer 1946; xviii. 319.
7. *Keep the Aspidistra Flying* (1936); iv. 7.
8. Cyril Connolly, *The Evening Colonnade* (1973); quoted in Crick, *Orwell*, 265.
9. *Wigan Pier*; v. 126.
10. Ibid. 145, 147.
11. Ibid. 153.
12. Ibid. 161. Here and in the concluding section of this chapter I draw upon some sentences from my essay 'Every fruit-juice drinker, nudist, sandal-wearer . . . : intellectuals as other people', in Helen Small (ed.), *The Public Intellectual* (Oxford: Blackwell, 2002), 203–23.
13. Friedrich Nietzsche, *Twilight of the Idols* (1889), trans. R. J. Hollingdale (Harmondsworth: Penguin, 1968), 92.
14. *Wigan Pier*, v. 162; cf. editorial note, x. 493.
15. Ibid. v. 30–1.
16. Ibid. 195.
17. Ibid. 156, 163, 166, 167, 169.
18. Ibid. 170–1.
19. Ibid. 152.
20. Orwell to Spender, 15 Apr. 1938; xi. 132.
21. Orwell to Connolly, 27 Apr. 1938; xi. 146.
22. Orwell to Nancy Cunard, 6 Aug. 1937; xi. 67.
23. 'Inside the Whale' (1940), xii. 103–4.
24. 'Political reflections on the crisis', *The Adelphi*, Dec. 1938; xi. 243–4.
25. 'Inside the whale', xii. 103–4.
26. See Crick, *Orwell*, 402–3.
27. *The Lion and the Unicorn: Socialism and the English Genius* (1941); xii. 405, 405–6.
28. *Lion and Unicorn*; xii. 406.
29. Ibid. 401.
30. 'Rudyard Kipling', *Horizon*, Feb. 1942; xiii. 160.
31. 'Kipling'; xiii. 159.
32. Annotations to Randall Swingler, 'The right to free expression', *Polemic*, Sept.–Oct. 1946; xviii. 443. Orwell's responses were printed as marginal annotations, and are reproduced in xviii. 439–43.
33. 'The prevention of literature', *Polemic*, Jan. 1946; xvii. 372–3. Swingler's article cited in the previous note was a response to this essay.
34. 'Prevention of literature'; xvii. 379.
35. 'Raffles and Miss Blandish', *Horizon*, Oct. 1944; xvi. 354.
36. 'Review of *The Two Carlyles* by Osbert Burdett', *The Adelphi*, Mar. 1931; x. 195–7.
37. 'Britain's left-wing press', *Progressive*, June 1948; xix. 296.
38. Orwell to Dwight Macdonald, 27 Jan. 1949; xx. 28..
39. See the admirably balanced editorial discussion of this in Appendix 9 of xx. 240–59. In my view, the recent discovery of the actual copy of this list in the Foreign Office files does not significantly alter this picture.
40. See, for examples, xx. 99–100, 105, 241, 247, 255, 256.

41. 'Poetry and the microphone', *The New Saxon Pamphlet*, Mar. 1945 [but probably written 1943]; xvii. 80.
42. Crick, *Orwell*, 439.
43. 'The intellectual revolt', *Manchester Evening News*, Jan. and Feb. 1946; the 'Afterword' was published in German in Aug. 1946; Orwell's original English text has not survived and this version is retranslated from the German by the editor of the *Complete Works*; xviii, 56–69, 70, 71.
44. 'Review of *Power: A New Social Analysis* by Bertrand Russell', *The Adelphi*, Jan. 1939; xi. 311–12.
45. 'As I Please', *Tribune*, 16 June 1944; xvi. 258–9.
46. 'Review of *The Edge of the Abyss* by Alfred Noyes', *Observer*, 27 Feb. 1944; xvi. 105–7.
47. See his correspondence with Koestler in Jan. 1946; xviii. 7–8.
48. Orwell to Koestler, 16 Mar. 1946; xviii. 154–5.
49. Swingler, 'Right to free expression'; Orwell, 'Annotations to Swingler'; xviii. 438, 439–43.
50. 'Inside the whale'; xii. 105.
51. e.g., x. 440; xii. 262; xvi. 36–7, 262; xvii. 50–1.
52. Orwell to Richard Rees, 3 Mar. 1949; xx. 52.
53. 'Appendix 4: Orwell's Reading List for 1949'; xx. 219–23.
54. *Tribune*, 30 Nov. 1945; xvii. 406–8.
55. 'Review of *The Novelist as Thinker*, ed. B. Rajan', *TLS*, 7 Aug. 1948; xix. 417.
56. Orwell to Fredric Warburg, 22 Oct. 1948; xix. 457; Orwell to Julian Symons, 29 Oct. 1948; xix. 461.
57. 'Review of *Portrait of the Anti-Semite* by Jean-Paul Sartre', *The Observer*, 7 Nov. 1948; xix. 464–5.
58. 'Review of *Barbarians and Philistines: Democracy and the Public Schools* by T. C. Worsley', *Time and Tide*, 14 Sept. 1940; xii. 261–2.
59. 'Review of *Cricket Country* by Edmund Blunden', *Manchester Evening News*, 20 Apr. 1944; xvi. 161–3.
60. These particular phrases, variants of which appear throughout his writing, are from 'London Letter', *Partisan Review*, Summer 1944; xvi. 159.
61. 'London Letter', *Partisan Review*, Mar.–Apr. 1941; xii. 354–5.
62. Ibid. winter 1944–5; xvi. 414.
63. Ibid. 415; 'Notes on nationalism', *Polemic*, Oct. 1945; xvii. 155.

16

Nothing to Say: A. J. P. Taylor

'As I once wrote about Bernard Shaw, I had a great gift of expression and nothing to say.'

I

The city of Wroclaw in Poland may be one of the less obvious locations in which to seek for understanding about the question of intellectuals in twentieth-century Britain. But in August 1948, Wroclaw, formerly Breslau in German Silesia, was the site chosen for a 'Congress of the Intellectuals', a gathering of leading cultural and scientific figures from both sides of the Iron Curtain, a gathering nominally intended to demonstrate cultural cooperation and thereby to attempt to diminish the strains of the Cold War, but one which was in practice little more than a Communist front. The ultimate purpose of the organizers of the conference was to orchestrate matters so as to produce a series of resoundingly unanimous condemnations of 'American Fascism'. The inviting of 'delegates' from the West seems to have been a somewhat haphazard matter; invitations had been sent to a range of 'intellectuals' who were assumed to be disposed to sympathize with Communism and to be critical of the policy of the United States. The selection of British delegates appears to have been largely left in the hands of the Polish cultural attaché in London. Those who accepted the invitations were mainly members of the Party or at the least fellow-travellers, although the organizers, as we shall see, had not been careful enough to ensure that only those who would toe the party line had been invited.

The British 'delegation' (not in fact delegated by anybody) included several of the obvious suspects: Ritchie Calder, Christopher Hill, Hewlett Johnson (the 'Red Dean' of Canterbury), and scientists such as J. D. Bernal, J. B. S. Haldane, and Hyman Levy. But it also included several figures less close to the Party such as the scientist Julian Huxley, the artist Felix Topolski, the novelists Richard Hughes and Olaf Stapledon, the journalists Kingsley Martin and Edward Crankshaw, the publisher George Weidenfeld, and the historian A. J. P. Taylor.[1] The opening address by the Soviet writer Aleksandr Fadeyev set the tone, attacking the 'reptilian Fascists' in the West, dismissing the worthlessness of 'Americanized' culture, and denouncing as 'hyenas' and 'jackals' such leading Western writers as T. S. Eliot and Eugene O'Neill, and even less plausible targets still, including Jean-Paul Sartre and André Malraux (all of whom were conspicuously not present). It was assumed that subsequent speeches would simply be variations on this agreed theme, but the next morning Taylor 'replied' on behalf of the British delegation in an unscripted speech.

He rejected the one-eyed simplicities of Cold War propaganda and urged that it was the special duty of intellectuals to uphold freedom of enquiry and of speech as well as to attempt to promote genuine tolerance and mutual understanding: 'In my opinion, it is our duty as intellectuals to preach tolerance, not to preach hate.' It was not the role of the intellectual to kowtow to power, including Soviet power: 'If we intellectuals are to work together, it must be on the basis . . . of truth.' He affirmed the classic Enlightenment ideal of the international republic of the mind: 'We intellectuals belong to the country of Voltaire and Goethe, of Tolstoi and Shakespeare.' And his peroration went for some of the highest notes in the repertoire: 'Without intellectual freedom, without love, without tolerance, the intellectual cannot serve humanity.'[2]

Taylor's speech caused something of a sensation: it disrupted the required unanimity and drew fierce denunciations from succeeding, pro-Soviet, speakers. The episode attracted widespread attention in the press. As one of his biographers puts it, Taylor's 'defiance at Wroclaw made him famous in the West, particularly when the story was written up in the *New York Times*'.[3] 'Famous' may be something of an exaggeration, and 'the West' meant principally in the United States, but still it was a notable act, an act immediately assimilable to one favoured model of the intellectual: speaking for truth and against power. Taylor was hailed as liberal democracy's idea of an intellectual. And his own account, written at the time, reinforced this identification. 'Julien Benda, who was himself at Wroclaw, must have acquired new material for "The Treason of the Intellectuals".'[4] This opening sentence of Taylor's article in the *Manchester Guardian* assumed his readers would be familiar with Benda's book, or at least with its thesis—or at least with its thesis as it had by then been most commonly misinterpreted—and would see its relevance to the Wroclaw congress. But no treasonous clerk he.

In fact, Taylor had briefly been a member of the Communist Party in the 1920s, and although he was so no longer, he still regarded himself as very much a 'man of the Left' (when his father died in 1940, his coffin was wrapped in the Red Flag, complete with hammer and sickle[5]). He was, moreover, critical of the very idea of the Cold War, for which he held the West primarily responsible.[6] He was in these respects an obvious invitee. But in the setting of the Wroclaw congress, Taylor had no hesitation in identifying himself and his colleagues as 'intellectuals' and in specifying their task in the most elevated of the terms which had, since the Dreyfus Affair, been available for underwriting the moral authority of that role. Taylor recognized that part of the problem at Wroclaw was the unrepresentative nature of the gathering in the first place: 'The fault lies with the British intellectuals who were invited to Wroclaw and would not trouble to go.' Still, there was quiet satisfaction in Taylor's conclusion that the actions of a few outspoken individuals, himself prominent among them, had made it impossible for the Russians to claim that the congress had unanimously condemned American fascism. As Kingsley Martin described the speech for *New Statesman* readers: 'Some people in England, and more in America, now said that the Soviet Union and Nazi Germany were indistinguishable. As intellectuals, Mr Taylor agreed that it was our business to refute such assertions. It was equally the business of the intellectuals at the conference to reject, instead of repeating, wild slogans about American Fascism.'[7] 'As intellectuals': Martin's use of the first-person plural betrays no unease about absorbing himself, Taylor, and the other delegates from Britain under this label.

Seen in the broader context of Taylor's career as a whole, however, this episode becomes less talismanic and more a tantalizing glimpse of one side of his complex character, in which genuine courage and mere provocativeness were blended in almost equal measure ('almost' because the provocativeness mostly seemed to dominate). At times he could be a very effective spokesman for liberal values, and he liked to see himself as a 'dissenter', championing unpopular ideas in the face of orthodoxy. As Martin put it after Wroclaw: 'Mr Taylor . . . is quite consistent. In England he attacks British policy; in the Eastern Zone he attacks Soviet policy.'[8] But this coexisted with what came to be almost an obsession with the 'realities' of power and a conviction that 'mere ideas' played little part in events. Moreover, he hardly made a natural recruit to the ranks of Benda's austere, priestly caste, largely removed from the world: he displayed an undiscriminating and apparently insatiable appetite for both celebrity and money, and he turned out so much popular journalism on such a wide variety of non-scholarly subjects that he was pilloried by his critics as 'the motoring correspondent of the *Sunday Express*'. His opinionatedness was one expression of his habitual counter-suggestibility: not for nothing did he call the book about the tradition of radical critics of Britain's foreign policy (with whom he so clearly identified) *The Troublemakers*. For Taylor, being mischievous could appear to be almost a test of intellectual vitality. On occasion, as in Wroclaw in August 1948, this could lead him to a notable outspokenness; on other occasions, thirsting for the extra little splash of attention it would bring, it could lead him to notable silliness. Taylor's shameless fluency in expressing his wilfully mischievous views lay at the heart of his vexed or paradoxical performance in the role of the intellectual—and hence of his representativeness for my purposes—not least because the opinion he expressed most forcibly was that the opinions of intellectuals were of very little consequence.

II

In narrating the bare outline of Taylor's career as an intellectual and public figure, large numbers must play an unusually prominent part.[9] His bibliographer's computations almost seem reminiscent of Soviet announcements of productivity figures for the last Five-Year Plan: twenty-three authored books; twenty-six books edited or introduced; thirteen pamphlets; forty-five essays in books; 115 historical essays in journals or periodicals; 459 newspaper articles; over 1,500 book reviews; 450 broadcasts on TV and radio. Whatever Taylor's limitations in the role of intellectual, they did not include failing to bend the public's ear.

After graduating from Oriel College, Oxford and spending some time on research in Vienna, Taylor was appointed an Assistant Lecturer in Modern History at Manchester University in 1930, at the age of 24. He began reviewing books for the *Manchester Guardian* four years later, and from 1935 onwards he was reviewing between twenty-five and thirty books per year. He moved to a Tutorial Fellowship at Magdalen College, Oxford in 1938, and in 1941 published his first book aimed at a broad readership, *The Habsburg Monarchy*. But it was only in the second half of the 1940s that his career really began to take off. In 1944–5 he helped A. P. Wadsworth with leading-articles for the *Manchester Guardian*, which were, hardly unusually for the period, strongly anti-German and pro-Soviet. He also began to take part in panel discussions on the radio about contemporary political topics (on which more below), as well as publishing regular reviews, mostly on historical subjects, in *The New Statesman*. By 1950, at the age of 44, he was well enough known to have a volume of his selected reviews reprinted in book form. The fact that he had thrown these pieces together without bothering to revise them, combined with the showy nature of the reviews in the first place, led to a lukewarm reception. Taylor's literary and public persona was already beginning to tell against him; noticing his first volume of collected reviews, even the *Manchester Guardian* expressed reservations: 'Perhaps one reason why so many judgments seem eccentric is that Mr Taylor has always been making judgments, and that, by his own confession, he now blushes for some of them.'[10] Throughout the 1950s, he wrote roughly a review a week, chiefly in the *Guardian*, the *Statesman*, and the *TLS* (there were eventually to be five volumes of his reprinted reviews).

But Taylor very quickly appreciated the burgeoning potential of media other than print: he accepted all opportunities to speak on the radio, and not just on the newly founded Third Programme which, as we shall see in Ch. 19, even some more orthodox academics recognized might be a valuable and appropriate medium for them; and he shamelessly pressed himself on the attentions of BBC television, finally in 1950 securing a place in the panel discussion programme 'In the News' (along with Robert Boothby, Michael Foot, and W. J. Brown). The success of this programme earned him the sobriquet in the press of 'the TV don', though he was to know much greater TV success towards the end of the decade. It has to be remembered, in considering Taylor's relation to different publics, that television played a much more minor part in the national culture at this date than it has come to do subsequently. As Burk puts it: 'Appearing on television . . . carried limited cachet: television sets for most of the 1950s were seen by many as something owned predominantly by the working and lower-middle classes rather than by the middle classes, and even less by the professional and academic middle class.'[11]

It was partly on the strength of this enhanced level of exposure that in 1951 Taylor was first asked to write regularly for the *Sunday Pictorial*. By this date, he had also started to write reviews for *The Observer*, and from 1952 he began to write regular articles for the *Daily Herald*. As his biographer puts it, speaking of the early 1950s: 'Alan was by now the most famous don in Britain.'[12] It is an index of his fame, as well as an expression of the manner which contributed to that fame, that he had a card printed which he used for refusing the numerous invitations to speak or write that now came his way.

All of this was, in the eyes of his professionally more austere colleagues, bad enough, and his journalism combined with his relatively unorthodox private life to attract more than his share of the usual narrow-minded tut-tutting in Oxford. And not just in Oxford: Kathleen Burk suggests he was turned down for the Stevenson Chair in International History at the LSE in 1952 because its Director, Sir Alexander Carr-Saunders, objected to Taylor's media activities.[13] But what was really to stamp him with the mark of Cain in the eyes of those given to such high-minded disapproval was his long association with *The Sunday Express*. This began in 1957 and he was soon contracted to write a fixed number of leader-page articles a year on all manner of subjects (it was the frequency with which he wrote on the topic of driving, notably the pleasures of driving fast, which earned him the mocking label mentioned earlier). The *Express* was a mass-market empire-celebrating newspaper, dominated by the views of its autocratic owner, Lord Beaverbrook: it was not only academic colleagues who wondered whether writing trashy, tub-thumping articles in such a paper was really the proper employment of the talents of an Oxford don, especially one supposed to be distinguished by his left-wing opinions. Taylor liked to respond to such eyebrow-raising by airily dismissing his articles as 'rubbish'—and by pointing out that whereas he was paid £12 for a review in the *New Statesman*, a leader of the same length in the *Express* would earn him £100.[14]

Taylor could sometimes show himself to be alert to the tensions which his dual life as academic scholar and popular journalist had installed at the heart of his career. When in 1954 he was invited to give the Ford Lectures in Oxford, one of the ultimate tributes a British historian can receive, he confided to Wadsworth, editor of the *Manchester Guardian* and long-standing friend: 'If I were asked to choose whether to be Ford's Lecturer or to return with the old team to "In the News", I'd hesitate. That no doubt is why some people wouldn't have me as a professor.'[15] Nonetheless, up to this point Taylor did continue to receive recognition as a scholar, as the Ford Lectures or (in 1956) election as a Fellow of the British Academy indicated. But 1957 proved to be something of a turning-point in Taylor's career in more ways than one. In June of that year he was passed over for the Regius Chair in History at Oxford (in favour of the less well-published but far better-connected Hugh Trevor-Roper): Taylor felt the Chair was his due and that 'the Oxford Establishment' had closed ranks in the face of his supposed political and personal heterodoxy, though it would have been hard by this point to say quite what his political identity was, beyond a reputation for a kind of left-wing populism. It would be an understatement to say the disappointment rankled: in the Preface to his *English History 1914–1945* which appeared eight years later, he still wanted the world to know that he was grateful for the support of G. N. Clark who commissioned him to write the book 'and sustained me when I was slighted in my profession'.[16] But an awareness of a different kind of explanation may be apparent when, later that year, he turned down his publisher's ideas for writing a popular book, claiming 'I've produced so much in recent years that I now need to restore my intellectual capital.'[17] Characteristically, he turned what might have been plausible defence into implausible attack: 'The more one writes, the more one is ignored or slighted in the academic world.'[18] It is, in any event, impossible to know how far his disappointment and resentment fuelled his acceptance of two other opportunities which were to shape his public reputation, but both occurred later that year. Not only did that autumn see the beginning of his association with the *Express*, but also the first of his appearances in a genre he was to make distinctively his own: the television lecture. These were remarkable tours de force: without script or autocue, Taylor would simply face the camera for thirty minutes and give a faultlessly fluent and clear lecture which he would bring to its neat conclusion at precisely the appointed time.

This was his apogee as a performer.[19] By the mid-1960s, he had given over forty such lectures on both ITV (which he, with characteristic perversity, favoured on principle) and the BBC, and at their peak the lectures attracted an audience of close to four million. He told an interviewer that he meant these talks to be just as serious as his university lectures only shorter.[20] This remark also gives some clue to understanding his role, and indeed that of the other academics who enjoyed media favour at the time. As I have already observed, there still existed very considerable cultural deference towards universities, and after 1945 there was an expanding audience eager to acquire some of the 'culture' they were supposed to have to offer. Part of the distinctiveness of this period comes from the fact that new media arose to meet these needs before this kind of deference was eroded by larger social and economic changes (the range of titles published by Penguin was one expression of this situation, the programming on both radio and TV was another). The kind of class deference at the heart of all this may be indicated from another angle by Sisman's comment that 'There was one irony about his screen success; Alan himself did not possess a television set.'[21]

A profile in the *New Statesman* in September 1957 recognized Taylor's unique standing, yet also, indirectly, raised the major question which would come to be asked about his career. 'There have been famous dons before him in politics or journalism. But dons like Keynes or Laski were famous for what they did or thought. Alan Taylor is famous for being Taylor.' It recognized that his position depended upon the expansion and the rise in visibility of popular media in the 1950s, but his fame could not be reduced to these conditions. 'There are many other television dons; several intellectuals write for the popular press. Few of them do it so well. None of them is a *star*.' (Falling into pastiche of his style was a common failing of writing about Taylor.) But the profile-writer struggled to identify what it was that Taylor wanted to say to the huge audiences he now commanded. As a teacher, he could be stimulating, but 'Taylor's pupils are . . . not handed the recipe for the good society.' Perhaps *The Troublemakers*, his Ford Lectures on the tradition of dissent against British foreign policy, was his most self-revealing book: 'For Taylor himself is a troublemaker. That is why he is a star, why he wants an audience in the first place, why he can get one and why he is able to excite it when he has got it.' Still, any sense of a 'message' or a consistent 'line', remained elusive. Perhaps the answer to the implicit question was too obvious or too simple to be wholly satisfying: 'Taylor does it because he enjoys it.'[22]

A notable example of the kind of media attention which some academics could command at the time came in the wake of the publication of Taylor's hugely provocative *Origins of the Second World War* in 1961. The book, with its emphasis on the accidental nature of the events leading up to war in September 1939 and its apparent refusal to regard Hitler as anything more than one partly incompetent statesman among others, provoked a storm of criticism. No critic was more telling than his old adversary Hugh Trevor-Roper in *Encounter*, in an article which developed into an exchange with Taylor through the summer and autumn of 1961. But what is more striking is that this exchange should have been thought likely to produce 'good television' in the form of a televised debate between Taylor and Trevor-Roper on 9 July, chaired by Robert Kee. Although the exchange seems to have been fairly restrained and scholarly, it attracted considerable attention, and the programme was in turn reviewed in the next day's newspapers.[23] Of course, the subject was undeniably a major one, and the experience of the war was still the dominating memory of British society in 1961. But cultural deference and a kind of cultural celebrity clearly played their part: it mattered that this was not a debate between just any two academics, but between the media-friendly Regius Professor of Modern History at Oxford and his even better-known local rival. The media like a prize fight.

Although Taylor was, especially in his early days, self-consciously a 'man of the Left' who missed no opportunity to criticize the selfishness and incompetence of the governing class, his direct involvement with contemporary British politics was, with one exception, slight. The exception, however, was a substantial and revealing one: his role in the Campaign for Nuclear Disarmament between 1958 and 1961. He was involved in this almost from the start, addressing the first public meeting of CND in February 1958 and being invited onto the CND executive in April of that year.[24] The question of the nuclear deterrent he regarded, quite simply, as 'the biggest issue in politics'. The sheer capacity of such weapons for destruction and mutilation was abhorrent to him, and he could see no situation in which their use, or counter-use, could be justified. But he also believed that the logic of the theory of 'deterrence' was faulty. This was an issue on which his view of the role of accident in history came into its own: if previous wars had in effect been started by a series of accidents, then the same could happen with nuclear war, and it is in this sense that the publication in 1961 of his *The Origins of the Second World War* could be considered 'a powerful propaganda stroke for CND'.[25]

From the outset, Taylor took a prominent part in the campaign, spending much time in 1958 giving speeches in town halls and similar venues up and down the country. He liked to think of himself as being in the tradition of previous 'troublemakers', in a direct line from the anti-slavery campaign and the Anti-Corn Law League of the nineteenth century, speaking in the same Birmingham City Hall where Bright had spoken, and so on. The showman in him responded to the challenge of public speaking on this scale, and he was evidently very good at it. The peak may have been reached on Easter Monday 1960 when, at the end of the Aldermaston March, he addressed a crowd estimated to be 100,000.[26] But Taylor had no sympathy with the policy of civil disobedience and 'direct action': his model of a single-issue pressure group was one which would argue its way to victory by persuading a large enough proportion of the electorate. As dissension among the various groups within CND became fiercer, Taylor felt increasingly out of sympathy with the newer generation; in the autumn of 1960 he resigned from the Executive Committee.

Taylor's involvement with the Campaign for Nuclear Disarmament was an important episode in his life, at once impressive, revealing, and tantalizing—tantalizing because it suggests something of the energy and capacity he could bring to an activity when he cared passionately about something outside himself, an issue on which he felt too strongly to be merely flippant or mischievous. One is reminded that *The Trouble Makers* was his own favourite among his books, though by no means the most successful or most important. One is also reminded of his Lancashire Dissenting inheritance, always most effectively reactivated by what he saw as the inanities of 'Establishment' foreign policy. Had he pursued the theme of his Ford Lectures in other writings of the late 1950s, his work might have occupied a place in relation to aspects of the radical Left discussion of foreign policy in that period somewhat akin to that occupied by, say, Raymond Williams's *Culture and Society* in relation to criticism of social and cultural policy, but the fleeting, hypothetical similarity only underlines how massive the contrasts between their two roles actually were.

Taylor was perhaps the first, and certainly the most widely known, of what came to be called 'the media dons', but in fact, from being an academic who did some reviewing and broadcasting on the side, he really became, by mid-career, a professional writer and 'media personality' who still continued to do a spot of teaching. Already by 1950 (when he was 44), his freelance income exceeded his university salary: it soon became more than three times greater.[27] From 1953 he held a University Lectureship (rather than college Tutorship) in Oxford which reduced his load of college tutorials, and he effectively gave up regular teaching in Oxford in 1963 when, on the expiry of his university post, he was elected to a 'Special Fellowship' at Magdalen ('I'm a rather special historian' was Taylor's characteristic—and almost self-defeating—argument in favour of this honour).

Through the 1960s and into the early 1970s, Taylor contrived to stay in the public eye and to enjoy his fame. When his university lectureship at Oxford came to an end after ten years, as such appointments usually did, he orchestrated the press coverage of his 'sacking'. His celebrity was such (and his Fleet Street contacts so good) that the news made the front pages of broadsheets and popular dailies alike.[28] Having left Oxford in the summer of 1963, he thereafter held a series of part-time or visiting academic positions, though for several years his principal appointment was as Honorary Director of the Beaverbrook Library, set up following the death of his patron in 1964. And he continued to publish, almost up to his death in 1990, though there was a strong sense from about the mid-1970s onwards that his star had waned. He played little part in public affairs, and although several of his works and compilations continued to sell well, attention within academia had been diverted to the new generation of social historians, such as Keith Thomas or Taylor's erstwhile comrade in CND, E. P. Thompson.

One question which the comparison with Thompson raises is what kind of difference it would have made to Taylor's role as an intellectual in mid-twentieth century Britain had he principally written about *British* history. Apart from *The Troublemakers*, Taylor was to write only one substantial work of British history, the concluding volume of what Oxford University Press still called 'The Oxford History of England', his *English History 1914–1945*, which was not published until 1965, when he was almost 60. The book was a great success: the initial print run was a remarkable 40,000 copies, testimony to Taylor's popularity in itself, and was soon sold out; sales of the Penguin edition were eventually to be greater still. And although the book was very much a detailed narrative history, concentrating on politics and war, it did express a view of English society, indeed a decidedly positive one. In particular, it spoke of the Second World War as 'a people's war', as the time when 'the British people came of age', and the famous concluding paragraph exemplified what Taylor meant by referring to his desire to 'reclaim patriotism' from its Right-wing appropriators.

> The British were the only people who went through both world wars from beginning to end. Yet they remained a peaceful and civilised people, tolerant, patient, and generous. Traditional values lost much of their force. Other values took their place. Imperial greatness was on the way out; the welfare state was on the way in. The British empire declined; the condition of the people improved. Few now sang 'Land of Hope and Glory'. Few even sang 'England Arise'. England had risen all the same.[29]

The stylistic tics are as intrusive as ever, the judgements as contestable as ever, but this was Taylor's most explicit attempt to win hearts as well as minds, a late bid for the kind of popularity enjoyed by Trevelyan or Bryant, a long application for the post of Historian Laureate.

The production of this book generated one vignette that is revealing of Taylor's divided reputation and his awareness of it. The initial design for the jacket departed from the normal sober OUP blue to incorporate a series of photographs, a design intended to attract booksellers and a wider public. Taylor protested: 'I have acquired, I think most undeservedly, the reputation of being a journalistic, unscholarly writer. This jacket will confirm that reputation. People will think that the book is another piece of provocative, paradoxical display by an elderly enfant terrible.'[30] Well, the book both was and was not such a display, just as he more generally both was a lifelong *enfant terrible*—and was something more than that. But it was a label he could not help but attract; as the *TLS* reviewer of *The Troublemakers* put it: 'It was at first an amusing trick to invent that *enfant terrible* (which may perhaps be anglicised as an intellectual teddy boy) to serve as the serious historian's *alter ego*; but the trick can well become an obsession, and the obsession can become involuntary and irreversible.'[31] In short, was Taylor a serious intellectual, or just 'an intellectual teddy boy'?

III

One of the recurring tropes of Taylor's writing is the disavowal of the intention to provoke or to shock. The more of his prose one reads, the more it becomes evident that this is a familiar part of what one might call 'the naughty-boy syndrome', the resort to a disingenuous literalism, the protestation that there really is less going on than meets the eye. (Sisman is perhaps pointing to something similar when he observes: 'Alan liked to undermine accepted ideas or beliefs by pretending not to understand them.'[32]) Consider three examples of this temperamental or stylistic tic. The first comes from the Preface to the third of his volumes of collected essays and reviews, *Englishmen and Others*, published in 1956. 'I am not a philosophic historian. I have no system, no moral interpretation. I write to clear my mind, to discover how things happened and how men behaved. If the result is shocking or provocative, this is not from intent, but solely because I try to judge from the evidence without being influenced by the judgements of others.'[33] The next example comes from the 'Second Thoughts' which prefaced the paperback edition of his hugely controversial *The Origins of the Second World War*. The book was taken, as he well knew it would be, as a piece of radical revisionism, practically exculpating Hitler from any responsibility for having brought about the Second World War.

I wrote this book to satisfy my historical curiosity; in the words of a more successful historian, 'to understand what happened, and why it happened'. Historians often dislike what happened or wish that it had happened differently. There is nothing they can do about it. They have to state the truth as they see it without worrying whether this shocks or confirms existing prejudices. Maybe I assumed this too innocently.[34]

The third example comes from his private response to the (anonymous) reviewer in the *TLS* of his *English History 1914–1945*, and shows him again denying that he had intended to be 'revisionist': 'I am neither revisionist nor orthodox—I don't think about the question one way or the other.'[35]

It is evident to the most cursory reader of Taylor's histories that he was, in fact, constantly concerned about whether what he wrote was 'shocking or provocative': his lapidary provocations only possessed any force because they challenged or reversed some 'existing prejudices'. These protestations are classic examples of trying to have things both ways. Taylor was, both as a man and as a historian, a compulsive attention-seeker: his writing visibly tried to be outrageous, irreverent, provoking. Yet at the same time he wanted to claim the authority of the purest empiricism: this is simply how things were, the facts speak for themselves, and Taylor wishes to represent himself as merely their amanuensis. In this respect, these stylized disavowals flirt with a kind of anti-intellectualism. They are a variant of the historian-as-plain-man credo: Taylor, in company with that sensible person the 'ordinary' reader, does not bother his head about fancy theories and counter-theories. That, he seems to imply, can be left to those people who make so much noise about such things—left, that is, to the intellectuals. Intellectuals, once again, are by implication always other people.

Yet in simultaneously combining this critical posture with a yearning to cut a figure in public debate in a way characteristic of the intellectual rather than of the 'mere' historian, Taylor embodied the fundamental tension which I analysed earlier. For example, reflecting in 1948 that 'a nation reveals its character in the way it seeks to impress foreigners', he praised the French for organizing 'a serious Congress of Historians', and then embarked on a little homily on the implications of this.

In England an historian is regarded as an impractical pedant, a tiresome necessity for teaching the young, and the title of 'professor' is a disqualification for public life. In France a professor, and especially a professor of history, enjoys the standing and influence of an elder statesman, and every historian assumes that his work contributes to the public life of France.[36]

As always, Taylor overstates for effect, but there is surely more than a hint here of that 'intellectuals envy' I diagnosed earlier. He clearly wanted his own 'work' to contribute to the 'public life' of Britain, but since his work tended to a kind of intellectual nihilism, it could mostly only have a negative effect, a denial of some larger or more coherent story told by others. This can, on occasion, be an indispensable task, and it is worth remembering that Taylor's was a consistently libertarian voice as well as a bracingly sceptical one. But by needlessly exaggerating his own freedom from ideas, principles, or even preconceptions, he ran the risk of undercutting his own authority. In practice, his writing constantly drew attention to its own performance, and that, combined with the reiterated insistence that history yielded no inferences or moral for the present as well as precious little pattern in the past, meant that it became harder and harder for the reader to resist the feeling that performance was all there was.

Six years later he again made use of the familiar contrast with France when deploring 'this soft lotus-land of English history' in which there was not enough 'bitterness and dispute'. In France historians felt that 'they have a vital duty to perform and [are] therefore eager to dispute over every historical question, great or small. To be an historian in France is to be a combatant, to be also a politician, and even (in the old-fashioned sense of the term) a prophet, a moral teacher.'[37] In one respect, this passage is characteristic of an ambivalence felt by many British intellectuals, caught between the desire to play a more prominent part in public debate and scorn for the kind of public debate which accords esteem to mere posturing and position-taking. But Taylor experienced this ambivalence with an intensity denied to his more modest or more consistent colleagues. He desperately wanted to be paid attention to in the way that he believed, or imagined, leading French historians were paid attention to, but at the same time he was always disavowing the role of prophet or moral teacher, indeed positively ruling that it was not one which the historian qua historian could legitimately occupy.

For all his enormous public success, therefore, the question about Taylor as an intellectual must remain whether he had anything to say which touched, in important ways, the general concerns of his publics. 'General', as I made clear in Ch. 2, does not for these purposes have to mean abstract or universal or even political. But it must be a way of talking which promises, on the basis of an acknowledged intellectual standing, to put specific and local concerns into some broader perspective. Taylor partly achieved this, it must be recognized, just by so brilliantly embodying the idea of the 'historian', the very clever person who knows an awful lot about the past and who can organize that knowledge into impressively clear and unfailingly interesting narratives. The past, simply in virtue of being the past, does always offer one kind of 'broader perspective'. But Taylor rarely attempted to connect that perspective to the concerns of his readers, or, rather, he denied that it could be done, even though some of his own writing—on, for example, the nineteenth-century critics of Britain's foreign policy or the changes in the condition of British society during the Second World War—did help people in the present to place themselves in a tradition or a development which offered to alter their self-understanding.

Taylor, however, did not appear to be particularly interested in such 'abstract' notions as 'self-understanding'. As he famously put it in reviewing Carr's *What is History?*, echoing J. B. Bury's famous dictum that history was a science 'no more and no less': 'Study of history enables us to understand the past; no more and no less.'[38] He seemed to suggest that he wanted people to read his own work in the same spirit in which they might read murder mysteries: to find out what happened, to take pleasure in the storyteller's art, to pass the time. On all the large and complicated questions about the relation of the past to the present, he allowed his mind to come to rest too easily and too quickly. There was in the end a kind of wilful refusal of seriousness in Taylor, an automatic repudiation of anything which smacked of reflective, generalizing analysis, a self-indulgent satisfaction in the merely clever or stylish.

But while that may be true 'in the end', along the way Taylor melded insight and scepticism in a manner which, though not wholly unique, did offer his readers and listeners, and eventually viewers, a perspective on the world, a perspective based on a deep grounding in the political and diplomatic history of nineteenth- and twentieth-century Europe. Here, he was the true successor to his mentor, Sir Lewis Namier, and the nearest parallel was possibly E. H. Carr, another historian much influenced by Namier, and one, like Taylor, also much given to sermons about the reality of 'power' and, more especially, the importance to Europe of Soviet Russia. Like both Namier and, to a lesser extent, Carr, Taylor was caught in the paradoxical position of the intellectual who wanted to be important but who professed to think that in general intellectuals were not very important. On this score, at least, he would have been particularly miffed by the mild criticism offered by former Prime Minister Clement Attlee in a review of *The Troublemakers*, when he observed that Taylor 'tends to over stress the importance of the intellectuals as is natural in an academic writer'.[39] (Perhaps a sentence in his *English History 1914–1945* was his revenge: there he described Attlee as 'a middle-class man, with considerable experience of the east end and some slight pretensions to be an "intellectual" '.)[40]

Certain themes or attitudes do recur throughout Taylor's writing. Hostility to Germany was one of the organizing nodes of his thinking about European history; hostility to America was practically a reflex in cultural and economic matters; support for the Soviet Union was, at least in the first half of his career, an axiom of his politics. He was, after all, a Left-wing Englishman of Nonconformist Lancashire stock. But he never really toed a party line, and his own exhibitionism frequently trumped his political convictions. Thus, although he was strongly pro-Soviet in the 1940s, he expressed his views very much in his own manner. He told a BBC Home Service audience at the end of 1945: 'Nobody in Europe believes in the American way of life, that is, in private enterprise; or rather, those who believe in it are a defeated party, which seems to have no more future than the Jacobites in England after 1688.'[41] It was not uncommon, of course, in the 1930s and 1940s to feel that market capitalism had failed and needed to be replaced by some kind of planned economy, but to say that 'nobody' believed in it was one kind of exaggeration and the parallel with the Jacobites was another (as the Hanoverians of collectivism might now ruefully acknowledge).

When he gave a series of talks in December 1946–January 1947 on what British foreign policy should be, he argued a vigorously anti-American line and went so far as to press for an alliance between Britain and Russia to resist American 'encroachment' in Europe. He received what he no doubt regarded as the accolade of being denounced in parliament. Henry Strauss, Member for the Combined English Universities, read out extracts from the transcript of Taylor's talks, calling them 'nauseous and contemptible', and Herbert Morrison, as Lord President of the Council, described them as 'anti-American, anti-British and not particularly competent'.[42] But perhaps what was in a way more revealing of the kind of response Taylor tended to generate was the next talk in the same series by R. C. K. Ensor, historian and journalist, who took the extraordinary step of beginning his own broadcast with a reproach to his immediate predecessor: 'What I disapproved in him was not merely the substance of his talks, but the manner. The substance to my thinking consisted too largely of shallow half-truths, more dangerous than plain untruths because more specious, yet not a bit more trustworthy to build on. But I also, if I may say so without needless discourtesy, objected profoundly to his jaunty cocksure manner.'[43] The making of such a criticism in the course of a broadcast on questions of foreign policy was striking enough in itself (and provoked at least one objection when printed in the *Listener*), but it is an admirably concise resumé of Taylor's characteristic faults, pinpointed at a relatively early stage of his career.

When in 1950 Taylor published his first collection of occasional pieces (mentioned earlier), he referred to this episode in his Introduction in his best tendentious manner. Quoting Morrison's denunciation, of which he was understandably proud, he suggested that this is what had led the BBC to drop him (which was not wholly true). He wanted to explain that not reprinting the talks in the present collection did not represent any acceptance of these criticisms on his part, and that he still held to the general tenor of the views expressed in them. But he risked jeopardizing the sympathy that might have accrued to him from this episode by the transparent excess of his description: 'At any rate I thought there was a use for a historian who would discuss Russian and Communist aims with the same detachment as he would discuss anything else. The BBC thought otherwise; they wanted those who would expound "the British way of life". I hope never to be numbered in this band of secular missionaries.'[44] The BBC wanted no such thing, and the romanticization of his own position was already becoming characteristic—and self-defeating. There are special difficulties involved in trying to make a whole career out of being an *enfant terrible*.

Indeed, reflection on the trajectory of his career (as on that of certain comparable figures) brings out unmercifully how the price of *remaining* constantly in the public eye is a level of overproduction of opinion which is bound to damage the initial cultural standing. In addition, the more one attempts to determine the *content* of Taylor's opinions, the more one sees that he was caught in a circle which may for a long time have been benign as far as securing further invitations to write or speak was concerned, but which was ultimately vicious if the aim really was to have a persuasive impact upon a public's beliefs. On most historical and political questions, what Taylor wanted to say was that it was a mistake to look for general explanations: things happened, people did things, chance was important, there was no pattern. This eventually became a kind of tic, a predictable, perhaps not wholly controllable, response, which meant that it lost its force. Once one becomes too easily parodiable, the mannerisms are in danger of becoming the message. (It surely says something about the ready recognizability of these failings that the parody of his style which won the *New Statesman* competition in 1965 was by fellow-historian Henry Pelling, not normally regarded as among the country's leading humorists.[45]) What mattered most to Taylor was to be arresting, but he was a classic illustration of how the search for arrestingness for its own sake is self-destructive. It made it too easy to conclude that in the end all he had was a manner, plus a lot of information: he deployed snippets of the information in the most mischievous or disruptive way possible. He wrote in very short sentences. He said that most of the things people believed were not true. But that that didn't matter because beliefs didn't really matter anyway. There were only actions. But they usually went wrong. And that didn't matter much either.

All this was absurdly contradictory, of course, since some, at least, of his abundant journalism was very much about expressing opinions the truth of which mattered to him, and among the striking virtues of his numerous substantial works of history was a capacity to identify a narrative or analytical thread which brought together causes and accidents, ideas and personalities, in some persuasive way. But all too often there could be a kind of intellectual nihilism about Taylor's performances, and 'performances' is precisely what they were—turns, forms of showing off, instalments of being A. J. P. Taylor. Those figures who are identified with a particular message or point of view can certainly suffer from one kind of exposure-fatigue, as people become bored with the sheer repetitiveness of the 'line', but they do at least have the content of their views to fall back on, so to speak, and they do have purposes external to themselves. But Taylor, especially as his fame grew and his left-wing credentials became more doubtful, was trapped in the vicious dialectic of celebrity in its pure form: he had to keep renewing his claim upon people's attention by saying attention-grabbing things. There wasn't something he indisputably 'stood for' other than being clever, knowledgeable, heterodox, fluent, amusing . . . for being, in short, A. J. P. Taylor.

His own reflection on this theme (quoted as the epigraph to this chapter) was characteristically terse—and dispiriting: 'As I once wrote about Bernard Shaw, I had a great gift of expression and nothing to say.'[46] The remark is vintage Taylor in several ways. It contains some truth; it's doubly self-referential, since he is also citing his own earlier writing; and it sacrifices measured judgement (about either himself or Shaw) to the pleasures of epigrammatic exaggeration. But reading his biography alongside his writings, it *is* difficult to identify consistent values or purposes animating his career, though certain themes do recur as we have seen. Taylor must, without question, be numbered among the prominent intellectuals of twentieth-century Britain, yet any attempt to distil a distinctive *content* out of his almost unfathomably copious writings seems misguided. In terms of the four dimensions or axes of the role of being an intellectual which I identified in Ch. 2 above, Taylor scored highly in terms of his initial scholarly and institutional standing, his access to media reaching broad non-specialist audiences, and his building of a reputation. In some ways, the synergistic effect that can be achieved by exploiting several different media and forms of cultural authority has rarely been better illustrated (for example, in the early 1950s when he was appearing on 'In the News', his by-line in the *Sunday Pictorial* proclaimed 'A million people see and hear this man on Friday nights').[47] What is less clear is whether, ultimately, he had anything much to *say* which touched the general concerns of his various publics.

When radical critics have needed to account for what they consider a leading left-wing politician's betrayal of principles and party, as with Ramsay MacDonald's formation of the National Government in 1931, they have frequently made reference to 'the aristocratic embrace', that metaphorical (and occasionally literal) seduction by wealth, status, and beauty. Critics of intellectuals who lose their way are sometimes tempted, in parallel fashion, to speak of falling victim to 'the journalistic embrace'. The failings of the metaphor are more apparent in this case. After all, exploiting the relevant media is a constitutive part of *being* an intellectual. But the idea does, perhaps, help us to understand something about Taylor, not so much on account of his well-documented infatuation with Beaverbrook, as his infatuation with the activity of journalism itself—the buzz, the money, the immediate gratification, the chance to use his considerable literary abilities. As a journalist, he was *plus royaliste que le roi*: writing to a deadline and a prescribed length, adapting the level to the readership, making it punchy and readable—these things came almost to be ends in themselves (Alan Watkins recorded that in all his years in journalism he had never known anyone who could write an article as quickly as Taylor[48]). His extraordinary fluency became his main failing. As the *Manchester Guardian* review of his first volume of essays damningly put it: 'Read as a collection the essays suggest a constant trailing of the coat, and the piling up of audacious opinion finally produces the effect of a firework display that has gone on too long.'[49] As time went by, more and more readers began to suspect that he was exercising his voice rather than having something to say. All he wanted, it sometimes seemed, was that people should be listening, and once it becomes obvious that that is all the speaker wants, then the listening tends to stop.

NOTES

1. By Taylor's own calculations: 'Of the British "delegation" sixteen were Communists and others were Marxist sympathisers'; 'Intellectuals at Wroclaw: a strange congress', *Manchester Guardian*, 2 Sept. 1948, 4; repr. in A. J. P. Taylor, *From Napoleon to Stalin: Comments on European History* (London: Hamilton, 1950), 223.
2. Quotations are taken from 'Speech of Professor Taylor at the Intellectuals' Congress', as quoted in Kathleen Burk, *Troublemaker: The Life and History of A. J. P. Taylor* (London: Yale University Press, 2000), 193–4; Burk suggests this text must have been a contemporary transcription of Taylor's unscripted speech.
3. Adam Sisman, *A. J. P. Taylor: A Biography* (London: Sinclair-Stevenson, 1994), 191.
4. Taylor, *Napoleon to Stalin*, 221.
5. Burk, *Troublemaker*, 161.
6. Sisman, *Taylor*, 162–3; for his early membership of the Party, see Burk, *Troublemaker*, 53.
7. Kingsley Martin, 'Hyenas and other reptiles', *New Statesman*, 4 Sept. 1948, 187.
8. Ibid. 187.
9. Details in the following paragraphs are taken from Chris Wrigley, *A. J. P. Taylor: A Complete Annotated Bibliography and Guide to his Historical and Other Writings* (Sussex: Harvester, 1980), as well as from Sisman, *Taylor*, and Burk, *Troublemaker*, especially the latter's detailed inventory of his freelance earnings.
10. R. T. Clark, 'History and politics' (review of *From Napoleon to Stalin*), *Manchester Guardian*, 18 July 1950, 4.
11. Burk, *Troublemaker*, 223; for further discussion of the role of television, see below, Ch. 21, Sect. III.
12. Sisman, *Taylor*, 213.
13. Burk, *Troublemaker*, 206. She also suggests that 'Carr-Saunders had proscribed all non-academic publication by anyone identifying himself as a member of the LSE'; no source is given, and although the School was known to have been embarrassed by some of Laski's activities in the 1940s, it would be surprising if such a ban had in fact been enforced. It does not appear to be mentioned in Ralf Dahrendorf, *LSE: A History of the London School of Economics and Political Science 1895–1995* (Oxford: Oxford University Press, 1995).
14. Quoted in Sisman, *Taylor*, 261–2.
15. Quoted ibid. 232.
16. A. J. P. Taylor, *English History 1914–1945* (Harmondsworth: Penguin, 1970 [1st pub. 1965]), 23.
17. Quoted in Burk, *Troublemaker*, 299.
18. Quoted in Sisman, *Taylor*, 286.
19. Cf. the judgement of Philip Ironside, *The Social and Political Thought of Bertrand Russell* (Cambridge: Cambridge University Press, 1996), 250: 'A. J. P. Taylor in his television appearances often came perilously close to being more "performer" than historian; indeed, his popular reputation was rather like that of a music-hall "memory man".'
20. Sisman, *Taylor*, 264–5.
21. Ibid. 265. It may not be irrelevant to recall the studied hauteur of Noel Coward's celebrated remark: 'My dear, television is for appearing on, not for watching.'

22. [Anon.], 'The seventh veil', *New Statesman* 28 Sept. 1957, 376–7.
23. See the accounts in Sisman, *Taylor*, 294–5, and Burk, *Troublemaker*, 285–6.
24. See Meredith Veldman, *Fantasy, the Bomb, and the Greening of Britain: Romantic Protest 1945–80* (Cambridge: Cambridge University Press, 1994), 133.
25. Sisman, *Taylor*, 288.
26. Ibid. 278.
27. See Burk, *Troublemaker*, 370, and the statistical appendix showing Taylor's quite extraordinary freelance earnings from 1957 onwards.
28. See Sisman *Taylor*, 318–23; Burk, *Troublemaker*, 220–2.
29. Taylor, *English History*, 727.
30. Taylor to OUP, 26 Sept. 1965, quoted in Sisman, *Taylor*, 334. Burk, *Troublemaker*, 305, quotes the letter in slightly different form, omitting the last sentence.
31. *Times Literary Supplement* (21 June 1957), 382; quoted in Wrigley, *Bibliography*, 92–3. According to the *TLS Contributors' Index*, the reviewer was C. M. Woodhouse.
32. Sisman, *Taylor*, 128.
33. A. J. P. Taylor, *Englishmen and Others* (London: Hamilton, 1956), p. vii.
34. A. J. P. Taylor, *The Origins of the Second World War* (Harmondsworth: Penguin, 1964 [1st edn. 1961]), 7.
35. Taylor to *TLS* reviewer, 18 Dec. 1965; quoted in Sisman, 335. The review, entitled 'Taylor Made', appeared in *TLS*, 16 Dec. 1965, 1169–70; the *TLS Contributors' Index* reveals that the reviewer was the Cambridge historian F. H. Hinsley.
36. 'The Europe of 1848: a congress of historians in Paris', *Manchester Guardian*, 17 Apr. 1948; repr. in *From Napoleon to Stalin*, 218.
37. A. J. P. Taylor, 'French history in dispute', *TLS*, 26 Mar. 1954, 3.
38. A.J.P. Taylor, review of E. H. Carr, *What is History?*, *Observer*, 22 Oct. 1961.
39. Lord Attlee, 'The dissidence of dissent', *Spectator*, 28 June 1957, 836.
40. Taylor, *English History 1914–1945*, 408.
41. Quoted in Sisman, *Taylor*, 187.
42. Quoted ibid. 171; cf. Burk, *Troublemaker*, 379.
43. R. C. K. Ensor, 'Difficulties of modern diplomacy', *The Listener*, 9 Jan. 1947; quoted in Sisman, *Taylor*, 171.
44. Taylor, *Napoleon to Stalin*, 10.
45. The parody is reprinted both in Sisman, *Taylor*, 337, and in Burk, *Troublemaker*, 308–9.
46. A. J. P. Taylor, *A Personal History* (London: Hamilton, 1983), 205; Taylor was referring at this point to his (justified) sacking in 1956 as a writer for the *Daily Herald*.
47. Burk, *Troublemaker*, 398.
48. Sisman, *Taylor*, 261.
49. Clark, 'History and politics', 4.

17

No True Answers: A. J. Ayer

'The new welfare state intellectuals . . . with their long-playing records and their ponytail-haired wives, their bottles of Spanish burgundy and volumes of A. J. Ayer.'

I

Another city, another year, another Congress of Intellectuals, another British delegation. Berlin in June 1950 was to be the setting for what one of the organizers intended as 'a gathering of all ex-Communists, plus a good representative group of anti-Stalinist American, English, and European intellectuals'.[1] The meeting was designed by its (American-financed) sponsors to be a riposte to the Communist-inspired gatherings of intellectuals in the previous two or three years, such as the congress at Wroclaw at which Taylor had made his protest. On this occasion the British participants included the historian Hugh Trevor-Roper, the art critic Herbert Read, the politicians Julian Amery and Harold Davis, the writer Christopher Hollis, the Germanist Peter de Mendelssohn, and the philosopher A. J. (Freddie) Ayer. (Their participation had been secretly financed by the Foreign Office, cooperating with its American counterpart to further the 'cultural war' against Communism.) But, as at Wroclaw two years earlier, several of the British delegates were appalled at the blatantly ideological harangues to which they were subjected by the leading American or American-backed figures. As Trevor-Roper later recalled: 'There was very little in the way of serious discussion. It wasn't really intellectual at all in my opinion.'

The British contingent started to make its dissent all too plain: Ayer and Trevor-Roper thumped the table whenever a delegate expressed support for further American military intervention in the world.[2] In the opening session, Ayer read a paper 'defending political tolerance, including even the tolerance of communists', and drew upon John Stuart Mill for support, none of which went down at all well with the organizers. Thereafter, the anti-Communist chorus sang in well-rehearsed unison, with Arthur Koestler providing the applause-provoking solos. After much struggle, the British delegation did manage to secure an amendment to the closing declaration, which would otherwise have been as dismissive of Marx's ideas as it was hostile to current Soviet policy. (This statement was to go on to become the basis for the work of the Congress for Cultural Freedom as it operated, secretly funded by the CIA, in Europe in succeeding decades.) Despite these blips, however, the Congress's sponsors pronounced themselves well pleased with the outcome of the event: according to one general in the US Defense Department, it had been 'unconventional warfare at its best'.[3]

Members of the British contingent reported the event in somewhat less glowing terms. Trevor-Roper published a decidedly acerbic account of the proceedings in the *Manchester Guardian*: The Congress was in no sense an intellectual congress. . . . It was simply Wroclaw in reverse—the Wroclaw of the ex-Communists.' In his own paper, prepared for the Congress but in the event not delivered, Trevor-Roper insisted on the duty of intellectuals to uphold truth in the face of ideological distortion, invoking Benda on the 'trahison des clercs'.[4] Ayer fully endorsed his colleague's account. It particularly mattered to Ayer that this blatantly ideological enterprise should not seem to be receiving serious *philosophical* support. Bertrand Russell, whom Ayer (selectively) admired and (even more selectively) identified with, was at this time going through a fiercely anti-communist phase, but after the Berlin meeting Ayer clearly felt that the great man was in danger of lending the prestige of his name to an unworthy enterprise, and 'did his best to persuade Russell to resign from his honorary presidency of the congress'.[5] After all, the good name of British philosophy was at stake. Ayer himself had been invited as a leading British philosopher (he was Professor of Philosophy at University College London at this point). When, as a result of the Berlin meeting, the Congress for Cultural Freedom was established to support the intellectual activities of 'the free world', all the eminent figures selected to be its honorary presidents were philosophers—Croce, Dewey, Jaspers, Maritain, and Russell. But what special authority did philosophers possess that made them the iconic champions of the intellectual life of the free world? In the eyes of the general public, philosophers were among the most obvious candidates for being classified as 'intellectuals'. In so far as Ayer occupied this role in Britain was it because his philosophical enquiries enabled him to instruct his fellow-citizens how to live?

II

'Contemporary philosophers may be divided into two classes: the pontiffs and the journeymen. As the names I have chosen indicate, the basis of this division is not so much a difference of opinion as a difference of attitude . . . a radically different conception of the method of philosophy and of the ends that it is fitted to achieve.' These were the opening words of Ayer's much-cited 1947 essay, 'The claims of philosophy', which was at once a summary of one of the main lines of philosophical argument in the previous decade or more and the declaration of a cultural identity. In Ayer's characteristically eye-catching classification, the pontiffs were the metaphysicians, a term generously interpreted to include all those who claimed to be identifying truths about 'ultimate reality'; these had been the dominant figures in philosophy until the last fifty years, and in some dark parts of the earth they pontificated still. Ayer ensured that British readers in the late 1940s would get the measure of this category by his choice of examples: he declared Hegel to have been 'the arch-pontiff of the nineteenth century', and he ruled magisterially (pontifically?) that 'the fate of the contemporary pontiff must be to go the way of Heidegger'. The journeyman, by contrast, is 'content to leave the scientist in full possession of the field of speculative knowledge' and tries 'rather to deal piecemeal with a special set of problems', broadly resumed under the heading of 'logical analysis'. Russell, Moore, and Wittgenstein were the chosen ancestors here, though none of them was exempt from criticism. Indeed, Ayer acknowledged a certain 'thinness of material' in the work of contemporary journeymen in general, but he airily suggested that this defect might be remedied through 'the reunion of philosophy with science'.[6]

Ayer directly confronted the charge that the conception of philosopher as journeyman was altogether too modest and involved abandoning what the man-in-the-street had always regarded as the role of philosophy, namely to help us understand the meaning of life and to give us some guidance on how we ought to live. Ayer conceded nothing: 'The reply to this is that there is no true answer to these questions: and since this is so it is no use expecting even the philosopher to provide one. What can be done, however, is to make clear why and in what sense these questions are unanswerable,' and having done this to his own (very considerable) satisfaction, he concluded with the memorable declaration:

> No more than the scientist is the philosopher specially privileged to lay down the rules of conduct, or to prescribe an ideal form of life. If he has strong opinions on these points, and wishes to convert others to them, his philosophical training may give him a certain advantage in putting them persuasively: but, whether or not the values that he recommends are found to be acceptable, it is not from his philosophy that they can derive their title to acceptance. His professional task is done when he has made the issues clear. For in morals, and in politics at the stage where politics become a matter of morals, there is no repository of truth to which only the learned few have access. The question how men ought to live is one to which there is no authoritative answer. It has to be decided by each man for himself.[7]

As with Russell's philosophical prose (which Ayer so admired), the decisiveness and clarity are constitutive elements of the argument here. Other writers may attempt to impress us with their vatic profundity or virtuoso technicality, but this presents itself as the voice of unillusioned, achieved reason: when confusion and irrelevance are cut away, the truth is relatively simple and relatively obvious.

The passage, like Ayer's writing more generally, is not in fact as self-effacing or transparent as it pretends to be. There is, on closer inspection, plenty of 'prescribing' going on here. The position it expounds is suffused with the existentialist pathos of *having* to choose and to take personal responsibility for one's choices, responsibility which cannot be offloaded onto superior intellectual authorities or even onto the nature of reality itself. It is also, of course, not as modest as it may at first seem: it claims there is no authoritative answer to the question of how men ought to live, but of course it is precisely offering an authoritative answer to the question 'can there be an authoritative answer to this question?' And it not only claims, in passing, to know at what stage 'politics become a matter of morals' (there have, after all, been some sharply contrasting answers to this question in the history of political thought), but it also presumes to know that the nature of 'truth' in morals and politics is, in one sense of the term, democratic, open equally to all. It implies, moreover, that this doctrine is the outcome of philosophical enquiry, that *this*, at least, is not something that 'has to be decided by each man for himself' (for what if I, obtusely, were to decide that morals *are* deducible from a metaphysical description of the nature of reality?). So the journeyman, it turns out, does a fair bit of pontificating after all.

To recapture the full cultural identity of this philosophical position would be to take a large step towards identifying the core of Ayer's role as an intellectual in post-war Britain. That process will involve a more extended exploration of the development of Ayer's reputation, including his reputation as a philosopher with something to say to non-philosophers, but a helpful preliminary may be to return to the scene of this particular essay's first appearance. It was published in March 1947 in the seventh (and, as it turned out, penultimate) number of *Polemic*, one of those short-lived, intellectually strenuous journals which tell us so much about the cultural landscape of the immediate post-war years.

The first number of *Polemic* (unnumbered and pretending to be a book in order to get round the ban on new periodicals which paper rationing had imposed) appeared at the beginning of 1946, with the ex-Communist Humphrey Slater as editor. It aspired to occupy the classic space of the 'general' or non-specialist intellectual periodical: 'From the beginning our intention was to print essays about ideas, written from a more general point of view than that of the particular sciences or of politics.'[8] Four features of the contemporary intellectual scene were singled out as needing particular attention: (1) the role of psychology and 'the discovery of the unconscious'; (2) 'the problem of verbal meaning'; (3) the success of Marxism; (4) 'the fundamental significance of the arts'. (From the third number, in May 1946, it was subtitled 'A magazine of philosophy, psychology, and aesthetics'.) The first number (which sold out in two days such was the hunger for serious reading-matter at the end of the war) contained essays by Russell, Ayer, Spender, Stephen Glover, Orwell, Henry Miller, Joad, and Rupert Crawshay-Williams. Several of these names were to reappear more than once in the journal's short life: out of a total of eight issues, Orwell had an essay in five and Ayer and Russell in four each. Orwell and Ayer, in particular, did much to set the tone, and the magazine soon developed a distinctive identity—in favour of a cool, liberal rationalism, sympathetic to science, hostile to the intellectual manifestations of romanticism, and markedly anti-Communist.

In this setting, Ayer's 'The claims of philosophy' essay (an earlier version of which had been delivered to a UNESCO gathering in Paris the previous year) had the character of a manifesto. But it announced its allegiances more by simply taking certain positions to be self-evident than by extended argument. For example, it ruled on the illegitimacy of all attempts to derive an ethics or a politics from an interpretation of history: the references to Hegel and his (alleged) deification of the Prussian state or to Marx and his 'historical determinism', by means of which this view was almost glancingly indicated, also carried a clear anti-totalitarian resonance in 1947. (As one might expect, *Polemic* had given a warm welcome to Popper's *The Open Society and its Enemies* which had been published in 1945.) Ayer's choice of examples, both positive and negative, might seem to suggest that the essence of his contrast could be stated in terms of the cultural cliché which was later to become so familiar, that of the contrast between a sober, sensible English philosophical tradition and an overheated, woolly-headed 'Continental' tradition. But, to do it justice, Ayer's essay was not really offered as a paean of nativist self-satisfaction, and Ayer could not at this stage of his career have been identified with British philosophical insularity: his debt to, indeed championing of, the Vienna Circle in particular was well known, and he frequently acknowledged the towering presence in modern philosophy of Frege and Wittgenstein. Ayer's overt allegiances were much more to modern science than to old England, though it is true that a preference for an identifiably national philosophical style was secreted as much through the elegant declarative prose as through the contrast between the tradition of Russell and Moore on the one hand and that of Hegel and Heidegger on the other.

As I remarked earlier, the conclusion to Ayer's 'Claims of philosophy' essay was suffused with the existentialist pathos of the responsibility of having to choose for oneself, and in this respect its tone, as well as the general cultural force of some of its conclusions, displayed obvious affinities with the one philosophical movement to enjoy a general cultural reputation in Europe, including Britain, in the decade after the war, namely Existentialism. In fact, it was to become an important part of Ayer's public identity in Britain in the late 1940s and early 1950s that he knew about Existentialism (he, for example, was later invited to write a review of Colin Wilson's *The Outsider* for *Encounter*, and, drawing upon his authority as a philosopher, wrote one of the few critical reviews that book was to receive).[9] Ayer, it is worth recalling, was nearly bilingual in French and English, and he had cultivated contacts with European philosophers since his first trip to Vienna in the early 1930s. Moreover, he had spent six months in Paris immediately after the Liberation, and had got to know Camus and several other French philosophers and writers. (Much later in his life, he represented this episode in characteristic vein: 'I don't know his work well, but he and I were friends: we were making love to twin sisters in Paris after the war.'[10]) He had not met Sartre, and when later, after Ayer's critical essays on him had appeared, a meeting was mooted, Sartre responded with uncharacteristic brevity: 'Ayer est un con.'[11]

Of course, interest in French Existentialism was much more a feature of the broader literary and intellectual scene in Britain than of academic philosophy, and it is telling that Ayer's earliest articles on the subject appeared not in a professional philosophy journal, but in Cyril Connolly's *Horizon* in 1945–6.[12] He ended his essay on Camus in characteristic fashion: he acknowledged that he found the Frenchman's moral attitude quite congenial, but he disagreed that it could be shown to be in any way the logical outcome of a process of philosophical argument. Such attitudes, Ayer insisted, can only appeal or not appeal to people as a result of 'their temperaments or their moral and aesthetic tastes'.[13] In this way, Ayer was always *plus Existentialiste que l'Existentialiste*. But he was not inclined, in the manner of Camus's parable about Sisyphus, to regard this situation as a kind of moral tragedy. As his biographer observes, Ayer concluded that the Existentialists 'had mistaken what is a logical necessity—the absence of transcendent meanings—for an empirical disaster'.[14] And this marked a decisive distance from Existentialism, not just on Ayer's part but on the part of that low-key self-consciously 'scientific' temper which he shared. Humphrey Slater, for example, criticizing, in the second issue of *Polemic*, 'the ubiquitous romantic reaction now showing itself in almost every sphere of intellectual and aesthetic life', had unhesitatingly singled out the current vogue for Existentialism as the leading instance.[15] Not only, it seemed, should philosophy not pretend to be able to offer authoritative guidance about the meaning of life: it ought not to make too much fuss about its incapacity, either.

This was the paradox at the heart of Ayer's career as an intellectual: the authority of his public role rested on his professional identity as a philosopher, but his declared philosophical position was that philosophy could have little to say on the issues that were of public interest. In this respect, Ayer's case illuminates a larger issue. Critics of various forms of so-called 'analytical' philosophy in the twentieth century have alleged that, precisely because these approaches all taught that philosophy was a limited, technical form of enquiry which could not provide authoritative guidance on the great questions of human life, they robbed the subject of its traditional public role. Indeed, it is further alleged that philosophers ceased to be intellectuals in Britain (by contrast to, shall we say, France?) because they espoused a style of philosophy which taught that they *could* not have anything significant to say.[16] The idea of an analytical philosopher with a public role thus comes to seem practically a contradiction in terms.

This is a common, revealing, and, in my view, mistaken belief about the operation of cultural authority: it precisely confuses the *content* of one particular set of ideas with the *role* of the intellectual more generally. To claim, on the basis of validated achievement in philosophy, that philosophers cannot settle the great questions of morals and politics is *not* to have nothing to say in public debate: it is, on the contrary, a position of very considerable power within such debate. Moreover, views cast in a negative form may not be, in any given situation, any less prescriptive than views cast in a positive form. To claim, on the basis of the best arguments of the most recent philosophy, that we could not in principle have any grounds for believing in the existence of such an entity as a 'god' may in some circumstances be to make no less influential an intervention in public discussion of life and morals than to claim that God teaches us that we may have sex only within marriage. There were several sources of Ayer's public standing, as I shall indicate, but his claim, as a leading philosopher, to know the limits of philosophy was certainly one of them.

Ayer is an interesting case-study for another reason too. His career provides a telling example—in some respects comparable to, but in the end quite different from, Taylor's—of the ways in which the capacity and opportunity to use various media to reach different publics is a finely balanced exercise, where the successive exposures are, so to say, cumulative and self-reinforcing while at the same time constantly threatening to dilute or destroy the primary professional or creative standing on which the broader cultural authority is supposed to rest. As a way of discriminating the sources of that authority in Ayer's case, it may be helpful to look chronologically at the stages in the growth and development of his reputation.

III

As a preliminary, we need to begin with a property which is more than purely personal, one which Ayer shared with others with a similar background and education as himself. Britain in the 1940s and 1950s, the period of the making of his fame, was still an intensely class-conscious society, one in which forms of cultural deference were hard to disentangle from forms of social deference. Ayer bore the stamp of one of the most prestigious educational trajectories which this society recognized: he was Eton and Christ Church. Moreover, with the development of radio and then of television as stages upon which intellectual standing could be exercised, Ayer's clipped upper-class accent, conservatively cut three-piece suits, and general air of social confidence and savoir-faire were not insignificant elements in his authority as a 'performer'. And of course in terms of public perception of assured quality, 'Oxford' was to philosophy what 'Harrods' was to department stores. In reality, Ayer was professor of philosophy at University College, London from 1946 to 1959, the period of his greatest success, and this metropolitan base, and the sense that this may have brought him into contact with more modern and less cloistered intellectual trends (especially scientific ones) than those associated with the ancient universities, may have helped rather than limited his standing with a broad lay audience. But he was no less clearly an Oxford 'product': he also taught there before 1939 and again after 1959, and that association, albeit in many ways an antagonistic association, with the headquarters of philosophy in England mattered.

The first step towards a more distinctive personal standing came with the success of *Language, Truth, and Logic*, first published in January 1936. Actually,

Ayer's social contacts and Oxford friendships played their part here, too: the fact that the book was published by Gollancz, one of the vogue publishers of the 1930s, was to secure it a certain amount of attention, but the unknown 23-year-old author obtained a contract only through the intercession of his friend Isaiah Berlin.[17] In addition, as I indicated in my earlier discussion of Collingwood, in the inter-war years even relatively technical works of philosophy were still reviewed in the periodical press. Thus, *Language, Truth, and Logic*, aided by a helpful puff or two, was reviewed in the *Observer*, the *Spectator*, the *New Statesman*, and the *Manchester Guardian*, as well as in more restricted but still relatively non-specialist journals such as Eliot's *Criterion* and Leavis's *Scrutiny* (very critically in the last two cases, as might be expected). In the next two or three years it attracted considerable attention from professional philosophers; on one count, *Mind* had by the end of 1939 published 'no fewer than ten articles and discussion notes directly relating to its central themes'.[18] But although in this way it achieved a considerable reputation, it could not be said to have been any kind of publishing success: it sold barely more than a thousand copies in Britain before the war. In these terms, its great period came after the war, and owed much, as did Ayer's career more generally, to the intellectual hunger of that period and its taste for plain, no-nonsense, English styles. The book was reprinted in a new edition in 1946, with an introduction in which Ayer responded to criticisms. *Language, Truth, and Logic* became one of the cultural reference-points of the next decade, and its timing meant that it was also one of the earliest beneficiaries of what I have termed the 'penguinification' of British reading. The Gollancz and Penguin editions sold 100,000 copies between them in the next thirty years, while it sold 300,000 copies in the same period in the USA, where it was published by Dover.[19]

The broad lines of the book's statement of the logical positivist position are well known and require no summary here.[20] In terms of its cultural impact, attention principally fastened on Ayer's classification, in the notorious chapter grandly titled 'Critique of ethics and theology', of all moral and theological statements as meaningless, expressions of attitude rather than of fact. Ayer was by no means the first emotivist in ethics, but he was perhaps the first to make it seem a liberating and energizing cultural battle-cry. For the book deliberately set out to dispossess various forms of authoritarianism of their weapons. And its crisp, conclusive style and confident sweep contributed to this effect. It simply was the case, it seemed to say, that the advance of modern science and philosophy had demonstrated not just the irrelevance but the obstructive function of traditional moral and religious teaching. The book's appeal to the educated young rationalist was correspondingly powerful: it was thrilling to be against nonsense, especially old and revered nonsense. As one commentator has put it: 'Ayer managed to make a vivid if imprecise impression on a wider public, who applauded him as a champion of modern scientific knowledge, and even of the oppressed social classes, against the deadly complacency of English cultural conservatism'.[21]

This was presumably the kind of appeal Richard Wollheim had in mind when he spoke of the book 'becoming perhaps the last Bible of British Nonconformity'.[22]

The next important, but usually wholly neglected stage in the making of Ayer's reputation involved his contact with the world of London literary journalism, which preceded his move to University College London in 1946. It started through Ayer's friendship with Cyril Connolly in the late 1930s: 'I think my entry into a wider world . . . was due to him' (he gave Connolly a copy of *Language, Truth, and Logic* bearing the revealing inscription 'To Cyril, who hates the same things as I do').[23] Whenever he was in London during the war he mixed with 'the *Horizon* crowd', which led to his contributing to several periodicals of general culture in the post-war years, including *Polemic*. This (and, it must be said, the rather glamorously 'fast' social life which he led, partly in literary circles, partly among the more bohemian fringe of the English upper class) meant that Ayer had, from an early stage, a dual public identity: he was a professor and a leading professional philosopher, but he was also a metropolitan man of letters. Wollheim later caught this feature of Ayer's sense of himself very well:

> With one part of himself Freddie thought that the literary side of his reputation *was* his reputation. He was not, after all, a mere teacher: a beak, an usher, a dominie, a hack. In London and Paris he moved amongst writers, some of his closest friends were poets, and, if he was to be circumscribed at all, it was to be, as with his great predecessor David Hume, as a citizen of the republic of letters.[24]

Wollheim and others remember, as a representative symbol of this dual identity, how Ayer would briefly come to the pub with everyone else after the departmental seminar, but would soon leave and catch a taxi, 'off to another world' (a taxi, note: one never imagines him waiting for a bus, still less putting on cycle clips). 'Freddie was a philosopher in London. It was only by some sort of accident, to which he felt it unnecessary to accommodate, that he was a philosopher *at* London.'[25]

Ayer was always what is conventionally described as 'well connected'. From Eton and Oxford onwards, he knew personally a considerable number of the social and political as well as the cultural elite of the country. He moved easily between London engagements with aristocrats (or fashion models), visits to Bertrand Russell at his Welsh hillside retreat, and holidays with the Gaitskells in Yugoslavia (it is a sign of the continuing integration and smallness of the various elites in Britain in the 1950s that these worlds were not then as far apart as their successors were to become in later decades). Ayer was also by inclination a cosmopolitan rather than a parochial figure, with the result that these connections were replicated internationally. He energetically attended congresses of philosophy from Leningrad to Latin America, but his standing always exceeded that of even the most distinguished professional philosopher. When he went on a lecture-tour to India in 1958 he was granted audiences with the President, the Prime Minister (Nehru), and the Defence Minister. When Arthur Schlesinger was arranging a series of evening seminars for members of the Kennedy administration in the early 1960s, Ayer seemed an obvious speaker.[26] Ayer made several visits to the United States, but his observation after spending some months there in 1948 indirectly says something about the role he took for granted in Britain, as well, perhaps, as reflecting the views of the *Partisan Review* circle with whom he socialized: 'The atmosphere seemed to me hostile to people like ourselves. I have always thought that the intellectual ought to dominate his environment . . . but during the months in New York I came for the first time to see how difficult this might be.'[27]

Ayer not only wrote well, he spoke well—sometimes very well—both in philosophical discussion and in general conversation (he always maintained that oral discussion was philosophy's essential medium). He was thus one of the British intellectuals for whom the Third Programme seemed tailor-made, and its launch in 1946 marked another key step in the making of his reputation. Ayer gave over twenty-five talks in its first decade, nearly always on philosophical topics, some of them fairly technical ('the physical basis of mind', and suchlike). The clarity and decisiveness of his prose were well suited to such talks, but he shone to still greater effect in debate (his style always tended to turn discussion into debate). In this vein, he argued about metaphysics and religion with Frederick Coplestone in 1949, and he regularly took part in discussions among a small group of scientists—Solly Zuckerman, Peter Medawar, and Julian Huxley—which were, remarkably, broadcast from Zuckerman's house in Birmingham. But perhaps the most striking example of the kind of cultural deference that could be accorded this level of intellectual activity in the early days of the Third was the occasion when 'a whole UCL departmental seminar was convened in Broadcasting House, and Ayer and his colleagues spent an hour and a half in live discussion of the issue of our knowledge of other minds'.[28]

But the medium which was to bring Ayer his greatest popular fame was television, and more particularly 'The Brains Trust'. This programme had started on the radio during the war, and remained there until 1955, with Julian Huxley, Cyril Joad, and 'Commander Campbell' as its regular panellists. It then transferred to television, and membership of the panel changed more often, though Huxley, Jacob Bronowski, Alan Bullock, and Marghanita Laski were among the most frequent contributors. Ayer made his first appearance on this programme in 1956 and was soon recognized as a great success on it: between 1956 and 1961 he appeared on forty-three occasions, including the final one, broadcast from New York. It was the kind of forum which suited Ayer: he was personable, quick-thinking, witty, dialectically adroit, and firmly committed to liberal, secular views which bore a faint penumbra of outrageousness, especially on topics connected to religion, sex, censorship, and so on. He was a producer's dream: a philosopher with opinions and plenty of 'em. In the course of the 1950s he replaced Joad not just on the programme but also as Britain's best-known professional philosopher (Russell's status was less clear by this point, though he was undoubtedly more widely known). It was a characteristic inaccuracy on the part of Colin Wilson to refer to 'the school of English philosophers' as being 'led by Professor Ayer', but it was also indicative of Ayer's reputation at that point and the lack of a plausible rival for the title.[29]

Ayer's appearances on the programme had as big an impact on his public standing as the appearance of *Language, Truth, and Logic* had had on his professional reputation. As his biographer records:

> Ayer's broadcasts before *The Brains Trust* had been mainly confined to highbrow matters—or to those and football—but the 'Trust' made him famous. His first newspaper profile appeared in the *Observer* in 1957, by his old friend Philip Toynbee. . . . Along with the profiles came the other trappings of fame—mail, abusive and admiring, invitations to talk at schools and literary societies, verses in *Punch* and cartoons in the *New Statesman.* Ayer now appeared on radio and television, talking on football rowdyism, Russell, cricket, the nature of truth, children's fiction, the non-existence of God. One could hear him *Talking Sport* with Tommy Steele, romantic literature in *Not So Much A Programme, More a Way of Life,* or the National Health Service on *Any Questions.* He even appeared on the early evening dictionary game, *Call My Bluff,* and the pop music show, *Juke Box Jury.*[30]

Ayer clearly relished his celebrity, but one has to ask, as with Taylor, how far his frequent and increasingly promiscuous media exposure began to erode his serious reputation. In Ayer's case, there was an intriguing disjunction between his professional and public standings. His forays into the media may have had less impact on his reputation among his fellow-philosophers than was true for Taylor among his fellow-historians. The beginnings of the decline in Ayer's position as any kind of pace-setter in his field may have dated from the late 1950s and early 1960s as other, less positivist or less Russellian, styles of philosophy came to seem more exciting to the rising generation of practitioners. In addition, Ayer was less given to being merely opinionated than Taylor; he tended to stick, often somewhat relentlessly, to a few familiar positions. In the eyes of a broad public, his election to the Wykeham Chair at Oxford in 1959 probably raised his standing, but in the course of the 1960s, and even more the 1970s and 1980s, there were signs that he was moving towards that kind of insolvency that threatens all those intellectuals who, through some combination of increasing opportunities and declining powers, find themselves beginning to make more withdrawals against their cultural capital than deposits. More generally, as I have already suggested, a delicate balance may be said to have obtained in the 1950s, when some leading dons became for the first time frequent contributors to popular journalism: they were still able to trade on old snobberies, that unspoken association of high culture with high social class, but in subsequent decades this source of authority diminished considerably as newly prosperous strata more and more determined the nature of media that owed no allegiance to the tastes of that cultivated milieu.[31]

IV

In terms of the content of the views which Ayer used these various media to advocate, he had a fairly consistent identity as spokesman for a secular, free-thinking liberalism, left-leaning in his politics, a vocal supporter of the Labour Party (especially when it was led by people like himself), a critic equally of Stalinist fellow-travellers and conservative cold-war ideologues. From his Christ Church days in the 1930s, Ayer had numbered several of the leading Oxford-educated Labour politicians among his friends, such as Roy Jenkins, Anthony Crosland, and, above all, Hugh Gaitskell. He was an outspoken sympathizer with the republican cause in Spain, and he campaigned against Quintin Hogg in the celebrated 'appeasement' by-election in Oxford in 1938; he served as chairman of his local Labour Party branch in London, and in 1945 he was briefly uncertain about whether to stand for parliament. Thereafter, his activities principally took the form of organizing and/or signing protests against various illiberal measures of both domestic and foreign policy (predictably, he signed a letter protesting against British intervention in Suez, and, no less predictably, it was a letter to *The Times*). Indeed, he eventually became such a common signatory of such letters in the 1960s (and must usually have taken alphabetic precedence over his co-signatories) that a cartoon of the period shows a character welcoming the chance to campaign against the construction of a motorway through the area of London inhabited by many leading literary and intellectual figures with the words: 'It's my great opportunity to be listed under the magical cross-heading "from Professor Ayer and others".'[32] The symbolic currency of his name is attested in another way by the heavy-handed mockery of the passage by Paul Johnson which serves as the epigraph to this chapter, where Johnson speaks of 'the new welfare state intellectuals . . . with their long-playing records and their ponytail-haired wives, their bottles of Spanish burgundy and volumes of A. J. Ayer'.[33]

In the course of the 1960s and 1970s Ayer became a member of the Great and Good, chairing committees, sitting on commissions, helping charities, and, on his 60th birthday in 1970, being knighted. His own views may not have changed very much, but his cultural role had altered. He was less and less seen as the iconoclastic, up-to-date voice of a scientifically minded philosophy—a cultural identity with considerable appeal in Britain between the 1930s and 1960s—and more and more as a 'name', a well-known writer, a pundit. A set of five articles in the *Evening Standard* in September 1968 on 'Rebels and Morals' was representative of this phase: his opinions on 'the permissive society' and related topics were far from reactionary, albeit somewhat bemused by the idiom of 'student unrest', but they were the merest punditry, with no pretence to being informed by his own 'serious' work in philosophy.[34] However, celebrity of this kind is brutally ephemeral. When the Social Democratic Party was launched in 1981, Ayer was an immediate and natural recruit on personal as well as political grounds. He was correspondingly miffed to find that when the new party published a large list of the impressive names of those who had joined, his was not included.[35]

Part of Ayer's role as an intellectual in Britain, especially in his heyday between the mid-1940s and the mid-1960s, consisted in his use of his celebrity and his considerable, though far from unchallenged, standing to give calm, confident utterance to basic liberal truths. In practice, Ayer tended to treat 'basic' and 'self-evident' as more or less synonymous where truths were concerned, but that note of philosophical authority probably enhanced his appeal. It is evident, for example, even in his earliest contribution to *Horizon* in 1944, in an essay on 'The concept of freedom'.[36] The argumentative pace is never less than brisk: a page or so of quick-footed analysis is sufficient for him to be able to declare: 'I conclude then that the assumptions on which the authoritarian view of freedom is based are manifestly false.' 'Manifestly false' is the authentic tone of the Oxford high-priori of that period: only the saddest of sad sacks could be taken in by something that was *manifestly* false. Unsurprisingly, the essay gives an altogether more indulgent account of 'the liberal view that the freedom of the individual is to be measured by his power to do what he himself actually wills'. But then it was an acknowledged part of Ayer's position that radically new values were not what a society such as Britain now needed, and anyway not something the philosopher qua philosopher could provide. As he got older, he more and more came to believe that the necessary values were already available and merely awaiting fuller adherence.

He gave a particularly bald and emphatic affirmation of this view in a public lecture on 'Philosophy and politics', delivered in 1965. Conforming to the common pattern, he began by contrasting the characteristic French assumption of the intimacy of the link between philosophy and politics with the habitual indifference of the English to the philosophical justification of political convictions ('our political life draws very little inspiration from political philosophy'). Most of the lecture was actually given over to a survey of types of political theory, understood as a series of answers to the question of why one should obey the law. With a typical show of analytical brio, he distinguished thirteen possible answers to this question, several of which fail to survive the opening minutes of tutorial investigation. Ayer could rarely resist this kind of philosophical showing off: those capacious tumbrils labelled 'trivial' and 'false' are repeatedly wheeled up, and a satisfying number of distinguished heads are distributed between them (the proposition 'that freedom consists in obeying a law which you impose on yourself' is 'a Puritan doctrine which became one of the cornerstones of Kantian morality, and one which I see no good reason to accept'). He acknowledges a general sympathy for the Utilitarian response, 'with one or two reservations', and concludes by affirming, in a rather downbeat way, the value of 'the old familiar liberal principles'. There was little constructive work for the philosopher, qua philosopher, to do. 'I do not really feel the need for anything to replace this mainly utilitarian, mainly tolerant, undramatic type of radicalism. For me the problem is not to devise a new set of political principles, but rather to find a more effective means of putting into operation the principles that most of us already profess to have.'[37]

Ayer could on occasion be an effective voice in combating the kind of moralizing conservatism and paranoid prejudice that often pass as justification for illiberal political measures, and although his own tastes and style of life always bore the marks of the privileged classes of the inter-war years, he refused to give aid and comfort to the cultural pessimism which could see the social changes associated with the welfare state and the 1960s only as evidence of decline. 'I believe that the average man is more humane, more pacific and more concerned with social justice than he was a century ago. This is not to say very much: we have very little ground for complacency; but since it is becoming the fashion to decry ourselves, I think it worth remarking that the belief in social progress is still empirically defensible.'[38] The unillusioned realism of tone is the chief carrier of the argument here, though 'empirically' may also indicate that hint of intellectual bullying into which this tone could sometimes descend.

Much of the service Ayer did to his readers and listeners who were struggling to formulate or justify their heterodox views, especially on religion and morals, was done precisely by means of this brisk matter-of-factness of tone. But this style was at the same time the marker of one of his greatest limitations: namely, the fact that the texture and distinctiveness of things did not interest him philosophically. They may in some cases have interested him humanly, though the evidence available to those who did not know him is not compelling here. Philosophically, he was drawn to clear, discrete, propositions: the historical or cultural quiddity of things received scant notice. Most of his writings on large moral, social, and political topics tended to take the form of cut-and-dried analyses of these issues into those (few) propositions which were demonstrably true and those (many) propositions which were demonstrably false or meaningless: and the fact that membership of these classes was, in his hands, so readily *demonstrable* was what deprived his analysis of some of the interest it might otherwise have had.

V

Finally, two vignettes which, for the historian of intellectuals, nicely illustrate different aspects of Ayer's position in British public life. The first combines Ayer's characteristic vigilance in defence of liberal principles with his powerful connections among the traditional elites. In 1960 he discovered by accident that boys whose fathers were not British by birth could not become Collegers (i.e. scholars) at Eton. He knew that this had not been true in his time at the school, otherwise he could not have been admitted (Ayer's father was born in Switzerland and came to England as a small child). He scented a whiff of anti-Semitism in this statute, so he wrote to the school's headmaster to enquire. His letter was passed to Sir Claude Elliott, who had been headmaster before the war. Elliott explained that the statute in question had been introduced in 1945: he defended it by saying that it was intended to try to avert the problems which might follow from having too large a foreign element at the school. Ayer replied that he would like the Fellows of Eton, the school's governing body, to reconsider the statute, adding that if they did not he would have to make its existence 'more widely known'. (Behind this thinly veiled threat, one can see Ayer's confidence that his name and his access to the media meant that this would be recognized as a serious danger by the Fellows.) In February 1961, Elliott, in a characteristic move of the English governing class, invited Ayer to lunch at his club to discuss the matter. The result of the lunch was a deal: Elliott agreed that Ayer's objections would be put to the governing body, and Ayer in turn agreed not to go to the press for a year (while reserving the right to lobby individual fellows). However, the Eton Fellows refused to change the statute. What then happened may seem like an exceptionally pure example of the 'a word in the ear' model; indeed, it is practically a radical conspiracy theorist's wet-dream. Ayer found himself alone in a train compartment (not a third-class compartment, one assumes) with Sir Edward Boyle, Tory minister, friend of Ayer, and, like him, an old Etonian. Ayer put the matter to Boyle, who promised to raise it with the Prime Minister, Harold Macmillan, himself an old Colleger, conveniently. Again, one would like to have been a fly on the wall when this item of national policy was discussed between the two men. In any event, Macmillan apparently wrote to Eton about the matter 'in a private capacity' (a wonderful fiction for a serving prime minister), and, unsurprisingly, the statute was repealed within a month. Ayer was thrilled at his success.[39]

Ironically, perhaps, for a man who resolutely refused to believe in the idea of an afterlife, Ayer's final performance in the role of intellectual in Britain was posthumous. Three days after Ayer's death in June 1989, Robert Jackson, the Minister for Higher Education in the Tory government of the day, could not resist exploiting the occasion to try to make an ideological point about the 'defeat' (by Mrs Thatcher) in the 1980s of the cultural values for which Ayer had stood. 'His is the voice of a dethroned hegemony—dethroned largely because of the poverty and superficiality of its thinking.'[40] It was a despicable and absurdly wrong-headed attack in a decade disfigured by despicable and wrong-headed pronouncements by government ministers: insofar as Ayer stood for liberalism in thought and behaviour, his cause remains in far better shape than the authoritarian 'national regeneration' idiocies trumpeted at the time by Jackson and his ilk (who seemed, incidentally, curiously insensitive to the hegemony of Leftish terms such as 'hegemony'). The published responses to Jackson's attack were indignant and properly severe. But the whole sorry episode did confirm two of the most salient aspects of Ayer's public identity. First, although at the close of the 1980s there still seemed several grounds on which to admire Ayer, his defenders would have had an easier task had his public performances in the later phases of his career been just a little less vulnerable to the charge of 'superficiality'. And second, the episode underlined that he had indeed been seen as an intellectual champion of precisely the secular, libertarian, social-democratic values against which Thatcherism was now attempting to wage its *Kulturkampf*; in other words, his philosophy did appear to many to issue in this kind of substantive teaching, even though he had constantly denied that it could do so.

NOTES

1. Quoted in Frances Stonor Saunders, *Who Paid the Piper? The CIA and the Cultural Cold War* (London: Granta, 2000 [1st edn. 1999]), 71.
2. Ibid. 80; cf. Ben Rogers, *A. J. Ayer: A Life* (London: Chatto, 1999), 236.
3. Quoted in Saunders, *Who Paid the Piper?*, 83–4. For the (self-satisfied) reflections of one of the principal American participants, see Sidney Hook, 'The Berlin Congress for Cultural Freedom', *Partisan Review* 17 (1950).
4. Hugh Trevor-Roper, 'Ex-Communist v. Communist: The Congress for Cultural Freedom', *Manchester Guardian*, 10 July 1950; cf. Saunders, *Who Paid the Piper?*, 91. Trevor-Roper referred to this experience in similarly disparaging terms in a 1968 lecture published as *The Past and the Present: History and Sociology* (London: LSE, 1969), 17–18. I am grateful to Blair Worden for generously making available to me Trevor-Roper's file of papers and correspondence relating to the Berlin Congress.
5. Rogers, *Ayer*, 236.
6. A. J. Ayer, 'The claims of philosophy' (1947), in *The Meaning of Life and Other Essays*, ed. Ted Honderich (London: Weidenfeld, 1990), 1–3, 6.
7. Ayer, 'Claims of philosophy', 16–17.
8. 'Editorial', *Polemic*, 2 [n.d., but 1946], 3.
9. A. J. Ayer, 'Review of *The Outsider*', *Encounter*, 7 (Sept. 1956), 75–7; see the fuller discussion in Ch. 18.
10. Quoted in Rogers, *Ayer*, 312.
11. Quoted ibid. 193. The *Larousse Dictionnaire Moderne Français-Anglais* (1960) endearingly, but perhaps euphemistically, translates 'con' as 'twerp'.
12. For *Horizon's* special affinity with French literary and intellectual life at the end of the war, see Michael Shelden, *Friends of Promise: Cyril Connolly and the World of 'Horizon'* (London: Hamilton, 1989), 122–5.
13. A. J. Ayer, 'Sartre', *Horizon*, 67 (1945), 12–26, and 68 (1945), 101–10; 'Camus', *Horizon*, 75 (1946), 155–68, quotation at 168.
14. Rogers, *Ayer*, 197.
15. 'Editorial', *Polemic*, 2 [n.d., but 1946], 3.
16. Perry Anderson's treatment of 'ordinary language' philosophy in his 'Components of the national culture' article of 1968 (discussed in Ch. 8 above) offers a particularly well-known instance of this; the article is reprinted in Anderson, *English Questions* (London: Verso, 1992), see esp. 67.
17. Rogers, *Ayer*, 106.
18. Cited ibid. 124.
19. Figures from ibid. 217.

20. For further discussion see A. Phillips Griffiths (ed.), *A. J. Ayer: Memorial Essays* (Cambridge: Cambridge University Press, 1991), and Graham Macdonald and Crispin Wright (eds.), *Fact, Science, and Morality: Essays on A. J. Ayer's 'Language, Truth, and Logic'* (Oxford: Blackwell, 1986).
21. Jonathan Rée, 'English philosophy in the fifties', *Radical Philosophy*, 65 (1993), 6.
22. Richard Wollheim, 'Ayer: the man, the philosopher, the teacher', in Griffiths (ed.), *Ayer: Memorial Essays*, 23. It is a nicely mischievous quip, though I wonder whether it was Wollheim or the typesetter who capitalized 'Nonconformity'.
23. Rogers, *Ayer*, 127.
24. Wollheim, 'Ayer: the man . . .', 22.
25. Ibid. 27.
26. Rogers, *Ayer*, 234–5, 215, 268, 249, 274–5.
27. Quoted ibid. 233; see the discussion of this theme in Ch. 10 above.
28. Ibid. 224; see the discussion of the Third Programme in Ch. 19 below.
29. Colin Wilson, 'Postscript', *The Outsider* (London: Gollancz, 1967 [1st edn 1956), 300.
30. Rogers, *Ayer*, 250–1.
31. This is discussed more fully in Ch. 21.
32. Rogers, *Ayer*, 247, 284.
33. Paul Johnson, 'Lucky Jim's political testament', *New Statesman* (12 Jan. 1957), 35.
34. Cf. the more blandly positive account of these articles in Rogers, *Ayer*, 294–5.
35. Ibid. 326.
36. A.J. Ayer, 'The concept of freedom', *Horizon*, 52 (1944); repr. in Ayer, *Meaning of Life*, 132–41, quotation at 135. The essay as a whole bears a notable resemblance to the thesis of Isaiah Berlin's much more famous inaugural lecture of 1958, 'Two concepts of liberty'.
37. A. J. Ayer, 'Philosophy and politics' (1965), in *Metaphysics and Common Sense* (London: Macmillan, 1969), 240–1, 247–8, 252, 256, 259–60.
38. A. J. Ayer, 'The humanist outlook' (1968), in *Meaning of Life*, 176.
39. The episode is recounted in Rogers, *Ayer*, 270–1, drawing on the original correspondence in the Eton archives.
40. Robert Jackson, letter to *The Independent*, 30 June 1989, 21.

PART FIVE

REPEAT PERFORMANCES

18

Outsider Studies: The Glamour of Dissent

'The Outsider has since made a living at writing.'

I

There is no denying the satisfying thrill, the subtly self-flattering frisson of excitement, involved in thinking of oneself as an 'outsider'. The immediate associations of the term suggest the bracing winds of freedom: being 'outside' is to be in open space, fresh air; it is to have freedom of movement, unconstrained, perhaps unsupervised; it is to be thrown on one's own resources, or even excluded, shut out; not belonging, not conforming, not tainted; different, unconventional, stirred by antagonism, disdaining tinselly rewards for which others abase themselves. To be an 'outsider' is at least to be one's own master, to have preserved a certain dignity: one has scorned power, but retained agency, sacrificed honours to maintain honour. The defining contrast is, of course, with the idea of the Insider: smooth of cheek and of manner, discreet and soft-footed, well-connected, well-thought-of, well-rewarded. The logic of the opposition must have it that the Insider is conformist, conventional, timid, unoriginal. His ('insiders' are nearly always figured as male) is a life lived in the shadow of a thousand compromises, of the gaze almost permanently averted; of truths not told and facts not faced. A favourite at court, a toady, a placeman . . . an *apparatchik*: the lexicon is updated, the charge remains.

So common is it for intellectuals to be described, and to describe themselves, as outsiders that we have almost ceased to realize what an absurd description this is. To be described as an intellectual in the first place is, by definition, not to be classed among those who are identified principally by their command of wealth and power. Spending a great deal of time in the (frequently solitary) pursuit of truth or aesthetic creation further nurtures a sense of being out of step with the broadly shared patterns of one's society. Nonetheless, these are, it ought to be needless to say, roles filled *within* society; or, to adapt a phrase, *il n'y a pas de hors-société*. Moreover, intellectuals in the cultural sense are individuals who have made some kind of mark in one field and then obtained the attention of a public not confined to that field: such figures are hardly the neglected and outcast of history.

If I am writing about someone by name in this book, it is probable that that person achieved a certain standing or recognition during their lifetime. What, then, does the claim to outsiderdom amount to?

It is principally a claim to a kind of glamorous validation, a way of pulling rank on those who are ostensibly in control of rank and its rewards. It hints, usually without really elaborating, at an epistemologically advantaged position: spurred by antagonism, pricked by the necessity to start from scratch, unconstrained by the conventional, the outsider perceives things the complacently comfortable could never recognize. One sees more clearly, speaks more freely, lives more honestly when unconstrained, and to be an outsider is to claim to be unconstrained in fundamental ways (though in reality it may simply represent being constrained in others). And the glamour of exclusion hovers over the status. A reverse 'Groucho principle' operates: who wouldn't want to be excluded from a club with members like that? The *salon des refusés* confers the real chic: academy painting is a byword for formal, lifeless conservatism.

As I have already remarked, metaphors of 'purity' and 'contamination' play a large part in the discourse about intellectuals, and claiming to be an outsider is also a way of laying claim to a kind of purity (I am an outsider, you are seduced, he is corrupted). The appearance of the trope is often a reaction to having experienced a degree of worldly success: one pulls back, keeping a prophylactic distance from the embrace of Mammon or Leviathan or Fama, each of them powerful creatures who notoriously have designs on the virtue of the susceptible intellectual. Conversely, the would-be intellectual who may be failing to command the attention of a general audience can fall back on outsiderdom as a consoling identity: was it not ever thus for those who are too advanced for the times, shut out by the mainstream media, reduced to flinging messages overboard in bottles, relying upon the greater discrimination of posterity?

The very prevalence of what one might call the 'outsider than thou' attitude among intellectuals indicates that there is a form of competition for a perceived cultural good at work here. Whether it is the Cambridge don and influential critic F. R. Leavis describing himself as an 'outlaw', or the old Etonian and widely published author and journalist George Orwell casting himself as a 'literary pariah', or the well-connected, well-heeled, well-reviewed novelist Virginia Woolf aspiring to found a 'Society of Outsiders' (or, more recently, the tenured professors-cum-media stars trying to lay claim to the prestige of the 'exile'), the very repetitiveness of the claims tells us that what we are dealing with here is a symptom of the logic of being an intellectual, not an objective description of a social or cultural location. As a self-ascribed status, outsiderdom is an empowering identity, an attempt to use the available media to address the relevant publics without, so the claim goes, succumbing to the seductions and self-deceptions of insiderdom.

Equally, the hypostasized opposite, the real insider, is, it turns out, a kind of mirage, the necessary postulate of a vanishing-point on the horizon which, whenever we start to get close to it, recedes, turning into just another moderately successful self-described outsider. And the same is true from the subjective viewpoint: insiders are nearly always other people, rarely oneself. For inside every apparently smooth, plump insider is a craggy, riven outsider waiting to be unmasked by 'genuine' insiders.

The larger truth upon which this dialectic rests is that no one is defined by just a single 'identity': a plurality of self-descriptions is always available, depending upon the purpose and perspective of the classification. Similarly, we are all inside some circles and outside others. Still, the glamour of outsiderdom persists. This chapter looks at two (very different) cases where a claim to outsiderdom was a constitutive part of each figure's understanding of the role of the intellectual. That the two cases are, in all obvious respects, so conspicuously different only makes the recurrence of a similar rhetorical element the more intriguing.

II

To decide who should be described as 'the best-known philosopher in Britain in the 1950s', one would clearly have to spend some time on the preliminaries of definition and boundary-setting. Probably the names of Bertrand Russell, Ludwig Wittgenstein, A. J. Ayer, and, more doubtfully, C. E. M. Joad would soon make an appearance. But there can be no doubt that if the criterion of being 'well-known' is commercial success, then the answer has to be, improbably, Colin Wilson. As to the other key matter of definition, there could obviously be more dispute as to whether 'philosopher' was the appropriate label, although he was described as such by himself and by everyone else—except, that is, by professional philosophers.[1] And one might even, less obviously, have to be precise about the period involved as well: before May 1956, no one had ever heard of Wilson, and by the end of 1957 it was almost true that no one wanted to hear of him again. If he was, briefly, British 'philosophy's' greatest star, he was, in a longer perspective, one of British culture's greatest mistakes. Still, he was at the time explicitly hailed as a genuine native version of that otherwise allegedly absent or exotic species, the philosopher-as-intellectual. No examination of the question of intellectuals in twentieth-century Britain can entirely ignore the Wilson episode, even if, to modify a celebrated phrase of Leavis's, he was an event in the history of literary publicity rather than of philosophy.[2]

It may now be difficult to appreciate just how sudden and extraordinary Colin Wilson's brief success actually was.[3] He had been born in Leicester in 1931; having left school at 16, he held a series of manual jobs, reading voraciously along the way; he then moved to London, and in 1954 he gave up paid employment to write. That summer and autumn he spent his days in the British Museum writing a novel, while at night sleeping rough on Hampstead Heath (facts which were to bestow an additional patina of glamour on him once he began to be lionized). He started work on the book he intended to call *The Pain Threshold* at the end of December 1954; in the course of 1955 it was accepted by Gollancz, the final version being completed by the autumn. (*The Outsider* was the publisher's shrewd suggestion for the title, a resonant label at a time when Camus was a widely read author in Britain.) Gollancz himself had something of a weakness for philosophical mysticism, as well the opportunist instincts of the good publisher scenting a very marketable young author. He authorized an optimistic initial print-run of 5,000 copies, while prudently underwriting his optimism with a dust-jacket quotation from Edith Sitwell calling it an 'astonishing' book and predicting that Wilson would be 'a truly great writer'.

On Saturday, 26 May 1956, two days before official publication, the London *Evening News* carried a very favourable review. But what really made the book was that the next day it was simultaneously acclaimed in lead reviews by the two presiding cardinals of the Sunday review pages, Cyril Connolly in the *Sunday Times* and Philip Toynbee in the *Observer*. Connolly's review called it 'one of the most remarkable first books I have read for a long time', while Toynbee's hailed it as 'truly astounding', 'an exhaustive and luminously intelligent study . . . of a kind which is too rare in England' (such books were more common elsewhere, apparently).[4] All 5,000 copies are said to have been sold out in the course of the following day. Other influential reviewers were no less enthusiastic: Elizabeth Bowen, for example, described the book in the *Tatler* as 'brilliant' and herself as 'thunderstruck' at Wilson's learning, while Kenneth Walker in the *Listener* called it 'the most remarkable book on which the reviewer has ever had to pass judgement'.[5] The media mill then began to whirr in earnest, and biographical notices and gossip-column pieces fastened on to the romantic story of the 24-year old homeless author and his major work of philosophy. These articles were not confined to the upper end of the newspaper market: at the beginning of June, Wilson appeared in the celebrated 'William Hickey' column in *The Daily Express*, while in July Dan Farson informed readers of the *Daily Mail* that Wilson's book had received 'the most rapturous reception of any book since the war'. Gollancz made as much publicity as possible out of the need for frequent reprintings ('Printings are so rapid that we are not certain whether the one in hand is the eighth or ninth'): by October, 20,000 hardback copies had been sold, and the book had already been selected as a Book of the Month in the United States. On royalties, foreign rights, and so on, Wilson earned £20,000 in the first year (approximately £400,000 at today's values).[6] He was immediately invited to contribute reviews and columns for various papers, and his supposedly 'bohemian' appearance became widely familiar through photographs and cartoons. As Harry Ritchie summarizes the book's initial reception: '. . . the acclaim was so spectacular that Wilson became a national celebrity overnight. . . . Wilson's fame as a philosopher was quite unique in the mid fifties, far outstripping that of the fashionably daunting Jean-Paul Sartre.'[7]

It is hard, in retrospect, to believe that this extraordinary success should be chiefly explained in terms of the positive qualities of *The Outsider* itself.

The book is difficult to summarize, partly because it is both rambling and self-contradictory; its subtitle gives fair warning of the flavour of what is to follow: *An Inquiry into the Nature of the Sickness of Mankind in the Mid-Twentieth Century*. At its core stands the figure of 'the Outsider', a romanticized individual who, liberated from the mundane preoccupations and social constraints of the common herd, dares to seek Truth (his liberal use of capital letters was a minor aspect of Wilson's tendency to overdramatize). In doing this, he (they seem all to be men) adopts an 'Existentialist' attitude: there are contexts in which this beguiling term can be used with some exactness, but Wilson's book is not one of them. The label vaguely gestures towards a kind of personal or mystical insight, the antithesis of the dreary, hamstrung empiricism of the professional philosophers or the obsessive prudence of science (or rather 'Science', which is one of Wilson's recurrent targets). Outsiders, we are told, are those who strive '*not* to limit the amount of experience seen and touched', who 'expose the sensitive areas of being to what may possibly hurt them', in an attempt to establish a greater hold on 'reality' and so enlarge the scope of their 'freedom' by a victory of 'the Will'.[8]

In practice, the bulk of the book consists of breathless summaries of the lives and ideas of a wide range of thinkers and writers, with a strong emphasis upon detecting hitherto unlooked-for similarities (Dostoevsky is 'the Russian Blake', and so on): among the proper names which recur most frequently are those of Blake, Dostoevsky, Gurdjieff, Hesse, Kierkegaard, Shaw, and, above all, the implicit presiding spirit of the book, Nietzsche (the mad politics of Wilson and his young associates were soon to be pilloried as those of 'the Spotty Nietzschean Tendency'). Whenever Wilson thought the reader might be in danger of failing to appreciate the distance that separated the book's soaring geniuses from the mere mass of mankind, he would toss in a few sub-Nietzschean asides about how the latter were sunk in their 'bovine swill'. In insisting, in the sequel published eighteen months later, on the urgent need to give practical expression to these insights, Wilson declared that 'the Outsiders must achieve political power over the hogs', and so on.[9] (It was presumably on account of such insights that the first reviewers spoke of his 'bracing sanity' and 'the strength and wisdom' of his views.) Wilson's thought (or, perhaps, 'Thought') is, as I mentioned, hard to summarize briefly, but Ritchie's terse phrase is not a bad epitome: 'grandiose blethering'.[10]

Even at the time, one or two reviewers stood out against the wall of enthusiasm sweeping through literary London, and recorded somewhat more sceptical judgements. Kingsley Amis in the *Spectator*, Burns Singer in *Time and Tide*, and the anonymous *TLS* reviewer had been a good deal less than ecstatic, while slightly later A. J. Ayer in *Encounter* for September 1956 and Raymond Williams in *Essays in Criticism* in January 1957 brought a more rigorous level of criticism to bear.[11] (In fact, as research for the *TLS Contributors' Index* now enables us to know, the *TLS* review was also by Burns Singer, though it says something about his estimation of the readerships of the two journals—or perhaps just something about his desire not to be caught in such flagrant pluralism—that the two reviews are by no means identical.[12]) Furthermore, a letter to the *TLS* in December 1956 by the critic John Carswell showed that 'a sample of 249 lines of quotation in Wilson's book had yielded 82 major errors and 203 minor errors'.[13]

Raymond Williams, in whose prose of this period the Leavisian cadence is still distinctly audible, made the general critical case: 'With literary journalism as it is, and with the application of techniques of commercial advertising and personal publicity to literature and publishing, certain books, which are capable of being immediately reduced to symptoms, can become, almost overnight, what passes for a literary or intellectual movement.' He itemized some of Wilson's 'blunders', his 'cavalier' way with both facts and judgements, his tendency to treat 'his own feelings as if they were self-evident general truths'. He also shrewdly noted that Wilson had been promoted 'with the aid of the Sunday thinkers', and that at this juncture being an 'outsider' 'may be one of the quickest ways to becoming an insider'.[14] In similar vein, A. J. Ayer, who, as we have seen, was sceptical of all attempts to repudiate the claims of reason and science in the name of 'higher' truths, and who, unlike most British philosophers of the time, was genuinely knowledgeable about Camus and French Existentialism, gently dismantled (some of) Wilson's confused assertions. Wilson, he reported with head-shaking weariness, never makes clear what the essential characteristics of the Outsider are supposed to be: 'As it is, he gives us various indications which do not make an entirely coherent picture', and so, damagingly, on.[15] In the course of 1957, Wilson's reputation was also shaken by a series of rather seedy revelations about his marriage and his monstrously inflated ego, the damage being compounded by his own ill-judged remarks to the press. But what did most to undermine his credibility were his own articles and reviews, which were of a superficiality and wacky, egotistical opinionatedness that even his admirers could not fail to notice. As Donald Davie observed in the *London Magazine* as early as February 1957: 'Mr Colin Wilson's activities become steadily more embarrassing.'[16]

A very different indication both of Wilson's sudden fame and of the scepticism with which he was nonetheless regarded in some quarters came in the form of a short story published at the time by his namesake, Angus Wilson, entitled 'A bit off the map'. Huggett, the central character, is a lightly disguised, and very amusing, portrait of Colin Wilson as seen by a young (and, as it turns out, psychotic) admirer. 'Huggett's writing a book that's going to go a long way to finding out the Truth, but it'll take him years to write because it's not only religion he's taking in but philosophy.' The group around Huggett call themselves 'The Crowd', and their chief activities consist in sitting in coffee bars talking about various (capitalized) abstract nouns. 'But The Crowd is not the same as the Angry Young Men which you read about. Someone said it was and Huggett got very angry, because it's by Love and Leadership that the Will works. And all these angry young men believe in democracy and freedom and a lot of stuff that Huggett says just gets in the way of real thinking.' But somehow 'real thinking' is precisely what Huggett and his followers never seem to get around to doing, and as the tale moves towards its macabre ending, the emptiness of Huggett's posturing and the social confusions of his young recruit become ever more apparent: 'He says real genius means Will Power. All this art and suffering is just cock, Huggett says (I don't like it when Huggett uses these words—cock and that. A lot of these intellectuals talk like that, "c–this and f–that").'[17] Ah, these 'intellectuals'!

Wilson's ranting piece in *Declaration*, the anthology of 'angry' essays which came out in the Autumn of 1957 (discussed in Ch. 7 above), further confirmed the dotty and unpalatable politics which his schoolboy Nietzscheanism involved. By the time his second book, *Religion and the Rebel*, was published in October 1957, the tide had definitively turned against him: the book was rubbished by almost every reviewer for its 'mixture of banality and incomprehensibility'. Picking up on this response, *Time* magazine carried a dismissive account of the book in November 1957; the caption under the accompanying picture of Wilson simply read: 'Egghead, scrambled'.[18] After the end of 1957, Wilson dropped from sight. He has continued to publish copiously, over thirty-five titles to date, both fiction and non-fiction, and he has continued to identify with his most famous creation while pursuing a relatively orthodox literary career: as he puts it in his entry in *Who's Who*, quoted as the epigraph to this chapter: 'The Outsider has since [*sc.* 1956] made a living at writing.'[19] But for the most part reviewers avert their eyes in embarrassment, like well-meaning shoppers trying not to notice the once-decorated war hero who has turned to drink.

III

In the best subsequent account of the episode, Ritchie asks the obvious question: 'Why, then, did such a patently bad and objectionable book as *The Outsider* receive such praise?'[20] Since my interest in Wilson here is focused upon the relation between intellectual achievement and media attention in forming cultural authority, we need, in considering this question, to ponder certain aspects of the book's reception in some detail, beginning with the dynamics of metropolitan literary reviewing in the mid-1950s. Ritchie notes that Wilson's fame was initially the creation of 'the Mandarins' those representatives of the old alliance between high status and high Modernism, the upper-class avant-garde, the heirs of Bloomsbury who were still so powerful in metropolitan literary reviewing, such as Edith Sitwell, Cyril Connolly, Philip Toynbee, Elizabeth Bowen, and John Lehmann. He divides the (much smaller) group of sceptical reviewers into two camps: first, 'the small band of academic reviewers—A. J. Ayer, Raymond Williams, and the *TLS* critic'; and second, a group who were themselves either young or 'middlebrow', such as Kingsley Amis or J. B. Priestley. (As I indicated above, we now know that the *TLS* review was by the 28-year-old poet and critic

Burns Singer, but perhaps this simply has the effect of moving that review from the first camp to the second.)

The Outsider, if not read too carefully, appealed to the Mandarins on several counts. To begin with, Wilson's manner of writing could seem to resemble theirs, to be intuitive and associative, not confined by academic protocols or tedious empiricism. Second, it abounded in references to *European* literature and philosophy at a time when their own cultural role rested heavily on their association with the glamour of 'Continental' ways in opposition to that dreary provincialism which a well-heeled bohemian set always affected to disparage in England itself. Third, the book took religion and mysticism seriously, as they did, and treated science condescendingly, as they also did. Fourth, they shared its Romantic elevation of 'the genius' above the mediocrity of the common herd: this appealed both to their Modernism and their snobbery. And finally, and perhaps above all, they were able to find in Wilson's book a counter to what they saw as the main threats to their own cultural authority in the mid-1950s, the resolutely English plainness of the 'Movement' writers, the tiresomely specialized knowledge of Redbrick lecturers, and the parochial *ressentiment* of the Angry Young Men. Wilson was young, thrillingly young (and available to be taken up and patronized, in both senses), while in his book one moved in the company of the giants of European culture without any hint of that pedantry and utilitarianism which spelt death for the old belle-lettristic Sunday reviewer.

But behind these cultural or temperamental affinities there surely hovered a shadowy presence who influenced their perception of the book, the figure of 'the intellectual'. As we have seen, the term itself was used with increasing frequency by this date, and the decade since the end of the war had seen a constant commentary on either the absence, or at the very least the muted presence, of this figure in Britain compared to the more glorious figure he (nearly always he) cut on the Continent. The extraordinary amount of attention focused during this decade on the iconic figure of Sartre cannot be irrelevant to the reception of *The Outsider*. This would have been the case even had Wilson not chosen to label his creed 'Existentialism', but that obviously helped: how many readers were in a position to judge what relation his vatic pseudo-profundities bore to the elaborate philosophical machinery which Sartre had derived from Heidegger? Wilson linked philosophy and literature; Wilson insisted on the necessity of rejecting one's upbringing and of *choosing* one's values for oneself; Wilson wore black rollneck sweaters: *ergo*, Wilson was an Existentialist. Scarcely twelve months after Annan and Shils had celebrated the uniquely 'integrated' and 'unalienated' state of intellectuals in Britain, the serious book-buying public had made an overnight best-seller out of an unknown 24-year-old for whom 'alienation' was a badge of honour.

This sequence is grist to my general analysis of the operation of cultural authority. On the face of things, Wilson appeared in 1956 to be ideally placed to exercise the role of the intellectual: he was given almost limitless access to the media, more than one public was paying attention to him, and he ostensibly had something to say which bore upon the general concerns of those publics, ultimately something about the meaning of life. But it very quickly emerged that he could not command the essential cultural authority which would have licensed performance in the role. It is important to remember that he had no history of creative or intellectual achievement behind him (this was his first book), and he could call upon none of the authority of qualifications or position. His standing depended entirely on the esteem accorded this one book and the attention given to his subsequent pronouncements: as the first of these came more and more to seem an error-strewn farrago, and the second revealed their fatuity even to the most casual observer, the claim to authority evaporated almost as quickly as it had been created.

The Wilson episode—in himself he scarcely merits being a 'case'—is instructive in several ways. To begin with, it was highly time-and-place-specific. The book would almost certainly have been a complete failure had it, *per impossibile*, been published in the mid-1930s or the mid-1970s. One cannot draw large conclusions from it about British culture's 'inferiority complex' (towards what?) or about how, in the absence of 'real' intellectuals, ersatz substitutes always arise to fill the vacuum. Second, the episode illustrates a particular feature of the dynamics of cultural authority in 1950s Britain. The Mandarin reviewers, such as Connolly and Toynbee, were, in one respect, fortunate in their moment: their aura of social as well as cultural status attracted a degree of deference from what was, thanks to the expansion of the Sunday papers, the success of the Third Programme, and a slowly democratizing system of secondary education, a wider public than that commanded by those who were their true predecessors—the Aesthetes and Bloomsberries of the inter-war period. High culture, high Modernism, and high social class were still closely associated: the Mandarins could not only tell a sonnet from a villanelle, but also a Chambertin from a Chateauneuf, and these were not always seen as merely contingently related capacities; the readership of the expanding 'quality' Sundays by and large still wanted their cultural tastes arbitrated by members of 'the quality' (I shall return to this issue in Ch. 21). And it was because Wilson had received this consecration that he became a best-seller, and it was because of his success that he became, briefly, fodder for Fleet Street more generally. An authoritatively vouched-for 24-year-old genius of bohemian appearance and outrageous views was newsworthy, in a way in which two-a-penny 50-year-old tweed-jacketed Redbrick lecturers in philosophy would not have been.

But, third, the episode showed that though the metropolitan reviewing scene in the early and mid-1950s may have come closer than that of many periods to meriting Leavis's strictures on 'coterie flank-rubbing', it was far from homogeneous even then. Sceptical voices did not have to struggle overmuch to make themselves heard, and they could do so in media which were of some consequence, such as the *Spectator*, *Encounter*, or the *TLS*. Moreover, these sceptical voices had their own, countervailing, sources of cultural authority to draw upon. It was surely predictable that a philosopher of Ayer's disposition would be resistant to Wilson's claims, but in 1956 Ayer's was, in its way, still a fashionable as well as a professionally validated voice. Similarly, the *TLS*, even under the editorship of a literary man-about-town such as Alan Pryce-Jones, was acknowledged to bring a certain scholarly rigour to the discussion of contemporary publications, and when its initial, and somewhat sceptical, review was followed up by the letter detailing the quite extraordinary scale of Wilson's misquotation, it could not pass unnoticed in the London literary world, or be discounted as the irrelevant pedantry of obscure provincial lecturers; at the very least, reviewers of his second book were encouraged to be a lot more cautious in their appreciation (as it turned out, they scarcely needed encouraging).

And finally, and most consequentially of all for my analysis, the episode surely suggests that even if a reputation for original thinking can in effect be manufactured by well-placed opinion-formers, it cannot be sustained for very long in the absence of independent evidence of intellectual or creative achievement. Even mere newsworthiness has to be parasitic upon something else, as the ruthless ignoring of Wilson by Fleet Street in subsequent years indicated. Leo Braudy is surely right to say, in his large study of fame and renown over the ages, that much of what passes for literary and cultural history is in reality the history of reputation, of what made a splash at the time.[21] On my analysis, the historian of intellectuals has no choice but to be attentive to matters of contemporary reception and standing, since a certain level of such response is constitutive of the role of the intellectual. But as the sorry story of Colin Wilson illustrates, the intellectual has to do more than merely make a splash. To retain any claim to be listened to on the meaning of life, it is not enough simply to be able to spell Nietzsche. The conceit of being 'the outsider' may have seemed, briefly, to serve Wilson well, but in fact in so far as he was listened to it was for reasons quite other than, indeed almost the opposite of, 'outsiderdom', and once those reasons ceased to operate, he ceased to be listened to.

IV

Every so often, a cultural episode which is in itself relatively minor acquires a kind of representative status as a moment when attitudes which are normally considered part of a familiar wisdom, or are in other ways so deep-lying as to escape contemporary analysis, are forced to the surface. The very fact that the content of these attitudes is derivative and their expression merely opportunistic only makes the occasion more valuable as a source of historical evidence. Where the question of intellectuals in Britain is concerned, one such occasion was the delivery of the BBC's Reith Lectures in June 1993 by Edward Said. The title of the lectures, and of the book in which they were subsequently published, was *Representations of the Intellectual.* Anyone who might have been inclined to think that the issues whose history I have been charting in earlier chapters would, by the final decade of the century, long have ceased to command attention, or anyone who might have assumed that the topic would by this date have been susceptible of a degree of exact and uncontentious academic summary, would do well to ponder what was revealed by this episode.

When it was announced in late 1992 that Edward Said would give the Reith Lectures the following June, there was some grumbling about the choice on the (highly disputable) grounds that Said's persistent and outspoken championing of the cause of the Palestinians in the Middle East conflict marked him out as someone who was too partisan, too much a propagandist, to be allowed to demean what, for all its faded glories and diminishing audiences, is still seen as one of broadcasting's most prestigious occasions. Said, Professor of English and Comparative Literature at Columbia University in New York, was himself a Palestinian by origin, educated in English schools in Egypt and thereafter at American Ivy League colleges, where he subsequently pursued a highly successful academic career. For more than two decades, his was an influential but independent voice commenting on Middle Eastern politics, drawing attention to the plight of the Palestinians dispossessed by the foundation of the state of Israel, contesting what he saw as the misrepresentation of that plight, and of Arab affairs more generally, in the Western press. In the United States Said had long had to contend with ill-founded charges of fomenting terrorism, encouraging anti-Semitism, and generally trashing Western culture, but the British press rehearsed these charges anew when his name was announced, and still more when the lectures were actually broadcast.[22] Much of the comment was ignorant and superficial, and even the supposedly 'in depth' profiles seemed more interested in his clothes than his ideas.[23] One of the few sympathetic articles rightly claimed that press coverage of the lectures had amounted to little more than a 'medley of smears, gossip, and ill-informed comment'.[24]

Nonetheless, the fact that Said *was* invited to give this still prestigious series of lectures is worthy of remark, and whatever the media debate about his (and his subject's) suitability, there was never any serious question of the invitation being withdrawn. Six lectures on representations of the intellectual were, therefore, broadcast at prime listening time on the most established of the mainstream national radio networks (it is, for several reasons, much harder to imagine the equivalent event taking place in the United States). The chorus of predictable comment about Britain being an un- or anti-intellectual society seemed to possess no means of coming to terms with these significant facts. And there was surely a certain piquancy in the sheer cosmopolitanism of the occasion: a lecture-series founded to honour the Calvinist Sir John Reith was being given by an American academic of Palestinian origin about a species widely supposed by his audience not to exist in their country.

Reviews of the lectures themselves expressed criticism, disappointment, and disdain in nearly equal measure. The response of *The Independent*'s reviewer, Robert Hanks, was representative:

> Two weeks into the 1993 Reith Lectures, and it seems fair to ask: what is Edward Said talking about? . . . This has turned out a deeply disappointing series. The argument is that the intellectual stands on the side of freedom and opposition, a lone voice standing out against orthodoxy (it's taken an hour to say this). But the distinction between the prescriptive and the descriptive has got blurred.

The crucial question, Hanks proposed, was 'Who is he talking to?' 'There's nothing remotely persuasive about these lectures, no attempt to pull you along with Professor Said's opinions, so you have to assume that he is consciously preaching to the converted, to his fellow dissident intellectuals. . . . Really, he is talking to himself. At the moment, there's little incentive for anybody else to listen.'[25]

Writing in *The Guardian* after the final lecture, Leslie Plommer put his finger on what was widely perceived as the chief weakness of the lectures:

> What he had to tell his tiny band of Reithers on the subject of intellectuals boils down, in 56 words, to this: that truth is a moveable feast and professional objectivity a pretence; that the intellectual's lifelong job is to tilt at orthodoxy and dogma with the overarching aim of advancing human freedom, knowledge, and rights for the underdog; that nine-to-five classroom technicians bent on pleasing their employer-patrons do not advance the cause of enlightenment. A good leader writer might pad this to 500 words, but only a lifetime of academic training equips a man to spin out fare ordinaire like this into, on my estimate, 21,500.

As this suggests, one of the stock responses triggered by Said's lectures was the sneer at the obscurity and verbosity of academic prose: whole estates of 'ivory towers' mushroomed in the reviews. Plommer noted that there had been a lot of talk, especially in advance, about 'violent controversy' surrounding the lectures, but that this was a considerable exaggeration: 'You might have thought the papers were full of hysterical Zionists baying for blood, as against the reality of less than a dozen non-review articles of any length, the majority sympathetic. Re-reading them, one is struck by how lazy much of the journalism is, and by contrast, how professional some radio reviewers are.'[26]

The laziness of much of the journalism is only the more depressing when reread several years later, not least for the way in which the topic itself, quite aside from whatever Said might have had to say about it, activated the familiar mechanisms of repetition and denial. 'It's a most un-English thing to be talking about,' observed one newspaper reviewer. 'In America, in France or elsewhere in Europe, debating the role of the intellectual over your cappuccino is a standard feature of cultural and cafe life; not so in Britain, where you only have to preface the word intellectual with Hampstead, and you have an all-purpose sneer.'[27] Certainly, an all-purpose column seems to be filed away in most newspaper offices under 'Intellectuals, lack of in England', though one might already begin to wonder whether this isn't really just the local form taken by those global over-the-cappuccino debates. One also notes yet again that, viewed from the defective 'here', America and the rest of Europe are confidently lumped together as so much more desirable 'elsewheres'.

In *The Times*, columnist Matthew d'Ancona resteamed the froth of many such debates in his meditations on the stereotype of 'the unintellectual English':

> The idea that the British [*sic*] are an unintellectual race is one of the great canards, spread by credulous Englishmen [*sic*] who get an inferiority complex every time they go to Paris. Why should we be any less proud of Bertrand Russell or Michael Oakeshott than the French are of Sartre or Foucault? Which country, after all, did Marx and Hayek choose to make their intellectual home? Britain has always had plenty of intellectuals, albeit of the tweedy don rather than the rive gauche variety. What we have managed to do without so far is an intelligentsia: although Britain produces the occasional Bloomsbury or *Encounter* group, our intellectuals are the most individualistic in the world. They do not function as an organised cohort or guild.

For this reason, suggested d'Ancona, Said's subject had little purchase in Britain: 'His approach may make sense in the salons of Manhattan, but in a country where there is no socially recognizable and distinct intellectual class, the idea that thinkers must be allotted a "role" doesn't ring true.' This is journalistic laziness of a high order: a quick visit to the cliché bank has allowed half a page to be furnished in the fashionable reproduction style. As a matter of fact, Said had precisely insisted upon the lonely, individualistic conception of the intellectual, but on such occasions no chance is missed to trot out the shallow pedantry of the intellectuals/intelligentsia distinction.

D'Ancona was on slightly firmer ground in challenging Said's assertion of the duty of the intellectual to side with the oppressed, and he suggested that such a restrictive definition of the intellectual would seem unpersuasive in Britain:

> Intellectuals may not be revered in Britain as they are elsewhere in Europe but they are protected from the delusion that their work is part of some grander moral scheme. If British scholarly life is too fragmented and undervalued, that is a price worth paying for intellectual independence. The minute that restrictions and conditions are imposed upon scholarship, scholarship ceases. In truth, the belief that thinkers must side with one group rather than another leads to the hateful culture of the Soviet writers' union. Alas for Professor Said, his ideas are all too orthodox.[28]

This is the 'plain and proud of it' tone which Orwell elevated into an ethic in its own right. It masks a nationalistic glorying in the supposed connection between liberty and a lukewarm public temperature: its defiant motto might be 'better unread than Red'. There is also a telling slide here between 'scholarship', 'thinkers', and 'writers': it suggests a fumbling recognition of the fact that 'intellectuals' signals some movement from 'inside' to 'outside', but the potential of this is lost as the mist of confident prejudice descends. The British have, characteristically, muddled through into inadvertent virtue, and we don't need to be preached at by any mere American professor, thank you very much.

The topic of 'intellectuals' was obviously thought to provide good copy at this time, since only four days later d'Ancona's colleague on *The Sunday Times*, Gilbert Adair, took up the issue, though in a less complacent manner. Ruminating on 'that peculiar cast of mind that has chosen to opt out of the history of ideas on the grounds that, while foreigners theorise about existence, we British simply exist and existence ought to be good enough for anyone', he recalled several episodes in which the British (led by the press) had displayed their traditionally dismissive attitude, including the response to Said's lectures, and asked:

> What is it with this country and the brain? Why is its characteristic attitude towards the intensest adventures of the intellect (and let me immediately add that I exclude the physical and natural sciences from the question) invariably reactive rather than, as in France or Italy or America, passionately active? Why are we so systematically dismissive of anyone with a real idea in his or her head?

The importance of contrastive elsewheres is again evident here: American intellectuals, in particular, are always astonished to find their country contrasted favourably with un- (or anti-)intellectual Britain. Adair professed to take comfort from the fact that anti-intellectual denials of the role of ideas were ineffectual, and he took as his example John Carey's book *The Intellectuals and the Masses*, which had attracted a good deal of comment, mostly unfavourable, when it was published the previous year.[29] Carey had denounced the snobbery and elitism of the great figures in literary Modernism, and declared that the hero of his book was Arnold Bennett who addressed the common reader, but, as Adair wryly observed, Carey's 'theoretical' validation of Bennett 'was not nearly enough to bring him back into existence': 'Now that the moveable feast of canapés that is the cocktail-party circuit has moved on, there's absolutely no sign of a Bennett revival.' By way of contrast, Adair listed the names of several contemporary foreign thinkers whose work, he affirmed, did indeed matter, and who could not be dismissed by habitual British anti-intellectualism; 'only someone willing to engage with the fundamental seriousness of those theories', he admirably insisted, 'will ever be able to present an intelligent critique of them'.[30] The constraints of weekly journalism allowed no room to pursue this potentially very fertile thought, but Adair's piece was at least a reminder that, even at this level, cultural attitudes are not monolithic, and that the best response to slack journalism is more rigorous, serious journalism.

Given this backdrop of largely dismissive, and sometimes downright bigoted, reaction to the Reith lectures, one naturally looks to the subsequent book to be a vindication of the highest intellectual standards. In himself, Said may seem to have been an excellent candidate for the role of champion of at least some of those values which have come to be associated with the concept of the intellectual in at least some of its senses. He clearly combined a deep personal culture with a spirited and wide-ranging engagement with public issues. He was by training a literary critic, committed to deploying the resources of criticism, in the widest sense, to challenge the power of coarse orthodoxies and ideological distortions both inside the scholarly world and out. His books, especially *Orientalism* (1978) and *Culture and Imperialism* (1993), have become points of reference in more than one academic field. And many observers have recorded their impression of a charismatic presence: serious, committed, articulate, and (perhaps not altogether irrelevant), good-looking. He was, as more than one commentator recorded, 'arguably the most influential intellectual of our time'.[31] He may seem in some ways, therefore, the ideal figure to 'represent' the late-twentieth-century intellectual.

V

For reasons that will become clear, it is not easy to summarize *Representations of the Intellectual*, brief though it is.[32] As reviewers of the lectures pointed out, a central theme is the insistence on the intellectual as a lonely, oppositional figure. But, as some of them also pointed out, it is not at all clear what the status of this insistence is supposed to be. That is to say, the book constantly slides without acknowledgement between the definitional—what the noun 'intellectual' means; the empirical—what people called 'intellectuals' have been like; and the prescriptive—what intellectuals should be like. To compound confusion, Said sometimes talks about the intellectual as a role, i.e. a set of structural relations with others, and sometimes as a character-type, i.e. possessing recognizable traits of temperament.

All this means it is more than usually difficult to summarize Said's argument by means of quotation. The book contains a large number of sentences where 'the intellectual' is the subject, followed by the verb 'to be', followed by a whole host of not obviously compatible predicates. The intellectual is someone who 'tells the truth'; the intellectual is 'the voice of the voiceless'; the intellectual is in 'permanent opposition to the status quo'; the intellectual is the real or symbolic 'exile'; the intellectual is someone who is both 'modest' and 'effective'; and so on. The argument, such as it is, exhibits a disabling reliance on simplistic binary alternatives. For example: 'I think the major choice faced by the intellectual is whether to be allied with the stability of the victors and rulers or—the more difficult path—to consider that stability as a state of emergency threatening the less fortunate with the danger of complete extinction, and take into account the experience of subordination itself, as well as the memory of forgotten voices and persons' (35). The stutterings of the syntax alone here suggest a thought over-encumbered by a kind of political free association, quite apart from the dramatization of the supposed alternatives. Or again: 'Even intellectuals who are lifelong members of a society can, in a manner of speaking, be divided into insiders and outsiders' (52). Not in an intellectually helpful manner of speaking, they can't. Or again: 'The *exilic* intellectual does not respond to the logic of the conventional but to the audacity of daring, and to representing change, to moving on, not standing still' (64). Some subliminal association between bravery and moving forwards haunts this sentence, but even that is not enough to rescue it from attempting to let tendentiously stacked alternatives do the work of argument.

Throughout, Said implicitly represents himself as resisting the glamour and seductiveness of official patronage, but he succumbs to a more insidious kind of glamour, that of being the champion of the wretched of the earth. Declaring the intellectual to be 'the voice of the voiceless' is one of his many acts of stipulative definition: the intellectual is someone 'whose *raison d'être* is to represent all those people and issues that are routinely forgotten or swept under the rug' (11), and again: 'There is no question in my mind that the intellectual belongs on the same side with the weak and unrepresented' (22). The 'unrepresented' do not seem to be given much of a say in team-selection here: the obvious danger is that they are being, in both senses of the word, patronized. And even if we feel that there is a generous or noble impulse at work, it clouds the task of definition. In so far as there is a persuasive ethical case here, it does not distinguish any role specific to the intellectual.

The contradictions into which Said is led are most economically encapsulated by the following sequence of sentences. Asking rhetorically whether the intellectual should endorse 'solidarity, primordial loyalty, [and] national patriotism' or should be 'a dissenter from the corporate ensemble', Said replies: 'Never solidarity before criticism is the short answer. The intellectual always has a choice either to side with the weaker, the less well represented, the forgotten or ignored, or to side with the more powerful' (32–3). The first of these sentences might seem an admirable motto for those genuinely committed to subjecting themselves to the ceaseless obligations of criticism (whether or not we believe that that has anything to do with being 'an intellectual'), but it is immediately betrayed by the second sentence, which is precisely to opt for 'solidarity' over 'criticism'. Choosing to 'side with' is the reflex of identification: the weaker, right or wrong. This is again a choice that anyone, intellectual or not, may choose to make and it has a certain emotional and political logic. But 'criticism' is precisely what it is not, since it is in effect to prejudge that the weaker are always right, or at least that their need for support overrides the question of whether they are, in this instance, right or not.

Said's book does not really confront, let alone resolve, these tensions between lonely individuality and axiomatic solidarity, in part because it never rises to a sufficiently analytical level. It is, in every sense, a romantic picture, concentrating on the talent and good faith of the isolated individual in his heroic struggle with the oppressive power of the conventional, the official, the established. It is culpably romantic, both in its damaging under-description of the actual social and institutional position of intellectuals in any period and society (and here the observation by some of his critics that Said himself held a well-funded named chair at one of the most prestigious American universities becomes potentially more than just a cheap jibe), and in its neglect of the enabling role of cultural tradition and intellectual community. This exaggerated individualism (remarkable in a self-described 'radical' critic) prevents him from taking the measure even of topics he himself introduces, such as professionalization and specialization. As the graceless abstract nouns themselves indicate, these are social processes, and not therefore susceptible to being reversed or overridden by an individual figure, no matter how resolute. 'By professionalism I mean thinking of your work as something you do for a living, between the hours of nine and five with one eye on the clock' (74). One may sympathize here with Said's implicit preferences without feeling that this too-ready redescription of the issue in terms of subjective attitude is likely to help us to grasp the nature and impact of professionalization. Similarly, what he has to say about specialization risks reducing the whole question to a matter of individual will and effort, whereas it is, of course, a structural issue, a matter of the relation between professional subgroups and their audiences, and so on. 'In the final analysis, giving up to specialization is, I have always felt, laziness, so you end up doing what others tell you, because that is your specialty after all.' This is a woefully thin response to the complex historical process which arguably has had a greater impact on the role of the intellectual than almost any other, and the tone is altogether too reminiscent of the genre of the spiritual pep-talk.

The classic analyses of Benda, Gramsci, Shils, and others are saluted in passing, but the book's own register remains that of the existential drama, with the solitary individual confronting the inescapable logic of choice. And the more one attends to the way so much of the prose is constituted by what can only be called a kind of existential rhetoric, the more one comes to feel that there is a very strong personal anxiety or fantasy at work here, an anxiety which is at least in part about being corrupted by success. Since this contention depends on a symptomatic rather than literal reading of the text, it may be best to start some distance away from the main point, by returning to a passage I have already partially quoted. In elaborating his 'outsiderly' ideal, Said writes:

> Even intellectuals who are lifelong members of a society can, in a manner of speaking, be divided into insiders and outsiders: those on the one hand who belong fully to the society as it is, who flourish in it without an overwhelming sense of dissonance or dissent, those who can be called yea-sayers; and on the other hand, the nay-sayers, the individuals at odds with their society and therefore outsiders and exiles so far as privileges, power, and honours are concerned. (52–3)

At first, the core of the distinction here appears to be between having and not having 'an overwhelming sense of dissonance or dissent', something which is a subjective or inward matter. But this is also supposed to line up with the distinction between having and not having the 'privileges, power, and honours' given out by that society. On closer inspection we find no necessary symmetry here: giving forceful expression to one's sense of 'dissonance' has been one of the surest routes to being garlanded with 'honours'. But one begins to wonder whether it is not important to Said, temperamentally, to try to maintain some such symmetry: those marked by their sense of dissonance *must* not succumb to the lure of 'privileges' and 'honours'. Once this suspicion is aroused, we begin to notice that the question of not 'succumbing' to the 'temptation' of 'honours' functions almost as a compulsive repetition in the text, intruding itself whether apropos or not. Thus, Said later stresses the importance of being one of those who 'are neither winning prizes nor being welcomed into all those self-congratulating honour societies that routinely exclude embarrassing trouble-makers who do not toe the party line' (59). Part of his case for the ideal of 'exile', whether literal or symbolic, is that 'exile is a model for the intellectual who is tempted, and even beset and overwhelmed, by the rewards of accommodation, yea-saying, settling-in' (63). Tempted, beset, and overwhelmed by rewards, the intellectual-as-refusenik has a near-impossible spiritual task. Thereafter, there are frequent little riffs on 'temptation', 'many intellectuals succumb completely to these temptations', and so on (e.g. 86). He at one point cautions that 'today's society still hems in and surrounds the writer . . . with prizes and rewards' (75); Sartre's public refusal of the Nobel Prize was surely for Said, as for many intellectuals susceptible to a similar fantasy, a deeply enviable moment.

His subjective, almost psychologistic, focus makes everything turn on the 'habits of mind' of the individual intellectual (100). And the worst habits, revealingly, are those which calculate worldly rewards. 'Your hope is to be asked back...; someday you hope to get an honorary degree, a big prize, perhaps even a professorship' (100–1). And he concludes in the register of the self-help manual. 'What strikes me as much more interesting is how to keep a space in the mind open for doubt and for the part of an alert, sceptical irony (preferably also self-irony).' A strict regime of daily doubt-exercises will presumably help keep one up to the mark, but it is hard to have much confidence in prescriptions for self-irony. Somehow, the very act of prescribing it seems to betoken its absence: 'be self-ironical' is the least self-ironical command. This highly *un*ironical upbeat tone becomes almost embarrassing in the final paragraph of the book: it is 'difficult to find a way to be consistent with your beliefs and at the same time remain free enough to grow, change your mind, discover new things, or rediscover what you had once put aside' (121). The prose here slides perilously close to a cross between that of the agony aunt and that of the tabloid astrologer: you will face difficult decisions, but you will discover you have inner strength; a good month to reassess your goals/relationships/travel plans.

One is, finally, forced to ask how one should understand and assess the fact that such a clever and sophisticated man could write such a poor book. There may, one must allow, be purely personal explanations, including the possibility that the relatively popular nature of the occasion led him to misjudge the level of discussion required. (It may be presumptuous to speculate about the impact of ill-health on someone's writing, but it seems appropriate to record that Said had recently been diagnosed as suffering from leukaemia.) There is also the possibility—something with which any writer or lecturer might sympathize—that by the end he found he had not made wholly clear even to himself exactly what the lectures were about: the sliding between different senses of 'representation' is only one possible symptom of this state. But I suspect that the confusions of this little book are in fact expressive of difficulties which inhere in the public discussion of the topic itself.

To begin with, the vexed and contradictory semantic history of 'intellectuals' (which I have been attending to throughout, above all in Ch. 1) makes itself felt in the constant instabilities in Said's usage of the term. His book is, in my view, one reminder among many others of how this variety of usage needs to be addressed explicitly and systematically if it is not to infect and disable one's own account. Absorbed, perhaps, by the pressing issue of how to *be* an intellectual in the contemporary world, Said as author has suffered the consequences of not giving the necessary time to the complexities of the term. The result is that at times he uses the word to denote certain prominent individuals (intellectuals 'represent achievement, fame, and reputation which can be mobilised on behalf of an ongoing struggle or embattled community' [43]), and at other times the term is applied to 'everyone who works in any field connected either with the production or distribution of knowledge' (9); at times the term indicates a subjective attitude ('the true intellectual is a secular being' [120]), at other times it stands for a set of occupations (intellectuals are 'the managers, professors, journalists, computer or government experts, lobbyists, pundits, syndicated columnists, consultants who are paid for their opinions' [68]); now it is used functionally (the intellectual is a figure who 'publishes certain views' and thereby 'enters the public world' [12]), and now it is used evaluatively ('an intellectual is fundamentally about knowledge and freedom' [59]); and so on.

Terminological strain is, as always, an index of deeper difficulties. Said's account is hobbled by his yoking together an enterprise that is ostensibly definitional (forms of the verb 'to be', as I have noted, bustle about, shamelessly trying to broker improbable semantic deals) with a commitment to using the noun 'intellectual' in a wholly positive way, as an honorific term which picks out a personal ideal. In addition, several of the problematic features of the large literature on intellectuals are also illustrated in its pages: the confusion of 'critical' with 'oppositional'; the presumptuousness of being the voice for the voiceless; the restriction of the objects of criticism/reflection to political actions and policies; the overemphasis on an antagonistic relation to the state; the neglect of the structural preconditions of the intellectual's activity; and, above all, the ahistorical framework which allows the characteristics of a few admired individuals to be passed off as constitutive of the category itself. Given all this, it is perhaps not surprising that Said never really manages to address the central issues about the historical variability of the operation of cultural authority, though one might think that the very fact of being invited to deliver the Reith Lectures would be bound to prompt some reflection on this matter. Instead, for Said the preoccupying dialectic is that between 'purity' and 'contamination' (this is one of his unlooked-for affinities with Benda, despite Said's bizarrely describing the politics of that anti-Fascist republican Dreyfusard as 'very much of the Right' [p. xii]). This dialectic helps to explain why, in the end, *Representations of the Intellectual* reads less like a work of sociological analysis or cultural history or even political advocacy, and more like a small treatise on character-formation, a self-help manual of spiritual exercises.

One is left to reflect somewhat ruefully on the familiar experience of how a figure whom one has defended, perhaps on rather high-principled grounds, against intolerant or dismissive attacks, turns out to be a disappointing representative of some of those very values one had tried to stand up for. Indeed, the more closely one studies Said's little book, the more it comes to seem a compendium of seductive delusions and, given the prestige of Said's name, a singularly unhelpful contribution to contemporary thinking about intellectuals. In this respect, therefore, the conjunction of Said's lectures and the media response to them encapsulates the nexus of attitudes and prejudices against which *this* book is directed. For this purpose, the fact that Said himself was not a British writer is of no great consequence, decisively important though it would be in many other contexts. Not only is the literature on this subject partly internationalized—anyone wanting to read about intellectuals in Britain will necessarily spend a considerable amount of time reading work written by non-British authors—but Said's lectures, and the response to them, were an event in British culture, one revealing of some of the deep-seated patterns of that culture as well as of the confusions which continue to dog this particular topic. An unexamined, glamour-garlanded ideal of 'outsiderdom' is not the least significant source of these confusions.

NOTES

1. See the perceptive discussion in Jonathan Rée, 'English philosophy in the fifties', *Radical Philosophy*, 65 (1993), 3–21.
2. In his *New Bearings in English Poetry* (London: Chatto, 1932), Leavis declared that 'the Sitwells belong to the history of publicity rather than of poetry' (73); the allusion may be the more apropos given that the first reputation-boosting puff which Wilson received was from Edith Sitwell.
3. For details of Wilson's success, see Kenneth Allsop, *The Angry Decade* (London: Owen, 1958), and, especially, Harry Ritchie, *Success Stories: Literature and the Media in England 1950–1959* (London: Faber, 1988), chs. 7 and 8. My own analysis differs from Ritchie's, but I am nonetheless indebted to his excellent account.

4. Cyril Connolly, *The Sunday Times*, 27 May 1956, 17; Philip Toynbee, *The Observer*, 27 May 1956, 13.
5. Both quoted in Ritchie, *Success Stories*, 145.
6. Details from ibid. 146; for current values I have extrapolated from the table itemizing A. J. P. Taylor's earnings from this period in Kathleen Burk, *Troublemaker: The Life and History of A. J. P. Taylor* (London: Yale, 2000), 416–19, and then checked that against the movements of the Retail Price Index for the intervening period, as given in the appendix to Robert Skidelsky, *John Maynard Keynes, a Biography*, 3 vols.: iii. *Fighting For Britain 1937– 46* (London: Macmillan, 2000).
7. Ritchie, *Success Stories*, 141.
8. Colin Wilson, *The Outsider: An Inquiry into the Nature of the Sickness of Mankind in the Mid-Twentieth Century* (London: Gollancz, 1956), 281. 'Subtitle' may be inaccurate: the quoted phrase appeared on the dust-jacket but not on the title-page.
9. Colin Wilson, *Religion and the Rebel* (London: Gollancz, 1957), 270.
10. Ritchie, *Success Stories*, 166.
11. Kingsley Amis, 'The legion of the lost', *Spectator*, 15 June 1956, 830–1; Burns Singer, 'The heavenly disease', *Time and Tide*, 9 June 1956, 686; 'Chosen Few', *TLS*, 8 June 1956, 342; A. J. Ayer, *Encounter*, 7 (Sept. 1956), 75–7; Raymond Williams, *Essays in Criticism*, 7 (January 1957), 68–76.
12. I am grateful to Deborah McVea of the Warwick-Leverhulme *TLS Contributors' Index* project for providing advance identification of Burns Singer.
13. 'Letters', *TLS*, 14 Dec. 1956; cited in Ritchie, *Success Stories*, 155.
14. Williams, 'Review of *The Outsider*', 68, 69, 71, 73, 75, 76.
15. Ayer, 'Review of *The Outsider*', 75.
16. Donald Davie, 'Letter', *London Magazine* (Feb. 1957), 61.
17. Angus Wilson, *A Bit Off The Map, and Other Stories* (London: Secker, 1957), 3–4, 6, 10. I am grateful to Kevin Jackson for bringing this story to my attention.
18. Ritchie, *Success Stories*, 154, 157.
19. See Wilson's entry in *Who's Who 2001* (London: Black, 2001).
20. Ritchie, *Success Stories*, 174.
21. Leo Braudy, *The Frenzy of Renown: Fame and its History* (New York: Oxford University Press, 1986), 17.
22. The *Sunday Telegraph* was a particularly culpable offender here: see e.g., ' 'Araby's chic apologist', *Sunday Telegraph*, 4 July 1993. One journalist who pointed out the belatedness of British comment, and who also offered a defence against these charges, was Christopher Hitchens, 'Defender of freedom in a culture lacking grace', *Guardian*, 3 July 1993, 25.
23. e.g. Lesley White, 'A highbrow hero storms the ivory tower', *Sunday Times*, 20 June 1993, sect. 2, 5; Brian Appleyard, 'Reflections from the tightrope', *Independent*, 23 June 1993, 23.
24. Ashok Bery, 'What Said really said', *THES*, 27 July 1993, 14.
25. Robert Hanks, 'The less Said, the better', *Independent*, 6 July 1993, 14.
26. Leslie Plommer, 'It's not all Reith on the night', *Guardian*, 28 July 1993, 18.
27. Anne Karpf, 'Hostile territory', *Guardian*, 23 June 1993, G2, 4 (note the slide between 'English' and 'Britain').
28. Matthew d'Ancona, *The Times*, 7 July 1993, 16.
29. See above, Ch. 5, n. 3.

30. Gilbert Adair, 'Unwilling to pause for thought', *Sunday Times*, 11 July 1993, sect. 9, 4.
31. Maya Jaggi, 'Profile: Edward Said', *Guardian* (1 Dec. 2001), Saturday Review, 10.
32. Edward W. Said, *Representations of the Intellectual: The 1993 Reith Lectures* (London: Vintage, 1994). I have used the American edition (New York: Pantheon, 1994); hereafter page references will be given in the text.

19

Media Studies: A Discourse of General Ideas

'The newspaper and periodical article is an indispensable form of the modern spirit, and whoever looks down on it from pedantry hasn't the faintest idea what is going on historically today.'

I

Periodical journalism, in the broadest sense, is not just the intellectual's natural habitat: it is also the noise made by a culture speaking to itself. It is the medium in which the question of intellectuals has been most frequently put, and the repetition in the answers is part of what makes this rather scorned source so evidentially valuable; this chapter's epigraph, from Ortega via Curtius, provides a weighty rebuke to the 'pedantry' which often underlies such scorn.[1] At the same time, what is involved here is not really a single medium: the actual forms of publication may be dizzyingly diverse, embracing almost everything that falls into the space between books at one end and daily newspapers at the other. For my purposes, the relevant kinds of publication that fall into this space are not best characterized by their material properties, but by the informing aspiration they share to provide 'a discourse of general ideas'. This, it seems to me, is the constant lying behind the shifting terminology used to pick out the emblematic occupant of this space—'a general cultural periodical', 'a review of ideas', 'a literary journal'.

A lot of work is being done here by the term 'general' as a qualifying description. The unstable, inherently contrastive, meanings attached to this word point up a series of structural tensions in twentieth-century culture, meanings which have included, though by no means been confined to, the following: not addressed exclusively to one segment of the reading population defined by age, gender, or occupation; not driven by the urgent but superficial demands of topicality; not confined to one school, movement, or group; not restricted to one department of knowledge or slice of experience. What has been understood by 'general' in any particular case has depended upon which of these contrasts has, negatively, been most pressing. Obviously, the substantive content of these categories changes over time: something viewed as threateningly 'narrow' in 1920 could look agreeably 'general' by 1980. It is the structure or space that is constant, not the particular cultural filling, and the ambition to conduct a 'general periodical' or 'review of ideas' has taken its character from the persistence of this structure.

One of the forms most commonly assumed by this ambition in twentieth-century British culture has been the founding of a 'literary' review which then continually protests that it should not be confined simply to 'literature'. There have been many editors who have shared the assumption behind T. S. Eliot's casual reference to the genre of 'the literary review—which might be called a review of general ideas'. The elasticity of the adjective 'literary' has been crucial here, allowing free movement between the broader sense of 'to do with books' and the narrower sense of 'imaginative writing'. But scarcely less important has been the residual character of the so-called 'literary review', its function as a no-questions-asked shelter for those on the run from periodicals with stiffer entry requirements. Britain has had (and, arguably, continues to have) a particularly rich culture of 'literary journalism', and at times this expansive label has provided a kind of protective colouration for some of those who, though their activities have undeniably been those of 'intellectuals', have been most squeamish about being so labelled.

This discourse about 'general' reviews—the desirability of their existence, the uncertainty of their definition, the repeated announcements of their disappearance—obviously replicates the discourse about intellectuals examined in this book. Indeed, in Britain, the former discourse may be said often to have substituted or acted as a disguise for the latter. In phrases such as 'the total intellectual' or, more recently, 'the public intellectual', the adjectives are pointing to the same aspiration to transcend conventional divisions and boundaries as does the term 'general' in the various specifications of the ideal of 'the general periodical'. And new attempts to realize that ideal continue to be made. Consider the self-description of the most recent of the long line of candidates: '*Prospect*, as a monthly magazine aimed at the intellectually curious, non-specialist reader, will occupy that large space between the "instant" and the "academic".'[2]

Much has been written about the rich harvest of periodicals in twentieth-century Britain, even though they have for the most part not yet received the kind of systematic, detailed scholarly attention which has been accorded to their nineteenth-century predecessors. Numerous examples of such publications have already made an appearance in this book; in addition, I have attempted to address the generic character of such publications on other occasions.[3] For these reasons, this chapter will not focus on such periodicals in their classic form; instead, it will track the ideal of 'a discourse of general ideas' as it migrated to a new and distinctively twentieth-century medium, albeit one which could still be described, borrowing from the traditional genre, as 'the country's best intellectual magazine'.

II

The relation between intellectuals and their potential publics in Britain changed at precisely 6 p.m. on Sunday 29 September 1946. Beginning, rather daringly, with a programme satirizing the pretensions of 'highbrow' cultural broadcasting, this moment saw the launch of the BBC's new Third Programme, a network that was to be devoted exclusively to the higher reaches of intellectual and cultural life. The founding of the Third provides an interesting example of how technological and, ultimately, social changes in the available media of expression can reshape the relationship which is at the heart of the intellectual's role. But, more strikingly still, much of the debate that has accompanied the Third Programme (and its successor Radio Three) during the half century or more of its existence has been one of the forms—one is tempted to say disguises—taken by discussion of the question of intellectuals in Britain. The paradoxes inherent in the cultural pattern of denial were displayed in particularly acute form in the programme's early years, just in the period when the most influential accounts of British exceptionalism in the matter of intellectuals were being published. Although the role or label of 'the intellectual' might be disowned, diffidently or aggressively, the Third Programme could at times seem to possess a unique power to stir passions about the importance of various kinds of cultural specialists addressing a wider public. How else, after all, is one to understand the fact that in 1957 fifteen of the country's leading intellectual figures should write to the *Times*, declaring: 'This is an issue which closely affects the interests of the . . . nation as a whole, and it vitally concerns the spiritual, cultural, and intellectual life of the community.' The 'issue' in question may now seem less than wholly cataclysmic—a moderate reduction in the broadcasting hours of the Third Programme.[4]

As we have seen, the first response of the educated class to the development of radio had tended to be a mixture of scorn and indifference, bracketing it with film and advertising as among the new 'mass' forms likely to threaten the position of traditional cultural activities.[5] In the 1920s and 1930s, the range of programming on the BBC's 'National Service' had been limited, concentrating principally on 'light' music and middlebrow drama, and although the repertoire of talks added in the late 1920s and early 1930s gave it a somewhat wider social purchase, it was still largely the case that by the late 1930s 'the "wireless" was regarded with scorn by most intellectuals, as yet another example of popular bad taste'.[6] Moreover, in radio's early days its reach was limited and its reception patchy, though things soon improved; in 1922 there was only 1 radio licence per 100 households, but by 1939 this had risen to 71 per 100.[7] Its importance as a source of news and official announcements was increasingly recognized, stimulated by its role at great moments of national crisis such as the Abdication or the outbreak of the Second World War. Indeed, the war was in many ways its finest hour, and made the cultural potential of the medium lastingly apparent. This led the BBC in 1945–6 to undertake a fundamental reorganization of its broadcasting, resulting in the establishment of three services that were defined as much by the educational and cultural profile of their intended listeners as by the thematic nature of their contents: the Light Programme, the Home Service, and—for want of any more acceptable label—the Third Programme.[8]

The terms of reference for the proposed new programme (called 'Programme C' in the planning stages) were confident and unapologetic about the nature of the intended audience:

> The Programme is designed to be of artistic and cultural importance. The audience envisaged is one already aware of artistic experience and will include persons of taste, of intelligence, and of education; it is therefore selective not casual, and both attentive and critical. The Programme need not cultivate any other audience, and any material that is unlikely to interest such listeners should be excluded.[9]

Both the style and the content of the new service marked it out as emanating from and addressing itself to the traditionally educated upper-middle class, but it was always one of the proud boasts of the Third that anyone could tune in and have new worlds opened up to them, whatever their social background. In this respect, the new programme partly shared in the social idealism characteristic of the second half of the 1940s. As one observer put it later: 'The Third Programme was founded on Labour England. Its imagined listener was a hard-working, Labour-voting schoolmaster in (say) Derby, who was interested in international theatre, new music, philosophy, politics, and painting, and who listened selectively to all these things on the Third. That's what everyone believed in.'[10] This, however, is to give a distinctively Leftish, and perhaps nostalgic, twist to an enterprise that at the time seemed even more obviously distinguished by its public-school diphthongs than by its grammar-school earnestness. Harman Grisewood, the Third's second Controller from 1948–52, was unabashed about concentrating on the traditionally cultivated class: he later confessed that 'we'd all been brought up by Reith to think that working men should appreciate Beethoven and that kind of thing, but I knew it was a lot of balls'. He was also unperturbed by the mounting criticism of the 'elitism' of the Third.

> The attacks on the Third reflect the kind of philistinism which Matthew Arnold and many others have accused the English of. (I don't think you'll find an equivalent of the pejorative English word 'highbrow' in any other language.) It's something to do with the prestige in England of the landed gentry—the people who we looked up to weren't intellectuals, in the way that the French and Germans have always looked up to their intellectual leaders. But I eagerly accepted the role of defender of the highbrow.[11]

At the time, Grisewood had recognized the network's appeal to would-be 'highbrows', dividing the audience into the 'habitués' and the 'aspirants' (terms which introduced the unfortunate suggestion that the first group spoke foreign languages while the second dropped their aitches).[12] As so often in British cultural history, charges of intellectual and social exclusiveness were hard to disentangle.

In its early Reithian days, the BBC as a whole inevitably reproduced many assumptions and practices of the governing class of the time. For example, one official justification given of the rule that announcers had to wear dinner-jackets was that they might be called upon to meet or interview important people for that evening's transmission, and that such people, 'coming on' from some earlier social engagement, would themselves already be in evening dress. A further striking instance of how the Third's programmers assumed that their listeners endorsed the traditional overlap between social and cultural status was furnished by the fact that for several years debates from the Oxford and Cambridge Unions were broadcast 'live'.[13] There was, in fact, considerable adverse comment on the closeness of the ties between the Third and Oxford and Cambridge, especially Oxford, and even self-consciously 'radical' programmes such as John Lehmann's 'New Soundings' automatically began its search for new talent at Oxford.[14] It seemed all too appropriate that the church in Langham Place, next to the Third Programme's home, was All Souls.

The terms 'highbrows' and 'intellectuals' appeared constantly in the early press comment, the more popular versions of which were sharply critical of the new service's relentless seriousness and its lack of appeal to all but a tiny fraction of the population. (The fact that there were to be no fixed time slots on the Third led at least one newspaper to play with the headline 'Timeless radio for intellectuals'.[15]) The early programming on the Third certainly reflected the confidence of a class secure in its possession of 'culture'. For example: the third evening of the new network was given over almost entirely to a full-length (over three hours) production of Shaw's *Man and Superman*, and in the following months T. S. Eliot's British Academy lecture on Milton was broadcast on the same evening as it had been delivered, there was an English production of Sartre's recent play *Les Mouches*, Gilbert Murray's translation of Aristophanes' *Frogs* was broadcast together with some scenes in the original Greek, followed later in the year by a series of Plato's dialogues, and so on.[16] It says much for the status of the new network that when in 1952 Michael Ventris wanted to announce the successful deciphering of the script of Linear B found on tablets at Knossos, he should have thought the Third Programme the appropriate place to do so—and that the BBC should have agreed with him.[17]

Talks on such learned topics were a staple feature of the early years of the Third, and they gave rise to that familiar dialectic between the twin dangers of 'talking down' and being 'over-specialized'. On the whole, the programme's actual listeners feared the first danger, while the second seemed more worrying to self-appointed spokesmen for the public at large. Indeed, in 1952 Noel Annan urged that there should be more talks he could *not* wholly understand: he wanted to hear scientists and other specialists addressing their peers without being forced to dilute and popularize. And in general he pleaded with producers and speakers

> not to underestimate their audience. The tiny fraction of the population which listens to the Third Programme listens because it already knows and understands a good deal about the matter which is being discussed. The Third is nothing if it is not highbrow: and I use that word in its most laudatory sense and do not associate it with unintelligibility for its own sake, or devitalised abstraction.[18]

It will already be clear that public discussion of the Third Programme provided the occasion for a particularly rich display of cultural attitudes grouped around the use of terms such as 'highbrow' and 'intellectuals'.

The size of the Third Programme's audience could be determined with somewhat greater accuracy than its social composition, though even here there was some dispute about the figures, as the BBC repudiated criticism from some sections of the press about the tiny proportion of the population who ever listened to a channel that was relatively expensive to produce. After its first few months, the Third was getting about 700,000 listeners, which was 6 per cent of the listening audience (the Light Programme attracted 50 per cent and the Home Service 44 per cent). By the end of the 1940s, the allegations in the press were that this had dwindled to no more than 250,000. The Parliamentary Broadcasting Committee concluded in 1949 that 'the average winter evening' audience for a Third Programme broadcast was 'in the neighbourhood of 90,000'. In 1953 a survey concluded that while individual broadcasts might reach over 100,000 listeners, the average audience for the Third was down to 45,000. By the 1970s, listening figures for the redesigned Radio Three fluctuated between 50,000 and 250,000. During the day the monitoring devices sometimes recorded 'no measurable audience', the term used when the numbers fell below an estimated 50,000. The further changes of the 1980s and early 1990s did not greatly alter this picture: 250,000 remained the largest audience reached by Radio Three, and it was usually considerably lower.[19]

The decline in the size of the audience from the peak reached in the network's early years has to be set against wider social changes. There was considerable pent-up hunger for all forms of cultural sustenance after the war—publishing benefited correspondingly, as far as paper shortages allowed—and radio listening in general peaked at this time. One indication of the cultural centrality of the activity was the remarkable fact that in these years the *Radio Times* outsold even the most popular Sunday newspapers. In 1950, when newspaper readership was at its all-time peak, a survey calculated that the *Radio Times* had a readership of just over 20 million (the figures for the *News of the World* were 17½ million and for the *People* 13 million).[20] The main change that displaced radio from this position was, of course, the growth of television, especially after the launch of 'Independent' (i.e. commercial) television in 1955. In 1946 there were only 15,000 TV licences, mostly in London, rising to 750,000 by 1951; by 1956 there were over 5 million and pretty much the whole country could receive transmissions; by 1960 this had doubled to 10 million, and by 1969 nine out of ten households had a television.[21] Later still, the BBC had to contend with the proliferation of independent radio stations, although the most direct challenge to the position of Radio Three (as the Third was renamed in 1967) was not to come until the launching of the commercial station, Classic FM, in September 1992. There were also broader social and technological changes, such as the great increase in music available on record and compact discs: where in the decades after the war many pieces of music could be heard outside the concert hall only on the Third, recordings of almost all such music became increasingly available from the 1970s onwards. And, more broadly still, the expansion of higher education had a double-edged impact on the audience for a network of this type. In principle, it enlarged the number of those whose education might have been expected to develop an appetite for the higher reaches of intellectual and cultural life, but at the same time it also meant that many were now getting from formal courses of education what a previous generation had acquired for itself from the airwaves. The setting up of the Open University in 1969 particularly usurped some of this function.

It is also worth recalling how closely the various programmes reflected what was still the comparatively rigid class structure of Britain in the 1940s: for example, a survey of listeners to all three BBC radio networks in 1947 classified 6 per cent of the audience as 'upper-middle class', 21 per cent as 'lower-middle class', and 73 per cent as 'working class'.[22] (There is a close correspondence here with a recent scholarly analysis of the census returns for 1951 which concludes that by 1951 only somewhere between 0.05 per cent and 0.1 per cent were classifiable as 'upper class', while 28 per cent of the population were 'middle class' and 72 per cent were 'working class'.[23]) Apart from the huge numerical preponderance of the third category, it is striking how confidently these traditional social categories were deployed in such surveys. In 1947 Britain's social structure was still, and was still perceived as, an irregular, squashed pyramid with a huge base and tiny apex. Intriguingly, a 1949 survey suggested that although the listener profiles of the other two networks were broadly what might be expected in class terms, the breakdown of the Third's audience was estimated to be 28 per cent 'upper-middle class', 37 per cent 'lower-middle class', and 35 per cent 'working class', although since by this point even the BBC's own optimistic estimate of the audience for the Third was only 100,000 people, these figures represented infinitesimal proportions of the latter two classes.[24]

However limited the size and social composition of the audience for the new network, its establishment undoubtedly provided the opportunity for certain intellectuals to reach a relatively wide, and potentially diverse, public—perhaps more diverse in some respects than that reached by any one periodical publication whose readership would usually be determined along professional or partisan lines. 'BBC producers are really the editors of the country's best intellectual magazine' was Noel Annan's judgement in 1952 (it was one of the best-paying, too, offering twenty guineas for a twenty-minute talk, 'a most welcome addition to the income of most intellectuals').[25] It is also important to recognize that speech programmes made up a far larger proportion of the Third's programming than of Radio Three's later: in its first ten years, for example, only a little more than half the broadcasting time was devoted to music.[26] Furthermore, the personal nature of a broadcast, even a formally delivered talk, increased the tendency to focus on the intellectual as a 'personality', where matters of accent, liveliness, and so on came into play as they had not on the printed page. The Third gave a new platform to some established intellectuals and helped to launch others. Interestingly, both the individuals whom I discussed in Ch. 5 as examples of ambivalent or reluctant intellectuals figured prominently in its early years. Bertrand Russell proved to be a particularly fluent and successful broadcaster, and his flourishing career on the Third added a fresh dimension to his reputation and surely helped to boost the sales of his commercially very successful *History of Western Philosophy*, published in 1947. G. M. Trevelyan's defining properties were not so obviously well adapted to the new medium, but the author of the best-selling *English Social History* was nonetheless in demand and by early 1947 he was reported as having 'held the attention of his radio audience for an hour'.[27] Two examples of figures who, in their contrasting ways, were enabled by the Third to achieve a degree of prominence they might not have reached by publication alone were Jacob Bronowski and Isaiah Berlin. The former had already cultivated the role of polymath, but some of the major steps along the path that were to lead to his becoming almost the public face of science on British television were taken on the Third, beginning with a five-part series on 'The Common Sense of Science' in 1948.[28] Berlin was the first person allowed to give unscripted talks on the Third (a case of *force majeure*, perhaps?), and he attracted particular attention for his six-lecture series on 'Freedom and its Betrayal' in 1952.[29] So successful was Berlin in this role that by 1955 the Assistant Controller of the Third, Christopher Holme, could propose that the difference between the Home Service and the Third Programme was best defined as that 'between Malcolm Muggeridge and Isaiah Berlin'.[30]

At first, the Third was markedly deferential to established literary reputations, so figures such as Shaw and Eliot were treated with great respect, but there soon came to be a category of writers whose reputations were partly made by their writing for radio, including Louis MacNeice and, most famously, Dylan Thomas. (As television assumed its dominant place in the culture from the 1960s onwards, there began to be a whole new category of figures whose status as 'intellectuals', such as it was, depended *primarily* on their success in that medium: this would arguably be true in different ways of such contrasting figures as Dennis Potter, Melvyn Bragg, and Michael Ignatieff.)

Academics, in particular, were beneficiaries of this greater 'exposure', as it was later to be called, leading several to establish far wider reputations than would otherwise have been possible. For example, in 1951 Grisewood calculated that forty of the eighty-eight talks given in a chosen month were by academics, including whole series of lectures by Herbert Butterfield, Fred Hoyle, E. H. Carr, and others (as well as broadcasting such established set-piece lectures as the Romanes at Oxford and the Rede at Cambridge). Grisewood did not fail to emphasize the size of the public these lectures were thus able to reach: 'Those who do in fact hear these lectures are in numbers to be compared with the crowds at one of our great sporting events, rather than with the numbers that can be admitted, for example, to the Sheldonian Theatre.'[31] Such lectures and talks were often repeated, and then made available to a further audience through publication in *The Listener*, which had been launched in 1929 and reached a circulation of 150,000 by the late 1940s.[32] But it was the informing conception of what made a talk suitable for the Third that revealed the (sometimes ghostly) presence of the notion of 'the intellectual'. As Annan summarized it: 'The Third Programme is a discourse of general ideas—ideas which relate to the great intellectual disciplines.' Merely topical or descriptive talks ('a commentary on the Budget, or a talk on the Health Service, or on cattle-ranching in Australia') belong on the Home Service, but 'they could be suitable [for the Third] were they related to the relevant group of general ideas, i.e. economic theory, sociology, agricultural science, or cultural anthropology'.[33] This may have been to accentuate the *academic* intellectual framework more than all those in Broadcasting House responsible for the network would have been entirely happy with, but it accurately pinpoints the structural role of the academic intellectual, journeying between specialism and 'a discourse of general ideas'. And as Grisewood had observed the previous year, there were many who 'feel concerned at the problem of specialization not only within a university setting, but in the broad context of our cultural life.'[34]

Even this, of course, still seemed positively cliquish to the Third's critics: in 1949 a Parliamentary report found that it had an 'academic atmosphere, relieved at times with a carefully diluted touch of Bloomsbury', and by the end of its first decade it was alleged to have combined some of the characteristics of 'a little magazine of the air' with being 'the radio High Table of British culture'.[35] At this time, such criticisms did not necessarily express a populist resentment of hearing educated voices on the airwaves. When, for example, *The Spectator* complained in 1951 that by failing to reach a wider range of listeners the Third was wasting the chance it gave 'to the intellectuals . . . to command spontaneously a huge audience',[36] it evinced an almost touching faith in both the intellectuals and their potential publics. In other words, part of the contradictory objection to 'High Tables' (here a metonymy for academic intellectuals more generally) is that the seating is limited: the talk is desiccated and pretentious, and, what's more, not enough people get to hear it.

III

Quite how far the Third did enable some of its contributors to operate in the role of 'intellectuals' is an interesting question. It became apparent almost immediately that distinguished academic and cultural figures could speak on the Third without forfeiting any of their existing status: they were addressing non-specialists without being asked to vulgarize their work, a situation which represents one ideal of the intellectual's function. At the same time, it was not a medium suited to the more hortatory forms of moral or political guidance. Intellectual controversy and debate were welcomed, but Third Programme talks were not expected to be overtly political manifestos: the BBC was far more sensitive about the need not to abuse its monopoly position and hence to maintain 'balance' or political neutrality than was the case with a more avowedly partisan newspaper or periodical. (One may speculate that elsewhere in Europe at this time such a service would surely have been much more thoroughly politicized, and accusations about the excessive power of the left or the right would have been commonplace.) This did not rule out certain sorts of cultural criticism: Bertrand Russell may have helped emancipate thousands of young listeners by insisting on the intellectually compelling nature of the arguments against the existence of God (especially in a memorable debate with the Jesuit philosopher Father Coplestone in January 1948), and other speakers similarly called into question the justification for a range of social and moral conventions. The Third also reinforced the supra-national claims of culture (and thus helped foster one sort of 'cultural capital' for its possessors): it maintained a strongly European profile in music and drama as well as, to a lesser extent, in literature and the other arts (its relations with American intellectual and cultural life were far sketchier in the early years).[37] And of course it mattered that it was a *national* radio network, not a private or sectarian enterprise; the status of those who spoke on it benefited correspondingly, even though the numbers listening to their talk might be small.

The place of intellectuals in British culture was also involved here in deeper if less direct ways. Throughout the life of the Third Programme and its successor Radio Three, the service has acted as something of a lightning rod for larger anxieties about 'exclusiveness' versus 'accessibility'. There has been a recurring pattern to debates over the role and future of the network (and of its successor), with some version of the following sequence being repeated each time: complaints build up about its 'elitist' or 'off-putting' character; the BBC proposes changes to make it more 'accessible' and 'inviting'; this provokes a chorus of protest about the 'dilution' of quality and the 'debasement' of standards; the BBC responds by emphasizing its duty to the payers of the licence fee and the need to adapt to social change; the service is modified very much along the lines of the original proposal; the regular audience for the service remains tiny and predominantly middle-class and middle-aged; after a while the complaints about its 'elitist' and 'outdated' character reach a new crescendo; and so on. Just as the increase of specialization and the increase in anxieties-about-specialization form an inevitable dialectic, so a similar pattern is bound to establish itself around the role of a self-consciously 'high-cultural' network in a national broadcasting system. The constant if uneven democratization of social life in mid- and late twentieth-century Britain repeatedly challenged the confident assumptions about culture and education that had been inherited from a less egalitarian era.

The pattern was set as early as 1948, when, after the Third had for the first time broadcast some 'light music', E. M. Forster went directly to William Haley, the Director-General of the BBC, to complain about the 'vulgarization' of the service.[38] (The sense of social confidence, of having access to other members of the elite, is marked here.) But the most revealing, and in some ways most decisive, of these episodes came in 1957 when the report on 'The Future of Sound Broadcasting' proposed substantial cuts in the Third's broadcasting hours, partly because the audiences were so small and the items broadcast so 'specialized'. It recommended dropping 'those programmes whose real place is in print, and more properly in the learned quarterlies than in the *Listener*'.[39] Instead, the target audience was revealingly specified in terms of periodical reading—'those people who read the political and literary pages of the *Observer* and *Sunday Times* and the more serious weeklies such as the *Spectator*, the *Economist*, the *New Statesman*, and the *Listener*'.[40] The proposals produced immediate protests, including, remarkably, a debate in the House of Commons on the motion that 'this House would deeply regret the passing of the Third Programme'.[41] In response, a Third Programme Defence Society was formed, and influential members of the educated class resorted to their ultimate weapon—a letter to *The Times* (the letter referred to earlier). A striking collocation of intellectual and cultural grandees signed this letter: Lord Beveridge, Sir Arthur Bliss, Sir Adrian Boult, the Bishop of Chichester, T. S. Eliot, E. M. Forster, Christopher Fry, Sir John Gielgud, Victor Gollancz, John Masefield, Harold Nicolson, Bertrand Russell, Vita Sackville-West, and Ralph Vaughan Williams. The chief common characteristic of these signatories seems to have been unremarked at the time, namely their age. By my calculations, their average age was 69, with Russell and Vaughan Williams leading the way at 85, followed by Masefield (79), Beveridge and Forster (78), and so on. (The campaign of protest was coordinated, it must be said, by the 42-year-old Cambridge historian Peter Laslett, who had until recently been a producer on the Third.)

At a meeting between the leading protestors and some of the Governors and officials of the BBC, T. S. Eliot made a withering attack on the proposed changes as a 'massacre', 'sheer vandalism', and a 'plan to pander to the more moronic elements in our society'. It's a fine moment: the (originally American) poet and critic haranguing Governors such as Sir Alexander Cadogan, Sir Phillip Morris, and Lord Rochdale who, as an observer later recalled, 'were being made to feel that they were nobodies in their own country'.[42] Public statements were issued; according to the report in the *The Times*: 'Mr T. S. Eliot demanded that a statement be issued to the public to dispel the fear that the BBC was preparing a catastrophic abdication of its responsibilities, lowering the standards of culture at home and lowering the prestige of Britain abroad.'[43] In one sense, all this may look like a fine example of cultural authority being wielded by a leading intellectual figure, and it could be said that the whole campaign represented a modest 'mobilization' of intellectuals to act publicly. But, from another angle, a reduction in a radio service's broadcasting time cannot but seem an issue of relatively minor and local importance, scarcely justifying the hyperbolic language of 'catastrophe', 'moronic', and so on. Moreover, the episode might equally be taken to represent the powerlessness of such figures: after all, the protesters lost, and from October 1957 the Third's hours were reduced by 40 per cent. Not for the first time, it was the BBC's side of the case that appeared to be both modern and 'popular': the intellectuals yet again seemed to be those who clung to a past supposedly less governed by either economic rationality or political democracy.

A similar pattern was to repeat itself at subsequent 'crises' in the network's life, notably in 1969 and 1992. It was the 1969 report on *Broadcasting in the Seventies* which finally led, in a general reorganization of BBC radio, to the recently renamed 'Radio Three' becoming principally a classical music network. (Existing networks had been renamed in 1967; part of the argument in support of such a change in respect of the Third Programme was that its previous title 'undoubtedly has connotations which discourage a large number who might have enjoyed many of its programmes from tuning in to it'.[44]) The letters of protest to the press this time included one signed by '40 members of King's High Table', and another signed by ten 'Fellows of Gonville and Caius College, Cambridge' which affirmed that the music programming of the Third 'makes a uniquely valuable contribution to the life of this country' and that 'in its attention to drama, literature, political and social discussion, it plays a vital role in upholding cultural standards, and providing cultural sustenance to the community at large'.[45] Those who supported the proposed changes precisely contended that in practice the 'community at large' was nowhere near large enough. Similar protests encountered similar defences after the new Controller, Nicholas Kenyon, introduced some sweeping changes in 1992. Another symbolic storm in the usual tea-cup was aroused by the decision in 1995 to buy in a popular announcer from Classic FM to present one of Radio Three's flagship programmes on the grounds that his manner and voice would be 'unintimidating'.[46] For once the protest from the network's listeners, spearheaded on this occasion by Gerald Kaufman, Chairman of the relevant Parliamentary Select Committee, succeeded in having this experiment aborted.

In the closing decades of the century, the higher management of the BBC, twitchily fearful of falling out with the *Zeitgeist*, displayed a mixture of nervous populism and accountants' philistinism in its dealings with its 'serious' network. As Hans Keller, the Third's abrasive and committed head of New Music and its musical conscience for many years, wrote in a bitter eve-of-retirement salvo in *The Spectator* in June 1979: 'The BBC rightly prides itself on not being commercial; the trouble is that again and again, it plans as if it were.'[47] Perhaps the nadir of the process by which the Corporation was rotted from within came with the attack on Radio Three by the Chairman of the Governors of the BBC himself, Marmaduke Hussey (formerly Rupert Murdoch's right-hand man in managing News International), who complained that the network was 'frankly elitist'.[48] As the network's historian, Humphrey Carpenter, observed: 'It is notable how, throughout the *Broadcasting in the Seventies* brouhaha, and indeed around the time of the 1957 cuts, the BBC consistently confused cultural programmes with broadcasting for minorities.'[49] From the confident assumption that 'culture' was unitary and was, in principle, a common possession even if in practice only a few had the education or leisure to cultivate it, the Corporation, like the world around it, has moved to the view that different groups in society have different but equally legitimate interests, and those who concern themselves with the traditional forms of 'culture' (now with obligatory scare quotes around it) are a minority with no greater claim on national resources than any other, a minority whom the BBC should treat, in Peter Laslett's scathing words, 'like other minorities: like the bridge players and the dog-fanciers, bird watchers and beginners in the Spanish language'.[50] It is surely impossible to imagine any BBC official saying in the early twenty-first century what John Morris, then Controller of the Third, said, and said with the assurance that the view would be widely endorsed, in the mid-1950s, when he affirmed that 'the BBC had a moral duty to improve taste and disseminate culture'.[51] It may be that the most significant change in recent years to the pattern of cuts-and-protests here described has been that the objectors to further alterations to the nature of Radio Three no longer have either the intellectual confidence or the social prestige that they still, just, enjoyed several decades ago.

Nonetheless, although social and cultural circumstances have changed hugely in the half-century since the Third Programme was launched, there are those among the present-day descendants of its first audience who feel that the BBC has panicked in its attempt to adapt to what it perceives these changes to be. Even the judicious prose of broadcasting's 'official historian', Asa Briggs, swells as he observes of the programmes broadcast on the Third: 'ambitious programming of this range was to be unknown in this country—or any country—after its demise'.[52] Certainly, many voices could be found to agree with that of the author (and former Third Programme presenter) John Spurling who wrote in 1996:

> My millennial dream is to see the Third restored, not just to its old excellence, but to a new glory as a real centre of international culture—tough, experimental, elitist, scholarly, argumentative, unmissable. Music would not dominate, as it does now, pushing everything else into gaps and corners, nor would the spoken material be PR chat *about* fiction or poetry, science, history, whatever, but the latest stuff itself, plus serious discussion and evaluation.

This offers an admirable prescription for a serious public broadcasting network that would recognize the increasing internationalization of culture while resisting its increasing commercialization, and not everyone would feel obliged to endorse Spurling's wistful conclusion: 'Impossible, of course.'[53]

This is a topic on which it is notoriously difficult to disentangle cultural pessimism, selective experience, and historical analysis. The style of the original Third Programme clearly reflected the mixture of intellectual confidence and social responsibility characteristic of certain sections of the educated class in the middle of the twentieth century. At the beginning of the twenty-first century, a different style reflects changes in all these elements. For example, Radio Three's current flagship cultural programme, *Night Waves*, is regularly broadcast on four or five evenings a week; it takes a much wider view of culture as its remit than would have been contemplated by the Third Programme's founders, including reggae as well as retrospectives, and it draws upon an extensive range of occasional contributors. On the other hand, following current media wisdom, it relies too heavily on the informal interview and hence on talk *about* a recent exhibition, film, or book rather than providing either some more direct presentation of a sample of the work in question or else a genuinely critical engagement with it. Producers and presenters can at times seem more anxious about the supposedly deterrent effect of articulate analysis than of inconsequential demotic chatter. Nonetheless, it is striking to see how from time to time changes either in a particular programme or in the network as a whole can still provoke cries of alarm and outrage that are almost identical to those that greeted alterations to the original formula of the Third Programme nearly half a century ago, and it is clear that debates about the function of such a service continue to be one of the ways, albeit a relatively minor and oblique way, of addressing the question of intellectuals in Britain.

NOTES

1. Ortega y Gasset as quoted in Ernst Robert Curtius, *Essays on European Literature*, trans. Michael Kowal (Princeton: Princeton University Press, 1973), 307.
2. David Goodhart, 'Editorial', *Prospect* 1 (1995), 1.
3. For a general survey, see 'The golden age that never was', *TLS* (18 Jan. 2002), 17–19; for a case-study of one influential attempt to exploit this medium, see also 'The critic as anti-journalist: Leavis after *Scrutiny*', in Jeremy Treglown and Bridget Bennett (eds.), *Grub Street and the Ivory Tower: Literary Journalism and Literary Scholarship from Fielding to the Internet* (Oxford: Oxford University Press, 1998), 151–76.
4. Letter on 'Future of Sound Broadcasting' signed by Lord Beveridge and fourteen others, *The Times* (26 Apr. 1957), 11. For the other signatories, see sect. II below.
5. See in particular D. L. LeMahieu, *A Culture for Democracy: Mass Communication and the Cultivated Mind in Britain Between the Wars* (Oxford: Oxford University Press, 1988); cf. the discussion in Ch. 5 above.
6. Humphrey Carpenter, *The Envy of the World: Fifty Years of the BBC Third Programme and Radio 3 1946–1996* (London: Weidenfeld, 1996), 5.

7. Ross McKibbin, *Cultures and Classes: England 1918–1951* (Oxford: Oxford University Press, 1998), 457.
8. See the detailed account in Asa Briggs, *The History of Broadcasting in the United Kingdom*, iv. *Sound and Vision* (Oxford: Oxford University Press, rev. edn. 1995 [1st edn. 1979]), 46–77.
9. William Haley, the BBC's Editor-in-Chief and subsequently Director-General, quoted Carpenter, *Envy of the World*, 11–12.
10. Alexander Goehr, interviewed in 1996, quoted in Carpenter, *Envy of the World*, 14.
11. Quoted ibid. 77–8
12. Quoted in Kate Whitehead, *The Third Programme: A Literary History* (Oxford: Oxford University Press, 1989), 50.
13. Carpenter, *Envy of the World*, 126.
14. Whitehead, *Third Programme*, ch. 10.
15. Quoted in Carpenter, *Envy of the World*, 24.
16. See ibid. 32, 52, 59, 64.
17. Ibid. 114.
18. Noel Annan, 'Talking on the Third Programme', *B.B.C. Quarterly* (Autumn, 1952), 144.
19. For the figures in this paragraph, see Whitehead, *Third Programme*, ch. 3, and Carpenter, *Envy of the World*, 48, 116, 303, 333.
20. Figures from McKibbin, *Classes and Cultures*, 503.
21. See Stuart Laing, *Representations of Working Class Life, 1957–64* (London: Macmillan, 1986), 141–2.
22. Whitehead, *Third Programme*, 57.
23. McKibbin, *Classes and Cultures*, 106.
24. Briggs, *Sound and Vision*, 74, 76.
25. Annan, 'Talking on the Third', 142.
26. John Morris (ed.), *From the Third Programme: A Ten-Years' Anthology* (London: Nonesuch Press, 1956), p. vii.
27. Briggs, *Sound and Vision*, 68–9.
28. Briggs describes Bronowski as 'one of the most accomplished and versatile broadcasters ever employed by the BBC'; *Sound and Vision*, 507.
29. In the Introduction to the recently published version of these talks, Henry Hardy cites examples of the impact they made at the time; Isaiah Berlin, *Freedom and Its Betrayal*, ed. Henry Hardy (Princeton: Princeton University Press, 2002),
30. Quoted in Carpenter, *Envy of the World*, 168.
31. Harman Grisewood, 'The Universities and the Third Programme', *Universities Quarterly* (1951), 367, 370.
32. Briggs, *Sound and Vision*, 521; cf. Alvin Sullivan (ed.), *British Literary Magazines*, iv. *The Modern Age, 1914–1984* (London: Greenwood, 1986).
33. Annan, 'Talking on the Third', 143.
34. Grisewood, 'Universities and the Third', 370.
35. For these descriptions, see, respectively, Briggs, *Sound and Vision*, 328, Whitehead, *Third Programme*, ch. 10, and Carpenter, *Envy of the World*, 303.
36. Quoted in Whitehead, *Third Programme*, 60.
37. In the network's first ten years, French contemporary theatre was said to have become its '*specialité de la maison*'; quoted in Briggs, *Sound and Vision*, 68.

38. Carpenter, *Envy of the World*, 87.
39. Quoted in Whitehead, *Third Programme*, 215.
40. Quoted in Asa Briggs, *The History of Broadcasting in the United Kingdom*, v. *Competition* (Oxford: Oxford University Press, 1995), 49.
41. Briggs, *Competition*, 53.
42. Quoted ibid. 57; Whitehead, *Third Programme*, 223, 175, citing the later article by Ved Mehta, 'Onward and upward with the arts: the Third', *New Yorker*, 18 May 1963.
43. 'B.B.C. hear plea for "Third" ', *The Times*, 19 July 1957, 7.
44. Carpenter, *Envy of the World*, 249, 238, 251; Briggs, *Competition*, 768–9.
45. 'Letters to the Editor', *The Times*, 4 June 1969, 11.
46. See Carpenter, *Envy of the World*, 357.
47. Quoted ibid. 306.
48. Quoted ibid. 356.
49. Ibid. 262.
50. Peter Laslett, 'An appeal to the absent', *Cambridge Review* (12 Oct. 1957), 7.
51. Quoted in Whitehead, *Third Programme*, 213.
52. Briggs, *Sound and Vision*, 921.
53. Quoted in Carpenter, *Envy of the World*, 363.

20

Long Views I: Specialization and its Discontents

'Elegy presents every thing as lost and gone, or absent and future.'

I

By the end of the twentieth century, it became common to single out two forces in particular as largely responsible between them for the 'death' or 'decline' of the intellectual. These two forces were taken to be distinctive of the present time, or at least to have assumed by this point a peculiarly intense and determining power. Indeed, so great was that power according to some accounts, especially of the two forces working in sinister combination, that it was held not merely to have led to the temporary or local disappearance of the intellectual but actually to have made the performance of the role impossible. The two forces were, first, the process of intellectual specialization, especially its subdivision of knowledge into an ever-multiplying profusion of mutually incomprehensible and inward-looking academic disciplines; and second, the rise of celebrity culture, with the dynamics of the popular media increasingly governing the public sphere of modern societies, leading to the displacement of the intellectual by the media personality. It is possible to see a relation at work between these two forces which, if not exactly dialectical, works by a logic of mutual repulsion, each stimulating the momentum, and exacerbating the effects, of the other. As these two juggernauts drive the relevant aspects of society in their opposite directions, the terrain on which the intellectual was supposed to have stood breaks apart and the species tumbles to its death in the resulting crevasse.

While all this can be presented as a dispassionate analysis of the cultural logic of market democracies, perhaps of modern societies of any description, it can also be seen as one of the most recent and most sophisticated of the guises assumed by the tradition of denial discussed in this book. Once again, the here-and-now is depicted as peculiarly unfavourable to the flourishing of the intellectual. It is typical of the alarmist and even apocalyptic character of such diagnoses to operate with only the skimpiest or most foreshortened sense of historical transition, in which an undifferentiated 'yesterday' of lush abundance suddenly gives way to an homogeneous 'today' of arctic scarcity. But where the topic of intellectuals is concerned, it is also characteristic of such accounts not just to ignore or understate the extent to which the two developments in question have long histories, but also to appear entirely oblivious to the fact that the despondent conclusions drawn from these developments also form part of a repetitive pattern themselves, stretching back over many decades.

In an attempt to mitigate some of the more pernicious effects of this kind of polemical amnesia, I have given a common structure to this and its companion chapter (Ch. 21). Each chapter sets its respective theme in a very long historical perspective, one which deliberately stretches back even beyond the beginning of the twentieth century. Each offers no more than a few illustrative instances, which are not always arranged in chronological sequence and which never pretend to be an outline or survey. Instead, in both cases, I concentrate on bringing out how the two main themes in question are, under different descriptions, defining elements in the operation of the cultural authority of the intellectual. For this, as I have argued throughout, requires both an element of achievement in a particular intellectual or creative activity (which can, seen from a particular angle, always appear as a form of 'specialization') and an element of acquiring a reputation for addressing a non-specialist public (which can similarly always be represented as a form of 'celebrity'). The role of the intellectual, on my analysis, is constituted by the movement between these two poles, and it is hardly surprising, therefore, if the very existence of intellectuals is always thought to be vulnerable to the overweighting of one at the expense of the other.

In principle, a process of specialization can be described as taking place in almost any area of life. There is always the same implication of a domain once held in common being broken up into smaller plots; a range of skills, functions, knowledge and so on that were, allegedly, at one time within the competence of a single individual now require the separate labours of several. Such a claim necessarily involves comparison across time, but the process itself never supplies an ur-state or external standard against which measurements can be made: the starting-point for comparison is always a matter of choice. Any state of affairs can be represented as more specialized than the state which preceded it, and there is no obvious terminus to the series.

Some degree of specialization of function must be present in any complex group or society. But just as there is no way of locating an original condition which is 'pre-specialization', so, by the same token, there is no general or a priori way to specify how much specialization is too much. It is one of those processes which, classically, each generation feels has gone too far in its own time. Of course, this can sit alongside recognition of the positive case: the benefits of the progressive division of labour can, in certain contexts, be enthusiastically saluted, and even the positive achievements of the most pertinent form of this—specialization in the pursuit of scientific understanding—can be acknowledged. However, not only is any such discussion always haunted by intimations of decline, but the standpoint from which such general evaluative assessments of the process are made is in effect assumed to be somehow outside the process. Commenting upon specialization, above all when deploring its harmful consequences, is not taken to be another specialism. So, the very act of identifying it is premised on the existence, if only for the duration of that act, of a perspective which is 'outside' it and hence more general.

There is thus an inherent and not merely contingent relation between reflections on specialization and the idea of the intellectual. The notion of 'specialization', as a developmental process, signals a movement from general to particular. The concept of the intellectual (to use for the moment a brutally truncated formula) signals a movement from particular to general. As a result, specialization, understood as a historically located sociological or cultural development, always simultaneously generates a need for the role of the intellectual and threatens to extinguish it. The very identification of specialization as some kind of *problem* is already premised on an intuition of loss, the loss of some more general perspective or capacity which is assumed to be desirable or even essential. Specialization and anxiety-about-specialization are joined at the hip, fated to hobble together across the landscape of cultural diagnosis. What, exactly, is alleged to be being lost will always be context-specific. Sometimes the emphasis falls on the deformation of the humanity of the specialist, sometimes on the disappearance from view of larger purposes, sometimes on the way the process cramps intellectual creativity, sometimes on the way communication between specialists or with some non-specialist audience becomes impossible, and so on. But what is constant is the presupposition that there is some more general perspective from which these dangers can be identified and perhaps resisted, as well as an implication that there was once, somewhere, a more desirable state of affairs not yet ravaged by this insidious process.

These rather abstract considerations bear on how the question of intellectuals has been asked and answered in twentieth-century Britain, but they do so, characteristically of this topic, in ways that are often oblique or disguised. Far from specialization being a force that has only recently begun to have destructive impact, diagnoses of the sickness of specialization have long been occasions for intellectuals to validate their function. For, as we shall see, the theme of specialization and its discontents is nearly always taken up by those who are already committed to bringing some more general perspective to bear in public debate. In this sense, the theme of specialization is at once an enabling trope and an alibi—and an alibi is, after all, an explanation of absence, of how one was 'elsewhere'.

II

One cannot identify a single point at which the intellectual division of labour was first perceived as a problem: the fear that the republic of knowledge becomes ungovernable as individual scholars and scientists each come to know more and more about less and less is of very long standing indeed, and predates its conceptualization in terms of 'specialization'. For example (and merely taking two of the more prominent cultural commentators in early and mid-nineteenth-century Britain), both Coleridge's idea of the 'clerisy' and Arnold's notion of 'criticism' can be seen as, in their different ways, attempts to reinstate something that was being lost with the advance of the division of intellectual labour. (Comte's conception of 'sociology', so influential among the leading minds of Victorian Britain, can be seen as an attempt to do something similar at a more theoretical level.) This may at first seem less obvious in Coleridge's case, but one only needs to recall that he saw the clerisy as 'transmuting and integrating all that the separate professions have achieved in science or art—but, with a range transcending the limits of professional views, or local or temporary interests, applying the product . . . to the strengthening and subliming of the Moral life of the Nation itself'.[1] A broadly similar ambition was announced in unequivocal terms in one of Arnold's early essays, where he declared that criticism's

> most important function is to try books as to the influence which they are calculated to have upon the general culture. . . . All these works have a special professional criticism to undergo . . . theological works that of theologians, historical works that of historians, philosophical works that of philosophers, and in this case each kind of work is tried by a separate standard. . . . Not everyone is a theologian or a historian or a philosopher, but everyone is interested in the advance of the general culture. . . . A criticism therefore which, abandoning a thousand special questions which may be raised about any book, tries it solely in respect of its influence upon this culture, brings it thereby within the sphere of everyone's interest.[2]

'Professional' was not yet to be equated with 'academic', but the attempt to resist or compensate for the damaging consequences of the division of intellectual labour clearly legitimated the broad judicial role Arnold assigned to the 'critic'.

Laments about the effects of specialization had become something of a critical commonplace by the second half of the nineteenth century, and by the early twentieth century universities were, with increasing vehemence, identified as the villains of the piece, accused of breaking up the fondly remembered 'common culture' supposedly displayed in the mid-Victorian periodicals. In part, this was a response to the closely-related notion of 'professionalization', as career patterns, genres of publication, and forms of recognition assumed a degree of autonomy from the mechanisms at work in the wider society, among the clearest indications of which were the formation of discipline-specific professional associations and the founding of the scholarly journals which corresponded to them, events heavily clustered in the last quarter of the century.[3] But just as the process could be deplored before it was given its modern name, so nostalgia for a form of public conversation that had been lost predated the currency of the term 'intellectuals' and the specific anxiety represented by the juxtaposing of this process to that role.

The terms 'specialism', 'specialization', and their cognates entered standard written English in the mid- and late nineteenth century; the earliest recorded uses of the relevant senses given by the *OED* cluster around the 1860s and 1870s. The first definition given of 'specialism' is 'restriction or devotion to a special branch of study or research', and similarly the second sense of 'specialist' is 'one who specially or exclusively studies one subject or one particular branch of a subject'. Appropriately enough, Herbert Spencer is quoted as lamenting and Mark Pattison as lauding the processes signalled by these terms, both in the 1860s.[4] The medical sense of 'specialist', the first sense given, acquired its autonomy at about the same time, and in most everyday circumstances it soon became the single, unambiguous sense, so that from the late nineteenth century onwards a reference to someone as 'an eminent specialist' could only refer to a physician, not to a physicist or philologist. (As always, such a notion entails a corresponding notion of the 'general' or unspecialized, as in 'General Practitioner' or GP, dated by the *OED* to the 1880s.) But any air of neologism the more encompassing scholarly sense might have had seems to have worn off by the time J. A. Symonds could write in the Preface to his *Shakespere's* [*sic*] *Predecessors in the English Drama* in 1884: 'I cannot pretend to be a specialist in this department [sc. Elizabethan dramatic literature]; nor have I sought to write for specialists.'[5] Clearly, Symonds assumed there was no danger that anyone would think he was disclaiming the intention of writing exclusively for an audience of doctors. Further derivative forms soon followed: in 1890 *The Times* still felt the need to hold its nose slightly in referring to measures 'to enable "specializing" students to follow their courses'. And, as always, some new coinages simply failed to take. For example, 'specialiser' makes only one appearance in the dictionary, supported by a suitably lofty quotation from *Fraser's Magazine* for 1878: 'Minds of the first rank are generalisers; of the second, specialisers.' Similarly, 'specialistic' did not survive a few brief outings, such as *The Athenaeum*'s reference in 1882 to 'The specialistic study demanded by modern philology'.[6] In any event, the now familiar dichotomy between the 'specialists' who devoted themselves to particular branches of knowledge and the 'non-specialist' public beyond, together with the anxiety this contrast was always prone to evoke, was already well established before the noun 'intellectuals' became current.[7]

The self-conscious cultivation, from the late nineteenth century onwards, of the identity of 'the man of letters' was itself a form of deliberate resistance to the perceived operation of specialization. As the ice-floes of history, philosophy, literary criticism, and so on broke off from the once mighty continent of 'letters', there came to be something rather wilful about the attempt to govern all these disparate territories armed with nothing more than a little belle-lettristic gracefulness.[8] Inevitably, the main divide came to be figured as that between the men of letters and the academics, although in practice specialization and resistance-to-specialization cut across this too easily identifiable divide. Nonetheless, as the twentieth century wore on, the history of the anxiety about the damaging consequences of specialization became largely a history of anxieties about universities, both their internal curricular organization and their external impact on the wider society. What may not be immediately obvious is the way in which those figures who have most prominently engaged with this anxiety have thereby instantiated the role of the intellectual while at the same time often disdaining it.

A useful starting-point may be provided by the fact that all those figures with whom we might associate this theme focused on its lamentable consequences. No one attracted any kind of attention or fashioned any kind of public role out of applauding and encouraging the process of specialization, since it is a process which is scarcely thought to require a helping hand. 'Specialization' is only constituted as a topic for public commentary by a pre-existing concern over what is being lost, neglected, or excluded. But since such matters are, by definition, not the professional focus of any one of the specializing disciplines in question, this concern tends to be voiced by those who have *already* positioned themselves as speaking from a wider perspective and to a wider public. Engaging with the issue of specialization is implicitly to occupy a role which is, structurally, that of the intellectual. But many of those who have taken up this theme in twentieth-century Britain have repudiated or scorned that role, at least when so labelled, providing us with several further examples of what I have been calling the paradoxes of denial.

The model for intellectual specialization has long been provided by the natural sciences. As one modern authority puts it: 'The primary fact of all scientific work is specialization. . . . By its very nature, scientific work is minutely specialized.' There is a degree of specialization in most walks of life, 'but no other occupation is so finely and distinctly sub-divided into "specialties" as science'. As a result, every scientific 'discipline', such as physics, chemistry, and so on, is actually divided into over a hundred 'specialties', and the research careers of the majority of scientists rarely engage with more than two or three of these.[9] In the course of the twentieth century, this model of 'research' imposed itself more and more forcefully on, first, the social sciences, and then, more awkwardly, on the humanities.

Interestingly, these subdivisions *within* the sciences are in themselves scarcely ever the occasion for general hand-wringing (as opposed to comment among the relevant scientists); attention has far more often been focused on the alleged divide *between* the sciences and the humanities, and then, more consequentially still, on the divide between the increasingly specialized humanities and general educated discourse. In practice, and despite many pious protestations to the contrary, it had already been accepted by the late nineteenth century that original work in the natural sciences was no longer part even of that fiction of the common educated conversation that sustained the general cultural periodicals. But this certainly did not mean that a kind of meta-discussion about the relation of the sciences to the posited general culture was excluded from that conversation. Thereafter, not only did certain individuals make names for themselves as intellectuals on the basis of their willingness to draw upon their scientific standing to address a non-specialist public on matters of general concern—and here a proud lineage stretches from figures such as J. B. S. Haldane, Lancelot Hogben, and J. D. Bernal earlier in the century to those such as Richard Dawkins or Steven Rose at its end—but, beyond that, one or two leading scientists or former scientists actually achieved a certain additional prominence by addressing the problem of specialization itself, including such names as C. H. Waddington, Jacob Bronowski, and Peter Medawar.

C. P. Snow provides a somewhat complicated instance of this pattern, partly because he might more accurately be described as a 'failed' rather than a 'former' scientist, partly because he achieved far greater standing as a novelist than as a scientist or administrator of science. Nonetheless, his 1959 lecture on 'The Two Cultures' has probably received almost as much attention as all other statements on specialisation across the century put together, even though that theme forms only a part of his lecture. (It is worth recalling that Snow thought this cultural divide was 'at its sharpest in England', partly on account of 'our fanatical belief in educational specialization, which is much more deeply ingrained in us than in any other country in the world, west or east'.) But Snow is, for my purposes, a revealing case, because his call to modern societies to find ways of overcoming the divide signalled in his title and to make the contribution of science more effective in the world was couched in the form of an attack on the group he thought principally responsible for the most pernicious consequences of the division, namely 'the intellectuals'. Usually, though not invariably, Snow qualified this term, speaking of 'the literary intellectuals', though he added somewhat resentfully that they had taken 'to referring to themselves as "intellectuals" as though there were no others'. It was the self-described 'intellectuals' who were resistant to the claims of science and hostile to the benefits brought by industrialization. Snow was very firmly talking about Other People when he concluded: 'Intellectuals, in particular literary intellectuals, are natural Luddites.'[10]

Although there have been recurrent calls, both before and after Snow christened it, for the division between the 'two cultures' to be overcome, in reality anxieties about specialization have not chiefly fastened themselves onto this single fault-line. For the most part, commentary has tended to dwell on the way the narrowness of focus entailed by disciplinary specialization within the 'literary culture' has cramped the capacities and interests of those subjected to it and rendered them less able or less willing to contribute to general public debate. In itself, therefore, this strain of lament actually posits the condition of participating in such debate as the norm, and the 'withdrawal' from it into a purely disciplinary concentration as the pathology. In effect, one might say, those who have decried specialization as a vitality-sapping affliction suffered by modern societies, especially Britain, as a result of their systems of education and research are actually asserting the desirability of such societies having an adequate supply of intellectuals. But that, as we have seen in earlier chapters in this book, is hardly how it has seemed to many of the participants in such discussions themselves.

One of the recurrent snares of polemics against specialization is the tendency to drift, or at the very least to seem to drift, into a sententious, intellectually vapid, mixture of holism and uplift which merely asserts that everything is connected to everything else. The pressure exerted by concentrating on the evils of specialization is necessarily towards generality; taking a stand on the basis of one specific form of enquiry or vocabulary or proposal too easily looks like a defeatist acceptance of another kind of specialization. In twentieth-century Britain, several of those whose identity as intellectuals was partly constituted by their self-conscious attempts to transcend specialism were to fall victim to this snare.

Aldous Huxley provides a particularly striking, and hence sobering, example. He once warned that even the man of letters might be prey to a form of specialization—'The man of letters is tempted to live too exclusively in only a few of the universes to which, as a multiple amphibian, he has access'—but that was not a danger by which his writing ever seemed seriously threatened. Few figures in the twentieth century have so insistently laid claim to the title of 'polymath'. In 1936 he was proposing to produce, in collaboration with Gerald Heard, 'a kind of synthesis, starting from a metaphysical basis and building up through individual and group psychology to politics and economics'. It is the kind of 'synthesis' that can make specialization start to look compellingly attractive. These ambitions led him to publish books with such titles as *Ends and Means: An Enquiry into the Nature of Ideals and into the Methods Employed for their Realization*, a title which was simultaneously wholly uninformative about the book's contents and dispiritingly accurate about its approach. His identity as a 'sage' allowed him to fill the book with such vatic profundities as 'Technological progress has merely provided us with more efficient means for going backwards', and his anti-specialist credentials were buffed up by his repeated assertion that 'causation in human affairs is multiple—in other words, that any given event has many causes'. (It seems appropriate that within the Peace Pledge Movement, which he joined in the 1930s, Huxley became Chairman of the wonderfully named 'Research and Thinking Committee'; the fact that Gerald Heard was its vice-chairman provided the sceptical with another clue to the likely rigour and practicality of its deliberations.)[11] It was an essential part of his role as a 'general intellectual' that Huxley should not be a specialist in any particular field, but it seems curious that the one thing he was always thought to speak with special authority about was the future. At times it is hard not to feel that it is the cultural *role* of the generalist that animated Huxley as much as the desire to occupy that role for specific purposes, but the danger, as Huxley's life indicates, is that 'the generalist' has to write too much, on subjects about which he is radically underinformed, undisciplined by the bracing effect of belonging to a critical community. Huxley was the consummate 'anti-professional', but it has to be said that some of his writings risked giving 'amateurism' a bad name.

A somewhat different set of dangers have beset those who have deplored the effects of specialization from secure positions within the university—indeed, necessarily from an original base within one particular specialism. Such figures always risk losing caste among their scholarly peers while simultaneously seeming to others to be practising a form of disciplinary imperialism, using the language and methods of one subject to make the general case. Understandably, this course is most often embarked upon by those who have least to lose professionally speaking, perhaps because their reputation has already been established beyond challenge, perhaps because they hold some post which takes them outside and in a sense 'above' everyday scholarly activity, perhaps because they have retired. Here, one could assemble a distinguished company, running from figures such as Gilbert Murray or H. A. L. Fisher in the early part of the century, through such names as A. D. Lindsay, F. R. Leavis, and Herbert Butterfield, up to individuals such as Noel Annan or George Steiner at its end. As I indicated earlier, each generation persuades itself that specialization has reached a particularly acute, even terminal, stage in its own time, so by way of a modest antidote to the alarmism and lack of historical perspective in the current versions of this anxiety, I want briefly to reconsider the salience of this theme at more or less the mid-point of the century.

III

The 1940s witnessed a surge in publications debating the nature and future of 'the university', focusing on the problem of specialization. A brief list of some of the titles which received considerable attention at the time (even if they have mostly now disappeared from view) would include Adolph Löwe, *The Universities in Transformation* (1940), 'Bruce Truscot' [E. A. Peers], *Redbrick University* (1943), and Walter Moberly, *Crisis in the University* (1949), as well as books which appeared to have a more modest scope though in practice they, too, drew up broader charges of over-specialization, such as F. R. Leavis's *Education and the University* (1943).[12] A symptom of the currency of this theme in Britain at the time, as well as a stimulus to further thought about it, was the English translation in 1946 of Ortega's influential polemic, *Mission of the University*.[13] In the second half of the decade the theme was aired in the press and debated in Parliament; the government announced its desire to find ways to make British universities less specialized.[14]

These books and the debates which they provoked were clearly not just addressed to other academics: the problem was presented as one which concerned society as a whole. In other words, the issue of specialization was thought to endanger precisely that level of *public* discussion which was taking place around this issue itself. An oblique illustration of this point is provided by an article (cited in Ch. 19) by Harman Grisewood, then Controller of the Third Programme. Writing in 1951, Grisewood could assume that the books published in the previous few years had established something of a consensus on the topic: 'It will probably be agreed that the dangers of specialisation are now to a large extent admitted and have been pretty well explored by recent discussions and factual evidence. The emphasis now seems to be upon the remedies, rather than upon diagnosis.' Grisewood's concern, as we have seen, was with the part to be played by the Third, which had then been in existence for nearly five years, and he emphasized that its ambitions embraced the universities and went beyond them: 'If, therefore, the Third programme has a part to play in diminishing dangers [*sic*] of specialisation, this role exceeds the university sphere.' He instanced the wide range of the talks and lectures that could be heard on the Third including whole series by such celebrated lecturers as Fred Hoyle or Herbert Butterfield. But he recognized that 'research' was increasingly a defining characteristic of academic life, and that these lecturers owed their cultural standing to the sense that they represented the highest achievements of their 'subject'. His remarks revealed the extent to which the Third depended upon recruiting such figures: 'In a recent month, taken at random, of the eighty-eight talks broadcast in the Third Programme forty were contributed by university professors or by other senior members of the universities speaking on their own subjects.' (In passing one should note not only the high proportion of academic contributors, but the sheer number of such talks—almost three per day at a time when the Third broadcast only during the evenings.)

Grisewood here touched lightly on one of the central tensions of the topic: as a way of combating the fragmentation assumed to be consequent on academic specialization, he was citing talks by figures whose standing rested on their achievements as specialists. His blithe assumption appeared to be that such specialization was not in itself a barrier to communication provided the listening public could be kept abreast of the latest research:

> It is hoped by those within the B.B.C. whose work serves the Third Programme that its contributors in the universities will establish a closer contact with the programme and will thus enable it to be shaped more and more in accordance with the pattern of research that prevails in each branch of learning; so that the audience for the programme can feel assured that it is in touch with the best minds in each field of knowledge and with the vital and sensitive points in the development of each specialised branch of study.[15]

Grisewood clearly assumed that it would be entirely proper for a national radio network to concern itself in this way with 'the development of each specialised branch of study': universities are here not being regarded as a distinct 'sector', but as part of a *single* national culture, perhaps as its apex. Indeed, the publication in which his article appeared, the *Universities Quarterly*, reflected similar assumptions: it was not the house organ of a single profession, carrying news of and to its members, but, rather, a forum in which the significance for society as a whole of ideas within and about universities could be debated.

If there was one academic figure who, in the middle of the century, was more closely identified than any other with the cause of combating specialization it was A. D. Lindsay. Lindsay provides a telling example of how the theme of specialization is mostly taken up by those *already* committed to trying to make their intellectual activities count with a non-specialist public. At the same time he is a rather poignant illustration of what I have been calling the paradoxes of denial since Lindsay's preferred headmasterly idiom of 'character' and 'judgement' gave short shrift to those who might be seen as members of 'a so-called intelligentsia'.

In one sense, Lindsay had never been a specialist. He had, it is true, initially made his mark as a philosopher, and that was the subject he had been appointed to teach, first as a Tutor at Balliol, then as Professor at Glasgow. But not only had he been reared in the Idealism of T. H. Green which, for all its rebarbative Hegelian vocabulary, conceived of philosophy as the broadest form of communal self-understanding, but it is also important that he had studied in, and went on to teach for, the Oxford 'Greats' school, combining philosophy with the study of classical civilization as a whole. In addition, Lindsay had an exceptionally strong sense of social duty which translated into what, for his time and class, were regarded as pronounced Left-wing views. From quite early in his career, he became a leading figure in the WEA, and he went on to become an active member of the Labour Party. His election as Master of Balliol in 1924, at the age of 45, gave him the perfect platform from which to promote his characteristic blend of educational and political good causes, as well as freeing him even further from conventional disciplinary pigeon-holing.

'The Master's Lodging in Balliol', Lindsay's daughter recalled in her biography of her father, 'has one door opening into the college and one to the street outside', neatly symbolizing the two sides of his subsequent career.[16] Lindsay was relatively unusual not so much in his combining of academic and public roles, but in the fact that although he was to prove notably effective in that kind of committee-work and behind-the-scenes lobbying and networking characteristic of the so-called 'Great and Good' in British public life, he also took bolder public stands on contentious political issues. The number of committees and boards which he chaired or sat on was wearyingly large, but it was his more outspoken public interventions that led to his being seen as a dangerous radical. For example, he made himself unpopular in some quarters in Oxford and outside by his attempts to secure some form of negotiation more favourable to the side of the workers in the General Strike of 1926 (not, of course, that he was alone among established figures, especially those imbued with some form of 'social Christianity', in taking this line). The most celebrated of his public protests came in the Autumn of 1938, just as he was completing a successful but trying three years as Vice-Chancellor. Lindsay was a strong opponent of the policy of appeasement, and he felt it his duty to do whatever he could to deflect the country from what he saw as a disastrous and shameful attempt at accommodation with Hitler.[17] There was to be a by-election that October in the Oxford City constituency, and at the last minute it was agreed that the official Labour and

Liberal candidates would stand down to allow Lindsay to run on the platform of opposition to appeasement. Lindsay campaigned vigorously; tempers ran high; meetings on both sides were disrupted (the young J. L. Austin, later renowned as the leading exponent of 'ordinary language' philosophy, was a notably unruly and persistent heckler of Lindsay's opponent). The issue polarized opinion in ways that cut across existing party lines: Lindsay received support from leading anti-appeasement Tories, including two future Prime Ministers, Winston Churchill and Harold Macmillan. In the event, the official Conservative candidate, Quintin Hogg, the future Lord Hailsham, won, if by a considerably reduced majority, but Lindsay's campaign, and the very fact of his being willing to come forward at this relatively late stage of his by now dignified academic career, was credited with helping to attract support to the anti-appeasement cause in the crucial months that were to follow. Thereafter, Lindsay continued his 'amphibian' existence, taking on various public roles during the war. In 1945 he accepted a peerage from the Labour government on the understanding that he would be a 'working peer', helping to guide government policy through the upper house, though his declining health prevented him from playing a prominent part.[18]

The attempt to combat the evils of specialization was the informing thread of Lindsay's more purely (though never very purely) academic career, from his earliest efforts to establish some modern equivalent for the Greats course at Oxford around the time of the First World War up to his founding of the new University College of North Staffordshire (soon to become Keele University) in 1951, a few months before his death. The Modern Greats school, better known as PPE (Philosophy, Politics, and Economics), set out to overcome disciplinary divisions and to study the modern world as a whole, with a broad Idealist notion of philosophy informing its approach.[19] But in time Lindsay came to acknowledge that no mere 'change in examinations is going to cure departmentalism'. He tried other means, such as instituting lectures on general culture at Balliol (not a success), and he always insisted that one of the virtues of the Oxford system was that 'our units of common life [i.e. the colleges] do not reflect the division and specialization of our studies'. 'As knowledge advances', he declared in 1936 at the end of his first year as Vice Chancellor, 'the need for specialization increases; as the boundaries of the various branches of knowledge grow less definite, the need for some corrective to specialization also grows.' He constantly reiterated his hope that 'all the men who come out of our universities should have some general understanding of our culture and institutions as well as some special and expert knowledge'.[20]

His earliest plans in the mid-1940s for what was to become Keele were based on this idea that more general studies were needed to counter the effects of disciplinary specialization, 'producing an appreciation of the relatedness of knowledge to the ends of a civilised society'. It is striking that the four things Lindsay thought principally wrong with existing universities (at least in his daughter's later recension of his thinking) were all forms of over-specialization:

1. the separation of specialist studies from the general understanding in which they should be rooted;
2. the separation of intellectual development from all-round development of the individual;
3. the separation of the 'intelligentsia' from ordinary life; of the privileged elite from the community which they should serve;
4. the separation of different specialist views of the world which should balance and correct each other.[21]

Accordingly, a general 'Foundation Year', providing an introduction to the characteristic approaches of various different disciplines, was to be a distinctive feature of the new university. Lindsay himself remained a committed, if increasingly beleaguered, champion of a conception of philosophy which attempted to provide this kind of general perspective, a conception which by this date was already finding more favour among educationalists and those proposing broad schemes for teaching in the humanities than among professional philosophers. Regretfully, he had to concede that 'philosophy . . . had become a specialty among other specialties, and he saw no place for it as a unifier of knowledge'.[22] Thus, although it was a strong presence in the original curriculum at Keele, it did not, as once may have looked likely, form the common unifying element.

One of the first students at Keele saw Lindsay, in a topical post-war comparison, as 'fighting to form a battalion of college Chindits so that he could lead them in a completely new strategy against the Imperial Guard of specialisation'. But Lindsay himself recognized that the rot of specialization set in even earlier, in the schools. Boys who came up too narrowly crammed 'were liable to become what he called "an intelligentsia in the worst sense of the term" or sometimes in rougher words, "Clever asses"'. (His commendation of the physically strenuous regime at Gordonstoun, quoted in Ch. 1 above, was couched in similar terms: 'If we adopted it we might save the universities from producing an intelligentsia.') Here, what may be seen, for all Lindsay's own Scottish origins, as a characteristically English inflection can be detected: the opposite of being too specialized is to be 'rounded', a state of character nurtured by and expressed in games and leadership as well as in studies, a state which always trumps that of being merely 'clever'. Expressing himself in this idiom, Lindsay, undeniably one of Britain's leading intellectuals at the time, could easily seem to be adding his voice to an always powerful native strain of anti-intellectualism. The last speech Lindsay made just before he died was at a school prize-giving: 'what he said at that prize-giving was his usual message about Keele; he talked to them about the evils of specialization and about what was needed in the modern world. "We have got to have people who know one thing frightfully well, but they must also have some general understanding"'.[23] No doubt both he and his audience would have been deeply affronted by the thought that this could be seen as a recipe for having more intellectuals.

The question of whether the Keele experiment should be judged a success lies beyond the remit of this book.[24] On the face of things, it has shared the fate of most other attempts to institutionalize some alternative to the dominant local pattern of single discipline-based courses: almost invariably, the departmental imperative has reasserted itself before too long. This has been true of Lindsay's earliest attempt in this direction, 'Modern Greats'; it has been true of Keele; it has been true of Sussex and those other 1960s universities which attempted to 'redraw the map of learning' in the 1960s, only to conform to the standard pattern by the end of the 1990s; and, more generally, it has been true of the Colleges of Advanced Technology and the Polytechnics, both of which were intended to offer alternatives to the existing idea of the university, but which ended the century renamed as universities and almost indistinguishable from their longer-established peers. And perhaps the fate of Lindsay's own reputation is emblematic of the cul-de-sac which apparently awaits all those who sally forth to slay the dragon of specialization. The relative obscurity of his name among philosophers half a century after his death, even among political philosophers, owes something to the fact that his brand of Anglicized Hegelianism has never again enjoyed real standing among professional philosophers, something to his having published almost no technical philosophy in the second half of his career, and something, too, to the tone of windy Christian uplift that suffuses his larger pronouncements. But specialization has a way of taking its revenge on those who would flout or repudiate its logic. This aspect of their careers is disregarded by subsequent generations of specialists and they come to be written out of an intellectual history conceived in terms of disciplinary contributions—left, perhaps, to be recovered by historians of intellectuals?

IV

There is scarcely a chapter in this book which does not include some reference, if often only in passing, to the process of specialization and to the threat it is said to pose to the role of the intellectual. Indeed, it could be said that the question of intellectuals does not arise until one can speak of figures deliberately bringing the cultural authority earned by some specialist endeavour *back* into the general sphere: the notion presupposes a degree of specialization. The modern concept of the intellectual represents, in part, an attempt to counter the limiting effects of specialization while drawing on the authority which the process confers. It is not surprising, therefore, that the theme itself has been a recurring preoccupation of reflection on this topic. We have seen instances of this, just to single out a few of the more obvious, in the contributors to the *Nation* and the *New Age* before 1914, in the ruminations of Eliot and Collingwood between the wars, and in practically every commentator on the question of intellectuals in the second half of the century, from Iris Murdoch or Perry Anderson to Russell Jacoby or Richard Posner.

The call for intellectuals to act as a counter or antidote to the damage caused by specialization had, in the first half of the twentieth century, more often emanated from those outside universities who represented themselves as having inherited the mantle of the older man-of-letters tradition. However, in the closing decades of the century this theme was increasingly taken up by certain categories of academic, among whom two main responses were discernible. The first was from those who not only aimed to write for a non-academic (or, in publishing terms, 'trade') readership themselves, but who also exhorted their colleagues to do so and berated those, always the vast majority, who did not, on the grounds that they were failing to discharge their responsibilities to 'the public'. The second was from those who imputed to their scholarly work, even in its densest and least accessible form, a 'political' character. This sometimes involved signalling an ambition to contribute, albeit by an extremely indirect route, to some larger movement such as feminism or multiculturalism, but it more often took the form of claiming a 'radical' or 'dissident' purpose for any work, no matter how abstract or recondite, that could be said to be disturbing conventional assumptions about reality and its representation. The second of these responses was almost exclusively cultivated by those who positioned themselves as 'oppositional' and on the Left. The first had no comparably clear political affiliation, and the stated aspiration to reach a non-academic public could have both progressive and conservative roots, though it is noticeable that those who evangelize for this course are very often hostile to theoretical or methodological innovations in their own disciplines and notably indulgent to the commercial and media interests which facilitate, if they do not wholly govern, access to non-professional publics, with the result that they are vulnerable to being characterised as belonging to the Right.

Both these responses have tended to be confined to scholars working in a relatively small number of subjects—above all, History or Literature; less commonly, Philosophy or Politics; and, just occasionally, some of the other social sciences. This obviously reflects the fact that the protocols of various disciplines stand at different distances from the relevant forms of non-specialist discourse. No research scientists would expect the publications in which their most recent findings were announced to be read by any but a highly specialized readership. The same scientists may, in some cases, also publish works of popular science that reach a wide non-professional readership, but this involves practising two clearly distinct forms of writing. Something similar is true of most scholars in the social sciences and humanities, but as one moves further away from the scientific model of 'research', the possibility that the same piece of writing may both be the foundation of professional recognition *and* be read by a wide non-specialist readership starts to raise its siren head. It is very rarely achieved in the social sciences: one or two sociologists with a high public profile manage something of this kind, whether because they are thought to be influential politically, such as Anthony Giddens, or because they deliberately cultivate a more literary mode of expression, such as Richard Sennett, and occasionally a piece of research by a less well-known figure that has clear policy application may attract attention, though even then it may be dependent on serious journalists to bring its findings to the notice of a wider public.

Politics may constitute something of a special case because it is intrinsically hybrid as an academic discipline, embracing extreme quantitative scientism at one end and traditional philosophical reflection at the other, with a good deal in between that is hard to distinguish from well-informed journalism. In its earlier, still less professionalized, forms it provided an academic home for several figures who would be included in most lists of twentieth-century British intellectuals, such as Ernest Barker, A. D. Lindsay, Harold Laski, G. D. H. Cole, Michael Oakeshott, and Isaiah Berlin.[25] Both political theorists and psephologists, as well of course as those who write about the ups and downs of the greasy pole in a more immediate way, can still aspire to attract the attention of a non-professional public, but the American model of positivist 'political science' increasingly renders this an unrealistic ambition for most of those who want to make a career in a university Politics department. Consistent with my general argument, it has been those who have already positioned themselves as 'intellectuals' who have been most prominent in decrying this development. For example, Bernard Crick argued that the professionalization of his subject had 'made complete nonsense of the old liberal model of intellectual influence: that intellectuals wrote books which were accessible to and read by literate and worthy common people, the non-graduates who used the public libraries.'[26] Actually, social change is already rendering even this sentiment somewhat dated, in that a growing proportion of those who use public libraries (where they still exist or have books in them) are university graduates, though the fact that they have stayed in formal education until 21 rather than 14, not to mention the greatly expanded numbers of 'mature students', does not make them any the less a non-specializt readership.

Within the humanities, it has been common to claim, even at the end of the twentieth century, that original work in philosophy and literary criticism can still be, and should still be, part of a general cultural conversation. However, in practice this has surely not been true for philosophy for a long time. The issues which philosophers habitually engage with are no doubt of deep and abiding human interest, and there remains some appetite among a non-professional readership for accessible accounts of philosophical ideas about these subjects. But it is surely significant that for several decades now the chief form of publication among professional philosophers, as among economists and almost all kinds of natural scientists, is the article in a specialist journal. It usually takes an intermediary, or a philosopher writing in deliberately popularizing mode, to engage a wider readership in understanding the significance of the debates carried on in these journals.[27] A figure with such diverse interests and superlative talents as Bernard Williams may be a partial exception, though it is notable that even his academic career was founded on a series of dauntingly professional articles; the more accessible and wide-ranging books came later.

'English' as an academic discipline—or 'literary studies', to use the more encompassing modern label—occupies a special place in discussion of this theme, since its overlaps with the practice of book-reviewing and the genre of biography give some of its practitioners the possibility of a purchase on the general reading public that is simply not available in most fields. But in practice works of literary criticism have come to be regarded as more or less unsaleable by trade publishers, unless they are by academics who already have an established presence in the general media, such as Frank Kermode or John Carey, and literary theory has become a byword in the broadsheet press for barbarous unreadability (especially among those who never read it). The structural position of literary studies ensures that cries of pain or rage directed at the myopia and aridity allegedly consequent upon specialization are particularly numerous in this area, especially those ventriloquized on behalf of a common reader who wants to know what is worth reading. By the end of the century, literary criticism clearly no longer occupied the kind of cultural centrality it had enjoyed in the years between about 1930 and 1960, when it could still seem like the only academic subject that had managed to install a generally intelligible evaluative discourse at the heart of its professional identity.[28] But it says something about the continuing generalist ambitions nurtured by at least some of its practitioners that general pronouncements about the effect of professionalization on the function or failure or future of intellectuals seemed much more likely to emanate from those with a past or present connection with 'English' than from almost any other source.

For good reason, the call for scholars to escape the crushing tentacles of specialization and to discharge their duty of addressing a broader public may, at the beginning of the twenty-first century, most often be heard among historians.[29] This is, after all, the one area in which suitably talented scholars can still aspire to write books that will simultaneously further their academic career and sell well to a non-professional readership, and the recent boom in 'TV history' has only accentuated this distinctiveness. The position may be more complicated in this case than first appears: there is, after all, a very considerable gulf between a figure such as Eric Hobsbawm, who has retained the high regard of fellow-scholars while helping to orient his fellow-citizens by identifying a number of main patterns in the kaleidoscope of modern world history, and a figure such as David Starkey, who, though continuing to undertake scholarly research, has become primarily a media personality and who chiefly gratifies an existing public taste for colourful details about distant monarchs. Be that as it may, the engagement of historians in broader public debate probably remains more noticeable than that of any other group of academics. A common refrain among those historians most eager to denounce specialization is that it is the historian's duty to provide an intelligible and compelling narrative of 'the national history' (though of course the majority of professional historians are not historians of Britain). Doing so has certainly been one way in which leading historians have in the past moved into the role of the intellectual, as suggested by earlier examples in this book such as G. M. Trevelyan and, in more limited and complicated fashion, A. J. P. Taylor, but the plurality of perspectives now rightly available on what was once called, with all the confidence of the definite article, '*the* national history' has made this a more complex assignment than it once was, not least politically.[30] Nonetheless, serious works of history, and not just of British history, do continue to command a relatively wide readership, and this enables the most visible members of the profession to denounce the narrowing effects of specialization with particular brio and confidence.

If the first response I identified—the call to write for a wider public—seems often to be hankering after appearances before the TV cameras and on broadsheet opinion pages, the second—the claiming of a 'political' character for even the least accessible work—tends to manifest itself in the very deepest recesses of academia at its most Masonic, in position papers at conferences and in prefaces to monographs, though the impulse at work in the two cases is not, ultimately, that dissimilar. In the last generation or more, especially in the USA, it has become increasingly common for academics in certain fields in the humanities and, to a lesser extent, the social sciences to represent their intellectual work as being intrinsically 'oppositional'.[31] When this impulse is combined, as it often is, with that style of reading that has been called the 'hermeneutics of suspicion', it bestows a special cachet on the activity of 'unmasking', that is, of revealing the hidden oppressiveness of narratives and categories which less enlightened or less critical sections of society are alleged to accept or take for granted. Such work may not actually aspire to be read by any but the few hundred other specialists in the given subfield, but it nonetheless represents itself as performing a political function by uncovering 'the discursive foundations of oppression'.

From one point of view, this can be seen as an attempt to provide a form of justification for work that can be directly of interest to none but a handful of colleagues, and hence a legitimation in the eyes of a wider public for a career that can at times seem uncomfortably privileged and functionless. But in that case it is an interesting question to whom this attempted legitimation is really addressed, since no sustained efforts are made to communicate it to a non-professional audience, most of whom would presumably be distinctly unimpressed by this as a justification anyway. It would certainly not be a great recommendation in the eyes of those who do largely control the power and wealth of the world. Of course, any scholarly work can draw attention to the social function it aspires to perform, and on occasion it needs to. In the past, for work in the humanities, this may most often have taken the form of claims about preserving and transmitting a cultural heritage, or extending and enriching people's experience, or upholding standards of accuracy and objectivity, and so on. These are still relevant justifications for the most part, but they could be mounted more persuasively, or at least with an easier conscience, when society was less insistently egalitarian in its cultural responses and judgements. The prevalence of the currently fashionable form of political self-legitimation for even the most arcane scholarly work in the humanities surely owes something to the sense that this is the most 'democratic', even 'radical', purpose one can serve. In effect, it accepts the constraints of specialization, but still seeks to move beyond them in the way the term 'intellectual' has traditionally signalled, not perhaps by speaking directly *to* a non-specialist public but certainly by speaking *for* one, especially that 'public' which confers a kind of automatic validity on the efforts of its champions, 'the oppressed'.

Reliance on the identity of being 'oppositional' can, it has to be said, represent a real impoverishment of intellectual and scholarly life. For one thing, to *set out* to be oppositional is to prefer a flattering self-description over a responsible assessment of the effects of one's activities. Not everything can be opposed nor should be, and to claim to take a stance against wherever 'power' resides in any society, institution, or relationship is simply to become irresponsible about outcomes. It is also logically self-defeating, for in so far as one's efforts are devoted to persuasion (as they cannot but be), one cannot really want to be successful. As soon as one's views did carry the day either by persuading those who have power or by contributing to a transfer or redefinition of that power, one would then, to remain consistently oppositional, have to oppose precisely those who now agreed with one's earlier position. The attempt to attribute an irreproachably democratic character to a career spent in the most specialized forms of research can produce paradoxes of its own.

In this chapter I have been arguing that instead of assuming that the process of specialization has finally, in our own generation, rendered the intellectual extinct, we would do well to recognize that lamenting the effects of that process has constituted a recurrent occasion for some individuals to speak out *as* intellectuals. We should also recognize that the perceived trend towards ever-narrower specialization has prompted one or two figures to attempt to counter it by undertaking heroic attempts at some form of synthesis. Perhaps the most striking example at the end of the twentieth century has been provided by someone who has already made several appearances in these pages, Perry Anderson. He has been a directing presence at *New Left Review* for over four decades, and even though he has for some time held a part-time appointment at an American university, he remains a proudly unclassifiable polymath. I earlier quoted from his linked pair of essays on 'A culture in contra-flow', published in *New Left Review* in 1990, but here it is worth remarking the ambition of these pieces. These two articles together total nearly 40,000 words: they break every rule of commercial periodical publishing, just as they give the lie to so many of the clichés about the unintellectual nature of British culture. Picking up from, but also correcting (and even partly apologizing for), his influential 1968 piece, 'Components of the national culture' (discussed in Ch. 8 above), Anderson again surveyed the structure of intellectual life in Britain, this time reporting in more positive vein. This analysis was buttressed by a magisterial (and therefore sometimes high-handed) survey of major intellectual 'fields'—sociology, aesthetics, philosophy, economics, history, and feminism, each construed in terms of the theoretical constructions of the leading practitioners—while acknowledging that in the culture as a whole the 'dominant structures of written production and communication' have become 'more specialized, segmented, stratified'.[32] In some ways, Anderson's own writing, both in *New Left Review* and in the *London Review of Books*, has been a calculated and often impressively successful attempt to overcome the effects of this specialization—or, in other words, to continue to fill the role of the intellectual.

At the beginning of the twenty-first century, with universities bulking ever larger in intellectual life, the revealing juxtaposition of anxieties about specialization and laments about the disappearance of intellectuals has become ever more common. Its continued prevalence could scarcely be better illustrated, by way of a conclusion, than by noting the simultaneous appearance of just that juxtaposition in three separate and quite unrelated reviews in a single issue of the *TLS*. In reviewing a biography of Tom Harrisson, anthropologist and founder of 'Mass Observation', Jeremy MacClancy observed that Harrisson had 'an unusual and variegated career for a British intellectual of his generation', and he went on to draw the contemporary moral. Harrisson would have liked to see himself as some kind of polymath: 'Instead, he came to be regarded as a brilliant amateur more and more out of place as specialization became the deadening academic norm.' A few pages further on, Richard Fardon, reviewing some books about Edmund Leach, announces the same theme in his opening sentence: 'Sir Edmund Leach was a towering figure in British anthropology, a public intellectual of the kind the discipline hardly produces nowadays.' And then Mark Garnett, reviewing the latest collection of Bernard Crick's essays (entitled *Crossing Borders*), observes 'Bernard Crick has been "crossing borders" throughout his professional career.' Crick, Garnett points out, admires

> the contributions of several authors who share Crick's own antipathy to 'mind-forged manacles'. Ernest Gellner, Hannah Arendt, Isaiah Berlin, Harold Laski, G. B. Shaw and Orwell all conformed to Crick's ideal of the public intellectual. They ranged widely in their thinking, and wrote in an accessible style in the hope of reaching as many readers as possible. As Crick notes (without labouring the point) they have very few successors, in Britain at least.[33]

And so a new generation takes up the old tune: there used to be intellectuals who were capable of reaching a wide public, but specialization is making them extinct in our time (no matter when that is). Only the presence of the modish term 'public intellectual' distinguishes these statements from comparable ones made at almost any point in the past century.

And now, wonderfully, as this book goes to press, even this new term is absorbed into that misty past which it implicitly celebrates: a reviewer notes that

James Wood, the author of the collection of critical essays under review, is 'not an academic but an old-style "public intellectual"'.[34] A term that only became current in Britain at the twentieth century's close acquires, when the contrast is with that threateningly modern figure 'the academic', the patina of age, confirming that laments about specialization are nearly always threnodies for a lost world, and that 'the intellectual' is one symbolic expression of what has supposedly been lost. Or, as Coleridge put it in the passage standing at the head of this chapter and which may serve as a commentary on so much writing about intellectuals: 'Elegy presents every thing as lost and gone, or absent and future.'[35]

NOTES

1. This summary is taken from Henry Nelson Coleridge's introduction to *On The Constitution of Church and State* (London: Pickering, 1839), p. xxviii.
2. Arnold, 'The Bishop and the Philosopher', in R. H. Super (ed.), *The Complete Prose Works of Matthew Arnold*, 11 vols. (Ann Arbor: University of Michigan Press, 1950–73), iii. 41.
3. On these developments, see Heyck, *Transformation of Intellectual Life*, esp. 'Conclusion', and Collini, *Public Moralists*, esp. chs. 1 and 6.
4. *OED*, 'specialism', *sb.*, 1; 'specializt', *sb.*, 2.
5. J. A. Symonds, *Shakespere's Predecessors in the English Drama* (London: Smith, Elder, 1900 [1st edn., 1884]), pp. viii–ix.
6. *OED*, 'specializing', *ppl., a.*, b; 'specializer', *sb.*; 'specialistic', *a.*
7. For further general discussion of this theme, see my 'Before another tribunal: the idea of the "non-specialist public" ', in *English Pasts: Essays in History and Culture* (Oxford: Oxford University Press, 1999), 305–25.
8. On the identity of the 'man of letters', John Gross, *The Rise and Fall of the Man of Letters* (London: Wiedenfeld, 1969) still provides the best starting-point; see also Neil Berry, *Articles of Faith: The Story of British Intellectual Journalism* (London: Waywiser, 2002).
9. John Ziman, *Knowing Everything About Nothing: Specialization and Change in Scientific Careers* (Cambridge: Cambridge University Press, 1987), 1, 56.
10. C. P. Snow, *The Two Cultures*, ed. Stefan Collini (Cambridge: Cambridge University Press, 1993), 16–17, 4, 22.
11. See Nicholas Murray, *Aldous Huxley, An English Intellectual* (London: Little, Brown, 2002), pp. v, 307, 298.
12. The debate in the mid-to late 1940s also gave new life to studies published a decade or so before, such as Eustace Percy, *Education at the Crossroads* (1930) and Abraham Flexner, *Universities: American, English, German* (1930).
13. Ortega y Gasset, *Mission of the University*, trans. H. L. Nostrand (London: Routledge, 1946).
14. For further discussion, see Noel Annan, *Our Age: Portrait of a Generation* (London: Weidenfeld, 1990), esp. 371; and John Carswell, *Government and Universities in Britain* (Cambridge: Cambridge University Press, 1985).
15. Harman Grisewood, 'The universities and the Third Programme', *Universities Quarterly*, 6 (1951), 368, 370, 367, 372.

16. Drusilla Scott, *A. D. Lindsay, A Biography* (Oxford: Blackwell, 1971), 111.
17. For a full account, see Scott, *Lindsay*, ch. 14.
18. Ibid. 292–6.
19. See Norman Chester, *Economics, Politics, and Social Studies in Oxford 1900–1985* (London: Macmillan, 1986), and Julia Stapleton, *Englishness and the Study of Politics: The Social and Political Thought of Ernest Barker* (Cambridge: Cambridge University Press, 1994), ch. 2.
20. Scott, *Lindsay*, 342, 226, 338.
21. Ibid. 348–9.
22. Ibid. 317, 370.
23. Ibid. 352, 341, 265, 383.
24. For interesting discussions, see W. B. Gallie, *A New University—A. D. Lindsay and the Keele Experiment* (London: Chatto, 1960); James Mountford, *Keele, An Historical Critique* (London: Routledge, 1972).
25. For a brief account of this succession, and a familiar lament about the failure of subsequent professors to occupy similar public roles, see Robert Wokler, 'The professoriate of political thought in England since 1914: a tale of three chairs', in Dario Castiglione and Iain Hampsher-Monk (eds.), *The History of Political Thought in National Context* (Cambridge: Cambridge University Press, 2001), 134–58. For some reservations about this lament, see my contribution to the same volume, 'Disciplines, canons, and publics: the history of "the history of political thought" in comparative perspective', 280–302.
26. Bernard Crick, 'Intellectuals and the British Labour Party', *Revue française de civilisation britannique*, 4 (1980), 12; see also Crick, *Crossing Borders: Political Essays* (London: Continuum, 2001).
27. Such as e.g. Bryan Magee, *Men of Ideas: Some Creators of Contemporary Philosophy* (Oxford: Oxford University Press, 1978).
28. See Stefan Collini, 'How the critic came to be king', *TLS*, 8 Sept. 2000, 11–13.
29. For representative examples, see David Cannadine, *History in Our Time* (London: Allen Lane, 1998); Niall Ferguson, 'On media dons', in Stephen Glover (ed.), *Secrets of the Press: Journalists on Journalism* (London: Allen Lane, 1999), 206–20.
30. For some interesting recent reflections on the general theme, see Peter Mandler, *History and National Life* (London: Profile, 2002); on the complexities of writing 'the national history', see also my 'Writing the national history: Trevelyan and after', in *English Pasts*, 9–37.
31. This is such a widespread phenomenon that it would be arbitrary to refer to any particular source, but for a perceptive discussion of some of the forms taken by this impulse, see the work cited earlier by Bruce Robbins, *Secular Vocations: Intellectuals, Professionalism, Culture* (London: Verso, 1993).
32. Perry Anderson, 'A culture in contraflow', *New Left Review*, 180 and 182 (1990), 41–78, 87–137; repr. in Anderson's *English Questions* (London: Verso, 1992), 193–301.
33. *TLS* (16 Aug. 2002), 3, 10, 28.
34. Philip Horne, 'The sacred Wood', *Guardian Review* (22 May 2004), 10.
35. Samuel Taylor Coleridge, 'Table Talk', in *The Collected Works*, 16 vols., ed. Kathleen Coburn and Bart Winer (London: Routledge, 1971–2001), xiv. 226.

21

Long Views II: From Authority to Celebrity?

> 'In place of thought, we have opinion; in place of argument, we have journalism; in place of polemic, we have personality profiles; in place of reputation, we have celebrity.'

I

Denial is adept at turning circumstance into opportunity. By the end of the twentieth century, it was becoming difficult to ignore the fact that intellectuals were an acknowledged presence even in Britain. But, fastening onto a prominent feature of contemporary cultural change, it was possible to drive a wedge between the recent past and the immediate future, turning the former, with its potentially flourishing intellectuals, into yet another lost or distant elsewhere. The upshot of current developments, it was argued, was so radically to alter the balance of the local cultural environment that intellectuals were on the point of becoming extinct. The species could henceforth be confined to a glass case in the museum of natural history: '*Homo intellectualis*: logophagic creature, found in the first three-quarters of the twentieth century; lived off cultural deference; habitat destroyed by plagues of game shows and celebrity gossip; ancestor of common-or-garden "media personality" (*Physiogia showbizia*).'

In other words, this chapter addresses the second of the two claims presented at the beginning of the previous chapter. That claim, in its simplest form, is that the kind of public presence once enjoyed by intellectuals is in the process of being displaced by the glitzy superficiality of celebrity culture. In its most commonly encountered guise, this claim rests upon assumptions about the role of intellectuals in the past which this book has been devoted to questioning. 'Real intellectuals', we are still told, are figures who, on the basis of their deeper insight into the nature of reality and the purposes of human life, are able to give guidance to others about what to believe and how to live. Such figures used to be accorded respect on account of the profundity of their insight, the power of their imagination, the depth of their learning, or the sheer unsettling force of their originality. Sustained by a public eager for enlightenment and willing to grapple with large and serious ideas—willing, even, to read large and serious books—they were what in France, the natural home of the species, are called *maîtres à penser*.

But in recent years, it is alleged, the structural supports of this authority have been washed away by a rising tide of commercialized popular culture. The public space in which intellectuals used to operate has been reconfigured so that the only people capable of commanding widespread attention are the creations of the popular media themselves, such as film stars, sports players, TV personalities, and other tabloid-familiar faces. This situation is, in turn, seen as part of a larger pattern of social change in which a once-confident educated culture finds itself besieged and defensive in the face of ever more assertive forms of cultural egalitarianism. If intellectuals are to be listened to at all, it is now said, they have to accept the constraints of this world, with the result that they abandon their historic role and give themselves over to producing soundbites accompanied by arresting visuals and good teeth. Instead of pronouncing on the meaning of life, intellectuals are now at best adjuncts to the lifestyle industry, an industry that can make use of a few good-looking wordsmiths who may thereby aspire to join the ranks of such contemporary grandees as bossy fashion advisers, cuddly gardeners, and scruffy chefs.

Once again I want to suggest that this apparently novel situation actually forms part of a larger and long-standing pattern of social lament whose very repetitiveness should alert us to the need for structural rather than merely local explanations. I am not going to attempt to engage directly with the overarching framework of alarmist cultural pessimism, something I have taken issue with on other occasions.[1] I shall instead concentrate here on the question of 'celebrity' itself in relation to the activities of intellectuals. For celebrity, like comedy, is a funny business, even though most commentary confines itself in practice to the mildly empirical (though also mildly contradictory) observation that there's a lot of it about.[2] As a result, it is fatally easy to assume that celebrity is such a familiar contemporary phenomenon that it does not call for much historical analysis. When the editor-in-chief of *Whitaker's Almanack* was quoted in the national press in 2003 as saying 'We are a nation obsessed with celebrity culture,' she was taken to be uttering a commonplace.[3] But what, if anything, is distinctive about the present situation in this respect, and what are the consequences for the activities of intellectuals in particular? Since I am suggesting that a longer historical perspective can help to correct for the temporal parochialism of contemporary chatter here, the next section of this chapter might be billed, in headline-speak, as '*Hello!* magazine meets the *English Historical Review*'.

II

The first edition of *Who's Who* was published in 1849. It consisted of an almanac followed by thirty-nine lists of ranks and appointments and the names of those holding them. . . . The range of lists was expanded over the next half century to more than two hundred and fifty. . . . [The change to the biographical format came in 1897 when the work covered] some five and half thousand leading figures of the day. Now as then the book aims to list people who, through their careers, affect the political, economic, scientific and artistic life of the country. . . . An invitation to appear in *Who's Who* has, on occasion, been thought of as conferring distinction: that is the last thing it can do. It recognises distinction and influence. The attitude of the present editorial board remains that of the editor of the 1897 edition who stated in his preface that the book seeks to recognise people whose 'prominence is inherited, or depending upon office, or the result of ability which singles them out from their fellows in occupations open to every educated man or woman'.

This comes from the 'Historical Note' which appears at the front of modern editions of *Who's Who*.[4] It is a confident as well as informative piece of writing. It is confident that it knows what the important aspects of the 'life of the country' are, confident that it knows what counts as 'distinction and influence', and confident in its ability to identify the bearers of these qualities. But it is also confident that its function and its governing principles have remained essentially continuous through the changes of the past century and a half. However well founded its confidence on the first three matters may be, on this last point it is surely self-deceived, for what it fails to recognize is that its operative criteria for inclusion are a historically layered accumulation reflecting the governing social principles of successive periods.

In practice, the four main criteria now at work in this symbolically important reference work are birth, office, achievement, and celebrity. Listing them in that order brings out how this is also a *historical* sequence: these have been the underlying principles that have chiefly determined prominence in successive stages of the development of modern society. Roughly speaking, birth is the eighteenth-century principle (to go no further back), office the nineteenth, achievement the twentieth, and celebrity the twenty-first. However, as with so much else in British history, the earlier stages have not been wholly superseded by the later ones, but have continued to coexist alongside them, and the weird mixture of criteria at work now faithfully reflects the confusion about who is 'somebody' in a still-snobbish country in the full throes of cultural democratization. It is worth pausing over these principles for a moment before focusing on the situation of intellectuals.

For the earliest stage of this sequence, the lists of who mattered were provided by Debrett's *Complete Peerage* and Burke's *Landed Gentry*, which are pure blood-stock catalogues. But in the Victorian period the notion that offices and positions of influence might be open to men (but for the most part not, *pace* the 1897 editor, to women) of talent rather than of birth began to make its mark. The earliest compilations of 'ranks and appointments', with the names of their occupants, were, in their way, an objective listing. It was a catalogue of roles, not a selection of famous individuals. Achievement, the officially acknowledged principle of the twentieth century, turns the spotlight on the individual, though it still assumes a degree of consensus about what activities are to count as significant. But although achievement requires recognition, it does not necessarily involve celebrity; moreover, the relevant recognition may come from a small and expert circle, and be on the whole retrospective. However, in the fourth age, which is now upon us, the celebrity is, notoriously, someone who is famous for being famous. The 'public eye' squints through the lens of a tabloid photographer's camera: the Top People have been joined by the topless. Being esteemed by a small circle, however distinguished, does not make one a celebrity, while conversely celebrity can, by definition, never be retrospective. As a result, current editions of *Who's Who* list not only a number of people whose inclusion would have been unthinkable to the Victorians, such as cooks and dressmakers, but some who would not have qualified in the eyes of their mid-twentieth-century successors, either—individuals whose distinction consists in such activities as asking intimate questions of other celebrities in public or looking composed while reading the news headlines from a teleprompter.

Such a reference work is, needless to say, erratic as well as symbolic: the forms of social and cultural change at issue are more systematic than its somewhat haphazard compilation can fully register. Some of the most widely recognized names in contemporary Britain do not appear in its pages—yet—while those of countless unknown minor gentry still do. Nonetheless, entries such as 'Black, Cilla, OBE 1997; entertainer', or 'Lynam, Desmond Michael; sports broadcaster' are expressive of a new world. But even if the Victorian *Who's Who*, and those most likely to appear in it or consult it, did not consider that mere public attention itself conferred any distinction comparable to that which they believed themselves to enjoy, it does not necessarily follow that celebrities (in some form that we could now recognize as such) did not exist in that period. And this thought helps us to refine the categories of our enquiry a little further.

When thinking about the uniqueness or otherwise of the form of 'celebrity culture' familiar by the end of the twentieth century, we need to ask three different questions of the preceding periods. First, we can ask about the distribution of public attention in any period, the forms and mechanisms of reputation or notoriety and the extent to which they did or did not correspond to what we now designate as 'celebrity' even if that term was not used. Second, we can ask about the development of the *term* 'celebrity' and the concomitant self-consciousness about the condition it describes. Third—and this will be a crucial question when we bring the discussion back to the issue of intellectuals—we can ask about the nature and extent of the cultural authority accorded to particular individuals simply in virtue of their celebrity, including the extent to which such figures are, for example, ranked alongside or even above traditional elites in terms of social esteem, or the extent to which the mechanisms which create celebrity become the most powerful mechanisms shaping the public life of the society more generally. As I suggested earlier, 'cultural authority' has become the accepted phrase in discussion of the role of intellectuals, though its essentially metaphorical character—and, therefore, the risk of its generating misunderstandings of its own—is emphasized the more one focuses on the kinds of attention commanded by sheer celebrity.

In any extensive society with moderately sophisticated means of communication, some figures will not just be better known than others but will become the object of attention and curiosity on the part of numbers of people whom they are never likely to meet face to face. But before we can talk about the existence of 'celebrities' in anything like the modern sense, various social conditions have to be in place, above all the means of extensively reproducing and rapidly disseminating information and likenesses, together with sufficient economic incentive to do so. In this respect, the celebrity shares with other commodities the property of being more or less infinitely reproducible to satisfy market demand and of having negligible use-value once that demand falls away. Unlike fame, which may be slow to build up and largely retrospective in its operation, celebrity is, by definition, of the moment, and is partly constituted by the sheer speed of the available media of circulation.

Only with what has been termed the 'birth of a consumer society' in eighteenth-century Britain did the mechanisms of such reproducibility begin to operate on the required scale. The actor David Garrick may have been one of the first figures from the cultural realm who attained in his lifetime a level of recognizability which far exceeded even that hitherto reserved for rulers and military leaders; his image was widely reproduced not just in paint but through newly developed techniques for exploiting the potential of other materials from print to porcelain.[5] More strikingly still, the Byronmania of the 1810s and 1820s bore many of the marks of more recent kinds of fan frenzy, complete with memento-hunting and sexual fantasy. But the Victorian era was the first to discover on a broad social scale how, as Leo Braudy puts it in his large history of the subject, 'success could easily be confused with visibility, celebrity with fame'.[6] In that period, certain royal, aristocratic, or simply very rich people sometimes attracted attention on the requisite scale; prominent actors, actresses, and singers particularly drew such followings; some sportsmen, explorers, and military heroes could occasionally sustain such a place in the limelight; and, more rarely still, certain leading political figures could also be treated in these ways. There are some interesting questions here about how these forms of celebrity could cut across divides of both class and gender in ways that could, on both counts, create anxiety in polite society. There are also continuities and discontinuities with the present, and the changes are not all in one direction. A headline such as '300,000 turn out in Manhattan to greet the Prince of Wales' may now seem to us to belong to the 1980s, though it in fact referred to the visit of Bertie, Prince of Wales, in 1860.[7]

The term 'celebrity' came into currency alongside these developments in the sense given by the *OED*'s compilers at the end of the nineteenth century: 'the condition of being much extolled or talked about; famousness, notoriety'.[8] This definition indicates the ambivalence that was built into the term from its early days: after all, being 'extolled' is a gratifying state, being much 'talked about' may not be, just as 'famousness' may be desirable but 'notoriety' not. Thus, when Matthew Arnold observed in the 1860s, speaking of Spinoza's now forgotten successors, that 'They had celebrity, Spinoza has fame,' the shift in tenses emphasized a defining contrast: celebrity is evanescent, fame endures.[9] But in this quotation, of course, the term refers to an abstraction, the state or condition of being widely known. The transfer of the sense to the use which refers to particular individuals first took the form (as with the parallel formation of 'intellectuals' itself) of playful or ironic experiments, referring to certain widely known, and perhaps slightly self-important, individuals as 'these "celebrities"' rather along the lines of references to 'these "dignitaries"', in both cases held at a distance in the tongs of quotation-marks. The earliest such uses, which date from the mid-Victorian period, all emphasize the topical, transient nature of such a status; celebrities are chiefly to be found in the worlds of wealth and fashion, and their status depends upon the attention of a larger audience. But at this stage of its development, the term could in principle be used of leading figures in any circles, and the usage might well specify the world in question.

For my purposes, a particularly illuminating stage in this history is reached with the arrival of the so-called 'New Journalism' of the 1880s and 1890s, or, what is at least as important throughout this discussion, the reactions of contemporaries to what they perceived as new in the New Journalism. The novelty was largely held to consist in a far greater and more intimate concentration on 'personalities' and the details of their daily lives, together with the more vivid or simply intrusive presence of the journalists themselves, a view sustained by modern historians: 'Daily and weekly papers were increasingly adopting the transatlantic techniques of the interview, the gossip column, the campaign, and the sensational news story'.[10] The emblematic genre of this fashion was the celebrity interview, staged in the individual's home, complete with photographs which the technology now allowed to be taken on the spot and quickly reproduced. The series entitled *Celebrities at Home*, which the journalist Edmund Yates conducted for over six years in the middlebrow journal *The World*, ran to more than 300 articles by the early 1880s.[11] (Already, the near-oxymoron of 'massed celebrities' begins to hover over such enterprises.) One might not have to have been an exceptionally jaundiced observer of contemporary mores at the beginning of the twentieth century to find oneself rather primly recalling, as a contributor to *The Cornhill Magazine* did in 1901, a time 'before the invention of the present fashion of demanding from perfect strangers answers to questions which one's most intimate friend would hesitate to ask'.[12] And consumerist curiosity was gratified in other ways, too: as one observer of the new genre asked rhetorically, 'Have you noticed how the ordinary interview, as it is known in England, is apt to read very much as if it were a catalogue of furniture?'[13] These developments impinged directly on leading writers and thinkers, and the tensions involved in attempting to address various kinds of broad public whilst protecting oneself from mere publicity provoked a certain amount of anguished analysis.

The details of the process by which an intellectual or literary figure is turned into a celebrity are always historically specific, but if we wanted a reminder that the *logic* of the mechanism has a longer history than current commentators allow, we could hardly do better than turn to Henry James's short story, 'The Death of the Lion', first published in *The Yellow Book* in 1894.[14] The story is narrated by a young man who, while working as a literary journalist, is sent to interview the reclusive author, Neil Paraday, and who, won over, abandons his trade and stays on to become the writer's companion and protector. The young man had initially been sent by his editor who sensed that there must be a 'story' behind such determined avoidance of publicity, and anyway, as James has his narrator report with ironizing fidelity: 'It struck [the editor] as inconsistent with the success of his paper that anyone should be so sequestered as that'—'wasn't an immediate exposure of everything just what the public wanted?' Actually, the young interviewer manqué has to be regarded as an unreliable narrator given his theme, for as he tells the reader at one point, if the account that the reader is now reading were ever published that would only confirm that 'the insidious forces that, as my story itself shows, make at present for publicity will simply have overmastered my precautions'. Or, as it might now be put it in slightly less Jamesian terms, 'Companion Tells All in *Yellow Book* Exclusive'.

In any event, no sooner is the young protector ensconced in his new role than what he calls 'a big blundering newspaper' discovers Paraday and writes him up, providing the occasion for more Jamesian purring: 'A national glory was needed, and it was an immense convenience he was there.' This article in turn leads to the prompt arrival at the author's retreat of another, far less sympathetic, journalist, a figure who, we are told, represents a syndicate of thirty-seven influential journals and, in addition, as he explains: 'I hold a particular commission from *The Tatler* whose most prominent department, 'Smatter and Chatter'—I daresay you've often enjoyed it—attracts such attention.' Needless to say, Paraday is soon turned into a celebrity despite himself—turned into, in the slang of the day, a literary 'lion', and such noble beasts were, by definition, pursued by zealous 'lion-hunters', as the slang of the day also had it, those society hostesses who feared their salons were not quite complete unless they could exhibit such a specimen. One especially pertinacious big-game hunter, we are told with a Jamesian wink, 'constantly made appointments with [Paraday] to discuss the best means of economizing his time and protecting his privacy'. She, like her fellow lion-hunters, is a little less persistent when it comes actually to reading his books, but then James knew from bitter experience that the social whirl was entirely compatible with small sales. Paraday's new book, we are told, 'sold but moderately . . . but *he* circulated in person to a measure that the libraries might well have envied'. His young would-be protector, still attempting to play the part of the little Dutch boy, is soon engulfed in the flood of publicity and talk.

'The people I was perhaps angriest with', he records in a passage that can seem eerily up-to-date, whatever the date, 'were the editors of magazines who had introduced what they called new features, so aware were they that the newest feature of all would be to make him grind their axes by contributing his views on vital topics and taking part in the periodical prattle about the future of fiction.' This is the respect in which the tale exhibits the continuing mechanism of celebrity with particular neatness; it is not because he is known to have relevant and well-informed views on such 'vital topics' that Paraday is called upon to express them and thereby enhance his reputation; rather, it is because he has become a 'personality', through the media's need to feed a hunger it creates, that he now seems an appropriate person to ask for opinions to fill up the columns of the new feature.

The cruel logic of the lion's existence is finally played out through a sequence in which he is invited to a grand country house to read from his as yet unpublished new book to a socially distinguished gathering. In advance of the event, his hostess persuades him to lend her the unique copy of this manuscript, which then starts to circulate among the guests, none of whom actually reads it, and, inevitably, is soon lost ('I haven't lost it', protests the last titled lady to have been entrusted with it, 'I remember now . . . I told my maid to give it to Lord Dorimont—or at least to his man'). Paraday himself falls ill in the course of the visit, too ill to read, but by now his hostess has recruited another lion to perform instead. Paraday stays long enough at the house to die, and his precious manuscript is never recovered. This ill-fated document serves, of course, as a figure for the fact that the lion's supplicating admirers have little genuine interest in the one thing they supposedly admire him for; and the whole process by which celebrities first become public property, and then interchangeable commodities, is lightly sketched by James, including a twist in the tail that readers may be left to discover for themselves.

This short story is one of several that James wrote in the late 1880s and early 1890s exploring the impact on the writer of what were seen as the unprecedentedly tawdry and intrusive new developments in the most powerful media of the day. These stories are shot through with ambivalence towards that public which James both cultivated and disdained, and the device of the unreliable narrator may be read as indicating his recognition that the various senses of 'public', 'publication', and 'publicity' are more than contingently related, so that any *writer* on this topic is necessarily complicit with the developments he is satirizing.

As these stories remind us, an essential precondition for the 'lionizing' of an author in the nineteenth century was the existence of 'polite society'. In other words, this was quite different from, say, the mass celebrity of the contemporary pop star: we are talking, rather, about someone who might be invited to one's select dinner party, where a complicated social mechanism was at work: the lion in question was a prize worth capturing and displaying, a trophy who conferred a kind of distinction on the dinner-table or drawing-room in question, but the person doing the capturing was very likely to be of higher social status than the author, most likely, indeed, to be a titled lady. Focusing on the metaphor of 'the lion' for a moment, once could say that James's story represents a stage in the long-drawn-out transition from the age of the patron to the age of the market: the patron no longer supports the writer as an ornament to his household, but it is still thought to be in a titled lady's social interest to capture and display such a beast once he (more rarely she) has already established his name with a wider public. The decisive part in the creation of this socially desirable object, however, is now played by the popular media of the day, and the lion-hunter, ever fashion-conscious, is wholly parasitic upon that process. And it is, after all, the journalistic imperative to fill the 'new features' that causes the author to be solicited to give 'his views on vital topics' (including the timeless 'periodical prattle about the future of fiction').

I do not propose to chart all the successive stages in the development of the media and concomitant shifts in the kinds of 'celebrity' they created in the course of the twentieth century, nor to document the repetitive litany of lament with which educated observers by and large greeted these changes. Two phases particularly stand out in this history. First, there was the impact of new media of popular culture in the 1920s and 1930s, especially film but to some extent radio, along with the expansion of forms of print aimed principally at a popular readership.[15] And second, there was the period of the dramatic expansion of television in the 1950s and 1960s, referred to earlier.[16] But it did not follow that these developments, and the reshaping of the forms of celebrity that went with them, simply resulted in the withdrawal of intellectuals from some previously unified public sphere. New forms, whether radio talks, paperback books, or broadsheet opinion columns, also represented opportunities to reach new publics, and the mechanisms of celebrity could partly work *for* intellectuals as well as against them.

Indeed, rather than assuming that the terms 'intellectuals' and 'celebrities' must represent some mutually exclusive or binary pair, it is worth remembering that many leading intellectual figures across the twentieth century have been treated like celebrities as that status existed in their day. The following short list is not necessarily a selection of the most important or interesting intellectuals in twentieth-century Britain, but simply a few of those who were truly lionized when at the peak of their cultural standing: George Bernard Shaw, H. G. Wells, Bertrand Russell, J. M. Keynes, Harold Laski, Aldous Huxley, C. P. Snow, A. J. P. Taylor—and I shall stop before getting to the more contentious territory of the living. The precise form of celebrity they enjoyed or endured varied, depending in part on the nature of the available media, but in all their cases it involved a level of public attention which went well beyond the receptiveness of a respectful readership. To take one of the less obvious examples, by the 1950s Aldous Huxley found himself the object of the kind of smitten curiosity normally reserved for the stars of the Hollywood industry which he served for so many years: on the evenings of his public lectures at MIT at the end of the 1950s extra police had to be drafted in to cope with the traffic jams, and the lectures themselves were relayed by loudspeaker to the crowds outside the lecture-hall.[17] Nor should it ever be forgotten that Huxley was to enjoy an apotheosis denied even to today's most pop-conscious intellectual celebrity, when he appeared in the collage that made up the sleeve of the Beatles' 'Sergeant Pepper' album.

At the same time, it is broadly true that the cumulative consequence of social changes across the second half of the twentieth century represented a major shift in cultural power: the creations and preoccupations of what is usually called 'popular culture' have come to enjoy a hugely enhanced presence in the public life of the whole society and especially in the media previously devoted to the doings and interests of the governing or educated classes. After all, however much observers at the end of the nineteenth century may have thrown up their hands in horror at the trivializing vulgarities of publications such as *Homes and Haunts of Famous Authors*, it was still *authors* who were the subject of this new form of attention, and even when they were commercially successful and artistically unambitious authors, their names usually meant nothing to the overwhelming mass of the population. But at the end of the twentieth century it was those figures with the largest popular following, especially figures drawn from film, television, and sport, who constantly appeared in even those sections of the media aimed at a relatively elite audience.

Indeed, what the phrase 'a celebrity culture' points to is the way in which simply figuring in the mass media becomes the chief claim on attention itself. Those earlier categories of 'celebrities' I referred to a few moments ago were certainly dependent on the media of their day, however restricted in their reach by modern standards, for the dissemination of their achievements and, in some cases, their likeness. But in a celebrity-culture, the causal power is reversed. Instead of the media functioning literally as a 'medium'—that is, a channel or conduit between an activity which exists before them and an audience that is independent of them—the media become the forum for the display of people who are their own creation: the media, in other words, become the determining cultural power in their own right. Thus, if, in earlier decades, a leading churchman was asked to contribute a column to a newspaper or a distinguished scientist was asked to take part in a radio discussion programme, the greater exposure the respective media conferred was in a sense secondary to and parasitic upon their prior standing in some other field. But when a TV presenter (with no particular literary leanings) is asked to act as one of the judges of a book prize, or when a film actor (with no particular academic leanings, to put it mildly) is asked to give a university's graduating address, it is the celebrity status itself that is primary.

The cultural significance of the media has been transformed both by the speed of impact of the information and images they generate and by the enhanced economic and political power of their audiences. For example, at the beginning of the twentieth century, 'serious' newspapers by and large reported things politicians had said to other audiences. The rhythm of politics still to some extent dictated the rhythm of the media addressed to the educated class: the calendar of the sittings of Parliament governed a large part of the contents of *The Times*. By the close of the century, the reverse had become true: politicians and their 'spin-doctors' are governed by the rhythms of the media. Announcements are timed to coincide with influential radio or television programmes; the media themselves are often the main initial audience for the political statements they report. Indeed, according to one well-informed observer, 'over the past half century there has been a huge change in the "balance of trade" between politics and journalism. . . . Today, compared with politicians, journalists are better educated, better paid, cleverer, more important, and quite often visibly more powerful.' This shift is strikingly manifested in salaries: *all* national newspaper editors now earn more than the Prime Minister, some of them four or five times more, while several columnists earn twice as much.[18] Similarly, 'performing' well in these media, again above all on television, becomes a determining ingredient in making a successful political career. And somewhat comparable patterns of change are discernible in the cultural sphere. The commercial success of certain writers depends to a great extent on their willingness and ability to be turned into media 'stars': looks are a more important ingredient in literary success than ever before. In other words, media celebrity creates its own kind of cultural authority.

Insofar as the definition which summarizes this development—'a celebrity is someone who is famous for being famous'—is attributed to a single source, it is to the American historian and social commentator Daniel Boorstin, but it is in fact a slight misquotation. What Boorstin wrote, now as long ago as the 1950s, was: 'The celebrity is a person who is well-known for his well-knownness,' which is more exact if less snappy.[19] That's to say, being 'famous' may suggest some idea of achievement, whereas 'well-known' emphasizes simply what the marketing consultants call 'brand-recognition', and the whole point of the quip was that in the case of the celebrity there is no prior achievement or other independent claim on attention. Of course, that remark and the many subsequent variants on it can simply register the more condescending judgement that such individuals are famous for something not worthy of being famous for, thereby expressing an underlying resentment at the larger triumph of popular culture that is involved. After all, most such celebrities initially make their mark as film stars, television 'personalities', professional sports players, and so on. It is repeated exposure in a widely received popular medium that gives them recognizability and in that sense imposes them upon the society as a whole; much of the sneering at the emptiness of their state precisely registers a disdain for this triumph of popular culture.

This triumph has brought in its train obvious changes in the rank order of culturally esteemed forms of achievement as well as a dramatic democratization of inherited notions of fame, changes which are reflected even in that ostensibly immutable cultural monument, *Who's Who*. As Tyler Cowen remarked in his recent study *What Price Fame?*, we now live in a 'fame-intensive society', and many people want a piece of the action, as recently evidenced in Britain by the surely remarkable fact that 'One hundred thousand members of the public applied to be on the last series of Big Brother.'[20] The original Hall of Fame for Great Americans was inaugurated in 1901; according to Cowen, there are now over 3,000 Halls of Fame in the United States, including separate ones for accountants, police officers, marble champions, dog mushers, and pickle packers.[21] How, we may ask, are intellectuals supposed to cut it in such company? By comparison to the first two-thirds of the twentieth century, there is now much less of that 'free transfer' of cultural authority simply on the basis of social standing or of possessing a certain level of education. The greater empowerment of an in-your-face social egalitarianism means fewer figures than ever are granted any kind of *a priori* claim to be listened to. We need, therefore, to consider whether, as a result of these changes, intellectuals are listened to by *anyone* now.

III

At this point, it may be helpful to sketch out a rough set of distinctions among three operative mechanisms of cultural standing as they impinge on the cases of intellectuals: expertise, celebrity, and reputation. In practice, these three mechanisms may overlap somewhat, but the differences among them may be briefly analysed as follows. Expertise is the possession of a validated form of skill or knowledge, one that is often signalled by the holding of a qualification or a particular office. A given individual may achieve standing as an expert, but the sustaining authority is clearly collective or institutional, and any one individual can, in principle, be substituted for another with the same training and experience without diluting that authority. By contrast, celebrity is irreducibly personal, even though the forces governing the making and unmaking of celebrities are those governing the production and circulation of market commodities more generally. Recognizability is the chief property possessed by celebrities; their opinions on various subjects are usually only supposed to be of interest because they themselves are already widely known. The operation of reputation is more complicated: it appears to be primarily personal, but it depends upon some standing or achievement in an activity which attracts cultural deference *independently* of that individual's contribution to it (unlike celebrity, where there may be no such 'prior' activity behind the individual). Reputation suggests that this achievement or display of capacity is known about in, or at least its existence is accepted by, circles much wider than those who actually understand or participate in the founding activity itself. For an individual's opinions to be solicited on account of their reputation, they must be thought by some people to be already respected by others and to have demonstrated their entitlement to that respect on previous occasions.

These different mechanisms may be illustrated by thinking of the different circumstances under which a scholarly or literary figure may be asked to appear in the mainstream media.

1. If some new Roman remains are discovered on a building site in London, and the Professor of Classical Archaeology at Oxford (whose name is largely unknown outside that discipline) is asked by a newspaper reporter for a quotable explanation of their significance, the operation of expertise that is involved is pretty clear. The reporter may have needed to establish that this individual did indeed know something about this branch of the subject, but what the paper's editors wanted was a title and a university that would carry unquestionable authority, not the views of an already known individual. They are not interested in the professor's opinions on subjects unrelated to this news item.

2. If a pop band is referred to by some junior minister as 'a marvellous advertisement for British culture', and an academic who frequently appears on television or in the newspapers is asked to come to a TV studio to comment, then the mechanism of the celebrity economy is operating here. The issue is entirely unrelated to the subject this individual professes in his or her scholarly capacity, but the academic in question is a known name and face who can be relied upon to express a provoking opinion of some kind (whether endorsing or confuting the original comment—tellingly, it doesn't much matter which). This particular scholar tends not to be too fussy about the details and rarely declines these invitations; such figures are what editors and producers call 'good value'.

3. If a major book appears which argues that academic economists have systematically misunderstood the functioning of the British economy and have been wrong in their analyses of every one of that economy's crises in the past 100 years, misleading both governments and the public, and if a senior academic economist who has also written in general periodicals about the public role of economists is asked to appear on a radio cultural magazine programme to discuss it, then that looks more like a case of reputation at work. The occasion calls for more than expertise as an economist, but a familiar 'media-friendly' academic who knows nothing about the topic will be worse than useless in this case. The individual in question is already known (by at least some of the people consulted by the programme's researchers) to have previously demonstrated a capacity for effective communication to a non-specialist public on this kind of topic, but the economist's professional standing and career to date also suggest a capacity to understand the technicalities of the subject without making the kinds of mistakes that would immediately discredit his or her opinions in the eyes of economically literate listeners.

In practice, many instances are not as clear-cut as these three examples (or at least the first two: the third is intrinsically more complex). Filling the role of intellectual can involve elements of all three mechanisms: at the heart of the role lies the attempt to deploy one's standing across a range of issues without thereby diluting it, though there is a natural tendency for individuals who are ambitious of success in the public media to pass from expertise through reputation to celebrity. Here the danger for such figures is that by constantly seeking exposure and agreeing to make such pronouncements they risk forfeiting much of the standing upon which their public role was initially founded, and so to maintain their 'visibility' they are forced into the vicious circle of pursuing celebrity itself through factitious controversy and sheer opinionatedness. They become more mouth than voice. And this is where, I believe, the most interesting aspect of the hackneyed claim about intellectuals being 'displaced' by the celebrity culture comes in. It may be those figures who enjoy most success in reaching a non-specialist audience who most need to be reminded that a condition of their status is the continued perception that they are also doing work in a specialized sphere which measures up to the highest standards of that specialism (whether literary, artistic, scholarly, scientific, or whatever). When that ceases to be the case, their media career may continue of its own momentum for some time, but quite soon they will either have to become full-time media celebrities, or they will find that the dry rot of repetition and overexposure does its deadly work and that the invitations to pronounce become rarer and rarer. As we have seen, intellectual capital needs to be constantly reinvested; a strategy of pure expenditure soon exhausts one's credit.

Some of the social changes which have undermined much of the deference from which Taylor, Ayer, and their academic peers initially profited have already been sketched. In addition to the impact of technological innovation such as the rise of visual and electronic media, they include increased prosperity and hence much greater market power for the bulk of the population. Historians have amply documented the rising prosperity of the immediately post-war decades, but it is not always realized how sharply this has increased in the final quarter of the century: according to the Office of National Statistics, 'the average income has doubled in real terms between 1971 and 1997'.[22] Increasingly egalitarian attitudes (notwithstanding the evidence of stark—and, in purely financial terms, worsening—inequalities) have deprived many of the old markers of social standing of their power. More specifically, there has been a loss of status for academics as a result of the huge expansion of higher education and what has been termed the 'proletarianization' of the profession of university teacher: a 'professor', whether of Tibetan or (more likely) of Tourism, is no longer automatically a substantial figure in the local or national community.

But perhaps at this point we should pause and question the very idea of there being a single 'national community' as far as cultural and intellectual life is concerned. Perhaps it was only ever a habitual complacency about their and their friends' importance which allowed leading public figures of earlier generations to think that they addressed, or even spoke 'for', such a community in the first place. Certainly, the increased recognition of the competing claims of various 'subcultures', whether defined in terms of ethnicity and gender or of musical taste and body-piercing, has made such complacency harder to sustain. This does not mean that the ambition to address some kind of broad, non-specialist public has disappeared, just that it may need, at certain points, to acknowledge its own social location (or, in practice, locations) and the legitimate interests of other, sometimes very different, locations. One useful piece of mental hygiene when talking about intellectuals is to get into the habit of speaking of 'publics' in the plural. Few things are more obstructive here than the unanalysed assumption that intellectuals used to reach a wide general audience drawn from society as a whole, but now they no longer do this. The truth is that the relevant publics have always been limited or segmented, by social class, educational level, gender, region, special interest, and so on. These defining properties are more important than sheer size, though it is also worth emphasizing just how restricted the audiences reached by earlier intellectuals often were.

This last point can be illustrated by referring once again to the figure who, in recent years, has probably been held up more often than any other as the model of the intellectual who writes for a broad general public, George Orwell. In his case, in particular, his great posthumous fame can easily lead us to assume that he must have been among the most listened-to at the time. In fact, until the publication of *Animal Farm*, little more than four years before his death, Orwell enjoyed only a rather limited reputation as a writer and journalist. His earlier novels had not been commercially successful, and even one of his finest non-fiction books, *Homage to Catalonia*, had still not sold its initial printing of 1,500 copies at the time of his death twelve years after its publication.[23] Of course, much of Orwell's most incisive commentary on his time was carried on in the pages of periodicals and newspapers, but even here the facts of their circulation can provide something of a reality check. His most regular contributions were as literary editor of *Tribune*, which came to be seen as the organ of the Bevanite Left within the British Labour Party, and as the author of the 'London letter' for *Partisan Review*, the house-journal of the ex-Marxist or *marxisant* critics and theorists known as 'the New York intellectuals', and in both cases the circulation was correspondingly restricted ('until 1945, circulation [of *Partisan Review*] was less than 5,000; by the early 1950s it had risen to well over 10,000; afterwards it began to drop again').[24] The greatest concentration of what are now regarded as his best essays appeared in two magazines, Cyril Connolly's monthly, *Horizon*, largely a journal devoted to upholding the highest aesthetic standards in literature and the arts, and Humphrey Slater's quarterly, *Polemic* (discussed in Ch. 17), the voice of the philosophically informed liberalism associated in the mid-1940s with figures such as Bertrand Russell, Karl Popper, and A. J. Ayer. The former sold between 7,000 and 10,000 copies during this period, the latter never more than 3,000 to 4,000 during its brief life between 1945 and 1947.[25] I am not suggesting that Orwell was particularly obscure: he had a growing reputation as a critic and essayist in the 1940s even before the publication of *Animal Farm* and *Nineteen Eighty-Four*. My point is, rather, that these statistics—and, still more, the cultural profiles of each journal—are indicative of the publics reached even by relatively successful intellectuals.

More generally, what we find when we look at the question historically is a plurality of overlapping publics reached by a plurality of overlapping media. Each phase in the development of these media since at least the early nineteenth century has nearly always been perceived as a threat to serious public debate while at the same time each phase has actually furnished intellectuals with new opportunities. And it should hardly need saying that different levels of cultural activity coexist within each of these media. For example, the widely denounced arrival of the new 'yellow press' of the early twentieth century, following the launch of the *Daily Mail* in 1896, coexisted with what is now often taken as one of the high peaks of serious political journalism, with the simultaneous flourishing on the Liberal side of the *Daily News* and the *Daily Chronicle*, as well as the transformation of the *Manchester Guardian* from a regional into a nationally influential daily, not to mention the flourishing culture of weeklies of the kind discussed in Ch. 4.[26] Similarly, the growth of radio in the inter-war years prompted jeremiads about its inevitably destructive impact on the nation's mental health, even as the founding of the Third Programme in 1946 was providing intellectuals with one of the most hospitable platforms they have ever known, and so on for each of the various media in successive periods.[27] Viewed from within this longer historical perspective, does the state of the media in contemporary Britain appear to be unique, even uniquely disastrous? Any response can only be selective at best, but there are good grounds for believing that the prospect is not so uniformly dark.

The historic medium through which intellectuals have operated most extensively is, of course, print—books, newspapers, and, perhaps above all, periodicals. Here, it does not seem at all obvious that the recent and current state of these media in Britain represent a contraction of opportunities for intellectuals to address their publics as a result of the enhanced power of the new form of celebrity culture. Certainly, giant publishing conglomerates and ghosted celebrity autobiographies are locked in a mutually needy embrace on the front tables of the chain bookshops, but if we are thinking of serious non-fiction publishing we have to remember that the later part of the twentieth century also saw the at least temporarily successful establishment of houses as different as Verso, Virago, Granta, Fourth Estate, Reaktion, and so on. It is true that the broadsheet press devotes more news space to the doings of celebrities than used to be the case, but it *has* much more space in the first place. There are as many national broadsheet titles as there have ever been, and they provide more room than ever for essays, columns, and book reviews. The enormous enlargement and diversification of Saturday editions has also made a difference here, with the recently launched *Guardian Review* providing a prominent example. It has to be recognized that several famous old journals have closed, and we are told ad nauseam that the general cultural periodical is dead, squeezed between the millstones of increasingly glossy lifestyle magazines and increasingly specialized scholarly journals. But somehow the genre refuses to die, and our own generation has seen the flourishing of new journals such as *Prospect* and the *London Review of Books*, as well as continued or renewed vitality in periodicals as different as the *Spectator, New Left Review*, and the *Times Literary Supplement*. Numbers, as I said earlier, are only a very small part of the story, but we should acknowledge that a journal as intellectually and politically serious as the *London Review of Books*, whose pages regularly carry long analytical articles by leading writers and scholars, now claims a circulation almost twice as great as the combined *total* of the circulations of the three periodicals in which most of Orwell's famous essays appeared: *Horizon, Tribune*, and *Polemic*.[28]

Another medium through which intellectuals have historically reached their publics but whose demise has been confidently predicted over many decades now is that of the public lecture and similar versions of the live word. The relative prominence of such occasions has declined somewhat, to be sure, but they continue not just to take place but to attract audiences, as the proliferation of lecture series, debates, and panel discussions and similar occasions bears witness, while new versions of the genre, such as the Oxford Amnesty Lectures (which began in 1992), have provided the occasions for some notable statements. The first series included Jacques Derrida, Frank Kermode, Edward Said, and others on 'Freedom and interpretation'; 1993 saw Jean-François Lyotard, John Rawls, Richard Rorty, and others on 'Human rights'; 1994 included Carlo Ginzburg, Eric Hobsbawm, and Emmanuel Le Roy Ladurie on 'Historical change and human rights'; and so on. And if the live word lives, albeit in somewhat altered circumstances, then the health of its younger sibling, the electronic word, is positively blooming. Indeed, it may be that, deep in the unregulated jungle of cyberspace, initiatives such as that of Anthony Barnett and his colleagues at OpenDemocracy in developing a truly global electronic forum for debate may signal the arrival of a medium through which intellectuals of the future will address incalculably diverse publics.[29]

But at present what lives in a more consequential way is the broadcast word—that is to say, the power of television and radio—and here we approach one of the cruces of the whole current debate about intellectuals and celebrity. A great deal of printer's ink has been spilt about this in recent years, so let me confine myself to making just three points.

First, it is noticeable how much the contribution, and still more the potential, of radio is neglected or underestimated. It is a medium well suited to the communication and analysis of ideas, as Orwell was not the only one to notice now over half a century ago.[30] This is particularly true of that distinctive subgenre the 20- or 30-minute radio talk—a form at which British radio has excelled over the years, and one that makes good use of the properties and powers of the medium itself. The relatively recent displacement of talks by talking (referred to above) does represent, it has to be conceded, a culpable loss of confidence on the part of radio producers and, above all, executives, ever fearful of charges of elitism and inaccessibility, rashly concluding that the informal interview format can 'get ideas across' without seeming forbidding. In practice, that format succeeds less well than a prepared talk; or, rather, it does something different. Instead of an author or scholar giving listeners an example of their wares, we tend to get question and answer *about* the book or idea—when did you write it, how did the idea come to you, who else was in the bath at the time? But whatever may be the virtues or limitations of the interview format, the general suitability of radio to serious intellectual discourse is undeniable, and it is far from obvious that we should write off a system of sound broadcasting that does, after all, still put out not just some excellent talks, but also such regular programmes as 'Analysis', 'Nightwaves', 'Start the Week', 'In Our Time', and so on.

Second, despite all the signs of life in various media that I have been pointing to, many commentators still appear to believe that the case about intellectuals and celebrity stands or falls on the evidence provided by television. So, let me here put forward a heterodox view that I realize risks being misunderstood or misreported, but which nonetheless seems worth saying, and it is this: television may indeed now be the medium with the greatest power in our society as a whole, but it does not follow that intellectuals do not flourish in our society if they do not flourish *on* television. That is not to say that they should in any way underestimate its influence and its reach, only that their analyses of that influence, like their contributions to our thinking on other topics, do not have to be disseminated through the medium of television itself. Television can do many things wonderfully well, but perhaps not so many things that matter in this particular context. The visual predominates, a tendency encouraged by the culture among professional producers and directors which emphasizes skill and inventiveness in using this distinctive dimension of the medium. It is less well suited to the oral exposition of ideas than radio, and less accommodating of nuance, complexity, and sheer length than print. A speaker's appearance and manner count for a lot; discussion is brutally abbreviated; liveliness, conflict, and sound-bites are over-valued.

A certain mutual wariness between intellectuals and television producers is, in these circumstances, understandable and not necessarily a bad thing. Consider, for example, the way in which Udi Eichler, producer of Channel 4's late-night discussion programme *Voices* in the 1980s, gave a distinctively televisual twist to the usual variations on the absence thesis. According to Eichler, British intellectuals distrust discussion, especially discussion on television. 'A large number of distinguished intellectuals, while wishing us well, have persistently declined our invitation,' and he listed 'such luminaries as Sir Karl Popper, Sir Peter Medawar, Michael Oakeshott, Richard Wollheim, Sir Isaiah Berlin, Edward Norman, Iris Murdoch', and others. He recognized that 'some of our most distinguished thinkers are at best wary of television in general', though he did not consider whether there might not be good reasons for this wariness, or indeed whether the style and format of programmes might not be changed to make them more hospitable venues. In Eichler's view, deeper features of the national culture were to blame: 'What is at stake here is the much lamented British tradition of empiricism or, to put it another way, the "pseud's corner" syndrome.' That sentence, properly staged, might make 'good television', but it offers little by way of analysis and explanation (quite apart from its extraordinary equation between empiricism and a style of mockery). 'The general hostility to speculative and theoretical thought is deeply embedded in our culture.' (This is presumably a different culture from the one in which Peter Medawar, Michael Oakeshott, Richard Wollheim, Iris Murdoch, and company enjoy 'seminal and authoritative stature'?) But once launched, Eichler seemed likely to leave no cliché unturned: 'This essential feature of British intellectual life has also resulted in a wholesale exclusion of, or, at best, a marginalisation of foreign thinking, both past and present.' One must charitably assume that he had had to spend too much of his life in television studios to have had a fair chance of learning what an ignorant and silly remark this was. Not only, he suggested, is intellectual life better elsewhere (France is his wholly unsurprising example), but it used to be better in the past, too, even the recent past of the 1960s when there were bold syntheses and utopian schemes around: 'The age of the instant theoretical panacea is, perhaps, over, and with it have gone the grand guru figures who set the agenda for public debate, who embodied whole systems of thought, and who made for very good television.'[31] One might have thought it would be impossible to use the phrase 'instant theoretical panacea' at all positively, but apparently not. It is the final phrase there, however, which really says it all. Ultimately, the trouble with all those seminal and authoritative British intellectuals is that they simply don't make for 'very good television'.

An oblique illustration of the fallacy of exaggerating the importance of television to the activities of intellectuals was provided by, dispiritingly, the *Times Higher Education Supplement* in the series it ran in 1996–7 on academics in the media. The selection seemed at first oddly arbitrary, mixing significant figures with others who appeared of much less consequence, but it all began to make more sense as soon as one realized the importance accorded to television appearances. In fact, nine out of their top ten choices were individuals who had principally achieved the level of public prominence that led them to be included in this list as a result of their appearances on TV, even if most of them had also done other kinds of journalism as well.[32] Such series principally reflect the media's own narcissism, which in turn generates an unassuageable anxiety about being 'out of date' and 'off the pace', with the result that the significance of short-term 'visibility' is exaggerated at the expense of long-term influence.

And third, it should be pointed out that even television is now old enough to have a history that conforms to the pattern I mentioned earlier in which developments which were at the time denounced for their vulgarity, irrelevance, or triviality come to be lauded retrospectively as evidence of a lost age of intellectual seriousness. It is worth recalling that, right up to the 1950s, 'because radio was believed by most BBC policy-makers to be the more important medium, the development of television was controlled by those whose interest and experience lay in radio.[33] At the beginning of the 1950s, as I mentioned earlier, only a few hundred thousand homes had television sets, and as one observer recalled: 'Few middle class people had them and certainly no intellectuals.' But the ironies start to become apparent when one discovers that that observer was A. J. P. Taylor.[34] Taylor was, as we have seen, the ur-'telly-don' of the 1950s and 1960s, and he, together with other examples of the species such as Freddie Ayer, were at the time dismissed and indeed denounced by fellow academics for shameless exhibitionism. The programmes in which such figures appeared are now fondly recalled as models of intellectually serious broadcasting.

The way in which dismissals of television's present are underwritten by nostalgic constructions of its past may be illustrated with a very recent example. Writing in *The Guardian Review* in November 2003, David Herman restated a by-now familiar case, a lament or dirge crooned over the coffin of intellectual life in Britain at regular intervals.[35] He suggested that between the late 1950s and the early 1990s 'the intellectual was a familiar presence on British television'. From John Freeman's 'Face to Face' interviews, through such regular series as 'Conversations for Tomorrow' and up to 'Voices' in the mid-1980s and 'The Late Show' in the early 1990s, there were discussion programmes that took ideas and their exponents seriously. His opening vignette recalled a 'Conversations' broadcast from 1964 in which Isaiah Berlin and A. J. Ayer argued over ideas with machine-gun velocity; licence-payers were certainly not being short-changed here, observed Herman, since 'Berlin and Ayer were probably the best-known intellectuals in Britain at the time' (it is interesting to note that celebrity is here presumed to amplify rather than threaten their status as intellectuals). Simply to list all the names mentioned as appearing on such programmes in these years would be to start to assemble a Who's Who of Britain's intellectuals (and not just Britain's): from Priestley and Russell through Berger and Brook, Steiner and Gellner, Hobsbawm and Giddens, to Sontag and Rushdie, and so on. But since the closing of 'The Late Show' in 1995, suggested Herman, this impressive sequence has been discontinued; hence his question 'Whatever happened to intellectuals on television?' To his credit, and unlike the authors of some of the more sweeping obituaries for the species, Herman acknowledged that in the culture at large 'there is no shortage of interesting philosophers, scientists, historians and cultural critics', but we no longer see them on our screens. 'The people who run British television today', Herman concluded, '. . . do not have the same passion for ideas and for the people who produce and create ideas. . . . [The] golden age is dead.'

Actually, what is usually dead when the phrase 'golden age' makes an appearance is any attempt at serious critical analysis, its place occupied instead by the familiar tropes of *Kulturpessimismus*. Not that anyone could deny that in recent years there has been, on the part of those who control television programming, a debilitating loss of confidence in the capacities and curiosity of their audiences, but, rereading Herman's piece, it is hard to decide whether his lament is based on the assumption that intellectuals need television or that television needs intellectuals. In either case the assumption may be false. Television pretty obviously doesn't *need* intellectuals: even at the height of the alleged golden age, there was a good deal of wailing and gnashing of teeth about how the various discussion formats tried in the programmes Herman now celebrates didn't make 'good television', and in later years they never enjoyed prime-time scheduling, even on BBC2 and Channel 4. But nor is it obvious, as I've already suggested, in what sense intellectuals *need* to be on such television programmes. Although the medium can be used in more creative ways, the truth is that being briefly interviewed by a professional presenter in a studio full of cameras is not a very effective way to get interesting ideas across, and all the evidence in relation to any of these programmes is that audience attention is largely distracted by questions of dress, mannerism, and fanciability. By and large it is people who work in the media themselves who are most touchily conscious of which figures are being courted or neglected by TV producers, but I doubt that, when a future historian is writing the history of Britain's intellectuals at the beginning of the twenty-first century, appearance on television will be a significant criterion for inclusion.

IV

As will by now be clear, I am trying to show how a particular contemporary concern both arises out of a set of long-standing conditions and also constitutes the latest instalment in an established tradition of commentary on this topic. But in doing so, I am assuming the understanding of the concept of the intellectual that was analysed in earlier chapters. I am assuming, that is to say, that that concept refers to a role or set of relations, a point of intersection between a reputation, a medium, a public, and an occasion. As this suggests, for an individual to occupy the role he or she must, by definition, have built a certain reputation, otherwise opportunities for addressing non-specialist publics will not have come their way, and, in addition, to reach such publics they must use forms of publication or other media that operate beyond the confines of their own specialism. But this means that they are bound to be vulnerable to the charge of 'selling out', in however minor a way, to the imperatives governing such media. This, I am suggesting, is not a matter of the ambition, misjudgements, and venality of any individual figure, though all those may indeed be involved in particular cases, but rather a structural truth about the role of the intellectual. And, in addition, we should not forget that some of the complaints about the impossibility of reaching a non-specialist audience now except through the distorting mechanisms of the celebrity culture have themselves been examples of serious social criticism successfully addressed to non-specialist audiences—as was, arguably, the case with the essay from which the despairing epigraph to this chapter is taken: 'In place of thought, we have opinion; in place of argument, we have journalism; in place of polemic, we have personality profiles; in place of reputation, we have celebrity.'[36] Another version of the Cretan Liar paradox tends to haunt this strain of lament.

Furthermore, we should recognize just how patronizing or condescending are those accounts that dwell exclusively on the diminished intellectual expectations of a celebrity-drugged public. One practical antidote to falling into such condescension, I would suggest, would be for such commentators to remember that they themselves are, most of the time, members of the audience rather than of the cast of performers. In other words, we are all of us general readers or part of a non-specialist audience most of the time, and we tend not to think of *ourselves* as entirely satisfied by gossip, glamour, and glibness.[37] Indeed, we think of ourselves as having quite sensitive antennae for detecting the failings of those would-be intellectuals so infatuated by the lure of publicity that we censure, distrust, and eventually stop listening to them—to the attempts to be provocative for its own sake, the unctuous parades of conscience or correctness, the opportunism and careerism, the superficiality, the vanity, the egotism. Perhaps we should acknowledge that such antennae may be possessed by many more people than the self-flattering cultural pessimists allow.

Of course, for most writers, scholars, or scientists, celebrity is hardly a pressing problem—and in that respect, at least, they may be classed among the fortunate many rather than the unlucky few. It is true that the power of celebrity culture does help to shape the conditions under which happily obscure figures may occasionally be asked to contribute to discussion beyond the limits of their special field, though even here the recurrently fashionable cultural pessimism seems to me misplaced. Through whatever combination of education, occupation, circumstance, talent, and luck, some individuals will have been able to devote an uncommon amount of time and resources to disciplining their analytical capacities or cultivating their imaginations or keeping themselves abreast of the best current thinking and writing in particular areas. When such individuals are invited to address a non-specialist public in some form, they can at least attempt to impose their standards of accuracy, adequacy, and complexity on the media through which they contribute rather than having that medium's standards imposed on them. In many cases, they may be only partially successful. Editors and sub-editors will cut, rewrite, and headline according to the prevailing wisdom of their guild; producers will have one eye on their time-slot and one on their audience ratings, quick on both counts to cut contributions they consider too long or too boring; presenters and interviewers will press to extract the memorable over the judicious, the partisan over the even-handed, the accessible over the daunting, the short over the long. While there is no point in such figures agreeing to contribute to these media unless they respect their defining properties—which are obviously not those of either an academic seminar or a work of imaginative literature—there may, nonetheless, be something to be said for their making an effort to slow things down, to start from somewhere else, to contest the tendentious or over-dramatic summary, and so on.

Beyond that, perhaps there are times when all such intellectual and literary figures, of whatever status, come to recognize that one of the most powerful weapons in their struggle to retain a degree of autonomy and control in such engagements is the word 'no'—no, I won't appear on your programme; no, I won't write 800 words on that topic; no, I won't review that book; no, I won't give you a sound bite on the state of modern literature, the state of our streets, or the state of David Beckham's marriage. Those eager to become the house-intellectuals of the media world may be afraid of saying no lest the phone not ring again, but nonetheless doing so can constitute the exercise of such industrial muscle as is possessed by the primary producers in this particular cottage industry. I realize, of course, that 'Just Say No' may sound like the slogan of 'Intellectual Virgins for Christ'—or perhaps, in this case, for Plato—but whatever drawbacks may be associated with the great increase in the proportion of intellectuals who are academics, the relative security such careers bring, by comparison to the freelance life, should at least mean that the sound of a ringing telephone does not *have* to induce the Pavlovian 'Yes, when do you want it by?'

Such thoughts, and the obloquy they are bound to attract in some quarters, are surely indications of complex reservations and ambivalences about the very role of the intellectual itself, a role perpetually tacking between the Scylla of timidity, hermeticism, and over-specialism, and the Charybdis of exhibitionism, philistinism, and over-exposure. We want our intellectuals to engage with the world, not to live in monkish withdrawal, but we also want them not to be tarnished by the vulgarity of the world. We want them to have achieved indisputable intellectual standing, but we also want them not to be narrow specialists. We want them to speak out, but we also want them not to be all mouth. As I argued in the Introduction to this book, I take these tensions and ambivalences to be indications that there is an object of desire at issue here, a barely acknowledged longing that disciplined intellectual enquiry or aesthetic creativity might yield us some guidance about how to live. Perhaps it's no wonder we are so resistant to allowing that someone who is more or less our contemporary could ever be getting this right.

We are, of course, never short of reminders of the vanity, gullibility, and irresponsibility often displayed by actual intellectuals, and eager commentators are always on hand to direct our attention to these failings. But in my view, better history is a liberating as well as a sobering force. Once we shed the unrealistic ambition nurtured by the illusion that previous generations of intellectuals reached and directed a public that was coextensive with society as a whole, then we are better placed to see how intellectuals can make use of existing media to reach those publics who, being neither as doped up nor as dumbed down as fashionable commentary suggests, *do* want to see issues of common interest considered in ways that are less instrumental or less opportunist, more reflective or more analytical, better informed or better expressed.

This will no doubt strike some as the most wilful kind of optimism and others as a dispiritingly unambitious job-description. It is true that, on the one hand, I have no wish to encourage that picture of the intellectual as condemned to do nothing more than putting messages in bottles and throwing them overboard, a picture that denies effective agency in the present and consoles itself with the prospect of vindication by a very select posterity. That picture surely bespeaks not just cultural despair but self-dramatization as well. But nor, on the other hand, do I think that much good can come from promoting that heavily romanticized conception of the intellectual as the acknowledged legislator of the world, marching at the head of mass movements, political or other programme in hand. Self-dramatization of another kind beckons here, and actually, for all their symbolic appeal, the barricades have never been a very good platform from which to try to conduct rational argument. Instead, I am suggesting that the sign under which the contemporary intellectual's rather more realistic dealings with the relevant media should be carried on may be that provided by Beckett's wry formula: try again, fail again, fail better.

NOTES

1. See particularly, 'The end of the world as we know it', *Guardian*, 'Saturday', 1 Jan. 2000, 1–3; 'From deference to diversity: Britain's cultural journey since 1945', *Guardian*, 'Dumb?', 28 Oct. 2000, 15–17; 4 Nov. 2000, 6–7; 11 Nov. 2000, 14–15; and 'Hegel in green wellies', *London Review of Books*, 8 Mar. 2001, 16–18.
2. For a more probing analysis of the phenomenon in broadly psychoanalytical terms, see Jacqueline Rose, 'The cult of celebrity', *New Formations*, 36 (1999), 9–20.
3. Lauren Simpson, quoted in *Guardian*, 3 Nov. 2003, 11.
4. e.g. *Who's Who 2003* (London: A & C Black, 2003), 'Historical Note'.
5. See Neil McKendrick, John Brewer, and J. H. Plumb, *The Birth of a Consumer Society: The Commercialization of Eighteenth-Century England* (London: Hutchinson, 1982); John Brewer, *The Pleasures of the Imagination: English Culture in the Eighteenth Century* (London: HarperCollins, 1997). But see also the recent questioning of this historical account of 'consumer society' by one of its earliest proponents: John Brewer, 'The error of our ways', cited at n. 63 in Ch. 11 above.
6. Leo Braudy, *The Frenzy of Renown: Fame and its History* (New York: Oxford University Press, 1986), 321.
7. See Tyler Cowen, *What Price Fame?* (Cambridge, Mass.: Harvard University Press, 2000), 52.
8. *OED*, 'celebrity', *sb.*, sense 3.
9. Matthew Arnold, 'The bishop and the philosopher', *Macmillan's Magazine*, 7 (Jan. 1863); this passage was reused in 'Spinoza and the Bible', *MacMillan's Magazine*, 9 (Dec. 1863); R. H. Super (ed.), *The Complete Prose Works of Matthew Arnold*, 11 vols. (Ann Arbor: University of Michigan Press, 1960–73), iii. 181.

10. Nigel Cross, *The Common Writer* (Cambridge: Cambridge University Press, 1989), 209.
11. My account of the development of 'celebrity' in the Victorian period is drawn chiefly from the following: Richard Salmon, *Henry James and the Culture of Publicity* (Cambridge: Cambridge University Press, 1997); idem. 'Signs of intimacy: the literary celebrity in the "Age of Interviewing" ', *Victorian Literature and Culture*, 25 (1997), 159–77; Nicholas Dames, 'Brushes with fame: Thackeray and the work of celebrity', *Nineteenth-Century Literature*, 56 (2001), 23–51. I am grateful to Sarah Wah for these references.
12. Lady Broome, 'Interviews', *The Cornhill Magazine*, 1901, 473; quoted in Salmon, 'Signs of intimacy', 161.
13. Anon, 'Interviews and interviewing', *All the Year Round*, 29 Oct. 1892, 425; quoted in Salmon, 'Signs of intimacy', 169.
14. 'The Death of the Lion' was first published in *The Yellow Book* in April 1894, and reprinted in the volume of James's stories entitled *Terminations* in the following year; I have used the text of the New York Edition (vol. XV, 1909).
15. This period is well covered in D. L. LeMahieu, *Culture for Democracy: Mass Communication and the Cultivated Mind in Britain Between the Wars* (Oxford; Oxford University Press, 1988).
16. See Ch. 19, Sect. II.
17. Nicholas Murray, *Aldous Huxley: An English Intellectual* (London: Little, Brown, 2002), 436.
18. Geoffrey Wheatcroft, *Media Guardian*, 12 Mar. 2001, 10.
19. The correction is noted in Braudy, *Frenzy of Renown*, 9; the original occurs in Boorstin's essay 'The Human Pseudo-event', reprinted in his *The Image, or What Happened to the American Dream* (London: Weidenfeld & Nicolson, 1962).
20. Piers Morgan, 'Celebrity nobodies', *Media Guardian*, 17 Nov. 2003, 7.
21. Cowen, *What Price Fame?*, 11, 7; see also P. David Marshall, *Celebrity and Power; Fame in Contemporary Culture* (Minneapolis: University of Minnesota Press, 1997).
22. Office of National Statistics' yearbook *Britain 2000*.
23. The details are given by Peter Davison in *Complete Works of George Orwell*, 20 vols. (London: Secker & Warburg, 1998), xi. 135.
24. Hugh Wilford, *The New York Intellectuals: From Vanguard to Institution* (Manchester: Manchester University Press, 1995), 36; see also Michael Foot, *Aneurin Bevan* (London: Gollancz, 1962–73); William Phillips, *A Partisan View: Five Decades of the Literary Life* (New York: Stein & Day, 1983.
25. For *Horizon*, see Jeremy Lewis, *Cyril Connolly: a Life* (London: Pimlico, 1998), 337 n.; for *Polemic*, discussed in Ch. 17 above, there is no existing secondary discussion, but there is some editorial commentary in the magazine itself.
26. For the rise of the 'yellow press', see Matthew Engel, *Tickle the Public: One Hundred Years of the Popular Press* (London: Gollancz, 1996); for the flourishing Liberal press, see Stephen Koss, *The Rise and Fall of the Political Press*, 2 vols.: ii. *The Twentieth Century* (Chapel Hill: University of North Carolina Press, 1984); David Ayerst, *The Manchester Guardian: Biography of a Newspaper* (London: Guardian Publications, 1971); and Alfred F. Havighurst, *Radical Journalist: H. W. Massingham (1860–1924)* (Cambridge: Cambridge University Press, 1974).
27. For the jeremiads, see LeMahieu, *Culture For Democracy*, part II; for the Third Programme, see Ch. 18 above.

28. According to the Audit Bureau of Circulation, the circulation of the *London Review of Books* in 2004 was 42,000.
29. see <opendemocracy.net>, accessed May 2004.
30. See e.g. his comments on the BBC's proposed new channel in 1946 (what was to become the Third Programme); 'London Letter' (Summer, 1946); *Complete Works*, xviii. 289.
31. Udi Eichler, 'Where have all the thinkers gone?', *Listener* (16 Feb. 1984), 10–16.
32. The *THES* series 'Celebrity Scholars' began on 16 Jan. 1996 with a profile of David Starkey; some seventy others followed over the succeeding eighteen months.
33. See Kathleen Burk, *Troublemaker: The Life and History of A. J. P. Taylor* (London: Yale University Press, 2000), 389.
34. Quoted in Burk, *Troublemaker*, 388.
35. David Herman 'Thought Crime', *Guardian Review*, 1 Nov. 2003, 18–19.
36. Taken from the article by Michael Ignatieff discussed at the end of Ch. 1, 'Where are they now?', *Prospect* (Oct. 1997), 4; a longer version of this article appeared as 'The decline and fall of the public intellectual', *Queen's Quarterly*, 104 (1997), 395–403.
37. I have argued this in relation to a different set of issues in 'Before another tribunal: the idea of the "non-specialist public" ', in Stefan Collini, *English Pasts: Essays in History and Culture* (Oxford: Oxford University Press, 1999), 305–25.

Epilogue. No Elsewhere

'After we have got all the facts of our special study, justness of perception to deal with the facts is still required, and is, even, the principal thing of all.'

I

A book which has so determinedly taken issue with one cherished belief about 'British exceptionalism', and which has attempted to expose some of the forms of parochialism that have helped sustain that belief, may perhaps be allowed to let the tone of its conclusion be set by an emphatically English voice, brooding on its own ambivalent sense of belonging. In his poem 'The Importance of Elsewhere', Philip Larkin, writing in 1955 and drawing upon the years he had recently spent working in Belfast, reflected on the way in which recognition of the foreignness of his surroundings there had made possible a kind of acceptance or coexistence. He may have been lonely, but 'since it was not home | Strangeness made sense'. He then went on:

> Living in England has no such excuse:
> These are my customs and establishments
> It would be much more serious to refuse.
> Here no elsewhere underwrites my existence.[1]

The poem points, in that characteristically Larkinesque tone of unillusioned realism, towards what is involved in facing up to the here and now, repudiating various forms of pretence and escapism. Part of what it means for somewhere to be 'home' is that one cannot maintain the kind of quizzical detachment from its 'customs and establishments' that comes from locating one's defining identity 'elsewhere'.

In this book I have tried to show how debate in twentieth-century Britain has constantly fallen back on a series of 'elsewheres' to underwrite its denial of the existence or authenticity or importance of intellectuals. Sometimes the elsewheres have been literal and geographical; sometimes they have been chronological (the past is another elsewhere); sometimes they have been idealized or projected or otherwise fantasmatic. Of course, one danger inherent in the approach adopted in this book is that of replacing claims about the distinctive absence of intellectuals with claims about the distinctiveness of the *claims* about the absence of intellectuals. However, I have also tried to show that these strategies of denial, far from being confined to British discussions, can be identified, albeit wearing appropriate local costume, in a variety of comparable countries, so that what may at first present itself as a distinctive national idiosyncrasy clearly needs to be understood as one manifestation of a more general logic. Where intellectuals are concerned, elsewhere is nearly always where it's at.

All this indicates, as I have already suggested, that we are dealing here with an object of desire, and it is in the nature of desire simultaneously to pursue and to resist total satisfaction. The stir of appetite is only ever temporarily stilled, the cycle of wanting is ceaseless and inexorable, and no reality can ever measure up to the reach of fantasy by which desire is powered. The here and now is bound to be always more or less inadequate. The figure of the intellectual is clearly invested with a form of desire: perhaps with the hope that thought and imagination should be powers in the world, perhaps with the longing that the reign of rationality and justice might finally begin, perhaps, most simply, with the wish that there should be sources of wisdom, somewhere, about how to live. The words and deeds of any actual individuals could only fall short of these yearnings. Any putative example pointed to in the here-and-now is inevitably bathetic: how could *that* limited, flawed, largely unoriginal individual possibly be the embodiment of the dream? So desire generates further fantasy, and fantasy, by definition, fastens on the not-here and the not-now.

Of course, from one point of view, all this may be taken to be encouraging. It may suggest that, behind all the defensive mockery and aggressive stereotyping, the notion of the intellectual represents something deeply valued, the existence of highly developed strategies of denial testifying, as so often, to the presence of strong wants. As the sources cited in this book have, I trust, amply documented, the question of intellectuals has not been a matter of indifference in British culture. But by the same token, the endless deferral involved in so many of the debates can also be seen as expressing the wish that the ideal should not actually be realized, lest it disturb other of our 'customs and establishments'. The deeply entrenched power of those forces has only been touched on intermittently in this book, but that does not mean that I underestimate them. It has been no part of my purpose to argue that intellectuals have found British culture a deeply welcoming environment, only that there is exaggeration in the opposite direction in portraying it as uniquely unfavourable.

So much of this book has been a prolonged act of attention to the *word* 'intellectuals' because it is a very remarkable case of the potency of a term itself, of its capacity to play almost an independent part in the story. It would, needless to say, be possible to write a book about intellectuals in twentieth-century Britain—about leading figures and groups of figures, their writings, their ideas, their lives—without paying much attention to this label, certainly without paying much attention to *their* use of it. But, as the sources quoted in this book have attested over and over again, the presence of the word transforms people's responses, including those of the people to whom it is applied: it acts like a chemical element that, when added to a stable compound, makes it change colour and become unstable.

As I have emphasized more than once, I have no wish to try to assume Humpty-Dumpty's legislative powers towards language; instead, I have sought to discriminate the various senses of the term 'intellectual' and to explicate the meaning of what, by common consent, has now become the dominant of those senses. Indeed, the fact that the term 'intellectual' *is* now so widely used in what I have dubbed the 'cultural' sense, and used without distancing quotation marks or sneering modifiers like 'so-called' tagging along, may be one of the preconditions for writing this book, the appearance of which may in turn be a confirmation that the Owl of Minerva is keeping to its usual flight schedule. For a variety of reasons, people in Britain at the beginning of the twenty-first century are becoming more familiar with the idea that the term and the roles it denotes have their place in this as in other cultures; this book attempts to contribute to that readjustment of our understanding of the past which always comes with shifts in our experience of the present.

More generally, it is surely true that at the beginning of the twenty-first century there are many signs that the grounds for the belief in British (or French or American or other) 'exceptionalism' are being reduced compared even with fifty, let alone one hundred, years ago. It is both a part and a consequence of such changes that historians in these different societies are beginning to identify an increasing convergence in both the actual position of intellectuals in their respective societies and in the cultural perceptions of them. In Britain, as in France and elsewhere, the publication of more detailed, sceptical, and comparative studies may perform one of the most valuable of history's traditional tasks by challenging stereotypes and eroding certainties, especially those long cherished as part of the nation's image of itself. It has been an immensely slow and painful business for Britain to come to realize, insofar as it yet has, that it is one medium-sized European country among others, with many similar interests and problems. It may be some small contribution to the successful resolution of this protracted identity-crisis if the cliché of the 'absence of intellectuals in Britain' comes itself to be seen as an idea with a particular and limited history within British culture, thus enabling the reality it has helped to mask to be analysed as no more than one distinctive variant of a larger international pattern.

II

There will, I realize, still be readers unpersuaded by this book's main arguments. Its self-restriction to debates *about* intellectuals, its preoccupation with senses of the term, its focus on intellectuals in the cultural sense, its deliberate broadening of attention beyond the political dimensions of the intellectual's role, its concentration on a particular level of sophisticated textual sources, its leanings towards a literary-critical engagement with those sources, and its polemical, revisionist intent—all these features may be seized upon by those who have reasons of their own for continuing to insist that intellectuals have been far less present, far less important, or simply far less interesting, in Britain than elsewhere. There may be little more that could be done, in any single book, to challenge this familiar insistence, and it may be necessary to wait until a richer historiography about intellectuals in twentieth-century Britain and elsewhere has accumulated to the point where, like a landslip or mudslide, it brooks no resistance in its reorganization of a familiar landscape.

That historiography, when it comes into being, may well challenge many of the arguments and judgements to be found in this book. In covering such a vast expanse, I have been more than ever mindful of the familiar ironic injunction 'Thin ice—skate faster'. But though no doubt my authorial vanity will be piqued when future scholars successfully dispute and correct statements made here, it will not require any implausibly Olympian detachment or wilful pollyannaism to regard such critiques as a sign of one kind of success. For, my principal aim in writing this book has been to open up a subject for proper historical investigation by removing what always functions as one of the most effective obstacles to serious enquiry, namely, the deeply entrenched cultural prejudice that we already know the answer and know that it is not very interesting. I have been conscious in writing this book that my sustained engagement with what I have called 'the absence thesis' may seem to have a potentially narrowing effect, that it might have seemed more rewarding to have explored in adequate detail some episodes of the intellectual activity that have been carried on in this society and to have attempted to draw therefrom some inductive conclusions about the distinctiveness or otherwise of its character. I like to think that, along the way, the book does include a good deal of that kind of exploration, but it is undeniable that any extended demolition of a view which, in its simplest form, is almost self-evidently false risks appearing a somewhat sterile exercise. I hope that the thick texture of this book will have gone some way towards mitigating that effect, as will my strategy of treating that claim symptomatically, using it to open up a hinterland of attitude and assumption, rather than simply concentrating on direct rebuttal. But whatever the judgement of readers on the success of those efforts, I remain convinced that the task of attempting to remove this formidable obstacle was a necessary one. If the kind of proliferation of scholarly research on the topic that I was imagining a few moments ago does take place in the future, then I would regard that, however revisionist it may be in relation to the arguments of this book, as a sufficient vindication. If, in the fullness of time, even political and journalistic comment on the topic starts to cast off some of the slacker clichés and stereotypes, then that will be an added bonus.

'Denial', however, is a cunning, feral beast, endlessly resourceful in protecting its wilful nescience. Having seen each of its usual tactics disarmed in the previous chapters, having been driven out of its preferred territory in the past and even dispossessed of its lands in the present, having finally been cornered in the Epilogue of a long book, it thrashes out in one last desperate bid: very well, it snarls, perhaps there have been intellectuals in Britain in the past and perhaps they are still functioning in the present, but (a triumphant gleam passes over its normally grim features) they will not survive in the future. They belong to a passing world, a world of unequal access to information, with a small educated elite extracting cultural deference from the unlettered, or less lettered, many. In a world of egalitarian social attitudes, widespread prosperity, near universal higher education, limitlessly available information, and an unprecedented abundance of competing distractions, no one will listen any more. The term itself will become an archaism. No less a figure than Pierre Nora recently suggested that this situation had already arrived in, of all places, France: 'L'époque à laquelle a correspondu la figure de l'"intellectuel" est sans doute aujourd'hui révolue. Le mot même, paré de tous les prestiges, flétri de tous les opprobres, chargé de confusions et de tant de malentendus, est devenu presque insupportable. On ne sait plus de qui ni de quoi on parle.' ['The epoch to which the figure of the "intellectual" corresponded is without doubt over today. The word itself, stripped of all prestige, branded with opprobrium, burdened with so many confusions and misunderstandings, has almost become unbearable. One no longer knows of whom or of what one is speaking.'][2]

Although the future forms, strictly speaking, no part of the historian's bailiwick, I believe that if the analysis pursued in this book is persuasive, then there are good reasons to believe that the role to which the cultural sense of 'intellectual' refers is not about to disappear, whether or not that particular word continues to be used to identify it. It is not just that, at the most abstract level, the structural relations which underpin the role will always be available to provide a corrective perspective, whether conceived as general/particular, disinterested/instrumental, specialist/non-specialist, or any similar contrasts. It is also that the kinds of major substantive issues that stir intellectuals to public utterance in the present are clearly not going to go away in any foreseeable future. I have already expressed my reservations about the glamorization involved in the much-quoted formula 'speaking truth to power', but I do not for a moment dispute that those with power of any kind display a constant and almost limitless tendency to control, doctor, and suppress the truth about their activities, and that there is therefore always call for those with the capacities, the education, the time, and the independence to attempt to tell the fuller and more accurate story. Similarly, the twenty-first century hardly seems likely to see a sudden abatement of global capitalism's relentless search for profits, and so the need to articulate and help make effective some alternative vocabulary of evaluation to that spawned by the 'bottom-line rationalism' of international corporations will surely continue. Again, the media's eager embrace, driven by the restless logic of commercialism, of the opportunities provided by the intersection of the democratization of cultural life and the development of new technologies will also continue to provoke the counterpoint of voices that are more reflective, more creative, more critical, and better informed. And nor, finally, does there seem any likelihood that the dialectic of specialization-and-laments-about-specialization will become a less marked feature of cultural reflection in the coming century. On all these counts, it does not seem probable that opportunities for intellectuals to make themselves heard are going to disappear any time soon.

With respect to the last of these points, what we may broadly call 'academia' will surely, for reasons discussed in earlier chapters, be even more central to the intellectual and cultural life of the twenty-first century than it has been to (at least the second half of) the twentieth. By no means all, or in some times and places even the majority, of those termed 'intellectuals' have been academics, nor should they be, but it seems highly likely that an increasing proportion of the coming century's intellectuals will have some kind of academic connection, and even those who do not will have to acknowledge and take account of the authority that academic scholarship in general will continue to possess. The very nature of disinterested scholarly enquiry provides a huge fund of resources to be called upon in criticizing all that is superficial, fashionable, and merely interest-driven in the agenda of the day. In this respect, academics do still have a deep well of resources to draw from, but such resources can only be made effective in the wider society if enough individuals are willing to try to tread the fine line (discussed in the last two chapters) between self-effacing specialism and self-promoting vulgarity. Academic intellectuals will have to continue to foster the rigour, the respect for evidence, the disinterestedness, and the wider perspective which are among the animating ideals of academic scholarship while at the same time managing to break out from its increasingly self-referring hermeticism to bring these qualities to bear in wider public debate. Doing this successfully would not mean trying to ape the street-cred of some strains of Cultural Studies, nor would it mean descending to the Sunday-paper opinionatedness of the occasional don with strong metropolitan literary connections. But the very processes which may appear to make it more difficult for reasoned argument, informed judgement, and a broad perspective to get a hearing in the public domain simultaneously generate a corresponding hunger for those qualities. A diet of media-degradable titbits and sound bites stimulates an appetite for something more substantial. Or, to switch metaphors, in a headline-swamped, opinion-heavy culture, the hard currency of well-grounded analysis becomes more valuable, not less. In attempting to meet these needs, academics, like other kinds of intellectual, can rely less and less upon the deference formerly accorded to irrelevant or merely contingent social attributes and connections. They have to prove their title to be heard by showing that they have something to say which is worth listening to.

It is certainly no part of my purpose in this book to suggest that in the matter of intellectuals we, whoever 'we' are in this case, should be satisfied with what we've got. I should like to think that no attentive reader of this book could be left feeling complacent about the state of public debate in Britain, now or in the past century. Recognizing our reality for what it is does not have to issue in complacency—it can, in some circumstances, have quite the opposite effect—but it does provide an infinitely better starting-point for thinking about improvement than the traditional mixture of prejudice and fantasy. It is a small but essential step towards that 'justness of perception' that Matthew Arnold called for in the passage which serves as the epigraph to this Epilogue.[3] Many years ago Raymond Williams wrote an influential essay entitled 'Culture is ordinary'.[4] Perhaps it's time that someone wrote an essay entitled 'Intellectuals are ordinary'. 'Ordinary' in the sense that they are indeed part of the cultural landscape of all complex societies; ordinary in the sense that it is neither unthinkable nor shocking to recognize that the noun 'intellectual' might regularly be applied to some of the contemporaries one reads, or occasionally to some of one's colleagues or friends, or even, in some circumstances, to oneself; and, above all, ordinary in the sense that carrying on the activities characteristic of intellectuals should not be seen as exceptionally heroic or exceptionally difficult or exceptionally glamorous or—and I realize that here I particularly lay myself open to misunderstanding—even exceptionally important. Important, yes, but not exceptionally important. Perhaps it's time to stop thinking of intellectuals as Other People, and to try not to fall so easily into the related tabloid habits of demonizing and pedestalling.

But maybe clichés never die? It is true that being possessed of a disheartening longevity is a defining characteristic of clichés, though they do sometimes come to be seen *as* clichés, and when that happens on any large scale they start to lose their power. Beliefs about the existence, nature, and role of intellectuals in Britain are not, it should hardly need saying, going to be determined by a single book on the topic. They are going, rather, to be determined by those countless acts of reading, thinking, speaking, and listening which, unseen by history, make and unmake cultural patterns: by arguments around dining-room tables and TV sets, by conversations in wine bars and workplaces, by what people choose to read in newspapers and by which magazines they choose to subscribe to, by what they pick up in the new mega-bookstores and what they click on on the ever-expanding Internet, and by people each making dozens of other barely conscious choices about what to attend to, who to listen to, how to respond, what to think. As I have argued throughout this book, the term 'intellectuals' names a relation, and whether there continue to be intellectuals in the twenty-first century and after will depend upon the behaviour of all parties to that relation.

For the present, the least we can do, though it is no small thing, is to understand and possess our own history. We need to work within 'our customs and establishments', which include the traditions of denial examined in this book. But by doing so in full historical self-consciousness, we cease to be the prisoners of those traditions, and that is the essential first step towards liberating us from the weary, unenquiring prejudice which insists that, where the question of intellectuals in Britain is concerned, there is simply very little to say. Living in Britain, now, there can be 'no such excuse' any longer. On this matter we cannot continue to pretend that some 'elsewhere' underwrites our existence.

NOTES

1. Philip Larkin, 'The Importance of Elsewhere', *The Whitsun Weddings* (London: Faber, 1964), 34. A date of composition of 13 June 1955 is given in Philip Larkin, *Collected Poems*, ed. Anthony Thwaite (London: Faber, 1988), 104.
2. Pierre Nora, 'Adieux aux intellectuels?', *Le Débat* (Summer, 2000), 14.
3. Matthew Arnold, *Literature and Dogma* (1873), in *The Complete Prose Works of Matthew Arnold*, ed. R. H. Super, 11 vols. (Ann Arbor: University of Michigan Press, 1960–77), vi. 158.
4. Raymond Williams, 'Culture is ordinary', in Norman Mackenzie (ed.), *Conviction* (London: MacGibbon & Kee, 1958), and frequently reprinted. For the following sentences I have drawn on my essay, '"Every fruit-juice drinker, nudist, sandal-wearer..."', in Helen Small (ed.), *The Public Intellectual* (Oxford: Blackwell, 2002), 221–2.

Acknowledgements

This book has been written in the interstices of other duties, other writing, other living, across an embarrassingly large number of years. I would particularly like to acknowledge the generous support of three institutions whose policies of enlightened patronage are still admirably resistant to those crude forms of short-termism and value-for-money-ism which require that support be confined to projects that will be completed during the underwritten period. The sabbatical leave policy of Cambridge University continues to guarantee regular spells of relief which only become more essential as the burdens associated with teaching and administration grow ever more pressing. Similarly, both the Institute for Advanced Study at Princeton, where I was a member in 1994–5, and the British Academy, which awarded me its 'Thank-Offering to Britain' Senior Research Fellowship for 1999–2000, recognize the individual's need for time in which to read and think and write other things. This book could not have been written without this kind of support.

I am more than grateful to my colleagues in the Faculty of English at Cambridge for bearing with my absences as well as (especially during the years in which I served as Chair of the Faculty) for bearing with my presence, too. The Faculty's tireless Administrator, Claire Daunton, exceeded her job-description in providing particularly thoughtful help and advice. Several of my former graduate students have readily reversed roles and tried to remedy the narrowness of my reading on various relevant topics: I thank Julia Stapleton, Hao Li, Ralph Jessop, Sean Matthews, Dan Burnstone, Peter White, Simon Grimble, Jason Harding, Daniel Williams, Sarah Wah, and Deborah Bowman. I am also indebted to Susan Manley, David Clifford, and, again, Simon Grimble and Jason Harding for research assistance. For two extended visits to Paris during which I somewhat fraudulently gloried in the title of 'Directeur d'études associé' at the École des Hautes Études en Sciences Sociales I owe thanks to the late Clemens Heller. I am also grateful to the Arts and Humanities Research Board for the award of a term's leave in 2004 during which this book was finally completed. At Curtis Brown, Peter Robinson had patience, and at OUP Christopher Wheeler had faith; I am sorry they both needed so much of these qualities in my case.

Unusually, perhaps, I have not published substantial portions of this book in advance in the form of essays and articles. Aside from certain passages indicated, with full references, in the text, the material is here appearing in print for the first time. The one exception is Chapter 13, the greater part of which appeared in two earlier essays 'The European Modernist as Anglican Moralist: the later social criticism of T. S. Eliot', in Mark S. Micale and Robert L. Dietle (eds.),

Enlightenment, Passion, Modernity: Historical Essays in European Thought and Culture (Stanford: Stanford University Press, 2000), 207–29, 438–44; and 'Eliot among the intellectuals', *Essays in Criticism*, 52 (2002), 101–25. In addition, several paragraphs that are now scattered throughout the book first appeared in my ' "Every fruit-juice drinker, nudist, sandal-wearer . . .": intellectuals as other people', in Helen Small (ed.), *The Public Intellectual* (Oxford: Blackwell, 2002), 203–23.

Some material has, however, been tried out in the form of public lectures, and I am very happy to thank the following institutions and individuals for invitations, hospitality, and stimulation: the Gauss Seminars in Criticism, Princeton University (Michael Wood and Hal Foster); the Sir D. Owen Evans Memorial Lectures, University of Wales, Aberystwyth (Gareth Williams and Lyn Pykett); the George Orwell Lecture, Birkbeck College, London (Bernard Crick and Sally Ledger); the 4th Humanities Research Centres' Joint Lecture, King's College London (Jinty Nelson); the Bateson Lecture, Oxford (Sir Tim Lankester and Stephen Wall); the Mary Parker Yates Lecture, Tulane University, New Orleans (Rick Teichgraeber); the inaugural annual lecture of the Bristol Institute for Research in the Humanities and Arts (Charles Martindale); as well as audiences at the following universities: University of California at Berkeley, University of British Columbia, Cambridge, Harvard, Johns Hopkins, Oxford, Paris, Princeton, Sussex, Swansea, Toronto, and Trinity College Dublin.

For specialized advice of various kinds, I am grateful to Jeremy Jennings, Dan Rodgers, and, generous beyond the call of any duty, George Craig. Any attempt to provide an amalgamated list of all those from whom I, like any scholar, have learned in the course of writing this book would be pointless, inaccurate, and insufficient—and anyway this book is quite long enough already. But my friends are another matter. My friends really *are* another matter, each of them pluralists several times over in occupying various combinations of roles as readers, critics, interlocutors, correspondents, models, supporters, counsellors, running partners, drinking companions, and more. They bear much of the responsibility for who I now am and so for the kind of book I have been able to write. Over and above that general responsibility, the following also read the typescript and are to blame for not getting me to change more of it: John Burrow, Peter Clarke, Tom Dunne, Geoffrey Hawthorn, Ruth Morse, Helen Small, John Thompson, Donald Winch.

Index